Everyday Women's and Gender Studies accomplishes what no one thought possible: It reinvents the introductory-textbook form to reflect the field's intersectional commitments. Organized around key concepts—from knowledges and identities to representation and places—it provides a flexible format to engage students in the challenges and pleasures of thinking critically about gender, race, and sex today.

Robyn Wiegman, *Duke University*

Braithwaite and Orr have given us that rare treat: an accessible, down-to-earth, yet still theoretically sophisticated guide to the ever-changing field of women's and gender studies. By focusing on key concepts and not star theorists, ordinary life and not iconic examples, this book provides a welcome and innovative introduction to the twisted and all-too-ever-present ways in which gender exerts itself on our bodies, our minds, our ideas, our identities. A welcome addition to the literature!

Suzanna Walters, *Northeastern University*

Everyday Women's and Gender Studies is an extremely welcome addition to the textbook landscape. Organized around key concepts rather than historical moments or cultural trajectories, it introduces students to the shifting, varied, and complicated discipline that is women's and gender studies. My colleagues and I have been searching for a textbook that offers students an organized and purposeful entrance to the field without relying on constrictive foundational assumptions or falsely unifying narratives; I am pleased to say that, with the publication of *Everyday Women's and Gender Studies,* we may have finally found our answer.

Tara Pauliny, *John Jay College, CUNY*

In *Everyday Women's and Gender Studies*, Ann Braithwaite and Catherine Orr take on the impossible—introduce, in very accessible language, first-time students, and quite possibly seasoned and new instructors to the vast and ever-evolving field of gender-based scholarly inquiries. In their organization by "concepts" rather than the conventional theoretical positions, historical periods, or cultural contexts, they succeed not only in providing information, but, importantly, modeling the field's evolution through interrogating the very idea of how we come to know, and what we do with that knowledge. A must for every student and instructor both in and outside of Women's and Gender Studies!

Sri Craven, *Portland State University*

This innovative textbook speaks directly to students and unpacks the knowledges, identities, bodies, representations, and places that motivate feminist pedagogy in Women's, Gender, and Sexualities Studies (WGSS). Rarely have I seen a text that helps students imagine and then explore how WGSS is put together in theoretical and practical terms. The transparency and clarity of the text is impressive. This accessible resource will assist feminist instructors in reaching a broad audience and communicate the significance of the feminist "knowledge project" for a new generation of students.

Nancy Naples, *University of Connecticut*

The authors have done something remarkable in creating *Everyday Women's and Gender Studies*. They have written a text that deeply engages students about six core concepts in the field in a sophisticated yet accessible way. This invitational and streamlined approach makes this book a game changer for teaching women's and gender studies undergraduates.

Michele Tracy Berger, *University of North Carolina–Chapel Hill*

Everyday Women's and Gender Studies is a refreshing, provocative, and creative alternative to standard introductions to the field. Challenging predictable origin stories and disciplinary basics, the volume offers an accessible approach to the field even as it destabilizes its most stubborn dogmas. The result is an intellectually rigorous yet practical guide not only to rethinking women and gender but, more importantly, to reactivating, with a twist, that ancient ethical question: how are we to live?

Lynne Huffer, *Emory University*

Written as a conversation with students about their everyday lives, *Everyday Women's and Gender Studies* introduces core concepts of the field and demonstrates how these help us to come to a richer understanding of the world around us. The text is superbly accessible, while holding onto the complexity of feminist thought, and it represents the very best of the lively debates that are the hallmark of Women's and Gender Studies classrooms.

Susanne Luhmann, *University of Alberta*

Everyday Women's and Gender Studies

Everyday Women's and Gender Studies is a text-reader that offers instructors a new way to approach an introductory course on women's and gender studies. This book highlights major concepts that organize the diverse work in this field: Knowledges, Identities, Equalities, Bodies, Places, and Representations. Its focus on "the everyday" speaks to the importance this book places on students understanding the taken-for-granted circumstances of their daily lives. Precisely because it is not the same for everyone, the everyday becomes the ideal location for cultivating students' intellectual capacities as well as their political investigations and interventions. In addition to exploring each concept in detail, each chapter includes up to five short recently published readings that illuminate an aspect of that concept. *Everyday Women's and Gender Studies* explores the idea that "People are different, and the world isn't fair," and engages students in the inevitably complicated follow-up question, "Now that we know, how shall we live?"

Ann Braithwaite is Professor and Coordinator of Diversity and Social Justice Studies at the University of Prince Edward Island. She is the co-author of *Troubling Women's Studies: Pasts, Presents, and Possibilities* (Sumach Press, 2005) and co-editor (with Catherine M. Orr and Diane Lichtenstein) of *Rethinking Women's and Gender Studies* (Routledge, 2012).

Catherine M. Orr is Professor and Chair of Critical Identity Studies at Beloit College. Her work has appeared in *Feminist Studies, Women's Studies Quarterly, Hypatia,* and *NWSA Journal*. She is co-editor (with Ann Braithwaite and Diane Lichtenstein) of *Rethinking Women's and Gender Studies* (Routledge, 2012). She lives in Madison, Wisconsin.

Everyday Women's and Gender Studies

Introductory Concepts

Ann Braithwaite, University of Prince Edward Island

Catherine M. Orr, Beloit College

Routledge
Taylor & Francis Group

NEW YORK AND LONDON

Please visit the eResource for this title at:
www.routledge.com/9780415536646

First published 2017
by Routledge
711 Third Avenue, New York, NY 10017

and by Routledge
2 Park Square, Milton Park, Abingdon, Oxon, OX14 4RN

Routledge is an imprint of the Taylor & Francis Group, an informa business

© 2017 Taylor & Francis

Library of Congress Cataloging in Publication Data
A catalog record for this book has been requested

ISBN: 978-0-415-53664-6 (hbk)
ISBN: 978-0-415-53666-0 (pbk)
ISBN: 978-1-315-64320-5 (ebk)

Typeset in Scala
by Servis Filmsetting Ltd, Stockport, Cheshire

Contents

Contents

Acknowledgments

No book is complete without recognizing all those who helped bring it to fruition. And like most books, this one is the product of more than the two names on its cover. We've presented many versions of our argument about what an intro course should introduce and have benefitted immensely from both the enthusiasm as well as the pushback. We've had numerous conversations with friends, colleagues, and students at conferences and meetings and workshops, over e-mail and Facebook and Skype. All of these encounters have demanded that we think in more complex ways about what to include in an introductory book and about the multiple needs of the students who show up in our first year WGS courses.

We want to especially thank Karlyn Crowley, Astrid Henry, Annalee Lepp, and Alison Piepmeier for their engagement with us at every step of this project and their whole-hearted support of it throughout. We may only see them in person once or twice a year, at WGSRF and NWSA, for our annual catching-up discussions about the state of the field. But electronic communication and social media have made it possible for them be part of this book's development nonetheless. They read and commented and mused aloud with us, and the book reflects their insights and observations for the better. Thank you, friends; you are the intellectual community that makes this profession so rewarding.

Ilya Parkins, Elizabeth Groeneveld, and Diane Lichtenstein all read early drafts of chapters and offered comments and insights that helped us focus and clarify and sharpen what we were doing. Robyn Wiegman was extremely supportive at the prospectus stage and offered insights that proved useful to the book's organization.

Acknowledgments

LeeRay Costa offered long detailed commentary at many stages of the project; the book is definitely the better for her willingness to give so much of her time to it and to us. And finally, our two student assistants, Andi Altenbach at Beloit College and Kaitlin Newson at UPEI, did much of the research for the online resources page. Many thanks to them all for being part of this process.

Our immense thanks also go to Samantha Barbaro, our current editor, and Leah Babb-Rosenfeld, our former editor at Routledge. Their enthusiasm for this project kept us motivated—and Sam's endless patience kept us on track. Much gratitude goes Olivia Hatt, who was indispensable in the production process. We also thank the many anonymous reviewers who read individual chapters and provided keen feedback that helped us hone our arguments. Finally, we'd like to thank Jaroslava "Jarka" Sobiskova for another beautiful cover for the book. Her art making continues to inspire us.

Ann thanks her friends and colleagues, and especially her students at the University of Prince Edward Island, for their boundless support of her work. Their willingness to listen—in formal and informal venues—as she tried out ideas exemplifies some of the best of academia and reminds her constantly why she loves doing what she does. She also thanks her partner for being her best sounding board and cheerleader, and her dog for getting her out of the house and clearing her head at least twice a day.

Catherine thanks her Beloit support network. Bill and Gayle Keefer funded the Keefer Senior Faculty Grant that paid for many books, airplane tickets, conferences, and a few good meals. Heartfelt thanks go to her faculty and staff colleagues at the college who think long and hard with her about what students really need to live lives of purpose and fulfillment. Finally, props to the Critical Identity Studies students and alums at Beloit whose enthusiasm and intellectual engagement regularly nourish and expand her faith about what is possible in higher education. She also thanks Gil, Wheaton, and the rest of her family for the foundation of love and care that make it all worthwhile.

And finally, as we did in a previous book, we thank each other. Every word of this book is ultimately written together, a long process made more difficult by time differences and our two very busy lives. We owe Skype a lot! But as complicated as it can be to write together over time and place, this is the kind of scholarly work that best exemplifies what we believe about the importance of intellectual community. We would do it all again—and already have plans to do so!

Note to Instructors, or, Is This the New Textbook for Your Intro Course?

Everyday Women's and Gender Studies (EWGS) is an opportunity to think otherwise about how to organize an introductory Women's and Gender Studies (WGS) course. While many introductory texts focus on a number of *topics*, often predominantly about women (or sometimes about gender more broadly), *EWGS* shifts the focus to some of the major *concepts* that organize the diverse work in this field. Concepts, in the broadest sense, are frameworks that allow us to weave together a range of disparate content, focusing on the connections between a wide variety of WGS interests. As a multifaceted discipline whose practitioners take up everything from sex chromosomes to sex work, global flows to girl cultures, social movements to sitcoms, war to the wedding industry, the prison industrial complex to pornography, fat bodies to female masculinities, and so much more, focusing on concepts allows us to follow the threads that connect the approaches, questions, languages, theories, actions, and topics we talk about in our introductory classes.

Our focus on "the everyday," in both the title and the many examples we provide throughout the text, speaks to the importance we place on students' understanding of the taken-for-granted circumstances of their daily lives. Precisely because the everyday is not the same for everyone, it becomes the ideal location for cultivating students' political investigations and interventions. In this book, then, we present six major concepts that structure much of the work done in the field—"Knowledges," "Identities," "Equalities," "Bodies," "Places," "Representations"—as well as a concluding chapter, entitled "Now What?"; our aim throughout is to both explore the idea that "People are different, and the world isn't fair" and engage students in the inevitably complicated follow-up question, "Now that we know, how shall we live?"

What Should an Intro Course Introduce?

A couple of the central questions we asked ourselves in thinking about how to write an introductory text (and not simply replicate the many others that already exist) was "Who is the audience?" and, perhaps more importantly, "What does that audience need from a textbook?" The introductory course is usually assumed to be a primary site for disciplinary training in "the basics," not just by the students who take the course, but often by the faculty who teach it. And, as a disciplinary artifact, the introductory textbook can play an outsized role not just in explaining what Women's and Gender Studies is to an uninitiated audience of undergraduates—the vast majority of whom will never take another WGS course—but in influencing instructors' understanding of what is critical to "pass on" to those students (and, by default, what is better left for the advanced courses that most intro students will never sign up for).

For example, when we were approached by an editor about writing an introductory text, she framed instructors' needs this way in an e-mail: "In my conversations with instructors on campus visits, etc., I've received quite a number of requests for a book that doesn't just assume that students know the basics of the history behind what they're reading." What struck us immediately was this notion of "the history." Two assumptions seemed implicit—and problematic—in this framing of what should be in an introductory text: there was only one history worthy of passing on to students and that history's content was—or should be—known to the rest of us in the discipline. But, we wondered, isn't this exactly the sort of assumption about history we would want our students to interrogate *even at the introductory level?*

We quickly dashed off what was, upon reflection, a rather snarky response to the editor: "To (re)produce a history that focuses only on women (as opposed to gendered identity formations), starts at Seneca Falls (thereby replicating race/class/U.S. privilege), then trots out 'waves' and 'generations,' and then wraps up with critiques by women of color and/or lesbians/queers [is not what this field needs]. This history has been done . . . and often roundly critiqued as highly problematic and/or not even true. The field does not need this history . . . again." Thus, from our first thoughts about this book, we took seriously the idea that we would not produce a dominant narrative about WGS origins and objects of analysis born of a singular history that privileges a singular identity category. Rather, like our own experience of this diversely constituted discipline full of complexity and interesting contradictions, we wanted to create an introductory text that encouraged students to see the value of WGS as a *knowledge project* that exposes the diverse impacts of difference and power in our lives, even in our lives as WGS practitioners.

Shifting the focus of the introductory course to WGS as a knowledge project means that we are freed up to ask critical questions about this course's purpose: What are the basics that should (some of us might say, must) be included? In other words, what do we feel duty bound to pass on to do the work of the discipline? How does this response shift if we instead ask, what knowledges from the discipline will be most provocative for our particular students? What can we let go of? For example, and apropos of our response to the editor, do we have to tell a story of something called "The Women's Movement," given that any number of WGS scholars have pointed out serious problems of race and class exclusions in this disciplinary narrative? If we find those claims about the problems with this "origin myth" of WGS compelling, why pass the myth on to our students? Likewise, do we need "waves?" After all, the value of this metaphor has been questioned repeatedly for constructing generational divides that sometimes do, but mostly don't, exist. And, do we have to make feminism the foundational—and singular—paradigm of the field when a significant number of practitioners in WGS might prefer to emphasize different intellectual traditions (think: womanist or trans or Xicanista or queer) and have pointed out the obvious: that there are multiple versions of feminism that fundamentally contradict each other? Too often, the women's movement or waves or feminism are the intro course artifacts that many of us return to in an advanced theory course or a fourth year capstone to "unteach." But, again, what if the students never take another course and thus never get the correction?

A New Approach, or, What Were These Authors Thinking?

Given our emphasis on rethinking the intro course as a knowledge project, this book is organized to highlight the richness of the many theoretical languages that inform contemporary thinking in Women's and Gender Studies. In this text, then, the concepts we introduce are informed by feminism(s), of course, but also by ethnic studies, critical race studies, queer theory and sexuality studies, disability studies, critical legal theory, cultural studies, and postcolonial studies. If Women's Studies (by its earlier name) was initially understood as the mobilization of feminism in the academy, WGS today has successfully put feminism in conversation with a broad assortment of thinkers and theoretical approaches in any number of disciplines that productively question its singularity. Those questions in the early context of the field's emergence about "which feminism"—and the successive questions about whether WGS is feminist/is about feminism/is where feminism is the object of study/is the study that feminists do—broadened the intellectual scope of the field such that passing on a singular, or at least uninterrogated notion of, feminism can no longer encompass the rich and productive set of debates and approaches that are mobilized under this disciplinary rubric. Rather, the knowledge produced in this field can only be reflected, we believe, if we refuse to invest in only one theoretical language as the focus of WGS. As such, the concepts laid out here derive from a wide variety of theorists and approaches that are, in a sense, translated from these debates about and beyond feminism(s), even as they maintain a common focus on questions of how we know, what we know, and what we do with the knowledges we have. Likewise, resisting feminism as the sole organizing concept of the introduction to the field means that the primary learning goal is not centered around a "conversion experience" for our students. In other words, we set aside questions about whether our success as faculty is measured by our students identifying themselves as feminists (or, indeed, anything else) as a result of taking this course. Instead, maintaining the focus on WGS as a knowledge project allows students to raise critical questions about the histories, political mobilizations, and limits of any identity category, theoretical approach, or field of study, including our own.

Obviously, we are evoking what is, to some, a rather profane line of thinking. But it is our suspicion that, as instructors of WGS intro courses, we don't always allow ourselves the critical space to question whether our classes are actually introducing what we think is most worthy of passing on from the discipline to our largest audiences. And we wonder: Why not introduce students to the version of the field we find most compelling? Why not, for example, introduce a version of WGS that raises more questions than answers; that develops habits of thinking through exploring issues from multiple perspectives; that emphasizes how understanding the world is contingent on the institutions, structures, and processes by which we are disciplined; and that is always doubling back to interrogate the assumptions implicit in its own knowledge production? What you have in your hands is, as best as we can pass it on to students in an accessible way, that version of WGS.

The question of who our students are in the intro class also frames our thinking about this book's organization. In many colleges and universities, the intro course serves double duty for any number of required credits (e.g., a general education or humanities or social sciences credit, a "diversity" or "cross cultural" credit, a "civic engagement" or "experiential learning" credit). What will capture the imagination of these heterogeneous student bodies in a way that makes this course worth their time and energy? And what, given the range of disciplinary training of people (like you) who teach this course, can be "covered" in this class? Starting with a recognition of who is in the classroom can—and perhaps should—challenge us to rethink both the pedagogical purpose and the received intellectual content ("the basics" or "the history") for any intro course. This is why we opted to write a text that focuses on key concepts in the broadest possible way but leaves aside the long, detailed, and varied intellectual heritage of those concepts. While this option runs the risk of lacking specificity about particular knowledges, it also provides instructors with the opportunity to present a version of the field that will be most meaningful to their own students and to themselves. Without a singular genealogy, history, foundational identity category, or movement named by us, our hope is that the need for performing resistant readings of the textbook or the labor of "undoing" the introductory version of the field for the few students who later take the advanced courses will be mitigated.

This open-ended approach to the field's history is both a political and an intellectual stance on our part, drawing on the thinking of writers, like Clare Hemmings and Sara Ahmed, who have warned against the ways in which scholars, despite their best attempts at open-mindedness, objectivity, and inclusiveness, nevertheless tend to assume a generalizable past to "secure a history as a *prelude* to the author's own particular insights" (Hemmings 2005, 117). As such, we see citational practices in introductory texts as fraught. They're "a catering system," as Ahmed terms it, "justified as a form of *reassurance*, a way of keeping things familiar for those who want to conserve the familiar" (2014). Because we are cautious about reproducing a version of the field that emphasizes what is familiar, we decided against using names of authors or citing works in the chapters themselves. We see this as a democratizing gesture that invites students to locate themselves as knowledge producers alongside recognized WGS scholars and practitioners, a move that also models WGS' challenge to hierarchies of knowledge that reinforce precisely the power relations we aim to question in this field. Since many intro students will not take additional WGS courses, it seems to us less relevant that their textbook cite authors and more important that they learn the critical thinking practices WGS emphasizes.

Of course, we realize that this may be another bit of profane thinking on our part. To be clear, the lack of in-text citations from this point forward is *not* an attempt to erase the discipline's intellectual history and present it as our own. (See "Chapter Genealogies" tucked away in the back of the book—where few students are likely to venture—to find out more about our intellectual debts.) Instead, we see it as a form of translation for students just wading into the challenging terrain of difference and power. As such, we distill a number of theories, approaches, languages, and ideas from across the breadth of this field into six approachable chapters for students. And many of you will no doubt recognize the provenance of our explications as belonging to people widely regarded as threshold thinkers in WGS: Jasbir Puar's homonationalism, Judith Butler's performativity, Michel Foucault's discourse/power/knowledge,

Kimberlé Crenshaw's intersectionality, Stuart Hall's representation, Andrea Smith's conquest, Donna Haraway's situated knowledges, Sarah Ahmed's killjoy, and many, many others. This text obviously benefits from discussions, debates, applications, and refusals from many important WGS thinkers ranging from academic stars to popular intellectuals to emerging scholars. Again, we think that focusing on these broad conceptual frameworks, without covering the who's who of WGS in the chapter itself, enables multiple points of entry into the discipline.

This is not to say that we don't provide some potential paths to launch what we think are some compelling WGS genealogies. Our selection of readings that accompanies each chapter, as well as the additional online resources, is offered as suggestions for some provocative ways to think about each concept. No doubt, seasoned instructors of WGS intro courses will have their own favorites, too—their "go-to" articles, chapters, films, lectures, and assignments that dependably do good work in their classroom. And we hope you will find our resistance of "coverage" allows for a nice balance of old and new, of our selections and yours, in shaping your course. That said, as with any text-reader, we clearly have preferences. Ours tend towards recently published, humanities-oriented materials that capture the multiplicity and instability of categories and meanings outlined in each chapter. The additional materials— both in-text readings and online resources available on the companion website (more articles, blog posts, podcasts, YouTube clips, videos, documentaries)—provide extensions, clarifications, illustrations, complications, and even "troublings" of what is in the chapters. We think of them as "exit ramps" to further explore these concepts depending on what individual instructors want to stress from any one chapter, given their own interests, areas of expertise, and learning goals. We hope this combination of broad conceptual frameworks along with a variety of possible directions for supplementary materials offers you the ideal combination of both structure and freedom to inspire your students to explore WGS.

Structure of Chapters, or, What's On Tap for Your Students?

In selecting six different but related concepts, we sought to ensure that the structure of each chapter was consistently reproduced as a means of developing some intellectual habits on the part of students. This book starts and ends with a declaration and a related question that we think are foundational to WGS. The declaration that *People are different . . . and the world isn't fair* is an easily made and yet complex observation that motivates the practitioners of this field to focus on a number of identity categories, explore the social worlds those identities create and inhabit, and challenge the ways in which they are reproduced. We then follow up with the (somewhat dauntingly open-ended) question, *Now that we know . . . how shall we live?* Ultimately, we want to encourage students to imagine alternative ways of being and acting in the world that are more just for a greater number of people. Our task in each chapter, then, is to both explain and complicate various layers of difference and unfairness and to demonstrate a method to think carefully about the effects that can accrue from trying to make change.

To organize this task, we divide the book into two even sections. Part One includes the chapters on "Knowledges," "Identities," and "Equalities," while Part Two consists of "Bodies," "Places," and "Representations." Part One is sequentially organized, and we suggest that students read "Knowledges," "Identities," and "Equalities" in that order as they lay the groundwork for what we then take up in the final three chapters. "Bodies," "Places," and "Representations" are more interchangeable and can be read in the order that works best for your course. Additionally, throughout the text, we note connections to previous examples or discussion points and indicate how some ideas are taken up further in other chapters. This strategy highlights for students and instructors alike the ways in which these concepts (and our examples) can connect in useful ways. To that end, we've also included a "Readings Chart" that points to alternative chapter-and-reading pairings. Finally, between each chapter and the readings that follow, we offer a "Preview of Readings" section that connects the topics covered in each reading with the concept outlined in the chapter.

Each chapter is organized in a similar way, opening with a hypothetical, but student-specific, illustration about how the concept circulates in their everyday lives. Using plenty of examples, each chapter develops an argument about differences and unfairness, exploring both the analytical potentials and limitations of the concept. Chapters then conclude with "The Concept at Work," which provides an extended example of its function in specific local, national, or transnational contexts. Our desire for these elaborated examples is to demonstrate that these concepts are big enough to frame any number of social issues and that they provide critical thinking tools for a wide range of topics in WGS and beyond. Finally, in order to emphasize the versatility of these concepts, we include a variety of "comments" in the margins that we call "Think about," "Know about," and "Talk about." These marginalia offer historical information, gloss key terms, ask students to think more in-depth about how to apply what they are learning to other contexts, and offer prompts that can be used for class discussions.

The idea of "fit," or the question of "Who fits where?," is central to all chapters. "Fit" is a handy heuristic at the introductory level, because it raises questions about belonging and inclusion—and their corollaries, not belonging and exclusion—in everyone's lived contexts. As such, this focus highlights the importance of identity categories (e.g., gender, race, class, sexuality, able-bodiedness, nationhood/citizenship, among others) and the ways in which they are constructed (as opposed to being the result of self-invention). Looking at the question of fit means that we are front-loading the roles of languages, social structures and institutions, and everyday practices in determining who fits where and rethinking what it even means to fit. For example, by whose definition do we or others fit somewhere, on what terms, and for what purposes? We realize that this could be a highly complex set of questions for introductory students. After all, they often ask, "Why isn't simply being included enough?" The aim of social justice, however—at least as we frame it in this book—is not simply the inclusion, visibility, or presence of otherwise excluded groups into existing social structures and practices. Instead, we point to instances where inclusion can also result in continued marginalization. In this way, our aim is to ask students to think about what we call the *terms of inclusion*, so as to constantly draw their attention to the idea that social structures and institutions are not neutral, but, instead, precisely that which need to be made visible, explored, questioned, challenged, and (often) changed. This shift turns the emphasis of social justice away from simply declaring inclusion to be the unquestioned goal. Instead, we ask students to both consider how exclusions occur (purposefully as well as inadvertently) and to explore how the very idea of inclusion might be something to be challenged and even resisted.

In addition, our explication of each of the six concepts is guided by what we call a "both/and" (as opposed to an "either/or") approach. We think that both/and approaches encourage students to see the multiple and contradictory ways in which identities are both structured by and yet also freed up to move within multiple discourses in our everyday worlds. While explicating the various ways in which identities are socially regulated, then, we also insist on people's abilities—albeit uneven and different—to challenge those regulatory regimes. The key, for us, is to identify this tension as productive and energizing, rather than depressing and immobilizing. In other words, recognizing one's social power doesn't mean overlooking one's own and others' simultaneous disempowerment, just as identifying moments of disempowerment doesn't just become a complete lack of agency. Rather than attempting to cast something only as "good" or "bad" for a particular group, we emphasize the multiplicity of potentially contradictory responses, again, always depending on questions like: For whom? Under what circumstances? To what ends? And with what consequences?

We believe that a recognition of the impossibility of being completely outside of power structures can be a transformative idea for students (and for all of us!), because the both/and assumption refuses to position them as simply resistant to or complicit with power relations. Instead, it recognizes that we are all in and of this world, accepting and perhaps benefitting—even as we are challenging and demanding change—from its structures, practices, and processes. And this recognition enables thoughtful action even as it demonstrates that our desires for change are an inevitably uneven and often fraught process. This both/and approach is especially highlighted in "The Concept at Work," where we raise questions of how we can engage with the world even while holding on to its contradictions and our own ambivalences about it.

Additionally, and importantly for students who are looking to this class for step-by-step instructions for solving the injustices they see around them, this recognition of a both/and approach leads us to complicate the often uneasy relationship between "how we think" and "how we act," or the relationship between knowledge and justice. How concepts help produce new knowledge about our worlds and what to do with new knowledge to bring about change in those worlds are clearly linked; yet, we argue, their connection is never linear nor easily mapped out, and certainly can never be prescribed in advance. In other words, we emphasize to students that activism never happens outside a set of powerful assumptions that frame our understandings of who we are in relation to others, assumptions that bear further investigation. We want them to think about how what we are acting for or against both draws on and is impacted by those relations, by what wrongs have been done to whom, by what kinds of justice we seek, and by how we might ethically and effectively bring about change. Each of these assumptions, of course, is potentially rife with contingencies and contradictions, even as we attempt to "do good" in the most obvious sense. As authors, then, we resist the idea that knowledge must be immediately instrumentalized into prescribed actions. Instead, we focus here on the necessity of thinking through the complexity of how we produce knowledge, how we can/should/might then act upon it, and on what the consequences of any action might be.

If knowledge is always multiple and situated, though, and there is no singular connection between our knowledges and our visions of or actions for social change, then related to that is the importance of recognizing that no dream of social change is ever applicable (or possible or desired) in every social location. We want to convey to students that social change is just as contextually specific as knowledge; senses of the possible are always framed by the time and place of one's circumstances and how we so differently occupy those locations. Again, this can be frustrating to students who look for simple solutions. But we contend that this attention to the difference that context makes is a necessary caveat to the social-change aspirations of this field. The advantage of emphasizing the contingent relationship of knowledge and action is that if instructors seek to make a specific connection for the benefit of their students' learning, then this book provides them with the critical thinking frameworks to ask about those contingencies and consequences.

If you have made it this far—and at least nodded at a few key points—then we hope this is your new introductory text. We realize it's a bit different: It leans a little more towards the humanities than most Women's and Gender Studies intro texts out there, it values critical perspectives over the discipline's more "sacred" objects, it seeks to instill intellectual habits more than it asks students to learn a single genealogy of the field's great thinkers, and it emphasizes complexity and ambivalence more than it seeks to prescribe conversion and "right" actions. We think this text-reader both offers students a set of concepts to unpack their everyday experiences and gives you, the instructor, a tool to convey your own passion for WGS to those students. Through our initial guiding observation that *People are different . . . and the world isn't fair,* which eventually gives way to the question *Now that we know . . . how shall we live?,* we hope that this text helps you to think otherwise about the possibilities for an introductory WGS course.

Introduction

People are different . . . and the world isn't fair.
Now that we know . . . how shall we live?

In so many ways, these are the guiding principles of the field of Women's and Gender Studies (WGS) and a number of other academic disciplines concerned with exploring social identities and social justice. It is these provocations—and the accompanying desire to make the world a fairer place for everyone—that mobilize the range of thinking, approaches, concepts, and practices in this field. Many of us locate ourselves here precisely because it is a place from which we can explore the differences between people and actively resist the all-too-common tendency to transform differences into exclusions. In WGS, we find a place to join with others in asking questions about identity categories such as gender, race, sexuality, class, ability, religious affiliation, and national identity: How are these categories variously defined? What do they mean in different contexts? What roles do they play in shaping our life choices and possibilities? How does what we know about the world change when perceived through different perspectives? What shall we do with the different knowledges we gain through this work? WGS is a place not only to ask questions but to work with others in attempting to rectify some of the unfairness we find as a result.

Like a number of disciplines in the university, WGS has recently engaged in numerous discussions about what its name means? Can it (or any name) adequately reflect all topics, ideas, and approaches that its practitioners undertake?

Originally called "Women's Studies" when it started over 40 years ago, the early work of the field was mostly compensatory; that is, it worked to include women in history, women in literature, women in, well, you-name-it. Noting that in so many of these areas of study, women (any women) were largely absent, people in Women's Studies tried to compensate for that by including them in courses, textbooks, and research projects. That early name, Women's Studies, has more recently been the subject of intense interrogation, as many of the discipline's practitioners believe that it doesn't reflect the contemporary breadth of what we do in this field. And as you'll have already noticed, we're calling this field "Women's and Gender Studies," or WGS, throughout this book, reflecting the most common name change in Canada and the United States. But WGS is not the only way programs have renamed themselves; other ways are variations on the words *women*, *gender*, and *sexuality*, for example, "Women's, Gender, and Sexuality Studies;" "Gender Studies;" "Gender and Sexuality Studies," as well as "Critical Identity Studies;" "Gender Equality and Social Justice;" "Gender, Race, and Culture;" and "Diversity and Social Justice Studies." How a program describes itself has a lot to do with the local needs and politics of its university or college; in this way it is different than History or Biology, but similar to other identity-based fields (e.g., "Ethnic Studies" or "Black Studies or Africana Studies").[1]

As WGS has expanded its range of concerns, it has also found more common cause with other academic disciplines working on related issues. What's important about the naming discussion for this book, though, is that it helps us talk about the variety of interests and research projects taken up by this field as it has broadened over that 40-year span. Topics discussed in your class could include: paid and unpaid work, religion, family structures, parenting practices, violence, settler colonialism, eating disorders, beauty culture, body modifications, reproductive justice, sexualities, war, sex work, girl culture, DIY (do-it-yourself) practices, media representations, and much more—along with how they are influenced by considering gender, race, sexuality, class, age, body size and shape, disability, national identity and immigration status, and religious affiliation. In WGS, as in this book, our shared aim is to develop critical approaches through which we can question, evaluate, understand, and change the world around us. WGS is a field that challenges us to always think in more complex

[1]**THINK ABOUT:** What is the program at your university or college called? What is the history of that name; has it undergone any changes, recently or historically? What were some of the debates around the name, and who was involved in those debates? Is the same also true for other programs, like the ones mentioned here? Do you have those kinds of programs? Why or why not? Obviously you probably don't know answers to all (or any) of these questions right now, but think about how you might go about finding out this information, and why it might be important to know.

ways about what we think we know about the world and to imagine what thinking about the world in other ways—or, "thinking otherwise"—could make possible. This is certainly not to suggest that everyone in WGS agrees on what to understand about that world, what to question, or how to change it—far from it! Indeed, the field is rife with debate over what a more just world would look like, for whom it would (and should) be more just, and how to bring that justice about. But one thing we are all passionate about—and we want you to be passionate about too—is the process of asking those questions, of looking for ways to know the world differently, and of working towards greater fairness, greater justice, for all of us.

Using This Book, or, Some Things to Pay Attention to as You Read

As you read this book and engage with the articles, websites, blog posts, and films that your instructor includes in the course materials, here are a few things to keep in mind.

1. You'll notice that we (authors) use the pronoun "we" (and "us") throughout this book. This use of "we" is a style of writing that recognizes that there is never a singular referent to that word; "we" doesn't (and couldn't) refer to any and all groups of people who may be readers, and certainly not everyone will recognize themselves in all of its uses. Instead, most of the time, the "we" references what seems to us like a common way of thinking about the world. We, the authors, want to leave open the possibility for you, the readers, to insert yourselves—or not—into any particular example used to illustrate a concept. And this is something that we hope you will pay attention to as you read: In what ways do the examples fit your experiences and understanding of the world? In what ways don't they fit? How do they lead you to think about how you are positioned in the world?[2] By not always specifying the "we," we authors hope to leave room for people to locate themselves directly ("That's me!"), to hang around the edges ("Not quite sure that's me"), or to refuse that "we" completely ("No way, they don't know who they are talking to!"). In short, we authors have tried to make the "we" a broad term that reflects a widespread position, but noticing when you do and don't feel included is instructional.

[2] **THINK ABOUT:** As you go through this class, and this book, keep track for yourself of the ways in which you become aware of your positionality in the world. How do your various identities open up ways for you to identify with the examples, readings, and class discussions you are having? What are ways in which your identities might lead you to have different perspectives? What are some points of class dissent and disagreement, and what are the places where it seems everyone is in agreement? Do you notice anything about those moments of disagreement or agreement, and can you draw any conclusions about them? This practice of taking a step back to think about how we come to know something is central to WGS. It emphasizes reflection and exploration of where and how knowledges of the world come about.

And of course, we also recognize that sometimes that "we" includes we authors, speaking to or reflecting our own positionalities too.

2. Most of our examples used to illustrate the concepts in this book are fairly ordinary and mundane. Focusing on the ordinary helps to illustrate how the kinds of conceptual knowledges we're introducing can be useful at every level of our lives. Our point in using what we call "the everyday" is to de-familiarize—to make strange—what otherwise goes unnoticed for many of us and to explore what's at stake in not noticing. And the everyday, of course, is never really the same for everyone. What goes completely unnoticed for some people is a defining episode or ongoing issue for others. Think, for instance, of how many times a day we are all faced with a set of steps to get into a building. For many of us, climbing those steps is so ordinary that we don't even think about it. Others of us notice over and over again the buildings with steps, because those steps impede us from entering or force us to find other ways to get in. Calling something "everyday" is a common way of distancing and even dismissing things in the world, of saying they are unimportant and not worthy of closer scrutiny. But in WGS, using the everyday is always a place to begin the work of recognizing how many ways there are to know the world and the potential consequences of acting on that knowledge.

3. As a field that covers so many topics, WGS has a huge, and ever-growing, intellectual heritage. This means that there are many scholars who have researched and written and contributed to our understanding of the concepts we present in this book. As authors, though, we have opted to not use their names or refer to their work directly in the main text, although we do provide curious readers with a list of some of the writers who have influenced our thinking about these concepts (see "Chapter Genealogies" at the end of the book, if you want to know more about them). In making this choice, we want to shift our readers' attention to the concepts themselves as opposed to inventorying who is known for what ideas. By not using citations or names in each chapter, our hope is that the focus stays with the idea of "thinking otherwise" that these concepts make possible. This is our way of inviting you into an ongoing conversation rather than imposing a kind of top-down, expert-driven thinking that positions WGS practitioners and professors as the ones with all the knowledge and WGS students as those without it. In a field where practitioners

take up everything from sex chromosomes to sex work, global flows to girl cultures, social movements to sitcoms, war to the wedding industry, the prison industrial complex to pornography, fat bodies to female masculinities . . . and so much more, there is plenty of knowledge already circulating in any WGS classroom. Keeping the focus on developing a conceptual knowledge base seems to us the best way to throw open the many possible topics to talk about in a class like this. And, of course, reading the articles following each chapter and exploring additional class materials will lead directly to many of the voices that are a part of the ongoing conversation in WGS. In the main part of this book, though, we want the "take-away" to be the usefulness of these concepts in making new sense of the everyday worlds we all inhabit.

In addition to the many examples we use throughout the book, each chapter ends with a short section entitled "The Concept at Work" that illustrates some of the ways that concept and the tensions around it were presented in the chapter. They're brief, and there is clearly much more to be said about the topics they cover. But they offer a quick case study of how elements of that concept can be brought to bear on a topic: how they can help unpack and begin to expose the many ways of thinking through that topic; what debates arise around that topic in doing so; and how that concept can aid in exploring that topic's range, from the local to the global. Not all "Concept at Work" sections take up every element of a concept, but they emphasize at least some of the ways that concept was explored in the chapter. As you read these sections, identify what ideas from the rest of the chapter are being mobilized. How do these extended examples use that concept in some way to further explore, question, and challenge a current issue?

4. Our focus throughout this book is on the complicated relationship between knowledge and social justice, between knowing the world and changing the world. As we will discuss in the "Knowledges" chapter, to say these are always intertwined is not to say that one leads to or from the other in any obvious way. Indeed, much of the debate in WGS revolves precisely around how to connect these two things. And there is plenty of disagreement! Thinking carefully about the connections (and, at times, disconnections) between knowledge and social change allows us to recognize that almost no social justice issue can ever be understood in "either/ or" terms, as either right or wrong, good or bad, about which everyone agrees.

Rather, the complexity inherent in such issues demands that we use what we're calling a "both/and" approach—that is, an approach that recognizes the partial perspectives we bring to any given situation, the complexity of our (and others') possible responses to it, and the need to negotiate our way through the inevitable uncertainty (and anxiety) of knowing that our best efforts might not "solve" the problem at hand. It is an approach that recognizes that we often hold contradictory views at the same time, and we often don't know how to (or whether we want to) resolve them. But it is also an approach that encourages us to think about how any well-meaning attempt at social change won't necessarily bring about the social justice we might want. Instead, as an approach, it demands that we articulate why, for whom, and under what circumstances some changes might be more justice-oriented than others, and it asks us what to do with that recognition.

Saying that knowledge and social change aren't inevitably connected highlights several major ideas in WGS, ideas you'll see woven throughout this book: (a) we all know the world differently; (b) our knowledges are at least partly influenced by our different social positions and identities; and (c) those differences often mean we don't agree on what constitutes an injustice nor on the appropriate or desired response to it. How to bring about social justice, then, or how to make the world more fair for more people, becomes a central question that is itself under investigation in WGS. We recognize that the connections between knowledge and social justice can never be simply mapped out and followed, but are also themselves the locus of intense deliberation and even acrimonious disagreement. This means that we must always be self-reflexive, challenging our own assumptions about where our ideas come from and how our personal investments in an issue are driving our responses to it.

5. Throughout the book, you'll find lots of focus on what we call "institutions," "structures," and "practices" in our exploration of the everyday. *Institutions* is a term that refers to formalized structures that organize social relations and govern individual behavior according to the dominant norms and values of a given community. Institutions include the family, education, medicine, media, religion, and the state. They are powerful because of their perceived "naturalness" in the world around us, and thus their invisibility in organizing a given social order. By

structures we mean the material and physical world around us: i.e., the architecture of buildings or the layout of a campus. Structures are important to point out, since they, too, usually seem "just the way things are," like, as mentioned previously, buildings that have steps. *Practices* is a term for talking about what people do, their activities and the ways those activities demonstrate how they fit (or not) into social structures and institutions. For instance, being a patient or a doctor, a student or a professor, reflects practices that shape our relationships to social institutions and structures, and, in turn, to each other. Our practices within those institutions and structures mean that we occupy our social worlds differently, with different levels of power and possibility. We'll return to many examples and more discussion of these terms.

One of the major reasons we use these terms throughout the book is because they force us to pay attention to how the world is constructed in ways that might seem natural, neutral, and even inevitable, but, upon closer examination, are revealed as products of social (although often unconscious) engineering of all kinds. Since we, as individuals, are always positioned diversely in the world, we need to also be aware of how much, and in what ways, that world shapes our sense of possibility. Take, for instance, an identity category that we all "have": gender. Just by looking around your classroom or your campus, you are aware of how many different ways there are to express gender: some variety of dominant or traditional femininity and masculinity for women and men, of course, but also masculine appearing women, feminine appearing men, transmen, transwomen, and genderqueer people. Individuals clearly have a lot of ways to think about and display their gender identities. And yet, when they move through the world, through a college campus for instance, that world is much more rigid about gender—insisting (usually) on only two gender categories, each very different from the other. In spite of the many differences between people, then, in our encounters with the institutions, structures, and practices of the world around us, we are all forced to choose which of the two rigid definitions of gender into which we fit.[3] That's why it's important to always focus on the social world around individuals, and not just individuals themselves. Otherwise, we miss how much the world not only reflects, but actually produces, the ideas we want to challenge.

[3] **THINK ABOUT:** Many universities and colleges have begun to reflect more expanded notions of gender, although in very uneven ways. What kind of gender options are available on your campus—on official paperwork, such as application forms or residence applications? What does the administration do with this information—that is, does it translate into changed structures, such as modifying residence arrangements? What about bathrooms on campus—how are they divided? Can you find other examples on campus where this idea of rigid gender options is still present or is being challenged and changed?

With these few preliminary ideas to keep in mind, we now invite you to explore the field of Women's and Gender Studies and what it has to offer. We, your authors, have obviously devoted a big chunk of our lives to this discipline. We've done so because we have found its concepts not just useful, but completely transformative to the ways in which we move through our own everyday lives. Obviously, we hope that WGS has the same potential for you! Whether this book is the only exposure you'll ever have to WGS or is just a first step in a long journey that makes it a big chunk of your life too, our aim is to demonstrate how these concepts help all of us "think otherwise" in productive and exciting ways about the very different worlds we inhabit.

Part One

Chapter One

Knowledges

Imagine the following: You're browsing the catalogs of a number of different universities and colleges as you try and decide which one to attend. You start noticing how varied the possible programs of study are: Women's and Gender Studies, African American Studies, Ethnic Studies, Indigenous and Aboriginal Studies, Sexuality and Queer Studies, Disability Studies. So many are new to you; you didn't have anything like this at your high school. You also notice Canadian Studies, American Studies, Peace and Conflict Studies, Human Rights Studies, Equity Studies, and Social Justice Studies. All of these are in addition to fields you do recognize: English, Math, History, Chemistry, and the like. And you wonder, what's so different about these new programs? Why do so many of them seem to be about "identity," and especially about identities that have been discriminated against in the past (and maybe even still today)? And even those that aren't as focused on identity still seem to focus on "rights" in some way.

You start thinking about why there are so many of these sorts of programs at the university level. Do these groups of people really need this kind of focused attention—since, after all, we live in a much more equal society now than, say, 40 or 50 years ago? And doesn't pointing out all these differences between people simply perpetuate feelings of resentment or guilt or prejudice or even hatred? Why bring it up? Who takes courses in these programs anyway? Are they just for people who identify with those groups, or can anyone take them? You wonder what exactly is being taught in these courses; how much could there be to say about any of these identities after all?

As you think about whether you would want to sign up for such a course, you realize that just debating with yourself about the existence of these courses is getting you to think about what is important to "know" at university or in your life beyond the university. These courses seem to suggest, just by way of their existence in the course catalogs, that there is something missing in those other courses that you've been taking in high school. Is knowledge of the world different if you look at it through different eyes, from different perspectives, at different times? And does knowledge itself change if it aims to promote something like social justice or human rights? All these questions! Now you want to find some answers. So you decide to give one of these courses a try.

Situating Women's and Gender Studies

As an academic discipline, Women's and Gender Studies (WGS) seeks to destabilize our everyday habits of thought and provide alternative visions about the ways we make meaning of, and subsequently shape, our worlds. It focuses mostly on exploring identity-based differences among people and examines the range of institutions, structures, and practices—both historical and contemporary—that perpetuate injustices toward individuals and/or identity groups. And WGS demands that we reflect on how we are differently positioned—sometimes in awkward and contradictory ways—with regard to privileges we possess as well as discriminations we experience. As such, WGS takes up questions that go beyond women and gender to consider race, sexuality, disability, social class, age, national origins, and more, all at the same time. Basically, WGS is an academic field that strives to create knowledge that reimagines human relations and seeks to bring about the ethical transformation of those relations in ways that both recognize and benefit broader numbers of people. As with any other academic discipline you encounter, then, WGS has an agenda. But, unlike many disciplines, it is more transparent and self-reflexive about what that agenda is.

As you may have noticed, WGS is offered in most colleges and universities, but hardly at all at the primary and secondary levels. There are many reasons for this, not the least of which is how we as a society tend to think about where and when knowledge transmission—as opposed to critical thinking about that knowledge—happens in our educational systems, and what we think is important to know at different stages of life and educational development. And, like all disciplines, WGS is slightly different in its various college and university locations. All academic knowledge projects reflect their specific geographical, historical, and cultural locations; they are, in other words, situated in local, as well as national and international, contexts that reflect certain ways of seeing the world[1]. So while it might seem obvious to say

[1]**THINK ABOUT:** Where is your university or college located? Are there courses or programs that seem specific to that location—about your particular province or state or region, for instance? What about programs that speak to particular issues or concerns—like *international development or entrepreneurship*? What are some of the newer programs and what are the ones that have been around for a long time? What seems to be missing altogether? This is a chance to take a look around your institution and see how it thinks about knowledge, what it identifies as important options for students and what it doesn't, and to ask yourself if you have any concerns about these options.

that what you are exposed to in this course as a way of introducing WGS is different from what someone else at another institution is exposed to for the same purpose, this difference is worth considering as a more general principle about knowledge itself. That is, thinking about knowledge as having a specific context in which it is produced and transmitted allows us to ask critical questions about how and why some things become important to know whereas other things are treated as all but unnecessary to consider.

These kinds of critical questions about knowledge are central to WGS. Thus, accounting for the specificity of knowledge contexts is also central to the task of this book and to how each of its major concepts is explored. A universal approach to knowledge would consider any bit of knowledge to be a "truth" no matter where it is located or who is making a knowledge claim. But if you are someone who moves between two or more locations, cultures, or perhaps even disciplines, you've probably learned that "the truth"—about what is most important, about the way the world works, about what success looks like, about who we are and why we're here—is anything but the same in all the situations you move through. Also, you've probably realized that people rarely agree on what constitutes any "truth," and that's especially the case when it comes to issues of identity. If disciplines like WGS are interested in producing knowledge that addresses people's lives, then it makes sense that they would seek to be contextually specific, both arising out of and reflecting the particularities of those places in which people find themselves. This book emphasizes the importance of this context and this specificity.

Knowledge and Invisibility

One of the ways to see this idea that all knowledge is situated—in other words, that it is reflective of the specific historical and contemporary contexts in which it was produced—is to consider how a discipline like WGS emerged as an academic field more than 40 years ago. The late 1960s was a time when a number of identity-based disciplines—Black Studies, Native Studies, Chicano or Latino Studies (especially in the United States)—were launched, in the wake of social movements to resist long-standing inequities and make visible both the presence and contributions of marginalized groups of peoples. Following this idea of identity-based resistance, the obvious case to be made for "Women's Studies" (the most common name for this field, up until recently) was the need to talk about women, to offset their absence throughout academia and just about every other facet of society. Within institutions of higher education, women, as an identity group, were barely present as professors, researchers, scientists, medical doctors, legal scholars, psychiatrists, religious authorities, critics, writers—in other words, as knowledge producers—let alone acknowledged as interesting objects of study in almost any field. Indeed, the major critique that became the impetus for this field's development was that the curricula across academia seemed to focus either exclusively on men, or, more troublingly, assumed men as the standard for every statement about humanity in general. And so, the early concern with the absence of women was (and still is in some contexts) a concern with both who is doing the studying and who is being studied. Thus, the call from early developers of this new knowledge project was to "add women" into existing fields, both as knowers and as that about which something more should be known. What quickly became apparent, though, especially to those women who didn't see their own identities and experiences reflected in this new project, was that any move to privilege one identity category—in this case, gender—regarding who and what should be known invariably created tensions around other identity categories: for example, race or class or sexuality. In other words, questions quickly arose (and continue to arise) around which women are being added in—which women become the knowers and the known, which women are made visible and stand-in for those who were previously absented, and which women still remain unseen or barely mentioned[2]?

This question of visibility and invisibility is central to how WGS thinks about the systems of knowledge it both critiques and produces. Indeed, much work in WGS continues to concern itself with identifying the many ways in which certain invisible, taken-for-granted ideas exist around us and then challenging those ideas for how they perpetuate a range of social inequities. Think, for instance, about how easily something as ordinary as our language reveals assumptions about a number of activities or occupations. Terms such as *nurse* and *male nurse* or *doctor* and *female doctor* suggest that these professions (along with their discrepancies in authority, pay, and status) are more naturally the purview of one gender and must thus be identified as different—by

[2]**KNOW ABOUT:** "Add women and stir" is a phrase that represents an implicit critique of the notion that social change happens by adding a few token members of an identity group without investigating and addressing the reasons for their initial exclusion. While the "diversity" achieved through adding different bodies to any given institution or organization is an important step, it rarely changes what we will talk about here and in subsequent chapters as the "terms of inclusion."

(3)**TALK ABOUT:**
Generate a list of other
common terms and
phrases where you see
this idea of invisible
adjectives at work. Don't
limit the discussion only
to gender as an invisible
adjective; think also of
sexuality (i.e., *marriage*
and *same-sex marriage*),
race, disability, and any
other identifier. How does
spotting these invisible
adjectives help you think
more about what gets
taken for granted as a
norm, and what gets
highlighted as different
than that norm? Here's
another example: *food*
and *organic food*.

making their descriptive adjective visible—when another gender occupies them(3). Of course, these designations of difference are partly historical; female nurses and male doctors were for a long time characteristic of the strict gender divides in the medical professions. But the persistence of these *invisible adjectives*, even today, reveals something about commonly held expectations about gender and about who seems to be more suited to particular kinds of work. Even more important, these early practices of identifying invisible adjectives also raised questions about whether these occupations remained the same when their gendered associations shifted. In other words, did those professions—what they involve, how they are conceived, the social value they are accorded—change when gendered barriers were crossed? What else might have been altered in what was assumed to be the work of "nursing" or "doctoring" when men and women (respectively) entered those professions? Asking questions about visible and invisible assumptions (by identifying some of those invisible adjectives, for instance) quickly led to exploring how knowledge itself can change when the knowers change, because new knowers bring different perspectives, different histories, and different investments to the same situation.

To explore the consequences of this practice in the historical context of our own location (the university or college), let's consider a course called "Canadian History" or "U.S. History," a course that is commonly offered (and in many places is required), and compare it to a course on "African Canadian History" or "African American History" (typically not required, and perhaps not even offered). What is the difference between these courses? What does the descriptor in front of these courses suggest to us about what is invisible in the first title that is made explicit in the second? What quickly becomes clear is that the "Canadian" or "U.S." history courses were always (and again, perhaps still are in some cases) preceded by any number of invisible adjectives—around race certainly, but probably also around gender, class, sexuality, and religion too—that just weren't named. What identifying invisible adjectives does is make apparent that those more commonly offered history courses have tended to assume whiteness as their primary subject—that is, the adjective "white" was always there in front of those other history courses, but almost always remained unspoken as the default assumption about the content of the course. Typically, such courses are not consciously about whiteness as a racial marker; rather, whiteness is not mentioned so much as simply assumed as the default for who is important to know about from the past.

Furthermore, we can see how deeply embedded a universalizing approach to knowledge is when we consider that, for the most part, these courses largely focused on institutions such as governments, wars, business, trade, and maybe education and medicine. That these courses were implicitly talking about whiteness (as well as maleness) becomes evident, since activities in these contexts were almost always conducted by those with (white) race and (masculine) gender privilege. Thus, it was whiteness and masculinity—or what white men were doing—that became the norm for what counted as historically relevant, and, therefore, what was worthy of exploring in a college course on U.S. or Canadian history. And even this observation could be—and was—further complicated by persistently accounting for invisible adjectives of even more identity categories. For instance, it wasn't just white men as a whole who were the default subjects of these histories, but a particular group of white men, who also embodied other dominant identities based on class, region, sexuality, citizenship status, religion, and ability. Noting these invisible adjectives renders categories of historical actors even more narrow and provokes still more questions: Where are the old men and the young boys, men of lower classes, gay or asexual men, men with disabilities (and any combination of these categories), who are also historical subjects from which we can learn something about our collective pasts?

What becomes apparent in this exercise of uncovering invisible adjectives is that attempts to make any group of previously invisible people visible involve more than just inserting marginalized groups into the universalizing histories of the past. And this realization has led us to think about knowledge differently, about what has counted as knowledge and where and how knowledge could be gleaned. So, for example, if the activities of marginalized groups—women, men of color, people with disabilities, children—were all but nonexistent in the histories of governments, wars, business, trade, education, and medicine, then researchers had to look elsewhere, to other kinds of activities, in other locations, to find these identity categories and their lived experiences. And looking elsewhere meant that completely new kinds of histories could come into view: histories of family and kinship structures, child care practices, food cultivation and preparation, consumer practices, the production of useable craft, housing design and use, adornment practices and cultures, and so much more. History, and historical thinking, became more expansive and more complex when both the subjects (the knowers) and objects (the known) of the past were no longer only a small minority of people and new knowledges could be generated by looking at other sites for other kinds of histories. And these new methods of seeking expansion and complexity by questioning invisible adjectives has become the goal of so much of the work in WGS and other identity-based fields.

Recognizing invisible adjectives, then, is central to the ways in which WGS produces and questions knowledge. WGS aims to make clear that knowledge, rather than merely reflecting some singular and universal truth, always reflects particular points of view, partial perspectives, and very specific ways of being in the world. As a result, becoming aware of what (and who) has been invisible means also becoming concerned with what (and who) is seen as neutral, universal, and dominant, and, by default, what (and who) is considered biased and partisan, and thus also is negated. By situating knowledge in the world, we can both destabilize its likelihood of being taken-for-granted and use those new insights to understand, talk about, and potentially act in the world differently.

The Power of Labeling

While identifying invisible adjectives is an important way to think about how our perspectives on the world are shaped, it also calls attention to the power dynamics that underlie this process. Universalizing the history and experience of a particular group—and thereby making the histories and experiences of everyone else all but invisible—produces what we call *normative* assumptions. As the term implies, the power of the normative is that it determines who fits in and who, by consequence, is rendered out of place. The normative, or normativity, becomes evident when we encounter any kind of social system—for example, an educational system, a popular media representation, a state-sponsored program, a religious institution—that doesn't account for our particular histories or experiences, and into which we do not fit. At that point, our sense of who we are, what we can contribute, the expectations made of us, and indeed our very life possibilities are positioned at the other end of a normative judgement produced by and reflected in that system, over which we might have very little control. It is in this way that some people fit or occupy "the norm," and others don't.

Think, for instance, of what seems to be a completely mundane example: using the terms "flesh-toned" or "nude" to describe the color of Band-Aids, pantyhose, crayons, or other consumer products. Clearly, these words only refer to particular colors of skin. They demonstrate at the level of our everyday language that some people seem to be naturally excluded from what is normal; they have skin colors that aren't those reflected in this phrasing and are thus deemed *other*. And while not having your skin color recognized in crayons or Band-Aids may seem trivial, being labeled based on the color of one's flesh has a long, ugly, and often violent history. What something is called (or how it is labeled) can thus be a form of *epistemic violence* (epistemic, from *episteme,* means relating to knowledge); it suggests that knowledge and the means we use to convey it are anything but benign. Rather, they can be—and often are—acts of discrimination and violence, reflecting (and resulting in) differences in social and political power.

One way to see the power of language to label and "other" is to consider a number of derogatory terms used to talk about different identities within U.S. and Canadian histories; as examples of epistemic violence, these are terms that have denigrated and insulted and thus also reinforced the idea that some people just don't—and should never—fit or belong. Words used to reference marginalized gender or sexuality or able-bodied or racial or national origin or citizenship status—*bitch, slut, queer, faggot, retard, psycho, lame, squaw, nigger, illegals*—are a few we know; you probably know others. These are words that, for many of us, are unbearable to hear or to use. That they invoke discomfort and anxiety—certainly for us doing the writing and probably for you doing the reading—says much about the violent power of such derogatory labels. In their very utterance, the very act of speaking them, they remind us—perhaps abstractly, perhaps quite intimately—of long histories and ongoing practices of exclusion and injury, no matter who is using them or in what context they are mobilized[4]. Of course there are other words that are sometimes used to insult someone's status: *cracker* and *breeder*, for instance, are also derogatory terms sometimes used about

[4]**THINK ABOUT:** That discomfort extends to us as authors, and our use of these words even in this context where our aim is to expose and challenge their workings. Because even if we believe that it is context that gives words meaning, we authors had long discussions about the risks of using these words to make even this point—wondering and worrying about their effects on different audiences in their own different contexts of reading and understanding. That we could not think of these words only intellectually or academically says a lot about their power, and the traces of those other uses they always carry with them, no matter how they might be alternately used. What kinds of responses did you have in reading these terms in a textbook? Are these responses shared by everyone in the class? Why or why not? (We'll talk more about the idea of "reclaiming" these terms below.)

(5)**KNOW ABOUT:**
Slutwalks first started
in Canada in 2011
in response to a
presentation at York
University (in Toronto)
at which a campus
police officer stated
that women could avoid
sexual assault if they just
didn't "dress like sluts."
Slutwalks are street
protests in which women
dress in a variety of ways
(short skirts, topless,
housecoats and slippers)
to draw attention to the
fact that how women
dress does not make
them responsible for
assault. Slutwalks are
now international, with
marches happening in
numerous countries
on every continent.
However, reclaiming the
word *slut* is not without
its critics, as many
groups of women point
out that since the word
has been differently
mobilized against them,
its reclamation cannot be
the same for all women
either.

people in dominant groups. But these words don't carry the same power and are much less likely to have the same kind of painful effects. They may be insults. But their power to other an entire group of people and, importantly, to have that othering reflected in histories, current social structures, and everyday practices—that is, to make that othering have consequences in people's everyday lives—is much less significant.

A powerful example to explore this complexity of labels is the word *slut*, a term that (re)gained a lot of attention in 2011 as "Slutwalks" occurred first in Canada and then internationally(5). And certainly, much social media over the past few years has talked about "slut-shaming." *Slut*, to most people, is easily recognized as an insult, a demeaning word used to put down women or girls, especially as it concerns their performances of gender and (hetero)sexuality. It often has little to do with how any specific woman or girl actually behaves, and speaks more to her status as an outsider, as non-normative because of class, race, or gender expression. And *slut* is more than just a word; throughout pop culture, in familial and peer contexts, in educational and medical structures, we constantly see a range of normative understandings about how women should look and behave. The word's power thus derives both from how it reflects expectations about appropriate (and thus also, inappropriate) gender and (hetero)sexuality and from the way those expectations are built into broader social narratives about what is appropriately feminine. *Slut*, then, isn't so much descriptive of any individual woman's behavior as it is a term that can be used to exclude by drawing attention to those normative assumptions(6); thus, it can't be easily countered by denying it or pointing out its descriptive flaws ("I'm not a slut!" is rarely an effective comeback for slut-shaming). And therein lies the power of this word; by accusing a woman of not fitting in with what is considered normative gender and sexuality, its aim and effect is to shame and other. The very utterance of this term, its very speaking, labels and excludes some women and girls through mobilizing all those norms of feminine behavior that are so ubiquitously reflected in the world around us(7).

Labels, then, are important to think about not just because our language about identity groups should be nicer or more "politically correct"; they are important because they illustrate how much normative assumptions are part of social institutions and everyday practices, in addition to our ordinary language. Wrapped up in these labels are the judgements about people's lives that are both built into and reflect a broad and discriminatory social order that has often been centuries in the making; they demonstrate that our pasts—and all their pain, injustice, and violence—are still very much with us in the present. Thus, actively denying or simply forgetting such histories, or calling for people to stop focusing on the past and move on—"just get over it!"—becomes yet another act of epistemic violence, another way in which normative judgements operate to obscure their power to label and other.

Given how we have been discussing knowledge, power, and language so far, it becomes clear that a term like *slut* is more than just a word; it is also a *discourse*, a concept which captures this recognition that labels are always more than simply talk. Instead, the term *discourse* is a way to signal that language or talk always references a range of other social structures, institutions, and practices that function to influence how we think and behave in our everyday lives. *Discourse* refers to what it is possible to say or do in any given context, at any given moment, or in any given circumstance; discourses frame our understanding of something and our experiences of it. For example, in the 1970s, feminist legal theorists introduced the term *sexual harassment* to describe what until then had been all-too-common behaviors in many kinds of workplaces (from factories to offices)—the experience for many women of being insulted, intimidated, and even groped (or worse) by male bosses and coworkers. Before the term *sexual harassment* was invented to describe these behaviors, they were more usually understood (if they were talked about at all) as simply part of what was to be expected in the workplace, part of what happened to women in that workplace, and part of the rationale for the idea that women didn't belong in that workplace anyway. (The past tense here is not to suggest that these behaviors have disappeared, nor that harassment and workplace bullying doesn't continue, around a range of identity categories—unfortunately!) The coining of the term *sexual harassment* led to a new way to understand and speak about those experiences. Insults and groping went from being business as usual to being named and understood as a form of gendered discrimination, something that could be legislated against. Thus, the term *sexual harassment* changed how people thought about these behaviors, how people experienced these behaviors, and how people responded to these behaviors[8].

[6]**KNOW ABOUT:** The term *performativity* refers to how language can actually do things like produce, regulate, and constrain certain identities. If you think about the power of a judge to declare a person guilty or a bully to use name calling to shame someone for how they look, act, or speak, then you have witnessed the performative power of language. What words have the power to make you feel special or to shame you? Does it matter who mobilizes (utters) these terms? How does that reflect issues of power in your relationship with the speaker?

[7]**TALK ABOUT:** What are some of the ways in which you see these normative ideas about gender and sexuality reflected in and perpetuated by the world around you? In many media representations, sure, but are there other sites where ideas of appropriate femininity are mobilized and sustained? What about

other identity categories, such as masculinity? Heterosexuality and homosexuality? Immigrant status? Think about education and medicine and religion and family, for example. How do all of these help make the point that perpetuating certain ways of being and acting in the world—certain norms—is about more than only how we talk about something?

(8)**THINK ABOUT:** Another good example to understand how discourse frames our knowledge and experience is that of hoarding—an example depicted in many current TV shows. As a term, *hoarding* connotes a particular way of thinking about people's behaviors: i.e., as a mental or psychological illness, as well as, often, a dangerous public health issue. Before the term hoarding was created, people probably spoke more in terms of clutter or messiness, and distinguished those from collecting (a more

In addition, the term *discourse* signals that these same labels that perpetuate normative understandings and actions can also be their sites of resistance and rejection. For example, when we say "the discourse" of something, such as "the discourse of femininity," the term references the normative language usually used to talk about women and girls as well the social institutions (like education or the family), the systems of representation (in art or women's magazines), and of course the everyday practices (such as adornment and leisure activities) that perpetuate common knowledges about what women and girls are or should be. However, lurking in the discourse of femininity are a number of labels that offer alternatives to those normative meanings. Much like the term *slut*, other terms—*diva, dominatrix, femme fatale, Jezebel, la vendida, butch,* and many other complications of femininity through race, nation, or sexuality—both refer to that which is not fully captured by normative femininity while simultaneously attempting to regulate it through insults and othering. When we speak of the discourse of femininity, then, we are also implicitly acknowledging a range of non-normative feminine identities that resist or confound the normative one. In this sense, discourses are resources of multiple and contradictory knowledges—some dominant and authoritative, some secondary or subversive, some just barely emerging, some all but forgotten—that also shape what can be thought or said or acted out as femininity. Recognizing a discourse, then, enables us to point to the ways in which the knowledge produced about something (or someone) is multiple and contradictory, always a both/and (as opposed to either/or) enterprise, and never fully contained by one meaning.

Finally, this idea of discourse is important to consider when people "reclaim" words, referring to themselves—consciously and confidently—with the very terms used to stigmatize and other them. Think of women who call their girlfriends "bitch," or of self-proclaimed "queers," or of "crip studies" in academia, or of the growing "mad pride" movements across the U.S. and Canada. These reclamations are about challenging systems of knowledge in that they attempt to shift the dominant meanings that accumulate around such terms. Using words like *bitch* or *slut* or *fag* or *nigga* to talk about oneself and others within the confines of one's own social group is a means to remove (or at least rework) the stigma, change the social relations, and shift the dominant meanings that give those words such power[9]. Remember the old adage, "sticks and stones may break my bones but words will never hurt me," an attempt to alleviate the sting of childhood insults? What we see in attempts to reclaim words—whether in daily use, comedy skits, hip-hop music, online memes, or through academic disciplines like "queer studies" or social movements such as Slutwalk—is that words do, in fact, matter. They hurt and they oppress precisely because their power is much more than just talk, both in how they evoke and potentially re-code meanings of who we are. They may not lose all their power when we reclaim them. But sometimes and in some contexts, reclaiming words implicitly demands some accountability for, and attempts to, offset the painful pasts out of which they emerged.

Social Change, Social Justice, Social Movements

In Women's and Gender Studies, one of the basic assumptions about producing new knowledge is that knowing the world differently will make the world different—more fair, more accessible, more just—for more people. In other words, alternative ways of knowing the world open up space for multiplying meanings in that world, for recognizing different ways of understanding the worlds we all occupy, and, most importantly, for then acting differently in those worlds. WGS, along with many other identity-based disciplines (such as African American or Black Studies, Ethnic Studies, Indigenous and Aboriginal and Native Studies, Sexuality and Queer Studies), entered the university over the course of the past 40 or so years as groups of people sought to use academically sanctioned forms of knowledge as the basis for social change. The discrimination and oppression experienced by these groups meant that they insisted on centering those identity-based perspectives in what they, and subsequently everyone else, should know about the world. Discussions about invisible adjectives that pointed to assumptions about gender, race, sexuality, dis/ability, indigeneity, nation; about labeling and fit; about how certain ideas become normative; and about resistance, shifting discourses, and reclaiming terms were all mobilized to analyze how a range of social institutions (including academia itself) have been sites of marginalization, exclusion, and othering. In this way, these disciplines have always sought to make the experiences of these groups intelligible in academic terms, as well as to transform the social conditions that created their marginal status in the

respected activity). Even if people also emphasized the need to organize and clean up the mess and clutter, there was no category called hoarder whereby a person was understood as sick, or a behavior was pathologized–understandings that both also invoke the idea of needing a "cure." Think about how the expression hoarding shapes us all, no matter what our behaviors; we frame ourselves in relationship to this category whether to identify with or against it. And that makes a difference to how we now think about clutter and collections of all kinds. And yet, this category probably also provides relief for some people, who now have a medicalized explanation for someone's (their own or other people's) behaviors. Can you think of other labels or categories that do the same kind of work as hoarding; what are the contradictions around those labels?

(9)**TALK ABOUT:** What do you think about this idea of "reclaiming"? What are terms you think have been easily reclaimed, or around which there is still much debate, or which can't be reclaimed at all? Who is authorized to reclaim terms and in what contexts? Can words really be "reclaimed" from their other historical usages? Why or why not? Note the differences (which there will probably be!) in the class around all of these questions. What do you make of these different responses?

first place. Clearly, then, the hope was—and still is—that multiplying our knowledges of the world will lead to alternative ways of organizing the worlds around us, and, thereby, lead to a more fair world for more people.

Academia, though, is just one of many possible locations of social change. The desire not just to know the world differently, but to change it has meant that these newer disciplines have emphasized the importance of various kinds of social activism outside of academia. The word *activism* usually signals the idea of direct involvement in bringing about social change. Its dominant representation evokes images of masses of people disrupting, challenging, and protesting in public spaces to win some concession from a powerful institution like the state or a corporation. But this is certainly not all activism can be. Writing letters and blogs, signing petitions, working (sometimes in highly tedious and bureaucratic ways) to change social policies and regulations in law or education, creating alternative images or stories about the world, constructing spaces hospitable to previously marginalized identities or taboo experiences, advocating for different treatment protocols for people in medical systems, providing food and other support for people doing this kind of work—these are examples of actions that change the world around us. Indeed, the belief in the importance of taking our new, altered, revised, multiple, sometimes contradictory, and previously invisible knowledges and using them to bring about social change for disenfranchised groups is so central to WGS that it is hard to imagine how it wouldn't focus on how our knowledges are connected (or should be connected) to changing the social contexts around us.

And yet, the focus on activism raises many of the questions about those invisible adjectives we discussed earlier. Activism for whom? Under what circumstances? With what goals or desired consequences? How are answers to these questions decided and by whom? And what about the complicated question of who can legitimately be involved in struggles? Does one have to be recognized as a member of a group in order to be involved in activist struggles undertaken by or for that group? And if one isn't, what are the effects of one's involvement on other activists, on strategies undertaken, and on perceptions from outside the group? For instance, if someone doesn't identify as a person with a disability, does their activism reflect an assumption that people with disabilities cannot (or even should not) advocate on their own behalf?

Does it perpetuate the power imbalance that is supposedly being challenged by suggesting that able-bodied people are needed in this struggle? Is the desire to "help" yet one more way of expressing the privilege that comes with being (if only temporarily) able-bodied? If our activism is from a position of embodying able-bodied privilege (even as we might also want to resist that privilege), what other questions are raised about the effects of activism? These kinds of questions about the *terms of inclusion* have generated numerous and sometimes even acrimonious debates over how shared desires to bring about social change can sometimes unintentionally express, and thereby make worse, unequal power relations.

In addition to the question of who can or should do what kind of activism is the equally thorny question of what counts as activism in the first place and of where it can and should happen? For example, if normative gender perpetuates the idea that men don't wear make-up, nail polish, and skirts in their everyday lives, then would these actions constitute activism, a challenge to gender norms that could also change them? And how would we know when the norms had been altered enough to count as effective social change? Determining what activism is raises questions about whether the way we live our individual lives is (or should be) activist, or whether activism only counts when occurring in a public context with other people. Think, as another example, about "fat activism." Fat activists work for changes to norms of body size and shape, to challenge dominant assumptions about health and healthy bodies, to alter social structures that don't easily accommodate bodies of many sizes, and to eliminate shame and stigma so often associated with fat bodies. For some people, resisting normative ideas about body size is manifested in how we dress and act: for instance, a large woman dressing in tight, revealing clothes or displaying sexual desires in ways that are presumed not to be appropriate (or normative) for fat bodies. These actions certainly resist the dominant discourse of shame around fat bodies, refusing stigma and instead insisting on their right to visibility and desire. Do these everyday actions constitute activism around fatness and body size? Who gets to decide that? And what happens when there are different ideas about the effectiveness of acts like these, even within the fat-activist community? In themselves, these kinds of actions do not obviously work to single-handedly eliminate fat oppression. But their presence can, and certainly does, alter perceptions of fat bodies. They are individual acts, and they may

(10) **TALK ABOUT:** This issue of what individuals do, and the effects of those actions, is explored again in more detail in "Bodies." But for now, can you think of other examples of individual actions that are presumed to have some larger social change consequences? For instance, through what we buy or consume or watch or listen to or go to? What are some of the debates—similar to the questions posed here—that come up among your classmates about these examples?

challenge norms about bodies over time(10). But is that enough—and for whom is it enough (or not enough)?

Clearly, knowledge and social change are intertwined. But their connection is never obvious and simply knowing something differently does not lead to a particular set of actions. Closer investigation of the ordinary and the everyday as important does not mean that a focus on "the big picture" isn't also important. It is! But a focus on the ordinary or everyday also reveals how much we live in many different worlds that don't all add up together to one overarching system of knowledge. Instead, it allows us to see contradiction and ambivalence as productive in that we're all unevenly invested in the knowledges within which we are situated and in the actions we undertake from those different positions. Learning to think with and work through complexities is always a process of negotiation with ourselves and with those around us. And we don't necessarily have to resolve those contradictions. Instead, the aim of WGS is to identify and bring to light those multiple perspectives and explore what and how they enable us to think and do otherwise in our everyday lives.

The Concept at Work: Love and Labor

Think about your knowledge of romance. What makes for a romantic encounter? Where was this knowledge produced, and what kinds of power relations are implicit in its production? How is romance tied into products for purchase: getting together for coffee, giving and receiving flowers or chocolate, even resulting (so the hope often is) in diamonds and weddings, artifacts that we recognize as part of the shared social rituals of love and commitment? But if we take a closer look at coffee, chocolate, flowers, and diamonds, we can ask questions that reveal how various groups of people are positioned quite differently in the production, circulation, and consumption of these artifacts. Asking questions about the everyday objects that populate our ordinary lives denaturalizes our knowledge of them and makes what is common instead very strange.

Think about coffee: Where does it comes from, who grows and harvests it and in what parts of the world, and how does it get to us? What roles do gender, nation, and age play in both its production "over there" and its consumption "over here"?

Why is coffee drinking so common as a social practice of getting together with other people (often in spite of its high cost and negligible nutritional content)? And why is there such investment on the part of coffee consumers to choose buying and drinking spaces that reflect our personal identities or senses of self (e.g., through music, decor, technology, ambiance, other patrons)? Think about the differences between Starbucks versus Dunkin' Donuts (or Tim Horton's in many parts of Canada and the eastern U.S.) versus small, independent cafes. Asking and exploring such questions can produce new knowledge about labor conditions in the global south where most coffee is produced, about the important gendered politics that inhere in local control over agricultural practices, and about how global flows of goods produce very different kinds of racialized identities in the production and consumption sides of the coffee trade. In short, our questions and the new knowledges they may produce can lead us to think about coffee and its everydayness quite differently than we did before.

Likewise, asking similar sorts of questions about diamond rings will lead us very quickly to histories of colonialism in much of Africa, to working conditions and social life for miners and their families (including in the Canadian north today where so-called "ethical diamonds" are produced), to century-long advertising campaigns by companies like DeBeers that seek to equate love, desire, and diamonds with marriage in popular culture. Or perhaps we might think of both grassroots and international campaigns against "blood diamonds" which have fuelled civil wars in various parts of the world. And raising the same questions about fresh-cut flowers as an expression of love can offer salient lessons in occupational safety (especially pesticide exposure), workers' rights (or lack thereof) to organize around their working conditions, child labor, and corporate influence in national politics. What these examples all point to is that our everyday familiar practices around cultural norms of love and relationships "here" are also deeply implicated in perpetuating all sorts of unintentional inequities "there"—and recognizing the depth of these intersections makes the familiar immediately strange and more complex.

These questions, and the new knowledge they produce, don't necessarily mean that we must stop drinking coffee, wearing diamonds, or buying flowers. For one thing, such actions would not necessarily mitigate the conditions of their production and consumption, nor remove our complicity in systems of domination. And alternatives such as drinking soda, wearing pearls, and buying plastic flowers have plenty of consequences, too! Determining the best course of action to address the inequities embedded in artifacts of romance is not necessarily clear. But having knowledge—current data, historical awareness, conceptual understandings—about our romantic attachments can have any number of effects. We might do nothing beyond reflecting on the fact that the everyday objects that populate our lives have a complexity that too often escapes most of us. Or, we might be more ambivalent about and even resist drinking any coffee that isn't organic or "fair trade." We might rethink our attraction to diamonds or our attachment to marriage. Or we might join with others to work to change trade policies around the importation and sale of flowers. There is no one necessary outcome that new knowledges leads to. But we do know this: social justice is all but impossible to aim for or achieve without asking these kinds of questions about our world and listening carefully to the knowledges that such questions produce. Knowing this complexity might lead us to think quite differently about the question "How shall we live?"

Preview of Readings

wallace, j. 2010. "The Manly Art of Pregnancy." In *Gender Outlaws: The Next Generation*, edited by Kate Bornstein and S. Bear Bergman, 188–194. Berkeley, CA: Seal Press.

Bailey, Moya. 2011. "'The Illest': Disability as Metaphor in Hip Hop Music." In *Blackness and Disability*, edited by Christopher Bell, 140–148. East Lansing, MI: University of Michigan Press.

Ingraham, Chrys. 2011. "One Is Not Born a Bride: How Weddings Regulate Heterosexuality." In *Introducing the New Sexuality Studies* (2nd ed.), edited by Steven Seidman, Nancy Fischer, and Chet Meeks, 303–307. New York, NY: Routledge.

Abu-Lughod, Lila. 2006. "The Muslim Woman: The Power of Images and the Danger of Pity." *Eurozine*. www.eurozine.com/articles/2006-09-01-abulughod-en.html

Pershai, Alexander. 2006. "The Language Puzzle: Is Inclusive Language a Solution?" In *Trans/forming Feminisms: Trans/Feminist Voices Speak Out*, edited by Krista Scott-Dixon, 46–52. Toronto, ON: Sumach Press.

In "Knowledges," we talk about the discipline of Women's and Gender Studies as a knowledge project that emerges out of historical, cultural, and social situations of exclusion. Instead of thinking of knowledge as "truth," we ask readers to think about knowledge production, that is, how some people and ideas become more visible—and thus more relevant and authoritative—than others. What is more visible tends to be regarded as normative and determines how people fit (or not) in various histories and institutional settings. This fit, or lack of it, has tremendous consequences for how people live—and can live—their lives. We then explore the ideas of language and othering, and introduce the term *discourse* to refer to the ways in which some ideas become common sense and others are rendered all but unthinkable. In this way, the names or labels we use to identify ourselves and others become ways to map various relationships of power, both oppressive and resistant. The chapter ends with a discussion of the complexities of the relationship of knowledges to efforts for social change and social justice.

In "The Manly Art of Pregnancy," j. wallace upends taken-for-granted assumptions that women are the only people who become pregnant and give birth. In this article, he argues that a pregnant body does not mark him as either feminine or woman, but rather produces new possibilities for masculine embodiment as well as the emergence of his identity as a dad. In its challenge to how reproduction is understood through a binary gender system, this article exposes some limits in popular discourses of gender, especially around the touchpoint of reproduction.

- How does seeing the role of "mother" and "mothering" as potentially being occupied by a range of different kinds of bodies and identities alter how we think about this role? How does it also shift perceptions of "father" and "fathering"?
- What ideas about gendered parenting might we need to let go of in a world of pregnant men?
- What are some other examples of shifting gender identities in the reproduction of families? (Think about housework, paid work, and care work.)

Moya Bailey's "'The Illest': Disability as Metaphor in Hip Hop Music" offers an exploration of how non-normative identity categories, in this case based on disability and race, produce tensions between difference and fairness. Particular forms of hip-hop (Hyphy) become vehicles for challenging invisibility based on race in a white-supremacist culture, even as these same forms make use of stereotypes about disability to express frustration with their marginalization.

- Is it justified when someone who uses derogatory language about a marginalized group is from another (or perhaps the same) marginalized group? For whom? What factors make a difference in who uses some words and language?

- How does Bailey resist labeling Hyphy "good" or "bad" for using terms like *retard* or *crazy*, terms that can be extremely offensive about people with disabilities? What are some of the results of this resistance to judge Hyphy (or any other pop culture form)?

"One Is Not Born a Bride: How Weddings Regulate Heterosexuality" is Chrys Ingraham's argument about a taken-for-granted social arrangement that normalizes particular notions of who women are and what they should want. She explores the deep cultural investment in weddings and marriage, especially for girls and women. As a result, the wedding industry functions as a heterosexual discourse that legitimizes certain kinds of gendered identities as natural, and thereby renders others as unnatural.

- Does same-sex marriage complicate discourses about the relationship of women to the wedding industry? Or does it simply extend weddings as the natural part of life's trajectory to more people?
- When you think about your future life trajectory, does it include marriage? If so, what investments are you making in this institution to punctuate your life's timeline? If not, what kinds of time, energy, and financial and emotional space does this decision allow for as compared to others who invest in marriage?

Lila Abu-Lughod cautions her non-Muslim readers in Europe and North America about what they think they know about Muslim women. In the context of international tensions and the march to war in Afghanistan, Muslim women's identities became hyper-visible even as their diversely lived contexts were fundamentally misunderstood. Such misunderstandings across difference too often lead to actions with tragic consequences.

- How can we think about our desires for change as emanating from and perhaps dependent on our partial knowledge of "others" we deem different from ourselves?
- How much of your sense of self is predicated on *not* being like others you perceive to be different?

Alexander Pershai's "The Language Puzzle: Is Inclusive Language a Solution?" complicates taken-for-granted ideas about how popularizing labels denotes, in and of itself, inclusion. Transgender as an identity might signify a break with binary notions of gender, but, like any other label for an identity category, it hardly allows for inclusion of everyone in that category on their own terms.

- How is it that labels for our various identities limit the way others think about us (and maybe how we think about ourselves)?
- Is it even possible to imagine ourselves outside of the categories we claim as our gender or our sexuality (or any other identity category)?
- What are some ways in which naming ourselves is connected to an argument for rights and visibility?

The Manly Art of Pregnancy

j wallace

There are many ways to go about acquiring what they call "a beer belly." I chose pregnancy. Beer and wings probably would have been an easier route, but I've never been one for the easy route, and I embraced the manly art of pregnancy. I'm a short, stocky guy who over the last year has gone from chunky, to having a great big gut, and back to chunky again. Along the way, I've also made a baby.

Judging by the resources available, one might assume that pregnancy is distinctly a woman's affair. Books have titles like *The Pregnant Mom's Guide*, *The Working Women's Guide*, *The Prospective Mother*, and *The Hip Mama's Survival Guide*. Most of the books for men make it clear that not only is pregnancy for women, but the only men interested in pregnancy are heterosexual males: *What to Expect When Your Wife is Expecting* is typical. Even books which say *Dad's Pregnant* in large friendly letters on the cover turn out to be written for cisgender men in heterosexual relationships, and about how to deal with your partner's pregnancy in your relationship. Books for pregnant men are hard to find indeed.

If the La Leche League can encourage women everywhere to embrace *The Womanly Art of Breast Feeding*, I'm going to put in a plug for the Manly Art of Pregnancy. For those of you not yet familiar with pregnancy as a manly art, let me introduce it. The pregnant person is at once a biologist, a mechanic, a weight lifter, and someone providing for hir family. Women can do those things, of course, but our culture still views them as masculine things, and in this way pregnancy made me more of a man, not less of one. Before I was pregnant, I feared that pregnancy would make me into a woman or a lady. But it didn't; it made me more

of a dude. I discovered that pregnancy is rife with things to worry about, and that after a while, gender stopped being one. Pregnancy became a manly act. Pregnancy helped me look, feel, and act more like an archetype of Man, and eventually lifted me to its pinnacle by making me a dad.

Let us begin with the aesthetics: Pregnancy is good for hair growth. Existing hair looks longer, darker, and thicker and new crops sprout up. I have new darker hairs on my chest, my leg hair is more visible, and even my beard is thicker. It's like taking testosterone all over again. Pregnant women often lament this, particularly when they are too pregnant to shave their own legs, but I loved it. The hair growth was so dramatic that I imagined pregnancy hormones being sold to people experiencing hair loss (because G-d knows they try to sell every other thing to people with hair loss). I imagined bald men rubbing Premarin on the tops of their heads, with bald Before, and hirsute After photographs.

When I took testosterone, not having a period was my favorite physical change. I loved the freedom it gave, the extra energy, not having to pay an extra tax for the femaleness I found miserable anyway. Pregnancy is the same. There is no bleeding. I can go about the world, safe in the knowledge that I will not have to beg a tampon from a co-worker. I no longer worry that a spare tampon will leap out of my bag at an inopportune moment. I don't worry that my period will stain my favorite date underpants. I skip the feminine hygiene aisle at the drug store entirely, and I am happier for it.

I recognize that these changes can be part of anyone's pregnancy, regardless of gender. The people that make maternity clothes clearly have thought about how masculinizing the physical changes of pregnancy can be and have therefore designed maternity clothes to re-assert femininity. Why else would they invest so much time and attention in making maternity clothes so very feminine? Seriously. Maternity clothes are pink, pastel, or floral, or all of the above, with liberal use of lace, bows, and ribbon. Maternity clothes flaunt curves, and they *flow*. It's very hard to look serious in most maternity clothes. In addition to all that, many of them make you look like you are four. When I first told my boss that I was pregnant she was very clear with me that if I showed up to work in maternity clothes, she would send me home to change. I can assure you that she meant it in good humor, but her point was well taken. So, I figured out what paternity clothes look like. As it happens, you can get through much of a pregnancy in larger shirts, larger jeans with suspenders, chef pants, and overalls. If the clothes make the man, the masculine art of pregnancy ignores the rack of maternity clothes. The secret advantage to this is that without the maternity clothes, no-one knows you are pregnant. You can walk around hiding a whole tiny person in your abdomen. Never once did a stranger put hir hand on my belly, gush about how I was glowing and ask how far along I was. The masculine art of pregnancy retains at least a little privacy.

Of course the challenge to this was changes in my chest. Pregnancy makes your chest grow. Before being pregnant I was a happy binder-wearing guy, smoothing my lycra undershirt down over my boxer briefs, but rapid growth in the chest department necessitated the first-trimester purchase of chest restraining devices. I put it off as long as I could. I tried shopping for things on my own, discreetly, like a shy straight guy shopping for a new girlfriend—but apparently these things are sized, and it's not like they encourage the "shy straight guy" to go into the change room and try things on. It became clear that I would need to be fitted, and I eventually resigned myself to this. I chose a local shop where I heard they had good fitters, walked up to the counter and asked in a manly, clear voice for assistance fitting me with maternity/nursing bras. Manly pregnant people ask for help with perfect confidence that they are entitled to good assistance, and I found I got good assistance in return.

And then there's this—I grew a penis. Transition-wise I've never really wanted to have genital surgery. Sure, there have been times, in beds and in kayaks, when a penis would have been handy, but for me it's not worth actually having one surgically attached. That said, at our twenty-week ultrasound they showed me grainy black and white pictures of a tiny penis I'm growing. I know not all pregnancies go this way, and it's not as if I decided to grow a penis rather than a vagina, but here I am, growing a penis. Had I known that exposure to sperm would awaken this ability in my body I might have spent more time in bathhouses and other seedy locations, but never mind, I can now add it to the list of things my body can do.

Pregnancy does mean making some life changes. I developed the art of seeming chivalrous while not lifting over forty pounds. I came to understand that sometimes, being manly is about knowing what tool to use. At seven months pregnant, the right tools to use to get a seized tire off one's car are a cell phone and roadside assistance. Crawling under one's car to strike at the tire with a hammer is not manly; protecting one's family and using a cell phone is. "Protecting one's family" is a manly pregnancy mantra. When the signs on the outside of a building warn that there has been an outbreak of fifth disease and pregnant people should not enter the building—you obey them, you do not enter, even when it means recruiting a nice lady to go inside and explain that you are not coming. Even when she goes inside and says "There is some guy, outside, who says he cannot come in because he is pregnant. . . ."

Pregnancy does not mean you lose access to your usual manly haunts, like the barber shop, and your local auto mechanic's. Even with the kid's kicks visible under the barber's towel, my barber did not notice my manly pregnant condition. We had the same conversation, and he gave me the same haircut and straight razor shave that he always does—and I gave him the same tip. The auto mechanics still called me sir and talked to me as if I know what the various engine parts are all supposed to do. It appears that if you're a guy, pregnancy does not make you a woman: it just makes you fat.

It's also easier to think about pregnancy as a manly activity if we butch up the language we use. I trained midwives, a doula, Ob/Gyns, and even a lactation consultant to talk about "pregnant people" not "pregnant women," or "pregnant ladies." A number of ciswomen friends had also complained that when they became pregnant they went from being "women" to "ladies" and they found the prissiness of the word uncomfortable. They too found "pregnant person" a better fit, especially if it meant not being referred to as a "lady" all the time. If we talk about "nursing," focusing on the action of providing for one's child rather than "breastfeeding," focusing on a body part assumed to be feminine, even this activity can sound more manly.

Pregnancy made me a dad. Pregnancy has been making dads out of men since about nine months after sex was discovered. I know fine men who have become dads in a variety of ways, some by love, some by adoption and fostering, some by other means, and I do not believe that there is any one traditional way of going about it. There are more common and less common ways, but all of them have a history and tradition. I became a dad through pregnancy and birth. Along the way, people who love me created the language of "bearing father" and "seahorse papa." We're queers, and we are well versed in creating the language we need to describe our realities. We will bring our world into being through words, as we bring babies into being through our bodies.

In the end, I gave birth to my son via a caesarean section. I have a small neat scar on my abdomen that I think of as "the baby escape hatch." Scars are manly. As I was recovering, I realized that the next time some intrusive person discovers I am trans

and asks me if I have "had the surgery," I can say "yes" and go on to describe my c-section. They never say what surgery they mean, and a c-section is generally recognized as a gendered surgery.

In the hospital, after the birth, I was snuggled up in bed in my pajamas, holding my small son, when the public health nurse strolled in. She looked at me in the hospital bed, at the baby in my arms, and around the room. Then she looked again, and clearly did not find what she was looking for. "Where's the mom?" she asked. The simple answer is that there is no mom. Children need love and support from a parent, not a gender. Parents, not necessarily moms and dads, raise children, whether they are boys or girls. The public health nurse stammered an apology, and fled. I've been rehearsing better answers to that question since—better answers that say his family is not your business, keep your assumptions to yourself.

I've become a dad changing diapers, holding a baby, reading books to someone who can't really focus his eyes yet, a dad who was up many times last night with the baby and who is now blurry-eyed from lack of sleep. I do dadly things, including many things other dads do, and things I remember my dad doing. I'm also a dad who nurses, who gets up in the night to feed the baby without having to heat bottles, which I understand is an uncommon dad kind of thing to do. But I do it for my small person. I want the best for my child, which I understand is a common desire of good dads.

I'm a dad you might run into in the library reading to my small child, a dad in the park carrying my baby on my front, explaining the world to him, a dad who plans to teach my child to love insects and look at ants and caterpillars, a dad who'll head off in a canoe with his small person. I look forward to being the dad helping my child bake cupcakes and discover the joy of gardening, and celebrating his artwork. When you see me, what you see, and who or what you think I am has been totally eclipsed by the dad my small person sees, knows, and loves. I'm his dad, and in the tiny world of our family, that is what really matters.

"The Illest"
Disability as Metaphor in Hip Hop Music
Moya Bailey

In this context, there's no disrespect, so when I bust my
   rhyme, you break your necks.
We got five minutes for us to disconnect, from all intellect and
   let the rhythm effect
'Bout to lose our inhibition. Follow your intuition. Free your
   inner-soul and break away from tradition.
            (will.i.am, "Let's Get Retarded" / "Let's Get It Started")

In 2003, the hip hop group the Black Eyed Peas released their
third album *Elephunk* which featured the controversial track
"Let's Get Retarded" (I. Am). The radio edit became "Let's Get
It Started" with only a few minor changes made to the verses
("cuckoo" becomes "wohoo"). The repackaged song went on to be
featured in several movie soundtracks along with being played
at the 2004 Democratic National Convention and was one of
the top 100 Pop songs of the year on Billboard's Hot 100 Chart
(Newman). The ARC Organization, formerly the Association of
Retarded Citizens, successfully lobbied the Pea's record company
arguing that the ubiquitous use of the word "retarded" is offensive and damaging to those who are medically labeled with the
term (Beckham). Others felt this was an example of the politically
correct language police gone too far. I'd like to offer an alternative reading through a *disidentification* with the lyrics as either
bad or of little consequence. Words have extreme power and it
seems that the persuasive but yet uninvestigated proliferation of
ableist language in hip hop begs further exploration. What work
are lyrics like "let's get retarded" doing and for whose interests?
Drawing largely on the intersectional analysis of Jose Muñoz, I
will demonstrate the synergistic properties of looking at this language through multiple lenses at once as a way to forestall the
limitations of a binary of good and bad, political correctness and
the protected right to free speech.

As I have begun to conceptualize my own research project,
I am very aware of the tension between the socially constructed
nature of identity and the political impetus to use identity to
make claims for adequate and equal treatment in society. I am
also interested in how the policing of identity through stigma
management impacts the ability of various groups to build coalitions and alliances for advocacy. Do these alternate connotations
of ableist language open up or foreclose these possibilities? What
follows is a short investigation of these queries.

Jose Muñoz's concept of disidentification is really useful in
thinking about people who inhabit the liminal spaces of marginalized categories by virtue of identifying with more than one
minority classification of embodiment (Muñoz). As the classic
Gloria Hull et al. title advances, *All the Women Are White, All
the Blacks Are Men, But Some of Us Are Brave*, existing within
the margins of the margins can produce a unique and valuable theoretical perspective (Hull, Scott, and Smith). One is both
inside and outside the already marginalized categories black
and woman but the combination can create a standpoint that
demonstrates the limitations of monolithic constructions of a
particular form of marginalization. Minoritarian discourses
generated by these multiply marginal subjects offer so much in
our attempts to theorize the body as it interacts with the world
around it.

By examining ableism in hip hop through the multiple lenses
of disability, queer, critical race, and feminist theories we can

go beyond the ineffective dichotomy of positive and negative representation and possibly discover useful theorizing derived outside the insulated world of academe. Ableism is the system of oppression that privileges able-bodied people and culture over and above those with disabilities. In the liminal spaces of hip hop the reappropriation of ableist language can mark a new way of using words that departs from generally accepted disparaging connotations. Though this project makes a case for a transgressée reading of ableism in hip hop, ableism in and of itself is still oppressive. Additionally, not all of it can be reimagined. Some of it is simply the vile invective that maintains hierarchies of oppression through able bodied privilege. Though other genres of music and popular culture generally reinforce ableism (Pop Music's love of "crazy" love), its presence in hip hop speaks, I argue, to centuries-old stigma management strategies of politics of respectability that remain futile.

Hip hop was born in 1970's New York City. The East Coast was the original home and as such became the dominant voice of hip hop (Kitwana). The emergence of the laid back yet violent rap sound of California made for the creation of a legendary and ultimately deadly east/west rivalry. This unfortunate history made way for the contemporary moment in which the "Diirty" South rules the landscape with its feel good club bangers. This constant reorientation allows for the emergence of different sounds. The Midwestern, i.e., Chicago sound and the newer, less violent sounds of the Bay Area and LA offer music that has been allowed to develop out of the mainstream's controlling gaze. The California derived sound of The Hyphy Movement's reappropriation of the derisive terms "retarded," "dumb," and LA Krump's dance styling both achieved their transgressive potential through their initial marginalization by mainstream hip hop.

The Bay, or Yay Area as it is sometimes known, along with Los Angeles, has been off the radar of the mainstream hip hop scene for a little over a decade. With the yet unsolved murder of the rapper 2Pac and the escalating violence associated with the genre,

so called California "gangsta rap" retreated from the popular scene. New art forms have developed most notably the hyphy sound and krumping dance style, with both making explicit claims to the importance of their regional location and histories of violence as major propellants of the styles.

Getting hyphy, characterized by exaggeration, overness, and overall extraness, offers opportunities for folks to let loose and get loose on the dance floor. Hyphy is also associated with "crazy" behavior like driving with no one behind the wheel with the car doors open or sitting on top of the car while it's moving ("ghost riding the whip"). The addition of whistle tips, a modified metal plate welded to the car's exhaust that makes a high pitched screeching sound, further demonstrates the need to be seen and heard within the hyphy movement. The social embrace of these ostensibly stigmatizing activities and performances are celebrated for their intentional transgressive power. By actively flouting societal conventions of quiet and sane behavior, black people connected to Hyphy music are challenging their marginalization in a culture that otherwise renders them invisible. They demand attention; even incurring the derision associated with ableism rather than be ignored.

> Sitting in my scraper, watching Oakland go wild . . . Ta-dow
> I don't bump mainstream, I knock underground
> All that other shit, sugar-coated and watered down
> I'm from the Bay where we hyphy and go dumb
> From the soil where them rappers be getting their lingo.
>   (E-40)

In "Tell Me When to Go," hyphy originator and most recognizable hyphy artist E-40 explains the unique and non-normative nature of the genre by connecting it to the location, as well as pointing out the appropriation of the language by rappers outside the Area. "Going dumb" is marked regionally as being something uniquely produced in California. The violence of California gang activity has been implicated in the production of this alternative culture.

The documentary *Rize* follows the practitioners of krumping from its origins in LA children's clowning parties to a dance form that has reached mainstream audiences through current hip hop choreography (LaChapelle et al.). Though beginning with Tommy the Hip Hop Clown's solo birthday performances, it quickly evolved to dance-battling clown troupes that served as alternatives to gangs for kids in the neighborhoods. As dancers got older the style continued to morph and the even more outrageous krumping was born.

To those unfamiliar, krumping looks violent with battles between dancers a central component. Krumpers hit each other to get amped up to dance in radically expressive and explosive ways. They connect the dance to African tribal warrior and spiritual rituals yet also invoke an internalized colonial gaze using words like primal, crazy, savage, and raw to characterize the link (LaChapelle et al.). So while celebrated and even exalted as a spiritual practice, it is simultaneously imbued with a primitive and barbarous ferocity that is connected to the loss of control.

We see this reappropriation in dance. One of the hallmarks of hip hop dance is the ability to look free form and accidental. Dancers are seemingly and often instructed in the music to lose control. This loss of control has been lyrically manifested in the seemingly ableist language of getting retarded and going dumb, though in the context of these songs, this is a good thing. Missy Elliot's 2005 hit featuring Ciara "Lose Control" invokes this sentiment (Elliot). The loss of control the freedom afforded to those who let go, who "wile out" is a momentary escape from the strictures of the everyday. The music itself, alcohol, and weed are used to allow people to slip out of their constraints and boxes and just be. There is an association of freedom with one's ability to go dumb and get hyphy. Ironically this ableist language further circumscribes the lives of those who are assigned these labels outside of the hip hop context. For those ascribed the labels

"dumb," "retarded," and "crazy," the liberatory nature of embracing these terms does not match their reality.

Dumb connotes a lack of intelligence that stigmatizes people and keeps people from being fully engaged in society. Similarly, those labeled retarded are tracked into special education classrooms and segregated from their peers. These acts of separation reinforce stereotypes about the value of people so labeled in a world that excludes them from formative participation. Crazy also serves to malign those ascribed with images of violent and uncontrollable behavior, in direct contrast to the state sanctioned controlled violence many people with mental health conditions describe experiencing.

The freedom that is expressed through the use of going retarded and dumb has the simultaneous effect of further foreclosing the freedom for those who are ascribed these terms by the medicojuridical system. While this language is a temporary escape for hyphy and hip hop practitioners, it presents many problems for those ascribed and held to these labels in the world. Beyond just being offensive, this ableism perpetuates stigmatization, marginalization, and oppressive structural hierarchies of human difference.

Like many other pejorative terms – lame, gyped, gay, bitch – "retard" and "dumb" have lost their referents, or rather the referent is purportedly discarded. When kids say "that's so gay" or "that's retarded" to mean something is bad or uncool, it is not supposed to reflect on the people who are ascribed those labels. Disability theorists argue that this is not true. These statements do in fact reinforce negative connotations on already marginalized groups effectively rein-scribing their liminality and Otherness. Disability Studies, like Women's Studies, illuminates the controlling normate in whose fictitious image we discipline our bodies. Part of the need for ableist language in hip hop is the erstwhile stigma that black bodies incur. In a futile attempt to manage their own societal stigma, black men in hip hop often target other marginalized groups including women, queer people, and people with disabilities. But the critical question is how do we congeal these often falsely differentiated populations into tandem resistance? What coalitions might be formed out of a reformulation of stigma management with an understanding of intersectionality?

Erving Goffman wrote extensively about stigma. Goffman researched the original Greek definition of "stigma" which meant a physical mark on the body that signaled some kind of moral failing in an individual (Goffman). This set the person apart and discredited him/her within the society. While this marking was a literal branding of the undesirables in ancient Greece (criminals, traitors, slaves, etc.), it has evolved to encompass minority groups whose physical characteristics set them apart from the norm (3). People with disabilities or "abominations of the body" were one of the three types of stigma Goffman identified who departed from the anticipated socially constructed norms of the group (5).

Goffman also described "stigma management" strategies employed by marginalized populations to mitigate their subjugated positioning in society. These techniques were employed by a wide variety of stigmatized groups including criminals, sex workers, racial/ethnic minorities, people with disabilities, etc. (20–23).

The autonomy myth is the undergirding societal assumption that all people are (or should be) independent autonomous beings that must provide for themselves (Fineman). This is indirectly coded as able-bodied white, wealthy, and male. This is what produces societal anxiety about people with disabilities, of color, and women, who are imagined as dependants who weigh on others (i.e., men's) autonomy (34). So many of the stigma management strategies of these marginalized groups center on making sure that they are perceived as important contributing members of society and not a drain on its resources.

People with cognitive disabilities are tangentially located within the broader disability movement that often centers physical impairments. People with physical disabilities may even try to distance themselves from this presumably even more stigma producing categorization. The documentary *Murderball* (2005) highlights wheelchair rugby players whose rough and tumble personas as well as sexual prowess are used to separate themselves from cognitive disabilities (Rubin et al.). Film and television often reinforce this problematic construction through the implementation of stereotypical roles and narratives that make the person with a cognitive disability the butt of a joke. The 2008 controversy over the Ben Stiller comedy *Tropic Thunder* (2008) illustrates this point well. In the film, Stiller plays a "retard" who is an actor who thinks that his real life capture by the local people is part of the filming (Stiller et al.). The film's tag line "once there was a retard" was pulled as a result of protests by various disability rights organizations within the US and abroad.

The blatant use of this offensive language speaks to the invisibility of ableism within popular culture. Disability activists have even taken to using the construction "the R-word" like the use of "the N-word." The n-word though has its own reappropriation story that is also connected to hip hop. But what this parallel structure presupposes is an analogous construction. Is Retard to Nigger what bitch is to queer? Vice versa? Are all of these words only as virulent as the person hurling them as an insult? Is it fundamentally different when someone who may identify with these words reappropriates them?

These questions remain as I continue to investigate the simultaneity of reclamation and reinscription that affect communities in such disparate ways. The seemingly celebratory power of language for one marginalized group impedes on the material reality for another and yet there are those who are multiply marginalized who traverse more than one group at the same time. The work of unpacking language that does not easily fit along the binary of positive and negative must propel our thinking into nonlinear dimensions. We must embrace the challenge of multi-dimensional complexity and uncover new models that can accommodate the contradictions of our language.

Works Cited

Beckham, Beverly. "Let's Not Use Words that Have Power to Wound." *The Boston Globe* 21 Mar. 2007.

E-40. *Tell Me When to Go*. BME, 2006.

Elliot, Missy. *Loose Control*. Atlantic, 2005.

Fineman, Martha Albertson. *The Autonomy Myth: A Theory of Dependency*. New York: New P, 2004.

Goffman, Erving. *Stigma: Notes on the Management of Spoiled Identity*. 1963. New York: Touchstone, 1986.

Hull, Gloria T., Patricia Bell Scott, and Barbara Smith. *All the Women Are White, All the Blacks Are Men, but Some of Us Are Brave: Black Women's Studies*. Old Westbury: Feminist P, 1982.

I. Am, Will. *Let's Get It Started*. A&M, 2003.

Kitwana, Bakari. *The Hip Hop Generation: Young Blacks and the Crisis in African American Culture*. New York: Basic Civitas, 2002.

Rize. Dir. David LaChapelle. Lions Gate Home Entertainment, 2005.

Muñoz, José Esteban. *Disidentifications: Queers of Color and the Performance of Politics, Cultural Studies of the Americas*. Minneapolis: U of Minnesota P, 1999.

Newman, Melinda. "NBA Dribbles with the Peas." *Billboard* 10 Apr. 2004. 11, 14.

Murderball. Dir. Henry Alex Rubin and Dana Adam Shapiro. Thinkfilm, 2005.

Tropic Thunder. Dir. Ben Stiller. Paramount, 2008.

One Is Not Born a Bride

How Weddings Regulate Heterosexuality

Chrys Ingraham

All aspects of our social world – natural or otherwise – are given meaning. Culture installs meaning in our lives from the very first moment we enter the social world. Our sexual orientation or sexual identity – or even the notion that there is such a thing – is defined by the symbolic order of that world through the use of verbal as well as non-verbal language and images. Heterosexuality as a *social* category is much more than the fact of one's sexual or affectional attractions. What we think of when we talk about heterosexuality or refer to ourselves as heterosexual is a product of a society's meaning-making processes. In reality, heterosexuality operates as a highly organized social institution that varies across nations, social groups, culture, history, region, religion, ethnicity, nationality, race, lifespan, social class, and ability. In America and elsewhere, the wedding ritual represents a major site for the installation and maintenance of the institution of heterosexuality.

The title of this chapter pays homage to French feminist Monique Wittig whose classic and provocative essay "One is Not Born a Woman" examines what she calls the political regime of heterosexuality and its requisite categories of man and woman. She argues that the category of woman and all of the meaning attached to that category would not exist were it not necessary for the political regime of (patriarchal) heterosexuality. For the purpose of this chapter, the same holds true of the taken-for-granted category of bride. While it may seem obvious to most that one is not born a bride, in reality many women see themselves as following a naturalized path toward heterosexual womanhood.

But how did this contrived and constructed social practice become naturalized? The task of examining this taken-for-granted social arrangement requires a conceptual framework capable of revealing how heterosexuality has become institutionalized, naturalized, and normalized. Any attempt to examine the institution of heterosexuality requires a theory capable of understanding how this institution with all its social practices such as dating, proms, and Valentine's Day, is often viewed by many of us as natural.

The heterosexual imaginary

French psychoanalyst Jacques Lacan's concept of the "imaginary" is especially useful for this purpose. According to Lacan, the imaginary is the unmediated contact an infant has to its own image and its connection with its mother. Instead of facing a complicated, conflictual, and contradictory world, the infant experiences the illusion of tranquility, plenitude, and fullness. In other words, infants experience a sense of oneness with their primary caretaker. Louis Althusser, the French philosopher, borrowed Lacan's notion of the imaginary for his neo-marxist theory of ideology, defining ideology as "the imaginary relationship of individuals to their real conditions of existence." The "imaginary" here does not mean "false" or "pretend" but, rather, an imagined or illusory relationship between an individual and their social world. Applied to a social theory of heterosexuality the *heterosexual imaginary* is that way of thinking that relies on romantic and sacred notions of heterosexuality in order to create and maintain the illusion of well-being and oneness. This romantic view prevents us from seeing how institutionalized heterosexuality actually works to organize gender while preserving racial, class, and sexual hierarchies. The effect of this illusory depiction of reality is that heterosexuality is taken for granted and unquestioned, while gender is understood as something people are socialized into or learn. The heterosexual imaginary naturalizes male to female social relations, rituals, and organized practices and conceals the operation of heterosexuality in structuring gender across race, class, and sexuality. This way of seeing closes off any critical analysis of heterosexuality as an organizing institution and for the ends it serves (Ingraham 1994, 1999). By leaving heterosexuality unexamined as an institution we do not explore how it is learned, how it may control us and contribute to social inequalities. Through the use of the heterosexual imaginary, we hold up the institution of heterosexuality as fixed in time as though it has always operated the same as it does today. This imaginary presents a view of heterosexuality as "just the way it is" while creating obligatory social practices that reinforce the illusion that, as long as one complies with this naturalized structure, all will be right in the world. This illusion is commonly known as romance. Romancing heterosexuality is creating an illusory heterosexuality for which wedding culture plays a central role.

The lived reality of institutionalized heterosexuality is, however, not typically tranquil or safe. The consequences the heterosexual imaginary produces include, for example, marital rape, domestic violence, pay inequities, racism, gay-bashing, femicide, and sexual harassment. Institutionalized heterosexuality and its organizing ideology – the heterosexual imaginary – establishes those behaviors we ascribe to men and women – gender – while keeping in place or producing a history of contradictory and unequal social relations. The production of a division of labor that results in unpaid domestic work, inequalities of pay and opportunity, or the privileging of married couples in the dissemination of insurance benefits, are examples of this.

Above all, the heterosexual imaginary naturalizes the regulation of sexuality through the institution of marriage, ritual practices such as weddings, and state domestic relations laws. These laws, among others, set the terms for taxation, healthcare, and housing benefits on the basis of marital status. Rarely challenged – except by nineteenth-century marriage reformers and early second-wave feminists – laws and public- and private-sector policies use marriage as the primary requirement for social and economic benefits and access rather than distributing resources on some other basis such as citizenship or ability to breathe, for example. Heterosexuality is much more than a biological given or whether or not someone is attracted to someone of another sex. Rules on everything from who pays for the date or wedding rehearsal dinner to who leads while dancing, drives the car, cooks dinner or initiates sex, all serve to regulate heterosexual practice. What circulates as a given in Western societies is, in fact, a highly structured arrangement. As is the case with most institutions, people who participate in these practices must be socialized to do so. In other words, women were not born with a wedding gown gene or a neo-natal craving for a diamond engagement ring! They were taught to want these things. Women didn't enter the world with a desire to practice something called dating or a desire to play with a "My Size Bride Barbie," they were rewarded for desiring these things. Likewise, men did not exit the womb knowing they would one day buy a date a bunch of flowers or spend two months' income to buy an engagement ring. These are all products that have been sold to consumers interested in taking part in a culturally established ritual that works to organize and institutionalize heterosexuality and reward those who participate.

Heteronormativity

A related concept useful for the study of the heterosexual imaginary and of institutionalized heterosexuality is heteronormativity. This is the view that institutionalized heterosexuality constitutes the standard for legitimate and expected social and sexual relations. Heteronormativity represents one of the main premises underlying the heterosexual imaginary, again ensuring that the organization of heterosexuality in everything from gender to weddings to marital status is held up both as a model and as "normal." Consider, for instance, the ways many surveys or intake questionnaires ask respondents to check off their marital status as either married, divorced, separated, widowed, single, or, in some cases, never married. Not only are these categories presented as significant indices of social identity, they are offered as the only options, implying that the organization of identity in relation to marriage is universal and not in need of explanation. Or try to imagine entering a committed relationship without benefit of legalized marriage. We find it difficult to think that we can share commitment with someone without a state-sponsored license. People will frequently comment that someone is afraid to "make a commitment" if they choose not to get married even when they have been in a relationship with someone for years! Our ability to imagine possibilities or to understand what counts as commitment is itself impaired by heteronormative assumptions. We even find ourselves challenged to consider how to marry without an elaborate white wedding. Gays and lesbians have maintained long-term committed relationships yet find themselves desiring state sanctioning of their union in order to feel legitimate. Heteronormativity works in all of these instances to naturalize the institution of heterosexuality while rendering real people's relationships and commitments irrelevant and illegitimate.

For those who view questions concerning marital status as benign, one need only consider the social and economic consequences for those who do not participate in these arrangements or the cross-cultural variations that are at odds with some of the Anglocentric or Eurocentric assumptions regarding marriage. All people are required to situate themselves in relation to marriage or heterosexuality, including those who *regardless of sexual (or asexual) affiliation* do not consider themselves "single," heterosexual, or who do not participate in normative heterosexuality and its structures.

One is not born a bride, and yet to imagine oneself outside of this category is to live a life outside of the boundaries of normality and social convention. To live outside this contrived and constructed social practice is to live on the margins of society, excluded from the social, legal, and economic rewards and benefits participation brings. To resist membership in the heteronormative social order – as bride or as groom – is to live with the penalties and challenges to all those who resist. It means living a life where you have to defend your sexual loyalties on a daily basis – are you straight or are you gay?

Weddings

To demonstrate the degree to which the heteronormative wedding ritual regulates sexuality we must begin with an investigation into the ways various practices, arrangements, relations, and rituals standardize and conceal the operation of institutionalized heterosexuality. It means to ask how practices such as weddings become naturalized and prevent us from seeing what is at stake, what is kept in place, and what consequences are produced. To employ this approach is to seek out those instances when the illusion of tranquility is created and at what cost. Weddings, like many other rituals of heterosexual celebration such as anniversaries, showers, and Valentine's Day, become synonymous with heterosexuality and provide illusions of reality that conceal the operation of heterosexuality both historically and materially. When used in professional settings, for example, weddings work as a form of ideological control to signal membership in relations of ruling as well as to signify that the couple is normal, moral, productive, family-centered, upstanding citizens and, most importantly, appropriately gendered and sexual.

To study weddings means to interrupt the ways the heterosexual imaginary naturalizes heterosexuality and prevents us from seeing how its organization depends on the production of the belief or ideology that heterosexuality is normative and the same for everyone – that the fairytale romance is universal. It is this assumption that allows for the development and growth in America of a $35 billion-per-year wedding industry. This multibillion dollar industry includes the sale of a diverse range of products, many of which are produced outside of the USA – wedding gowns, diamonds, honeymoon travel and apparel, and household equipment. Ironically, the production of these goods frequently occurs under dismal labor conditions where manufacturers rely on a non-traditional female workforce, indirectly altering cultural norms in relation to heterosexuality and family. In Mexico, Guatemala, and China, for example, the effect has been to shift the job opportunities away from men with the consequence of significant levels of domestic violence and femicide. Sexual regulation in these locations is directly related to the gendered division of labor working to produce goods that support the American heterosexual imaginary. Veiled in the guise of romance and the sacred, these social relations conceal from view the troublesome conditions underlying the production of the white wedding.

When you think of weddings as "only natural," think again! This process of naturalization begins with children. By targeting girls and young women, toy manufacturers have seized on the wedding market and the opportunity to develop future consumers by producing a whole variety of wedding toys, featuring the "classic" white wedding, and sold during Saturday morning children's television shows. Toy companies, generally part of large multinational conglomerates that also own related commodities such as travel or cosmetics, work to secure future markets for all their products through the selling of wedding toys. Mattel, the world's largest toymaker and a major multinational corporation, has offices and facilities in thirty-six countries and sells products in 150 nations. Their major toy brand, accounting for 40 percent of their sales, is the Barbie doll – all 120 different versions of her. Mattel's primary manufacturing facilities are located in China, Indonesia, Italy, Malaysia, and Mexico, employing mostly women

of color and at substandard wages. Annually, Mattel makes about 100 million Barbie dolls and earns revenues of $1.9 billion for the California-based company. The average young Chinese female worker whose job it is to assemble Barbie dolls lives in a dormitory, sometimes works with dangerous chemicals, works long hours and earns $1.81 a day.

The staging of weddings in television shows, weekly reporting on weddings in the press, magazine reports on celebrity weddings, advertising, and popular adult and children's movies with wedding themes or weddings inserted, all work together to teach us how to think about weddings, marriage, heterosexuality, race, gender, and labor. Through the application of the heterosexual imaginary, the media cloak most representations of weddings in signifiers of romance, purity, morality, promise, affluence or accumulation, and whiteness. Many newly-weds today experience their weddings as the stars of a fairy-tale movie in which they are scripted, videotaped, and photographed by paparazzi wedding-goers, not as an event that regulates their sexual lives and identities along with those of the laborers who make their wedding possible.

The contemporary white wedding under multinational capitalism is, in effect, a mass-marketed, homogeneous, assembly-line production with little resemblance to the utopian vision many participants hold. The engine driving the wedding market has mostly to do with the romancing of heterosexuality in the interests of capitalism. The social relations at stake – love, community, commitment, and family – come to be viewed as secondary to the production of the wedding spectacle.

The heterosexual imaginary circulating throughout the wedding industry masks the ways it secures racial, class, and sexual hierarchies. Women are taught from early childhood to plan for the "happiest day of their lives." (Everything after that day pales by comparison!) Men are taught, by the absence of these socializing mechanisms, that their work is "other" than that. If they are interested in the wedding it is for reasons other than what women have learned. The possibilities children learn to imagine are only as broad as their culture allows. They are socialized to understand the importance of appropriate coupling, what counts as beauty, as appropriate sexuality, what counts as women's work and men's work, and how to become "good" consumers by participating in those heterosexual practices and rituals that stimulate their interests and emotions and reap the most rewards.

One is not born a bride. One learns to comply with the social and cultural messages that flow to and through the wedding ritual. It is the rite of passage for appropriate heterosexual identity and membership. It is everything but natural.

References

Ingraham, Chrys. 1994. "The heterosexual imaginary", *Sociological Theory* 12 (2): 203–19.

—— 1999. *White Weddings: Romancing Heterosexuality in Popular Culture*. New York: Routledge.

The Muslim Woman

The Power of Images and the Danger of Pity

Lila Abu-Lughod

In the common Western imagination, the image of the veiled Muslim woman stands for oppression in the Muslim world. This makes it hard to think about the Muslim world without thinking about women, sets up an "us" and "them" relationship with Muslim women, and ignores the variety of ways of life practiced by women in different parts of the Muslim world. Anthropologist Lila Abu-Lughod emphasizes that veiling should not be confused with a lack of agency or even traditionalism. Western feminists who take it upon themselves to speak on behalf of oppressed Muslim women assume that individual desire and social convention are inherently at odds: something not borne out by the experience of Islamic society.

Focal Point: Post-secular Europe?

From the cartoon crisis and minaret ban to the multiculturalism debate: on the politics of post-secular Europe.

What images do we, in the United States or Europe, have of Muslim women, or women from the region known as the Middle East? Our lives are saturated with images, images that are strangely confined to a very limited set of tropes or themes. The oppressed Muslim woman. The veiled Muslim woman. The Muslim woman who does not have the same freedoms we have. The woman ruled by her religion. The woman ruled by her men.

These images have a long history in the West but they have become especially visible and persistent since 9/11. Many women in the US mobilized around the cause of the Afghani women oppressed by the fundamentalist Taliban – women who were represented in the media as covered from head to toe in their *burqas*, unable to go to school or wear nail polish. An administration – George W. Bush's – then used the oppression of these Muslim women as part of the moral justification for the military invasion of Afghanistan.[1] These images of veiled and oppressed women have been used to drum up support for intervention. Besides the untold horrors, dislocations, and violence these US interventions have brought to the lives of Muslim women in Afghanistan and Iraq, I would argue that the use of these images has also been bad for us, in the countries of the West where they circulate, because of the deadening effect they have on our capacity to appreciate the complexity and diversity of Muslim women's lives – as human beings.

As the late Edward Said pointed out in his famous book, *Orientalism*,[2] a transformative and critical study of the relationship between the Western study of the Middle East and the Muslim world and the larger projects of dominating or colonizing these regions, one of the most distinctive qualities of representations – literary and scholarly – of the Muslim "East" has been their citationary nature. What he meant by this is that later works gain authority by citing earlier ones, referring to each other in an endless chain that has no need for the actualities of the Muslim East. We can see this even today in visual representations of the Muslim woman. I have been collecting such images for years, ones that reveal clearly the citationary quality of images of "the Muslim woman". The most iconic are those I think of as studies in black and white. One finds, for example, impenetrable Algerian women shrouded in ghostly white in the French colonial postcards from the 1930s that Malek Alloula analyzes in his book, *The Colonial Harem*.[3] This kind of photography, Alloula argues, was dedicated to making Algerian women accessible, if only symboli-cally, to French soldiers, tourists, and the people back home. And then one finds in the late 1990s covers of American media, even highbrow, such as the *New York Times Magazine* or the *Chronicle of Higher Education*, that similarly depict women whose faces are hidden and bodies covered in white or pale Islamic modest dress. These are women from Jordan or Egypt whose lives and situa-tions are radically unlike those of women in colonial Algeria, and unlike many other women in their own countries. One also finds in Alloula's book of postcards images of women dressed dramat-ically in black, with only eyes showing. Again, almost identical images appear on the covers of the *New York Times Magazine* and even *KLM Magazine* from 1990 to the present, despite the fact that the articles they are linked to are on different countries: Saudi Arabia, Jordan, and Yemen. There is an amazing uniformity.

Why should we find this disturbing? I certainly feel uncom-fortable with my collection of media images because my twenty-five years of experience doing research in the Middle East, especially Egypt, has taught me that images like these do not reflect the variety of styles of women's dress in those countries and do nothing to convey the meaning of these differences. My own family albums include photos of my Palestinian grand-mother and aunt in one of these countries – Jordan – my aunt wearing a blouse and slacks, her long straight hair uncovered; even my grandmother has just a simple white scarf draped loosely over her hair. They also include an old photo of my grand-mother and aunt and two of my uncles taken sometime in the 1950s, the men in suits and the women in neat dresses, their hair nicely coiffed. Even if one turns to recent news items from these countries, take Jordan for example, again, one finds small photos that include the national women's basketball team in shorts or the Queen dining with a group of other cosmopolitan women, European and Jordanian, and you can't tell the difference. Why are these not on the cover of the *New York Times Magazine*, repre-senting Jordan, instead of the shrouded woman?

Moreover, it is odd that in many of the images from the media, the veiled women stand in for the countries the articles are about. None of these articles in the *New York Times Magazine*, for example, was about Muslim women, or even Jordanian or Egyptian women. It would be as if magazines and newspapers in Syria or Malaysia were to put bikini clad women or Madonna on every cover of a magazine that featured an article about the United States or a European country.

Burqa or Chanel suits?

There are several problems with these uniform and ubiquitous images of veiled women. First, they make it hard to think about the Muslim world without thinking about women, creating a seemingly huge divide between "us" and "them" based on the treatment or positions of women. This prevents us from think-ing about the connections between our various parts of the world, helping setting up a civilizational divide. Second, they make it hard to appreciate the variety of women's lives across the Muslim or Middle Eastern worlds – differences of time and place and dif-ferences of class and region. Third, they even make it hard for us to appreciate that veiling itself is a complex practice.

Let me take a little time over this third point. It is common knowledge that the ultimate sign of the oppression of Afghani women under the Taliban-and-the-terrorists is that they were forced to wear the *burqa*. Liberals sometimes confess their sur-prise that even though Afghanistan has been liberated from the Taliban, women do not seem to be throwing off their *burqas*. Someone like me, who has worked in Muslim regions, asks why this is so surprising. Did we expect that once "free" from the Taliban they would go "back" to belly shirts and blue jeans, or dust off their Chanel suits?

We need to recall some basics of veiling. First, the Taliban did not invent the *burqa* in Afghanistan. It was the local form of covering that Pashtun women in one region wore when they went out. The Pashtun are one of several ethnic groups in Afghanistan and the *burqa* was one of many forms of covering in the subcontinent and Southwest Asia that has developed as a convention for symbolizing women's modesty or respectability. The *burqa*, like some other forms of "cover" has, in many settings, marked the symbolic separation of men's and women's spheres, as part of the general association of women with family and home, not with public space where strangers mingled.

Portable seclusion

Twenty-some years ago, the anthropologist Hanna Papanek, who worked in Pakistan, described the *burqa* as "portable seclusion".[4] She noted that many saw it as a liberating invention since it enabled women to move out of segregated living spaces while still observing the basic moral requirements of separating and protecting women from unrelated men. Ever since I came across her phrase "portable seclusion", I have thought of these enveloping robes as "mobile homes". Everywhere, such veiling signifies belonging to a particular community and participating in a moral way of life in which families are paramount in the organization of communities and the home is associated with the sanctity of women.

The obvious question that follows is: if this is the case, why would women suddenly become immodest? Why would they suddenly throw off the markers of their respectability, markers, whether *burqas* or other forms of cover, that were supposed to assure their protection in the public sphere from the harassment of strange men by symbolically signalling that they were still in the inviolable space of their homes, even though moving in the public realm? Especially when these are forms of dress that had become so conventional that most women gave little thought to their meaning?

To draw some analogies, none perfect: why are we surprised when Afghan women don't throw off their *burqas* when we know

perfectly well that it wouldn't be appropriate to wear shorts to the opera? Religious belief and community standards of propriety require the covering of the hair in some traditions – Muslim, Jewish, and Catholic until recently. People wear the appropriate form of dress for their social communities and are guided by socially shared standards, religious beliefs, and moral ideals, unless they deliberately transgress to make a point or are unable to afford proper cover. If we think that American women, even the non-religious, live in a world of choice regarding clothing, all we need to do is remind ourselves of the expression, "the tyranny of fashion".

What had happened in Afghanistan under the Taliban is that one regional style of covering or veiling, associated with a certain respectable but not elite class, was imposed on everyone as "religiously" appropriate, even though previously there had been many different styles, popular or traditional with different groups and classes – different ways to mark women's propriety, or, in more recent times, religious piety. Although I am not an expert on Afghanistan, I imagine that the majority of women left in Afghanistan by the time the Taliban took control were the rural or less educated, from non-elite families, since they were the only ones who couldn't emigrate to escape the hardship and violence that has marked Afghanistan's recent history. If liberated from the enforced wearing of *burqas*, most of these women would choose some other form of modest head covering, like all those living nearby who were not under the Taliban – their rural Hindu counterparts in the North of India (who cover their heads and veil their faces from relatives by marriage) or their Muslim sisters in Pakistan. Some there wear gauzy scarves, some the newer forms of Islamic modest dress.

I want to make a crucial point about veiling here. Not only are there many forms of covering which themselves have different meanings in the communities in which they are used, but veiling itself must not be confused with, or made to stand for, lack of agency. As I have argued in *Veiled Sentiments*, my ethnography of a Bedouin community in Egypt in the late 1970s and 1980s, pulling the black headcloth over the face in front of older respected men is considered a voluntary act by women who are deeply committed to being moral and have a sense of honour tied to family. One of the ways they show their self-respect and social standing is by covering their faces in certain contexts. And they decide for whom they feel it is appropriate to veil. They don't veil for younger men; they don't veil for foreign men. They don't even veil for Egyptian non-Bedouin men because they don't respect them and don't, in the latter two cases, consider these men as part of their moral community.

To take a very different case, the modern Islamic modest dress that many educated women across the Muslim world have started to wear since the late 1970s now both publicly marks piety and can be read as a sign of educated urban sophistication, a sort of modernity. What many people in the West don't realize is that the women in Egypt who took up this new form of head-covering, and sometimes even covering their faces, were university students – especially women studying to become medical doctors and engineers. I remember very well that the only girl in the elite but rural Bedouin family I lived with in the 1980s to have achieved a high school education was also the one who wanted desperately to take on this new form of veiling. She also wanted to marry an educated man so that she could express her newfound knowledge and modern values. She was delighted that her father arranged a marriage with an engineer and she moved to the provincial city of Marsa Matruh. When I next saw her, she was indeed wearing this new form of *hijab* or headcovering, not the traditional headcovering of married women among the Bedouin, her community.

In an important study of women in the mosque movement in Egypt – where since the 1970s women have been going to learn about their religion, attending lessons at the mosque, often by women preachers, and insisting that they have a place there – the anthropologist Saba Mahmood has shown that this new

form of dress is perceived by many of the women who adopt it as part of a bodily means to cultivate virtue.[5] They talk about it as a choice resulting from their desire, their struggle in fact, to be close to God. I will discuss Mahmood's book, *Politics of Piety*, below to explore more fully how we might think differently about freedom and constraint. But here I just want to point out that Saba Mahmood refuses to give functionalist reasons why in the 1980s women all over the Muslim world began taking on this form of modern Islamic modest dress – covering their hair and wearing long robes, whereas since the 1930s women had been joining feminist organizations and wearing Western clothing. Some of these functionalist explanations have been that they are protesting against the West and finding authentic culture, or going backward in time to protect themselves against the onslaught of modernity, or devising comfortable ways to move into public and work with men in offices, or to ride the buses without being harassed. Instead, Saba Mahmood says that we should consider the terms of the women themselves: and they say that they want to be close to God, that they want to be good Muslims. They now do so through veiling and through teaching themselves about their religion, whether how to pray properly or how to be a good person.

Two points emerge from this very basic look at some of the many meanings of veiling in the contemporary Muslim world. First, we have to resist the reductive interpretation of veiling as the quintessential sign of women's unfreedom. What does freedom mean if we know that humans are social beings, always raised in certain social and historical contexts and belonging to particular communities that shape their desires and understandings of the world? Isn't it a gross violation of women's own understandings of what they are doing to simply denounce the *burqa* as a medieval or patriarchal imposition? Second, we shouldn't reduce the diverse situations and attitudes of millions of Muslim women to a single item of clothing. Perhaps it is time to give up the black and white Western obsession with the veil and focus on some serious issues that feminists and others concerned with women's lives should indeed be concerned with.

Beware pity

I have argued that the power of these images of veiled women is that they dull our understanding and restrict our appreciation of complexity. The second half of the subtitle of this essay is "the danger of pity". What does pity have to do with Muslim or Middle Eastern women? It seems obvious to me that one of the most dangerous functions of these images of Middle Eastern or Muslim women is to enable many of us to imagine that these women need rescuing by us or by our governments.

I first began to think about pity when I ran across a book many years ago at the Princeton Theological Seminary; it was the proceedings of a Presbyterian women's missionary conference held in Cairo, Egypt, in 1906. It was a collection of many chapters on the sad plight of the Mohammedan woman (as she was known then) in countries from Egypt to Indonesia, detailing the lack of love in her marriage, her ignorance, her subjection to polygamy, her seclusion, and the symbolic evidence of her low status in her veiling. In the introduction to this book, graphically called *Our Moslem Sisters: A Cry of Need from Lands of Darkness Interpreted by Those Who Heard It*,[6] Annie Van Sommer, speaking on behalf of her fellow women missionaries (and of course appealing for financial support for the good works of these women missionaries), explains: "This book with its sad, reiterated story of wrong and oppression is an indictment and an appeal [. . .] It is an appeal to Christian womanhood to right these wrongs and enlighten this darkness by sacrifice and service." She goes on to say: "It seems to some of us that it needs the widespread love and pity of the women of our day in Christian lands to seek and save the suffering sinful needy women of Islam. You cannot know how great the need unless you are told; you will never go and find them until you hear their cry." Western Christian women at the turn of the century thus saw themselves as voicing what Muslim women cannot, or amplifying the stifled voices of these "others" in the service of Christian salvation. This, of course, is in Victorian times when women didn't have the vote, were rarely in the public sphere, were supposed to have been angels in the house. The missionary women were unusually independent and adventurous, though often they went as wives.

One can worry about the echoes of this rhetoric in contemporary liberal feminist concerns about women around the world. One need only think of the American organization the Feminist Majority, with their campaign for the women in Afghanistan, or the wider discourse about women's human rights. Like the missionaries, these liberal feminists feel the need to speak for and on behalf of Afghan or other Muslim women in a language of women's rights or human rights. They see themselves as an enlightened group with the vision and freedom to help suffering women elsewhere to receive their rights, to rescue them from their men or from their oppressive religious traditions.

If one constructs some women as being in need of pity or saving, one implies that one not only wants to save them from something but wants to save them for something – a different kind of world and set of arrangements. What violences might be entailed in this transformation? And what presumptions are being made about the superiority of what you are saving them for? Projects to save other women, of whatever kind, depend on and reinforce Westerners' sense of superiority. They also smack of a form of patronizing arrogance that, as an anthropologist who is sensitive to other ways of living, makes me feel uncomfortable. I've spent lots of time with different groups of Muslim women and know something about how they see themselves, how they respect themselves, and how I admire and love them as complex and resourceful women.

My point is that perhaps we ought to be more aware of different paths in this world. Maybe we should consider being respectful of other routes towards social change. Is it impossible to ask whether there can be a liberation that is Islamic? This idea is being explored by many women, like those in Iran, who call themselves Islamic feminists. And beyond this, is liberation or freedom even a goal for which all women or people strive? Are emancipation, equality, and rights part of a universal language? Might other desires be more meaningful for different groups of people? Such as living in close families? Such as living in a godly way? Such as living without war or violence?

There are other perspectives, some of which question Western superiority. For example, addressing himself to the United States, one notorious Islamist accuses: "You are a nation that exploits women like consumer products or advertising tools, calling upon customers to purchase them. You use women to serve passengers, visitors, and strangers to increase your profit margins. You then rant that you support the liberation of women [. . .] You are a nation that practices the trade of sex in all its forms, directly and indirectly. Giant corporations and establishments are established on this, under the name of art, entertainment, tourism, and freedom, and other deceptive names that you attribute to it."[7]

More moderate Muslim apologists also defend Islam against accusations by Westerners of sexism. In a new global studies textbook on Islam, the section called "Islam is sexist" contains a twenty-eight-point rebuttal of this charge. This rebuttal gives explanations of Quranic verses, describes the Prophet Muhammad's position on various aspects of women's status, provides observations about how late women were given the vote in some European countries (Switzerland in 1971, for example), and notes how many Muslim women have governed countries (five prime ministers or presidents in Pakistan, Bangladesh, Turkey, and Indonesia) compared to none, for example, in the United States.[8]

Is what these apologists describe by way of sexual exploitation or lack of public power a reason to pity American or European women? We would find this either absurd or annoying. We have a million answers to their charges. Even if we are critical of the treatment of women in our own societies in Europe or the United States, whether we talk about the glass ceiling that keeps women professionals from rising to the top, the system that keeps so many women-headed households below the poverty line, the high incidence of rape and sexual harassment, or even the exploitation of women in advertising, we do not see this as reflective of the oppressiveness of our culture or a reason to condemn Christianity – the dominant religious tradition. We know such things have complicated causes and we know that some of us, at least, are working to change things.

Similarly, we need to appreciate that all kinds of women in the Muslim world might also see the charges of the oppression of Muslim women as absurd, or annoying. This would include ordinary women like those I've lived with in rural areas and the feminists and other reformers who have, since the late nineteenth century, seen problems in their own societies regarding the position of women. We have to be careful not to fall into polarizations that place feminism only on the side of the West. There are plenty of Third World feminists, including in many parts of the Muslim world. Some call themselves Islamic feminists, some do not. But such feminists face dilemmas when Western feminists initiate campaigns that make them vulnerable to local denunciations by conservatives, whether Islamist or nationalist, as traitors. Middle East scholars like Afsaneh Najmabadi, originally from Iran, now argue that not only is it wrong to see history simplistically in terms of a putative opposition between Islam and the West, but it is strategically dangerous to accept the cultural opposition between Muslim fundamentalism and Western feminism. The many people within Muslim countries who are trying to find alternatives to present injustices, those who might want to refuse the divide and take from different histories and cultures, who don't accept that being feminist means being Western, will be under pressure to choose – are you with us or against us? Just as we are all being cowed into this.

Free choice and tradition

But I want to make another point: not only are Muslim women engaged in projects for women's rights in terms that we recognize, but many women in other parts of the world don't necessarily see their lives as deficient in terms of rights. I'm not talking about self-delusion and false consciousness – that the women don't see their own oppression. I'm arguing that we need to recognize and perhaps even be able to appreciate the different terms in which people live their lives. In my book *Writing Women's Worlds*,[9] which I think of as an experimental "feminist" ethnography of the Awlad 'Ali Bedouin women in Egypt I lived with in the early 1980s, I tried to tell women's stories in the terms they used. I also tried to capture the criteria they used for judging others and putting forward claims.

Stories of marriage offer the best evidence both of the inaptness of the opposition between choice and constraint that dominates our understanding of the differences between Western and Muslim women and of the importance of recognizing different constructions of "rights". Girls I knew in this Bedouin community resisted particular marriages that were arranged for them but never the basic principle that families should arrange marriages. They might sing songs about the kind of young men they wanted to marry – those who were not cousins, those who were educated, those riding in certain kinds of cars and trucks – but they assumed that it was up to their families to choose such matches for them. They even made trouble when they didn't want a particular husband, often subverting or undermining a marriage arranged for them. But even the love poems that I wrote my first book about, *Veiled Sentiments*,[10] poems that registered their longings and frustrations, were a mode of expression fully within a system, not a rebellion against a system that arranged marriage, that required women to preserve their honour by not showing any interest in men, or that expected men and women not to show affection in public, even when married. Many girls

and mothers told me about the dangers of love matches; all valued the protections and support afforded by their families in arranged marriages. More interesting, women in marriages often asserted "rights"– based on some sense of Islamic and customary law but mostly derived from a keen sense of justice they had internalized through watching community practices but also from ingrained expectations about their self-worth and their responsibilities. This happened in cases when husbands treated them badly.

An even better example of the problem of assuming we know what rights women want is the case of polygyny in this community. A whole chapter of my book *Writing Women's Worlds* attends to the shifting relationships, solidarities, angers, and sorrows in one polygamous marriage that I knew intimately. It wasn't the fact of a husband marrying more than one wife that was ever the issue for these particular co-wives. This practice was supported in Islamic law and recognized as something that happened for various reasons, including a desire for children or providing for unsupported women. Instead, it was the particular personalities, histories, behaviours, and feelings for each other that mattered to the women. The reproach and claim of one co-wife, after telling me a long story about an infuriating situation that she found herself in just after her husband married his third wife, was different from what I would have imagined or expected. I had asked her, sympathetically, at the end of this story, if she'd been jealous. She answered right away: "No I wasn't jealous. I was just angry that we were being treated unfairly. Aren't we all the same?" This is hardly a liberal argument for women's human rights or an argument about the oppressiveness of polygyny. It is an argument that co-wives have the right, according to the Qur'an and Bedouin ideals, to be treated with absolute equality.

What is the point of these stories I am telling about particular women in the Middle East, or feminists in the Muslim world? The late Susan Moller Okin, a well-known American liberal feminist thinker who wrote a widely publicized essay entitled, "Is multiculturalism bad for women?"[11] made a statement that provoked much criticism. She proposed boldly that women in "patriarchal" minority cultures (her essay was about cultural minorities in the United States but extended to the world's "patriarchal" cultures) "might be much better off if the culture into which they were born were either to become extinct (so that its members would become integrated into the less sexist surrounding culture) or, preferable, were encouraged to alter itself so as to reinforce the equality of women."[12]

To suggest that someone's culture should become extinct is a strong statement. It reminds one of the Presbyterian missionaries I mentioned above, who were so sure that Christianity was the only answer for women. I think we have to be more respectful. We have to recognize that people don't necessarily want to give up their cultures and their social worlds – most people value their own ways of life. They don't like to be told to give up their religious convictions. Again, we can come back to the work of Saba Mahmood on the young women in the 1980s and 1990s in Egypt who are trying to figure out how to live good Muslim lives, taking on the veil in the process. Mahmood refuses the ideals of liberal philosophers who insist that individual choice is the prime value. She describes these Egyptian Muslim women's strong desires to follow socially-prescribed religious conventions "as the potentialities, the 'scaffolding' [. . .] through which the self is realized", not the signs of their subordination as individuals. She argues that their desire to take the ideals and tools of self-reference from outside the self (in Islamic religious practice, texts, and law) challenges the usual separation of individual and society upon which liberal political thinking rests. She tells us we need to question the (modern American) distinction that underlies most liberal theory between "the subject's real desires and obligatory social conventions". As I noted above, she describes the women who want to pray and be "close to God" by veiling and being modest as involved in a project of deliberate moral cultivation. Are we to say it is not?

Choices for all of us are fashioned by discourses, social locations, geopolitical configurations, and unequal power into historically and locally specific ranges. Those for whom religious values are important certainly don't see them as constraining – they see them as ideals for which to strive.

I want to add one more crucial detail to the ideas of Saba Mahmood regarding these women and how we should best think about them. These women are not somehow completely other, completely unconnected to us, living in this totally separate world, in their own reality. They may be living their realities, but all are, in one way or another, shaped by the interconnections between the parts of the world that the now popular civilizational discourse defines as West and non-West, Judeo-Christian and Muslim. Many of the differences that exist today are products of different but intertwined histories, histories of interaction and reaction. They are products of different circumstances that have been created through our interactions, whether in the era of the Crusades or colonialism, or now the global hegemony of the United States.

We may want justice for women but can we accept that there might be different ideas about justice and that different women might want, or choose, different futures from what we envision as best? And that the choices they see before them are in fact a product of some situations we have helped foist on them? My conclusion is that if we do care about the situations of women different from white middle class Western women, we would do well to leave behind veils and vocations of saving others and instead train our sights on ways to make the world a more just place. The reason my argument for respecting difference is not the same as an anthropologist's position of cultural relativism – that is, anything goes or it's just their culture so we have to let them be – is that the position I'm advocating doesn't stop us asking ourselves how we, living in this privileged and powerful part of the world, might examine our own responsibilities for the situations in which others in distant places have found themselves and the choices now open to them. Islamic movements themselves have arisen in a world shaped by the intense engagements of Western powers in Middle Eastern lives. Some of the most conservative movements that focus on women in these parts of the world have resulted from interactions with the West, including 3 billion dollars funnelled by the CIA into the conservative groups in Afghanistan that undermined a Marxist government that was engaged in forced modernization, including mass education for women.

It seems to me that if we are concerned about women, including Muslim women, maybe we can work at home to make US and European policies more humane. If we want to be active in the affairs of distant places, maybe we should do so in the spirit of support for those within the communities whose goals are to make women's (and men's) lives better. Whatever we do, we should begin with respect and think in terms of alliances, coalitions, and solidarity, rather than salvation, or pity. Above all, we need to resist the power of the limited and limiting black and white images of Muslim women that circulate in our midst.

Notes

1 See: Lila Abu-Lughod, "Do Muslim Women Need Saving? Reflections on Cultural Relativism and its Others", *American Anthropologist*, 104.3 (2002), 783–790; Charles Hirschkind and Saba Mahmood, "Feminism, the Taliban, and Politics of Counter-Insurgency", *Anthropological Quarterly*, 75.2 (2002), 339–354.

2 Edward Said, *Orientalism*, New York: Pantheon 1978.

3 Malek Alloula, *The Colonial Harem*, Minneapolis, MN: University of Minnesota 1986.

4 Hanna Papanek, "Purdah in Pakistan: Seclusion and Modern Occupations for Women", *Separate Worlds*, Hanna Papanek and Gail Minault (eds.), Columbus, OH: South Asia Books 1982, 190–216.

5 Saba Mahmood, *Politics of Piety*, Princeton, NJ: Princeton University Press 2005.

6 Annie Van Sommer and Samuel W. Zwemer, *Our Moslem Sisters: A Cry of Need from Lands of Darkness Interpreted by Those Who Heard It*, New York: The Young People's Missionary Movement 1907.

7 Osama Bin Laden, *Messages to the World: The Statements of Osama bin Laden*, Bruce Lawrence (ed.), James Howarth (trans.), London: Verso 2005, 166–68.

8 Mir-Zohair Husain, *Global Studies: Islam and the Muslim World*, Dubuque, IO: McGraw Hill/ Dushkin 2005, 61–62.

9 Lila Abu-Lughod, *Writing Women's Worlds: Bedouin Stories*, Berkley, CA: University of California 1993.

10 Lila Abu-Lughod, *Veiled Sentiments: Honor and Poetry in a Bedouin Society*, Berkeley, CA: University of California 1986.

11 Susan Moller Okin, *Is Multiculturalism Bad for Women?* Joshua Cohen, Matthew Howard, and Martha Nussbaum (eds.), Princeton, NJ: Princeton University 1999.

12 Ibid. 22.

The Language Puzzle
Is Inclusive Language a Solution?

Alexander Pershai

No matter what terms one uses, negotiates or invents to talk about transgender issues and experiences, they are sure to suffer from a linguistic deficiency of one kind or another. There are no adequate terms and categories to define and discuss transgender, trans(s)exuality, gender-queer, cross-dressing, et cetera. Every time we try to find such terms, we fail—partly because transgender is very diverse and cannot fit into traditional categories of "the world of men and women" and partly because language offers us a limited set of terms and meanings of gender-related identities and practices.

Some transgender persons try to avoid traditional definitions and categories because these definitions lock them into spaces they don't belong. For them, the application of traditional names and definitions (such as he, she, man, woman) would be violent and offensive. To them, being transgender means freedom from an identity that is defined by such terms. Other transgendered people are happy to be defined and recognized by and within a female/male binary and would find it derogatory if anything else apart from the terms of women and men were used to address them.[1] No matter what position one takes, one ends up with an artificial and unsatisfactory homogenization of transgender people into a generalized "common" category.

Tackling the issue of language means dealing with individual choice of self-identification, limited linguistic resources and the desire to develop a new language that would give a place and an adequate category for everyone. In this essay, I address the concept of inclusive language regarding transgender and question what would be gained and lost by introducing new terms.

*

The question of language reform has been central to feminist thought for about thirty years. Current language structures are viewed as androcentric (male-oriented), sexist formations that exclude and oppress women, as well as other marginalized groups, and make them invisible.[2] Feminist language reform aims to change exclusive "man-made" language into non-sexist language. Some projects, such as *The A–Z of Non-Sexist Language* by Margaret Doyle, suggest inclusive language as an alternative to exclusive language.[3] Inclusive language provides a space and a place for all groups of people and makes everyone visible and (self)identifiable in adequate and respectful terms. Following that logic, it is possible to assume that inclusive language would make space for transgender experience.

However, inclusive language is complicated and contradictory. Linguist Deborah Cameron points out two basic problems of the projects of feminist language reform. The first one is a "lack of inclusiveness." The second is "inoffensiveness as a political goal." The result is a list of "words to avoid rather than discussing shades or meaning within current feminist usage," and an inclusive language that gives a space only for normative women, ignoring minorities of all types.[4] At the same time, "non-sexist language is one of those feminist ideas that has somehow managed to achieve the status of orthodoxy, not just among feminists, but for a great mass of well meaning people and vaguely liberal institutions."[5] That is, using non-sexist language became a matter of sensitivity and being up-to-date when inclusive language itself is reduced to polite and inoffensive definitions of the norm.

The inclusive language project challenges the representation of linguistic resources of and within a male/female binary. Sexism in this context is women's disadvantaged position in society. The creation of non-sexist categories still concern a binary of women and men. The issues of transgender are still erased and so is the repressive mandatory character of sex and gender.

Language has an infinite creative capacity, but at the same time this freedom of creation has to follow particular rules of grammar and semantics. Linguistic freedom is ambiguous; everybody is free to create but only within the spaces and resources that the existing language provides. Feminist thinker Dale Spender defines this duality of language, the freedom of creation and its limitations to linguistic sources as a language trap.[6] "Once certain categories are constructed within the language, we proceed to organize the world according to those categories. We even fail to see evidence which is not consistent within those categories . . . New names systematically subscribe to old beliefs, they are locked into principles that already exist, and there seems no way out of this even if those principles are inadequate or false."[7]

The lack of terms for transgender means we have to generate semantic hybrids by putting together the notions of *sex*, *sexuality* and *gender* together with prefixes such as *trans-*, *inter-* or *cross-*. Language locks us up within the structure that, first, demands that one have a sex/gender, and second, gives us a limited number of categories for that sex/gender, namely, male or female. Of course, to some degree one could use *person* or *one* as a substitute. But such substitutions are problematic because as soon as we come to defining one's relationships to the world the grammar pushes us to use personal pronouns *he* and *she*, *his* or *her*.

Transgender goes beyond the limits of socially and culturally constructed spaces and categories. Transgender shakes up and subverts the "usual," culturally acceptable visions of sex and gender, male and female, femininity and masculinity, normativity and deviation and so on. Transgender is a much more complicated notion than just crossing borders, changing sex or playing with cultural stereotypes. Still we (have to) define transgender by available and not necessarily applicable linguistic resources. We keep on following pre-given meanings and visions of sex and gender and try to inscribe transgender into normative spaces.

As the definitions of normative and culturally recognizable sex and gender are not acceptable for some transgender people, trans communities coin new terms such as *hir* and *s/he* to identify and define transgender. Using such terms helps to make transgender people definable, recognizable and visible, and includes them in social and cultural structures. *Hir* and *s/he* provide transgender individuals with the possibility of a proper self-identification, and of having a name. But *hir* and *s/he* also turn transgender into a social category that can result in mechanisms of both recognition and marginalization. It is possible that the use of *hir* and *s/he* might become mandatory in speech to signify the "correct" gender of a transgender individual. Will a transgender person *hirself* be happy to expose (or be exposed) that *hir* sex and/or gender is modified? Would it be equally desired by all members of a trans community?

The category of transgender emerges into already functioning social structures of male-oriented society where positions of sex and gender are normative, well-definable and recognizable, and where the category of "male" is supreme and all the rest is subordinate. Having a recognizable category for transgender, and unmistakable relevant pronouns such as *hir* and *s/he*, will indicate peoples' place in a social hierarchy. From this perspective *hir* and *s/he*, from the very beginning, would indicate the *difference from the male norm* and signify a subordinate position of transgender in society.

The question of emphasizing difference thus accompanies the construction of a new category. *Hir* and *s/he* help to create a canon, to homogenize the category. Is there a linguistic canon of transgender? No, there is none; transgender is so diverse that even in a rough sense, we can hardly find common ground. Does transgender need a canon? If yes, then what for? Why is there a desire to give transgender a proper, unmistakable definition? Why does one need to know who exactly—he, she or s/he—one is talking to?

Sheilla Jeffreys, specialist in sexual and queer politics, points out that gender is necessary for the construction of heteronormative male supremacy and patriarchal structures. Gender as a category is used to underline the power of heterosexuality and normative society.[8] Transgender as a settled social category might become another resource to create and reinforce patriarchal discrimination. *Hir* and *s/he* will be another position in a hierarchical heterosexual structure; instead of a binary of *he* and *she*, there will be the triplet *he, she* and *s/he,* in which *he* would still be in a supreme position. Trying to invent a new category in and for the already existing structure doesn't change anything in terms of meanings, it just clarifies definitions of the Other, while positions of power remain the same.

At the same time, even without proper definitions, transgender already exists and occupies the very same space as gender. It uses the infrastructure of gender—the basic male/female border—and bodylines, particularly visual, behavioural, verbal and sexual cues. What is unique to transgender is that it uses the cultural abstractions of gender and its individual applications as empty shells, which it then fills with new meanings. And in some cases, the introduction of new terminology or of better, more appropriate and more precise definitions is not necessary; because existing social structure allows manipulations with gender. Thus, this is not a question of outdated meanings. It is a matter of their reappropriation by some transgender individuals who are happy to stay within existing frameworks. It might be the case that transgender could do without "proper" labels.

What is clear is that the choice of introducing, negotiating and using definitions should belong to trans communities. More attention should be given to self-definitions of transgendered people. As anthropologist Don Kulick points out, it is important "to start collecting data about how transgendered persons actually talk—how they use language in a wide variety of social situations to engender themselves and others."[9] And for these purposes it is important that transgender individuals could use adequate definitions such as *hir* and *s/he* but not on a mandatory basis. It should be a matter of individual choice.

I support the desire of the transgender community to have adequate terms to talk about themselves, to be recognizable as transgender individuals, if desired. My doubt concerns the practical outcome of creating a common category of transgender. By creating or negotiating categories, we exercise existing power relations: new categories cannot exist on their own when they are given meanings and conditions within functioning social structures.

As Deborah Cameron points out, instead of replacing sexist terms with non-sexist ones it is more important to focus on meaning and to try to understand the functioning of linguistic resources.[10] Thus far we've discussed the introduction of new definitions and the recreation of already existing categories. By doing so we have not addressed the social system that oppresses transgender, but have merely tried to upgrade it. Perhaps it is more reasonable to focus our efforts on creating a community that would be structured along categories other than sex and gender; a society where the question of having a mandatory gender would be removed or possibly replaced by something else, where the pronouns *he, she* or *hir* would be less important in terms of interpersonal communication and social organization.

However, this is clearly a long-term project since our very language is structured along the gender binary in which existing linguistic meanings stand for the specific division of resources of who one can and cannot be or become according to one's gender. I am not sure if it is possible to outline a clear-cut solution for this problem: language and the social infrastructure that marginalize transgender cannot be changed overnight. My concern is to recognize the problems and potential dangers of creating a "homogenized" category for transgender. I believe that gender (self-) identification—both for transgendered and non-transgendered individuals—should not be categorized and should be a voluntary decision for everyone.

Notes

1 See, for example, works by David Valentine, where be argues the problem of violence of categories for transgender people and gives examples of how identities and practices could be understood differently within a transcommunity. David Valentine, "'The Calculus of Pain': Violence, Anthropological Ethics, and the Category Transgender," *Ethnos* 68, no. 1 (March 2003), 27–48; David Valentine and Riki Anne Wilchins, "One Percent on the Burn Chart: Gender, Genitals and Hermaphrodites with Attitude," *Social Text* 52/53 (Winter 1997), 215–222.

2 Sexism in language is a complicated and heterogeneous issue. There are different and contradictory tendencies look at the possibilities, advantages and disadvantages of non-sexist language reform. See, for example, Dale Spender, *Man Made Language* (London: Routledge and Kegan Paul, 1930); Deborah Cameron, *Feminism and Linguistic Theory* (New York: St. Martin's Press, 1985); Deborah Cameron, *Verbal Hygiene* (London: Routledge, 1995); and Ann Pauwels, *Women Changing Language* (London: Longman, 1998).

3 See Margaret Doyle, "Introduction to *The A–Z of Non-Sexist Language*," in Deborah Cameron, ed., *The Feminist Critique of Language: A Reader* (London: Routledge, 1998), 149–154.

4 Deborah Cameron, "Lost in Translation: Non-Sexist Language," in Cameron, ed., *The Feminist Critique of Language*, 161, 156, 159.

5 bid., 155.

6 As Dale Spender puts it: "This makes language a paradox for human beings: it is both a creative and an inhibiting vehicle. On the one hand, it offers immense freedom for it allows us to 'create' the world we live in . . . But, on the other hand, we are restricted by that creation, limited to its confines, and, it appears, we resist, even though they are 'arbitrary,' approximate ones. It is this which constitutes a language trap." Dale Spender, "Extracts from *Man Made Language*," in Cameron, ed., *The Feminist Critique of Language*, 96.

7 Ibid., 96, 98.

8 Set Sheila Jeffreys, "Heterosexuality and the Desire for Gender," in Diane Richardson, ed., *Theorizing Heterosexuality: Telling it Straight* (Buckingham, UK: Open University Press, 1996), 75–90.

9 Don Kulick, "Transgender and Language: A Review of Literature and Suggestions for the Future," *GLQ: Journal of Lesbian and Gay Studies* 5 (1999), 615.

10 Cameron, "Lost in Translation," 160–163.

Chapter Two

Identities

*I*magine the following: The student union at your university has proposed establishing a "men's center" on campus, to offer a separate space for men to gather and to respond to "men's issues." There's already a women's center on your campus, one used by many students (and some faculty and staff), albeit almost exclusively women. In fact, from what you've heard, the women's center has had a lot of discussion recently about who their space is for: Is this space only for women? Or are men welcome too? And if so, in what capacity? Can they, for instance, staff the space alone, or do they always have to be there with a woman? And even if the space is for women, which women are included? Is it welcoming to transwomen? Does one have to have always identified as a woman, or simply identify as a woman now? Or, is the question instead how other people perceive a person (irrespective of how they identify themselves)? And what about women who feel like their specific concerns aren't really reflected in what the women's center does—Muslim women or Aboriginal women, who tend to use other spaces on campus that address their religious practices and cultural connections? You wonder if the same sets of questions will arise about the proposed men's center. And what about people who identify as genderqueer or as not having a gender identity— will there be a center for them too?

Even more, though, you're intrigued by the different responses on campus to this proposal: the students who wonder why men need a specific space on campus and what a men's issue is; people on and off campus who laugh at the idea, suggesting "there's something wrong with men who want such a space"; some people at the women's center who are adamantly against this idea, insisting that the entire campus is already implicitly men's space and that this proposal is insulting to women and to what a women's center is trying to accomplish. Even some faculty and staff are speaking up against this idea, arguing that it makes light of the differences between women's and men's experiences on campus and attempts to equalize histories of exclusion that aren't the same (or don't even really exist). And you find yourself moving back and forth between different positions, seeing merits in many of these claims and attempting to negotiate your way through them to figure out what seems fair. Then you find yourself wondering about still other spaces on campus that seem specific to particular "identities": e.g., the First Nations/Native students center, the GLBT or Rainbow Alliance group, the Chinese students' association. What about them? Does the existence of those identity-based spaces raise and provoke the same reactions? And, as some critics of this idea have also asked, what if the proposal was for a "white students" association or "heterosexual students" center—questions you feel really conflicted about? Would the reactions be the same?

It's becoming very clear to you that that there are a lot of questions raised by this proposal for a men's center that circulate around understandings about identity categories. And the level of heightened reaction to this proposal demonstrates that so much seems at stake for all the parties involved. How, you wonder, are these various claims to identity, and the different needs of the groups represented by these specific spaces, to be negotiated? And how can you figure out where you stand in this complex and sometimes conflicting set of claims about what seemed at first like a fairly ordinary proposal?

Rethinking "Identity"

The question of what we mean by the term *identity* is central to Women's and Gender Studies, because it is central to how people think about themselves and the worlds they inhabit. Identity is evoked in the ways we talk about oppression and privilege, or about who is included and who is excluded in any number of social contexts. There are many ways to conceptualize identity. We often think of it as something core to who we are, as something biological or psychological that is then expressed by how we look or talk or move. Or, we might think about identity as something we possess or come to acquire, as if it's our own personal property that no one else can take from us. Or we might even think about it as something we actively choose for ourselves—like picking clothes off a rack—and then cultivate like a sense of style. But identity in WGS is much more than an individual characteristic. Rather, identity refers to a number of categories and the many ways in which those categories are used to define and regulate people. Common identity categories that WGS explores include gender, race, sexuality, class, ability, body size, age, religion or secularity, and nationality or citizenship status.

Focusing on how identity categories are defined and regulated allows us to think of identity as something that is produced. It also means that each of us must always negotiate the various contexts that reflect dominant ideas about those identity categories.

To speak of identity as produced is important, because it shifts our attention away from thinking about it as something that belongs to an individual person and instead demands that we think about how the broader society understands and gives meaning to an identity category. This shift also allows us to ask about and explore how those identities are produced—historically, politically, structurally, culturally, and linguistically. Our identities—man, young, black, gay, Christian, able-bodied—always have different meanings in different circumstances; they become meaningful (and even meaningless sometimes) in certain contexts, and those meanings change over time and location. For example, think about how much the social meanings of "black" have changed historically in both Canada and the United States, with resultant differences for how people have been defined (as falling within or outside of that category), what has been expected of people defined as such, and the opportunities that have been available to people based on that definition. These identities are constructed through various social institutions and structures—e.g., family, media, education, law, economics, religious institutions, the state, housing, transportation, architecture—that position us not just differently but inequitably as well. Thus, identity categories affect our sense of self as well as our life chances profoundly. And, finally, to think of identities as produced means being mindful that the ways we see ourselves are always negotiated in relation to other people, both as individuals and as groups. In this way, identity is also always relational, always constructed and experienced as a relationship to other people and to social institutions and structures. So rather than thinking that identities are "facts" about people that simply explain who they are in some obvious way, the approach we take in WGS suggests that identities are more like shifting terrains upon which we both locate ourselves and are positioned by others—sometimes comfortably, sometimes uncomfortably—and that the meanings of those terrains are always in flux.

Also important to remember is that identity is never singular (in spite of the word being used most often in the singular). It is not as if people only claim one identity category at a time: woman, straight, Latino/a. Rather, identities are always intersectional[1]—a term we use in WGS to describe the ways that we occupy many identity

[1]**KNOW ABOUT:**

Intersectionality is a term that has sparked much important theorizing about identity in WGS, but also much debate. For some people, a focus on intersectionality is a way to talk about women's—often women of color's—multiple oppressions, especially around gender and race (among other identity categories) taken together. For others, intersectionality is more descriptive of everyone—a way to think about both *oppression* and *privilege* (terms discussed more in the "Equalities" chapter) by acknowledging how we all have intersecting identities. How this term has been conceptualized and used has often moved researchers in different directions.

categories at a time: we are all gendered, but also belong to (or are presumed to belong to) race, class, and sexuality groups, too. Intersectionality doesn't only describe the idea that we are all many identities, though. It also recognizes that each of those categories is reflective of hierarchies of oppression and privilege and always crosscut by the others, thereby changing the definitions, understandings, and experiences of any one category. It allows us to ask new questions about how identities are formed and experienced, especially by those whose experiences of oppression are often silenced or rendered invisible to others. Intersectionality, therefore, is a framework for thinking about how identity categories are produced. For instance, think about the differences that age makes to how women might be positioned over a lifetime (as youthful and desirable versus no longer "on the market") or how race changes perceptions about masculinity in men (as responsible providers versus potential threats[2]). Think also about how these assessments of which aspects of identity are visible and meaningful shift depending on various contexts and locations that one might move through in a given day (e.g., neighborhood, school, work, social gathering). Intersectionality is thus a concept that describes the mutuality of identities. It is a recognition that the intersection of categories such as gender, race, class, sexuality, ability, nation makes a difference to how each person is positioned in the world and, in turn, experiences the world around them[3].

This understanding of interconnectedness is especially useful because to speak of identities as intersectional means to acknowledge how multifaceted we are—gendered and raced and sexualized and classed; some of our identity categories may be dominant in relation to others (e.g., white, male, citizen) and some may be marginal (e.g., working class, disabled, migrant)—and that these different positions may occur simultaneously, with different effects. Each of us always occupies a complex combination of dominant and subordinate positions that vary as we cross into different contexts: social institutions or structures (such as education or medicine), sets of practices and relationships (such as parent, student, supervisor), and locations (such as home, workplace, public spaces, cyberspace). Thus, *intersectionality* is an important term because it demands that we always conceptualize the simultaneity of multiple identity categories that everyone occupies, with the result that we can never generalize broadly about any individual or any group; this means that we can never simply

[2]**TALK ABOUT:** Generate more examples of how identities intersect to change understandings of any single category. How do many of these intersections become stereotypes and generalizations? What are some of the ways in which you see these arising in the world around you, for example, in pop culture, news reporting, educational texts? How are the consequences or effects of these stereotypes different for different groups of people? How would you go about countering some of these?

[3]**THINK ABOUT:** Notice how both of these examples—the age of women or the idea of men as providers—also reflect assumptions about (hetero)sexuality. If the category of sexuality shifts, then our understandings of gender and race tend to shift too: for instance, questions of women's age and desirability are socially understood quite differently when

say something like "men are . . .," "Asians like . . .," or "people with disabilities think . . .," since each of these identities also has plenty of other differences—differences that make a difference—within them.

Constructing Identity Categories

What difference might it make to think about major identity categories—gender, race, ethnicity, sexuality, disability—as constructed, or as socially produced historically, institutionally, relationally, and intersectionally[(4)]? Where does that get us? One response has to do with how it fundamentally shifts our understandings of who people are, why the world works the way it does, and what we might to do change things for the better for a greater number of people. Think, for instance, of statements that seem to describe people's identity categories: he is black; she is disabled; they are straight. While these statements might seem obvious, simple descriptions of who people are or how they reflect various identity categories, our focus here suggests that these are in fact quite complex statements. What *black*, *disabled*, and *straight* mean differs radically over time and location, as well as in relation to other identity categories. In the West, for instance, they are categories that have been produced through historical events and policies (like colonialism and immigration), through social structures and stereotypes (about how people's bodies are supposed to look and move), and through institutions such as law and religion (with their mandates about who can marry whom and what is recognized as constituting a family[(5)]).

Thinking about an identity category as historically constructed can shift our thinking in fundamental ways. For instance, understanding the category of race as historically constructed means acknowledging that there is no biological feature (genetic or otherwise) that all the people whom our society identifies as a particular race have in common. Rather, both the idea of race itself as well as particular examples of race (such as white or black or Asian) are products of specific encounters of different groups of people and the subsequent exploitations of lives, lands, and other resources through imperialism, colonialism, war, and genocide. Indeed, many scholars suggest that before about the early Renaissance period in the West, race was not a concept that was particularly meaningful. While violent invasions of other lands have been going

that woman's sexuality is assumed as lesbian; likewise, presumptions about men as providers, no matter their racial designation, also tend to alter for gay rather than straight men. Thus, we can see that intersectionality, more than just a way to think about identity, is also a kind of tool that allows us to "root out" those invisible adjectives we talked about in the "Knowledges" chapter.

[(4)]THINK ABOUT: The terms *social constructionism* and *essentialism* refer to two primary ways in which identity categories can be understood and explained. *Social constructionism*, the approach we authors take here, refers to the idea that definitions of and meanings attributed to identity categories are specific to time and place, arising out of the environment and culture in which they are embedded. So to say that an identity category such as "homosexual" is socially constructed is to on throughout human history, and such invasions often included the enslavement of whole groups of people considered "other," the notion that those people were perceived to be a different race was not salient until quite recently (historically speaking). This understanding of how an identity category has developed helps us recognize that even contemporary differences in wealth, social standing, health, life chances, educational access, and social precarity or resilience might be attributable less to "natural" differences of identity than to the historical legacies and contemporary practices that (re)produce that identity category itself.

In much the same way as race, we can argue that both sex and gender, as identity categories, are also historically produced. For example, in the West, the notion that men and women are of the "opposite" sex or that masculinity and femininity constitute complete contrasts is also, historically speaking, a relatively new idea. The dominant way of thinking about sex and gender—that is, about biology (sex) and about the social roles (gender) attributed to biology—is that one is born male or female and then becomes masculine or feminine based on their biology. Even more, biology is assumed to be fairly unproblematic; external genitalia, reproductive organs, secondary sex characteristics, hormones, and genetics all line up with each other as clearly male or female. So not only do sex and gender align, but one's sex, or biology, is always clear and clearly different from the other sex. And, of course, one's gender always follows (as if in a causal relationship) one's sex and each is clearly differentiated from the other[6].

Taking a more historical approach to this set of assumptions raises a number of points that allow us to see how much these distinctions have also been produced or constructed, rather than simply existing in nature. For a long time, for instance, women were simply regarded as "less perfect men." Sexual dimorphism—the division of the human species into two distinct and opposite categories of male and female biologies—didn't take hold until late in the modern era, into the eighteenth century. This doesn't mean that people didn't see or think there was a difference between the people they called men and the people they called women. But it does mean that the basis for that belief was not grounded in the notion of two distinct biological sexes, clearly aligned with two distinct genders. And even today, there are many instances where these beliefs in sex and gender cannot account for the varieties of either of

say that its definition, its social meanings, how it is viewed by a particular society, are all specific to time and place. On the contrary, *essentialism* refers to the belief that the meaning of an identity is static and universal, and doesn't change across time and place.

[5]**KNOW ABOUT:** The term *heteronormativity* refers to the ways in which particular ideals of heterosexuality and gender are privileged or become the "norm" in our society: the belief that women and men, clearly distinguished from each other, "fit together" or complement each other, and that their sexual relationships express that complementarity through a number of norms that include monogamy, living together, and sharing lives and bank accounts. But think of examples of heterosexuality that don't fit the norm: paid sex work (more on that at the end of this chapter)

or polyamory/multiple partners or partners who don't live together or share lives in expected ways. While these might be heterosexual, they are not heteronormative; that is, they don't fit the ideals attached to only particular practices of gendered heterosexuality. Thus, many people argue that it is possible for same-sex partners to also be heteronormative: to fit into most of those ideal heterosexual norms (except for the idea of a sexual relationship between two "opposite" sexes/genders). The concept of heteronormativity helps us broaden our understanding of how central particular understandings of sexuality and gender are to a range of social institutions such as family and marriage, and helps us also understand the basis for struggles to redefine each of these so they aren't based on the sex/gender of the people involved.

these categories or for the ways in which they don't always align. Think, for example, of the dominant approach to intersex in Canada and the United States. *Intersex* is a term used to describe any number of physiological anomalies to the sexual dimorphism largely taken for granted: genitalia that differs from the "norm" in some way (such as "too small" a penis, "too large" a clitoris, a urethra that doesn't extend to the tip of the penis), gonads (reproductive organs) that don't align with external genitalia (a difference often discovered at puberty), hormonal conditions (which also usually show up later in life around puberty) that result in secondary sex characteristics that don't match genitalia (and gender), and chromosomal incongruities that often underlie other anomalies[7]. The medical diagnosis of intersex, then, is a way to mark variations of biology that don't fall easily into one of the two categories of male or female.

The diagnosis of intersex, at birth or later, generally results in medical interventions, surgical and/or hormonal. These medical interventions to "correct" or "fix" anatomies that don't clearly fall into one of two categories demonstrates how much a belief in (and an attachment to) sex dimorphism actually overrides human variation. Indeed, the belief that there are two sexes, separate and opposite from each other (and two genders aligned with those sexes), imposes a binary structure on biology even when nature is much more complex—a binary structure that the medical establishment then works to perpetuate. Knowing some of the ways in which ideas about gender and sex are constructed, then, is a way to destabilize ideas about the naturalness of either. Femininity cannot be considered an inevitable or natural outcome of people with vaginas, nor can masculinity be seen as an inevitable or natural outcome of people with penises.

Thinking about the identity category gender as constructed also means turning our attention to the various ways that understandings of that category are built into the world around us, focusing on the role of social structures and institutions, language and representation, and everyday practices in upholding particular definitions of identities. Identity categories are not just historical occurrences, but are constantly being (re)produced by various social structures and institutions in ways that are often limited/limiting and invisible. Take, for example, that idea expressed above—that gender is a dichotomy, or that there are only two genders, opposite from each other and usually existing in a hierarchical relation to each other[8]. Think about how something as common as public bathrooms consistently reflects this idea of only two genders and insist that everyone fit into one or the other category; there are generally only two doors to go through, represented by symbolic figures that we are all supposed to recognize, and there are definite sanctions against people who go through the "wrong" door. Or think about the many ways in which the idea that there are two opposite genders is embedded in the world around us—from gender specific products of all kinds to food and colors and styles to sports and leisure pursuits and activities (we'll return to the implications of this idea shortly). No matter the complexity of people's gender presentations or how they identify themselves, the world around us reflects and attempts to impose a rigid structure of gender dichotomy on all of us[9]. And some of us fit more readily than others, in some circumstances, into that mold—although all of us will probably "fail" at some point to uphold the rigid definitions of that dichotomy.

But as argued above, no identity category exists in isolation; all identities are relational and intersectional, combining in a myriad of ways with others. And yet, it is often difficult to remember this, as dominant definitions of any category always appear as if they exist in isolation from other identities, obscuring the ways in which one always changes another. Think, for instance, of the organization of a toy store into the "pink" aisles—clearly intended for girls, and the "blue" aisles—clearly intended for boys (and sometimes for either sex/gender). Understanding identity as intersectional, as well as constructed through institutions and everyday practices, helps us think more critically about gendered toy aisles. In looking closely at the toys in the pink aisle, for instance, the centrality of blonde hair specifically, and whiteness generally, in most of the images on packaging that model what kids should do with these toys is overwhelmingly present. While girls of color may be featured on the packaging when groups of children are shown (to increase diversity), the primary reflections about femininity that most children, no matter their race or ethnicity, will see through these toys are reflections of white femininity—that is then also able-bodied and with a specific body size and shape. And this isn't just the case for toys, but is also evident in cartoons, movies, children's literature, and textbooks. When an institution consistently produces femininity as white, able-bodied, and thin, it becomes easier to see the ways in which an idealized understanding of gender is also always marked

(6)KNOW ABOUT:
The term *biological determinism* is also used to talk about this belief that biology is "destiny," that is, that one's biological make-up always leads to particular social outcomes. This belief in biological determinism, one that is still around today, is not limited to thinking about gender, but has also been used to talk about race and class, among other identity categories. Many people who oppose this belief point out how it always seems to end up upholding status quo social relations and hierarchies.

(7)THINK ABOUT:
Many scholars argue that intersex is a fluid category that depends on how one defines *anomaly*. This definition then influences how prevalent intersex is considered to be, with statistics ranging from about 1 in 500 births to 1 in 2,000 or more births. As with all identity categories,

definitions clearly matter for thinking about frequency. Likewise, scholars also argue that the belief that there are two genders informs the belief that there are only two biological sexes; as long as sex and gender are supposed to align, then all biological variation is "forced" into a binary in order to keep a gender binary in place, too.

(8)**KNOW ABOUT:** Although the idea of gender dichotomy is predominant in contemporary Canada and the U.S. (and many other countries in the world), this isn't always the case. Since 2007, Nepal, for example, has recognized the category of "third gender," and several countries today offer an option outside of male/female to their citizens for documents such as passports. Additionally, many Indigenous peoples in both Canada and the U.S. have long recognized gender designations

by other taken-for-granted identity categories. "Gender" is thus highlighted as the central defining feature of the pink aisle, while all the ways in which that gender is also about race and ability and body size are almost completely obscured.

Meanwhile, over in the blue aisles, toys frequently make use of war and other kinds of "action" as a context for play. This range of toys' representations of masculinities is also clearly set up relationally to those femininities, presented as oppositional (as if men and women were on opposite ends of any continuum of human traits), hierarchical (men aren't just different from women but each is valued differently in all kinds of institutional contexts), and mutually exclusive (to be a man is to not be a woman and to be a woman is to not be a man). Likewise, these various kinds of gun-toting, action-oriented masculinities demonstrate that our cultural imaginaries of weapon-clad cops and soldiers are often racialized quite differently than our imaginaries of weapon-clad gangsters, pirates, and terrorists, where the former are usually presented as white and the latter are not. And again, masculinity is taken for granted as a singular category, although it clearly intersects with and reflects particular ideas about class, able-bodiedness, and national identity.

This normalizing of particular identities as static and singular can be pushed even further, though, to see how powerfully institutions shape our understanding of these identity categories and ourselves in relation to them. As suggested above, for example, it doesn't just make a difference which boy (e.g., white, citizen, Christian) picks up an action figure and which girl (e.g., Asian, thin, disabled) picks up a doll; it also makes a difference that guns and dolls come to be seen as representative of ideas about gender across any number of contexts—intimate and public, local and global. Domestic spaces then come to be seen as feminine spaces, regardless of which gender occupies them; militarized spaces come to be seen as masculine, regardless of which gender is a soldier. And this is the case whether we are talking about the literal sense of "home"—that private, intimate location of familial relations and personal expressions, or about the "home front"—that geopolitical entity which might be said to be under threat and in need of protection by military campaigns in faraway lands.

The implications of deviating from these ideals of femininity or masculinity become especially visible when people reach across the gender divides that these institutions produce. For example, women in the military (or, girls with guns) present a conundrum in a number of contexts, not the least of which is being soldiers who also happen to be mothers. What does it mean—practically and symbolically—to send mothers to war, to ask mothers to potentially sacrifice their lives for their country? Can we simply assume that mothers as soldiers are perceived in the same way as fathers as soldiers? While they might both be parents, socially what it means to "mother" a child is often perceived quite differently than what it means to "father" a child. As this example illustrates, then, the military is an institution that both reflects and produces particular ideas about gender as an identity category, precisely because it is itself also a "gendered institution." And it's not just a gendered institution; it's a gendered institution that is racialized and reflects ideas about able-bodiedness, class, sexuality, and nation.

Likewise, think about how concepts of dominant masculinity are breached when men occupy domestic and familial spaces. Are men who are, for example, nannies or preschool teachers regarded as having the same motivations for their career choices as women? Are they scrutinized or rewarded in different ways than women in the same occupations? And how do our responses to these questions shift as the race, class, sexuality, and national identities of these men shift? Again, it is not just that people in various institutions are gendered but that the institutions themselves are gendered, in turn shaping people differently and with different effects. And it's not just that people are racialized, but that institutions themselves are also racialized, reflecting particular ideas about racial hierarchies and when they matter more (or less). No matter how varied people are, then, the focus on institutions and structures illustrates how rigid ideas about identity markers are. Characteristics of identity categories come to be attributed to, and defining of, inanimate objects, places, and activities in ways that constantly communicate who we are or should be. Of course, most people don't fit easily (or at all) into these categories and are, therefore, in some ways (ironically) always "failing" at identities they claim to be.

To sum up, then, identity categories are always produced, constructed historically and institutionally as well as through everyday practices, in ways that often remain invisible, especially to those who fit easily, most of the time, into them. Gender, race, sexuality, disability, nationality—those markers of identity that play such an important

outside of this binary. The belief in gender as dichotomous is clearly not the only way for a society to organize gender as an identity category. What remains common here, though, is the underlying belief in demarcating separate and distinct genders as part of the category of gender.

(9)**TALK ABOUT:** Generate a list of examples of this kind of gender dichotomy around you. How are the same products produced and marketed so differently for men and women—i.e., razors or soaps? What else is being suggested by the gendering of food or leisure activities—that is, what is that saying about supposedly appropriate feminine and masculine behaviors? Keep thinking about the ways in which assumptions about gender dichotomy are built into the world around us in small and large ways as you read through this chapter.

role in answering the basic question of who we are—have a constantly changing set of definitions and parameters that position us in some relationship to the world around us. These locations frame—or attempt to delimit—many of our possibilities for being and acting at any given moment in any given context. But that's hardly all there is to say about identity, especially when we think about the ways in which all of us in some way or another fall outside of, openly resist, and even consciously subvert the rigidity of identity categories in small and big ways.

The Limits of Identity Categories

The above section explored the idea that identity categories are constructed in a variety of ways, so that their meanings and definitions are not natural so much as constantly being (re)produced. But the irony—or tragedy—of how identity categories are defined through this process is that they rarely adequately reflect the diversity of people's experiences or ways of being in the world. Indeed, quite the opposite. Too often, these categories seem like, and are experienced as, attempts to force people into rigidly defined boxes that limit their life choices, often with disastrous effects. But these identity categories don't just exist "out there" in the world; they are also something we identify with or claim as our own. Put differently, we are always negotiating our lives in relation to the demands of these categories, sometimes desiring the categories, sometimes refusing them. And that those categories are rarely adequate to meet the complexities of our lives raises a number of additional issues to consider.

Let's return to an earlier example. Think about how restricted the idea of gender dichotomy is and the ways in which so many people do not fit the most rigid understanding of that binary at least some of the time ("failing" at those identities): women who do construction work or men who are the primary caretakers of children. Or, in another example, think of a category like race, with its fairly rigid ways of identifying and demarcating lines of difference between groups of people—black, white, Latino, Asian—that cannot account for the myriad of ways in which people identify themselves racially far outside of the dominant constructions of this category (as mixed race, *mestiza,* hybrid identities). If no one ever fits completely within the rigid norms and boundaries of a category, what does this suggest to us about the categories themselves and about their limitations? Clearly, there is often a disconnect, or at least a tension, between how these identity categories exist in the world around us and our (in)ability to fit into them. And while not fitting into categories might seem like a good thing—a form of pointing out their limitations or expressing our individuality—it is also the case that not fitting, or refusing categories altogether, has consequences: again, contemplate something as ordinary as public bathroom use, where the consequences of being perceived to be in the wrong bathroom can range from expressions of disapproval to verbal abuse to violence.

Even if identity categories are limiting and too limited for most people, it is also clear that they still play a central role in how many people define themselves and others, and in how people come together to create communities that are assumed to share some commonalities. But then there are potential issues that can arise from this gathering around a presumed shared identity. If no one ever fits completely, if everyone fails at identity assumptions and norms at least some of the time (and sometimes much of the time), then how and when is someone assumed to fit "enough" to be counted as part of that identity category? Who decides, and on what basis and with what power to make that decision stick, that someone "really is" a particular identity or "really belongs" to a particular category? The moment an identity category is established as a means to differentiate between people, locating and regulating the borders of that category also becomes part of its definition. Consider, for example, something like sexuality, so often understood as a binary between heterosexuality and homosexuality; at what point, on what basis, and by whose definition(s), is that distinction made? Is the distinction based on people who have sex exclusively with the other sex or gender (presuming there are only two of each), or only some of the time? People who identify as one category, or who are identified by others? People who only think about particular sexual encounters, or who have them? Or, as another example, think about something like disability and the social debates that ensue over whether someone is disabled "enough" or "in the right ways" that then allow for access to various resources[10]. Even as people identify themselves with identity categories, and identify with others through those categories, there are also clearly concerns about the borders and parameters of all categories too—and those borders are not just benign differences.

[10]**TALK ABOUT:** Can you think of other examples where this idea of regulating the borders of identity categories occurs, and what the consequences of that might be for who is included and who isn't? Think back to the examples that opened this chapter—of a men's center or other seemingly identity-specific spaces or organizations. What is gained and what is lost by focusing on identity in this way—and for whom? If there is disagreement in this class discussion (as there probably is!), what is the basis of that disagreement, or what do you notice about those differences of opinion?

One example to further explore the complexities of identity categories is the term *queer*. A term that used to be used derogatorily to refer to same-sex desire, queer has, over the past twenty or so years, been (re)appropriated as a means to challenge the identity categories of gender and sexuality through its proud adoption. Its meanings are complex and debated, though, with implications for who and what is defined as queer and for how "queer community" is understood. On the one hand, queer is often used as a catch-all term for a specific set of identities. So instead of listing gay, lesbian, bisexual, transgender, the word queer becomes a shorthand; it becomes an identity category that brings together many sexuality and gender identities that are considered non-normative, in the process becoming a term which many people then claim. This is the sense of queer as a synonym for a range of sexuality and gender identities, a term that then also demarcates a border between non-normative and normative expressions of gender and sexuality. Of course, as suggested above, if this is the case, then there are also both benefits and costs to this identity category. Queer becomes a means of bringing people together or forming community and common identity (and thus also the basis of possible political struggle or shared leisure activities); but as with all identity categories, it also becomes a site of debate over who and what counts as queer, and who and what doesn't—with all the attendant issues of which definitions are being mobilized, who and what is making those distinctions, and what the costs are of naming some people as queer and others as not.

On the other hand, the term queer (especially as used in academic settings, in "queer theory" or "queer studies") also references a politicized dissent from how dominant (and limited) definitions of any kind of sexuality and gender identities are embedded in the world around us. This understanding of queer doesn't point to an identity category, but rather aims to ask questions about how all identity categories are constructed. As such, we can talk about practices, acts, and cultural forms as "queering" understandings of sexuality and gender—that is, as calling attention to their production or construction and attempting to destabilize their definitions. Queer, in this usage, is not an identity so much as a way to challenge identity, to point out the construction of and consequences in making distinctions between supposedly queer people and non-queer people; it is a term that calls our attention to asking questions about how and why and for whom queer is taken on as an identity, about how the borders of queer are patrolled and regulated, and about its consequences.

One way to conceptualize the difference between these two notions of queer is to think of the first usage as a noun (referring to an identity category) and the second as a verb—"to queer" (to challenge and subvert categories and identities). So someone can identify as queer: "I am queer"—meaning that they fit into some definition of or understanding of a category called "queer." But they can also "queer" a category like gender—by questioning the foundations of such a category, exposing its hidden assumptions, and exploring the limitations of binary gender definitions in numerous ways: presenting themselves in ways that don't align with social expectations for that category or identifying in ways that fall outside that binary, such as genderqueer or transgender[11]. The term queer, then, recognizes that sexuality and gender are historically and institutionally constructed and provides, for many people, an identity category that is often experienced (as with all identity categories) as a source of strength, affinity, and pride. At the same time, queer (as in *queering*) can resist those same constructions by constantly pointing out how limited dominant definitions of sexuality and gender are, and, in the process, destabilize their taken-for-grantedness. And people can and do hold onto both of these meanings at the same time, identifying as queer for everything it gives them, while simultaneously "queering" it as an identity category.

For all its attention to the subversion of dominant histories and social structures, for many people queering also runs the risk of forgetting that all identities are intersectional and that how sexuality or gender are socially defined and positioned depends a lot on their intersection with other identity categories: race, class, national identity, disability. Think, for instance, of how much stereotypical perceptions of men's sexuality are altered by representing them as either white men or black men—with the latter so often calling on longstanding imaginaries of black men's hyper (and thus more dangerous) sexuality, whether they are gay or straight. Or, think of stereotypical perceptions of Asian women's sexuality as more "exotic" than white women's. Or, finally, think about stereotypes of people with disabilities as being asexual, neither desired nor desiring. Queering gender and sexuality, then, has to always draw attention to and challenge the ways in which genders and sexualities (in the plural) are produced; it means recognizing that challenging dominant definitions also means challenging

[11]KNOW ABOUT:
Like queer, the term *transgender* has a complicated genealogy. Some people use transgender as an umbrella term for a variety of non-normative gender expressions: e.g., effeminate men, butch women, drag queens and kings–that is, for gender expressions that fall somewhere outside the normative expectations of the more usual gender binary. As this kind of umbrella term, transgender can be thought of as challenging not only gender norms, but gender dichotomy itself, not by creating a third category, but by pointing out how limiting and limited binary categories are. We could, then, speak of

the differences that other factors like race and social class make to these categories. Otherwise, queering may resist and subvert some categorizations of gender or sexuality, but it may also run the risk of reifying and perpetuating others. To queer, thus, means something quite different than using queer as a shorthand for a number of excluded or non-dominant identities.

As this chapter has explored, identities—or identity categories—are both regulatory and productive; they discipline us by trying to force us into rigid boundaries, but they're also the ways in which we identify ourselves, and thus are also sites of various kinds of resistances and subversions as we struggle over their meanings. Emphasizing that identities are products of history, negotiated among and within institutional settings, and always intersectional means that we can identify the complex ways in which definitions of identities are constantly being (re)produced—and that we can also imagine ourselves and others in new ways as we point out the limitations of those categories. Acknowledging the complexity of historical and institutional legacies, along with recognizing the variety of ways their limited definitions are resisted and subverted provides a deeper understanding of the centrality of this concept in our lives, denaturalizing its taken-for-granted status and allowing us to see it as a complex set of processes of ongoing definition and negotiation in our daily lives.

The Concept at Work: Queering Heterosexuality

Imagine that you're watching television one night, one of those crime drama shows, and the plot line circulates—again—around the serial murder of female sex workers (except they're always called prostitutes, or even whores or hookers—even by the police/FBI/crime scene investigators in the show). Of course, by the end of the hour, the serial murderer is caught, and throughout the show he (and it is almost always a he) is represented as a dangerous and vilified character who is no doubt a criminal in his desire to murder these women. But what fascinates you throughout—and what you start recognizing as a pattern in so many of these shows—is the way in which the sex workers are also represented as "other" in some way. Variously presented as poor, addicted, desperate women doing survival sex work to women who have chosen this kind of work, the overall approach to these women always strikes you as a mixture

"transing" in the same way as "queering" is being discussed here. For other people, though (and perhaps increasingly so), transgender is being taken up and understood as a third possibility for gender identification or as a separate identity category—with all the same issues of then defining and deciding inclusion and exclusion. One current debate around transgender is whether this term replicates some of the same issues of identity categories or whether it offers new possibilities for thinking about gender. Of course, both the thinking about this debate, and its consequences, might be very different for individuals' own identification or for how societies think about gender as an identity category.

of pity and horror. No matter how they got there, the sentiment seems to be, they're really not doing what "good" women should. They always need some kind of "rescuing," not only from their lives of crime (because in most places, sex work is largely a criminalized activity) but also from their desperation and exploitation. What these shows draw on is a dominant understanding of sex work that positions women who exchange money for sex on the "bad" side of a "good girl"/ "bad girl" binary. This attitude towards sex work is so embedded in the culture that in almost every representation, sex work by women is stigmatized and criminalized.

However, suppose we think of sex work as a way to queer heterosexual femininity rather than simply an identity category that illustrates an inappropriate (or "bad") kind of heterosexuality. Seen in this way, sex work becomes a way to expose how heterosexuality (and ideas about heterosexual romance) is also a series of resource transactions that involves the same give and take, the same assessment of benefits and costs, as sex work or any other kind of economic exchange. Think about cultural expectations for an unaccompanied woman in a bar, for example. If a man buys her a drink, what kinds of responses seem to be expected (or demanded) of her—and how do we know them so readily (whether we agree with them or not)? What are the likely sanctions if she doesn't comply (and again, how do we know these so readily; where do we repeatedly see them around us)? And how might such expectations be intensified based on her age, her race, her body shape and size, her dress and appearance? In other words, all women have to negotiate some form of potential sexual stigmatization if they don't perform heterosexual femininity in particular ways, even in situations not of their choosing. And those stigmatizations are exacerbated depending on their race, class, age, and national identities—again demonstrating how idealized heterosexual femininity is always intersectional.

Yet, if we consider sex workers, those who demand cash for meeting the dominant culture's expectations for heterosexual femininity's roles in this exchange, we could argue that such demands for cash are a dissent from that sexual economy. Sex workers resist heterosexual femininity by positioning themselves clearly as the "bad girl" and extracting direct and immediate payment for it. In this process, they also queer heteronormativity, in that their practices of heterosexuality don't fall into the dominant sexual and gender definitions of that category with its emphases on particular forms of monogamy, love and relationship, marriage and family. Thinking queerly about sex work, then, means understanding both the potentials and limits of "deviance" and "conformity." It allows us to identify with more complexity the range of transactions that are part of all heterosexual relationships: for instance, the deals (albeit usually not called *deals*) women make with themselves and with men for partnerships, family, shared childcare, economic possibilities, among other benefits. Queering heterosexuality can lead us to think more carefully about that which is rarely acknowledged—that is, that men also negotiate exchanges in relationships (a negotiation that is probably even more invisible and unacknowledged). Thinking queerly—about heterosexuality or any other category—means paying attention to how the categories we have for identities—man, woman, black, white, fat, thin—both construct boundaries and make room for ways to desire to do and to be otherwise: embracing hybridity, living on borders, claiming what is reviled. Seeing identity categories with more complexity, nuance, and ambivalence opens up the question of "How shall we live?" in the most intimate parts of our lives.

Preview of Readings

Angel, Buck. 2013. "The Power of My Vagina." In *Feminist Porn Book: The Politics of Producing Pleasure*, edited by Tristan Taormino, Celine Parreñas Shimizu, Constance Penley, and Mireille Miller-Young, 284–287. New York, NY: The Feminist Press.

DeMello, Margo. 2014. "Racialized and Colonized Bodies." In *Body Studies: An Introduction*, 99–116. New York, NY: Routledge.

Gavey, Nicola. 2011. "Viagra and the Coital Imperative." In *Introducing the New Sexuality Studies* (2nd ed.), edited by Steven Seidman, Nancy Fischer, and Chet Meeks, 119–124. New York, NY: Routledge.

Walters, Suzanna Danuta. 2014. "The Medical Gayz." In *The Tolerance Trap: How God, Genes, and Good Intentions Are Sabotaging Gay Equality*, 81–96. New York, NY: New York University Press.

Pascoe, C. J. 2011. "'Guys Are Just Homophobic': Rethinking Adolescent Homophobia and Heterosexuality" In *Introducing the New Sexuality Studies* (2nd ed.), edited by Steven Seidman, Nancy Fischer, and Chet Meeks, 175–182. New York, NY: Routledge.

"Identities" introduces the term *intersectionality* as central to the way we think about the confluence of identity categories—including race, class, gender, sexuality, ability, age, nationality, citizenship status, and body size—sometimes positioning us as dominant and sometimes as subordinate as we move through various contexts. We talk about how identities are relational, the ways in which they change throughout time, and how identity categories themselves are always limiting in some ways, even though they play a significant role in how we define ourselves. *Queer*—as a noun and a verb—allows for specific kinds of resistance to dominant understandings of sex and gender.

Buck Angel's "The Power of My Vagina" illustrates the ways in which identities—like man or transman—are both productive and policed. In producing porn that displays both his hyper-masculine body and the pleasure he experiences from vaginal penetration, Angel taps into the anxieties and elations of how people relate to their own sense of masculine selves.

- In what ways is pornography a source of identity and power for Angel?
- How does Angel's age, race, and able-bodiedness provide him access to privileged forms of masculinity (in spite of his identity as transman) that might not be available to others who embark on a similar journey?

"Racialized and Colonized Bodies" by Margo DeMello argues that race matters, a lot, in the North American historical context and the present moment. As she points out, identities based on race have no biological foundation, but instead form an arbitrary set of hierarchal categories. Even though race (was and still) is a social construct, it nevertheless shapes many factors that touch people's everyday lives, including beauty standards, sexual desires, employment, and life chances within particular racialized categories.

- What does documenting the overwhelming racism embedded in the identity categories prevalent in societies like ours (contemporary Canada and the U.S.) do to change understandings of the present—and possibilities for the future?
- In what ways does the racialization that colonialism launched still play out around us?
- Does being a member of the identity group change how we might think and communicate about that group? How might we think about responsibility and accountability in depicting the experience of others?

Nicola Gavey's "Viagra and the Coital Imperative" offers a critical assessment of how Viagra and its marketing produces particular kinds of heterosexual masculinity through emphasizing the "failure to perform." She argues that Viagra both reflects and produces normative understandings of heterosexual identity for men and women.

- What is the impact of heterosexual men's expectations on the sex lives of their women partners?
- In what ways might we see the "coital imperative" as a product of the marketplace? That is, what does Viagra both reflect and perpetuate?
- What are some other examples in the world around you where you see this "coital imperative" at work?

Suzanna Walters offers a skeptical take on how gayness is constructed in popular culture as "natural" instead of socially, culturally, and historically mediated. Although the "born that way" stance has also recently coincided with unprecedented levels of acceptance for gay rights, it also reveals assumptions about that acceptance as making few allowances for actually choosing to belong to a marginalized identity category.

- What is at stake when society seeks a biological basis for our desires and behaviors? Can you think of other examples of biological claims about behaviors?
- Does naturalizing identity categories like gayness and lesbianism through the use of scientific methods do anything to address how these identities are valued (or not) in the larger culture?

In "'Guys Are Just Homophobic': Rethinking Adolescent Homophobia and Heterosexuality" C. J. Pascoe researches how adolescent boys use what she calls "fag discourse" to police each other's performances of masculinity. With the quotidian use of homophobic slurs recast as a mandate about gender (as opposed to sexuality), the way these boys treat the bodies of girls—demeaning them, dominating them, groping them—emphasizes the relational characteristics of masculine identity formation.

- Are Pascoe's descriptions of gender relations in school settings familiar to you?
- In what ways are boys and men around us rewarded for their masculine performance (or lack thereof)?
- How might "fag discourse" help us understand the prevalence of men's and boys' sexual harassment and assault of women and girls?

The Power of My Vagina

Buck Angel

Buck Angel was born female and survived a tumultuous and anguished youth to become the successful self-made man he is today. Parlaying the self-esteem and confidence he garnered through his sex change, he made history as the world's first female-to-male transsexual (FTM) porn star. In 2007, he became the first FTM to win the prestigious Transsexual Performer of the Year Award from AVN. Buck Angel is also a groundbreaking filmmaker who has produced a series of public service announcements on seldom discussed topics, and a unique pair of documentaries about trans men's sexualities, one for the mainstream, and the other for an adult audience. He's an entrepreneur who has gone from pioneering a new adult-industry niche, FTM porn, to appearing in mainstream media. More recently, he's become a motivational speaker, educating people about sexuality and gender, with a universal message of learning to love one's self.

My name is Buck Angel. I am a man. I have a vagina and I work in the sex industry.

From the moment we're born, our culture tells us that genitals determine gender and not all genitals are created equal: we are taught that having a vagina makes you weak. Many women grow up feeling like it is not okay to be sexually at peace with their vaginas. I certainly felt that way for many years. I had a very hard time with my vagina; I could not touch it or really look at it. I was ashamed of it—not so much because I was "female," but more because I didn't like my vagina. It made me feel like I was less of a man.

Through my sex change and the use of testosterone, I became more sexually aware and my body became more sensitive. I felt compelled to explore my body in ways I hadn't before I transitioned from female to male. Then, one day while masturbating, I just slipped my fingers inside myself. What a powerful feeling to be able to have an orgasm with a part of my body I had never fully experienced before. Eventually, I became comfortable engaging in penetration with a partner. I became so excited and positive about my vagina that I decided I wanted to share it with everyone!

I couldn't find any role models of guys like me in the porn world, so I decided to step up to the plate myself. When I first started my work in the adult industry, I wanted to represent myself as a transsexual man who was sexual and confident. I wanted to show that I could enjoy my vagina as a man, and that I didn't have to feel ashamed or disgusted. Porn isn't afraid of showing you everything, and I wasn't going to be either.

But when I first began, I had no idea that my work would ignite such a firestorm of controversy. The negativity and hate that my porn unleashed was primarily from biological men, I think perhaps because they are so attached to the idea that "the penis makes the man." But some women and trans men also spewed hate and venom at me. Some said that sexually explicit films are degrading, especially toward women. Plenty of trans men were horrified that I showed the world that there are men like me out there. They were concerned that I was trying to represent all trans men, and make everyone think that all trans men enjoy their vaginas and use them in the same way.

My intention was only to represent myself, and to show that I took pride in myself and my vagina—to demonstrate that I wasn't any less of a man because I enjoy being penetrated (by both men and women). To be able to experience sexual gratification from my vagina on film has been hugely liberating and empowering. It has provided me with even more self-confidence, along with a great deal of pleasure.

Some trans guys contacted me to thank me. Before seeing my porn, they didn't feel comfortable with their bodies, and they thought they would have to get a penis to be a "complete man." Many of these guys denied themselves sex because they were unable to enjoy the bodies that they—and the majority of trans men—have. (The surgery to create a penis is very expensive, risky, often unsuccessful, and, in my opinion, lacking in aesthetics and function.) They saw me as a man, having sex, using my vagina, and receiving great pleasure.

Obviously, the barrage of hate has upset me, but the positive feedback made me realize that I do not make pornography simply for people to get off. I do educational work, too. I challenge people to examine how our society defines gender on the basis of genitals alone. I change the way they look at what it means to be a man. I promote the idea that having a vagina is powerful, no matter who it is attached to. I inspire many trans men who have vaginas to feel safe to explore and enjoy sex. I show the public that guys like us exist and that we are sexy and sexual. My latest projects are educational and include interviews with different trans men about their sex changes, and how their sexuality has transformed along with their gender and their bodies. I want to provide trans men with a voice—and for more of us to speak loudly and be heard.

When men do adult work they are considered "studs." There is no reason that it should be any different when women do the same work. This double standard of sex work is appalling. I have chosen this line of work not because (as the stereotype about women with vaginas goes) I am abused, coerced, or incapable of doing something else. I make porn because I am passionate about educating about sex and gender. The message of being *empowered* through sex work is a very important one.

To use the word "vagina" in my life now makes me feel like Superman. I see that other trans men are starting to feel the same way. We no longer have to feel like that word makes us weaker, but that we can own and use it to feel and express our personal power. I believe that making my films has helped to open doors for people (no matter their gender) who have always felt some sort of shame about their bodies, or dissociation from them. That's my kind of feminism: taking control of our bodies, naming them on our terms, and being unafraid of using our power, especially sexually. Taking back the word "vagina," using it as a symbol of power, and showing it on film has changed my life. In turn, by being so open and public about that, I have also changed the world.

Racialized and Colonized Bodies

Margo DeMello

In 2008, the United States elected its first African-American president, Barack Obama. (Actually, he's bi-racial, but according to the American racial classification system, which we will discuss in this chapter, he's classified as black or African-American.) Many observers and commentators thought that his election would usher in a post-racial America; a new era in our nation's history marked by a decline in racism and a movement away from the concept of race.

Unfortunately, this did not occur. During the 2008 election, a huge number of racist jokes and images emerged, equating Obama and his wife with apes, or associating him with watermelons, fried chicken, welfare, and other stereotypical African-American images and items. After the election, hate watch groups noted a rise in the number of white supremacist groups operating throughout the country. In the 2012 election, race continued to play a role in the election, with Mitt Romney supporters seen wearing shirts reading "Put the white back into the White House," or "Don't Re-Nig in 2012." Photographs have surfaced of effigies of the president being lynched in people's front yards, and prominent celebrities like Donald Trump continue to assert that Obama is not an American or a Christian, suggesting that he's both Muslim and from Africa (and also demonstrating how very different concepts like race, culture, and religion are often confused and conflated in the minds of many Americans). Such accusations and attacks have never been aimed at other presidents in our history. Even without those elements, racism, and race, certainly did not disappear in the United States.

As Ta-Nehisi Coates writes in the *Atlantic* (2012), President Obama needs to be "twice as good and half as black," meaning that in order to appeal to white Americans, he needs to work harder and be twice as successful as everyone else, but must also appear minimally black so as to be unthreatening to those same whites. As (now Vice President) Joe Biden had said, during the 2008 primary season, "I mean you've got the first sort of mainstream African-American, who's articulate and bright and clean." If Obama was not so "bright and clean," he certainly would not have been elected. And yet, his blackness is still a major threat to a great many Americans.

A recent study demonstrated that successful African-American businessmen tend to have "baby faces," or faces with smaller facial features than other African-Americans, and that those features made their wearers seem warmer and less threatening, which led to their success. This demonstrates that for many whites, African-Americans are still considered to be threatening, and it is only when their features are "less African" that they can be successful. Even though President Obama does, in fact, have relatively small facial features, his relative blackness is still quite threatening to quite a few Americans.

The reality is that in the United States, as is the case elsewhere in the world, race matters; it is among the most salient features that we notice in another person, and more importantly, we attribute meaning to our understanding of race. And while anthropologists, sociologists, and other scholars now know that race is a social construct, rather than a biological fact, it still lives on in the minds of most as a biological feature. For that reason, no understanding of the body in society can be complete without looking at how race is embodied, and how that embodiment plays out on the social level.

What is race?

Most people think that races are biological divisions, or sub-species, of humanity; sort of like breeds of dogs. Most natural and social scientists today, however, see race as a social construct, rather than something that exists in nature. In other words, while we may look different from each other, those differences do not translate into sub-groups of humans the way we think of races. They are simply superficial physical differences.

Races are artificial categories of people that are distinguished from each other on the basis of arbitrary criteria – like skin color or eye shape. Those groups are then ranked in a graded hierarchy; those at the top of the hierarchy – in Western countries, that would be people of northern European descent – are then granted more privileges and opportunities than those at the bottom of the hierarchy. Race is a social, economic, and political system of division and inequality.

We know that racial categories are artificial because each year that the United States has taken a census (every ten years since 1790), there has never been a census that has used the same racial terms from a previous census. Each census a different set of terms are used, showing that the United States government cannot even agree on what the racial terms should be.

But while we are arguing that race is a social construct, race does have roots in the body, and in a misunderstanding of bodily difference. Humans look different from each other because our ancestors evolved in regions of the world with differing environmental conditions. Those conditions led to populations evolving with different physical features, which are better adapted to those environmental conditions. For example, skin color is created through a combination of genes and environment. Variation in skin color is determined primarily by the amount of **melanin** in the skin cells. Melanin protects the skin from too much ultra-violet radiation, so people whose ancestors come from environments with a great deal of sunlight have darker skin than those whose ancestors come from areas with little sunlight. Facial features, too, evolved in specific populations as a result of the environmental conditions in the region in which those people evolved. For example, longer noses develop in areas where temperature is cold and dry; shorter noses where temperature is hot and moist. The **epicanthic fold** of the eye developed in far northern climates like North Asia, North Europe, and the Arctic, because it protects eyes against harsh sunlight and cold.

But just because our ancestors passed on traits to us that make us look different from each other does not mean that we can be broken into subgroups on the basis of those differences. And more importantly, just because we look different from each other does not mean that we *are* different – especially on a group level. "Racial" differences are superficial and are not correlated with how smart a person is, whether a person is musically inclined, or even whether a person is athletic. Furthermore, there is no way to say that a whole population of people who share a number of physical characteristics also share intellectual or emotional characteristics. There is simply no connection between external physical traits and other characteristics. However, thanks to racial stereotyping and discrimination, once people begin to believe that certain people are smarter, thanks to their skin color, those perceptions can become self-reinforcing, as lighter-skinned people will get hired and promoted more often, leading to more light skinned people in positions of power and authority.

If race is not biologically real, how did the concept develop, and why is it so pervasive in social thought today?

Interesting issues: the shooting of Trayvon Martin

Trayvon Martin was a 17-year-old African-American boy who was shot to death by a neighborhood watch coordinator named George Zimmerman in a gated community in Florida in 2012. Martin was walking to his father's fiancée's home, wearing a hoodie, from a convenience store where he had purchased a fruit drink and a bag of

Skittles, and Zimmerman spotted him and thought he looked suspicious. Zimmerman called police to report his behavior, telling them that he was going to follow him; the 911 dispatcher told him not to do so. Zimmerman followed Martin and at some point the two got into a physical altercation which ended with Martin hitting Zimmerman and Zimmerman shooting Martin, who was unarmed, in the chest. Zimmerman was not charged with a crime thanks to a Florida law known as "stand your ground," which means that someone can shoot someone, and does not need to back off, if they feel that they or their property is being threatened. The case caused a national uproar over an unarmed black youth being shot by an adult Hispanic man who was not even charged in his murder. Supporters of Zimmerman claimed that he legitimately acted in self-defense while supporters of Martin claim that the law allows any young black person wearing a hoodie to be shot to death without provocation. Martin's supporters held a number of "Million Hoodie Marches" in his honor and even President Obama weighed in, saying that if he had a son, he would look like Trayvon. On the other hand, reporter Geraldo Rivera blamed Martin for his death, saying that because of the "thug wear" that he was wearing, he was killed. Eventually, Zimmerman was charged with second degree murder, after having allegedly racially profiled and shot an unarmed Martin, and in July 2013, after a 19-day trial during which the jury could have found him guilty of either second degree murder or manslaughter, they found him not guilty of all charges.

Colonialism and the emergence of race

Race emerged as a concept during the age of European expansion which brought Europeans into contact with, and dominion over, people from the Americas, Asia, and Africa. As the Spanish, English, French, and other European superpowers began to establish colonies around the world, and especially with the rise of the African slave trade, the idea began to emerge that non-Europeans were not just culturally different from Europeans, but were biologically different as well. One of the many world-alter-ing results of colonialism was the birth of the system of **racialization** whereby groups of humans are categorized and ranked by a new concept known as "race."

During the centuries of European colonial expansion, the peoples of Asia, Africa, and the Americas were not just dominated, with their land, resources, and labor taken from them, but were assigned places within a new hierarchy of races with Europeans placed on top. Different systems of classification emerged which attempted to categorize the variety of people on the planet – but especially those under European control – by skin color and facial features, but also by religion, language, and culture. By overemphasizing the similarities within these groups, and de-emphasizing the differences, Africans, Asians, and Native Americans started to be thought of as cohesive, and inferior, "races." From here, the physical characteristics were correlated with what were thought to be the intellectual and cultural characteristics of each group. This became the basis for the racial system of classification that we have inherited: the idea that we can predict human behavior from something as simple as the color of one's skin or the shape of one's eyes.

The trans-Atlantic slave trade was another major impetus for the development of racial thinking. In the United States, the notion of creating a permanent category of enslaved people was not compatible with its ideology of equality for all that our founding fathers shared. However, the system of racial thinking which said that some groups are biologically inferior to others provided an easy exception to the American ideology of equality. If Africans were truly inferior to whites, then they could not be given the same treatment as others, and thus, by this thinking, slavery – which, like colonialism, developed to further European and American economic gain – was not inconsistent with the ideals of the founding fathers. So a system of racial inequality emerged to justify a system of economic greed, and to reconcile the practice of inequality alongside of a philosophy of equality for all.

The artificiality, and indeed ludicrousness, of the race concept is especially visible in concepts like **hypodescent**. Hypodescent (also known as the "one drop rule"), is the way in which children of mixed-race parentage are classified. In this system, any child born of a white and a black parent is automatically assigned the race of the socially subordinate parent, i.e., the black parent. This system arose to keep the children of slaves and their masters black, and thus enslaved. This rule allowed white men to have sexual access to black women (but not the reverse) and at the same time, did not threaten white domination. Hypodescent explains why Barack Obama, Tiger Woods, and Halle Barry are all considered to be black, even though all have parents from different backgrounds.

Ultimately, the physical differences that we call race mean really very little biologically. However, they mean a great deal culturally and socially.

The display and eroticization of racialized bodies

Colonialism and racialism were also enabled by the **World Fairs** which started in the nineteenth century and were used to display to the world the new technological and cultural developments of the West.

One of the major elements of these fairs was the national pavilion, created by participating countries, in which participants could expose international audiences to the best their countries had to offer in terms of culture, food, music, dance, and art. Related to the national pavilions, but quite different in spirit, were the **human zoos**. At these displays, visitors could gawk at native people from colonized nations in reconstructed villages. Circus showman P. T. Barnum was a major promoter of native people, whom he displayed as anatomical and cultural oddities, as was Robert Ripley, who founded the Ripley's Believe It or Not shows. German animal trader and zoo founder Carl Hagenbeck also played a major role in finding and displaying native people

in zoo-like conditions for a paying public to watch. Sometimes the people actually *were* displayed in a zoo. Hagenbeck, for example, displayed his collection of Inuit peoples at the Hamburg Zoo, Geoffrey de Saint-Hilaire exhibited Nubians, Zulus, and Bushmen at the Paris Zoo, and in 1896, one hundred Sioux lived at the Cincinnati Zoo. In 1906 the Bronx Zoo exhibited an African pygmy man named Ota Benga with the chimpanzees until the city's African-American community protested. He was billed as a "missing link" between chimpanzees and humans.

At the 1876 Centennial International Exhibition in Philadelphia, native people were for the first time exhibited in the United States in what was called the "ethnographic display." "Negro villages" were found at the 1878 and 1889 fairs in Paris, the Chicago Expo in 1893 had exhibits showcasing the lives of Algerians, Apaches, Navajos, Samoans, Japanese, and Javanese, the 1900 Exposition Universelle in Paris had a living diorama featuring natives from Madagascar, the 1901 Pan-American Exposition in New York had both The Old Plantation, depicting the lives of happy slaves, and Darkest Africa, an African village, and in 1904, the St Louis World's Fair had displays of such recently conquered people as people from Guam and the Igorots of the Philippines.

The exotic appearance and behaviors of the natives served to draw in paying customers. The Igorots of the Philippines, for example, were both tattooed and were known to eat dogs. Even though they only ate dogs for ceremonial occasions at home, the organizers of the St Louis Expo fed them dogs daily so that Americans could watch the spectacle. Human zoos and other native exhibits like this were contrasted with the highest achievements of Western society to both accentuate the primitiveness of the natives and to emphasize the civilization of the Western world. While these displays were both reflective of, and contributed to, the colonial ideology, they were also influential in constructing a narrative about native people as savages and racial inferiors. The exhibitions not only promoted the colonial agenda, but helped to implement it, as Christian missionaries visited world's fairs in order to learn about the cultures that they planned to "civilize."

While these displays largely disappeared by the 1960s, a current example exists in Thailand, where Padaung refugees from the civil war in neighboring Burma are living in refugee camps set up like human zoos, where tourists can pay the Thai government to take photos of the Padaung women, who are known for wearing long coiled brass rings around their necks. Another example is found in India's Andaman Islands, where women from India's Jarawa ethnic group dance for visitors who, according to at least one report, throw bananas and biscuits at them.

Outside of the world's fair, native men and women were showcased in sideshows at carnivals, dime museums, and circuses. When women were displayed, their sexuality was often highlighted. One of the saddest and most notorious examples was the case of Saartjie Baartman, a Khoi San woman from South Africa with steatopygia, a condition whereby a large amount of fat accumulates around the buttocks; she also had elongated labia, both found commonly among Khoi San women. She was a slave owned by Dutch farmers who was exhibited throughout Europe and billed as the "Hottentot Venus." She was displayed in 1810 and 1811 in a cage in London where customers were invited to pinch her butt, and then sold to a French animal trainer who exhibited her in France. After her death in 1815, anatomist Georges Cuvier dissected her body, giving special attention to her labia. He preserved her body parts for future study, comparing them to those of white women. Her skeleton, along with her preserved brains and genitals, were displayed in a French museum until 1974. In 2002, her remains were finally returned to South Africa where they were buried.

The notion that people of color are more sexual than whites has a long history. In the slave colonies of the New World, black men were seen as hypersexual and dangerous, and were kept far from white women, who needed to be protected from them. Asian men, too, were once seen as sexually threatening. The practice of smoking opium in the United States was criminalized in the late nineteenth century in many locations because Chinese men were said to lure white women into opium dens, where they would be defiled. Black women, on the other hand, were considered to be ready sexual objects for white men's use; already degraded, constantly available. In addition, there were few white women in many of the colonies; they were not encouraged to travel from the safety of their homes in Europe, which meant that European men used slaves for sexual services, especially in the Caribbean, where white men took black women as concubines. Anthropologist Verena Martinez-Alier (1974) calls this the **dual marriage system**, whereby in the Caribbean, even after the arrival of European women, white men had a legal white wife, and a black concubine.

The threat posed by black men was controlled by beatings and other measures, while after slavery, it was controlled by lynchings. Between 1882 and 1946, it is thought that almost 5,000 black men were killed by lynching; many of those men had been accused of raping, accosting, or, in some cases (like that of teenager Emmett Till, killed in 1955), whistling at a white woman. Even today, the notion that black men pose a special danger to white women is still an extremely persistent belief. Black women's virtue, on the other hand, was not similarly protected, and during slavery, black women could be legally raped by their masters. In other words, this racialized and sexualized system has two equal and opposite poles: at one pole lies the sexual exploitation of black women by white men, and at the other pole, the extreme concern with purity of white women, and the threat posed to them by black men.

Even today, non-white women are often thought to be more sexual, erotic, and exotic than white women. Black women in particular are represented through advertising, pornography, and art as more primitive, savage, and sexual than other women. Asian and Latina women, too, are often considered to be more sexual than white women; the international sex tourism industry is built on the stereotypes of women from various cultures. Men, generally from Western countries, travel to the Caribbean, Asia, and Latin America in search of the exotic, hypersexual fantasy woman, to contrast to the uptight white woman back home. In places like Bangkok, where poverty and desperation (as well as human trafficking) forces young women and girls into prostitution, tourists tell themselves that these girls are "hot for it," and are naturally more sexual than the women back home are. The mail-order bride business, too, is built upon stereotypes of foreign women; Asian women are sexual, yes, but will make obedient wives to American husbands fed up with the feminism of Western women. Black men, too, are still thought to be more "naturally" sexual than whites; in fact, blacks in general continue to be defined more by their bodies – they are natural dancers, natural athletes – while whites continue to be defined by their intellects.

In the twenty-first century, the term "bootilicious" has come to refer to a woman, either black or Latina, with a curvy body and a large butt. This woman, represented by celebrities like Jennifer Lopez, Beyoncé, and Kim Kardashian, has been fetishized in our culture, ogled by men, and seen with jealousy, fear, and perhaps disgust by many women. That women of color are more hypersexual than white women is also thought to be confirmed in the higher rates of teenage pregnancy among young African-American and Latina women, and the way that poor women of color are featured on television shows like *Jerry Springer*, where their sexuality is made into a public spectacle.

Interesting issues: good hair

Race is also an important factor in what different cultures consider to be beautiful. Especially in those regions of the world that once experienced either European colonialism or slavery, people with Caucasian facial features and hair are seen as more attractive than those with features and hair associated with Africans. For African-Americans today, hair continues to be an area where standards of beauty and acceptability are strongly racialized. Long, straight, silky hair has long been considered to be not only the most beautiful but most feminine form of hair in the United States, which leaves African-Americans, who typically have curly or kinky hair, automatically excluded from this standard of beauty. Thus the importance and proliferation of hair-straightening products (a $45 million annual market) aimed at African-Americans; products that demand a great amount of time, money, and sometimes pain, as the chemicals in these products can often burn the skin. But curly vs. straight hair (known as "good hair") is not just a question of beauty for many African-American women. It's also a question of fitting into a society that is still dominated by white people and white values. Comedian Paul Mooney, in the 2009 Chris Rock film Good Hair, said that "if your hair is relaxed, white people are relaxed; if your hair is nappy, they're not happy." Today, many African-American women choose to wear straightened weaves, sometimes made from human hair (which itself comes from poor women in India), camouflaging their own hair. Oprah Winfrey, one of the most powerful women in the world, only just wore her hair "natural" for the very first time on her own magazine cover in 2012. In every other issue in the 150 issues on which she has appeared, she has either had her hair straightened or worn a wig. On the other hand, many African-Americans embrace hair styles that signify their ethnic heritage, such as braids, cornrows, or the "Afro," although in many places – especially at work – these styles are seen as "too ethnic" and still too threatening to white people.

Mapping and measuring bodies in the era of biological racism

With the rise of biological science in the seventeenth century, scientific theories were harnessed into the new racial thinking, leading to the emergence of scientific racism and the hardening of racial thinking in the West.

Carolus Linnaeus, for example, who is credited with creating the taxonomic system used to scientifically catalog plants and animals today, came up with the idea that there were five biological races, each with their own physical and intellectual characteristics, while naturalist Georges Cuvier felt that there were three races; of course both Linnaeus and Cuvier placed Europeans on top of their new scientific racial hierarchies. All of the other scientists throughout the nineteenth century agreed with these early thinkers, and all saw Europeans as being biologically superior; the debate primarily centered on how the races developed, and who – Native American or African – was the most inferior. In all of these cases, the idea of racial superiority and inferiority was a given, and was used to justify slavery, since, after all, Africans were thought of as being biologically suited for slavery. After the end of slavery, scientific theories of race continued to be used to deny rights to people of color in the United States and around the colonial and post-colonial world.

A number of pseudosciences developed which were used to prove the superiority or inferiority of the races. For example, eighteenth-century Dutch anatomist Petrus Camper claimed that the races could be distinguished by the angle at which the forehead slopes to the nose and jaw; whites had the most refined angle with Africans having an angle closer to apes, demonstrating their evolutionary inferiority.

Another approach was called **physiognomy.** Physiognomy refers to discerning the character of a person from their facial features or body parts. An Italian doctor named Cesare Lombroso was an advocate of this approach and examined the bodies of hundreds of criminals in the nineteenth century in order to ascertain the physical characteristics shared by criminals and what he called "primitive man." He found that those primitive traits were found most commonly among Africans, a group he knew to be inferior to whites. Another nineteenth-century theorist who subscribed to this theory was Francis Galton, who was also, not coincidentally, a leading eugenicist. Whether the subjects were Italians, Irish,

Jewish, or African-Americans, the result was the same – those groups deemed racially different were seen by the scientists at the time as racially inferior in character, intelligence, and morality.

Physiognomy has also been practiced in the twentieth century. For instance, the Nazis used special calipers to measure the facial features of Jews and those who were suspected to be Jews; Nazis thought that Jews had larger, more animal-like facial features, so the size of a person's nose, ears, or brow ridge could mean the difference between life and death. The Nazis were advocates of what they called **criminal biology,** based on Lombroso's theories. They used this approach to detect who was more likely to become a criminal based on their facial features. They taught criminal biology alongside courses in racial hygiene, and used their data to show that Jews were more likely to be criminals and murderers than Aryans. The irony, of course, is that the Nazis were the real murderers.

More recently, evolutionary psychologist Satoshi Kanazawa has revived Lombroso's theories and claims that criminality really can be detected by facial features. As in the nineteenth century, physiognomy continues to be linked to racism, with many proponents, such as Kanazawa, continuing to find in non-white facial features evidence of criminality, aggression, or bad character.

Another scientific approach to racism was **craniometry.** Promoted by anthropologist Samuel Morton, this approach was based on the comparison of human skulls. Morton compared the skulls of Native Americans, African-Americans, and European Americans in order to show that the group with the largest cranial capacity, and thus the largest brains, was the most intelligent. Morton's research showed that, not surprisingly, Europeans were the most intelligent race, followed by Native Americans, and finally African-Americans. His theory was used to prove the theory of **polygenism:** that the races were created separately. In the twentieth century, however, biologist Stephen Jay Gould (1996) showed that Morton used faulty data in order to prove his thesis. One result of Morton's work, and the work of others like him, was that American natural history museums were at one time full of the skulls, bones, and artifacts of Native Americans. In fact, at one time it was perfectly legal to dig up Native American graves and use the bones and other items found therein for scientific purposes or display. It was not until the passage of the **Native American Graves Protection and Repatriation Act**, which passed in 1990, that Native American bones were finally given back to Native Americans, and that grave looting of this type was prohibited.

Race, health, and race purity

In racialized cultures like the United States, on every health and mortality measure, including life expectancy, infant mortality, maternal mortality, prenatal care, infant birth weight, cancer survival rates, and more, whites have better health and survival prospects than other groups.

These differences are due to lifestyle differences between racial groups, the fact that people of color are disproportionately poor, and thus lack access to health insurance and quality health care, the fact that poor people of color will have less healthy living and working conditions, the higher rates of violent crime in non-white communities, and racial discrimination by health care providers.

Because historically African-Americans have had worse health outcomes and higher rates of mortality than whites, thanks to the horrors of slavery and the post-slavery inequalities experienced by blacks, some took that as proof of their natural inferiority. On the other hand, during slavery, it was also thought that blacks suffered less from some diseases, such as yellow fever, than did whites. This was used to justify slavery, since whites would suffer more severely from working in the swampy hot conditions in which diseases like this flourished.

A similar process occurred with Chinese Americans. It was said that the Chinatowns in which Chinese immigrants lived in the United States were cesspools of filth, crime, overcrowding, and disease. Animals were raised alongside humans and were slaughtered openly, in the streets. But it's not thanks to Chinese preferences that Chinatowns exist – they were created by white Americans as a segregated site where Chinese people were forced to live and work, because they were excluded from living and working in white communities. Similarly, when the Chinese were blamed for the spread of Avian Flu in 2003, or Mexican slaughterhouse workers were blamed for the Swine Flu epidemic of 2009, both groups were blamed for conditions of poverty that were not of their choosing.

Sexually transmitted diseases are another good example of how health and illness can be racialized. In the nineteenth century, when doctors realized that African-Americans in the south had contracted syphilis in high numbers, this was used to further the belief that African-Americans had lower morals, and were more promiscuous, than other groups. AIDS is another example. While in the 1980s, AIDS began in the United States as a disease largely confined to two groups – men who have sex with men and injection drug users – it has spread throughout the population into new groups. Today, one of the groups with the highest infection rate is people of color. Here too, it is sometimes thought that blacks (like gays before them) lack the self-control that is necessary to fend off sexually transmitted diseases. The reality is that poverty, lack of education, lack of access to health care, and a lack of information about AIDS (which is, after all, supposed to be a "gay disease") all contribute to the spread of AIDS in the black community.

Another example is addiction. We know that drug consumption patterns exist within racial and ethnic groups, such that, for example, African-American men have more alcohol-related problems than do whites, and Latino men are more likely to have alcohol abuse issues than both blacks and whites. One reason why people of color are more inclined than whites to use harmful substances is because they are targeted by tobacco and alcohol companies. Another reason has to do with the higher rates of poverty and unemployment, combined with the lack of good schools and access to health care. On the other hand, contrary to popular assumptions, blacks do not use crack cocaine in greater numbers than whites. However, in the United States, they are arrested and imprisoned in far greater numbers for crack cocaine use than whites, pointing towards the racist nature of the criminal justice system.

One result of these differentials in health outcomes between racialized groups is the race purity movement, or the eugenics movement. This was a European and American movement, which began in the nineteenth century, that was concerned with keeping the "white race" pure, and controlling both the intermixing between the races as well as the reproduction of the non-white races. One of the reasons for its emergence was the idea that non-whites were diseased, compared to whites. For instance, in Germany, Jews were medicalized: they were turned into a health threat that needed to be solved, through segregation, sterilization, and ultimately, extermination.

In the United States, one of the driving forces behind the development of the race purity movement was the waves of immigrants who began arriving in the late nineteenth century. Attracted by the new industrial jobs, these immigrants, who were mostly uneducated and unskilled people from eastern and southern Europe, arrived in American cities and were forced to live in crowded urban ethnic neighborhoods which quickly became filled with crime and disease. The result was a series of laws enacted to both restrict immigration from non-white nations and to control the immigrants once they had arrived. The 1920s and 1930s were possibly the most racist period in the American nation's history. Immigration laws, intelligence tests, **anti-miscegenation laws**, segregationist policies, and even forcible sterilization laws which mandated sterilization for the "unfit," were all examples of the racist nature of the period. As long as non-whites' existence was seen to threaten the health of white people,

and more generally, the health of the body politic, then non-white bodies needed this type of intensive control.

The animalization of non-white bodies

Another way in which racial control operates on a bodily level is through **animalization**. People of color have been compared to animals since at least colonialism, and certainly since the African slave trade emerged in the seventeenth century. By the nineteenth century, with the rise of evolutionary thought, some people felt that while humans may be related to apes, some humans were *closer* to apes than others, and Africans in particular were thought to be the "missing link" between apes and humans. By using animals – especially monkeys and apes – to refer to Africans, and by implying or stating that Africans and African-Americans were closer to these animals than whites, whites asserted their superiority over them.

In addition, African-Americans were not just thought of as animals; they were treated like animals. Treating a human like an animal is a way to degrade and dehumanize them. African slaves were shackled and muzzled like animals, beaten like animals, branded like animals, bought and sold like animals, had their children taken from them like animals, and had their humanity and individuality ignored, just as humans do with animals. They were property just as animals were, and could be legally killed by their property owner, just as animals could. Huge numbers of Africans died in transit from Africa to America; a loss of life that was absorbed into the prices of the remaining men and women. (Animals who are transported to pet stores in the United States also experience high rates of what the pet industry calls "shrinkage," and those losses are also figured into the prices of the remaining animals.)

Marjorie Spiegel's 1997 book, *The Dreaded Comparison*, makes clear the similarities in the ways that African slaves were treated, and how animals were then, and are still, treated today.

Further, she shows that whites justified their use of, and treatment of, slaves with many of the same justifications that humans use today to justify their use of animals as food or medical subjects. Blacks were thought to not feel pain, they were thought to not feel love towards their children, and they were thought to be happier under slavery than living on their own. In addition, slavery was an important part of the economy of the American south – how could plantation owners expect to do without it?

Other groups have been animalized too. Both the Chinese and the Japanese were called vermin and were compared to rats in the nineteenth century by white Americans, and during World War II, the Japanese described the Chinese as pigs during their invasion of Manchuria. Even Disney's animated cartoons play a role in this animalization. If we look at Disney cartoons over the years, you can see how animal characters are racialized. Crows, monkeys, and apes are played by African-Americans, Chihuahuas by Latinos, and cats by Asians, and all are negatively stereotyped.

But perhaps most well known is the treatment of the Jews by the Nazis in the 1930s and 1940s. The German word for "race," *rasse*, is also the word for a purebred animal, demonstrating not only the Nazis' tendency to animalize people but also their concern with maintaining "blood purity" in both animals and people, Jews were called vermin, rats, and cockroaches in Nazi speeches and in the German media. Minister of Propaganda Josef Goebbels said, "It is true that the Jew is a human being, but so is a flea a living being – one that is none too pleasant . . . our duty towards both ourselves and our conscience is to render it harmless. It is the same with the Jews," while the Nazi Party Manual had the following line: "All good Aryans should squash Jews and members of other 'inferior races' like 'roaches on a dirty wall.'" The Nazi propaganda film *Der Ewige Jude* (1940) included the following line: "Rats . . . have followed men like parasites from the very beginning . . . They are cunning, cowardly and fierce, and usually appear in large packs. In the animal world

they represent the element of subterranean destruction . . . not dissimilar to the place that Jews have among men."

But as with slavery, the animalization of Jews went far beyond name calling. During the eugenics movement in the United States and Germany during the early part of the twentieth century, the practice of animal breeding – breeding those with the desirable characteristics and killing and sterilizing the rest – became the inspiration and example for eugenic efforts to upgrade the human population in both countries. These efforts led to compulsory sterilization of the disabled in the United States and compulsory sterilization, euthanasia killings, and, ultimately, genocide in Nazi Germany.

From 1942 to 1945, European Jews were transported in cattle cars to the camps, some were tattooed with ID numbers like livestock, and millions were slaughtered en masse, with their humanity and individuality completely extinguished. The camps themselves were modeled on American stockyards and slaughterhouses: Nazis borrowed features intended to make the processing of Jews at the camps as speedy and efficient as possible, and to streamline the final part of the operation which took the victims to their deaths. In the gas chambers, Zyklon B, a pesticide normally used on mice, was used for the mass killings. Rudolf Höss, the commandant of Auschwitz, called that camp "the largest human slaughterhouse that history had ever known" (Patterson 2002: 122). Jews, Gypsies, and others were also experimented on in the infamous experiments of Josef Mengele, who called a group of Polish women who were subject to grotesque experiments the "rabbit girls."

In this chapter, we have discussed what to many of us is one of the most common-sense ideas of all: the idea of race. But in reality, race is not common sense at all; it is a term and a system of classification that was created just a few hundred years ago in order to divide humans and to provide privileges and benefits to some, at the expense of a great many. As we have seen, the consequences of that system have been devastating. In Chapter 7, we will look at another system, that of gender, which will probably seem even more natural to you, but which may be just as socially constructed as the racial system discussed in this chapter.

Key terms

Animalization
Anti-Miscegenation Laws
Craniometry
Criminal Biology
Dual Marriage System
Geishas
Human Zoos
Native American Graves Protection and Repatriation Act
Physiognomy
Polygenism
Racialization

Further reading

Blanchard, Pascal. (2008). *Human Zoos: Science and Spectacle in the Age of Colonial Empires*. Liverpool: Liverpool University Press.

Gould, Stephen Jay. (1996). *The Mismeasure of Man*. New York: W.W. Norton & Company.

Herring, Cedric, Keith, Verna, and Horton, Hayward Derrick. (2004). *Skin Deep: How Race and Complexion Matter in the "Color Blind" Era*. Chicago, IL: University of Illinois Press.

hooks, bell. (1990). *Yearning: Race, Gender and Cultural Politics*. Boston, MA: South End Press.

Spiegel, Marjorie. (1996). *The Dreaded Comparison: Human and Animal Slavery*. New York: Mirror Books.

Viagra and the Coital Imperative

Nicola Gavey

Anyone encountering Viagra for the first time through direct-to-consumer promotions of the drug could be forgiven for thinking they had stumbled onto a miraculous new elixir of relational health and wellbeing. Viagra, according to drug company advertisements, will generate not only sex, but also the restoration of closeness, romance, love and intimacy. It will, in fact, protect against the very breakup of relationships threatened by "distance" – a distance born, it is implied, of the ailing self-esteem and crumbling masculinity caused by "failure to admit" and therefore to overcome the condition of "erectile dysfunction" (see Gavey 2005). And what is the route to such happiness and harmony? It is the biotechnological production of a penile erection with all the qualities – of firmness and duration – required for vaginal penetration and "successful" intercourse.

As critics have pointed out, the promotion of Viagra as a magic-bullet remedy to this host of personal and relational troubles relies on a whole array of contemporary assumptions about sex and gender. So too, of course, does the construction of the very problem (erectile dysfunction) it is designed to fix. Most blatantly, the whole phenomenon of Viagra relies on a hard-core "coital imperative" (Jackson 1984). This is the widely shared presumption that heterosexual sex *is* penis–vagina intercourse; and that anything else is either a preliminary to – or an optional extra beyond – real sex.

In magazine advertisements targeted at potential consumers, notions like "satisfactory sexual activity" and "making love" are premised on the requirement of a penis erect enough for penetration that lasts (see Gavey 2005). (Hetero)sex, within the Viagra promotion industry, *is* penetration – of the vagina by the penis. And the penetrating penis must be capable of reliable and durable action to avoid pathologization. According to a "sexual health inventory" on the drug company's website, even the man who reports he is able to maintain an erection that is firm enough and lasts long enough for "satisfactory" intercourse "most times" and reports "high" confidence in his ability to "get and keep an erection" scores the advice that he "may be showing signs of erection problems" (see Gavey 2005). The possibility that sexual activity or making love could happen without penile penetration of the vagina – which conceivably might be an option that some heterosexual men with erectile changes (as well as some without), and their partners, might otherwise consider – is completely obscured within the promotional advice.

Of course drug companies did not invent the coital imperative. Contemporary culture is thoroughly saturated with the commonsense assumption that (hetero)sex is coitus. In fact, to question that mature heterosexual sex could be otherwise – that it might not require intercourse – is likely to generate bemused and/or dismissive responses emphasizing the power of *nature* to determine the proper form of sexual practices and desires. From this perspective, the coital imperative might be seen as simply the way things are; as a taken-for-granted feature of human nature. However, in this chapter I argue not only that the coital *imperative* in its current form is highly problematic, but also that it is neither simply natural nor immutable.

The dangers of the coital imperative

Feminists have long debated the symbolic meaning of intercourse. Some have portrayed it as a key site of women's oppression (e.g., Dworkin 1987), while others have sought to resurrect it as a viable sexual practice for heterosexual feminists (e.g., Segal 1994). However, despite these exchanges about the politics of coitus, the coital *imperative* which casts intercourse as an *essential* part of heterosexual sex, unquestionably has a downside – for women in particular. Heterosexual intercourse is a sexual practice that has life-changing implications, in particular pregnancy and the transmission of sexual infections (some of which have lasting complications and/or are life-threatening). While a myriad of techniques and technologies exist for circumventing potential consequences like an unwanted pregnancy or an STI, they are widely perceived and/or experienced as difficult or adverse in their own right. For example, the most technically effective methods of birth control, such as oral contraceptives and IUDs (intrauterine devices), are well known for their "dangerous or troubling side effects" that lead many women to discontinue use (e.g., Petchesky 1990: 189). Also, while many women report enjoying intercourse (see Segal 1994), others go through with it in the absence of their own desire or pleasure (e.g., Gavey 2005) because of the assumption it is normal and, therefore, required. Some women continue to have intercourse even despite routinely experiencing outright pain and discomfort. One 51-year-old woman, for instance, said she was sometimes unable to "disguise how much discomfort" she experienced during intercourse due to her own advanced illness; yet she persisted because of her belief that it was not good for men to go without regular intercourse (e.g., Potts *et al.* 2003: 706).

Given the potential for intercourse to have serious adverse consequences for (particularly women's) health and wellbeing, it would be reasonable to assume that it might be better regarded as a choice within sex rather than as a taken-for-granted act if "sex" is to occur. However, by and large this is not the case. Elsewhere I have discussed the poignant case of Romanian women who continued to engage in coital sex with their husbands, in the absence of their own pleasure, and despite the painful consequences associated with unwanted pregnancies, which were difficult if not impossible to avoid during the extreme pronatalist regime under Ceausescu. One woman, who had had seven illegal abortions, said: "When I was asked by my husband to make love with him I began to feel pains in my stomach because of fear" (cited in Gavey 2005: 123). Despite the especially harsh social conditions these women were living under, which exacerbated the stakes of engaging in unwanted intercourse, the fantasy of sexual and reproductive choice does not necessarily play out fully even in neo-liberal societies in which the notion of choice seems to be fetishized above all else. Girls and women commonly report having sexual intercourse even when they don't want it and/or gain no pleasure from it (e.g., Gavey 2005). Intercourse, it would seem, is part and parcel of sex; not an item that can freely be chosen *or* discarded from the (hetero)sexual menu. Sanders and Reinisch (1999), for instance, found that while virtually everyone in their study regarded penile–vaginal intercourse as constituting having "had sex," 60 percent were of the view that oral–genital contact (if it was "the most intimate behavior" they engaged in) would not.

The coital imperative is not natural

One of the interesting insights gained from historical studies of sex is the finding that some of the assumptions that currently operate as taken-for-granted truths about (hetero)sexuality are not in fact historically constant. For instance, historians write of a "sexual revolution" in the eighteenth century during which the whole nature of what heterosexual sex *was* changed radically. According to Tim Hitchcock (2002), drawing on data from England and Western Europe, it became increasingly phallocentric at this time, moving away from a set of practices that encompassed mutual masturbation, kissing and fondling, mutual touching, and so on. Instead, "putting a penis in a vagina became the dominant sexual activity" (Hitchcock 2002: 191). By the nineteenth century, "proper" marital sex in the United States not only centered on the act of coitus, but reference to noncoital sex was rare in publications of the era, and when it was mentioned it was always associated with prohibitions (Seidman 1991). Perceptions of women's sexuality also changed markedly over this period. From being seen as sexually aggressive (Hitchcock 2002), women came to be seen as sexually passive. Their pleasure during sex, and their orgasm in particular, became increasingly less important (see also Laqueur 1990). More recent changes over the twentieth century include the shift away from seeing (hetero)sex in primarily procreative terms. Through the "sexual revolution" of the mid-to-late twentieth century, women's sexual pleasure has come back onto the agenda – at least in theory.

It seems ironic, then, that at a time when the procreative function of sex has perhaps never been less important, the sexual act "designed for" procreation has not only persisted as the defining feature of hetero(sex); but, with the Viagra moment, it is increasingly being stretched across the lifespan. Most men using Viagra and similar products are beyond a procreating stage of life. Yet, while the reproductive function of coitus is no longer valorized, the particular heterosexual act for reproduction is. Apparently, in the nineteenth-century United States when the reproductive function of sex was still of primary importance (D'Emilio and Freedman 1988), and sex was based even more narrowly around the procreative act of coitus than it is today, it was assumed that sex between a husband and wife would generally diminish over the course of their marriage (Seidman 1991). By the age of fifty, it was thought, men's sexual life would be over: the "sex drive" being "either absent by that age or enfeebled to a point where it would have little significance in the marriage" (Seidman 1991: 25). Today, when men's bodies give up on producing the kind of rigid penile arousal required for "successful" intercourse, it

is considered to be a sexual dysfunction (even though to some extent statistically normal, as the drug company promotions like to reassure people). Such trends might have been predicted by Jeffrey Weeks's (1985) diagnosis of the colonization of sex by capitalism since the beginning of the twentieth century. As part of a more general "commoditisation and commercialisation of social life," Weeks (1985: 22, 23, 24) pointed to an "expansion of perceived sexual needs, particularly among men." This was fertile ground for the "proliferation of new desires as the pursuit of pleasure became an end in itself." Not only the pursuit of pleasure; for sex has become increasingly entangled with all sorts of "higher" psychological and relational meanings, such as intimacy and identity (e.g., Seidman 1989). Intercourse is practiced not simply as a (possible) means to physical pleasure, but as an expression and/or confirmation of love and closeness (e.g., Gavey *et al.* 1999).

The coital imperative is not immutable

Attention to the historical antecedents of our contemporary sexual norms, as we have seen, suggests that there are no single cultural or biological determinants of human sexual behavior that are rigidly prescriptive over time and place. Further support for this contention exists in contemporary evidence that (at least) some people do act otherwise, to embody alternative forms of (hetero)sexuality (not to mention those who escape the strict confines of hetero-normativity through lesbian, gay, or other forms of queer sexuality). One example of this comes from the accounts of women and men who have faced erectile difficulties only to find that it enhanced their sexual relationships (Potts *et al.* 2004: 497). As one man who did not have erections commented:

Matter of fact . . . in some ways our sex life has been, in a *different* way, better since . . . It was a matter of adapting to suit the occasion rather than giving all away, which I suppose . . . some people give it all away, but we were determined not to . . . And she can get me to a climax and sort of keep me going, you know, far more than I used to before . . . so in that way the sex is . . . different and arguably better than what it was before.

Stories such as this – and there were more – disrupt the pharmaceutical company's uni-dimensional hype about the devastation that erectile difficulties (necessarily) cause for heterosexual relationships, as well as for sex itself.

Viagra's intervention

As part of the increasing medicalization (e.g., Tiefer 1995) and commercialization of sexuality, "Viagra" is a cultural phenomenon rather than simply a (set of) biotechnological products; a phenomenon that relies on, reinforces, and extends existing sociocultural norms. The impact of Viagra can be felt at several different levels, from the intimate lives of individual women and men to the broader public domain of popular culture. Given that the promotion, and presumably the appeal, of Viagra trades on the coital imperative, it is not surprising that it can intervene within people's private sexual lives in ways that directly (re)assert this imperative. For instance, a 48-year-old woman described how Viagra enforced the coital imperative within her sexual relationship, with the unwelcome extinction of noncoital sexual activities (Potts *et al.* 2003: 704–5):

> [Viagra use began] during a time when I was trying to impress upon him that foreplay would be a nice thing. After twenty-odd years of marriage, foreplay is one of those things that goes by the way; however, I was trying to maintain that this was, you know, quite an important part of making love, so when Viagra came along the whole foreplay thing just *vanished*, I mean it wasn't even a suggestion, it was: "OK, I've taken the pill, we've got about an hour, I expect you in that time to be acquiescent."

Not only does Viagra intervene in men's bodies, minds, and sexuality (and, therefore, in women's experience of heterosex and in relationships between men and women), but the Viagra phenomenon intervenes in culture itself This phenomenon is more than just the chemical compound sildenafil citrate. It is the potent mix of the drug itself (as well as newer similar drugs) and their promotion within drug company marketing, professional endorsements, and various popular cultural representations. The promotion of Viagra as a biotechnological miracle for restoring men's potency, and with it personal and relational happiness, plays with culture. It shifts the meanings of intercourse – not by inventing new meanings, but by reinforcing and intensifying existing ones in ways that move to squeeze out any comfortable spaces for alternative meanings around having or not having intercourse. At the same time, it prescribes new norms for coitus by extending normative expectations for its place in the lives of aging men, and those with health conditions that threaten erectile reliability. In these ways the Viagra phenomenon shifts the cultural conditions of possibility for (hetero)sex, in ways that are both prescriptive and restrictive.

Some of the interviewees in Potts *et al.*'s research observed that the cultural phenomenon of Viagra involved the *construction* of a problem. That is, it represented the invitation to understand erectile changes as pathology rather than simply a natural change or as an expression of acceptable corporeal and sexual diversity. For example, as one 60-year-old woman explained (Potts *et al.* 2003: 712):

> Yes, it would definitely be different for everybody, I guess, but I think you'd probably find that . . . a large percentage of women in my age group would say that . . . the desire decreases as you get older and . . . Possibly, if I think about it, it'll come up *because* Viagra has been brought up, right? Because I think Viagra has made a lot of people feel inadequate . . . everybody's on the defensive about how often they have sex and so on, in the older age group.

Even for women and men who already do see erectile changes as a problem to be fixed, Viagra delivers one solution (pharmaceutically restoring the erectile capacity) with such force that other potential "solutions" are either obscured or devalued. In the case of men for whom Viagra poses a serious health risk (e.g., those taking nitrates in medication prescribed for angina or those using recreational drugs that contain nitrates), this fixation with an erect penis and coitus *as* sex is potentially fatal. In these ways, we can see how the Viagra phenomenon works both prescriptively, to install new needs for intercourse, and at the same time restrictively, to close down other legitimate possibilities for sexuality.

In this chapter I have argued that the Viagra phenomenon reinforces and hardens the coital imperative. Not only does it potently work to re-naturalize and re-normalize the centrality of intercourse to heterosexual sex, but it extends its reach to areas of society that previously were able to slip it by (that is, men and women beyond middle age, and those with certain health conditions). And, on the way, it pathologizes bodies and people who cannot, or prefer not to, engage in sexual intercourse on every, or even any, sexual occasion.

In the midst of a Western cultural moment that is arguably open to all sorts of possibility for progressive social change around sexuality, the Viagra phenomenon is profoundly *disappointing*. Social constructionist perspectives (e.g., Foucault 1981; Tiefer 1995) which draw attention to the shifting and contextual nature of human behavior and experience have become highly influential within sexuality studies. Moreover, even recent trends within biology emphasize the co-constitution of organisms and their environments (see Gavey 2005). The convergence of these constructionist perspectives from biology, social science and history permits a cautious optimism that the plasticity of human sexuality might allow for shifting and less rigid norms that promote increased tolerance and an ethic attentive to difference and power. It is just possible that these trends within the academy, as well as within the queer margins of culture, might have signalled broader movements towards new cultural understandings and practices. Were such an ethic brought to bear on questions relating to health, wellbeing, and equality, the coital imperative would surely be due for some wider critical scrutiny. Instead, such potentially radical cultural shifts have arguably been stalled by the escalating medicalization of sexuality within the corporate thrust of pharmaceutical companies hungry for new markets in which to expand profit. Through then prominent co-option of the coital imperative, which is strategically necessary in order to create a new market for a costly erectile fix, the disappointing spin-off is that many men and women are likely to be deprived of the cultural conditions for realizing diverse sexual and reproductive choices that might have enhanced their health and wellbeing.

References

D'Emilio, John and Estelle B. Freedman. 1988. *Intimate matters: A history of sexuality in America*. New York: Harper & Row.

Dworkin, Andrea. 1987. *Intercourse*. New York: The Free Press.

Foucault, Michel. 1981. *The history of sexuality* (*Volume 1: An Introduction*) (R. Hurley, trans.). Harmondsworth, Middlesex: Penguin.

Gavey, Nicola. 2005. *Just sex? The cultural scaffolding of rape*. New York and London: Routledge.

Gavey, Nicola, Kathryn McPhillips, and Virginia Braun. 1999. "*Interruptus coitus:* Heterosexuals accounting for intercourse", *Sexualities* 2 (1): 35–68.

Hitchcock, Tim. 2002. "Redefining sex in eighteenth-century England." In Kim M. Phillips and Barry Reay (eds), *Sexualities in history: A reader*. New York and London: Routledge.

Jackson, Margaret. 1984. "Sex research and the construction of sexuality: A tool of male supremacy?" *Women's Studies International Forum* 7: 43–51.

Laqueur, Thomas. 1990. *Making sex: Body and gender front the Greeks to Freud.* Cambridge, MA and London: Harvard University Press.

Petchesky, Rosalind P. 1990. *Abortion and woman's choice: The state, sexuality, and reproductive freedom (Revised Edition).* Boston, MA: Northeastern University Press.

Potts, Annie, Nicola Gavey, Victoria Grace, and Tiina Vares. 2003. "The downside of Viagra: Women's experiences and concerns", *Sociology of Health and Illness* 25 (7): 697–719.

Potts, Annie, Victoria Grace, Nicola Gavey, and Tiina Vares. 2004. "'Viagra stories': Challenging 'erectile dysfunction'", *Social Science and Medicine* 59: 489–99.

Sanders, Stephanie A. and June M. Reinisch. 1999. "Would you say you 'had sex' if . . . ?" *Journal of the American Medical Association* 281 (3): 275–77.

Segal, Lynne. 1994. *Straight sex: Rethinking the politics of pleasure.* Berkeley and Los Angeles: University of California Press.

Seidman, Steven. 1989. "Constructing sex as a domain of pleasure and self-expression: Sexual ideology in the sixties", *Theory, Culture & Society* 6: 293–315.

—— 1991. *Romantic longings: Love in America, 1830–1980.* London and New York: Routledge.

Tiefer, Leonore. 1995. *Sex is not a natural act and other essays.* Boulder, CO: Westview Press.

Weeks, Jeffrey. 1985. *Sexuality and its discontents: Meanings, myths and modern sexualities.* London and New York: Routledge & Kegan Paul.

The Medical Gayz

Suzanna Danuta Walters

In a 2010 episode of the late, great medical drama series *House*, a young man faints, has a heart attack, and generally decomposes on his wedding day. His problem? He's gay and has gone through the full reparative-therapy regime. Blunt Dr. House assures him that "like so many other things, you were born that way," but the sick man insists, "we get to choose how we live our lives," and he has chosen heterosexuality and marriage. Of course, the dear doctor is dead on, and the dude gets dumped by his fiancée and embraces the queer inevitable, for the price of not acceding to that "truth" may just be his own death by dishonesty. This episode—unusually dramatic in its depiction of the perils of bucking biology—is by no means anomalous: it is rare indeed to find *any* contemporary depiction of gay identity that doesn't represent sexuality as predetermined in some fundamental way.

If marriage is conjured as the Oz of queer liberation, then biological and genetic arguments are the yellow brick road, often providing both the route and the rationale for civil rights. There does seem to be some evidence that increasing numbers of people are buying into the immutability arguments, although that may very well be more about the rapid popularization of genetic arguments for everything from happiness to shyness than it is about ideas of sexuality per se. But the polls are dramatic: in May 2013, Gallup reported that 47 percent of Americans believe that gays are "born that way," while 33 percent believe being gay is due to "factors such as upbringing or environment"—the largest gap ever seen since these polls have been conducted.[1]

Just as we have come to take it for granted that right-thinking people believe homosexuality is innate and hardwired (either through genetics or through some broader combination of genes and hormones), we have also come to believe that wrong-thinking people—either vicious homophobes or simply ill-informed onlookers—insist on gayness as choice and volitional "lifestyle." Or as sympathetic columnist Ellen Goodman reports, "Well, it turns out that the more you believe homosexuality is innate, the more accepting you are of gay rights. A full 79 percent of people who think human beings are born with a sexual orientation support gay rights, including civil unions or marriage equality. But only 22 percent of those who believe homosexuality is a choice agree."[2] It has become something of a truism in popular perception that a belief in immutability leads to more "accepting" (less homophobic) ideas. For example, a 2011 Gallup poll reported that Americans were evenly split on homosexuality's cause, but those who agreed that "people are born gay/lesbian" (a proxy for genetic or biological causation) were less anti-gay than those who agreed that "being gay/lesbian is due to environment." This same poll confirms that 87 percent of people who think homosexuality is inborn support civil unions or marriage equality, compared with 43 percent of those who believe it is caused by environment. For those who believe that sexuality is a choice, 65 percent stated they think lesbian and gay relations are morally wrong.[3]

Gays themselves are no strangers to the lure of the biological; many contemporary advocacy groups state quite explicitly that "born that way" is the way to go in arguing for gay rights. Truth Wins Out, an organization that focuses primarily on fighting the reparative-therapy movement (a constellation of activists and therapists committed to "turning" gays straight), argues that "at the core of these anti-gay efforts is a central truth: Polls show that people who believe homosexuality is a choice are significantly more likely to vote against gay rights. . . . The right wing has realized that the key to winning the culture war is convincing Americans that homosexuality is a frivolous and malleable lifestyle choice."[4] As sociomedical scientist Rebecca Jordan-Young points out, times have changed such that "the notion of innately different preferences in men and women was once politically suspect, [but] it is now often suggested that accepting these innate differences will encourage a more rational approach to equality."[5]

Indeed, the turn of the century seems to have provided a "perfect storm" moment in which the idea of immutability has taken hold of the public imagination. As Kate O'Riordan argues in an article detailing "the life of the gay gene," this idea, regardless of its scientific veracity or replicability, has taken on a life of its own, from newspaper articles and databases to T-shirts and song lyrics.[6] There is, inarguably, an overwhelming "born with it" ideology afoot that encompasses gay marriage, gay genes, and gayness as "trait" and that is—of course—used by both gay rights activists and anti-gay activists to make arguments for equality or against it.

At the heart of this debate are any number of erroneous assumptions, many of which I've discussed earlier. But underlying the "born this way" framework is a core commitment to an absolute "nature versus nurture" dichotomy. As Sarah Wilcox summarizes in her review of the media's contributions to the biological mantra,

> The dominant theme of biological discourse about sexuality was a dichotomy between being born gay and choosing to be gay. In this dichotomy, biology, genes, and being born gay are defined in opposition to choice and the possibility of change in sexual orientation. Key assumptions behind this dichotomy include: 1) biological determinism, or the idea that biology can only mean direct determination of a characteristic; 2) a conceptualization of homosexuality and heterosexuality as mutually exclusive and dichotomous categories; and 3) the idea that political and social change is dependent on proof that homosexuality is an innate and unchanging characteristic.[7]

So choice is configured as absolutely opposite to, or the inverse of, biological predestination, a framework which flies in the face of even the most conservative scientists, who generally believe in some level of "interplay" between social/cultural/historical factors and genetic and biological ones.

This is tricky, and I am well aware that I am heading into some rocky terrain here. A belief in biological immutability is now, much to my chagrin, the mother's milk of gay rights discourse. I have rarely been able to raise this issue—with gays or with allied straights—without causing an angry response and an insistence on both the truth of biological immutability and the necessity of framing it thus to access rights and social tolerance. If the public debate is set up so that "tolerance" is dependent on immutability and predetermination, it is hard to argue against both the larger frame of tolerance and the explanatory rubric of biological destiny. But argue we must. For while it is true that there appears to be a real correlation between believing in the born-gay thesis and supporting gay rights, that same thesis allows heterosexuals to, as historian John D'Emilio puts it, "quell their moral reservations about our lives and push aside their personal squeamishness about what we do"[8] because gayness is configured as something that just *is*, not something one actually *does*. The tolerance framework depends on these immutability arguments to embrace gays who just can't help themselves. Tolerance as a theme of contemporary gay rights is dependent on biological arguments much as plants need sunshine to flourish.

Biology Is Destiny (Again)

Biological (and, more specifically, genetic and neurological and endocrinological) explanations for sexual orientation have a long history and have been thoroughly examined by any number of feminist and gay scholars, who have diligently detailed the rise and fall and rise again of these debates.[9] Surely, gays have been placed under the medical gaze since gayness itself was invented as a category not of behavior but rather of full-fledged and demarcated identity. The medicalization of sexual identity—and the search for a cause, if not a cure—has a long and infamous history, a history that includes well-meaning attempts by social activists to create a safe life for same-sex desire through the designation of inevitable and unstoppable difference but also, more ominously, includes the long and sordid history of incarceration, medication, electroshock "therapy," and numerous other attempts to rid the body (and mind) of its same-sex desires.

Notions of homosexuality as "inbred," innate, and immutable are therefore not new and were endorsed by a wide variety of thinkers and activists, including progressive reformers such as Havelock Ellis (who was also, of course, a devout eugenicist) and not so progressive doctors and scientists, eager to assert same-sex love as nature's mistake. Karl Ulrichs in the 1860s and '70s, Richard von Krafft-Ebing in the 1880s, and Magnus Hirschfeld in the 1910s and '20s—all pioneer sexologists and generally advocates of "toleration" or at least decriminalization—came to believe in some notion of innate homosexuality, whether through theories of a kind of brain inversion or through vague references to hormonal imbalances and other (unsubstantiated) anomalies. For Ulrichs, homosexuality was a congenital condition in which the gay or same-sex-desiring man (and most folks did completely ignore women in the search for causation; this lacuna continues today) is essentially psychically hermaphroditic: a female mind trapped in the wrong (male) body. Krafft-Ebing came to similar conclusions, seeing homosexuality as evidence of a sort of brain inversion. Ellis made a distinction between "true" inverts, who were characterized by some kind of biological immutability, and "homosexuals"—a rarer form of behavioral and situational identity. Even the designation of gays as a "third sex," a theory that

held much appeal among a wide range of thinkers and activists, was premised on some reference to a biological substratum that produced such anomalous identities.[10]

The motto of Hirschfeld's Scientific Humanitarian Committee was actually "Per Scientiam ad Justitiam," or "through science to justice," an indication that for many of these early scholar-activists, science was understood to be the key not only to unlocking the "mystery" of sexuality but to opening the prison doors of criminalized "perverts" around the globe. And science itself was understood then—and even more so now—as the conduit to tolerance; if you are born that way, then you are worthy of freedom. In the early days of this nascent field of sexology, the supposed objectivity and "truth" of science provided a twofer: a justification of the inevitability of gayness for sex reformers and a justification for the field of sexology itself, now bolstered and propped up by the cultural authority of science. These ideas mostly had little traction—either within scientific communities or in the larger reform movements—and of course no reliable evidence whatsoever. And, needless to say, sexual science provided no immunity from persecution, particularly when the Nazis came calling.

These and other theories of the heritability or genetic or biological origins of gayness have ebbed and flowed during different historical and social moments, most obviously intersecting with the rise of eugenics and other determinist frameworks but also with reformist efforts both here and abroad. Arguments for immutability and biology are less popular, however, in historical periods that evince a broader skepticism toward scientific answers to social problems. For example, in an era that saw the emergence of gay liberation (and a challenge to older medicalized models of social identity more generally) like the 1960s and 1970s, heritability was not particularly on the radar screen for either gays or their opponents, and it was the *anti-gay* forces at the time that insisted on a sort of biological aberrance. As D'Emilio rightly points out, "In the literature produced by gay liberationists and lesbian feminists in the late 1960s and early 1970s, there is virtually a consensus that heterosexuality and homosexuality do not exist in nature, so to speak, but instead are products of culture . . . that emanate from an oppressive society."[11] Early gay rights groups such as the Mattachine Society didn't focus on issues of causation but rather on *rights,* explicitly defining gays as an oppressed minority group. Indeed, in the opening salvo of the 1971 manifesto "The Woman-Identified Woman," the authors declare that "a lesbian is the rage of all women condensed to the point of explosion."[12] Even further, they state that "lesbianism, like male homosexuality, is a category of behavior possible only in a sexist society characterized by rigid sex roles and dominated by male supremacy. . . . Homosexuality is a by-product of a particular way of setting up roles . . . on the basis of sex; as such it is an inauthentic . . . category."[13] So much for warped genes and predetermined desires. Thus, the early gay movement was committed to undermining the designation of homosexuality in pathological and medical terms, exemplified in the long battle to remove "homosexuality" as a disease category in the *DSM* (the *Diagnostic and Statistical Manual of Mental Disorders,* long the gold standard of classification for psychologists), finally achieved in 1974.[14] Implicit in that demedicalization—and *explicit* in much of the political organizing and thinking of the time—was an insistence that the question of "origins" (biological or otherwise) was the wrong question.

Not all post-Stonewall gay activists and thinkers were anti-essentialist or opposed to a biological perspective. Attenuated versions of essentialist[15] arguments have cropped up in the unlikeliest places. Even radicals such as lesbian-feminist poet and writer Adrienne Rich—through her concepts of the lesbian continuum and woman-identified woman—managed to make lesbian sexual desire less about desire for another woman per se and more about a kind of a political desire or even a biological drive. For Rich and some others of this period, lesbianism was less a "preference" than a force or, as queer theorist Jennifer Terry describes it, "somewhere between a natural drive and a

moral imperative, while retaining elements of both."[16] Rich's position illustrates the many—often contradictory—sides of this equation. For, on the one hand, she offered up a naturalized version of lesbian desire that derived from a sort of primal mother-daughter bond or a continuum of woman identification and connection. On the other hand, she was one of the first to really articulate the idea of "compulsory heterosexuality" as essentially forcing women into traditional forms of intimacy premised on male domination. Her response to this compulsory heterosexuality, and the response of a vital branch of early radical feminism, was what became known as "political lesbianism," offering up same-sex desire as a positive and pro-woman *choice* that explicitly rejected both compulsory heterosexuality and medicalized models of homosexuality. For these activists, sexual and emotional *choice* was the radical mode that promised a freedom beyond mere tolerance. That there was really no gay male counterpart to this forceful notion of choosing lesbian sexuality speaks to the ways in which gender profoundly shapes the entire debate around gay etiology. This lack of symmetry between lesbians and gay men on the "choice" issue carries over into contemporary debates and even scientific research, as we will see later on. So a figure like Rich illustrates well this contradiction between ideas of choice and a belief in some determining "force," because she herself seems to have held both positions simultaneously.

There is no question, however, that the romance with biological causes for sexual "orientation" (really *same-sex* orientation, as the search for the hetero gene or the straight hypothalamus goes largely unexamined) has ratcheted up in recent years, due in no small part to the combined force of the gay-marriage debates and the increasing "medicalization" and "geneticization" of behavior and identity more generally. The public and scientific obsession with genetic origin stories, in particular, was spurred on by the initiation of the Human Genome Project in 1989, which furthered the already booming business—both popular and scientific—in genetic bases for behavior, personality, disease, and so on. The search for a gene for nearly everything (from shyness to sexiness) became a lucrative industry, and the early nineties produced a wave of studies that moved from the science journals quickly into the public eye.

Some of this impetus toward discovering "hard" scientific evidence of homosexuality has emerged as a reaction to social/psychological theories that predominated in the 20th century and that attributed homosexuality to some version of pathogenic family life: stunted development, bad mothering, absent fathers, or failed Oedipal resolutions. For many scientists—especially gay ones—this new science of sexual orientation was seen as a corrective to the glib psychology of the day, which tended not only to assume homosexuality as an emotional and sexual disorder of some kind but to place "blame" firmly on the already overburdened shoulders of mothers. In addition, this new moment has been marked by the (relatively unique) phenomenon of openly gay scientists conducting this research. Not only does this give added legitimacy to these studies, but many, if not all, of these researchers claim that they are doing this "for" gay people and in the service of furthering tolerance, if not gay rights. We will come back to this claim later.

Girly Brains and Macho Digits

The two scientists most commonly cited in regard to the biological determinist theory of homosexuality are Simon LeVay and Dean Hamer, both of whom are openly gay and published their initial salvos in the "born gay" battle in the early 1990s. LeVay, a neuroscientist, and Hamer, a National Institutes of Health geneticist, have often explicitly presented their research as ammunition in the war for tolerance of gays and lesbians. In what independent scholar Nancy Ordover calls "The Great 1990s Medicalization of Queerness," both LeVay and Hamer published studies that ostensibly "proved" that homosexuality was biologically determined.[17] In 1991, LeVay published "A Difference in Hypothalamic Structure between Homosexual and Heterosexual Men" in the journal *Science,* announcing that a cell group in the interstitial nuclei of the anterior hypothalamus was twice as large in heterosexual men as in gay men, on the basis of an analysis of the brain tissue taken from the autopsies of forty-one subjects in New York and California. The subjects consisted of eighteen gay men with AIDS, one bisexual man with AIDS, sixteen "presumed heterosexual" men (six of whom died of AIDS-related deaths), and one woman with AIDS—a skewed sample whose problematic features did not go unnoticed. In 1993, Hamer and colleagues published their gay-gene manifesto, "A Linkage between DNA Markers on the X Chromosome and Male Sexual Orientation," which argued that a gene (which they suspected more than isolated) on the X chromosome influences male sexual orientation. Several other significant studies in the 1990s and early 2000s connected homosexuality and gender identity to biological origins, focusing on brain and finger size, various hormones and endocrine systems, maternal womb environment, and every permutation therein.[18]

Studies of twins have also played an important role in the medicalization of homosexuality and have become a highly debated area of experimentation. One of the most significant studies of this type was undertaken in 1991 by psychologist J. Michael Bailey and his collaborator, Richard Pillard, a psychiatrist. According to this initial study, "52% of identical (monozygotic) twins of homosexual men were likewise homosexual; 22% of fraternal (dizygotic) twins were likewise homosexual; 11% of adoptive brothers of homosexual men were likewise homosexual."[19] Bailey has since become one of the central, and most controversial,[20] players in the "born gay" debates and in sexuality studies more broadly construed, both for his methods—which have come under scrutiny from study subjects and researchers alike—and for his conclusions about gender, sexuality, desire, and identity. Bailey's research has been widely criticized for reinvigorating stereotypes of gay men as gender "inverts" and for claiming scientific definitions of sexual identity based solely on levels of penile arousal. And his work on transsexuals and bisexuals is equally reductive and controversial.

Another hypothesis that has garnered a great deal of popular press attention is the argument that men with older brothers are more likely to be gay. This is based (at least in part) on two studies by sexologist Ray Blanchard in 1997 and 2001 which found that "the more older biological brothers a man has, the more likely he will be gay because mothers become immunized against male-specific antigens by each male fetus so her anti-male antibodies interfere with the sexual differentiation of each successive male fetus's brain,"[21] suggesting that male homosexuality is "caused" by some event in the womb, perhaps the levels of circulating testosterone (although, of course, these can't be measured in the fetus, so this is just—in the end—guesswork). Other scientists have tried to link (male) homosexuality to female fecundity, as did Italian evolutionary psychologist Andrea Camperio-Ciana when he published studies suggesting that "homosexuality is a sex-linked trait" and that "female relatives of male homosexuals . . . produce more children."[22]

Without going into detail here, suffice it to say that these studies have presented any number of problems—from small sample size and constitution to embedded assumptions and unsubstantiated generalizations and the problem of replicability. Sexual desire and gender identity have often been conflated and confused and both have been understood as relatively clear and unambiguous categories. As Jordan-Young notes in her wide-ranging critique of the "science" of sex differences, the studies were deeply inconsistent and contradictory, particularly concerning the very unit of analysis (the "homosexual"), such that "one scientist's heterosexuals are another scientist's homosexuals."[23]

The past decade has seen the publication of similar studies linking homosexuality to genes or other biological factors, resulting in arguments concerning the effects of prenatal stress and the assertion that lesbians don't menstruate, have asymmetrical faces, and are good whistlers. It can get pretty silly: there have also been several studies linking sexuality to visible physical features such as the hands. One of these is called the 2D:4D effect, which claims that straight men and lesbians have shorter index fingers than ring fingers, but gay men and straight women have a smaller digit-ratio difference. The trend is more pronounced in supposedly "effeminate" gay men and also apparently indicates whether he will be a "top" or a "bottom." And as if our deformed fingers and our whistling capacities weren't enough of a problem, in 2000, Martin LaLumiere and Kenneth Zucker published a study in the *Psychological Bulletin*, which concluded that homosexuals are more likely to be left-handed. While Zucker says the research provides empirical evidence that links homosexuality to left-handedness, he also adds, "we don't have a definitive answer as to why the relationship exists."[24] This caveat is repeated by many scientists linking homosexuality to genetics, including LeVay and Hamer. It seems that the difficulty lies in proving cause and effect: does homosexuality cause handedness, hypothalamus size, and strange little fingers? Or are left-handed people with varying finger length more likely to desire members of their own sex? And more to the point, do we want to limit the richness of our desires and identities to the discrete markers of the physical body?

Bad Science, Bad Reporting, Bad News

There was a flurry of activity when these big studies of the 1990s came out, breathless reports in the weeklies and newspaper coverage extolling the "breakthrough" discovery of the "cause" of homosexuality. But at the same time, there was also a significant amount of critical and even skeptical attention, particularly from gay activists and scholars. In more recent years, however, the critical edge has worn down or moved solely into the academy, and the oft-repeated "most scientists believe" claim has become our collective common sense. Although many people have remained skeptical, the gay-gene story has come to have a "just so" quality, in which "references to the critique of the gay gene became diminished [and] the idea of the gay gene conversely became stronger."[25]

While scientists themselves are often culpable for overstating or misstating their findings, more often than not the problem lies in the reporting, which is quick to make (false) generalizations in the desire to promote a headline-grabbing "sea change" in research and findings. No scientists worth their salt claim a single determination (a gene, a hormone), yet this small cluster of studies has produced both a journalistic and a popular perception that gayness (specifically male homosexuality) is innate, immutable, predetermined in some finite and marked and knowable way. All nuance is thrown to the wind as evolutionary biologists such as David Barash declare that the "ship has sailed, and the consensus among scientists is that same-sex preference is rooted in our biology."[26] Note here the focus on *same-sex* preference as biological—no one seems to care much about *opposite-sex* origin.

The gap between a suggestion of possible biological *factors* and wholesale biological *determination* is narrowed to the point of invisibility. Stephen Jay Gould and other critics of deterministic and socio-biological frameworks have long insisted that we distinguish between *potentiality* and *determination*. This distinction, like that between heritability and immutability, is often lost in the public discussion of gay origins. Kate O'Riordan rightly points out that "the slippage between terms like *genetics, heritability, familial,* and *biological* is not only a feature of science news or popular science writings, but also of scientific databases, maps, and catalogues."[27]

Clearly, biological explanations have an enduring hold on our popular imagination, especially when it comes to sexuality and gender, and popular journalists have played a major role in this fascination, feeding "a popular appetite for deciphering human sexual relations by drawing parallels between animal mating patterns and human experiences of sexual attraction, dating, marriage, divorce, promiscuity, and homosexuality, often humorously simplifying or exaggerating the actual scientific findings."[28] Unfortunately, both the gay press and the mainstream media seem to take this stuff at face value. Given the motivation to promote tolerance, and the assumption that determinist ideas do this, it is unsurprising—albeit depressing—how few differences there are between the gay popular press and the mainstream popular press in this regard. But while some reporters attempt to modulate the "gay gene" mania—and do justice to the nuance and tentativeness with which many scientists make any assertions—most have jumped on the determinist bandwagon with fervor. This is due, in part, to the procedures of mainstream news reporting, in which bold headlines and controversial assertions are de rigueur and modulated ambivalence is a bad news day.

Even when reporters use numerous qualifiers (e.g., using words like "tend" and "appears"), the headlines—which almost always state categorically that gay brains or desires or preferences are ineluctably different from non-gay ones—mitigate against the more nuanced and tentative text of the article. One such piece in *Discover* magazine opens with a welcome willingness to assert that "the question remains unresolved."[29] Yet in the next sentence, this honest ambivalence is thrown to the wind because now we are told, "Whether or not a gay gene, or a set of gay genes, or some other biological mechanism is ever found, one thing is clear: The environment a child grows up in has nothing to do with what makes most gay men gay. Two of the most convincing studies have proved conclusively that sexual orientation in men has a genetic cause."[30] "Genetic" is thus set up in opposition to "environment" in a simple nature/nurture dichotomy in which behaviors are either singularly "caused" by genetic or other "predetermined" factors *or* behaviors are singularly "caused" by factors seen as social, cultural, or familial. Even more curious, this research apparently leaves open the possibility that *lesbians* may actually be "influenced" by environment and not, therefore, genetically programmed, a conclusion which seems rather incongruous, to say the least. Logically speaking, if sexual orientation is singularly produced through biogenetic factors, then women should not be left aside in the deterministic frameworks.

Not all studies, of course, have received the same attention. Indeed, one critic has argued that one study in particular has been sidelined because, "in contrast to LeVay's findings, which reiterated a traditional framework for equating homosexuality with femininity in men and with masculinity in women, [Dick F.] Swaab and [Michel A.] Hofman's research indicated that while the brains of homosexual men were different from those of heterosexual men, they did not resemble those of heterosexual women."[31] As Peter Conrad notes, "by trumpeting genetic discoveries on page one while relegating disconfirmations to back pages (if noting them at all), the media misrepresents the state of genetics. It amplifies the impression that genes for particular problems are being discovered, but is unlikely to correct that view when a disconfirmation occurs. This ultimately presents an overoptimistic view of the role of genetics in social problems and misinforms public knowledge."[32] Even here, though, gayness is easily situated as a "social problem" that merits attention as such, whether scientific or otherwise.

A Homo Mystery Wrapped in a Gay Enigma

So many of these studies—and their reporting—begin with the designation of homosexuality as a "problem," a mystery to be solved. The assumptions and perspectives of most popular representations and reporting on the "gay gene" are informed and framed by socio-biological and evolutionary psychological precepts and norms, such that, as anthropologist Roger Lancaster succinctly puts it, "sociobiology has become common sense."[33] It is surely the case that, as sociologist Martha McCaughy argues,

"sociobiological explanations of human homosexuality wind up naturalizing heterosexuality by holding up homosexuality as a challenge for evolutionary theorists to explain—as if the legitimacy of evolutionary theory itself depends upon an evolved heterosexual human nature!"[34]

For those sociobiologists whose theories of evolution and zero-sum games often rule the day, the language can be even more stark. For psychobiologist Qazi Rahman of Queen Mary College in London, "Homosexuality is effectively like sterilization. . . . You'd think evolution would get rid of it."[35] In other words, since homosexuals don't reproduce (supposedly), then—evolutionarily speaking—they should have gone the way of the dinosaurs. Or maybe we'll just find out that all dinosaurs were a little light in their prehistoric loafers.

The immutability arguments not only set up a problem to be solved but rely on some sort of analogy to figure out this supposed problem: is gayness like handedness or hair color or height? Or is it more like intelligence or taste? Are gays like blacks or other minority groups? Or is it just set in stone? For some popular writers, homosexuality is not just a preference, but more like a compulsion, ineradicably written in our genetic codes and hormonal flows. *Washington Post* writer Marguerite Kelly claims that "most scientists think that a person's sexuality is the work of nature, not nurture; that it is as innate as the color of his eyes and just as immutable. A homosexual can no more be attracted to a member of the opposite sex than he can be attracted to a lamppost."[36] Tell that to all the attractive lampposts out there.

The arguments run in many directions; it is not as simple as social constructionists versus geneticists or biological determinists; social constructionists also find themselves at odds with the perspective of evolutionary psychologists who "hold that homosexuality is a naturally selected adaptation, or at least a trade-off for such an adaptation."[37] Some have tried to find a "solution" to this debate by proposing a sort of combined thesis, which often goes under the heading of "evolutionary social constructivism," in which distinctions are made between same-sex sexual behavior and sexual identity, and the Darwinian hypothesis of "alliance formation" is utilized to "explain how a socially constructed homosexuality is embedded in our evolved nature."[38] The "alliance-formation" folks, say two academic critics of the biological position, "argue that same-sex sexual behavior is an adaptation that has been preserved in the gene pool because it promotes reciprocal altruism."[39] Others claim that it simply makes no sense to be gay because it doesn't aid in the reproductive imperative and would have, therefore, been weeded out over time. Some have solved this dilemma by recourse to some variant of kin-selection hypothesis, in which gay relatives are understood to aid in the reproductive success of their close kin, "thus enabl[ing] the gay gene to proliferate through collateral lines of descent, even if its bearers did not reproduce at all. In this model, homosexuals would be 'helpers at the nest.'"[40] This handy-gay-uncle argument has very little evidence to go for it and has the added problem of being wholly wedded to a rather overly determinist reading of evolutionary theory, as well as a particular view of family formation.

Both scientists and science reporters are often eager to prove both the stability and always-thereness of gays at the same time that they assert their minority status, their relative smallness in relation to the general population. So gays are a stable but small population, always there but always a minority. Timeless but bounded. Transcultural but not transient. Of course, all of this work accepts the notion of homosexuality as a mystery (or, in some cases, a Darwinian puzzle) to be figured out. As one scientist opines, "If there is one thing that has always seemed obvious about homosexuality, it's that it just doesn't make sense. Evolution favors traits that aid reproduction, and being gay clearly doesn't do that."[41]

Notes

1. Gallup, "Gay and Lesbian Rights": 47 percent in May of 2013, up from 31 percent in 1996 and 35 percent in 2009.
2. Goodman, "Vatican Retreat on Homosexuality."
3. J. Jones, "Support for Legal Gay Relations Hits New High." In this poll, 42 percent believe people are gay due to "factors such as environment and upbringing," 40 percent believe being gay is something "a person is born with." Of those who believe it is not inborn, 54 percent are against legalizing same-sex marriage.
4. Truth Wins Out, "History."
5. Jordan-Young, *Brain Storm*, 5.
6. O'Riordan, "Life of the Gay Gene."
7. Wilcox, "Cultural Context and the Conventions of Science Journalism," 231; Lancaster, *Life Is Hard*.
8. D'Emilio, *World Turned*, 163.
9. See especially the work of Jennifer Terry, Anne Fausto-Sterling, Roger Lancaster, Edward Stein.
10. See especially Hirschfeld, *Sex in Human Relationships*; Ulrichs, *The Riddle of "Man-Manly" Love*; Krafft-Ebing, *Psychopathia Sexualis*; Ellis, *Sex in Relation to Society*.
11. D'Emilio, *World Turned*, 155.
12. Radicalesbians, "The Woman Identified Woman."
13. Ibid.
14. UC Davis Department of Psychology, "Facts about Homosexuality and Mental Health."
15. Essentialism is a highly debated concept, but here I am using it to refer to a notion that something (say, gender or sexual desire) has a fixed "essence" or nature that is basically unchanging and not the product of social and historical forces. So essentialism is contrasted with various versions of constructionism, which understands bodies, desires, identities as existing in specific places and times and not expressing some underlying and unchanging "given."

16 Radner, "Compulsory Sexuality and the Desiring Woman," 96.

17 Ordover, *American Eugenics*, 64.

18 These include Jiang-Ning Zhou, Michel Hofman, Louis Gooren, and Dick Swaab's "A Sex Difference in the Human Brain and Its Relation to Transsexuality," which discovered "a region in the hypothalamus that is 60% larger in men than in male-to-female transsexuals" (69), and Cheryl McCormick and Sandra Witelson's 1994 study, which argued that "the communication conduit between parts of the brain used for understanding speech and perceiving objects is bigger in gay men than straight men." McCormick and Witelson, "Functional Cerebral Asymmetry and Sexual Orientation in Men and Women," 528.

19 Bailey and Pillard, "Genetic Study of Male Sexual Orientation," 1093.

20 For examples, see Carey, "Criticism of a Gender Theory"; Burt and Jorgensen, "NU Panel to Investigate Prof's Research Tactics"; R. Wilson, "Transsexual 'Subjects' Complain about Professor's Research Methods."

21 Bering, "Sneaky F*cker Theory."

22 Barber, "Could Homosexual Genes Be Naturally Selected?"

23 Jordan-Young, *Brain Storm*, 168.

24 Quoted in Bode, "Sexuality at Hand."

25 O'Riordan, "Life of the Gay Gene," 364.

26 Barash, "Evolutionary Mystery of Homosexuality."

27 O'Riordan, "Life of the Gay Gene," 364.

28 Terry, "'Unnatural Acts' in Nature," 153.

29 Abrams, "Real Story on Gay Genes."

30 Ibid.

31 Terry, *American Obsession*, 240.

32 Conrad, "Public Eyes and Private Genes," 146.

33 Lancaster, *Trouble with Nature*, 12.

34 McCaughy, "Perverting Evolutionary Narratives of Heterosexual Masculinity," 273.

35 Quoted in Kunzig, "Finding the Switch."

36 Kelly, "Daughter's Friendship with Effeminate Boy Isn't Hazardous."

37 Adriaens and de Block, "Evolution of a Social Construction," 573.

38 Ibid., 574.

39 Ibid., 576.

40 Ibid., 583.

41 Kunzig, "Finding the Switch."

"Guys Are Just Homophobic"

Rethinking Adolescent Homophobia and Heterosexuality

C. J. Pascoe

Teenage masculinity

Kevin, a high school student in suburban San Francisco, sits at an IHOP, short of money for dinner. His friend, Craig, agrees to lend him money, but only on the following condition – that Kevin repeat a series of confessional phrases which Craig can videotape and place on YouTube. Kevin buries his head in his hands asking, "You're going to take a video of this and post it on YouTube aren't you?!" Craig ignores Kevin's plea saying, "Anyway, repeat after me. I Kevin James Wong."

KEVIN: I, Kevin James Wong.
CRAIG: 17 years old.
KEVIN (WHO AT THIS POINT STARTS TO GIGGLE EMBARRASSEDLY):
    17 years old.
CRAIG: Senior at Valley High School.
KEVIN: Senior at Valley High School.
CRAIG: In Santa Clarita.
KEVIN: In Santa Clarita.
CRAIG: Am now confessing.
KEVIN: Am now confessing.
CRAIG: That I, Kevin Wong.
KEVIN: That I, Kevin Wong.
CRAIG: Am a homosexual male.
KEVIN: Am a homosexual male.

They dissolve into laughter as their friend Jesse jumps into the frame behind Kevin. Craig posted the video on YouTube and eagerly showed it to me as I interviewed him in a local Starbucks.

He and his friends giggled as they continued to show me other YouTube videos, one of which featured them imitating men engaging in anal intercourse and then bursting into fits of laughter.

About two years before I watched Craig's video in that Santa Clarita coffee shop I found myself two hours away, at a high school in Riverton California, where a group of fifth graders had been bussed in for the day to participate in the local high school's performing arts day. As I looked around the outdoor quads decorated with student artwork and filled with choirs singing and bands playing, a student from River High, Brian, ran past me to the rear quad yelling to a group of the elementary school boys. He hollered at them, pointing frantically, "There's a faggot over there! There's a faggot over there! Come look!" The group of boys dashed after Brian as he ran down the hallway, towards the presumed "faggot." Peering down the hallway I saw Brian's friend, Dan, waiting for the boys. As the boys came into his view, Dan pursed his lips and began sashaying towards them. He swung his hips exaggeratedly and wildly waved his arms on the end of which his hands hung from limp wrists. To the boys Brian yelled, referring to Dan, "Look at the faggot! Watch out! He'll get you!" In response, the 10-year-olds screamed in terror and raced back down the hallway. I watched Brian and Dan repeat this drama about the predatory faggot, each time with a new group of young boys.

Kevin, Craig, Brian and Dan enacted similar scenes containing similar messages: men or boys who do not conform to normative understandings of masculinity and sexuality should be mocked, humiliated and possibly feared. I have spent the better part of the last decade interviewing teens about and observing their behavior around definitions of masculinity and sexuality. Across a variety of geographic settings, boys from a range of class and racial/ethnic groups report sentiments much like those expressed by Kevin, Craig, Brian and Dan. Conversations with and observations of these boys indicate that homophobic taunts, jokes, teasing and harassment are central to the ways in which contemporary American boys come to think of themselves as men.

The homophobia articulated by Kevin, Craig, Brian and Dan seems representative of many American youth. Nationally, 93 percent of youth hear homophobic comments at least occasionally and 51 percent on a daily basis (National Mental Health Association 2002). Interestingly, in one state, 80 percent of youth who have been targeted with anti-gay harassment identify as heterosexual (Youth Risk Behavior Survey – Washington 1995). While this harassment is primarily directed at boys, girls suffer from sexualized harassment as well. The American Association of University Women (2001) documents that 83 percent of girls have been sexually harassed at school. These cursory statistics point to an educational experience in adolescence characterized in part by sexualized and gendered aggression directed from boys at other boys *and* at girls.

This type of joking and teasing can have dire consequences. Ninety percent of random school shootings have involved straight-identified boys who have been relentlessly humiliated with homophobic remarks (Kimmel 2003). For instance, Michael Carneal and Andy Williams, both involved in rampage school shootings, had been harassed for being gay (Kimmel 2003; Newman et al. 2004). Michael Carneal's school newspaper actually published a report outing him as gay (though he did not self-identify as such) (Newman et al. 2004). Eric Mohat, a 17-year-old high school student in Ohio who enjoyed theater and playing music, shot himself in 2007 after hearing homophobic taunts. Similarly, Carl Joseph Walker Hoover, an 11-year-old middle school student in Massachusetts, suffered homophobic harassment from his classmates for performing well academically. He hung himself as a desperate response to the teasing. Lawrence King, having been bullied relentlessly since third grade for his non-traditional gender presentation, was shot and killed by a fellow student in 2008 whom he had asked to be his Valentine.

While certainly the sort of joking and minor humiliation exhibited in the two opening stories does not match the level of violence in these examples, a problematic intersection of gender and sexuality undergirds all of them. Practices that seem to reflect basic homophobia – imitating same sex eroticism, calling someone queer or mincing about with limp wrists – are also about policing gendered identities and practices. Through making homophobic jokes, calling other boys gay and imitating effeminate men boys attempt to assure themselves and others of their masculinity. For contemporary American boys, the definition of masculinity entails displaying power, competence, a lack of emotions, heterosexuality and dominance. Says Kevin, for instance, to be masculine is to be "tough." The ideal man is "strong" and he "can't be too emotional" adds Erik. Maleness does not confer masculinity upon a given boy. Rather masculinity is the repeated signaling to self and others that one is powerful, competent, unemotional, heterosexual and dominant.

This signaling appears in two ways, through practices of repudiation and confirmation. Repudiatory practices take the form of a "fag discourse," consisting of homophobic jokes, taunts, and imitations through which boys publicly signal their rejection of that which is considered unmasculine. Boys confirm masculine selves through public enactments of compulsive heterosexuality which include practices of "getting girls," physically confining girls under the guise of flirtation and sex talk. For many contemporary American boys masculinity must be repeatedly proven, as one's identity as masculine is never fully secured. This essay unpacks adolescent boys' public enactments of homophobia and heterosexuality, examining them as sexualized as well as gendered processes which have ramifications for all teenagers – male, female, straight and gay.

The fag discourse

Boys repeatedly tell me that "fag" was the ultimate insult for a boy. Damell stated, "Since you were little boys you've been told, 'hey, don't be a little faggot.'" Jeremy emphasized that this insult literally reduced a boy to nothing, "To call someone gay or fag is like the lowest thing you can call someone. Because that's like saying that you're nothing." Indeed, much like the boys terrorized by Brian and Craig, boys often learn long before adolescence that a "fag" is the worst thing a guy could be. Thus boys' daily lives often consist of interactions in which they frantically lob these epithets at one another and try to deflect them from themselves.

Many boys explained their frequent use of insults like queer, gay and fag by asserting that, as Keith put it, "guys are just homophobic." However, analyzing boys' homophobic practices as a "fag discourse" shows that their behavior reflects not just a fear of same sex desire, but a specific fear of *men's* same sex desire. Many told me that homophobic insults applied primarily to boys, not to girls. While Jake told me that he didn't like gay people, he quickly added, "Lesbians, okay, that's good!" Now lesbians are not "good" because of some enlightened approach to sexuality, but because, as Ray, said, "To see two hot chicks banging bodies in a bed, that's like every guy's fantasy right there. It's the truth. I've heard it so many times." So their support of lesbians is more about heterosexual fantasy than about a progressive attitude (Jenefsky and Miller 1998).

Furthermore, several boys argued that fag, queer and gay had little to do with actual sexual practices or desires. Darnell told me "It doesn't have anything to do with being gay." Adding to this sentiment, J. L. said, "Fag, seriously, it has nothing to do with sexual preference at all. You could just be calling somebody an idiot, you know?" As David explained, "Being gay is just a lifestyle. It's someone you choose to sleep with. You can still throw a football around and be gay." David's final statement clarifies the distinction between popular understandings of these insults and teens' actual use of them. That is, that they have to do with men's same sex eroticism, but at their core discipline gendered practices and identities (such as the ability, or lack thereof, to throw a football). In asserting the primacy of gender to the definition of these seemingly homophobic insults, boys reflect what Riki Wilchins (2003) calls the Eminem Exception, in which Eminem explains that he doesn't call people "faggot" because of their sexual orientation, but because they are weak and unmanly. While it is not necessarily acceptable to be gay, if a man were gay *and* masculine, as in David's portrait of the football-throwing gay man, he does not deserve the insult.

What renders a boy vulnerable to homophobic epithets often depends on local definitions of masculinity. Boys frequently cited exhibiting stupidity, femininity, incompetence, emotionality or same sex physicality as notoriously non-masculine practices. Chad, for instance, said that boys might be called a fag if they seemed "too happy or something" while another boy expounded on the dangers of being "too smiley." Ironically, these insults are pitched at boys who engage in seemingly heterosexual activities. Kevin, when describing his ideal girlfriend said, "I have to imagine myself singing, like serenading her. Okay, say we got in a fight and we broke up. I have to imagine myself as a make-up gift to her singing to her out of her window." Kevin laughed as he said that when he shares this scenario with his friends "the guys are like, 'dude you're gay!'"

Because so many activities could render a boy vulnerable to these insults, perhaps it is little surprise that Ben asserted that one could be labeled for "anything, literally anything. Like you were trying to turn a wrench the wrong way, 'dude you're a fag.' Even if a piece of meat drops out of your sandwich, 'you fag!'" While my research shows that there are particular set of behaviors that could get a boy called the slur, it is no wonder that Ben felt a boy could be called it for "anything." In that statement he reveals the intensity and extent of the policing boys must do of their behaviors in order to avoid the epithet.

The sort of homophobic harassment detailed above has as much to do definitions of masculinity as it does with actual fear of other gay men (Corbett 2001; Kimmel 2001). Being subject to homophobic harassment has as much to do with failing at masculine tasks of competence, heterosexual prowess or in any way revealing weakness as it does with a sexual identity. Homophobic epithets such as fag have gender meanings *and* sexual meanings. The insult is levied against boys who are not masculine, even momentarily, and boys who identify (or are identified by others) as gay. This sets up a very complicated daily ordeal in which boys continually strive to avoid being subject to the epithet, but are simultaneously constantly vulnerable to it.

This sort of homophobia appears frequently in boys' joking relationships. Sociologists have pointed out that joking is central to men's relationships in general (Kehily and Nayak 1997; Lyman 1998). Through aggressive joking boys cement friendship bonds with one another. Boys often draw laughs though imitating effeminate men or men's same sex desire. Emir frequently imitated effeminate men who presumably sexually desired other men to draw laughs from students in his introductory drama class. One day his teacher, disturbed by noise outside the classroom, turned to close the door saying, "We'll shut this unless anyone really wants to watch sweaty boys playing basketball." Emir lisped, "I wanna watch the boys play!" The rest of the class cracked up at his imitation. No one in the class actually thought Emir was gay, as he purposefully mocked both same-sex sexual desire and an effeminate gender identity. This sort of ritual reminded other youth that masculine men didn't desire other men, nor did they lisp or behave in other feminine manners. It also reminded them that men who behaved in these ways were worthy of laughter and derision.

These everyday joking interchanges, however, were more than "just jokes." For some boys, such as Lawrence King, the intolerance for gender differences espoused by these joking rituals has serious, if not deadly, consequences. Ray and Peter underscore this in their conversation. Ray asserted "I can't stand fags. Like I've met a couple. I don't know. The way they rub you. Gay people I don't care. They do their thing in their bedroom and that's fine. Feminine guys bother me." Peter, his friend, continued "If they try to get up on you. I'll kill you." Ray and Peter illuminated the teenage boys' different responses to gay and effeminate men as Ray espouses tolerance for the presumably gender normative former and Peter threatens violence against the latter. In this sense the discourse runs a continuum from joking to quite violent harassment. While boys said that the "fag" insult was more about failing at masculinity, than about actually being gay, it seemed that a gay and unmasculine boy suffered the most under this "gender regime" (Connell 1987).

As a talented dancer who frequently sported multicolored hair extensions, mascara and wore baggy pants, fitted tank tops and sometimes a skirt, Ricky violated norms of gender *and* sexuality. He told me that harassment started early, in elementary school. "I'm talking like sixth grade, I started being called a fag. Fifth grade I was called a fag. Third grade I was called a fag." Though he moved schools every two years or so, this sort of harassment continued and intensified as he moved into high school. At his school's homecoming game (for which Ricky had choreographed the half time show) he was harassed until he left after hearing things like "there's that fucking fag" and "What the fuck is that fag doing here? That fag has no right to be here." When watching him dance with the school's all female dance team other boys reacted in revulsion. Nils said, "It's like a car wreck, you just can't look away." J. R., the captain of the football team, shook his head and muttered under his breath, "That guy dancing, it's just disgusting, Disgusting!" shaking his head and stomping off. Even though dancing is the most important thing in his life, Ricky didn't attend school dances because he didn't like to "watch my back" the whole time. He had good reason for this fear. Brad said of prom, "I heard Ricky is going in a skirt, it's a hella short one." Sean responded with "I wouldn't even go if he's there." Topping Sean's response Brad claimed, "I'd probably beat him up outside."

The harassment suffered by Ricky featured none of the joking or laughter exhibited in other interchanges. Very real threats of violence undergirded boys' comments about him. Ricky told me that he walked with his eyes downcast in order to avoid guys' eye contact, fearing that they'd see such eye contact as a challenge. Similarly he varied his route home from school each day and carried a rock in his hand to protect himself. For many boys, in order to maintain a sense of themselves as masculine, they felt they had to directly attack Ricky, a symbol of what they feared most, of unmasculine nothingness.

Compulsive heterosexuality

If daily life for many boys entails running a gauntlet of homophobic insults, how do they avoid being permanently labeled as Ricky was? Boys defend against homophobic teasing and harassment by assuring others of their heterosexuality. By engaging in a number of cross-gender rituals, a boy can relatively successfully defend himself against ending up in Ricky's position, the object of harassment, derision and violence. In the same way that boys' homophobia is not specifically about a sexual identity, compulsive heterosexuality[1] is not only about expressing love, desire and intimacy, but about showing a sexualized dominance over girls' bodies. The sort of gendered teasing in which boys engage in takes a toll on girls as well as other boys. In my research I found three components of compulsive heterosexuality: rituals of getting girls, rituals of touch, and sex talk.

Perhaps the most obvious example of "getting girls" is having a girlfriend. Having a girlfriend seems a normal teen behavior.

For boys who are identified as feminine and teased for unmasculine practices, having a girlfriend functions as some sort of protection against homophobic harassment. Justin told me that some boys have girlfriends "so they look like they're not losers or they're not gay." David told me that a lot of the kids at his high school think that he is gay because of his preppy clothing choices and his lisp such that for him "it's better to have a girlfriend . . . because people think I'm gay. I get that all the time." In order to defend against teasing and harassment boys like David need to establish a sort of baseline heterosexuality by proving they can "get a girl." Because of the difficulty in avoiding all of the behaviors that might render one vulnerable *to* teasing, having a girlfriend helps to inure one to accusations of the "fag discourse."

Similarly, cross-gender touching rituals establish a given boy's heterosexuality. These physical interchanges may first appear as harmless flirtation, but upon closer inspection actually reinforce boys' dominance over girls' bodies. The use of touch maintains a social hierarchy (Henley 1977). Superiors touch subordinates, invade their space and interrupt them in a way subordinates do not do to superiors and these superior–inferior relationships are often gendered ones. Boys and girls often touch each other as part of daily interaction, communication and flirtation. In many instances cross-sex touching was lightly flirtatious and reciprocal. But these touching rituals ranged from playfully flirtations to assault-like interactions. Boys might physically constrain girls under the guise of flirtation. One time in a school hallway a boy wrapped his arms around a girl and started to "freak" her, or grind his pelvis into hers as she struggled to get away. This sort of behavior happened more often in primarily male spaces. One day for instance, in a school weight room, Monte wrapped his arms around a girl's neck as if to put her in a headlock and held her there while Reggie punched her in the stomach, albeit lightly, and she squealed. A more dramatic example of this was during a passing period in which Keith rhythmically jabbed a girl in the crotch with his drumstick, while he yelled "Get raped!" These examples show how the constraint and touching of female bodies gets translated as masculinity, embedding sexualized meanings in which heterosexual flirting is coded as female helplessness and male bodily dominance.

While people jokingly refer to boys' sex talk as "boys will be boys" or "locker room" talk, this sex talk plays a serious role in defending against acquiring an identity like Ricky's. Boys enact and naturalize their heterosexuality by asserting "guys are horndogs" or by claiming that it is "kind of impossible for a guy" to not "think of sex every two minutes" as Chad does. Thinking about boys' sexual performance in terms of compulsive heterosexuality shows that asserting that one is a horndog and cannot help but think about sex is actually a gendered performance. Boys' sex talk often takes the form of "mythic story telling" in which they tell larger than life tales about their sexual adventures, their bodies and girls' bodies that do not reflect love, desire or sensuality, but rather dominance over girls' bodies. Pedro, for instance, laughed and acted out having sex with his girlfriend by leaning back up against the wall, legs and arms spread and head turning back and forth as he continued to say proudly "I did her so hard when I was done she was bleeding. I tore her walls!" The boys surrounding him cheered and oohed and aahhed in amazement. Violence frequently frames these stories. Much like the touching rituals in which boys establish dominance over girls' bodies, these stories show what boys can make girls bodies do. Rich, after finishing lifting weights in his school's weight room, sat on a weight bench and five boys gathered around him as he told a story, after much urging, about sex with his now ex-girlfriend. He explained that they were having sex and "she said it started to hurt. I said we can stop and she said no. Then she said it again and she started crying. I told her to get off! Told her to get off! Finally I took her off," making a motion like he was lifting her off of him. He continued, "There was blood all over me! Blood all over her! Popped her wall! She had to have stitches." Boys start cracking up and moaning. Not to be outdone, other boys in the circle begin to chime in about their sexual exploits. Even those who don't have stories about themselves, asserted their knowledge of sex through vicarious experiences. Troy joined the discussion with a story about his brother, a professional basketball player for a nearby city. He "brought home a 24 year old drunk chick! She *farted* the whole time they were doing it in the other room! It was *hella* gross!" All the boys crack up again. Adam, not to be outdone, claimed "My friend had sex with a drunk chick. He did her in the butt! She s*** all over the place!" The boys all crack up again and yell out things like "Hella gross!" or "That's disgusting!" These graphic, quite violent stories detail what boys can make girls bodies do – rip, bleed, fart and poop.

To understand the role of sexuality in maintaining gender inequality it is important to look at sexuality, and specifically heterosexuality, not as a set of desires, identities or dispositions, but as an institution. Adrienne Rich (1986) does this when she argues that heterosexuality is an institution that systematically disempowers women. Similarly, compulsive heterosexuality is a set of practices through which boys reinforce linkages between sexuality, dominance and violence. This heterosexuality is a defensive heterosexuality, not necessarily a reflection of an internal set of emotions.

Conclusion

Many boys' school-based lives involve running a daily gauntlet of sexualized insults, as they simultaneously try to lob homophobic epithets at others and defend themselves from said epithets. In this sense masculinity becomes the daily interactional work of repudiating the labels of fag, queer or gay. Unpacking the definition of what appears to be homophobia clarifies the gender policing at the heart of boys' harassment of one another and of girls. Homophobic epithets may or may not have explicitly sexual meanings, but they always have gendered meanings. Many boys are clearly terrified of being permanently labeled as gay, fag or queer, since to them such a label effectively negates their human-ness. As a part of boys' defensive strategy, girls' bodies become masculinity resources deployed in order to stave off these labels.

The practices of compulsive heterosexuality indicate that control over girls' bodies and their sexuality is central to defi-nitions of adolescent masculinity. If masculinity is, as boys told me, about competence, heterosexuality, being unemotional, and dominance, then girls' bodies provide boys the opportunity to ward off the fag discourse by demonstrating mastery and control over them. Engaging in compulsive heterosexuality also allows boys to display a lack of emotions by refusing to engage the empathy that might mitigate against such a use of girls and their bodies. It is important to note that many of these boys are not unrepentant sexists or homophobes. In private and in one-on-one conversations, many spoke of sexual equality and of tender feelings for girls. For the most part these were social behaviors that boys engaged in when around other boys, precisely because they are less reflections of internal homophobic and sexist dispo-sitions and more about constituting a masculine identity, some-thing that is accomplished interactionally.

This gendered homophobia, as well as sexualized and gen-dered defenses against it, comprises contemporary adolescent masculinity. Fear of any sort of same sex intimacy (platonic or not) polices boys' friendships with one another. The need to repudiate that which is not considered masculine leads to a very public renunciation of same sex desire. Heterosexual flirtation becomes entwined with gendered dominance. What this means is that the public face of adolescent sexuality is rife with repro-duction of gender inequality, through processes of the fag dis-course and compulsive heterosexuality.

References

A.A.U.W. 2001. *Hostile Hallways*. Washington, DC: American Association of University Women.

Connell, R. W. 1987. *Gender and Power*. Stanford, CA: Stanford University Press.

Corbett, Ken. 2001. "Faggot = Loser." *Studies in Gender and Sexuality* 2(1): 3–28.

Henley, Nancy. 1977. *Body Politics: Power, Sex, and Nonverbal Communication*. Englewood Cliffs, NJ: Prentice-Hall.

Jenefsky, Cindy and Diane H. Miller. 1998. "Phallic Intrusion: Girl-Girl Sex in Penthouse." *Women's Studies International Forum* 21(4): 375–85.

Kehily, Mary J. and Anoop Nayak. 1997. "'Lads and Laughter': Humour and the Production of Heterosexual Masculinities," *Gender and Education* 9(1): 69–87.

Kimmel, Michael. 2001. "Masculinity as Homophobia: Fear, Shame, and Silence in the Construction of Gender Identity." Pp. 266–87 in *The Masculinities Reader*, ed. S. Whitehead and F. Barrett. Cambridge: Polity Press.

——. 1987. "The Cult of Masculinity: American Social Character and the Legacy of the Cowboy." Pp. 235–49 in *Beyond Patriarchy: Essays by Men on Pleasure, Power and Change*, ed. M. Kaufman. New York: Oxford University Press.

Kimmel, Michael S. 2003. "Adolescent Masculinity, Homophobia, and Violence: Random School Shootings, 1982–2001." *American Behavioral Scientist* 46(10): 1439–58.

Lyman, Peter. 1998. "The Fraternal Bond as a Joking Relationship: A Case Study of the Role of Sexist Jokes in Male Group Bonding." Pp. 171–93 in *Men's Lives . . .*, Fourth ed., ed. M. Kimmel and M. Messner. Boston, MA: Allyn and Bacon.

National Mental Health Association. 2002. *What Does Gay Mean? Teen Survey Executive Summary*.

Newman, Katherine, Cybelle Fox, David J. L. Harding, Jal Mehta and Wendy Roth. 2004. *Rampage: The Social Roots of School Shootings*. New York: Basic Books.

Rich, Adrienne. 1986. "Compulsory Heterosexuality and Lesbian Existence." Pp. 23–74 in *Blood, Bread and Poetry*. New York: W.W. Norton.

Wilchins, Riki. 2003. "Do You Believe in Fairies?" *The Advocate,* February 4, pp. 72.

Youth Risk Behavior Survey – Washington. 1995. Washington, DC: NYRBS.

Note

1 This concept draws upon Adrienne Rich's (1986) influential concept of "compulsory heterosexuality" as well as Michael Kimmel's (1987) notion of "compulsive masculinity."

Chapter Three

Equalities

icture the following: You're looking forward to a visit from a friend who wants to see where you go to school. But your friend just texted, very disappointed, saying they sprained their ankle, are walking around on crutches, and won't be able to go out dancing tonight as you had planned. "No worries," you say, "come anyway! I'll be in class when you arrive, but just make yourself at home in the library until I get out of class, and I'll meet you there." Later, walking across campus, you notice someone ahead of you walking up the steps to the door of the library. They're carrying two big bags, and a backpack is slung over their shoulder. They stand in front of the building, trying to juggle their bags so they can open the door. You race up the steps to open it for them. But as you pull it open, it strikes you that this is a really huge and heavy door, one of those big, old, imposing ones with carved wood and embossed glass. It is heavy to open, certainly for people with big bags and probably, you realize, for your friend with crutches, too. And you start to wonder, what about people who are small or who aren't very strong? What about people with mobility, balance, or fatigue issues? What about people who couldn't even get to the door because of all those steps? The rest of the day, you find yourself looking around campus and thinking about the people who could quite easily be shut out of many of its buildings. The built environment around you clearly makes basic access more difficult for some people.

Thinking about stairs and doors is just the beginning, though. You note other issues around access to buildings: elevators—or lack of them, hills—or lack of them, sidewalks—or lack of them. This gets you speculating about how accessible your campus really is and about whom your campus really seems to serve. How, you wonder, are some people disadvantaged by an architecture that makes it harder for them to move between buildings, get to places on time, or just participate in the everyday life of the campus? And what about the insides of the buildings, with those tiered lecture halls and bad acoustics? What about the bathrooms, with their narrow doors and stalls? Is this campus really a place where everyone is equal (as the university brochures and school administrators are constantly saying)? How could everyone's experience of it be equal, if some of its basic structures seem so inhospitable to so many people?

But what does equal really mean in this case? After all, aren't there lots of differences between people on campus—of ability and mobility, sure—but also of gender, race, class, sexuality, age too, each presenting different kinds of needs? And people have different learning preferences, and academic strengths and challenges. Don't those various attributes make a difference to people's experiences on campus? You start to notice the ways in which campus experiences really aren't the same for everyone: class differences mean that some students have to work to afford their tuition while others have more time for extracurricular activities; gender differences mean that some people feel less safe walking around campus, which in turn influences their choice of courses and of out-of-class activities; some students have caretaking responsibilities at home, impacting their ability to participate in activities outside of regular course hours. But, you think: does equal mean that everyone has the same experience of campus? How could that ever be possible—or even desirable? After all, people are different from each other, and most people feel quite strongly about holding on to those differences in their own lives. And while you hear a lot about how your university is dedicated to equality, you wonder more and more what that term actually means and whether everyone could even agree on what that looks like. Clearly, you recognize, *equality* is a term that many people are passionate about. But it's also one that seems to raise a number of questions!

Two Definitions of a Term

Equality is an idea thoroughly embedded into our everyday thinking about what will make the world more just and fair. Most of us probably can't understand why or how it should even be questioned as a value or goal. Indeed, many people think of it as something that has largely been achieved. Equality is the result, so the story goes, of changes brought about by social movement struggles over the past 60 or so years to have people's differences recognized: civil rights, feminism(s), gay and lesbian rights, disability rights. It is through movements like these, we maintain, that people attain "equal rights," and that injustice, discrimination, and exclusion are overcome.

This shared belief holds that the quest for equality has made the world a fairer place, a place that is more inclusive, in spite of those many differences. Thus, it seems, even if our society is not (yet) perfectly equal, the basic foundation required to get there has been laid. And yet, considered from the perspective of groups who have historically been excluded—or who see themselves as still only nominally included in society—this widely held ideal immediately provokes a set of difficult questions: Equal to whom? Included how, and at what cost? Who decides when equality or inclusion has been achieved and by what standard? And what happens when the desire to belong and the terms of belonging don't line up: for instance, when some groups seem to be both included and excluded at the same time—e.g., First Nations or Native peoples in Canada and the United States, or immigrants who have yet to obtain official citizenship papers—part of "us" and yet also "them"?

In theory and in practice, many people consider equality to be about basic fairness; that is, it's about ensuring that everyone has the same possibilities in their lives or is treated the same way. As a result, we assume that removing barriers (i.e., those laws and policies that say only certain people can apply for jobs or only some people can move about in particular public areas) has moved us closer to that equality. But has this worked? Have such changes in laws and policies brought about an end to exclusion, discrimination, and injustice for everyone? Is it enough to say that if everyone is treated the same, then what might seem to be "unequal" can be explained simply by differences in hard work or self-discipline[1]? That doesn't seem quite right. Perhaps there is something limiting in how we think of this path to equality, something that might not allow us to talk about what seem to be continuing differences and inequalities between groups of people.

In order to think more complexly about equality, we need to think about how this term is understood and mobilized. There are at least two major ways to think about the concept of equality—not just in the legal sense but in everyday life. Probably the most common understanding of equality is *formal equality*, or what is also called *equality of opportunity*. This understanding of equality emphasizes the idea of treating everyone in the same way, or giving everyone the same chances. Formal equality thus largely focuses on removing barriers that get in the way of those opportunities, that is, on changing laws or workplace policies or rules for membership in organizations.

[1] **THINK ABOUT:** Consider how a term like *colorblindness* exemplifies this kind of explanation. It is a word that refers to the notion that "we are just people" and is communicated in phrases like "I don't see color" or "People are just people." The problem with this particular investment in treating everyone the same is that it tends to invalidate people's pride in their culture, history, and heritage at the same time as it seems to equate one's color with something negative that shouldn't be discussed. Colorblindness doesn't work as a way to address racism, because it de-emphasizes the importance of people's experiences of racism. It is an ideology that some white people embrace to reformulate ignorance about how race is embedded in the world around us. Think also about how the term itself is implicitly ableist in its negative assumption about what it means to be blind.

Some recent examples include legalizing same-sex marriage (throughout Canada in 2005 and in the United States in 2015), or guaranteeing equal pay for equal work so that differences of sexuality, gender, or race no longer make a difference in people's paid work. Once the laws and policies are in place, according to a formal-equality approach, the barriers that led to discrimination are removed, more people are now able to have the same opportunities in life, their rights are recognized, and equality is achieved.

But as many of us know—or have experienced firsthand—simply having the same opportunities or being treated the same doesn't necessarily result in the same outcomes. In fact, when we look around, it often appears that differences in outcomes continue to exist between groups of people, even when there is nothing written into any law or policy to produce those differences. Some quick examples: think, for instance, of the fact that in both Canada and the United States, women, as a group and irrespective of race or class, still earn less than men overall. Or, consider that the imprisonment rates for black and Aboriginal people are much higher than for the white population. Or, look at how lesbian/gay/bisexual/transgender youth are more likely to be homeless and less able to find shelter than non-LGBT youth. There are no laws or policies in place that mandate different treatment in pay, or different rates of imprisonment, or different access to shelter systems. But these are differences that persist nonetheless. Obviously, then, simply saying that everyone is being treated the same is no guarantee that people will achieve the same results. Recognizing these patterns of differences in outcomes—and that they closely replicate the historical disenfranchisement of some groups of people—is key to understanding the limits of formal equality.

To explore this idea more, contemplate this familiar example: public bathrooms. Imagine you're at a concert, during which there is a 15-minute intermission. Everyone races to the bathroom, where, usually, there are only two possibilities, two doors from which to choose: men or women. On the other side of those doors, there is the same number of toilets (or toilets and urinals together)—that is, five possibilities for people to urinate. And at the end of the 15 minutes, many of us already know what happens: the number of people in the line-up for the women's bathroom far exceeds the number left in the men's (of course, this example assumes that there was a similar number of people in each line). And yet, each bathroom provides the same opportunity; each treats everyone who enters the same way, giving them the same number of possibilities to urinate. So how do we make sense of this different outcome at the end of intermission[2]?

There are many possible explanations for this disparity in outcomes: most women sit to urinate, which sometimes means wiping the seat first and having to manoeuvre more clothes than many men; many women menstruate, and taking care of that sometimes takes a little longer; women are often the ones to take kids into bathrooms with them, which requires negotiating two people's bathroom needs simultaneously. Indeed, sometimes the structure of bathrooms seems to insist that it be women who accompany children—for instance, if changing tables are only in the women's bathroom and not the men's, and are only located inside a stall. (We're not counting time at mirrors and sinks here, even if gendered bathroom culture might point to differences in time spent primping or socializing in the bathroom.) The point is that because of particular customs of toilet design in Canada and the United States (sit-down toilets are not universal in every culture), because of clothing and dress practices, because of biology, and because of childcare arrangements, men often move through bathroom lines faster than women. Of course this bathroom example makes broad generalizations; not all men stand up to urinate, some men take kids to bathrooms with them, and so forth. But the generalizations work here to make a simple point about some easily observable differences in outcome: beginning with the same opportunity for everyone can, and often does, end with different outcomes that disadvantage one group of people more than another. The result here is that some people see the concert in its entirety, and some people don't.

The second major definition or approach to equality, then, shifts our attention away from thinking about opportunity and instead focuses on results. *Substantive equality* or *equality of outcome* (also called *equity*) recognizes that even with the same opportunities, different groups of people will nonetheless experience different outcomes. Of course, removing legal or policy barriers that blatantly discriminate (e.g., when newspaper classified sections were divided into "jobs for men" and "jobs for women" or when signs on public facilities that read "white only" or "colored only" were common) is always a necessary first step. But, as substantive equality approaches illustrate,

[2]**THINK ABOUT:** The WTO (World Toilet Organization) notes that public washrooms are an issue for a large number of people and their availability and accessibility can impact many people's lives. Think, for instance, what the dearth of public washrooms in urban areas means for people with small children (whose ability to control their bodily functions is less than that of many adults), or for adults with bladder issues, or for people with chronic illnesses such as Crohn's or Irritable Bowel Syndrome, who might need more regular and easy access to bathrooms during a flare-up. Clearly, the perception that bathrooms aren't an important issue is only true for some people.

simply changing these kinds of policies and laws is often not sufficient to actually achieve equality. In the bathroom example, then, while the reasons for the differences in outcome are partly biological and partly cultural, the important observation is that those differences aren't surmounted by simply ensuring that everyone has the same opportunity. Identifying both this difference in outcome and recognizing the reasons for it can then help us see how something as seemingly neutral as the design of bathrooms may in fact inadvertently benefit some people more than others.

If we want to achieve a more equal outcome, then, what could be done to alter the results in this bathroom example? One potential solution might be to simply have more toilets available in the women's bathroom, giving women more opportunities to urinate and thereby allowing everyone to return to the concert at the same time. Or, another solution might be to eliminate gendered distinctions between bathrooms altogether and simply allow anyone to queue up in any line. This last solution would also provide a more equitable outcome for anyone who is scrutinized for being in the "wrong" bathroom: transmen, transwomen, genderqueer people, or simply those people who have to pee and don't care about the appropriate door to enter to do so. What this focus on outcomes does, though, is shift attention beyond a concern with providing the same opportunities to everyone to explore the multiple reasons for why those might still inadvertently perpetuate different outcomes and to consider ways to then alleviate their impact[3]. A substantive equality approach to this issue thus demands that we: (a) look beyond only providing the same opportunities in our quests for equality; (b) understand the ways that some differences between people (no matter the reason) really do make a difference, not just to individuals but, more importantly, to entire groups of people in patterns that become obvious; (c) investigate the ways that social structures, institutions, architectures, policies, and practices are not neutral but reflect a set of assumptions that benefit some people more than others; and (d) focus on responding in ways that rethink all of these points in order to achieve more equitable outcomes for everyone.

What the argument here so far demonstrates, then, is that the question of inclusion or exclusion of particular identity groups involves more than simply calling for people to be treated the same or to have the same rights. Instead, it turns our attention to identifying how social structures and institutions themselves might work to benefit

[3]**TALK ABOUT:** Look around your campus. Can you identify other examples where equality of opportunity results in a difference of outcome? For instance: how does the classroom you are in fit only some people? What can be or has been done to mitigate those differences? By individuals? By the school administration? Have these worked—and how? What do you think of those actions?

some people over others, simply because they fit more readily into those structures. There is no doubt that recognizing patterns of differences in outcome is difficult, since it involves challenging a deep investment in understanding ourselves as autonomous individuals with "free choice," individuals who bear the sole responsibility for what happens in our lives (good and bad). We don't want to think of ourselves as being either advantaged or disadvantaged by things outside of our control—such as the structures and institutions around us; instead, we usually (want to) believe that these seemingly more intangible things can be surmounted by our own individual efforts. Shifting our attention to outcomes, though, means learning to account for other factors that influence and limit inclusion and asking more challenging questions about those factors. It helps us recognize that exclusions beyond the level of individual choices and decisions instead are always systemic.

Norms and Standards and Invisible Adjectives (Again)

While the above example of public bathroom access might seem to be a fairly inconsequential issue for many people, it works well to illustrate that the same opportunities might not lead to the same outcomes, that those different outcomes might reveal that some groups are more affected than others, and—most importantly for this chapter—that those differences in outcomes might be the result of social structures themselves, and especially, of the unseen norms that these structures reflect. Consider another fairly common example that helps explicate this idea of the invisibility of norms. At many places of employment (especially white- or pink-collar office jobs), the workday is assumed to be approximately 9:00 a.m. to 5:00 p.m. And yet, when we think of the hours of most K–12 schools, the schedule is different, usually starting and ending earlier. For parents who work outside the home and have children to care for, this means finding alternative child care during those hours that don't align; but afterschool programs and babysitters cost extra money, take time to arrange, and have the potential to fall through on any given day (especially if kids get sick, which happens quite often). This situation causes parents to scramble to make other arrangements or they have to use a sick day (if their employer provides them). This situation is even more aggravated in shift work or service industry jobs where the hours change more frequently or in jobs where employees are required to be on call. The structure of the nine-to-five workday thus seems predicated on a worker who either does not have these other responsibilities, or who has someone else to take care of them at little or no charge[4]. While most commonly the people who are often disadvantaged by this schedule are women—who, statistically, still do more childcare and more coordinating of the care of children—it's clearly not just women who deal with the consequences of these differences in schedule. The standard of this workday schedule also disadvantages men who are primary caretakers for children (or elderly people or animals), as well as women and men who cannot afford (or can't find) alternate care arrangements. This bind that so many parents experience—between being an engaged parent and a good worker—reflects that workplace norms and the norms for (re)producing the next generation are often at odds; they are not neutral nor universally accommodating, but, rather, reflect sets of competing assumptions.

Another way to think about this idea of how norms are built into the workday schedule is to return to the terminology of the invisible adjective (introduced in the "Knowledges" chapter). Think about how this workday reflects a set of invisible adjectives about workers: i.e., "no care responsibilities," "availability for any hour of the day," "able to pay for child care." While it's obviously a stretch to call these phrases adjectives (and, of course, such phrases would never show up in employment ads or job descriptions, because formal equality laws make that illegal), they nonetheless reveal a set of assumptions that benefit particular ways of being in the world and thus particular groups of people. A substantive equality approach, though, encourages an ongoing process of examining the ways that these norms become the subtle (and often even inadvertent) ways that fit continues to be elusive for particular identity groups, by recognizing that social structures and practices themselves are never neutral.

By suggesting that the norms reflected in social structures lead to patterns of exclusion, substantive equality also challenges how we typically think of *discrimination*. Consider, for instance, how many university campuses have anti-bullying educational initiatives in place to counter verbal and physical violence against those who identify as or who are perceived to be lesbian, gay, bisexual, and transgender (LGBT).

[4]**KNOW ABOUT:** Up until recently, this arrangement of the work day was premised on assumptions about men as the people in the paid work force, and women as the ones doing the unpaid work (e.g., housework, child care) in the home. Men were also supposedly paid a "family wage," that is, a wage that was enough to cover the costs of caring for an entire family. While this pattern of familial arrangements has certainly changed immensely, the underlying assumptions about this division of labor, and the structures of the workplace that reflected it, haven't changed as much. And of course, even this idea of the family wage rested on presumptions about heterosexuality, class and, often, race: families were assumed to consist of a man and woman; many families were never able to afford to not have both parents in the paid work force; and many people had to find alternate child-care arrangements, through trading time with neighbors, for instance.

These programs usually focus on changing people's attitudes about—and thus, behaviors in regards to—sexuality and gender. They highlight the goal of ending discrimination by increasing knowledge about and acceptance of differences of gender and sexuality on campus, and, thus, of making life easier for people who are otherwise targeted as outsiders. And on some level, programs like these definitely can and do work, often educating people, encouraging them to change their attitudes and behaviors, and creating possibilities for more people to more comfortably go about their everyday lives.

But think also about how the university, through its structures and practices, continues to produce norms that only reflect some people's gender and sexuality: for instance, having only two boxes to choose from to identify one's gender in the paperwork for students, faculty, and staff, or referring to "husbands" and "wives" on invitations to campus events in ways that clearly reveal assumptions about heterosexuality and gender differences in these titles. These assumptions, mirrored in such ordinary institutional practices, ironically support and perpetuate the very set of attitudes and behaviors that are being targeted by these anti-bullying programs, thereby reproducing dominant norms about gender and sexuality that exclude LGBT people. And when institutions like universities assume that traditional patterns of discrimination are "taken care of" by awareness programs, the burden of pointing out ongoing forms of discrimination (and inequality) then most often falls to those for whom they are not invisible, that is, to those who experience the discrimination. This too often puts LGBT people (and anyone else who wants to draw attention to this) in a difficult position: either ignore the institution's ongoing discrimination towards them—which functions as one more affirmation that the problem is taken care of—or point out the discrimination and run the risk of being seen as the problem, as ungrateful and hypersensitive, or as a "trouble maker." When people's livelihoods depend on being collegial or being perceived as a team player, the risks of speaking out become all the more daunting. The understanding of bullying that these kinds of programs attempt to alleviate, therefore, must extend beyond people's behaviors to focus on the more invisible—and perhaps more powerful—discriminations in the everyday world around us.

This focus on how structures and practices around us tend to favor particular ways of being in the world leads to the important concept of privilege. *Privilege* is a word that helps us identify how some groups of people fit easily into the norms of existing social structures and practices; it is a term that helps us talk about the difference that considering identity categories makes by pointing out those invisible adjectives around us. Noting that a particular group of people have privilege is not an accusation that they are deliberately taking advantage of or maliciously mistreating others; indeed, what's so helpful about this concept is precisely the opposite. Privilege focuses on how it is that factors outside of individuals—social structures, practices, and norms—give some groups of people advantages that they usually don't notice. In this way, noting privilege can also mitigate responses such as guilt or defensiveness from those who benefit, because it moves us beyond merely looking at individual actions and attitudes and instead directs our attention to how inclusions and exclusions so often happen in spite of individuals' intentions (good or bad).

Let's explore the following example to see how discrimination and privilege shift the focus beyond looking only at people's interpersonal behaviors and intentions. Some innovative middle managers at a diverse, fast-growing company attempt to boost morale and create more worker cohesion by instituting an informal get-together after work on Fridays at a nearby tavern. Everyone is invited, although, obviously, attending isn't a job requirement. The managers organizing these get-togethers see only their positives: the work week is over, everyone is ready to relax, the managers are willing to buy everyone some food and the first round of drinks, and people can "talk shop" in more free-flowing ways than at the office. It's a good time to debrief, brainstorm, and build community—all laudable goals. But now, use the concept of privilege to think about the potential exclusions in this scenario. In other words, think about who might be left out of this plan: people with caregiving responsibilities at home or strict deadlines to pick up children at daycare or who share caretaking duties with those who have jobs that start when theirs ends; people with conditions or chronic illnesses for whom extending the day's activities just isn't possible; people who struggle with addiction and may not be comfortable at a bar; or people who have Friday religious observances. If this is just a social event, then perhaps such exclusions don't matter that much. But if this is an occasion when managers get to know those employees in line for promotion or bonuses, or when ideas for the workplace are encouraged and discussed more informally, then this well-intentioned event presents a situation where its very structure is clearly making it impossible for everyone to be included, with very real effects on their work lives.

Using the concept of privilege allows us to think about how the event itself reflects and thus fits some people and not others, regardless of the good intentions of its organizers. And while it is impossible to be all-inclusive all the time, the point is about developing awareness of the privilege embedded in structures and practices like this one. Clearly the exclusions listed above often reflect broader ideas about some identity groups. Rethinking exclusions and inclusions as the result of norms and invisible adjectives in the world around us thus leads us to see both discrimination and privilege as two sides of the same coin. In other words, instead of talking only about how one person knowingly discriminates against another through their attitudes and behaviors, we can now talk about how it is structures and practices that discriminate through their seemingly neutral norms that invisibly privilege some groups over others[5].

Of course, individuals' actions happen within, and often are sanctioned by, those larger structures, institutions, and practices, and the norms they produce. For instance, at its most extreme, individual violence, such as sexual assault or gay bashing, is clearly aberrant behavior of some people, and obviously people who commit such violence should be held accountable. But assault and bashing are not simply the atypical behaviors of a few people. Rather, they emerge out of particular ways of thinking about identity groups—ways of thinking that are then embedded in those structures and institutions, such as media, education, politics, religion, health care—in the same way as the anti-bullying example discussed above demonstrated. Or, think of how something like the disproportionate percentage of black and Latino men in prisons supports the assumption that these men are somehow more criminal, which, not coincidentally, leads to more surveillance, profiling, prosecution, and imprisonment of black and Latino men, at a greater rate and for longer periods than less surveilled and profiled and prosecuted white men. Yet, only focusing the attention (or blame) on individual police officers or judges or lawyers remains the dominant way of thinking about the consequences of social differences. It is much easier to speak of and seek to eliminate "a few bad apples" than to rethink the larger foundations of our society.

[5]**THINK ABOUT:** This argument about discrimination and privilege occurring through institutions and social structures also challenges more common understandings of racism or sexism (or any "ism") too, by shifting attention away from behaviors and attitudes and onto invisible norms and standards; with this new understanding, we can talk about institutions and practices as racist or sexist, rather than using these words simply to talk about individuals. It is not enough for individuals to say they're not racist or homophobic, as long as the institutions and structures around us perpetuate racial and sexual and gender inequities.

Equality's Debates

While substantive equality shifts attention to social structures as the locations of both exclusion and discrimination *and* inclusion and privilege, attempts to change these outcomes can lead to a number of conflicts. Think back to our earlier example about public bathrooms and the suggestion that changing their structure—for instance, having more stalls in the women's bathroom than the men's—would lessen the differences in one group of people's ability to return to the show at the same time as another. For some people, altering the architecture of public bathrooms might not seem very controversial. Why not treat women and men differently in bathroom construction and add a few more stalls to the women's bathroom in order to move towards more similar outcomes? But this well-meaning gesture to mitigate an apparent inequality, by treating different groups of people in different ways, can expose a number of tensions between recognizing social differences and working towards fairer or more equitable outcomes for everyone.

Consider this example, for instance, to see how working towards more equal outcomes can also lead to often-contentious debate. Many of us in Canada and the United States live in areas that get a lot of snow and ice during the winter. The result is that sidewalks and walkways between buildings on many college campuses become more difficult to traverse, especially in the limited time between classes, meetings, and campus-wide activities. And snow and ice become issues for different people manoeuvring around campus: people with physical impairments who use mobility aids (crutches, wheelchairs, walkers) or who have balance issues; older people for whom a fall would be very dangerous; pregnant people[6]; people pushing baby strollers; people wearing footwear not suitable to snow and ice, and (as our opening example illustrated) anyone with an especially large load of books to lug around—that is, a lot of us! One solution to this moving-around difficulty could be to install sidewalk heaters beneath the major walkways on campus. The heaters would melt the snow and ice and enable everyone to negotiate their way around in the winter the same as they do in the non-winter months. Wouldn't a much greater number of people be better off with this change? More people could be out and about, there would be fewer injuries from falling, students and faculty would less likely be late for or miss classes,

[6]**THINK ABOUT:** Women are not the only people who get pregnant. Some transmen, who clearly identify as men (but who have retained female reproductive organs), stop taking hormones in order to become pregnant and have children, after which they return to taking hormones. Think about how much our everyday language perpetuates assumptions that might also exclude some people from a range of experiences: saying "breastfeeding" rather than "nursing," for instance, perpetuates an image of whose body is doing the feeding of infants. Abortion rights language also often references "women" in its advocacy for access to this reproductive service.

and more people would be involved in on-campus activities (with the result that more activities could be planned to get everyone through the long winter[7]).

Presumably, few people would argue against this kind of initiative, at least initially, especially when they recognize how much we all could benefit from this change. But let's continue to think about what would be required to make this happen. Suppose the university administration announced that in order to accomplish this modification, tuition for all students would have to increase and there would be an additional deduction from employees' pay. Suddenly, for many people (and perhaps especially those for whom manoeuvring around campus isn't a big issue, even in snow and ice), what appeared to be a good idea now seems more like a response to "special interests." Such a change is regarded as an attempt by one group of people to receive a benefit at the expense of others, as unfair for the people who don't need these changes, and as giving some people more or different rights than others. In short, this kind of response is often accused of being unequal and even of causing inequality[8]. Thus, while the recognition of differences between people may often not seem controversial, taking differences into consideration to diminish their negative impacts can soon become quite controversial. And this same kind of debate is at play when it comes to any number of other examples: retrofitting old buildings to be wheelchair accessible, paid maternity leave and state funding for birth control and abortion, investments in public transportation, and Affirmative Action programs—all changes that are often dismissed as responding to special interests regardless of their potential for more equitable (and positive) outcomes for large numbers of people. It is often difficult to negotiate the idea that assumptions about the neutrality of social institutions, structures, and practices needs to be questioned, let alone reach an agreement that we should share responsibility for change that might benefit us all.

Taking differences between groups of people into account brings up another set of contentious debates that resonates with the troubled histories of "separate but equal" laws and social practices. Historically, differences of gender or race or sexuality or ability too often meant that some groups were stigmatized and excluded from access and benefits that dominant groups enjoyed. Think of the long history in both Canada and the United States of legislating separate schooling for different racialized groups, usually black and white, but also Aboriginal and Native peoples in the residential

[7]KNOW ABOUT: This idea of heaters built into sidewalks is common in many Scandinavian countries, leading to positive results. As sidewalks are rebuilt, heaters are inserted under the pavement and more walkways become snow and ice free. These countries report that overall it costs less to make this infrastructural change than the time and money lost in accidents and time off work amounts to; additionally, the result of people of all ages and abilities being able to move around town more easily has benefitted cities' commerce and people's social lives.

[8]TALK ABOUT: Let's make this even more complex. Does it matter how much tuition is raised or how much the pay deduction is? What about those for whom even the smallest tuition increase becomes a burden? Suppose the tuition increase or pay deduction were proposed only for those who "need" this school system. And it wasn't too long ago that children with disabilities were separated into different classrooms, often travelling on different buses and entering the schools through different doors. Although this history of separation was often the result of prejudice and fear, in some cases separation was (and is) done with the intention of protecting groups deemed different from a norm, a response known as *protectionism*, which raises a number of challenges. Consider, for instance, the following example. In many large urban areas (e.g., Tokyo, Cairo, Mexico City, Mumbai) around the world, local authorities have implemented "women only" subway cars or buses to address complaints by women about being harassed and groped by men. While voluntary (in that women don't have to use them and they are also usually open to young boys and men with disabilities), they have proven to be popular options to address the realities of harassment. But in both recognizing a social difference and attempting to respond to the difference it makes, such accommodations can inadvertently bolster the perception that women (in this case) are different and need to be treated differently—in turn, perpetuating their exclusion from a social structure into which they don't easily fit (crowded subway cars). For many critics, then, providing women-only public transit is either a special right—favoring one group by giving its members something that others don't have—or an example of a protectionist approach that accommodates rather than challenges the initial problem[9].

A substantive equality approach thus means paying attention to multiple issues of difference simultaneously. First, it obviously incorporates formal equality or eliminating barriers to everyone having the same kinds of opportunities. Second, it means recognizing that social differences are both created by and perpetuated through social structures and practices, because they reflect norms that privilege some ways of being over others—usually both unintentionally and invisibly. Finally, and importantly, it requires that we double back on attempts to accommodate different groups, no matter the intention, to ensure that the result is greater equality of outcome. Ultimately, then, equality is always more complicated than simply looking at how groups of people are treated, whether the same or differently. Even in well-intentioned responses to inequalities, it is the questions of "Equal to whom?" "On what terms?" and "At what cost?" that can lead us to a more just world.

change—would that make a difference? Why or why not? How do we, as a diverse group of people who share this campus space, go about negotiating this desire for more ease of movement for more people and the various costs of achieving that desire?

[9]**TALK ABOUT:** What are some other recent attempts to address perceived differences through segregating groups? Consider examples such as girls-only math classes or schools for black children only that feature an Afrocentric curriculum. Does it make a difference if these are argued for by members of these groups rather than, as is the history in both Canada and the U.S., their occurring as the result of policies of gendered or racial segregation? What is perceived to be gained by these kinds of separations? What is thought to be lost? How would you argue for or against these kinds of separations?

The Concept at Work: Marriage and Sexual Citizenship

Citizenship has always been a contested category, meaning that who counts as a citizen of any given country has often been the source of much debate. In the nineteenth century, for example, in both Canada and the United States, the qualification for citizenship was owning property, meaning that women of any age or racial group and all people of color—none of whom could legally own property—did not qualify as citizens. Citizenship was thus restricted to a particular category of people: white, property-owning men over a specific age. Over time, as the result of resistance, protest, civil disobedience, and uprisings, laws changed and women and other groups were able to purchase property. And more importantly, this criterion for citizenship was removed so that owning property is no longer a necessity to be considered a citizen of either country. However, even though this particular qualification for citizenship is now gone, other criteria remain that have also been invisible adjectives in front of "citizen."

The recent legalization of same-sex marriage, for example, exposes how a series of presumptions about relationships and family life have also been central to notions of the citizen. Legalized in Canada since 2005 and in the United States since 2015, same-sex marriage seems, on the one hand, to clearly be about achieving equality, that is, extending the same opportunity for a social rite to more people. It expands the possibility to marry to a group that has historically been excluded from its many benefits, which include insurance coverage, pensions, wills, hospital visitation, child custody, income tax deductions (in the United States), and power of attorney, not to mention the social recognition of one's relationship and family as legitimate. With the state's extension of marriage rights to these relationships, the privileges of social recognition and monetary reward are now extended to another group of people. There are, however, many critics of same-sex marriage in LGBT communities, who see it as perpetuating heteronormative social norms that emphasize these exclusionary ideals of monogamy, two-partnered relationships, gendered roles, shared households, the production of children, family-oriented consumption, and lifelong, public commitments (and coining a new word—homonormativity—to describe this).

Marriage—no matter between whom—is thus a practice that privileges some relationships over others, conferring a set of understandings about both what kind and whose commitments matter, over what kind and whose can be ignored or even violated. This newly acquired legal status recognition for same-sex marriage does nothing for those who live their romantic/sexual lives outside of marriage. For example, what about couples, regardless of their sexuality, who choose not to marry? What about people for whom relationships are composed of more than two partners (polyamory)? What about people who don't live together in the same household out of choice? Or what about those who do live together but don't share bedrooms or bank accounts? What about parenting practices that bypass biology or legal marriage, and instead raise children within a community of blended families or child-care cooperatives, or rely on other people with whom they trade off child minding—none of whom have legal rights as partners or parents? There are a number of other ways of having fulfilling relationships and committing to other people that do not fit the marriage model. But, of course, neither do they reap the systemic privileges accorded through the dominant model of marriage. Marriage of any kind, then, is a practice that can perpetuate inequality, not by denying some people the right to marry, but by embedding so many benefits of citizenship in this one privileged social status.

The term *sexual citizenship* refers to this idea that there are always invisible assumptions about "appropriate" practices of sexuality and gender built into what the state considers the ideal kind of citizen—and thus, who is thought to belong more easily or naturally, and who is othered or excluded. Marriage is thus not simply the marker of a particular type of relationship between two people, but a marker of a relationship to the state, and to the larger society of any country. And this is not simply a benign observation or one that simply recognizes a difference in how people in any country live their lives. Notions of sexual citizenship extend to a number of state practices and laws, including immigration and refugee policies and asylum claims, regulating what kinds of relationships and families are recognized as belonging to that state and what kinds are not; think about how both U. S. and Canadian immigration policies reflect these ideas of sexual citizenship in their restrictions about how people must be related to each other in order to be granted admission to the country.

Ideas about sexual citizenship also influence how nation-states see themselves in relation to other nation-states. For example, both Canada and the United States have

Chapter Three

increasingly mobilized their extension of marriage rights to same-sex couples as a way to position themselves as more tolerant than other countries. In holding up the recognition of same-sex marriage as a symbol of their progressiveness and even exceptionalism, though, what continue to remain unacknowledged are the ways other cultures might think about relationships, family, sexuality, and gender differently (a stance known as *homonationalism*). But that taken-for-grantedness of our particular notions of sexual citizenship as more progressive has also increasingly been used justify to state policies, such as sanctions or even invasions of other countries, in the name of exporting those supposedly better (more modern) relationship practices.

Preview of Readings

Carbado, Devon W. 2013. "Privilege." In *Readings in Diversity and Social Justice* (3rd ed.), edited by Maurianne Adams, Warren Blumenfeld, Carmelita Castaneda, Heather W. Hackman, Madeline L. Peters, and Ximena Zuniga, 391–397. New York, NY: Routledge.

Huff, Joyce L. 2009. "Access to the Sky: Airplane Seats and Fat Bodies in Contested Spaces." In *The Fat Studies Reader*, edited by Esther Rothblum and Sondra Solvay, 176–186. New York, NY: New York University Press.

Spade, Dean. 2014. "Their Laws Will Never Make Us Safer." In *Against Equality: Queer Revolution Not Mere Inclusion*, edited by Ryan Conrad, 165–175. Oakland, CA: AK Press.

Titchkosky, Tanya. 2011. "'Where?': To Pee or Not to Pee." In *The Question of Access: Disability, Space, Meaning*, 71–81 [excerpt]. Toronto, ON: University of Toronto Press, 2011.

Abbas, Ali. 2012. "Death By Masculinity." In *Why Are Faggots So Afraid of Faggots? Flaming Challenges to Masculinity, Objectification, and the Desire to Conform*, edited by Mattilda Bernstein Sycamore, 33–38. Oakland, CA: AK Press.

"Equalities" introduces the terms *formal equality* and *substantive equality* to talk about how working towards fairness and justice must go beyond the mandate to treat everyone the same way. Although we tend to think about equality as individuals having the right to make choices, a more comprehensive quest for equitable outcomes would have to include the ways in which social structures, systems, and processes construct norms that shape those choices. In considering ways to eliminate discrimination, we usually think about the need to pass laws. However, it is also important to think about how privilege perpetuates all sorts of inequitable outcomes without any deliberate or conscious discrimination taking place.

In "Privilege," Devon W. Carbado asks readers to consider how both privilege and oppression can operate simultaneously in our everyday lives. Because our identities are always already implicated in systems of oppression, acts of deliberate discrimination account for very little of the inequity experienced in our societies. In accounting for the ways in which he benefits from unearned gender and heterosexual privilege as well as the ways he is penalized on the basis of race, Carbado concludes that resistance to discriminatory systems requires more than mere acknowledgment, but must include a refusal to acquiesce to such systems.

- In what ways do Carbado's lists help us think intersectionally about privilege?
- According to Carbado, how is attending a hetero wedding in a location that prohibits gay marriage perpetuating discrimination?
- In what other areas of our lives does the exercise of privilege indirectly support discrimination against other identity categories?

Joyce L. Huff's "Access to the Sky" uses airplane seats to think about how fat bodies fit, or (in many cases) don't fit, in broader social contexts. She wonders why being "overweight" becomes an excuse for discriminatory treatment by corporations like Southwest Airlines when over half of Americans fit into that category. The terms *minoritizing* and *universalizing* are discourses used to explain how arbitrary decisions that profit a private company are accepted as fair by members of the general public.

- According to Huff, what do airlines and other transportation companies tend to assume about the bodies of their passengers?
- How do social stigmas about bodies (and identities) function in discussions about rights?

- In what ways would our everyday environments change if a wider array of body types were accommodated into the built environment?

Dean Spade opens his article, "Their Laws Will Never Make Us Safer," by noting the ironies in play when highly policed communities demand accountability for the murder of a child, in this case Trayvon Martin, from the very system that is otherwise so unjust to them. Spade argues that hate-crimes legislation, which can take up vast amounts of activist energies, does very little to quell the violence and injustice experienced by marginalized communities on a daily basis. Criminalization and imprisonment actually produce and perpetuate the violence that most communities seek to escape while profiting elites who run prisons as private business ventures.

- How might we talk about the paradoxes produced in our society's tendency to police bodies that are thought to be dangerous? How are those same bodies put in danger in a larger quest for safety?
- According to Spade, how do law enforcement and protection perpetuate a "false promise"?
- How can abolishing prisons address the safety issues of poor communities of color or queer and trans communities?

Tanya Titchkosky, in the excerpt from her article "'Where?': To Pee or Not to Pee," wants disability to be "knowable" as something other than a series of undesired difficulties in public locations like colleges and universities. Her research was borne of a series of interactions with her built environment at her university as well as the encounters she had with others in that space. Titchkosky offers five stories that are often used as rationales for why the exclusion of any consideration of disability is "justified."

- What do the five stories assume about disability as a category of identity?
- In what ways does understanding disability as produced by built environments help us think about where to locate responsibility for producing more equality? What are some difficulties that might still arise in this shifting of questions of responsibility?

In "Death By Masculinity," Ali Abbas condemns the under-interrogated privilege of some gay white men in the United States for the ill-informed sexist and nationalist orientations that measure queer identities and equalities through little more than their own experiences. Abbas raises concerns about a narrow vision of sexual citizenship that leaves out issues of poverty, health care, immigration, and military policy.

- What is the problem, according to Abbas, with sexual desire for "straight acting" men?
- How is sexuality evoked in talking about a nation's progress toward democracy?
- What is assumed about what makes a nation good or bad in these notions of progress, and what is accounted for?

Privilege

Devon W. Carbado

. . . This essay is part of a larger intellectual project to encourage a shift in—or at least a broadening of—our conceptualization of discrimination. My aim is to expand our notion of what it means to be a perpetrator of discrimination. Typically, we define a perpetrator of discrimination as someone who acts intentionally to bring about some discriminatory result. This is a narrow and politically palatable conception; it applies to very few of us. In this essay I suggest that those of us who unquestionably accept the racial, gender, and heterosexual privileges we have—those of us who fail to acknowledge our victimless status with respect to racism, sexism, and homophobia—are also perpetrators of discrimination.

Informing this privileged-centered understanding of discrimination is the notion that taking identity privileges for granted helps to legitimize problematic assumptions about identity and entitlement, assumptions that make it difficult for us to challenge the starting points of many of our most controversial conversations about equality. We simply assume, for example, that men should be able to fight for their country (the question is whether women should be entitled to this privilege); that heterosexuals should be able to get married (the question is whether the privilege should be extended to gays and lesbians); that white men should be able to compete for all the slots in a university's entering class (the question is whether people of color should be entitled to the privilege of "preferential treatment").

While a privileged-centered conception of discrimination usefully reveals the bidirectional effects of discrimination—namely, that discrimination allocates both burdens and benefits—the conception may prove entirely too much. After all, all of us enjoy some degree of privilege. Are all of us perpetrators of discrimination? The answer may depend on what we do with, and to, the privileges we have. Each of us makes personal and private choices with our privileges that entrench a variety of social practices, institutional arrangements, and laws that disadvantage other(ed) people.

For example, many of us get married and/or attend weddings, while lesbian and gay marriages are, in most parts of the United States (and the world), not legally recognized. Others of us have racially monolithic social encounters, live in de facto white only (or predominantly white) neighborhoods, or send our kids to white only (or predominantly white) schools. Still others of us have "straight only" associations—that is, our friends are all heterosexuals and our children's friends all have mommies and daddies. These choices are not just personal; they are political. And their cumulative effect is to entrench the very social practices—racism, sexism, classism, and homophobia—we profess to abhor.

In other words, there is a link between identity privileges, and our negotiation of them, on the one hand, and discrimination, on the other. Our identities are reflective and constitutive of systems of oppression. Racism requires white privilege. Sexism requires male privilege. Homophobia requires heterosexual privilege. The very intelligibility of our identities is their association, or lack thereof, with privilege. This creates an obligation on the part of those of us with privileged identities to expose and to challenge them.

Significantly, this obligation exists not only as a matter of morality and responsibility The obligation exists for a pragmatic reason as well. We cannot change the macro-effects of discrimination without ameliorating the power effects of our identities. Nor can our political commitments have traction unless we apply them to the seemingly "just personal" privileged aspects of our lives. Resistance to identity privileges may be futile, we cannot know for sure. However, to the extent that we do nothing, this much is clear: we perpetuate the systems of discrimination out of which our identities are forged.

But precisely what constitutes an identity privilege? Further, how do we identify them? And, finally, what acts are necessary to deprivilege our identities and to disrupt their association with power. These questions drive this essay. . . .

Heterosexual Privileges

Like maleness, heterosexuality should be critically examined. Like maleness, heterosexuality operates as an identity norm, the "what is" or "what is supposed to be" of sexuality. This is illustrated, for example, by the nature versus nurture debate. The question about the cause of sexuality is almost always formulated in terms of whether homosexuality is or is not biologically determined rather than whether sexual orientation, which includes heterosexuality, is or is not biologically determined. Scientists are searching for a gay, not a heterosexual or sexual orientation, gene. Like female identity, then, homosexuality signifies "difference"—more specifically, sexual identity distinctiveness. The normativity of heterosexuality requires that homosexuality be specified, pointed out. Heterosexuality is always already presumed.

Heterosexuals should challenge the normativity and normalization of heterosexuality. They should challenge the heterosexual presumption. But heterosexuals might be reluctant to do so to the extent that they perceive such challenges to call into question their (hetero)sexual orientation. As Lee Edelman observes in a related context, there "is a deeply rooted concern on the part of . . . heterosexual males about the possible meanings of [men subverting gender roles]" (1990, 50). According to Edelman, heterosexual men consider certain gender role inversions to be potentially dangerous because they portend not only a "[male] feminization that would destabilize or question gender" but also a "feminization that would challenge one's (hetero)sexuality" (1990, 50). Edelman's observations suggest that straight men may want to preserve what I am calling the "heterosexual presumption." Their investment in this presumption is less a function of what heterosexuality signifies in a positive sense and more a function of what it signifies in the negative—*not* being homosexual.

And there are racial dimensions to male investment in heterosexuality For example, straight black male strategies to avoid homosexual suspicion could relate to the racial aspects of male privileges: heterosexual privilege is one of the few privileges that some black men have. These black men may want to take comfort in the fact that whatever else is going on in their lives, they are not, finally, "sissies," "punks," "faggots." By this I do not mean to suggest that black male heterosexuality has the normative standing of white male heterosexuality. It does not. Straight black men continue to be perceived as heterosexually deviant (overly sexual; potential rapists) and heterosexually irresponsible (jobless fathers of children out of wedlock). Still, black male heterosexuality is closer to white male heterosexual normalcy and normativity than is black gay sexuality. Consequently, some straight (or closeted) black men will want to avoid the "black gay [male] . . . triple negation" to which Marlon Riggs refers in the following quote: "Because of my sexuality I cannot be Black. A strong, proud, 'Afrocentric' black man is resolutely heterosexual, not even bisexual. . . . Hence I remain a sissy, punk, faggot. I cannot be a black gay man because, by the tenets of black macho, a black gay man is a triple negation" (1999, 307) . . .

Keith Boykin, former director of the Black Gay and Lesbian Leadership Forum, maintains that "heterosexual sexual orientation has become so ingrained in our social custom, so destigmatized of our fears about sex, that we often fail to make any connection between heterosexuality and sex" (1997). Boykin is only half right. The socially constructed normalcy of heterosexuality is not due solely to the desexualization of heterosexuality in mainstream political and popular culture. It is due also to the sexualization of heterosexuality as normative and to the gender-norm presumptions about heterosexuality—that it is the normal way sexually to express one's gender.

Moreover, it is not simply that homosexuality is sexed that motivates or stimulates homophobic fears about gay and lesbian relationships. These fears also relate to the fact that homosexuality is stigmatized and is perceived to be an abnormal way sexually to express one's gender. The disparate social meanings that attach to gay and lesbian identities on the one hand and straight identities on the other make individual acts of heterosexual signification a cause for concern.

Recently, I participated in a workshop where one of the presenters "came out" as a heterosexual in the context of giving his talk. This sexual identity disclosure engendered a certain amount of whispering in the back row. Up until that moment, I think many people had assumed the presenter was gay. After all, he was sitting on a panel discussing sexual orientation and had participated in the Gay and Lesbian section of the American Association of Law Schools. There were three other heterosexuals on the panel, but everyone knew they were not gay because everyone *knew* them; they had all been in teaching for a while, two were very senior, and everyone knew of their spouses or partners. Everyone also knew that there was a lesbian on the panel. She, too, had been in teaching for some time and had been out for many years. Apparently, few of the workshop participants knew very much about the presenter who "came out." Because "there is a widespread assumption in both gay and straight communities that any man who says something supportive about issues of concern to lesbian or gay communities must be gay himself," there was, at the very least, a question about his sexual-

ity. Whatever his intentions were for "coming out," whatever his motivations, his assertion of heterosexuality removed the question. . . .

I became sensitized to the politics of heterosexuals "coming out" in the context of reading about James Baldwin. Try to find a piece written about Baldwin and count the number of lines before the author comes out as heterosexual. Usually, it is not more than a couple of paragraphs, so the game ends fast. The following introduction from a 1994 essay about Baldwin is one example of what I am talking about: "The last time I saw James Baldwin was late autumn of 1985, when my wife and I attended a sumptuous book party" (Forrest 1994, 267). In this case, the game ends immediately. Independent of any question of intentionality on the author's part, the mention of the wife functions as an identity signifier to subtextually "out" his heterosexuality. We *read* "wife," we *think* heterosexual. My point here is not to suggest that the essay's overall tone is heterosexually defensive; I simply find it suspicious when heterosexuals speak of their spouses so quickly (in this case the very first sentence of the essay) when a subject (a topic or a personality—here, James Baldwin) implicates homosexuality. . . . The author engages in what I call "the politics of the 3Ds"—disassociation, disidentification, and differentiation. The author is "different" from Baldwin (the author sleeps with women), and this difference, based as it is on sexual identity, compels the author to disassociate himself from and disidentify with that which makes Baldwin "different" (Baldwin sleeps with men).

Heterosexual significations need not always reflect the politics of the 3Ds. In other words, the possibility exists for heterosexuals to point out their heterosexuality without reauthenticating heterosexuality. Consider, for example, the heterosexual privilege list that I give below. While each item on the list explicitly names—outs—heterosexuality, in none of the items does heterosexuality remain unproblematically normative.

As a prelude to the list, I should be clear that the list is incomplete. Nor do the privileges reflected in it represent the experiences of all heterosexuals. As Bruce Ryder observes: "Male heterosexual privilege has different effects on men of, for example, different races and classes. . . . In our society, the dominant or 'hegemonic' form of masculinity to which other masculinities are subordinated is white, middleclass, and heterosexual. This means that the heterosexual privilege of, say, straight black men takes a very different shape in their lives than it does for straight white men" (1991, 292). My goal in presenting this list, then, is not to represent every heterosexual man. Instead, the purpose is to intervene in the normalization of heterosexual privileges. With this intervention, I hope to challenge the pervasive tendency of heterosexuals to see homophobia as something that puts others at a disadvantage and not something that actually advantages them.

Heterosexual Privileges: A List

1. Whether on television or in the movies, (white) heterosexuality is always affirmed as healthy and/or normal (black heterosexuality and family arrangements are still, to some degree, perceived to be deviant).

2. Without making a special effort, heterosexuals are surrounded by other heterosexuals every day.

3. A husband and wife can comfortably express affection in any social setting, even a predominantly gay one.

4. The children of a heterosexual couple will not have to explain why their parents have different genders—that is, why they have a mummy and a daddy.

5. (White) heterosexuals are not blamed for creating and spreading the AIDS virus (though Africans—as a collective group—are blamed).

6. Heterosexuals do not have to worry about people trying to "cure" their sexual orientation (though black people have to worry about people trying to "cure" black "racial pathologies").

7. Black heterosexual males did not have to worry about whether they would be accepted at the Million Man March.

8. Rarely, if ever, will a doctor, on learning that her patient is heterosexual, inquire as to whether the patient has ever taken an AIDS test and if so, how recently.

9. Medical service will never be denied to heterosexuals because they are heterosexuals (though medical services may not be recommended to black people because they are black).

10. Friends of heterosexuals generally do not refer to heterosexuals as their "straight friends" (though nonblack people often to refer to black people as their "black friends").

11. A heterosexual couple can enter a restaurant on their anniversary and be fairly confident that staff and fellow diners will warmly congratulate them if an announcement is made (though the extent of the congratulation and the nature of the welcome might depend on the racial identities of the couple).

12. White heterosexuals do not have to worry about whether a fictional film villain who is heterosexual will reflect negatively on their heterosexuality (though blacks may always have to worry about their racial representation in films).

13. Heterosexuals are entitled to legal recognition of their marriages throughout the United States and the world.

14. Within the black community, black male heterosexuality does not engender comments like "what a waste," "there goes another good black man," or "if they're not in jail, they're faggots."

15. Heterosexuals can take jobs with most companies without worrying about whether their spouses will be included in the benefits package.

16. Child molestation by heterosexuals does not confirm the deviance of heterosexuality (though if the alleged molester is black, the alleged molestation becomes evidence of the deviance of black [hetero]sexuality).

17. Black rap artists do not make songs suggesting that het-

erosexuals should be shot or beaten up because they are heterosexuals.

18. Black male heterosexuality does not undermine a black heterosexual male's ability to be a role model for black boys.
19. Heterosexuals can join the military without concealing their sexual identity.
20. Children will be taught in school, explicitly or implicitly, about the naturalness of heterosexuality (they will also be taught to internalize the notion of white normativity).
21. Conversations on black liberation will always include concerns about heterosexual men.
22. Heterosexuals can adopt children without being perceived as selfish and without anyone questioning their motives.
23. Heterosexuals are not denied custody or visitation rights of their children because they are heterosexuals.
24. Heterosexual men are welcomed as leaders of Boy Scout troops.
25. Heterosexuals can visit their parents and family as who they are, and take their spouses, partners, or dates with them to family functions.
26. Heterosexuals can talk matter-of-factly about their relationships with their partners without people commenting that they are "flaunting" their sexuality.
27. A black heterosexual couple would be welcomed as members of any black church.
28. Heterosexual couples do not have to worry about whether kissing each other in public or holding hands in public will render them vulnerable to violence.
29. Heterosexuals do not have to struggle with "coming out" or worry about being "outed."
30. The parents of heterosexuals do not love them "in spite of" their sexual orientation, and parents do not blame themselves for their children's heterosexuality.
31. Heterosexuality is affirmed in most religious traditions.
32. Heterosexuals can introduce their spouses to colleagues and

not worry about whether the decision will have a detrimental impact on their careers.

33. A black heterosexual male does not have to choose between being black and being heterosexual.
34. Heterosexuals can prominently display their spouses' photographs at work without causing office gossip or hostility.
35. (White) heterosexuals do not have to worry about "positively" representing heterosexuality.
36. Few will take pity on a heterosexual on hearing that she is straight, or feel the need to say, "That's okay" (though it is not uncommon for a black person to hear, "It's okay that you're black" or "We don't care that you're black" or "When we look at you, we don't see a black person").
37. (Male) heterosexuality is not considered to be symptomatic of the "pathology" of the black family.
38. Heterosexuality is never mistaken as the only aspect of one's lifestyle, but is perceived instead as merely one more component of one's personal identity.
39. (White) heterosexuals do not have to worry over the impact their sexuality will have personally on their children's lives, particularly as it relates to their social lives (though black families of all identity configurations do have to worry about how race and racism will affect their children's well-being).
40. Heterosexuals do not have to worry about being "bashed" after leaving a social event with other heterosexuals (though black people of all sexual orientations do have to worry about being "racially bashed" on any given day).
41. Every day is (white) "Heterosexual Pride Day."

Conclusion: Resisting Privileges

I have argued that one of the ways to contest gender and sexual orientation hierarchy is for heterosexual men to detail their social experiences on the privileged side of gender and sexual orientation. In advancing this argument, I do not mean to suggest that the role of these men is to legitimize "untrustworthy" and "self-interested" victim-centered accounts of discrimination. There is a tendency on the part of dominant groups (e.g., males and heterosexuals) to discount the experiences of subordinate groups (e.g., straight women, lesbians, and gays) unless those experiences are authenticated or legitimized by a member of the dominant group. For example, it is one thing for me, a black man, to say I experienced discrimination in a particular social setting; it is quite another for my white male colleague to say he witnessed that discrimination. My telling of the story is suspect because I am black (racially interested). My white colleague's telling of the story is not suspect because he is white (racially disinterested). The racial transparency of whiteness—its "perspectivelessness"—renders my colleague's account "objective." . . .

Assuming that the identification/listing of privileges methodology I have described avoids the problem of authentication, one still might wonder whether the project is sufficiently radical to dismantle gender and sexual orientation hierarchies. Certainly the lists I have presented do not go far enough. They represent the very early stages in a more complicated process to end gender and sexual orientation discrimination.

The lists, nevertheless, are politically valuable. . . .

None of this is to say that awareness and acknowledgement of privilege is enough. Resistance is needed as well. But how does one resist? And what counts as resistance? With respect to marriage, for example, does resistance to heterosexual privilege require heterosexuals to refrain from getting married and/or attending weddings? It might mean both of those things. At the very least, resistance to identity privilege would seem to require "critical acquiescence": criticizing, if not rejecting, aspects of our life that are directly linked to our privilege. A heterosexual who gets married and/or attends weddings but who also openly challenges the idea that marriage is a heterosexual entitlement is engaging in critical acquiescence.

In the end, critical acquiescence might not go far enough, It might even be a cop out. Still, it is a useful and politically manageable place to begin.

References

Boykin, K. (1997). *One More River to Cross: Black and Gay in America*. New York: Doubleday.

Edelman, L. (1990). "Redeeming the Phallus: Wallace Stevens, Frank Lentricchia, and the Politics of (Hetero)sexuality." In J. A. Boone and M. Cadden (eds.), *Engendering Men: The Question of Male Feminist Criticism*. New York: Routledge.

Forrest, L. (1994). "Evidences of Jimmy Baldwin." In L. Forrest (ed.), *Relocations of the Spirit*. Emeryville, CA: Asphodel Press/ Moyer Ball.

Riggs, M. T. (1999). "Black Macho Revisited: Reflections of a SNAP! Queen." In D. W. Carbado (ed.), *Black Men on Race, Gender, and Sexuality: A Critical Reader*. New York: New York University Press.

Ryder, B. (1991). "Straight Talk: Male Heterosexual Privilege." *Queen's Law Journal*, 16, 287–303.

Access to the Sky

Airplane Seats and Fat Bodies as Contested Spaces

Joyce L. Huff

As Michel Foucault (1979) has pointed out, since the eighteenth century Euro-American cultures have conceived of the body as adaptable, able to achieve and maintain socially prescribed standards. In the twenty-first-century United States, this body has come increasingly to be seen as capable of adapting itself to spaces constructed to meet the needs of corporations rather than those of individuals. For example, mass production, a process that accommodates manufacturers' desires to maintain high profit margins by producing goods quickly and cheaply, assumes that the consumer's body is mutable and will alter to fit into pre-constructed spaces, such as off-the-rack, rather than tailor-made, clothing. In *Enforcing Normalcy*, Lennard J. Davis (1995) notes how easily the notion of the adaptable body, with its supposed ability to conform to norms, comes to serve as the basis for a social imperative that compels individuals to strive for normalcy. Although Davis articulates his critique of coercive social norms in relation to disability, his insights could just as easily apply to anyone whose body falls outside the parameters of today's narrowly defined notion of the "normal." In fact, the very notion that individual bodies are adaptable endorses a fiction of absolute corporeal control, when, in fact, our bodies resist our control in numerous ways.

Although it is frequently argued that niche markets are currently replacing mass markets, and that consequently products are now tailored to meet the needs of specific targeted groups rather than those of a hypothetical average individual, the notion of an adaptable body remains central to the manufacturer's vision of the consumer. Clothes marketed specifically to larger women, for instance, still come in standard sizes with fixed proportions to which individual bodies must adapt. In fact, such clothing is usually marketed along with products such as "foundation garments," which are designed to facilitate this adaptation.

The recent debate over Southwest Airlines's decision to enforce a long-standing policy requiring large passengers to pay higher fares highlights the ways in which the imperative to normalize may serve corporate interests at the expense of those of individuals. In June 2002, Southwest Airlines announced its intention to make passengers with hips spanning over seventeen inches pay for two airline seats. Southwest claimed that the policy was created in response to customer complaints: "Nine out of 10 customer complaints are from passengers who get squeezed in their seats by obese neighbors" (Nielson, 2002, p. E4). An anonymous ticket agent echoed this reason when she told the *San Francisco Chronicle*, "Probably 90 percent of the people who complain to us in writing are people who say they paid for a whole seat but didn't get it because the person next to them was so large" (St. John & Zamora, 2002, p. A17).

Southwest's decision sparked a national debate over the rights of fat passengers. In fact, when fat activist Sandie Sabo discussed the policy on the *Fight Back! Talk Back!* radio show hosted by consumer advocate David Horowitz (not to be confused with the conservative pundit of the same name), the issue prompted 407 posts to the show's online forum. Southwest defended its policy by proclaiming its dedication to serving its customers: "It is certainly not safe, comfortable, or fair for a person who has purchased a ticket to be left with only a portion of a seat or no seat" (Barrett, 2002). But fat activists challenged the sincerity of the airline's commitment to their customers—when the customers in question happen to be fat ones. For example, the National Association to Advance Fat Acceptance (NAAFA) took the airline to task for failing to meet the needs of fat passengers. "We feel that today's aircraft simply are not equipped to deal with larger passengers," said NAAFA spokesperson Jeanette De-Patie. "We at NAAFA don't want to take anyone else's space and don't believe anyone should have to be uncomfortable, but at 17" to 20", airline seats are very small" (Blickenstorfer, 2002). Southwest's reasoning obscures the fact that the limitations on the amount of space allotted to each airline passenger are artificially constructed by both the airlines themselves and their regulatory agencies to suit their own needs. Thus, far from being limited to a discussion of the safety, comfort, or rights of individual passengers, fat or thin, the ensuing controversy raised questions about the definition of the "normal" body in a world in which space is commodified.

In the debate, supporters of Southwest Airlines frequently employed a "minoritizing" discourse that cast limited space on airlines as a "fat people's issue." Here I am borrowing Eve Kosofsky Sedgwick's terminology. In *Epistemology of the Closet*, Sedgwick (1990) uses the terms "minoritizing" and "universalizing" to describe two opposing views of sexuality: one that represents sexual identity as "an issue of active importance primarily for a small, distinct, relatively fixed homosexual minority," and one that characterizes it as "an issue of continuing determinative importance in the lives of people across the spectrum of sexualities" (p. 1). These terms have since been appropriated by disability studies scholars, such as Rosemarie Garland Thomson (1997a), to discuss the ways in which the compulsory "norming" of bodies has been represented as a disabled person's problem (minoritizing), when such issues should be central to current discussions of identity politics (universalizing).

I employ Sedgwick's terms to discuss the way in which fat people are imagined as embodying the problems of corporeal identity in a twenty-first-century consumer culture. I find these words particularly useful in discussing the Southwest debate,

because they emphasize the active nature of perception in structuring reality and thus implicate discursive and material practices, which are grounded in perception and the process of minoritization. To employ a minoritizing discourse is a political action, one that particularizes a societal issue and attempts to turn it into a private, individual problem, which then can, and should, be solved through individual, rather than social, action.

In the case of Southwest Airlines, minoritizing rhetoric classifies lack of space on airplanes as a fat person's problem, the implied solution to which is weight loss. Southwest represents the problem in terms of individual passengers fitting into individual seats—"an issue of active importance primarily for a small, distinct, relatively fixed" minority that does not fit their definition of the average customer. Most posters on *Fight Back's* forum presumed that seats were designed to accommodate this hypothetical average customer, which they assumed represented the statistically average American. As L.A. Chung (2002) of San Francisco's *Mercury News* points out, Southwest has a "carefully cultivated image of being the airline for the average Joe." When the issue is represented in this way, it seems obvious that the solution should also be an individual one, adopted by the few who are directly affected by the problem. As one participant on the *Fight Back* forum, "malfunctionbob," states, "I think instead of taking the common American approach of making the world adjust to the few [sic] Perhaps the few might adjust to the many" (2002b, p. 1). Such language makes it the responsibility of the individual to find ways of adapting to the policy or to pay for special accommodation.

Fat activists have countered the effort to minoritize the issue with a more universalizing discourse, one that presents airplane seating as a problem for the majority of individuals. They argue that airlines should be held accountable for creating seats that are uncomfortable for most passengers, be they fat or thin, tall or short, with physical disabilities or temporarily able-bodied. For example, on *Fight Back*, when a supporter of Southwest's policy employs the rhetoric of special needs, stating that larger seats for fat passengers would amount to "special accommodation that is subsidized by all," Sabo responds in a universalizing manner: "Why on earth should passengers larger than 17" across have to subsidize the airline's choice to use seating that is uncomfortable for almost all of the flying public?" (2002b, p. 1). The idea that some bodies' needs should be labeled "special" highlights what is really at stake in this debate: the definition of the normal, as opposed to the "special," body.

Similarly, lawyer and activist Sondra Solovay employs a universalizing discourse, this time one of universal human rights, when she argues, "It's an issue of fundamental civil rights when people are prevented from traveling because of their personal attributes" (Wastell, 2002, p. 18). Solovay echoes disability rights activists in focusing on the ways in which the culture is constructed to meet the needs of some individuals and not others: "There is nothing inherently limiting about blindness, deafness or wheelchair usage. These conditions are viewed by the court as limiting because they occur in the context of a society that has constructed structural and communication barriers that restrict people with these conditions from participating in daily activities" (2000, p. 148). She here implies that what is needed is a reconstruction of the physical and social environment to meet the needs of a greater number of people.

Sabo also universalizes, or at least, majoritizes (if I may invent a term) the issue when she points out that since 55–60% of Americans have been deemed overweight by the National Institutes of Health, the fat customer has become statistically average, and that, therefore, there is nothing special about the accommodation sought in this case (*Fight*, 2002b, p. 1). Of course, in both fat and disability studies, it is now a commonplace that the idea of the "average" or "normal" individual represents not a statistical average, but rather a cultural ideal, which carries the weight of an ideological imperative. Davis's (1995) analysis of the development of the bell curve highlights the eugenicist ideology of human perfectibility that underpins the hegemony of such notions. Indeed, disability studies scholars have cited the current obsession with thinness in American culture as an example that unmasks the ideological nature of social norms in general. Thomson (1997b), for example, has reported that her female students' "struggle with the tyranny of slimness enables them to recognize that bodily aberration is relative to a cultural and historically specific standard that serves particular interests" (p. 302). It is not surprising, then, that the "average" customer, for whom Southwest presumably designs its seats, represents an ideological construct rather than a statistical average.

The underlying ideology that determines the size of the so-called average customer to whom Southwest supposedly caters is a capitalist one. Although airlines and their supporters may invoke average customers who represent cultural ideals, in fact seat sizing has a lot more to do with profit margins and maximizing the number of paying customers. After all, tallness is a trait that is culturally valued in the United States today, and airline seating does not accommodate the tall, as a lawsuit filed by the Tall Club of Silicon Valley in 2001 attests (Chung, 2002).

Southwest's press release presents airline seat size as absolute. "Our policy," they explain, "isn't about a person's weight . . . If a person occupies his/her *seat* and a portion or all of the adjoining *seat*, then that Customer will need to purchase the additional *seat* he/she is occupying" (italics mine) (Barrett, 2002). Here, the space taken up by passengers is quantified using the term "seats," as if this term designated a standard unit of measurement. It is passenger size, not seat size, Southwest implies, that is malleable.

But seat size is not immutable. Indeed, Sabo charges that when profit was the primary concern, Southwest itself has altered the size of its seats. She states, "There is no accident that Southwest Airlines is currently the only profitable airline, and the only airline that did not ask for federal bailout after 9/11. They did away with any options for larger seating, (business and first class), and made all their seating the smallest in the industry." And *Fight Back* poster Rosalie Prosser puts it more succinctly: "First they shrink the seats and then blame large people for not fitting" (2002a, p. 1). On their official website, Southwest responds to the question, "Why not make your seats wider or add a few wide seats on your aircraft?" by stating, "Our ongoing goal is to operate a low-fare, low cost airline, and the costs of reconfiguring our fleet would be staggering and would ultimately reflect in the form of higher fares for our customers" (2006). But, as Sabo notes, "this would all be academic if they would pull the price for 'lost' seats, or for supplying some real-sized seating, from their Executives' salaries" (*Fight*, 2002a, p. 1).

Cost-cutting measures that affect the distribution of space on airplanes, however, are not limited to the shrinking of seats. Fewer flights mean more crowded conditions as well. As journalist Carrie Levine (2006) states, "Since the number of available flights offered by troubled airlines has been shrinking, overcrowding is worsening the problem." And *USA Today's* Chris Woodyard (2003) attributes the problem to Southwest's streamlined boarding policy, another cost-cutting tactic: "Sometimes the airline simply finds [fat passengers] a row that isn't expected to sell out . . . Southwest's problem appears to revolve around its policy of not reserving seats." In the case of Southwest's seating, then, it is corporate needs, rather than concerns for the comfort of any customer, average or not, that are accommodated when seating is designed. In fact, when a Southwest representative told members of the NAAFA at the 2002 conference that the policy was intended for the comfort and convenience of fat passengers, NAAFA members replied by asking, "Do you intend to also make using the restrooms more comfortable for large passengers?" (Blickenstorfer, 2002). The answer, not surprisingly, was no.

In a corporately constructed environment, space is not merely a limited resource, but also a purchasable resource, a commodity. As journalist Kathleen Parker (2002, p. 13A) concedes in her critique of Southwest, "Though space is less a tangible commodity than food, it is no less a 'product' if you happen to be in the airline business. Airlines sell space." Renee Wynne (2002, p. B5) writes a letter to the *Seattle Times* stating, "You use more space, you should pay more for it. Same thing with any other commodity." In this particular case, space on a plane is assigned a monetary value. The determining question revolves around the maximum number of bodies that can be placed into a mass produced airplane to maximize airline profit.

To define seat space as a commodity, however, is a misrepresentation that serves airline interests, according to Sabo. She asserts, "When you purchase an airline ticket you are purchasing a ticket for a trip, not a ticket for a seat." She goes on to explain, "The reason that the airline contracts with you for a trip (not a seat) is so that they have the legal right to change your seat (without your permission), bump you, over book flights (the key to their existence) or even cancel your flight." If the trip and not the space is indeed the true commodity, presumably fat customers should be provided with the space that they require to make their purchased trips: "If we are purchasing a ticket for a trip, then it seems to stand to reason that the airline is liable to provide that trip what ever it takes" (*Fight*, 2002a, p. 1).

In countering customer demands for larger and more comfortable seats, Southwest has responded that larger seats would mean fewer seats and fewer paying customers: "If we were to replace just three rows of three seats with two seats, each being one and a half times wider, we would have to significantly raise our fares to maintain our profit margin" (Barrett, 2002). But this logic denies the fact that, like seat size, fares are not fixed quantities—they vary according to customer demand—and, as specific flights are not always sold out, the overall profit margin on a flight is also constantly variable.

Southwest's policy assumes an audience accustomed to capitalist modes of thought, one that will endorse the premise that businesses need to continually increase profit margins, one that will believe that this need is sacrosanct to the degree that they will subordinate their own needs and desires to it. In fact, on the *Fight Back* forum, many respondents posted in defense of what one woman called "the needs and rights of a business to cater to the 'average' customer." According to this person, a 4'11" woman who labeled herself "The Short Poster," individuals can and must adapt themselves to suit corporate needs: "When I need to make an accommodation, I make it. If I don't fit in, I choose again, meaning I accommodate the need or go elsewhere. I don't demand that a riding stable have a saddle and stirrups short enough to fit me. I don't go to crowded museum exhibitions if it means I can't see over people to view the displays. The list is endless. So bloody what? I adapt . . ." (2002a, p. 2).

The Short Poster's response reveals the stigmatizing potential of minoritizing discourses. If individuals, or minority groups, are responsible for solutions to social problems, then it follows that they are also to blame when solutions are not found. For instance, Susan Nielson (2002) writes in the *Sunday Oregonian*, "We've outgrown our seats, and that's not Southwest's fault . . . let's not blame the airlines for size discrimination. Our appetites are insatiable, and our airplanes are only so big." Nielson claims that what is at is at stake is "why Americans got so big, and who's to blame" (p. E4). Here, the body visibly marked as unable or unwilling to adapt bears the responsibility for societal failures (in this case, airlines that fail to provide adequate seating), and is thus stigmatized. In his groundbreaking work on the subject, Erving Goffman (1963, p. 5) defines "stigma" as a negative attitude about a specific personal trait or "an undesired different-ness from what we had anticipated." Southwest appears to have anticipated flying only customers with hips spanning seventeen inches or fewer when the seats were built; fat thus represents a differentness that they neither anticipated nor desired.

Indeed, many of the published responses to fat flyers seem to have less to do with space than with stigma. For instance, Jenn Cornall, quoted in the *New York Daily News,* says, "It was disgusting to have to share my seat with someone else's fat." Interviewer Lenore Skenazy responds that "whining flyers can complain about people with double chins in a way they could never complain about, say, moms with lap children, because there is nothing immoral about motherhood. Can you imagine a business traveler moaning, 'Toddler flesh spilled into my seat'?" (2002, p. 33). In fact, one of the questions asked of Southwest representatives by NAAFA members at the 2002 convention was: "Do you intend to deal with other customer complaints in the same manner? Do you anticipate charging mothers with crying babies more? Or parents of children who kick the seat in front? How about loud people or those who use offensive language? Or those who talk too much or drink too much?" The Southwest representative replied that the NAAFA members were comparing "apples and oranges" (Blickenstorfer, 2002). Clearly, for NAAFA members, the comparison contrasted Southwest's differing treatment of a variety of customers who encroached on others, physically or audibly. For Southwest, however, what mattered were customer complaints, which were frequently grounded in stigma against fat people. NAAFA members did not demand that customers stop complaining or question the legitimacy of any complaint, including the ones about space; they merely pointed to the dis-similar ways in which complaints were handled by the airline when the grievance involved a stigmatized individual as opposed to a "normal" one.[1]

In effect, the airline expected the stigmatized group to be responsible for resolving the problem. Goffman states that in response to stigmatization, one might "make a direct attempt to correct what he [sic] sees as the objective basis of his failing" (1963, p. 9), as the Short Poster does when she accepts socially prescribed limits on her participation in the public sphere rather than challenge a corporation's right to construct public spaces to which she cannot adapt. Stigma can thus be exploited to shame minorities into compliance with dominant ideologies. In fact, for some supporters of Southwest's policy, the point was exactly that; Southwest's policy was lauded for providing a new way to humiliate those with bodily differences into compliance with the norm. Aptly named obesity expert Mike Lean, for example, states: "Someone who weighs 260lb hangs right over into the next seat. If that's the sort of penalty you're facing, it might persuade a few more people to be more thoughtful about their diet" (Timms, 2002, 4). But, as one poster on *Fight Back* points out, the policy is about body size, not about diet; "Hipster" states, "A policy that makes this distinction would only punish fast food eating couch potatoes larger than 17" and not the smaller fast food eating couch potatoes" (2002b, p. 1).

The tendency to defend, rather than to contest, the corporate right to allocate and commodity space can be seen in a discussion regarding passengers on the Washington, D.C., subway, or Metro. In this conversation, Southwest was invoked to make a distinction between publicly funded services and private businesses. The discussion began when passenger Lynn Wood wrote a letter to the *Washington Post* suggesting that fat Metro riders pay double fares. Metro spokesperson Lisa Farbstein responded by affirming the responsibility of public transportation to serve all members of the public. "Metro is a public transit authority" she begins. "That means that everybody has a right to use it, and it's subject to all the things people like and don't like about public spaces. The people who wrote in might not like sitting next to a larger person, but there are also folks who don't like sitting next to someone who wears perfume and scented products." She continues with a list of other inconveniences encountered in public spaces: "children who are squirming or screaming," "people who disturb the peace with inadequate headphones," and people who engage in "loud conversations, many on cell phones." She concludes, "Metro is not in the business of promoting prejudice and bigotry. People come in all sorts of different bodies, and they all have every right to ride Metro" (Shaffer, 2005). In response, some posters contrasted the rights of Metro riders with those of Southwest flyers. "Could I just suggest," says one poster, "that 'standards' for a public transportation system might be inclusive enough to allow any person to travel on its system for a fare; as opposed to a private airline which can set its own standards and price system as long as it doesn't unfairly discriminate?" (Shaffer, 2005).

Southwest employs the stigmatizing potential of minoritizing discourses when they frame the problem of limited space as one in which, according to a *Fight Back* poster, fat people crowd "NORMAL Sized [*sic*]" people (2002a, p. 7). Or, as David Stempler, president of the Air Travelers Association, puts it, "If passengers have supersized themselves and are encroaching on the space of others, fairness says you should be paying for the space" (St. John & Zamora, 2002, p. A17). Note that he uses supersized as a transitive verb, suggesting that the situation is caused by passengers and should be remedied by them.

Through stigmatizing rhetoric, the contested site becomes not the airline seat itself, but rather the body potentially occupying that seat. In making fat people the source of the problem—and thus responsible for its solution—Southwest has forestalled complaints from "normal" customers by displacing their aggression onto fat passengers. They have essentially attempted to erase the possibility of a scenario in which this aggression would be directed at airlines for failing to meet the general population's needs. Sabo goes so far as to state, "It is my allegation that SWA is pitting thin people against fat people . . . in a way to draw the attention away from their continuing attempts to jam as many passengers into an airline [*sic*] as they can. They are playing up the great disdain and prejudice that many thin Americans have against fat people" (*Fight*, 2002a, p. 1), An article in the *Sacramento Bee* even referred to the debate as a "mini-war between fat and thin passengers." The author, Anita Creamer (2002), goes further than Sabo, claiming that policies like Southwest's are an attempt to scapegoat fat people to forestall all sorts of complaints:

Meanwhile, what a fine distraction all this has been from the fact that most of the annoyances of airline travel today have nothing to do with the overweight passenger sitting next to you. No, the airlines themselves are to blame for the lost kids and lost luggage, for frequent flyer miles that are all but impossible to redeem and for seats measuring only 18 inches across. And the airlines are to blame for overbooked flights, for delays and for ridiculous security policies that seem to require public officials to be searched nearly every time they fly. No matter how hard we try, we can't pin the bad business practices necessitating the $15 billion federal bailout of the airlines on fat people either.

Creamer concludes, "Trying to distract us by blaming even a small part of those inconveniences on fat people is an insult" (p. E1).

Such universalizing discourse prompts a search for more universal solutions. Parker (2002) humorously states, "Fat and Skinny Unite (FASU) and stop flying until the airlines give us bigger seats" (p. 13A). Solovay (2006), however, takes seriously the search for more universal solutions. She states, "This is an issue that affects most travelers, and it is important for travelers to stick together on this issue and hold airlines accountable for the space choices they make." It is important to note that neither Parker nor Solovay is suggesting that customers have no right to speak up when they feel that their rights or comfort have been infringed upon. Rather, while acknowledging that crowding on airplanes is a problem, they challenge the assumption that the cause necessarily lies in fat bodies and that the sole solution depends on the idea that individuals can and should adapt their bodies to meet the needs of corporations. Instead, they call for all consumers—fat and thin—to join together in demanding that the needs of *all* be met.

What activists are advocating amounts to a reconfiguration of the public sphere to allow the participation of a greater number of people. Sally Smith, editor in chief of *BBW* (Big Beautiful Woman) magazine, advocates such a universal solution when she asserts that "for most other things in this society, costs are amortized so that everyone can be included. It costs more to put wheelchair ramps on buildings, but we don't make people with disabilities subsidize the costs" (Payne, 2002, p. D1). And Sabo agrees: "Why wouldn't it be fair for everyone to share the cost of adding some larger seats for larger flyers? We share the cost for changing tables in restrooms, for handicapped parking, for ramps, and for all sorts of public assistance programs. The whole point of sharing the cost for accommodations between all members of society is specifically so those people needing those accommodations don't wind up forced out of society" (*Fight*, 2002a, p. 1). The rhetoric employed here presents the problem as not simply a problem of fat people and airline seats, but rather a universal one relating to how we wish to structure our society and who will be included in it.

And this, in the end, is the real question raised by the Southwest debates. The move from seat to body as contested site raises issues regarding how much space a body can inhabit in an environment constructed by twenty-first-century corporations. It is true that airlines have historically been considered bastions of size oppression because of weight restrictions on flight attendants; in fact, they have also been taken to task recently for perpetuating other forms of discrimination, such as banning female flyers who wear clothing considered promiscuous or gay couples who publicly display their affection for each other. But airlines are not the source of the problem; rather, their practices are symptomatic of the consequences that can result when the public sphere is designed in manner that excludes certain members of that public. What is needed in the case of fat bodies and airline seats is not simply larger seats but also an interrogation of the very notion of both the adaptable body and the corporate logic that deploys this concept in the distribution of public space.

The critique of bodily norms that is already taking place within disability studies is essential to this project. Southwest clearly saw their policy as a potential "disability issue" and were quick to point out on their website that "interstate airline travel is specifically excluded from Title II of the Americans with Disabilities Act" (Southwest, 2006). One commentator on *Fight Back* attempted to draw a distinction between "good" disabled people, who are supposedly willing to pay for their own accommodations, and "bad" fat people, who refuse to pull their own weight, so to speak. "Pay the money," "malfunctionbob" urges. "And before you go talking about disabled people and the like I'd like to say that they pay considerable expense adapting to the world of the many" (2002b, p. 1). This statement ignores current disability rights movements and wrongly casts people with disabilities as a "model minority." The strategy is to pit two relatively disempowered groups against each other, when a coalition would be beneficial to both groups, who share an interest in both the deconstruction of the notion of the normal body and the reallocation of public space.

References

Barrett, C. (2002). A Message from Southwest Airlines. Retrieved May 31, 2003, from http://web.archive.org/web/20020802161757/http://www.southwest.com/about_swa/press/additional_seat.html.

Blickenstorfer, C.H. (2002, August 9). NAAFA Think Tank: Airlines and Fat Passengers. Retrieved May 31, 2003, from http://web.archive.org/web/20021014025007/http://www.naafa.org/Convention2002/airlines.html.

Chung, L.A. (2002, June 25). Southwest's Policy Poses Big Questions. *The Mercury News*. Retrieved May 31, 2003, from http://www.accessmylibrary.com/coms2/summary_0286-6864223.ITM.

Creamer, A. (2002, July 1). Real Issues of Weight for Fliers. *Sacramento Bee*, E1.

Davis, L.J. (1995). *Enforcing Normalcy: Disability, Deafness, and the Body*. New York: Verso.

Fight Back! Feed Back! Forum. (2002a). 2 Seat Policy. Retrieved May 21, 2006, from http://forums.fightback.com/forumdisplay.sort=lastpost&order=desc&pp=25&daysprune=-1.

Fight Back! Feed Back! Forum. (2002b). Weight and Diet Dialogue Triggered by Airline Announcement. Retrieved May 21, 2006, http://forums.fightback.com/forumdisplay.php?f=3&page=2&sort=lastpost&order=desc&pp=25&daysprune=-1.

Foucault, M. (1979). *Discipline and Punish: The Birth of the Prison*. A. Sheridan (Trans.). New York: Vintage.

Goffman, E. (1963). *Stigma: Notes on the Management of Spoiled Identity*. New York: Simon and Schuster.

Levine, C. Man Has Weighty Problem with Airline. *Boston Bay Chronicles*. Retrieved May 22, 2006, from http://web.archive.org/web/20040909084415/http://eyetrack.morris.com/story_pages/5_a/03.shtml.

Nielson, S. (2002, June 23). This Battle of the Bulge Doesn't Fly. *Sunday Oregonian*, E4.

Parker, K. (2002, June 25). Skinny Seats the Real Culprits. *Milwaukee Journal Sentinel*, 13A.

Payne, M. (2002, June 22). Weigh More? You Pay More. *Sacramento Bee*, D1.

Sedgwick, E.K. (1990). *Epistemology of the Closet*. Berkeley: University of California Press.

Shaffer, R. (2005, September 26). Transcript: Dr. Gridlock. *Washington Post*. Retrieved May 22, 2006, http://www.washingtonpost.com/wp-dyn/content/discussion/2005/09/23/DI2005092301029.html

Skenazy, L. (2002, June 26). Extra Fares for Fat Folk are Flighty, *New York Daily News*, 33.

Solovay, S. Red Alert: Southwest Campaign. Retrieved May 21, 2006, from http://www.fat-shadow.com/SW.htm.

Solovay, S. (2000). *Tipping the Scales of Justice*. New York: Prometheus.

Southwest Airlines (2006). Customer of Size Q&A. Retrieved

May 21, 2006, from http://www.southwest.com/travel_center/cos_qa.html.

St. John, K., & Zamora, J.H. (2002, June 20). Southwest to Make Overweight Buy 2 Seats. *San Francisco Chronicle*, A17.

Thomson, R.G. (1997a). *Extraordinary Bodies: Figuring Physical Disability in American Literature and Culture*. New York: Columbia University.

Thomson, R.G. (1997b). Integrating Disability Studies into the Existing Curriculum. In L.J. Davis (Ed.), *The Disability Studies Reader*. New York: Routledge.

Timms, P. (2002, June 25). Paying for the Excess. *The Scotsman*, 4.

Wastell, D. (2002, June 23). Fatties Bite Back. *London Sunday Telegraph*, 18.

Woodyard, C. (2003, September 25). When It Comes to Weighty Flyers, Why Can't We All Just Get Along? *USA Today*. Retrieved May 22, 2006, from http://www.usatoday.com/travel/columnist/woodyard/2003-09-25-woodyard5_x.htm.

Wynne, R. (2002, June 22). Northwest Voices: A Sampling of Readers' Letters, Faxes, and E-mails. *Seattle Times*, B5.

Note

I would like to thank Robert McRuer, Abby Wilkerson, Pam Presser, Lisbeth Fuisz Randy Kristensen, Nolana Yip, and Todd Ramlow for their feedback on early drafts of this chapter.

1 Solovay and Vade point to similarities in the treatment of fat individuals and members of other stigmatized groups in their chapter in this collection on fat and transgender individuals.

Their Laws Will Never Make Us Safer

Dean Spade

An Introduction

At many transgender Day of Remembrance events, a familiar community anecdote surfaces. The story goes that convicted murderers of trans people have been sentenced to less punishment than is meted out to those convicted of killing a dog. In Istanbul, where trans sex workers have been resisting and surviving severe violence, criminalization, and displacement caused by gentrification, recent advocacy for a trans-inclusive hate crime law has included sharing stories of trans women being raped by attackers who threaten them with death and openly cite the fact that they would only go to prison for three years even if they were convicted of the murder. These stories expose the desperate conditions faced by populations cast as disposable, who struggle against the erasure of their lives and deaths.

The murder of Trayvon Martin in 2012 raised related dialogues across the U.S. The possibility that Martin's murderer would not be prosecuted, and the awareness that anti-black violence consistently goes uninvestigated and unpunished by racist police and prosecutors, led to a loud call for the prosecution of George Zimmerman. In the weeks after Martin's murder, I heard and read many conversations and commentaries where people who are critical of the racism and violence of the criminal punishment system struggled to figure out whether it made sense to call on that system to make Martin's murderer accountable for his actions.

On the one hand, the failure to prosecute and punish Zimmerman to the full extent of the law would be a slap in the face to Martin's family and everyone else impacted by racial profiling and anti-black violence. It would be a continuation of the long-term collaboration between police and perpetrators of anti-black violence, where the police exist to protect the interests of white people and to protect white life and operate both to directly attack and kill black people and to permit individuals and hate groups to do so.

On the other hand, given the severe anti-black racism of the criminal punishment system, what does it mean to call on that system for justice and accountability? Many people working to dismantle racism identify the criminal punishment system as one of the primary apparatuses of racist violence and probably the most significant threat to black people in the U.S. Opposing that system includes both opposing its literal growth (the hiring of more cops, the building of more jails and prisons, the criminalization of more behaviors, the increasing of sentences) and disrupting the cultural myths about it being a "justice" system and about the police "protecting and serving" everyone. For many activists who are working to dismantle that system, it felt uncomfortable to call for Zimmerman's prosecution, since the idea that any justice can emerge from prosecution and imprisonment has been exposed as a racist lie.

The tensions inside this debate are very significant ones for queer and trans politics right now. Increasingly, queer and trans people are asked to measure our citizenship status on whether hate crime legislation that includes sexual orientation and gender identity exists in the jurisdictions in which we live. We are told by gay and lesbian rights organizations that passing this legislation is the best way to respond to the ongoing violence we face—that we need to make the state and the public care about our victimization and show they care by increasing surveillance of and punishment for homophobic and transphobic attacks.

Hate crime laws are part of the larger promise of criminal punishment systems to keep us safe and resolve our conflicts. This is an appealing promise in a society wracked by gun violence and sexual violence.[1] In a heavily armed, militaristic, misogynist, and racist society, people are justifiably scared of violence, and that fear is cultivated by a constant feed of television shows portraying horrifying violence and brave police and prosecutors who put serial rapists and murderers in prison. The idea that we are in danger rings true, and the message that law enforcement will deliver safety is appealing in the face of fear. The problem is that these promises are false, and are grounded in some key myths and lies about violence and criminal punishment.

Five realities about violence and criminal punishment are helpful for analyzing the limitations of hate crime legislation (or any enhancement of criminalization) to prevent violence or bring justice and accountability after it has happened:

1. *Jails and prisons are not full of dangerous people, they are full of people of color, poor people, and people with disabilities.* More than 60% of people in U.S. prisons are people of color. Every stage and aspect of the criminal punishment and immigration enforcement systems is racist—racism impacts who gets stopped by cops, who gets arrested, what bail gets set, which workplaces and homes are raided by Immigration and Customs Enforcement (ICE), what charges are brought, who will be on the jury, what conditions people face while locked up, and who will be deported. Most people in the U.S. violate laws (like traffic laws and drug laws) all the time, but people of color, homeless people, and people with disabilities are profiled and harassed and are the ones who get locked up and stay locked up or get deported. Ending up in prison or jail or deportation proceedings is not a matter of dangerousness or

lawlessness, it's about whether you are part of a group targeted for enforcement.

2. *Most violence does not happen on the street between strangers, like on TV, but between people who know each other, in our homes, schools, and familiar spaces.* Images of out-of-control serial killers and rapists who attack strangers feed the cultural thirst for retribution and the idea that it is acceptable to lock people away for life in unimaginably abusive conditions. In reality, the people who hurt us are usually people we know, and usually are also struggling under desperate conditions and/or victims of violence. Violence, especially sexual violence, is so common that it is not realistic to lock away every person who engages in it. Most violence is never reported to police because people have complex relationships with those who have hurt them, and the whole framing of criminalization where "bad guys" get "put away" does not work for most survivors of violence. If we deal with the complexity of how common violence is, and let go of a system built on a fantasy of monstrous strangers, we might actually begin to focus on how to prevent violence and heal from it. Banishment and exile—the tools offered by the criminal punishment and immigration enforcement systems—only make sense when we maintain the fantasy that there are evil perpetrators committing harm, rather than facing the reality that people we love are harming us and each other and that we need to change fundamental conditions to stop it.

3. *The most dangerous people, the people who violently destroy and end the most lives, are still on the outside—they are the people running banks, governments, and courtrooms and they are the people wearing military and police uniforms.* Fear is an effective method of social control. Prison and war profiteers fuel racist and xenophobic fears by circulating images of "terrorists" and "criminals."[2] In reality, the greatest risks to our survival are worsening poverty and lack of access to health care, adequate housing, and food. This shortens the lives of millions of people

in the U.S. every day, along with the violence of police and ICE attacks, imprisonment and warfare that the U.S. government unleashes every day domestically and internationally, and the destruction of our climate, water, and food supplies by relentlessly greedy elites. If we really want to increase well-being and reduce violence, our resources should not be focused on locking up people who possess drugs or get in a fight at school or sleep on a sidewalk—we should be focusing on dismantling the structures that give a tiny set of elites decision-making power over most resources, land, and people in the world.

4. *Prisons aren't places to put serial rapists and murderers, prisons are the serial rapists and murderers.* If we acknowledge that the vast majority of people in prisons and jails are there because of poverty and racism, not because they are "dangerous" or violent, and if we acknowledge that prisons and jail utterly fail to make anyone who spends time in them healthier or less likely to engage in violence, and if we recognize that prisons and jail are spaces of extreme violence,[3] and that kidnapping and caging people, not to mention exposing them to nutritional deprivation, health care deprivation, and physical attack is violence, it becomes clear that criminalization and immigration enforcement increase rather than decrease violence overall.

5. *Increasing criminalization does not make us safer, it just feeds the voracious law enforcement systems that devour our communities.* The U.S. criminal punishment and immigration enforcement systems are the largest prison systems that have ever existed on Earth. The U.S. imprisons more people than any other society that has ever existed—we have 5% of the world's population and 25% of the world's prisoners. Our immigration prisons quadrupled in size in the decade after 2001. This hasn't made us safer from violence, it is violence.

The fundamental message of hate crime legislation is that if we lock more bad people up, we will be safer. Everything about our current law enforcement systems indicates that this is a false promise, and it's a false promise that targets people of color and poor people for caging and death while delivering large profits to white elites. Many might hope that queer and trans people would be unlikely to fall for this trick, since we have deep community histories and contemporary realities of experiencing police violence and violence in prisons and jails, and we know something about not trusting the cops. However, this same ongoing experience of marginalization makes some of us deeply crave recognition from systems and people we see as powerful or important. This desperate craving for recognition, healing and safety can cause us to invest hope in the only methods most of us have ever heard of for responding to violence: caging and exile. Many of us want to escape the stigmas of homophobia and transphobia and be recast as "good" in the public eye. In contemporary politics, being a "crime victim" is much more sympathetic than being a "criminal." By desiring recognition within this system's terms, we are enticed to fight for criminalizing legislation that will in no way reduce our experiences of marginalization and violence.

In recent years, these concerns about hate crime legislation have gotten somewhat louder, though they are still entirely marginalized by the corporate-sponsored white gay and lesbian rights organizations and mainstream media outlets from which many queer and trans people get their information about our issues and our resistance. More and more people in the U.S. are questioning the drastic expansion of criminalization and immigration enforcement, and noticing that building more prisons and jails and deporting more people does not seem to make our lives any safer or better. Many queer and trans people are increasingly critical of criminalization and immigration enforcement, and are unsatisfied by the idea that the answer to the violence we experience is harsher criminal laws or more police.

Three kinds of strategies are being taken up by queer and trans activists who refuse to believe the lies of law enforcement systems, and want to stop transphobic and homophobic violence. First, many people are working to directly support the survival of queer and trans people who are vulnerable to violence. Projects that connect queer and trans people outside of prisons to people currently imprisoned for friendship and support and projects that provide direct advocacy to queer and trans people facing homelessness, immigration enforcement, criminalization and other dire circumstances are under way in many places. Many people are providing direct support to people coming out of prison, or opening their homes to one another, or collaborating to make sex work safer in their communities. This kind of work is vital because we cannot build strong movements if our people are not surviving. Directly helping each other during our moments of crisis is essential—especially when we do it in ways that are politically engaged, that build shared analysis of the systems that produce these dangers. This is not a social service or charity model that provides people with minimal survival needs in a moralizing framework that separates "deserving" from "undeserving" and gives professionals the power to determine who is compliant enough, clean enough, hard-working enough, or quiet enough to get into the housing, job training, or public benefits programs. This is a model of mutual aid that values all of us, especially people facing the most dire manifestations of poverty and state violence, as social movement participants who deserve to survive and to get together with others facing similar conditions to fight back.

The second kind of work is dismantling work. Many people are working to dismantle the systems that put queer and trans people into such dangerous and violent situations. They are trying to stop new jails and immigration prisons from being built, they are trying to decriminalize sex work and drugs, they are trying to stop the expansion of surveillance systems. Identifying what pathways and apparatuses funnel our people into danger and fighting against these systems that are devouring us is vital work.

The third kind of work is building alternatives. Violent systems are sold to us with false promises—we're told the prison systems will keep us safe or that the immigration system will improve our economic well-being, yet we know these systems only offer violence. So we have to build the world we want to live in—build ways of being safer, of having food and shelter, of having health care and of breaking isolation. Lots of activists are working on projects to do this, for example, on alternative ways to deal with violence in our communities and families that don't involve calling the police, since the police are the most significant danger to many of us. Many people are engaged in experimental work to do what the criminal and immigration systems utterly fail to do. Those systems have grown massive, built on promises of safety. But they have utterly failed to reduce rape, child sexual abuse, poverty, police violence, racism, ableism, and the other things that are killing us. Their growth has increased all of those things. So, we have to look with fresh *eyes* at what actually does make us safer. Some people are building projects that try to directly respond when something violent or harmful happens. Others are building projects that try to prevent violence by looking at what things tend to keep us safe—things like having strong friendship circles, safe housing, transportation, not being economically dependent for survival on another person so you can leave them if you want to, and having shared analysis and practices for resisting dangerous systems of meaning and control like racism and the romance myth.

Some people who are identifying prisons and borders as some of the most significant forms of violence that need to be opposed and resisted by queer and trans politics, are calling for an end to all prisons. For me, prison abolition means recognizing prisons and borders as structures that cannot be redeemed, that have no place in the world I want to be part of building. It means deciding that inventing and believing in enemies, creating ways of banishing and exiling and throwing away people, has no role in building that world. This is a very big deal for people raised in a highly militaristic prison society that feeds us a constant diet of fear, that encourages us from early childhood to sort the world into "bad guys" and "good guys." Our indoctrination into this prison culture deprives us of skills for recognizing any complexity, including the complexity of our own lives as people who both experience harm and do harm to others. Working to develop the capacity to even imagine that harm can be prevented and addressed without throwing people away or putting anyone in cages is a big process for us.

In the growing debate about whether hate crime legislation is something that will improve the lives of queer and trans people, and whether it is something we should be fighting for, we can see queer and trans activists working to develop important capacities to discern and analyze together. This form of discernment is familiar to prison abolitionists, and it is also visible in other areas of queer and trans politics. It is an ability to analyze the nature of an institution or system, rather than just to seek to reform it to include or recognize a group it targets or harms. Abolitionists have long critiqued prison reform, observing that prison expansion usually occurs under the guise of prison reform. Important complaints about prison conditions, for example, often lead to prison profiteers and government employees proposing building newer, cleaner, better prisons that inevitably will result in more people getting locked up.[4] Queer activists have engaged this kind of discernment about reforming violent state apparatuses in our work to oppose the fights for same-sex marriage and the ability to serve in the U.S. military. In this work, we have questioned the assumption that inclusion in such institutions is desirable, naming the existence of marriage as a form of racialized-gendered social control and the ongoing imperial and genocidal practices of the U.S. military. This work is complex, because so many queer and trans people, conditioned by shaming and exclusion, believe that getting the U.S. government to say "good" things about us in its laws and policies, no matter what those laws and policies actually exist to do, is progress. This framing asks gay and lesbian people to be the new face of the purported fairness and liberalism of the United States, to get excited about fighting its wars, shaping our lives around its family formation norms, and having its criminal codes expanded in our names. The ability to recognize that an enticing invitation to inclusion is not actually going to address the worst forms of violence affecting us, and is actually going to expand the apparatuses that perpetrate them—whether in Abu Ghraib, Pelican Bay, or the juvenile hall in your town—is one that requires collective analysis for queer politics to grasp.

The Against Equality book projects, of which this section makes up the third and final, offer us a bundle of tools for building that analysis and sharing it in our networks, for trading in the dangerous ideas that the Human Rights Campaign and the other organizations that purport to represent our best interests are not likely to disseminate. This section, in particular, focuses on how criminalization and imprisonment target and harm queer and trans people, and why expanding criminalization by passing hate crime laws will not address the urgent survival issues in our lives. The most well-funded and widely broadcast lesbian and gay rights narratives tell us that the state is our protector, that its institutions are not centers of racist, homophobic, transphobic, and ableist violence, but are sites for our liberation. We know that is not true. We are naming names—even if you wrap it in a rainbow flag, a cop is a cop, a wall is a wall, an occupation is an occupation, a marriage license is a tool of regulation. We are building ways of thinking about this together, and ways of enacting these politics in daily work to support one another and transform the material conditions of our lives.

Notes

1   A 2011 study published in the *Journal of Trauma-Injury Infection & Critical Care* reported that "[t]he U.S. homicide rates were 6.9 times higher than rates in the other high-income countries, driven by firearm homicide rates that were 19.5 times higher. For 15-year olds to 24-year olds, firearm

homicide rates in the United States were 42.7 times higher than in the other countries."

Richardson, Erin G. S.M.; Hemenway, David PhD, "Homicide, Suicide, and Unintentional Firearm Fatality: Comparing the United States With Other High-Income Countries," 2003, *Journal of Trauma-Injury Infection & Critical Care*, January 2011 – Volume 70 – Issue 1 – pp 238–243. http://journals.lww.com/jtrauma/Abstract/2011/01000/Homicide,Suicide,_and_Unintentional_Firearm.35.aspx.

Every year, approximately 100,000 people in the U.S. are victims of gun violence, and about 85 people per day die from gun violence in the U.S. "Gun Violence Statistics," Law Center to Prevent Gun Violence, http://smartgunlaws.org/category/gun-studies-statistics/gun-violence-statistics/. An average of 207,754 people age 12 or older experience sexual assault every year in the U.S. Approximately every two minutes, someone is sexually assaulted. 54% of assaults are not reported to the police, and 97% of rapists do not serve any jail time. "Statistics," Rape, Abuse & Incest National Network, http://www.rainn.org/statistics/. According to the Colorado Coalition Against Sexual Assault, in the U.S. one out of every six women and one out of thirty three men have experienced an attempted or completed rape. Citing National Violence Against Women Survey, "Prevalence, Incidence, and Consequences of Violence Against Women," November 1998. The Colorado Coalition Against Sexual Assault also reports that "the United States has the world's highest rape rate of the countries that publish such statistics—4 times higher than Germany, 13 times higher than England, and 20 times higher than Japan" citing NWS, "Rape in America: A Report to the Nation," 1992. See http://web.archive.org/web/20100822123802/http://www.ccasa.org/statistics.cfm.

2   It is helpful to remember that people in the U.S. are eight times more likely to be killed by a police officer than a terrorist. "Fear of Terror Makes People Stupid," Washington's Blog, http://www.washingtonsblog.com/2011/06/fear-of-terror-makes-people-stupid.html citing National Safety Council, "The Odds of Dying From . . ." http://web.archive.org/web/20080508135851/http://nsc.org/research/odds.aspx.

3   By conservative estimates, 21% of people in men's prisons are estimated to experience forced sex while imprisoned. Cindy Struckman-Johnson & David Struckman-Johnson (2000). "Sexual Coercion Rates in Seven Midwestern Prisons for Men" (PDF). *The Prison Journal* 80 (4): 379–390.

4   Angela Davis lays out this argument succinctly and effectively in *Are Prisons Obsolete?* Angela Y. Davis, *Are Prisons Obsolete?* (New York: Seven Stories Press, 2003). In 2012, these dynamics were visible when anti-prison activists in Seattle started a campaign to stop the building of a new youth jail that the local government was promoting as a way of resolving long-term complaints about horrible conditions of confinement in the existing youth jail. The anti-prison activists argued that the old jail should be closed, but not replaced. The campaign is ongoing. See, http://nonewyouthjail.wordpress.com.

"Where?"
To Pee or Not to Pee
Tanya Titchkosky

Where Access and Inaccessibility Meet

My workplace is the setting for my analysis; first, let me say a few words about this 'where.' I work in a twelve-storey university building of 350,000 square feet. It is the third-largest building on Canada's largest and arguably most diverse university campus. The building's main entrance is ramped and the building has state-of-the-art elevators with audio indication (although the announcement of the floor number and the opening of the door are not well synchronized). I began to work in this building in July 2006 and discovered that there were no washrooms in my place of work that met either university or provincial minimal disability accessibility standards.

Ironically, some of these inaccessible washrooms were marked with the universal icon of access. One such icon, for example, was on a women's washroom door that opens about sixty-one centimetres, or twenty-four inches. This narrow opening meant that almost anyone trying to enter this washroom would have to nimbly squeeze through the doorway. I was disturbed by the lack of access. In the round of daily life, I talked to many people in this setting about the lack of an accessible washroom and the obviously incorrect signage. I did not set out to make this trouble into a research project and I was not covertly collecting data. I was, however, attempting to live with, understand, and ultimately fix a problem. Simply telling those in authority that the signs were incorrect did not bring the signs down. So, I tried to learn about how and when the access signs were posted as a way to get them taken down – and I attempted to figure out how this might relate to the absence of accessible washrooms and the possibility

of changing that, too. As a newly hired disability studies professor these washroom quandaries became an essential aspect of *where* I was working.

Through the act of drawing attention to these barriers, I was given a plethora of stories regarding why there were no accessible washrooms, as well as stories regarding why such inappropriate access signs were posted. I was struck by the various *stories-at-the-ready* that are part of this workplace environment. Even as accessibility features of one top-floor washroom were improved, there remained a wealth of justifications for why there were no 'wheelchair washrooms' and justifications as to why there were signs that said otherwise. I was incredulous and returned again and again to the scenes of exclusion, thinking perhaps that I was wrong, that maybe my dyslexic ways got the measurements all mixed up. Not being someone who uses a mobility device, I find the confrontation between me and these washrooms a strangely surprising reminder of my dyslexia. Still, this exclusionary environment is where I was finding signs of disability, experiencing its poignant absence, as well as encountering many stories. A professional environmental audit was conducted, confirming inaccessible washrooms throughout the building.

Since collecting the stories found in this chapter, the physical environment has continued to change. First, plans were made for a 'really' accessible washroom. In 2007, OISE built its first standard accessible washroom on the main floor. However, this washroom is located within the library and is available only during regular library hours. In 2009, the second such washroom was built on the fifth floor, a floor that has many classrooms. This washroom is not subject to any time restrictions. At the time of this writing, the main floor public washrooms have also been made accessible. Nonetheless, narratives that justify a lack of access to facilities remain present in my workplace.

The Relation of Where to Whom and to What

Inaccessibility is disquieting. In *Writing the Social,* Dorothy Smith (1999b: 8–9) says of her research that

> . . . I have not started writing on the basis of research data. Rather, I have started with a sense of problem, of something going on, some disquiet, and of something there that could be explicated. [Inquiry] . . . profits from dialogue between what we mean to say and what we discover we have said, and, of course, the work of rewriting to embrace what we find we have said that is beyond or other than our intentions.

The daily experience of inaccessibility represents a 'sense of disquiet' for me from which the work of inquiry can spring. Such inquiry does not necessarily require the generation of traditional forms of social scientific data, but it does require attending to where we find ourselves and how people and places can be said to be as they are.

Thinking about the intersections of social differences in public spaces – even washrooms, whose taken-for-granted status is almost necessary – is essential for gaining an understanding of how everyday embodied experiences are managed by discourses regarding competition for scarce resources, hetero-normative expectations, colonizing powers, and by neo-liberal demands. Here I focus on ordinary stories that attempt to justify 'what is' – stories which manage a sense of disability as something that need not be part of where we find ourselves working. This analysis follows a fundamental assumption of interpretive social inquiry, namely, that how people justify 'what is' is an interpretive social

act. The interpretive act of justification is intimately tied to collective understandings of the meaning of what is, thus defining a ground between people and places and producing a sense of the real – not to mention the 'really important.' Justification is not second order to the fact of exclusion; it is our 'facticity,' it is a 'form of human life,' it is how we *do* exclusion as well as *generate* its everyday sensibility (Gadamer, 1991: 216, 220). This means that justifying what is *governs* imaginative relations to our lives as embodied beings.[1] What is and its justification through narrative are what I call the 'say-able.' It is through engaging the say-able that we can find a way to uncover the meaning we are making of our lives together. The say-able, of course, occurs between people in a social space – in the 'where.'

In some places and at some times, we are required to provide a justification for what is – for what we say this particular 'where' means. I am not interested in trying to determine what 'really' caused people to say what they said. Instead, my interest is in revealing how we perform the meaning of our lives together as we talk about the reasons for the shape of this life. Examining justification as it represents the meaning of where disability is and is not located raises the possibility of making something *new* of the collective from which these say-able things emanate. This is pursuing research with a purpose (Barton et al., 2002, 1997). I turn now to justificatory accessibility talk as where we can encounter a space of questions representing the complicated interpretive nature of our embodiment (Titchkosky, 2007a, 2007b).

The Say-able

Here is an ordinary something that was said: 'You know, I mean, things just weren't built with people with disabilities in mind. That's why there are no accessible washrooms here.' There is nothing necessarily spectacular about this narrative. Even if such a saying was taken to be spectacular, rare, inflammatory, or innocuous, it is nonetheless sensible since it is say-able. Once said, it is a story that remains (Arendt, 1994, 1958; Clough, 2002; King, 2003; McGuire and Michalko, 2011). The apparent and obvious ease of a statement like 'things just weren't built with people with disabilities in mind' is a way to make inaccessibility sensible under contemporary conditions. This ordinary 'truth claim' is a type of say-able thing in relation to disability that I have heard many times, in both rural and urban environments across Canada, and in reference to all sorts of structures. It is a comment so ordinary that survey data collection processes might never solicit it since surveys require respondents to reify ordinary experience.

Noticing and collecting things – especially ordinary things – said in the stream of daily life regarding the justifiable character of exclusion requires a different relation to 'data' than is usual in the social sciences. Narratives such as 'You know, I mean, things just weren't built with people with disabilities in mind' are so routine and common that it would be difficult to attribute them to a particular individual speaker. The mundane efficacy of the merely say-able allows such sayings to slip past individuality. Indeed, speakers of the say-able are perhaps better regarded as a conduit of types of cultural understandings. An understanding that the say-able is where cultural understandings reside is what grounds my methodological decision to return to and address the say-able, shaped as an amalgam of narratives. My data here is an amalgam, or a composite, of people's justifications for why in 2006 there was not a washroom in this large university building that met minimum accessibility requirements.[2]

I have created five stories, five say-able justifications, from a variety of comments encountered through my everyday experiences where I work. All the say-able things I recount in this chapter were said in the presence of others, some of whom sometimes treated these things as wrong or distasteful, but who were not oriented to see them as baffling. In this creative amalgam, sheer *sensibility* is what interests me. Thus, I have grouped or amalgamated fragments of narratives spoken by people to compose stories that represent typical ways of saying that exclusion is justified.

Insofar as everyday language can, following Alfred Schutz (1970: 96–7), be understood as a 'treasure house of ready-made pre-constituted types,' the 'whole history of the linguistic group is mirrored in its way of saying things' and there is no need to individualize these words. From an interpretive sociological perspective, all say-able things are representative of the cultural grounds of possibility from which they emanate; or, as Maurice Merleau-Ponty (1958: 214) says, every 'word is a gesture, and its meaning, a world.' Now that I have provided a justification for my use of taken-for-granted justifications that readily circulate through the rounds of daily life, the question is: What are our say-able things doing in the places where access and exclusion meet? Here are five stories.

Five Stories

1 Some faculty and staff say that they fought hard, some twenty years ago, just to get a ramp for the front door of the building. They suggest that is probably when the signs of universal access were posted everywhere, including on inaccessible washroom doors. Once posted, 'How were we to know any better?'

2 People say that in the distant past, human rights lawyers used to rent space to meet here. It is said that some of these lawyers were wheelchair users. This group began to push for accessible washrooms. They failed and took their meetings elsewhere. Still, the inaccessible washrooms got the universal sign of access posted on them. A lawyer wonders, 'Maybe a cubicle inside the inaccessible washroom got a wider door?'

3 Those responsible for the building say that others keep talking about how students in wheelchairs are going to come to school here, but they never show up. 'Why go through the expense?' As for the signs being posted, 'Isn't something better than

nothing?' Agitated by the suggestion that people are getting stuck attempting to enter these washrooms, someone pointedly reasons, 'If they can't use the washrooms *what are they doing* here anyway?'

4 Administrators, officially responsible for making structural decisions and allocating funds, say that they are working on it. You can't do everything in a day. In fact, maybe we need to just slow down. Thirty years ago, in good faith, the signs were put up and it is possible that, within a decade, we might be moving to a new building. 'Remember,' they say, 'we did secure the special fund to build a fully equipped accessible showcase classroom. Maybe some of that fund could be used to build a washroom?'

5 All sorts of people are perplexed to find out about the inaccessibility and that those in authority do not seem to take it as a crisis that we are working in a building that does not have a washroom that meets minimum accessibility standards. This perplexity, verging on incredulity, conditions what it means to work in this building. 'My Department requested that those in charge at least take down the misleading signs. But the signs are still there. What should we do?'

Examining locally produced, everyday narratives which justify the exclusion of disabled people requires the social theorist to act, as Hélène Cixous (Cixous and Derrida, 2001: 6) advises, like 'a little nail stuck in the gap' *between* the various things that are say-able about disability. Feminist disability studies scholar, Rosemarie Garland-Thomson (1997:10–12), has also emphasized the gap – one productive for critical inquiry – between how disability is represented and the lived actuality of disability. Our lives with disability are certainly informed by the representations they receive, but they always already exceed any representational confine. Sara Ahmed (2006: 161) speaks of a gap, too: a gap requiring a mixed orientation able to proceed obliquely between 'reception and possession.' Proceeding from the gap between received stories of

justified exclusion and the possession of disquiet, inquiry can be a little nail in this gap, exploring its meaning. The gap of interest here lies between the everyday reception of ways of saying that disabled people are justifiably excluded from university environments, and the conflicting versions of 'normal bodies' that we come to possess in these encounters.

Let us now proceed as a little nail stuck in the gap between the stories we have just received and discern what kind of sense they represent.

Making Exclusion Reasonable

In the round of everyday life, and in places where people come to notice that there are barriers preventing the participation of some, comments about such exclusions erupt. 'Justification' is one dominant type of comment. People say, *because* of the past, *because* of the passage of time, *because* of ten, twenty, thirty years, *because* it won't make a difference, *because* we don't know what to do . . . the washrooms remain inaccessible. Or . . . *in order to* fight for ramps, *in order to* balance costs and benefits, *in order to* take care of who belongs, or *in order to* make plans for the future while living with a harsh paradox of the inaccessible labelled accessible . . . the washrooms remain as what is – inaccessible. Some reasons are not agreeable, some unjust. Still, this situation of inaccessibility is say-able in the language of causality, that is, the taken-for-granted logic of 'if A, then B' obtained in every narrative fragment. This language paints the radical lack of access in an ordinary hue, which glosses the issue of human rights, questions of belonging, and other consequences that accompany the power to exclude. Moreover, justifying *what is* can hold at bay considerations of *what is not* and all this participates in constituting a sense of where we find ourselves.

Even if people oppose the offered reasons, it remains an unexamined 'fact' of social life that it is reasonable to seek a reason for the lack of access. Giving reasons is a possible, even expected, response, and no one seems surprised by this social practice. Whether or not the reasons for lack of access are judged good or bad, the social activity of people seeking reasons fosters the sensibility that lack of access is reasonable. Thus, lack of access is a space for and of reason. We could adopt a more social scientific approach and take an interest in what caused people to give this or that reason; or investigate the veracity of the claims behind the reason given; or even measure the prevalence of this or that reason. But such an approach does not address the social 'fact' that these washrooms and signs bar some people from participating and, so, narrations of this 'fact' are doing the job of maintaining the status quo. Recall Thomas King (2003:2), 'The truth about stories is that that's all we are.' These stories reflect established relations between people and social space. 'Justification giving' is one thing shared between these stories. The question now is: what sort of reality, or definition of the situation (McHugh, 1968), is being produced from such reasoning?

A sensible explanation functions to make the on-going exclusion of disabled people appear more or less ordinary. Such explanations enter the context of exclusion, making it seem part of a rational project. Reasoning such as 'because of our past and in order to move in to the future' is a way to achieve the ordinary sense of what is and is not going on. *Giving* reasons achieves the ordinariness of inaccessibility; all such reasoning relies upon and sustains the common-sense understanding of *disability as excludable*. Just as radical inaccessibility is not unique to this particular university building, or to any building anywhere for that matter, everyday uses of 'because-of and in-order-to motives' are also not unique to this setting (Schutz, 1970). The provision of reasonable motives flavours *any* social situation with sensibility. This means that the *particular* meaning achieved by these justification narratives remains a poignant question worthy of consideration if we are to re-think where we find ourselves. What, then, has been made sensible?

Including Disability as a Justifiably-Excludable-Type

The giving of reasons achieves the inaccessible washroom situation as sensible through a tacit reliance on 'including disability as an excludable type' (Titchkosky, 2003b: 518). The building is missing accessible washrooms and yet it is not; the building is not missing disabled people and yet it is. The building's missing washroom is made sensible through the seemingly justifiable conception of disability as excludable. Disability is included as justifiably absent, and when it is present it appears in the form of an unimagined or unwanted question, that is, 'What are they doing here anyway?' In such a situation, 'accessibility' becomes a space for reasoning how the appearance of missing disabled people can be accounted for as a reasonable exclusion.

The inclusion of disability as a justifiably-excludable-type is one way disability *is* represented in everyday life. This poignant paradox is not unique to my workplace. The phrase 'oh, she's gone on disability' attests to the structured ubiquity of the inclusion of disability as an excludable type. I am not arguing against disability insurance. Rather, I am arguing for a consideration of ordinary talk as a constitutive power making up the meaning of people. The power of this form of inaccessibility is demonstrated by the absence of disabled people in my place of work.[3]

Some ways of making disability present as reasonably excluded require an understanding of people living with disability as a justified absence. The conception of disability as a justified absence *acts as a barrier* to inclusion for some disabled people – a barrier that is not necessarily recognized as such. Unless the relation between environment and its participants is theorized and thereby disturbed, disability will continue to be included as an excludable type even as the physical environment changes. The discursive act of making something 'justifiably absent' ultimately has much to do with how we delimit the shape of possible worlds – or, in Judith Butler's (2009: 2) terms, justifying absence performs, and makes present, what counts as 'viable and non-viable' lives. This means that any conception of 'where,' such as the social and physical environment, needs to be understood in relation to things possible to say about it.

Acting like a little nail in the gap between the multiple stories of justifiable exclusion entails a restless reflexive engagement with these ordinary ways of living with the paradox of disability as an excludable type. I return to the justification narratives with the aim of finding some difference in the same (Bhabha, 1994); to live otherwise than ordinary (van Manen, 1990); and to offer an alternative relation to the alterity (Cixous and Derrida, 2001) in the discursive space that disability represents. The question now is: 'How does included-as-excludable appear as a sensible and justifiable understanding of the lives of disabled people?'

Extra-Ordinary Exclusion

The narratives display different ways to do justification while constituting a sense of place as well as governing relations between place and people. Through utilitarian cost-benefit rationality, through bureaucratic sequencing of tasks, through partial fights and unmade decisions – through these ways and many more like them, justification is accomplished. While the end results might be common to these narratives, the justificatory processes depicted in them are not. The third narrative, the one that suggests that disabled people are neither desirable participants nor imbued with rights, seems different; it is the most obviously egregious of the stories and sticks out as most in need of interrogation. Yet I am uneasy with focusing on where it seems most obvious to do so. I now proceed with this disquieting 'preliminary, inarticulate understanding,' as Hannah Arendt (1994: 310) calls it, of an obvious offense, as well as a need to seek the non-obvious in the obvious.

Again, the third story:

Those responsible for the building say that professors keep talking about how students in wheelchairs are going to come to school here, but they never show up. 'Why go through the expense?' As for the signs being posted, 'Isn't something better than nothing?' Agitated by the suggestion that people are getting stuck attempting to enter these washrooms, someone pointedly reasons, 'If they can't use the washrooms *what are they doing* here anyway?'

In this story resides 'a treasure house of ready-made types' (Schutz, 1970: 96–7) – there are those who belong; those who do not; and those who can explain the situation of belonging to and for all. Professors are characterized as unrealistic, but are still oriented to as a type who belongs in the workplace. On the condition that they are not wheelchair users, or that they can use inaccessible washrooms, professors, like students, are part of this story since they are 'obviously' part of the university setting – they are depicted as belonging where they are. Professors who hold the expectation that disabled people belong in the setting, in contrast, are dealt with by raising the idea of false expectations. Wheelchair users are depicted as 'never showing up,' as an 'expense.' When they do show up, they are also depicted as a questionable type, that is, 'what are they doing here anyway?' 'They' are a type who does not belong and so can never really be present, but if present, 'they' are only questionably so, a 'maybe participant,' since 'something is better than nothing,' because nothing is the only alternative on offer. As partial participants, disabled students are typified as visitors who have overstayed their welcome, rather than as desired or necessary members.

Interestingly, story number three does not claim that it is unrealistic to have an interest in accessible washrooms in public buildings. The inaccessible washrooms are not the targets of this justification. Instead, the targets are disabled students; it is disabled students whose absence is justified and whose presence is made questionable. Notice also that disabled professors or staff members remain unimagined types. 'Students with disabilities' are taken as the type who do not belong and as never really present anyway. The type that does not belong, the disabled type, is far removed from the imagined possibility of belonging to any of the other 'ready-made types' common to this workplace, such as professor or staff member (Michalko, 1999: 41ff). All this combines to give a sense of where 'we' are, as well as how we are to be there – whatever else 'place' is, it needs to be understood as a governing power.

The third story suggests that professors have an unrealistic interest in disability since it is rare, transitory, not present, expensive, and only found in students of whom it is not clear 'what they are doing here anyway.' This story participates in rearticulating an extraordinarily common belief that disability is not only rare but is also nothing other than limit and lack, unexpected and undesirable, or simply 'trouble' (Abberley, 1998; Hughes, 2007: 673). This narrative, then, represents an extreme example of including disability as an excludable type where exclusion is *made* normal because disability is *made* not-normal. Disability is not normal, not imagined, not needed, not common, not necessary, and not going to come to mind as the type for whom buildings are built or services provided. Disability is not, as the saying goes, 'where it's at.'

Arguing against the inclusion of a type by invoking the type itself is a straightforward act of discrimination. The open discrimination of story three makes it stick out, but is there not some connection between this obvious discrimination and the other stories' more ordinary use of histories of the environment to narrate justifiable exclusion? What possibilities arise if we treat story three not as aberrant prejudice (a bad apple), but instead as the heart of the consciousness of embodiment in this setting?[4] Recall, as well, that the third story is composed of narrative fragments spoken among people who did not respond as if they were confused. If people are always a 'consciousness among consciousness' (Merleau-Ponty, 1958: xiv), then this suggests

the necessity of treating what is said in relation to other say-able things, and not treating what is said as a symptom of a bad apple or some other individualized state of affairs. By resisting individualization of the say-able, the interrogation of the wider cultural grounds of embodiment can continue. Let us continue, then, to explore the contradictory sensibility of these say-able things about disability as this constitutes a sense of 'where.'

Notes

1 For further consideration of the governance of embodiment/ disability and imagination, see, for example, Ahmed, 2006; Bhabha, 1994; Butler, 1997; Diprose, 2005; Frazee, 2005; Foucault, 1988; Goodley, 2010, 2007; Lindgren, 2004; Michalko, 2002; Parekh, 2006; Shildrick and Price, 1996; Stiker, 1999; Thomas, 2004; Tremain, 2005 [not referenced in this book—please seek original article for further information].

2 An amalgam of narratives is related to Peter Clough's (2002: 8) suggestion that bringing together various narrative fragments that arise in a given locale is a method that protects the anonymity of the speakers while allowing the theorist to 'speak to the heart of consciousness.' Acknowledging Canadian tri-council ethical concerns, my narratives harm no one since no individual is represented and the narratives stem from my daily round of life where no collection of narratives was embarked on (see van den Hoonaard, 2000; Canadian Institutes of Health Research, 2005; Gubrium and Holstein, 2002). What are represented in these narratives are things that are say-able and treated by all involved as sensible (, 2003; Gadamer, 1996, 1991; Sacks, 1984; Scott, 1998, 1995; Smith, 1999b, 1990; van Manen, 1990).

3 For empirical documentation regarding exclusion, consider the Canadian government's own representations of it (HRDC, 2006; Canada, 2004; or Prince, 2009; McColl and

Jongbloed, 2005), which shows the combined unemployment, underemployment, and non-labour force participation rate for 'persons with disabilities' to be around 80 per cent. The United Nations (2003–04) has characterized the fate of disabled people around the globe as a 'silent crisis.' For the severity of the exclusion and marginalization of disabled people, please consult Barnes, 1998; Charlton, 2003; Dossa, 2009; Erevelles, 2000; Jones, 1994; Oliver, 1996, 1990; Rioux, 2002.

4   Mairtin Mac an Ghaill (2000: 314) says that '[a]n idealist analysis of the curriculum that reduces the heterosexist structuring of schooling to aberrant teacher prejudice is insufficient to explain the complex social interaction of white male and female teachers with black male students in racialized, male dominated institutions.' I follow through on this understanding as it connects with other physical and ideological educational structures. In this way, I avoid the need to say that really it is strong or weak curriculum, or really it is good or bad physical structures that lead to the radical devaluation of disability in the Canadian educational milieu. Instead, having been made by culture, disability – in relation to textbooks *or* washrooms – is a good place to examine culture.

Death By Masculinity

Ali Abbas

In 2007, I was expected to attend an LGBT leadership conference in order to maintain a scholarship that helped to pay for my undergraduate degree. I was anxious to meet other scholars and activists who had been selected based on their concern for social justice. While sitting down with a fellow attendee, I became engaged in a conversation about current projects we were pursuing. The conversation started out light but soon turned serious when the focus shifted to the Middle East. As a self-identified Arab, I quickly found myself the target of interrogation and criticism. At one point, I was asked how I could still be proud of my heritage and simultaneously "identify with the politics of the LGBTQ community." According to the other scholar, "the Muslim world just isn't ready for it." I was not just offended at his obviously loaded and prejudiced comments, but I felt pressured to fit either the stereotype or the demand: I could be an Arab or an advocate of the LGBTQ community, but never both.

"You really are playing into your culture. Think of the possibilities of reform!"

Because this individual asked me where I got off still "playing into" my culture, he assumed that somehow his upbringing as a white middle-class US American (as opposed to those Americans who are immigrants, non-US citizens, or otherwise choose not to identify with the US) was the norm. This gung-ho attitude resonates with the masculinist attitudes ubiquitous in gay spaces, where men who are "nelly" are routinely denigrated, and paranoid fantasies about feminine men trying to "take over the community" are commonplace. Of course, this is a community that drag performers, butch dykes, and men who patronized dark, damp bars in basements fought for after they were ostracized by employers, friends, family, and society—a battle that was later appropriated by upstanding white men who came out years after they made their money. The argument voiced by the man at the conference had a no-less-hateful intention than the all-too-common hatred directed at queeny men. Just as traditional gay masculine men must protect their (stolen) personal property—bars, gyms, gayborhoods, etc.—from repulsive feminine invaders, a new generation of *liberal* gay masculine men must defend their cultural property, the LGBTQ (most often just G and sometimes L) community.

Those on the top will claim that identity is dead only insofar as this releases them from any responsibility for their words or actions. All over the internet, gay personals websites valorize "straight acting" as a universal value that is both desirable and positive, linking it to a set of norms that eerily imitate moral code in religious law (thou shalt be butch). In bar scenes, men stand in lock-step formation, patrolling the behavior of those who stray outside the borders of masculine performance, imposing fear of social deportation. Likewise, the largest LGB organizations prioritize the privileges and choices long upheld by patriarchal US American society, like the right to receive benefits through marriage or the right to kill under order of government.

"Straight-acting" does not only prioritize a certain gender presentation, but also inherently assumes whiteness and ableness of body (people of color or anyone using a wheelchair need not apply). Personal profiles use the words "masculine" and "feminine" as a way to marginalize, though the authors claim that they are simply helping out the browsers to narrow search results. By claiming that "Hey, it's just what I prefer, dude," the writers fail to realize that, in a community formed by and built upon identification with the body and its practices, the simplest marginalization becomes a vehicle for exclusion and opens new channels for bashing. Not only should a gay man prefer someone masculine (one who avoids "playing into" other value systems), but also someone clearly US American. Supposedly, by laying claim to the pride of stars and stripes, one can overlook years of US segregation, oppression, and imperialism of the body, in favor of something more fitting—like a shiny new BMW in which to cruise ethnically-cleansed parks.

"Not that I think they're backwards or anything, I just wish the gays of the Middle East could learn from the gays of America."

Why? So publications purporting to be LG (again, sometimes B, less often T, almost never Q) can advertise expensive watches and handbags while discussing privileged politics in articles positioned next to images of young fit white men? The "Dude, I just don't do femme" hypocrisy of gay men (last time I checked the lexicon, sex with men was society's ultimate act of femininity) is echoed in these claims of intercultural "dialogue." It is as though the "I just" or "but" placed in compound sentences somehow relieves the speaker of any accountability for racism, misogyny, femme-phobia, or hate.

Somehow, the existence of gay bars in urban and usually expensive geographies becomes proof of social equality. Yet how secure can a space be if it will inevitably be out-gentrified by rich straight white couples? Only then does migration to new under-privileged areas become trendy, and the cycle begins again. I am terrified at the thought that social justice can be measured by the size of a bar or the make of a car. Even with the protection of "historical landmark" status for gay bars and dives, there is no guarantee that individuals in the LGBTQ community will ever find their own sanctuary in a relationship between body and society.

Why are gay bars so crucial to LGBTQ politics in other countries? Why is the amount of repetitive dance music produced and distributed in bars dominated by men the marker of queer activism?

On the basis of my upbringing in the Middle East and from what I've observed during recent trips back, I can assure those afraid of not having a welcome vacation spot that bars with a multitude of same-sex interactions are alive and kicking. Yet I unapologetically declare that they are not a mirror of the bars in major US cities. If a community strives for autonomy and individuality, then why is it so important that every space emerge as identical? Why is it so hard to believe that queerness can exist outside the model we have come to know in the United States? Perhaps it could be that liberal gay masculine men, as often as they pretend to be strong in singularity, depend upon the masses. No one would buy into the hype of mass gay consumerism if they were sure that alternative modes for living and creating culture existed and were easily accessible without shelling out the cash.

"I just feel bad for them, you know? They live in these conditions where they cannot even speak out without fear of death. If their relatives believe so strongly in suicide bombings and honor killings, they can't help but fuck things up for the gays."

It is inevitable that with the performance of masculinity comes a strict belief in nationalism. How can one imitate the white, US American, able-bodied, middle-class, masculine lifestyle without including extreme and often violent patriotism? With the rise of anti-Arab/anti-Muslim (anti-brown) sentiment outside the gay community, it was only a matter of time before gay men and their allies aligned themselves with the politics and hateful policies of the normative public. Rather than fight to uphold human rights and dignity, LGBTQ politics remain narrowly focused on civil rights and privileges linked to citizenship (e.g. gay marriage). Liberal masculine gay men assume that gay marriage is a sign of equality because it allows for (limited) mobility in a system that distributes health and tax benefits based on the state-recognized relationship between two people. Everyone, both citizen and "alien," contributes labor into this system, yet there is no room within it for the undocumented, or anyone who poses a threat to "national security."

Liberal masculine gay men wholly support the US American marriage complex and the "right to serve" in the military, a right that currently leads to the murder of millions of people of color and the illegal detainment of many more. Political gay bloggers valorize their "out" lives in rich urban neighborhoods, while speaking of the threat of radical gay-bashing Islamo-Fascists. They claim that anyone who has been following the headlines should realize that men and women of color who happen to hold citizenship in developing nations are out to blow themselves up in order to target Americans, and in this attack they might take out rich gay urban men! These men are obsessed with the word "terrorism" (politically far-removed from poverty, war, occupation, and sickness—leading causes of death, but not connected to marriage and the right to serve) and safeguarding of American traditions. Ironically, I see that masculine gay men have very much in common with the bodies they name as threats to their freedom. Perhaps the racist, essentialist, and Orientalist remarks about "Middle Eastern" culture aren't personal fabrications but a projection of the current climate in the US American LGBTQ community.

"You're just being an apologist [for Arabs]. You really need to be honest with yourself."

The word "apologist" surfaces quite often in these heated conversations. In the classroom, it is used against those who challenge misguided statistics with real-world narratives. In the social scene, it is used to silence those who might speak out. It is a an accusation that forces one to "be grateful that you just live here, many people would die to have the opportunities you have."

How ironic that an LGBTQ movement should focus its liberation on equality and freedom by comparison. As long as there is someone out there living in much less desirable conditions, then somehow our oppression is more tolerable; I personally see no correlation between the two. Yet the white gays and lesbians who reside at the top of the privilege food chain identify their current surroundings and experiences as universal goals that everyone else just fails to realize.

The growing trend of "tolerance" demands that leaders direct funds into the legalization of gay marriage, which could otherwise be used to fight hunger and homelessness; the benefits of gay marriage, like tax breaks and healthcare, only benefit a particular minority of LG people who hold a majority of power. Why fight for the ability to receive health benefits through a state recognized partnership when we should be pressuring the state to pay for everyone's healthcare? Who benefits most from partnership tax cuts and will that bring an end to financial inequality? These are the questions that are never raised when the subject of gay marriage is discussed. It makes me wonder: who exactly is the apologist?

"Some cultures just have a problem with the way they treat their women."

Perhaps the women of "some cultures" should be liberated so that they may become excellent producers and consumers like their US American sisters. Why should women have the freedom to choose a *hijab* or language preference in school when proper French and English educations would dictate otherwise? It seems that liberal masculine gay men, who ordinarily take no interest in the well-being of women, have no problem using women (as inherently feminine victims of circumstance) to demonize others. This dichotomy of us/them and right/wrong somehow always positions the liberal and masculine as the civil, the hero, and the master, while everyone else is tolerable at best.

The same gay men support overcharging women at gay bars (if they let them in at all), and the removal of locks on women's bathroom doors. These men not only target feminine gay men, but any female body, in their war to gender-cleanse the bars. Women are able to access these bars, but only as specifically indicated guests who will accessorize the male body. The very same gay men will justify their actions by claiming that women, both straight and queer, should patronize their own bars or that the traditional resentment towards women in gay bars is a reaction to the homophobia of straight bars. Both excuses are simply ways of justifying a subculture that continues to mistreat women. By pretending that "some cultures" ultimately have a problem with the way they treat women, rather than all cultures (including gay culture), gay men, riding high on the homo-nationalist bandwagon, can sleep soundly.

"Why don't they just come out of the closet?"

This question arose after my biography and interests were carefully examined by a group of fellow scholars. It is the essence of the problem. How can gay white men who wear designer suits to work and drink designer cocktails at night sleep knowing that my consciousness may not be completely focused on granting them approval? How can anyone be a legitimate LGBTQ activist while defending cultures that the media portrays as anti-queer? Masculinity (often resulting in hyper-patriotism) requires our undivided attention. Because liberal masculine gay men claim to be the crusaders of the LGBTQ community, they can decide who is and who isn't acceptable—not only in body, but in action.

It is inconceivable to US American gays that there are men and women in the world who engage in same-sex sexual practices yet don't identify as L, G, B, T, or Q. Yet there are infinite ways that relationships exist everywhere. All these relationships come fully assembled with as much joy, sadness, anger, love, and violence as traditional US monogamous relationships (gay or otherwise).

I have to wonder what our masculine liberators intend to do with the people of the Middle East de-rooted from their "savage ways." Will they be free to assimilate into US American LGBTQ culture and take a backseat in bars like their counterparts of color? Will they be free to serve the masculine power structure that claims to "know what's best"? I sense that as long as they wear the nicest clothing, patronize the trendiest bars, and keep their mouths shut about the injustices their newly paid taxes commit, they are more than welcome to join the LGBTQ community in the United States.

Part Two

Part Two

Chapter Four

Bodies

Imagine this scenario: It's the weekend, and you're getting ready to go party with a group of friends. You're looking forward to getting away for a few hours and not obsessing about your schoolwork. You start thinking about how partying plays such a huge role in so many students' lives. It's time away from studying, sure. But it's also a kind of event that stirs up anticipation that is so energizing. Whether on campus, at a nightclub, or at someone's house, partying is explicitly about bodily pleasures: dancing, drinking and eating, displaying and expressing desire (and watching others do the same, of course), flirting and sexual suspense, feeling the music pulse, letting go and losing control for a while; it's all part of the intense gratification of partying that you want to experience.

But you start wondering more about this idea of bodily pleasures and possibilities, as you reflect on whom you do (and don't) expect to see tonight. How do different groups of people display their bodies? Whose bodies are watched and flirted with and by whom? And whose bodies just aren't welcome? You recognize that even if these events are about letting go, they are also a space where only some people can (are allowed to?) let go. Others have to be more cautious: women who leave their drinks unattended or who get drunk; gay men and lesbians who flirt and display their sexuality openly; fat people who dress in tight, sexy clothes and love dancing; or racialized minorities who show up in groups in predominantly white spaces. These bodies are not read in the same ways as those who fit certain expectations; their presence too often results in suspicion, harassment, or even violence. Clearly, you start to recognize, different bodies have different senses of possibility in party spaces.

But as you think about where you want to go tonight—maybe a club off campus— you start wondering about how this problem might be about more than simply how people control, or don't control, their bodies. How, for instance, do places themselves regulate the bodies that are there? Is there a high cover charge just to get in? Is there a single genre of music played or a single language spoken, welcoming some groups and not others? Does the majority of the crowd have a connection to a specific institution, workplace, or neighborhood? Is the crowd marked by specific gender, racial, or sexual identities? Could this space, for instance, accommodate—in every sense of this word—the bodies and pleasures of older people, of people with mobility issues, or of people who display their religious devotions by what they wear? Who blends in, and who is (and is made to feel) out of place and with what consequences? In short, you recognize, some bodies and pleasures are acknowledged and some are clearly ignored in locations that purport to be open to all. This raises complex questions!

Bodies and Identities

In Women's and Gender Studies, bodies are central to thinking about identities, social structures and institutions, systems of representation, and everyday practices. Bodies of all kinds—gendered, racialized, national, classed, immigrant, disabled, aged, fat (among others)—are consistently judged, scrutinized, surveilled, controlled, and patrolled from any number of angles. But they are also the medium through which we encounter the world and live out our very different lives. Our bodies are defined in innumerable and often contradictory ways, both by others around us and by ourselves. And most of us have ambivalent relationships to our bodies and the multiple meanings attached to them.

One of the predominant assumptions made about bodies is that they reflect the "truth" of the people who inhabit them—their individual personality, characteristics, morality, intellectual worth, capabilities—in addition to their membership in broader identity categories, such as gender, race, or disability. This assumption suggests that one can know who a person is by "reading" what is visible on their body as if it were a kind of "text." In that sense, we tend to think about bodies as always reflecting the truth about people's identities in unproblematic and easy-to-discern ways. But how do bodies speak, or how are they read, sometimes in spite of our conscious intentions to have them say something about ourselves? Finally, what are the consequences when what the body is speaking and what others read from it don't align?

Perhaps one of the most obvious (and high-stakes) examples of this kind of speaking-body assumption is that a person's sex and gender can be "read" off their body as they move through the world. This assumption leads many people to think that men and boys exhibit and can be defined by one range of appearances and behaviors, while women and girls exhibit and are therefore defined by another, and that both their biological sex and gender identity (how they identify their own gender) are obvious by way of their bodies' expressions. Of course, for many of us, the gender attribution made of us—that is, the gender we are presumed to be based on those external bodily expressions—doesn't necessarily line up with our gender identity; and as we discussed in the "Identities" chapter, neither necessarily aligns with our biological sex. In other words, how people identify themselves isn't always the same as how other people understand and read their bodies, and their biological sex may not necessarily line up with what that reading might assume either. The pervasiveness of these beliefs, then, tells us a lot more about how prevalent ideas of gender (and sex) dichotomy are in the world around us than it does about the truth of people's identities.

Think, for instance, of how unreliable these beliefs can be and the fraught and damaging consequences they can lead to. In almost any circumstance, the bodies of people who identify as transgender or genderqueer, or even, sometimes, butch women and effeminate men, can be read in ways that might be counter to their own gender identity—with the all-too-frequent result that they are thought to be "lying" about their identity or "passing" as something they are not[1]. And consider how much more fraught and indeed potentially dangerous this assumption is in scenarios of heightened surveillance: airport X-ray scans or emergency rooms in hospitals. But it is not only people outside of that dichotomy who worry about and attempt to control how their bodies are read. People who identify themselves clearly on one side or the other of that sex and gender dichotomy also desire to control how their body is read by others, in order to ensure that they are not misread and that people address them in ways with which they identify. Looking at the various ways one can be a man or a woman, recognizing that not everyone who appears as masculine or feminine identifies as a man or a women, and acknowledging that not all gender expressions or identities align neatly with biological sex, should, then, lead us to question larger social investments in these binary notions of sex and gender.

Bodies that are read as ambiguous, though—as not fitting this binary system—are not simply benignly interpreted as different. They too often become targets of

[1]**KNOW ABOUT:** *Passing* is a term that has been used to talk about people whose bodies are interpreted as speaking an identity with which they may not themselves identify. Used most often to talk about race—that is, for black people who have been (or have been able to be) read as white—the term has also extended to talking about gender, and to people who pass as the gender they identify as, rather than the gender they were assigned. Note here, of course, how much the language of passing depends on the idea that there really is a "true" identity, but that the body can be convincingly led to "lie" about that identity. And the use of the word *lie* here is important; the history of both racial and gender passing being "found out" is one that has most often led to violence, imprisonment, or even death.

increased surveillance, high levels of violence (especially in public spaces), and even medical, legal, and other institutional attempts to regulate and control them. What might begin with being called a sissy or a tomboy on the playground, then, can turn into incidences of bashing and physical assault, legal interventions (e.g., being stopped for being in the "wrong" washroom, being delayed at airports, being denied medical treatment, or even being institutionalized), and unwanted medical and psychological attempts at gender "corrections."[2] These interventions into the lives of people who don't, or don't want to, conform to a gender binary demonstrate how much gender nonconformity is so often viewed as threatening to any number of social institutions, as well as to people who have much invested in maintaining this alignment. The effective message of the binary system of sex and gender, and the belief that this must be clearly and truthfully imprinted on bodies, is that anyone who does not fit neatly into predetermined categories is both at risk and a risk—a response that both "blames the victim" and perpetuates the belief that sex and gender are individual characteristics and not simultaneously built into the world around us. In other words, people see ambiguous bodies as "wrong," but don't consider the various ways in which that "wrong" is culturally produced and perpetuated.

This discomfort with bodily ambiguity doesn't apply only to gender. Think, for instance, of the way in which one's racial or ethnic identity is also so often presumed to be obvious on the body. The statement that someone "doesn't look" Jewish or Native American or Mexican demonstrates the popular assumption that a particular bodily appearance—stereotypically, a nose shape or hair texture or skin color—must reveal a particular racial and ethnic identity. Likewise, the (always rude) question "What are you?" (or the purportedly more polite, "Where are you from?") implies that someone's perceived racial or ethnic identity, especially if that seems ambiguous, is something about which others have the right to know. And again, these assumptions are far from benign in the national histories of both Canada and the United States. Historically, assumptions about intelligence, morality, and criminality—and the belief that bodies revealed these truths about people—have been part of the justifications for colonialism, slavery, and segregation laws and practices in both countries.

The production of racial and ethnic identity categories and their use in justifying various forms of exclusion and violence demonstrate all too well that reading race off

[2]**KNOW ABOUT:**
Conversion therapy is a term that describes various types of attempts to "correct" people's gender expressions and sexuality identities by changing their behaviors and thus also, it is believed, their desires. While today mostly practiced by some fundamentalist religious groups in Canada and the U.S., the idea of correcting gender was until recently the aim of much psychological intervention and backed by large associations such as the American Psychological Association and the American Psychiatric Association. Recently some states and provinces have outlawed attempts to change or correct gender, in children especially.

bodies is still central to our perceptions of who people are. Contemporary versions of this form of reading bodies for truths about identity are evident in practices such as "racial profiling," or, more colloquially, captured in phrases such as "driving while black" or "flying while Muslim." This passing of judgement on bodies, based solely on assumptions about bodies speaking a truth about identity, makes clear that some bodies are accorded status as belonging in a variety of everyday contexts, while others are defined as out of place, suspicious, and threatening[3]. The belief that the bodies of these "others" speak different truths is then used to justify a variety of regulations and mechanisms of control about who belongs and who is to be kept out, in contexts that range from the corner store to the nation.

While there is a long history to this idea that bodies speak truths about people, what was thought to be known about those bodies has changed throughout history. In the mid-nineteenth century, for example, "sciences" such as phrenology and physiognomy attempted to identify criminals or people with lower intellectual capacity by noting some kind of bodily difference about them—e.g., bumps on the head, the slope of the forehead, the space between the eyes, or the curve of the nose. And, perhaps not accidentally, people whose foreheads and eyes and noses seemed "too big" or "too wide"—thus signalling their "nature" as less intelligent or more criminal or too "primitive"—were not coincidentally people colonized by the cultures out of which such sciences emerged. Of course, what those scientists rarely questioned was how the normative standard of comparison usually reflected (their own) white, male, able, and urban bodies. Instead, the scientific "discovery" of people's criminality or intellectual incapacity was read as proof of just how different some people were from those doing the measuring of these differences, a conclusion that of course simply reinforced existing social relations and the hierarchical organization of bodies in colonial contexts[4].

As the range of examples mentioned thus far—sexed and gendered bodies, racialized bodies, nationalized bodies, religious bodies—makes clear, reading the body as a reflection of the truth of a person's identity is a fairly commonplace method for organizing dominant ideas about (and knowledge of) people in any society, even as it reflects a series of problematic assumptions. And the dominant (albeit usually unconscious) belief in this equation means that there is both a constant pressure to ensure

[3]**TALK ABOUT:** Generate a list of examples—in the news or in pop culture representations—where this idea of bodies "out of place" seems to be at work. What are the ways in which these examples have been talked about—and by whom? What are debates around them? How have various groups responded to these examples and what they say about particular bodies, and thus groups of people? For instance, one recent example is the increased focus on the death of so many black people at the hands of the police and the #BlackLivesMatter response.

[4]**TALK ABOUT:** Think back to the idea of "othering" first explored in the "Knowledges" chapter. What are some consequences of othering in people's lives? How is othering also reflected in social structures and practices around us? Besides bodily appearances, can

that bodies speak desired truths as well as a constant attempt to challenge the truths produced about bodies.

Discipline and Agency

Now let's think about what happens to different bodies in certain spaces. For example, think of the spaces where your classes are held. As you walk into your classroom, a fairly typical arrangement probably greets you: chairs and tables or possibly a large lecture hall with fixed seating facing the front of the room. There is no doubt a board of some kind at the front too, some digital technology (a computer, screen, and projector), maybe a table and podium, and signs that say "no eating or drinking" or that display the phone number of the university security services. Lighting on the ceiling projects a uniform brightness and is controlled by several switches situated at the front of the room on the wall, about four feet up from the floor. It's an apparently neutral and unassuming (if not very comfortable) space used to organize learning and teaching, similar to thousands of other colleges and universities.

And yet, as many of us know from experience, the classroom is anything but a neutral space. Instead, the organization of classrooms reflects particular expectations of everyone who enters them: about how we should learn and teach, about how we are to behave, and about how to comport ourselves during a given period of time. In other words, these neutral and unassuming spaces actually reflect taken-for-granted ideas about how to sit—and that sitting is the way to learn, about where to focus attention, and about where authority and safety are located inside and outside of the classroom. When we walk into a classroom like this, then, and take "our place" in it, our bodies are being regulated simply by doing what they are expected to do in that space; even more, we are self-regulating, in that we don't even stop to question what to do, knowing what is expected of us and simply then doing that, thus perpetuating those ideas about teaching and learning. However, to say this is not to say that any of us is being forced to do something "against our will." Rather, the example of the classroom simply recognizes that the spaces we all occupy, and the social institutions and structures we are a part of, organize our experiences in ways of which we are hardly aware. We know how to behave in these spaces, and, importantly, we

you think of other ways in which othering takes place today—and about and around whom? For instance, what kinds of assumptions does the above expression "flying while Muslim" both depend on and help perpetuate?

monitor ourselves to meet social expectations associated with the spaces we encounter. As such, we internalize their demands, usually without requiring anyone to tell us to behave in a particular way (at least after the first grade). We are, in other words, "disciplined" by that social institution into practices of self-surveillance, regulating our own bodies, and thinking about our relationship to particular social structures and institutions.

What this example demonstrates, then, is the central role that bodies play in perpetuating power relations. Rather than working through some external threat of punishment, it is the more subtle mechanisms within the space itself that encourage us to control our own bodies and adapt them to the demands of that space. As such, we become aware that any situation produces a (limited) range of possible actions and helps us identify why those actions, and not others, are followed. For instance, in the classroom, we generally get something out of meeting the demands of the space: satisfaction, pleasure, knowledge, sense of self, belonging, to say nothing of material benefits, such as passing grades and paychecks. These responses are "productive"—both for us and for the institutions that sanction such spaces—since our bodies behaving in particular ways are the product (the output) that in turn justifies the existence of such spaces (consider what would colleges and universities be if they didn't produce graduates). But, of course, these same spaces produce other responses at the same time: boredom, frustration, alienation, and resistance. These responses speak to ways that we don't always fit—or don't fit completely—that institution's demands; they are responses that resist the demands of that space even as they are produced by it.

For example, as a student, you may sit quietly, looking intently at your professors while they are lecturing. But you may also be daydreaming, doodling, or dismissing out of hand what is being said in class. Recognizing this gap between what is expected by the space and how we fit into it shifts our focus to thinking about institutional spaces like classrooms as something we co-create through relations of power that circulate in that room; our various positions here (professor, student), as well as the space itself, contribute to those power relations. To say this, however, is not to say that everyone exercises the same power in that institution—indeed, quite the opposite. There are clearly repercussions for not fitting oneself into institutions in the ways deemed most appropriate for different bodies. Institutions reflect particular (often unseen) ways of being in the world, and those benefit some people more than others. To say it this way recognizes that bodies don't seamlessly align with expectations of that space and that those misalignments can themselves be productive (even if differently productive) in their implications.

Educational institutions are, of course, not the only institutions or social structures that discipline bodies. Media, the state, religion, family, law, the leisure industry, and medicine (among others) operate on bodies as well. But not all institutions regulate bodies in the same ways. The differences are important to recognize, since the ways in which our bodies are defined and regulated often conflict. Think, for instance, of the differences between how medical institutions tend to define and regulate childbirth versus how a midwife is likely to define this experience. In a hospital, the birth schedule is run on a very different clock than midwifery's, with resulting different sets of expectations for the actions (or non-actions) of the person giving birth in a hospital than those for a midwife-led birth[5]. The person giving birth in a hospital is constructed as a "patient" who undergoes a risky medical procedure that requires expertly trained personnel to intervene with treatment for pain management and constant monitoring for information deemed vital to the successful outcome of the birth. In this framework, that person becomes a source of data, rather than the source of expert knowledge. Additionally, medicine has developed standards about the ideal time for gestation, about how long birth should take, and about what steps should happen in what order, regardless of the vast amount of variation between bodies and how those bodies birth.

Midwifery, on the other hand, tends to regard birth as a "natural" process, that is, focused on a body that exists outside medicalized understandings of pathology and pain. This means that the birthing process centers on the body of the person giving birth; how much time they take, who is present during the process, what intervention is needed and when, the best location of the birth (at home, a birthing center, a hospital) are decisions for them to make, rather than a medical professional. Thus, birth and the bodies of the parent and child(ren) are often regarded in midwifery outside of medicalized practices and their scientifically based technologies. And each of these sets of practices leads to different perceptions of how bodies should fit into

[5]**THINK ABOUT:** Women are not the only people to give birth. Transmen can—and have—given birth, a process that usually involves halting hormone therapies for a length of time in order to become pregnant. We deliberately avoid saying "women" here, opting instead for some variation of "the person giving birth," in order to avoid the link between biological sex and gender identity and social role. As we have argued elsewhere in this book, language matters. And the reality of transmen giving birth is further explored in one of the readings in this book.

them, different expectations made of those bodies, and, thus, different experiences for those bodies.

Each of these approaches to birth thus represents a set of assumptions about processes, data, and the truth about bodies in the birth process, although neither is necessarily more true or even necessarily better than the other. The point we are emphasizing here is that bodies are always being defined and regulated by various institutions. Clearly, one approach is more accepted as the authoritative standard than others (as is the case with the more medicalized approach to childbirth in much of the United States and Canada). But other ways of defining bodies constantly challenge—and thus change—those standards too. And people experience, at least to some extent, their bodies as disciplined within these competing institutional definitions and regulations. To say that bodies are disciplined through a variety of social structures and practices, then, is not to suggest that we have no control, or that we are coerced into particular ways of behaving. As both this and the above classroom examples demonstrate, people don't just quietly acquiesce to the disciplining of their bodies, and this is especially true when those bodies are marked as undesirable or insubordinate in some way in that context.

This recognition that bodies are both disciplined by, and able to nonetheless move within, structures and institutions is described as *agency*, a term that points to the capacity for people to act within these structures that also shape (and thus delimit) their options. *Agency* is different than *choice*, a term more suggestive of freely determining what one does, choosing among an endless number of possibilities. *Agency* recognizes limits and recognizes how people manoeuvre within those limits. The difference between these two terms is subtle but important. As an example, it might help to think of a supermarket aisle with dozens of breakfast cereals. Instead of emphasizing the choices available, the concept of agency demands that we think about the limits that are always already in place in such a situation. In other words, it asks us to consider how our set of choices came to be: how did we, for example, get to the point of assuming that cereal is what's for breakfast? Deciding between twenty types of cereal is indeed a kind of choice, but one that, like any choice, is circumscribed[6]. This situation produces the normative response—the everyday practice of selecting some kind of cereal for breakfast—but it also produces a number of other possible responses that can challenge that normativity: eating ice cream or

[6]**THINK ABOUT:** Of course, the completely taken-for-granted background of this example is the idea that our choice of cereal is also circumscribed by the larger and constant emphasis on consumerism and the presumed need to always consume something; indeed, too often our discussions end with what consumer choices someone has made, leaving in place that emphasis on consumption as unquestioned. Think about how consumer capitalism is (among other things) a system for translating human needs (e.g., love, acceptance, community, recognition) into products that can be bought and sold. In this way, things that have clear use-value (e.g., food, clothes, shelter) are transformed into things that also have a highly skewed exchange-value (e.g., gourmet cuisine, designer jeans, gated communities). Thus expressing ourselves—our beliefs, our politics, our identities—usually takes place within this context, that is, around what our individual consumer

ribs or sushi at 7:00 a.m. or skipping breakfast altogether. Choice, then, is never as open-ended as we might initially think, but neither are our actions determined or completely controlled. We choose from among a limited set of options, and those choices in turn both reflect normative expectations and potential opportunities to challenge those expectations.

This distinction between choice and agency helps us "make strange" all kinds of everyday practices. Think, for instance, of whether or not you really have the choice to shower before entering that supermarket with that cereal aisle, or any other public space. Does everyone in contemporary Canada and the United States—in your class-room, say—really have the choice *not* to practice this form of personal hygiene at least several times a week? What kinds of broader social structures contribute to this self-discipline? What are the ramifications of not participating in this regulation of bodies, our own and others? How much do we, individually and collectively, have invested in partaking of this social definition of, disciplining of, bodies? And how is something like regular showering differently enabled by other factors such as loca-tion and socioeconomic status and able-bodiedness and cultural identification, all of which might make this disciplining practice easier or harder, more or less available, desirable or onerous? Our choice to shower, then, is clearly circumscribed by any number of other factors, all of which contribute to defining that activity in particular ways and then disciplining us into following along.

In short, we don't "choose" from an infinite number of possibilities unhindered by the many contexts we are in; rather, we exercise a delimited amount of agency from within contexts that make some actions more possible than others. Put differently, when we speak of agency, we're pointing to the ways in which bodies are always circumscribed, drawing attention to how they are simultaneously subjected to these disciplinary regulations, as well as to how those contexts make possible multiple ways of acting, resisting, redefining, reworking, tweaking, and making new meanings.

Negotiating Discipline

Another good example to explore the complexities of agency is what is commonly called "beauty culture." Beauty culture includes a range of regulations around bodily

choices are, rather than challenging the idea that consumption is the route to that expression. And we also have emotional attachments to both the values we express and the things through which we express them—and these are sometimes contradictory. More on this last point in the final chapter.

appearance: makeup, hair styling, fashion and adornment, body size and shape, cosmetic surgery, exercise, and dieting, where each of these involves a range of practices that are deeply embedded in our everyday lives. Through such practices our bodies are continually defined, surveilled, regulated, and disciplined, albeit in different ways and with different effects. Both participation in and access to beauty culture are further impacted by other identity categories, so that not just gender, but race, age, class, and mobility also become part of our varied relationships to its practices.

To various extents, we all participate in beauty culture; we monitor our bodies in ways that are expected of us and take part to greater or lesser degrees in the myriad of practices that reflect common assumptions about normative bodily appearance. And certainly, we can recognize the numerous ways in which we are called to participate in our own constant self-monitoring—mirrors in bathrooms, health magazines at the checkout counter, celebrity endorsements of cosmetics, clothes, and diets—and often feel (sometimes intense) pressure to fulfill the definitions of beauty and appearance they endorse. Notice again how these practices perpetuate consumerism as the primary way in which we are to participate in beauty culture. These expectations come not just from media, but from family, peers, and various social locations that expect certain looks (note, for instance, all those job ads that ask for a "professional" appearance). And there's no doubt that sometimes the definitions of bodies in beauty culture are incredibly homogenous; the dominant norms of feminine beauty, for example, are represented within an extremely narrow range of race, age, facial features, hair texture, skin color, body size and shape, implied sexuality, and able-bodiedness. And the bodies that reflect hegemonic masculinity are just as rigidly delimited, again producing ideals that are clearly racialized, able-bodied, and about particular body sizes and shapes.

Regardless of beauty culture's limitations on our life choices, if we follow our new understanding of power, we must also recognize that its demands are nevertheless productive; that is, it produces the range of responses from us that, in turn, allows us to shape a recognizable identity. Thus, while beauty culture definitely is a mode of regulating everyone's bodies, it is also a primary way in which we come to identify ourselves. Think, for instance, about when you dress up for a special occasion.

In many ways, you are fulfilling the expectations around you about the appropriate appearance for that event. You regulate yourself to meet those demands because you know that you are being watched, surveilled, by others around you for how well you fit, and so you also watch or survey yourself to ensure you're meeting those expectations. And yet, to simply say that your body has been disciplined and that you're just falling in with dominant standards doesn't seem adequate to capture the ways you participate in that process. No doubt, you feel a sense of satisfaction with or pleasure in this accomplishment and with other people's recognition of your success. Those reactions aren't because you've simply been taken in or "duped" by beauty culture, nor because you somehow failed to recognize that your responses are produced and manipulated by that industry. Because even as you're fulfilling a set of expectations, you are also manoeuvring through them, negotiating what you do and don't do, and altering some expectations while following others; you are using your body to define yourself, to speak something, in ways that don't necessarily line up completely or seamlessly with that larger set of expectations.

There is no clear distinction between these poles that argue capitulation versus strategic adoption of beauty-culture norms. The line drawn between what we're being coerced to do and what we're choosing to do is blurry, especially when we become acutely aware of the ways in which, upon close inspection, the vast majority of us "fail" to meet dominant definitions of beauty. Instead, what's important to emphasize here is that both these apparent successes and failures are part of the same mechanism of power relations. They are how we seek to express ourselves as individuals and as members of groups. We cultivate our bodies into fashionable selves, professional selves, desirable selves, casual selves, as well as against the values reflected in those selves (e.g., anti-fashion selves[7]). In other words, beauty culture is definitely a mode of regulating our bodies. But it also provides a number of ways to fashion an identity, either with or against those dominant definitions of beauty, and often, by doing both at the same time. None of this is to suggest that we may not have concerns about and want to critique the dominant set of expectations for bodies, or challenge the variety of industries and organizations through which those are disseminated. Beauty culture—its institutions, practices, ideals—produces hierarchies, exclusions, and violences that no doubt limit the possibilities for many people. It creates uneven

[7]**TALK ABOUT:** How is "anti-fashion" still a style that depends on consumption of various kinds? What happens when "high" fashion industries pick up "street styles," that is, when elements that were initially conceived of as challenging the fashion industry become part of that industry: think about ripped jeans, safety pins as jewelry, tie-dye t-shirts? Is it possible to get outside of consumption and consumer capitalism in order to express something about ourselves? What about other examples where we use our consumption choices to express something about our values or political beliefs: recycled paper, pink ribbons, tiny houses, for instance? What are the advantages or disadvantages of a politics expressed through our buying of particular products (rather than lobbying efforts or other kinds of agitations)? Are there differences of opinion in your class around these questions—and if so, around what points do those differences revolve?

expectations that are clearly marked by race, age, and gender. But it is important to recognize that agency—the power to act within limits—is always a negotiation between those larger disciplining mechanisms and our own desires to shape the ways we identify ourselves and others.

But let's push this notion of negotiation a little further. No doubt we display our own bodies all the time (with greater or lesser senses of investment in how people are reading them), and much of the time we find pleasure in that display. But of course we're not only seen or watched when we want to be. Our bodies are also surveilled, displayed, and exhibited for public consumption at unwanted times. Consider, for instance, "mug shots" that circulate online or those tabloid "caught on camera" photos of celebrities or politicians going about their daily lives, unprepared for their public display. Or think about how sexually explicit photos that enhance the pleasure within a relationship where trust is established can sometimes become a source of power, control, and potential humiliation if that trust between people is broken. The tension evident in these examples—between the desire to be seen and the anxiety (horror, even) about being seen or being misread—illustrates well the conflicts around agency in bodily displays.

A good example to explore these tensions is the body adornment practice of tattooing. In the last 20 years or so, tattoos have become fairly commonplace in Canada and the United States—so much so that they barely register as something about which to comment. Most people with tattoos want to display them to the world, at least some of the time. They are both personal statements and meant for public consumption, marking something that we perceive to be unique about ourselves that often has (and demands) an audience. We may use tattoos to mark experiences and what those experiences mean to us, to signify our belonging to some groups (or not belonging to others), and to be recognized as particular kinds of people[8]. In short, through our tattoos, our bodies speak our identities in a variety of ways. Looking at the history of tattooing, however, reveals how much the meanings of what tattoos say are inflected by classed, gendered, racialized, and nationalized identity categories. For example, the "tattooed lady" in the nineteenth-century "freak show" was no doubt exhibited for audiences' entertainment or even for their purported education (i.e., about her otherness from middle-class feminine norms, and thus, by comparison,

[8]**THINK ABOUT:** If tattoos (and other body modifications) are ways in which we often signal a "belonging," think about what groups are the most desirable–and which ones never make the list. The popularity of styles such as "tribal" or Celtic, the references to symbols considered "Native" (feathers, wolves, eagles), even the ubiquity of kanji (Japanese or Chinese characters) all seem to position belonging to some groups/cultural heritages as more desirous than others. Why do these seem so much more evident today than other possibilities–tattoos of Egyptian hieroglyphics or of ancient West African symbols (known as *Adinkra*)? And why do most of these also seem to draw on perceptions of a particular group in history (and whose telling of that history is it)? Think about who claims these belongings (and what identities are not claimed) through body modifications.

the audience's normality). Yet this -xhibition also offered her opportunities for travel and work; in this context, she no doubt thought about the display of her body quite differently than do many of us exhibiting our tattoos today. Understanding women's agency in any historical (or cross-cultural) context, then, means looking at the multiple possibilities for understanding women's bodies that existed at that particular time and place, and how women negotiated their way through those possibilities. It means recognizing that that tattooed lady may have felt all kinds of tensions and contradictions in her display (as do many of us in any of our contemporary bodily displays), but within a different set of social constraints and possibilities for individual expression.

The contemporary popularity of particular types of tattoos also reveals how this body modification practice continues to produce meanings through various classed, racialized, and even colonial histories. Sixty years ago, a pin-up girl tattooed across a bicep tended to mark one's gender and class position fairly concretely as white, working class, and male. Today, the pin-up girl is a popular choice for many young (predominantly white) women's biceps. Likewise, "tribal" tattoos reflect historical legacies of location, identity, and belonging that may be different than their desired meanings on contemporary middle-class bodies in Canada or the United States. The gap between these histories and contemporary meanings raises a number of provocative questions: Does it matter whether or not we have specific knowledge about the cultures who produced these tribal patterns as long as others read the meaning we want to communicate? Can a tattoo be simply an aesthetic choice, that is, just a matter of style[9]? Or, what does it mean when someone gets a tattoo of a word or character in a language not their own? If one doesn't speak any Chinese or Japanese languages, what is the meaning of writing something like *courage* in kanji (Chinese and Japanese characters)? Does it make a difference if one identifies as Chinese or Japanese, even if they don't speak either language? And what if one doesn't identify as such, but speaks the language nonetheless?

Bodies are central to WGS, because they allow us to ask questions about identity categories and power relations and to explore the ways in which we negotiate our own senses of self through encounters with larger social structures and institutions. They are the medium through which we encounter and live in the world even as they are

[9]**THINK ABOUT:** One critique of some bodymodification practices, including tattooing but also branding, scarification, and some kinds of piercings, is that they are examples of *cultural appropriation*: the adoption of something from one culture by people from a different cultural group, especially when that adoption is of a marginalized or historically oppressed group's practices and artifacts by members of the more dominant culture. The issue of cultural appropriation is explored in more detail in the "Representations" chapter.

also constantly defined and scrutinized in that world. As such, our relationships to bodies—our own and those of other people—are often contradictory and ambivalent. From the idea that bodies speak truths about ourselves and others to the assumption that those truths can then be (accurately) read off bodies, and from an understanding that all bodies are regulated and disciplined to the recognition that they also have agency to define themselves (albeit in different ways), focusing on bodies in WGS means that we interrogate both assumptions about self-expression and concerns about social control.

The Concept at Work: Fat Bodies and Obesity Crises

Think about the way in which fat bodies—bodies that are bigger or heavier than normative expectations for bodies—are consistently regarded as a problem that needs solving. Headlines in the news media or online entertainment sites celebrate famous people who "overcome" obesity, thereby suggesting that obesity is a state of being which must definitely be left behind. The fat body is the object of social scrutiny and anxiety in contemporary Canada and the United States (and many other places as well), as it is talked about with derision, ridicule, pity, and embarrassed sympathy. It is imagined to be devoid of self-discipline and to be a signifier of laziness, moral lack, bad health, diminished possibilities, outsized medical costs, and early death. And it is the locus of constant intervention—through unsolicited suggestions, diet aids and workout programs, familial input, and medical advice. As such, it is the site of social panic about the health, not just of the individual body but of the larger society as well. And fatness is thought to have different causes and effects depending on its gender, age, class, race, and national identity. Think of how the "obesity crisis" is talked about differently for children versus adults, poor communities versus rich ones, women versus men, and various racialized communities, where notions of responsibility and the consequences of fatness are assumed and perpetuated so unevenly.

The fat body, though, is so much more, especially for those of us who are labeled fat. It is the body through which people live rich personal lives, socialize, work, play, desire, and love. Because the fat body is typically pathologized in

Canada and the United States, making it the site of individual self-expression, pleasure, and pride transforms that body into a site of resistance—a key tenet of fat activism. For some people, then, the fat body is the very location of a political expression that challenges both social norms about bodies and the structures, practices, and institutions (e.g., medicine, education, media, work, transportation) that keep those norms in place. As such, fat becomes an identity that is claimed and applauded rather than rejected and feared. Its very existence is transgressive, resisting the normative perceptions of desirability, health, and belonging that shape all bodies.

At the same time, we can say that there is no such thing as a fat body so much as there is a culture that produces specific definitions of fatness into which some bodies then fit. Again, it is important to complicate assumptions about fat, asking: What counts as fat and who is doing the counting? How is fatness made meaningful, by whom, and in what contexts? Whose fat body is being talked about and whose is not; that is, do gender, race, or age make a difference to that talk? The answers to these questions change immensely over different times and places. Note that these are very different questions than what makes a person fat and what is to be done about it, the more usual focus of popular discourses about fat. Rather, these broader questions reveal how fat bodies are defined, monitored, and sanctioned in sites as disparate as law, insurance industries, and the economy.

The construction of the fat body as a problem to be managed is also increasingly exported, seen as a concern far beyond the borders of Canada and the United States. International NGOs and health organizations have expanded their focus to include fat bodies around the world, generating worry about a growing international obesity crisis. What are the consequences, though, of understanding fat through the same frameworks that dominate Canada and the United States, irrespective of particularities of geographies, food practices and availability, lifespan, familial arrangements, beauty standards, and cultural differences of desirability and sexuality? Seeing obesity as the same everywhere—both as understood in similar ways and as leading to similar consequences—opens up yet another occasion for greater bodily surveillance and regulation that constructs "others" as problems to be managed and controlled by "us."

Preview of Readings

Coyote, Ivan. 2014. "The Rest of My Chest." In *Gender Failure*, Rae E. Spoon and Ivan Coyote, 67–74. Vancouver, BC: Arsenal Pulp Press.

Wilson, Bianca D. M. 2009. "Widening the Dialogue to Narrow the Gap in Health Disparities: Approaches to Fat Black Lesbian and Bisexual Women's Health Promotion." In *The Fat Studies Reader*, edited by Esther Rothblum and Sondra Solovay, 54–64. New York, NY: New York University Press.

Guthman, Julie. 2011. "What's on the Menu?" In *Weighing In: Obesity, Food Justice, and the Limits of Capitalism*, 185–196. Berkeley, CA: University of California Press.

Gerschick, Thomas J. 2011. "The Body, Disability, and Sexuality." In *Introducing the New Sexuality Studies* (2nd ed.), edited by Steven Seidman, Nancy Fischer, and Chet Meeks, 75–83. New York, NY: Routledge.

Falcón, Sylvanna. 2006. "'National Security' and the Violation of Women: Militarized Border Rape at the US–Mexico Border." In *The Color of Violence: The Incite! Anthology*, edited by Andrea Smith, Beth E. Richie, and Julia Sudbury, 119–129. Boston, MA: South End Press.

The "Bodies" chapter begins by interrogating the assumption that bodies "speak" truths about individual people and can be "read" like texts. When bodies are read as ambiguous—especially in terms of gender—the question of fit (as in the example of public bathrooms) can become a high-stakes encounter with consequences ranging from mild sanctioning to physical violence. We discuss the ways in which bodies are restricted (or "disciplined") in various spaces while simultaneously having agency to negotiate those spaces in ways that benefit us. The examples of body modifications and beauty culture allow for an extended discussion of the ways in which those negotiations between capitulation and resistance complicate common understandings of "choice."

In Ivan Coyote's "The Rest of My Chest," they (Coyote uses they/them/their as pronouns) recount how perceptions of their body—in particular their breasts—are morphing, such that that part of their body seems to be less and less their own. However, if Coyote wants top surgery (to remove their breasts), they must submit to medical authorities (in this case a psychologist and a psychiatrist) who can authorize that surgery. They must present themselves as sufficiently "broken" (with a "gender identity disorder") and therefore judged to be in need of "fixing."

- How are the medical authorities reading Coyote's body? What truths do they seek?
- Why do some bodies need to come under the authority of the state for medical procedures and some do not? For instance, why are breast-reduction surgeries easily authorized in some cases and not as easily in others?
- In what ways do we tend to talk about our bodies as being or not being part of who we are? How does that talk affect our sense of self or our relationship to our bodies?

As a researcher in both academia and her own black lesbian/bisexual community, Bianca D. M. Wilson raises critical questions about whose bodies are "targets" for public health interventions in "Widening the Dialogue to Narrow the Gap in Health Disparities: Approaches to Fat Black Lesbian and Bisexual Women's Health Promotion." Wilson emphasizes the need for interventions to promote a "full ecology of human well-being" as opposed to the elimination of disease and dysfunction. This more culturally grounded approach would render the "obesity crisis" more complex as well as illuminate a useful appreciation for more diverse body sizes than current medical and dominant discourses provide.

- In what ways is "health" associated only with particular kinds of bodies? What are examples of where you see this association made?
- Following Wilson, what are some ways that we can intervene in the discourses that target some bodies as sites of pathology?
- How might conversations about public health promotion shift if we spoke of wellness instead of disease prevention?

"What's on the Menu?" is Julie Guthman's look at the intersection of food politics and the so-called obesity crisis. She wants readers to consider the ways in which this intersection is made even more complicated when considering issues such as: wage inequalities that make more expensive "healthy" foods harder to come by; our binge–purge economy that pays off for both the cheap food and the alternative food economies; pesticide use that may have large impacts on health outcomes for those forced to eat cheaply; and the stigmatization of fatness, even as the definition of that category is itself endlessly changing.

- In considering the connections that Guthman makes about various people's health, what are some key questions that you might ask about the next meal you eat?
- What are the political investments that need to be made if we want better-fed and healthier societies?
- How do individual choices to eat organic, eat local, or eat vegetarian/vegan have an impact on food politics and food policy? Who can make these choices and what is needed for people to be able to make them?

Thomas Gerschick's "The Body, Disability, and Sexuality" notes that because bodies serve as a kind of social currency, normative and attractive bodies signify worth, whereas non-normative bodies—because of disability or age—are deemed less worthy of social recognition. This assessment produces asymmetrical power relations in which entire facets of disabled people's lives are ignored or deemed secondary to their bodily or mental impairments, especially when it comes to sexuality. Gerschick advocates for the importance of creating and nurturing sexual subcultures.

- Where do we get our ideas of what sexy is? What kinds of bodies aren't seen or heard from in those ideas?
- How do our bodies function as commodities? What determines their worth in the various contexts through which we move?

In "'National Security' and the Violation of Women: Militarized Border Rape at the US–Mexico Border," Sylvanna Falcón discusses how the rape of women's (and sometimes men's) bodies is a common practice in militarized locations and war zones, which include, since 9/11 especially, the U.S.–Mexico border. The near total institutionalized power that agents of state authority have over non-citizens means that seeking redress for these assaults is a nearly impossible task. Yet, as Falcón demonstrates, women who have been victims of rape do file complaints and have organized with various non-governmental organizations to both raise awareness and seek justice.

- How does the ubiquity of sexual violence in war zones shape both the behavior of women as potential victims and men as potential perpetrators?
- Why is it important to give the victims of sexual violence opportunities to tell their stories?
- How might the author's use of the victims' names and sharing the details of their bodily and psychological violations affect attitudes about sexual violence by state actors such as the border patrol?

The Rest of My Chest

Ivan Coyote

When I was young, they were way littler. In my early twenties, all I had to do really was bench press a bit of weight here and there, and they almost disappeared, I worked them down to muscly little apricots with nipples on them, easily hideable with a tight tank top and a t-shirt over top, then a long-sleeved shirt and a sweater and maybe a jacket. Then for a while I used Saran wrap, if you can believe that, in the good old days, back in the early nineties, Saran wrap but only for special occasions, of course, not for everyday, just for a fancy dinner or dress-up when you didn't want them messing up the line of your dress shirt like they do.

Then came the ACE bandages, but lucky for me those didn't last too too long before I started dating the dancer, and see, dancers mostly dance their breasts right off themselves, but also they have these flat elastic shirt things that the costume designers sew up for them to wear so they all look like androgynous willow trees, and once I got my hands on one of those elastic dancer shirt things, well, I never looked back.

Until my late thirties, at least, when all of a sudden they got so much bigger, and then it was onwards to the double front compression shirt which sounds really heavy and constricting because it fucking is, right, and it is not made for guys like us, nothing really truly is made for us, it is mostly designed for cis-gendered men and their man boobs and not really built to hold these ladies like mine, this pair that I went and grew myself somehow in the last six or seven years or so.

So. So. Nineteen years, I have been binding. Yes, thank you. I realize some of you are thinking, holy fuck, Saran wrap. That dude is old. And that is okay by me.

Where was I? Anyways, so all of a sudden a guy wakes up on the verge of forty-something years old and now not only do I have kind of big tits somehow but God being the joker that they are, I also have really nice big tits seriously sweet Jesus I wish it weren't so. Some days I look in the mirror and I think, whose are those? They are sweet but whoever left these here will hopefully come and take them away now because I need to put a shirt on and go outside.

That's the thing, right? I am totally fine with them when I am naked, well, mostly okay, unless you stare or take a side-view picture or touch them like this instead of like this or this, right, and so mostly I am okay with them naked, I suppose, unless you get all weird about them, in which case then I will definitely counter with feeling way weirder, but what I for sure all the time now definitely am not okay with is having these breasts on me unbound with my clothes on. Hard to describe, I guess, for those of you who feel actually attached in some way to all the parts of your body, or okay with every part of your body, because please, I know that it is not just trans people who feel like this about our bodies, but if you in fact feel perfectly okay with all the parts of the body you are travelling in right now then I say good on you, sincerely, I am glad for you, but it is not like that for me, you see, and I have tried and tried and tried for so long now and, well, I am pretty much certain it almost goes without saying at this point that chances are I am most likely not going to wake up one morning and say, okay, turns out it was all just a phase and only today I decided that I am totally fine having tits. In fact, look, look at my tits, I just love having them around.

This is probably not going to happen. And now, just lately, these three fingers have started tingling and going numb and the only thing that makes that tingling dead feeling go away is to take off the binder, and I am hoping it is not permanent nerve damage because I can't leave the house now at all with the ladies not tended to properly, just can't do it, can't really say why and don't need to anymore, so.

So I finally called my doctor. She referred me to a psychologist for a mental health assessment and diagnosis. I went to talk to that psychologist in her office downtown. I had never done anything like that before. That psychologist, she was way cooler than I thought she would be. I cried a lot more than I thought I was going to, and she asked a lot of questions about depression, general happiness, and my body. I tried to act not suicidal but not way too happy and well-adjusted, either. I am supposed to be here to get fixed, I know this already. So there has to be something wrong enough with me but not too wrong, not so wrong that I need different help from someone else that isn't her with something more pressing than I hate having these tits. Have to find that balance.

See, the thing is, I want top surgery, but I am not on hormones. Well, news flash, every single one of us is technically on hormones right now, but I am not taking any hormones, right, and this is not how it is supposed to go. I forget who wrote these rules, who decided the order of things, and why, and who decided hormones first then off come the tits, I don't know why there seems to be that rule, but I had to make a special case for myself that I was trans enough. In British Columbia, the province in Canada where I live, this surgery is covered by our health care system, provided you qualify. And by qualify, they mean be diagnosed. They, being the government. The government will pay for you to get fixed, but only if they decide you are broken in the right way. The other they being, in this case, the medical establishment. Before the bureaucrats can sign off on the form and send it to the surgeon, a psychologist and a psychiatrist must first decide if they believe me that I am who I say I am. In order to do this, I must fill out a long multiple-choice questionnaire, which the psychologist that my doctor referred me to will read through and assess, and then refer me to a psychiatrist for a proper diagnosis. Because someone who is trained in this stuff has to sign off that I do in fact have a bona fide gender identity disorder, but that someone cannot be me, because I am not qualified. And by gender identity disorder, they all mean that you want to be a man. Or a woman, as the case may be. It is not enough to just feel that you are not a woman or a man. You must want to be not the box that they have all previously put you in. There is no box to check for not wanting a box at all. No one knows how to fix that.

I had to be diagnosed with gender dysphoria, or gender identity disorder, and think about it, how would that feel to be told that just being yourself is a disorder, but if I don't say the right things and they don't say those words gender identity disorder, then I pay for everything out of pocket myself and I don't know about you but nine thousand dollars is a lot of money, and the question I keep on thinking but not asking that shrink is why can my cousin have two breast augmentations and get her lips filled with silicone, and no judgments here from me, because lord knows my poor cousin has received enough of it from our Catholic family, and she has been asked plenty of questions regarding who is paying for it all and why and what it might cost her in the long run, and ask her, just what exactly she feels it has all cost her in the end, but my question is, how come nobody makes her see a shrink first, yeah, but I don't ask that question because I need to catch more flies with honey or it's nine thousand bucks for me and I am already the wrong kind of trans guy because I don't want the hormones, I just want the breasts gone, well, not just gone, but the chest reconstruction too.

When I tell the psychologist that I use the "she" pronoun for work and in media interviews, she furrows her brow and writes faster on her pad of paper. When I tell her I have no intention of going on testosterone, she looks up at me, then down again and writes a bunch more stuff. I am starting to think about what I am not going to be able to do with that nine thousand dollars and how exactly am I gonna come up with it anyways. When the psychologist, who is actually pretty cool, asks me if I pack. As in a dick. As in, in my pants.

She asks me like she thinks I am going to say no. I can tell she doesn't think I am trans enough for this. Not to get it funded anyway.

Yes, I do, I say. I have been packing for over ten years easy, I tell her, maybe closer to fifteen. We used to make our own out of condoms and cheap hair gel and nylons. I told you. Fucking old school, man.

Well, then. She sits up straighter in her chair, starts writing some more.

I can't believe this, I say. Don't tell me this all comes down to whether or not I carry a dick in my pants.

She considers the implications of this for a minute.

I guess I am saying that, she admits.

I found this shocking at the time, but later, I had to admit it made a lot of sense. Just like the whole fucking world, and all those cocks, those cocks on people who want them on them anyways, and then I got to thinking about big cities all full of skyscrapers and hello, patriarchy, of course it comes down to my dick. Of course, having a dick in my pants and identifying on the masculine end of the spectrum makes all the difference. Especially when it comes to getting what I want.

The psychologist refers me to a psychiatrist for a formal diagnosis. Acquiring this diagnosis quickly became complicated for me, because there are very few psychiatrists in my province who the bureaucrats have certified to be allowed to make such an important decision about me, for me. On top of this, I have been writing about the gender binary and my place in it, or outside of it, for many years now, and one by one the psychiatrists that the bureaucrats had deemed qualified to decide if I was indeed transgendered enough to proceed with surgery were all forced to recuse themselves from making any decisions about me on ethical grounds, because they had read my work on gender in

their how-to-be-nice-to-trans-people sensitivity workshop when they were going through the process of being trained to be certified to be allowed to make such decisions about people like me.

Make sense? I didn't think so. To sum it up, most of the psychiatrists who the government looked to so they could decide whether or not I was trans were unable to assess me because I had written about being trans, and they had read some of my work while learning about how to deal with trans people, and so were no longer objective enough to decide fairly if I was trans or not. This resulted in delays, and probably more paperwork. Conflict of whose interest, exactly? Interesting question.

Finally, the bureaucrats found a psychiatrist in a suburb who hadn't read any of my work on gender, and was thus naturally better equipped to understand and assess my gender for other professionals. Forms were filed. Letters were written. Decisions were made by those obviously more qualified than I am to understand myself.

I'm not saying it's a perfect system, but it's a health care system, and I am still grateful to reside in a country that possesses one.

As for this psychiatrist, I wanted to dislike him on principle but I could not seem to muster it up once we met in person. He had an Arthur Eames office chair, which I coveted very much, and we bonded over furniture (mid-century Danish teak modern) for a while before getting down to business. He proceeded to ask me a bunch more questions about my gender history, and my relationship with my father. He asked me how long I had been binding my breasts. I told him nineteen years.

His eyebrows shot up. Why so long? he asked, incredulous. Most of my patients come to me after about two weeks of that torture.

I don't like to rush into things, I told him.

He laughed so hard at that, a real genuine belly laugh too, and slapped his desk with a flat palm, so that I couldn't help but like him a little, despite myself. Couldn't help but wonder, though, just who else had been in my chair, because I knew tons of guys who had been binding for this long or even longer, guys who couldn't afford the cost or the time off, or who didn't have any health insurance at all, or who didn't jump through the right hoops or say the right things to the right suits. Turns out this guy mostly worked with adolescent trans kids.

Anyway, he wrote down stuff about my father issues, noted among other things that I was dapperly dressed and very punctual, which I appreciated, and sent me a copy of everything he wrote about me, which I also appreciated, and recommended me for gender reassignment surgery, without the usual pre-requisite hormone treatments.

My next question is for you. Am I trans enough now? Or, conversely, do you now feel that I no longer belong in the sisterhood? Did your feelings change at all for me over the course of this story? Do you find me more or less attractive? If so, why?

Please rate the strength of your feelings from one to five, one meaning you feel not very strongly about it all, to five meaning you have very strong feelings about me getting top surgery. Now, please fold up your answers and put them in your pocket. Please keep them to yourself, as I will try to do with my feelings about your breasts. Thank you so much for participating.

Widening the Dialogue to Narrow the Gap in Health Disparities

Approaches to Fat Black Lesbian and Bisexual Women's Health Promotion

Bianca D. M. Wilson

... perhaps you question the size of my hips—
the second largest continent in the world sired these hips
of course they would be as large—
the oldest civilization on earth gave birth to these hips
of course they would be as wide—
... make you release before you were ready to hips—
when you want to hold a woman's hips
when you want to feel the difference between you and my hips
when hard hips want to be soothed by charmine hips
these are my hips—so let the legacy live on
    —C.C. Carter, "Herstory of My Hips"

This poem, written by C.C. Carter, a contemporary Afro-Latina lesbian artist, deeply resonates with me. My personal experiences as a fat woman who participates in Black lesbian and bisexual women's communities have shown me an appreciation for body diversity that is atypical of mainstream American culture. I use the term fat to refer to anyone who sees themselves as larger, heavier, or rounder than average, as well as to refer to the population of people who are categorized as "overweight" or "obese" according to medical guidelines (which change periodically). In a Black lesbian and bisexual women's cultural context, we see evidence through Web sites, photos, and poetry that there is a consciousness that women of all sizes need to be valued and respected, and that larger women can represent ideals of beauty, health, and spiritual-physical balance. My empirical research on Black lesbian sexual culture has also echoed these sentiments, as I have found desire and attraction to larger body sizes as a key domain of Black lesbian sexual life (Wilson, 2006). As such, it is

not surprising that I experience a stark contrast between my life and work in Black lesbian and bisexual women's communities and that of my professional life within health behavior and health promotion research. The dominant perspective within my professional settings would suggest that the deterioration of health among women in ethnic minority and lesbian communities is in large part due to their being fatter than other communities. That I reside at the intersection of these two worlds informs my attempt to craft a response to public health institutions' efforts to address the "obesity epidemic" in the various communities to which African American lesbian and bisexual women belong.

Introduction: Personal, Political, and Scientific Arenas Converge

As a health researcher working both in academia and community-based health settings, I am frequently informed of the high rates of "obesity" in the United States, and the even higher rates within African American and lesbian communities. Indeed, it has been reported that African American women as compared to European American women (Flegal, Carroll, Ogden, & Johnson, 2002), and that lesbians as compared to heterosexual women (Aaron et al., 2001; Cochran et al., 2001; Dibble, Roberts, Robertson, & Paul, 2002; Mays, Yancey, Cochran, Weber, & Fielding, 2002; Valanis et al., 2000), are heavier and more likely to be categorized as "overweight" and "obese" when using standardized measurements such as the body mass index (BMI). Further, a few studies have also reported higher weights among African American lesbians as compared to lesbians of other ethnic groups (Cochran et al., 2001; Mays et al., 2002). The simple reporting of these demographics is not problematic. My concern is the tone, language, and content of scholars' presentations that use these data as a starting point for their collection of "fat-is-bad" statements. Many public health scholars routinely provide an oversimplified message regarding the relationship between weight and health, clearly communicating the idea that to be overweight or obese inherently translates to being ill or on the verge of illness.

When these statements about weight and health are made, I often find myself reacting viscerally. I look around and am reminded that, at this level of education and profession, I am often the only large person in a given room, and am typically the only Black or gay person of any gender or size. Immediately my awareness of the differences between me and my colleagues is heightened, and I am reminded that I belong to the "target populations" of fat Black or lesbian people being discussed. I try my best to appear unaffected, but I am affected. Their talk about my impending early death due to my body size is juxtaposed with my experiences and work in Black gay communities, which demonstrate that there are far greater enemies to the health and well-being of Black lesbian and bisexual women than the fat on our bodies, such as violence, poverty, and psychological oppression. I acknowledge and embrace the emotionality behind this reaction. Such emotions have been a catalyst to considering alternative ways to view the issues of weight and health in Black lesbian and bisexual women's communities.

Reshaping the Problem: A Black Feminist Ecological Framework for Examining Health among Fat Black Lesbian and Bisexual Women

My position on how to approach health promotion among fat Black lesbian and bisexual women is informed by Black feminist theory and is complemented by my training in community

and cultural health psychology. Although typical scholarship informed by these theories have not applied a critical perspective to the dominant fat-is-bad health research paradigm, their major tenets have been useful for my own translation of a fat positive perspective into health research and practice. A Black feminist framework is broadly characterized by one that is asserted through the lived experiences of Black women, but which also seeks to understand and dismantle the power of interlocking oppressive systems (Combahee River Collective Statement, 1977; hooks, 1984). Synthesizing Black feminist thought as expressed through writing, activism, academic scholarship, and art, Patricia Hill Collins (1986; 2000) highlights the importance of both acknowledging the intersections of multiple oppressions and respecting and valuing the existence of Black women's culture as key dimensions. I apply this to Black lesbian and bisexual women's health work by privileging a "bottom-up" over a "top-down" approach to health promotion in which Black sexual minority women are active leaders in determining needed paths to maintain or improve their communities' health. Additionally, the oppression that Black lesbian and bisexual women face as a result of fat hatred, racism, sexism, heterosexism, and classism within and outside of the medical industries must be dismantled as an integral component to health promotion within fat Black lesbian and bisexual women's communities.

These domains of Black feminist thought are congruent with the salient components of my approach to health research rooted in theories of community psychology and cultural health psychology. Community psychology emphasizes the importance of collaborative approaches to research and the significance of developing applied research programs that account for the full ecology of human well-being (Wilson, Hayes, Greene, Kelly, & Iscoe, 2003). Within an ecological approach to health, there is an emphasis on both understanding the social processes that promote wellness and maintaining features of community settings, such as community norms and institutions, that serve as resources for healthy development. Cultural health psychology uses an integrated approach to health that seeks a balance of emotional, mental, and physical health, and specifically views cultural values and norms as a major factor in how health is constructed and practiced (Kazarian & Evans, 2001). A key feature of both of these areas of psychology is the view that individual and community wellness, rather than the absence of disease and dysfunction, is the ultimate goal,

Weaving these perspectives together, I advocate for approaches to Black lesbian and bisexual women's health that respect the self-definition and lived experiences of Black women. Additionally, I aim to apply frameworks for health research and practice that define health holistically, integrating our mental, emotional, and physical well-being. When we examine fat Black lesbian and bisexual women's health from this perspective, several directions for health research and practice become illuminated. Namely, we should attend more to the direct and indirect effects of oppression due to size, race, gender, and sexuality on the health of fat Black lesbian and bisexual women. Examining the full ecology of fat Black lesbian and bisexual women's health, we ought to study and address the physiological and psychological effects of oppression on the body. At the interpersonal levels, we could examine the impact of interactions within a health care system that is generally anti-fat. Finally, at the intersection between individual and cultural levels, I argue for an approach to healthy lifestyles that is respectful of existing cultural values for size diversity in Black lesbian and bisexual women's communities.

Oppression in the Lives and Deaths of Fat Black Lesbian and Bisexual Women

A contemporary perspective on public health research posits that empirical and intervention endeavors ought to examine factors affecting health at multiple levels of the ecology (Laverack &

Labonte, 2000). Examples of current efforts to think ecologically with regard to health among fat people include those who have turned their attention to structural factors that they believe affect weight levels among members of certain communities (particularly those who are African American or Latino and poor). These structural factors include lack of access to open, safe space for exercise, and over-access to high-fat, high-caloric food chains (Hill, Wyatt, Reed, & Peters, 2003), as well as the negative effects of experiences with oppression on eating behaviors among African American women (Lovejoy, 2001; Thompson, 1994).

Though ecological and anti-oppression thinking is evident in these scholars' important efforts to account for the interaction between individual behavior and structural systems, this line of research tends to focus on weight or BMI as the final health outcome of interest. This is a limited framework; examining and eliminating structural barriers to better foods and creating opportunities for movement ought to be seen as independent healthful goals regardless of impact on weight. In this way, much of the previous research examining structural barriers to healthy foods and activity perpetuate a simplistic fat-is-bad health model and assume without strong evidence that body weights categorized as "overweight or obese" are highly predictive of poor health outcomes. Further, they tend to assume that weight loss (or prevention of weight gain) is key to maintaining health across all populations. Detailing research that points to problems within the traditional paradigm for studying weight as a predictor of mortality and morbidity, however, is not the focus of this chapter. But there is a growing body of research highlighting the limitations of a simplistic "fat-is-bad" and "weight loss-is-good" approach to health research and practice that indicates that weight is not an ideal outcome for testing the effectiveness of health promotion programs (see, e.g., Campos, Saguy, Ernsberger, Oliver, & Gaesser, 2006; Ernsberger & Koletsky, 1999; Miller, 1999, for empirical reviews documenting that the relationship between weight and health is not causal, and is in fact more complex than typically reported; see Mann et al., 2007, for a review demonstrating that calorie-restrictive dieting is not effective for weight loss; and see Stevens et al. 1992; 1998, for studies illustrating that weight is not a significant predictor of African American women's cardiovascular health).

Although the relationships between weight and health are unclear, major systemic factors experienced by many Black lesbians and bisexual women, such as racism, anti-fat discrimination, sexism, poverty, violence, and heterosexism, are powerful detractors from health (physical, emotional, and mental) and should be considered in a meaningful way as targets for public health intervention. The health consequences of various intersecting oppressions on the lives of Black lesbians and bisexual women can be understood and addressed at individual, interpersonal, and systemic levels. At the individual level, it may be fruitful to examine empirically the moderating effects of psychological stress due to the experience of intersecting forms of oppression on the physiological health of fat Black lesbian and bisexual women. That is, what are the psychologically mediated health effects of discrimination due to being a fat, Black, sexual minority woman? Drawing from the broader research on the psychophysiological effects of stress, Black scholars have studied the direct relationships between racism and various indicators of health among African Americans (see Bowen-Reid & Harrell, 2002, for review; see also Clark, Anderson, Clark, & Williams, 1999). Through these studies, they have illustrated that in addition to genetics and behavior, structural forces such as discrimination and systemic oppression affect health, potentially through the physiological effects of stress (McEwen & Seeman, 1999). An ecologically valid approach to fat Black lesbian and bisexual women's health would avoid a narrow focus on weight loss and expand the levels of analysis to identify additional important factors affecting health within this community. Once we commit to studying the effects of contextual factors on health in African American and lesbian/bisexual women's communities, thereby

expanding a medical model that is currently neither focused on nor equipped to address systemic factors associated with health, we will increase our capacity to develop effective health promotion programs. Public health researchers and interventionists can work with community, health, and social psychologists, as well as community organizers, to promote oppression coping and resistance strategies that optimize our chances of buffering the physiological effects of systemic discrimination due to size, sexuality, race, and gender.

Research that accounts for the effects of oppression on the lives of fat Black lesbian and bisexual women through physiological responses would then hopefully also lead to contextually focused interventions that directly target structural roots of oppression that serve as barriers to those women's wellness. Such interventions may be in the form of legislative and political action, such as targeting discriminatory health insurance company policies that deny insurance to people who are categorized as overweight or obese regardless of other markers of health. These policies leave many fat Black lesbian and bisexual women un- or underinsured (which is particularly troubling because these individuals are already at high risk for being underinsured as Blacks, sexual minorities, and women). Other forms of structural interventions include culture work through the arts to raise awareness and encourage critical dialogue about the ways that fat Black lesbian and bisexual women exhibit health in their everyday resistance to oppression. Although suggesting these strategies for social change is not in and of itself innovative on my part (as I have borrowed these ideas from the many activists in my life), it would require a radical shift in current public health strategies to view environmental, power structure, and cultural change as equally, if not more, important work than discrete health behavior change. For example, over twelve years ago Angela Davis (1994), in her essay "Sick and Tired of Being Sick and Tired: The Politics of Black Women's Health," advocated for structural health interventions that increased access to health care and opportunities for overall well-being, such as the eradication of poverty and the creation of a universal health care system. Specific to the effects of racism on health, but relevant to the study of the effects of multiple forms of oppression on Black lesbian and bisexual women's health, Krieger (2003, p. 197) similarly argued, "The point is that neglecting study of the health impact of racism means that explanations for and interventions to alter population distributions of health, disease, and well-being will be incomplete and potentially misleading, if not outright harmful."

For fat Black lesbian and bisexual women, it is important to note that in addition to racism, we must also negotiate the realities of heterosexism (Eliason & Schope, 2001), sexism (Krieger & Fee, 1994), and anti-fat bias (Harvey & Hill, 2001) within the health care system. The fact that fat Black lesbian and bisexual women sit at the intersections of all these marginalized identities cannot be overlooked in our efforts to acknowledge the ecology of our health care experiences. Typically, however, larger-than-average weight among Black women is viewed as a symptom of the deleterious effects of other forms of oppression, and the effects of anti-fat bias within society (including within the health professions) on Black women's health are often ignored. I have heard numerous fat Black lesbian and bisexual women say that health providers willingly ignore their reported symptoms and concerns, choosing instead to reduce all health complaints to symptoms of their weight or a combination of being Black and fat. Anecdotally, this type of dismissive and frustrating experience that fat patients have with their health providers appears to lead to poor care, and in many cases patients eventually choose to stop accessing the health care system altogether. Research claiming that weight is highly predictive of the health statuses of people of any group systematically discriminated against by health providers is incomplete without an analysis of the confounding effects of low-quality healthcare. To what extent does poor treatment in health care systems due to size, race, gender, or sexuality account

for previously identified correlations among weight, disease, and death for fat women? How do problematic, as well as positive, experiences with health care providers affect health care access rates among fat Black lesbian and bisexual women? In turn, do limited health care access behaviors in response to negative experiences with providers predict future health problems? These are some of the questions that researchers would be asking if they approached the study of health among fat people without an anti-fat bias and if they considered the full ecology of fat Black sexual minority women's health care. Research addressing questions like these can also help inform health provider-focused interventions designed to reduce negative biases against any and all of the communities to which fat Black lesbian and bisexual women belong.

Currently, there are various forms of cultural competency trainings that have been designed to address heterosexist, racist, and sexist policies and procedures in the health care system. A next step would be to develop and disseminate trainings that also address the stigma experienced by fat people, particularly because contemporary fat prejudice is partially justified through medically based arguments (Campos, 2004). With adequate health care and freedom from oppression, what would fat Black sexual minority women's health look like? A paradigm shift whereby health is truly constructed as a sociocultural phenomenon as much as a physiological one would lead to systemic-level interventions in which social justice work becomes a viable form of public health intervention.

Neither Placating nor Destroying Black Lesbian Women's Culture

Though moving toward a social change paradigm in public health is an ideal that I hold, I recognize that this may be, at the least, a slow-moving shift. Given this, we still must determine appropriate ways to pursue various forms of individual-level interventions that promote health and well-being in Black women's communities. I argue that our efforts to target health behaviors, however, should be grounded in the cultural values of Black sexual minority communities. Research suggests that both African American and lesbian communities, separately and at their intersections, have greater appreciation for women of larger-than-average sizes than that of the dominant, patriarchal, Euro-centered, heterosexist society. African American women have been found to exhibit lesser levels of body dissatisfaction as compared to White women, despite being generally heavier than White women (Celio, Zabinski, & Wilfley, 2002; see also Lovejoy 2001, for review). Also complementing the perspective that "big" is or can be beautiful, my own anecdotal experiences in Black communities have illustrated that heavier women have often been noted to be associated with health by the use of the term "healthy" to describe larger-than-average, attractive women. Similarly, lesbian participants in body image research have reported lower levels of body dissatisfaction as compared to heterosexual females (Owens, Hughes, & Owens-Nicholson, 2003; Rothblum, 2002). Although these studies' representations of African American and lesbian communities as accepting of large body sizes may not fully capture the complexity of esteem and body image among these groups, the empirical literature does suggest that there may be existing cultural values among these minority groups that support a higher value of body size diversity than found in mainstream U.S. culture.

As such, the relationship between the public health industry and African American and lesbian communities' culturally based values regarding body image is at a contentious place. Although many African American lesbians may appreciate body diversity and even view larger bodies as healthy, we are constantly confronted with the medical industry's view of our large bodies as inherently diseased and problematic. Several researchers examining weight among African American women and lesbians have called for culturally specific approaches to health promotion efforts that take this tension into account, but their intent appears to be to identify ways to *sensitively* get Black women to be *thinner* (Lovejoy, 2001; Yancey, Leslie, & Abel, 2006). Yet scholars have not adequately provided evidence that smaller bodies will equal greater health among African American or sexual minority women, which would justify the risk of changing a community's healthy norms toward body diversity. Though the practice of culturally grounding health promotion work may involve challenging cultural norms and values that promote illness and disease transmission (Wilson & Miller, 2003), the goal of public health work should not be to convince a group of people that their sense of themselves is inherently unhealthy and problematic. Rather than a focus on weight loss, an approach that balances cultural beliefs of beauty and health with well-intended health promotion messages to encourage healthy nutrition intake and physical activity would be most appropriate. For example, health promotion programs that facilitate all Black lesbian and bisexual women, not just those who are fat, to maintain physically active lives and to eat foods that help them maintain that lifestyle would be a start in the right direction. This type of program communicates the importance of nutrition and activity in the lives of all people, and does not make erroneous assumptions of health status based on weight, categorizing fat women as "needing" healthy foods and exercise while categorizing thin women as "fine the way they are."

Health programs may consider encouraging healthy behaviors and viewing actual health status, not weight, as markers of success. I view approaches such as these as commensurate with two of the main themes of Black feminist thought proposed by Patricia Hill Collins (1986; 2000)—respecting Black women's right to define and value ourselves, and acknowledging the existence of a Black women's cultural experience. At this time in public health research, however, the dominant paradigm consists of an externally defined health problem that produces an image of health and wellness for Black women that reduces the possible variations in healthy body sizes. Further, it focuses almost entirely on the reduction of weight as a remedy to disease. It would be more ethical to improve the scientific knowledge base regarding factors associated with health within the communities in which African American lesbians and bisexual women participate, than to find culturally "palpable" intervention strategies based on skewed interpretations of problematic data. Interventions focused on physical activity independent from weight loss as a means of achieving health have a stronger scientific evidence base (Miller, 1999) than interventions focused on weight reduction (see, e.g., Mann et al., 2007). Therefore, efforts aimed at balancing the cultural milieu of African American lesbian and bisexual women's communities, as well as the separate African American and lesbian communities in which they may participate, with the commitment to health promotion may do this best by targeting the ecological factors described above as well as individual barriers to physical activity and well-rounded nutrition. An example of such an intervention that has been found effective is Health at Every Size (Bacon, Stern, Van Loan, & Keim, 2005), which promotes body acceptance and healthy eating and activity without the goal of weight loss.

Conclusion

Looking ahead to future research, a more nuanced and ecologically valid examination of fat Black lesbian and bisexual women's health is required for the development of culturally grounded health programs intended for this community. Yet, given the data available today, it appears well advised to move away from approaches that seek to change the body sizes of Black women as a means of health promotion. As a fat woman who works in and is a part of Black lesbian and bisexual women's communities, I hope to never see the beautiful respect for body diversity that exists among many of us destroyed by the public health industry in the name of an uncritical acceptance of research that uses a

problematic and oppressive "fat-is-bad" bias as its starting point. In the face of multiple forms of oppression that attack our sexuality, size, skin color, race, and femininity, the reality that even some of us have maintained at least small amounts of love for our bodies is an amazing act of resilience that should be cherished. A health movement in Black women's communities that prioritizes respecting internally defined conceptualizations of health and quality of life, improving access to nutrition and physical activity for all individuals, and eradicating our subjugation to oppression at structural levels would be an exciting and liberating next step.

References

Aaron, D., Markovic, N., Danielson, M., Honnold, J., Janosky, J., & Schmidt, M. (2001). Behavioral risk factors for disease and preventive health practices among lesbians. *American Journal of Public Health, 91*, 972–975.

Bacon, L., Stern, J.S., Van Loan, M.D., & Keim, N.L. (2005). Size acceptance and intuitive eating improve health for obese, female chronic dieters. *Journal of American Diet Association, 105*, 929–936.

Bowen-Reid, T., & Harrell, J.P. (2002). Racist experiences and health outcomes: An examination of spirituality as a buffer. *Journal of Black Psychology, 28*, 18–36.

Campos, P. (2004). *The Obesity Myth: Why America's Obsession with Weight Is Hazardous to Your Health*. Gotham Books: New York.

Campos, P., Saguy, A., Ernsberger, P., Oliver, E., & Gaesser, G. (2006). The epidemiology of overweight and obesity: Public health crisis or moral panic? *International Journal of Epidemiology, 35*, 55–60.

Carter, C.C. (2003). Herstory of my hips. *Body Language* (pp. 84–85). Kings Crossing Publishing: Atlanta.

Celio, A.A., Zabinski, M.F., & Wilfley, D.E. (2002). African American body images. In T.F. Cash & T. Pruzinsky (Eds.),

Body Image: A Handbook of Theory, Research, and Clinical Practice (pp. 234–242). Guilford Press: New York.

Clark, R., Anderson, N., Clark, V., & Williams, D. (1999). Racism as a stressor for African Americans: A biopsychosocial model. *American Psychologist, 54,* 805–816.

Cochran, S., Mays, V., Bowen, D., Gage, S., Bybee, D., Roberts, S., et al. (2001). Cancer-related risk indicators and preventive screening behaviors among lesbian and bisexual women. *American Journal of Public Health, 91,* 591–597.

Collins, P.H. (1986). Learning from the outsider within: The sociological significance of Black feminist thought. *Social Problems, 33,* 14–32

Collins, P.H. (2000). *Black Feminist Thought: Knowledge, Consciousness, and the Politics of Empowerment.* Routledge: New York.

Combahee River Collective Statement (1977). In B. Smith (Ed.), *Home Girls: A Black Feminist Anthology* (pp. 272–282). Kitchen Table Women of Color Press: New York.

Davis, A. (1994). "Sick and tired of being sick and tired: The politics of Black women's health. In E.C. White (Ed.), *The Black Women's Health Book: Speaking for Ourselves* (pp. 18–26). Seal Press: Seattle.

Dibble, S.L., Roberts, S.A., Robertson, P.A., & Paul, S.M. (2002). Risk factors for ovarian cancer: Lesbian and heterosexual women. *Oncology Nursing Forum, 29,* E1–7.

Eliason, M.J., & Schope, R. (2001). Does "don't ask don't tell" apply to health care? Lesbian, gay, and bisexual people's disclosure to health care providers. *Journal of Gay and Lesbian Medical Association, 5,* 125–134.

Ernsberger, P., & Koletsky, R.J. (1999). Biomedical rationale for a wellness approach to obesity: An alternative to a focus on weight loss. *Journal of Social Issues, 55,* 221–259.

Flegal, K.M., Carroll, M.D., Ogden, C.L., & Johnson, C.L. (2002). Prevalence and trends in obesity among US adults, 1999–2000. *JAMA, 288,* 1723–1727.

Harvey, E.L., & Hill, A.J. (2001). Health professionals' views of overweight people and smokers. *International Journal of Obesity, 25,* 1253–1261.

Hill, J.O., Wyatt, H.R., Reed, G.W., & Peters, J.C. (2003). Obesity and the environment: Where do we go from here? *Science, 299,* 853–855.

hooks, b. (1984). *Feminist Theory: From Margin to Center.* South End Press: Boston.

Kazarian, S., & Evans, D. (2001). *Handbook of Cultural Health Psychology.* Academic Press: San Diego.

Krieger, N. (2003). Does racism harm health? Did child abuse exist before 1962? On explicit questions; critical science; and current controversies: An ecosocial perspective. *American Journal of Public Health, 93,* 194–199.

Krieger, N., & Fee, E. (Eds.). (1994). *Women's Health, Politics, and Power: Essays on Sex/Gender, Medicine, and Public Health.* Baywood Publishing: New York.

Laverack, G., & Labonte, R. (2000). A planning framework for the accommodation of community empowerment goals within health promotion programming. *Health, Policy, and Planning, 15,* 255–262.

Lovejoy, M. (2001). Disturbances in the social body: Differences in body image and eating problems among African American and White women. *Gender & Society, 15,* 239–261.

Mann, T., Tomiyama, A., Westling, E., Lew, A., Samuels, B., & Chatman, J. (2007). Medicare's search for effective obesity treatments: Diets are not the answer. *American Psychologist, 62,* 220–233.

Mays V, Yancey A, Cochran S, Weber, M, & Fielding, J. (2002). Heterogeneity of health disparities among African American, Latina/Hispanic, and Asian American women: Unrecognized influences of sexual orientation. *American Journal of Public Health, 92,* 632–639.

McEwen, B.S., & Seeman, T. (1999). Protective and damaging effects of mediators of stress: Elaborating and testing the concepts of allostasis and allostatic load. In Adler, N.E., Marmot, M., McEwen, B.S., & Stewart, J. (Eds.), *Socioeconomic Status and Health in Industrial Nations: Social, Psychological, and Biological Pathways* (pp. 30–47). Academy Sciences: New York.

Miller, W.C. (1999). Fitness and fatness in relation to health: Implications for a paradigm shift. *Journal of Social Issues, 55,* 207–219.

Owens, L., Hughes, T., & Owens-Nicholson, D. (2003). The effects of sexual orientation on body image and attitudes about eating and weight. *Journal of Lesbian Studies, 7,* 15–33.

Rothblum, E. (2002). Gay and lesbian body images. In T.F. Cash & T. Pruzinsky (Eds.), *Body Image: A Handbook of Theory, Research, and Clinical Practice* (pp. 257–265). Guilford Press: New York.

Stevens, J., Keil, J.E., Rust, P.F., Tyroler, H.A., Davis, C.E., & Gazes, P.C. (1992). Body mass index and body girths as predictors of mortality in black and white women. *Archives of Internal Medicine, 152,* 1257–1262.

Stevens, J., Plankey, M.W., Williamson, D.F., Thun, M.J., Rust, P.F., Palesch, Y., & O'Neil, P.M. (1998). The body mass index-mortality relationship in white and African American women. *Obesity Research, 6,* 268–277.

Thompson, B.W. (1994). *A Hunger So Wide and So Deep: American Women Speak Out on Eating Problems.* University of Minnesota Press: Minneapolis.

Wilson, B.D.M (2006). African American lesbian sexual culture: Exploring components and contradictions. *Dissertation Abstracts International: Section B: The Sciences and Engineering, 66,* 4003.

Wilson, B.D.M., & Miller, R. L. (2003). Examining strategies for culturally grounding HIV prevention: A review. *AIDS Education and Prevention, 15,* 184–202.

Wilson, B., Hayes, E., Greene, G., Kelly, J., & Iscoe, I. (2003). Community psychology. In D. K. Freedheim (Ed.), *Comprehensive Handbook of Psychology,* Vol. 1: *The History of Psychology* (pp. 431–449). Wiley Publishers: New York.

Valanis, B., Bowen, D., Bassford T., Whitlock E., Charney P., & Carter R.A. (2000). Sexual orientation and health: Comparisons in the Women's Health Initiative sample. *Archives of Family Medicine, 9,* 843–853.

Yancey, A., Leslie J., & Abel, E. (2006). Obesity at the crossroads: Feminist and public health perspectives. *Signs, 31,* 425–443.

What's on the Menu?

Julie Guthman

The Obamas' Garden

Upon assuming the role of First Lady in 2009, one of the first things Michelle Obama did was to plant an organic garden on the White House lawn. This was not too long after Michael Pollan (2008a) had written his open letter to the president-elect, whom he dubbed farmer-in-chief. The letter provided a long list of recommendations for food and farming policy reform to reduce the use of fossil fuels and wean the US food system off the logic of cheapness.[1] For this, Pollan was himself informally crowned farmer-in-chief, and a huge swell of grassroots support arose to name him secretary of (food and) agriculture. The White House must have been listening. After all, it was one of Pollan's recommendations to "tear out five prime south-facing acres of the White House lawn and plant in their place an organic fruit and vegetable garden."

The garden wasn't without its critics. The Mid America CropLife Association, which represents chemical-agribusiness interests, sent an angry letter to the White House claiming that only conventional agriculture can feed the world. For the most part, though, the garden encountered little resistance and was widely heralded, especially by the alternative-food movement. If nothing else, this demonstrates the huge success of the organic farming and gardening movement in communicating its *ideas*, which used to sit on the countercultural margins, to a much wider audience. To wit, as Pollan also pointed out in the same letter, there is room for food and farming across the political spectrum. "Reforming the food system is not inherently a right-or-left issue: for every Whole Foods shopper with roots in the counterculture you can find a family of evangelicals intent on taking control of its family dinner and diet back from the fast-food industry—the culinary equivalent of home schooling. . . . There is also a strong libertarian component to the sun-food agenda, which seeks to free small producers from the burden of government regulation in order to stoke rural innovation. And what is a higher 'family value,' after all, than making time to sit down every night to a shared meal?" Therein lies the problem: an approach that appeals to all parts of the political spectrum cannot challenge the political-economic forces that are producing cheap, toxic, and junky food—and making some people dependent on it.

Since the Obamas planted their organic garden, the rest of the food and agriculture agenda has remained the same, more or less. For example, the Obama administration, under the guidance of the EPA and the USDA, has been pushing the use of coal waste containing gypsum (a form of calcium) on fields, despite its containing traces of lead, mercury, and arsenic; Obama has been championing immigration reform, which includes paths to citizenship but also tighter border controls, which will continue making the undocumented workers who slip through easily exploitable (see chapter 6); and he has already signed into law a reduction in food assistance to go into effect in 2014. In December 2010, he signed a bill extending the Bush tax cuts, exacerbating the nation's increasing economic inequality. This is not an argument with gradualism—it is painfully evident that the Obama administration has had to seriously tamp down expectations in view of an intransigent and increasingly virulent Right. And it's not even necessarily about scale, that this small garden is a drop in the bucket amid the vast farms and factories that produce cheap food. There is definitely something to be said for creating a highly visible model. My concern, rather, is the absence in the policy agenda of any move that would begin to undermine a food (and industrial) system that simultaneously brings hunger, danger, and unremittingly undercompensated toil; it's the absence from public discussions of acknowledgment that our food system is part of a political economy that systematically produces inequality; and it's the reluctance of much of the alternative-food movement to take on the big fights, instead promulgating the notion that education will change how people eat—and thus transform the food system. Obama's garden, in other words, throws into sharp relief the limitations of alternative food as a change strategy.

Yet, it is the appeals to obesity to which I draw your attention. Naturally, in his open letter Pollan also discussed the health costs and dangers of type 2 diabetes and obesity, which he said could be avoided with changes in diet and lifestyle. In promoting the garden, Mrs. Obama was quick to point out that it would not just "provide food for the first family's meals and formal dinners; its most important role will be to educate children about healthful, locally grown fruit and vegetables at a time when obesity and diabetes have become a national concern" (Burros 2009). How is local, organic, and seasonal garden-grown food a tenable solution to obesity?

In the face of insurmountable evidence that traditional dieting rarely achieves lasting results, exposing people to attractive fresh food, like the kind found at farmers markets and in gardens, does seem a kinder, gentler approach. Even *The Biggest Loser,* a medium for advertising all manner of commodified diet food, has not edited out one of the trainers' recommendations to eat more *organic* vegetables. At one level, it's hard to take issue with this recommendation. After all, who could be against fresh, visually appealing vegetables? And such an approach certainly couldn't hurt, so it seems.

Nevertheless, in urging people to make better "choices," those who advocate for fresh, organic, and local produce as a means of weight loss are not wholly unlike those who want to combat global warming by getting consumers to swap their incandescent light bulbs for fluorescent ones. (Incidentally, buying fresh, local, organic foods at farmers markets roughly covers five different suggestions listed in the top fifty things you can do to stop global warming as listed at http://globalwarming-facts.info/50-tips.html.) These suggestions are based on a singular hegemonic understanding of the cause of the problem: calories and carbon dioxide emissions, which to some degree forecloses efforts to search for other causes (and, remarkably, the proposed solutions to both obesity and global warming have to do with energy). They educe individual, consumerist solutions based on those singular causes, which tends to neglect the sources of the problem in production and lets off the hook those most responsible for the problem (corporate bad actors and policy makers). And they don't consider the consequences of defining problems and solutions in ways that may be damaging to those most vulnerable to the problem (whether resource-poor subsistence producers or very fat people).

In these ways, the current conversation about obesity and good food shares many characteristics of environmental orthodoxies (such as global warming), in which taken-for-granted assumptions are built into explanations and solutions, and urgency to do *something* trumps careful scientific examination (Forsyth 2003: 37–38). Forsyth emphatically does not deny that environmental problems such as global warming exist. Rather, he argues that conventional ways of understanding such problems can be "intellectually constraining in that they delimit the universe of further scientific inquiry, political discourse, and possibly policy options" (originally in Jasanoff and Wynne 1998: 5). As antidote, he proposes what he calls a critical political ecology approach that pays attention to (a) how existing framings shape scientific understandings of the problem; (b) how those framings foreclose or leave out other explanations; and (c) the social consequences of the framings. Looking beyond the standard explanations does not necessarily reveal other certain explanations or falsify myths, he argues, but it can illuminate problems in new and meaningful ways.

Back to the Problem

This critical political ecology approach is what I have tried to take in this book. The orthodoxies I have examined are about obesity and alternative food separately and as they articulate in efforts to address obesity as a health problem. My goal has not been to deny the increase in obesity prevalence, the idea that obesity *can* cause illness, that certain environments lack access to the good life, or that the existing food system produces nutritionally suspect food (quite the reverse). Instead, it has been to challenge the assumptions along various links of the explanatory chain—and particularly at the point at which these two discourses intersect. I have done this in the interest of *opening up the conversation* to other ideas, contending not only that current rhetorical and practical efforts may be ineffective but also that they may do harm in the name of "doing good." With that in mind, let me now review and cross-fertilize the key concerns I have raised, which, following Forsyth, I roughly categorize as representational, causal, and consequential.

There is little question that the significant increase in size between 1980 and the early 2000s is worthy of explanation, keeping in mind that fatness itself is not new. Yet, the ways in which this phenomenon has been measured and represented can obscure as much as they tell. First, as an indicator of obesity, high BMI is crude and doesn't adequately represent aspects of adiposity that may be more or less detrimental to health—for example, differences between subcutaneous and visceral adiposity. Second, the particular ways of categorizing BMI values into definitive ranges of normal, overweight, and obese inflects some

of these changes with more drama than they perhaps warrant. Third, because they rely on conventions of averaging to define normal phenotype, they tend to confuse the normal with the normative, "what is" with "what ought to be." The reliance on averages is particularly odd, given that BMIs in the "overweight" range are actually the new normal.

Nor do these BMI ranges match up neatly to health outcomes. Not only is a much broader range of BMI values than those in the "normal" range associated with relatively low risk for mortality; the use of probabilistic risk factors is also a crude and often confusing way to understand and represent how particular body morphologies (i.e., shapes) may lead to disease. One reason is that any given disease or risk factor is associated with a multiplicity of others, and the direction of causality is often indeterminable. Obesity and type 2 diabetes, for example, are risk factors for each other, poverty is a risk factor for both, and obesity is also a risk factor for poverty. It is certainly reasonable to think that poverty leads people to eat too much low-quality food, and that causes obesity, which then causes diabetes-related death. But it is also plausible that poverty presents an obstacle in seeking preventative health care—or, more likely, is nested in a host of complicating factors that affect health outcomes. It is also possible that toxic exposures are causing both obesity and type 2 diabetes, with each a symptom of the other. The point is that the relevant psychological, economic, social, cultural, biological, and ecological factors are inextricably coconstitutive, and risk factors appear a highly reductive way to represent a problem that is very difficult to sort out. Insofar as the medical costs of treating obesity also incorporate such risk factors in the calculations (as attributable fractions), the idea that obesity is a cost to the nation is sketchy. Rarely do we hear that poverty is a huge cost to the nation. And, of course, rarely do we hear about the calculations of health care costs related to efforts to be thin.

The heart of the representational problem, then, is reliance on epidemiology as a basis of health knowledge and diagnosis.

As "surveillance medicine," detached from actual bodies, epidemiology cannot take the place of clinical medicine and laboratory science in determining and treating what exactly is pathological, for which obesity may be a very weak proxy. Although it may be true that the tools of epidemiology are the best available for noting trends in population-level public health, they should nonetheless be understood for what they are and what they can and cannot do.

Moving into the questions about obesity's causes, the period of growth in BMI has seen enormous nutritional changes. To the degree that rising BMIs reflect nutritional changes, at least some of these are for the better. Although many Americans are food insecure, these days few truly go hungry. Many good foods have been made more available, such as fresh fruits and vegetables, and foods that have made people taller, such as milk, seem to generate far less concern than those that have putatively made us fatter, notwithstanding the increasing prevalence of lactose intolerance. Nevertheless, we shouldn't assume that differences in nutritional intake solely explain body size difference along class, race, and gender lines. The assumption that obesity inheres to people with low socioeconomic status because they lack income to buy healthy food, live in food-insecure environments, or are beset with stress-eating and self-medication is belied by data that show little difference in caloric intake among different income groups. In general, steadfast loyalty to a nutritional explanation, via the energy balance model, neglects other possible explanations that may lie in the enormous environmental changes that occurred just in advance of the period when mean BMI began to creep upward. Furthermore, aspects of the increase in size such as the increase in extreme obesity are not well explained by the energy balance model. The increase in infant obesity is most definitely not. Some of these shifts in body size could well have resulted from exposures to endocrine-disrupting chemicals and food ingredients (both related to class but not through the vehicle of "consumer choice") that affect body size in ways other than

through caloric intake and expenditure. Conversely, the emphasis on obesity tends to occlude the many diseases and conditions associated with poor nutrition and toxic exposures that don't happen to manifest in fatness.

The discourse of obesity has articulated with efforts to redirect blame for poor health toward certain built environments instead of those who live in them. Pointing out the inequities in access to nutritious food and pleasant outdoor environments is laudable. Nevertheless, since the food side of the obesogenic environment thesis, with its emphasis on the ubiquity of cheap, fattening food, appears to apply to just about all food environments in the United States, it paradoxically provides support to those who say that obesity results from personal choices. For, if some people remain thin amidst the plenty, they presumably are more effective in mediating these environments. More fundamentally, the thesis assumes the energy balance model of obesity causation. Again, to the extent that obesity prevalence does cluster geographically, it could also be a consequence of place-specific toxic exposures or simply that people of the same race and class also tend to cluster geographically.

Even accepting the energy balance model, the obesogenic environment thesis tends to ignore how inequalities in income, employment, and wealth, as well as regressive tax policy (such as reliance on sales tax, which causes the poor to bear a relatively larger portion of the tax burden than a progressive income tax does), give rise to the character of these environments. To be sure, in addition to the many uncertainties and absences in these discourses, the current conversation about obesity and food is remarkably indifferent to the dynamics of capitalism and the long-term production of inequality—and how urban environments reflect the buying and investment power of people who inhabit them. In that way, the current conversation is very much in the vein of what Robbins calls "apolitical ecologies," in which explanations of ecological problems (and obesity *is* that) focus far too much on individual behavior and choices and far too little on the broader political and economic context in which choices are made. This is particularly clear in the discussions of the food system. To the extent that food system activists focus on policy, they attribute far too much to the role of commodity subsidies and too little to the broader geopolitical concerns and political-economic conditions that have encouraged overproduction of commodities and compelled food processors and manufacturers to cut costs to compete. Additionally, in their desire to support small, agrarian producers, they have almost entirely neglected that the rest of the food system has been a source of tremendous inequality. American agriculture was built on racialized land and labor relationships—many whites received land nearly free, while others were prohibited, discouraged, or disenfranchised from owning land, and worked as slaves, sharecroppers, indentured servants, or undocumented workers, depending on migration histories and the particular racial character in which they were slotted. Since the legacies of unequal access to land and high-paying jobs are far from erased, neglecting the issue of income—and thus whether different groups even have a choice to buy the kind of food they want—is shameful. Eschewing the use of regulatory "sticks" in ways that might curtail the use of some of the worst materials and practices in agriculture and other industrial production is shameful, too.

Altogether, much of the current conversation about obesity and good food is an expression of the ideology of healthism. Healthism makes personal health attainment the highest goal, sees poor health outcomes as a result of behaviors, and conflates personal practices of self-care with empowerment and good citizenship. Recall that healthism is itself a reflection of neoliberal norms of governance, since it concedes the rollback of public-sector responsibility for supporting and protecting the health of all and instead places responsibility on individuals for their own health outcomes. In doing so, healthism tends to neglect—or write off—those without the means or the desire to share in these norms. The way healthism filters both understanding of obesity and conceptualizing of food system transformation has consequences—consequences that can work against social justice and well-being.

First, no matter how worthy the intentions behind it, obesity talk makes fat people a problem and renews the stigma of a population that has had to endure much of it. Healthism gives additional cover for expressing distaste for fat bodies. Swipes at obesity, especially coming from those who have never been subject to such scrutiny or objectification, or the pain and frustration of weight loss, are insensitive at best and seriously damaging at worse. The intense social scolding of fat people (or people who believe themselves too fat) can be costly, too, and can work at cross-purposes to health and well-being. Besides the fact that many fat people are reticent to seek care for fear of embarrassment, scolding, or self-doubt, blaming fat people for health care costs is leading to the denial of health care in the name of health. To the extent that healthism reinforces fat discrimination in jobs, education, and access to health care, it can worsen inequality, adding to ways in which socioeconomic status can be an outcome of size as well as a cause of it.

Second, many of the approaches to redressing obesity and improving the food system exacerbate racial and class inequalities, regardless of body size. This is most obvious with the obesogenic environment thesis, which takes healthism's notion of the good life and projects particular ideals and aesthetics onto the built environment. Such accounts do not address the political-economic circumstances that make some places desirable and allow disinvestment in others. Not only are the ideal, leptogenic environments financially unattainable to most; disparaging certain types of neighborhoods as "obesogenic" does little for those who live in them, including many working-class whites, since such disparagement could contribute to more devaluation. Conversely, trying to solve the problem by making obesogenic places more like wealthy, leptogenic places can push poor people out through gentrification.

Third, the unrelenting emphasis on the putatively tight relationship between calories and adiposity misses serious dangers in food, including those that don't manifest as fatness. The inattention thus far to environmental obesogens is the most telling of all. While there is much discussion about the injustice in access to fresh fruits and vegetables, food movements continue to pay relatively little attention to the daily dousing of pesticides in fields and agricultural communities, which lead to cancer and birth defects, and now, it appears, to fatness (Harrison 2008b). While there is much talk about supersizing and other ways food marketers get people to eat more, there is much less discussion of the ways that cheap food, including many diet foods, alter physiological processes in other potentially debilitating ways. That foods which are nutrient-depleting, cancer-causing, or just hard on the body are promoted for weight loss suggests once more that aesthetic displeasure with fat is driving much of the conversation and even affecting political priorities. I don't say this lightly. Studies have shown that people would rather have heart disease, be legally blind, or have a leg amputated than be fat (Puhl and Brownell 2001). We know that people smoke cancer-causing cigarettes to avoid getting fat.

Finally, the implicit linking of good food, good bodies, and political activism allows those who are already privileged to achieve even higher status by virtue of their bodies and food-purchasing habits. Fat stigmatization necessarily accords higher status to those who are not fat (Julier 2008). Bolstered by the ideology of healthism, which suggests a lack of personal responsibility and knowledge among the fat, those who are not fat are positioned as more responsible and knowing, regardless of what, if anything, they do to be thin (LeBesco 2004). Owing to its abiding association with upscale eating, organic, local food also accords higher status to those who buy and eat it (Guthman 2003). With the appearance of alternative-food participation as the paradigmatic way to transform the food system, and food transformation as the social movement issue of the day, eating well (and having a thin body) begins to be equated with creating positive social change. In effect, the alternative-food movement attaches political citizenship and ethics to personal investments in body and health. Those who have already done well in wallet and body get to feel as though they've done even more. It is this most self-congratulatory aspect of the alternative-food movement that is perhaps most consequential for social justice, since it limits what is put on the table politically.

What to Put on the Table

Precisely in this vein, I ask you, the reader, to reconsider where the problem lies. We have a political economy that produces and makes available cheap food and goods, underpays people, and urges them to buy this food and these goods to keep the economy afloat—and then a culture that blames them for consuming this food and these goods after all. A large part of this political economy involves barely regulated food, chemical, and pharmaceutical industries that produce materials not all of which are willingly ingested, inhaled, or absorbed but which modify our bodies in ways we barely understand.

And the broadest social force against these, the alternative-food movement, has focused on providing good food and has nearly abandoned changing the regulatory environment to reduce toxic exposures. Nor has it ever really engaged with issues of wages and entitlements so that all people can afford to eat well. To the contrary, the influence of healthism has helped justify individualistic approaches to food system change, and even allowed food injustice to be defined merely as unequal access to high-quality food rather than also including unequal incomes in food work and unequal exposure to pesticides.

That the more radical food justice movement (at least in rhetoric) addresses the access problem but for the most part steers clear of labor and to some extent income issues speaks to a self-perpetuating narrowing of political possibility. Precisely because social movement possibilities are so constrained by neoliberal logics of the market, many dedicated activists barely see other ways forward besides educating people to the qualities of food and bringing good food to low-income people in acts of charity or through nonprofit subsidies and in the name of health and empowerment. The charitable act of bringing good food to others is in no way comparable to transforming the increased class disparities that neoliberal capitalism has produced. To be sure, having come into being in a neoliberal context, the current trend in food activism writ large tends to reflect and uphold neoliberal forms of governance, despite the fact that the particular confluence of problems, in many (but not all) ways, stems from neoliberal economic policy. Accordingly, the alternative-food movement puts a great deal of emphasis on the market rather than the state, on consumption rather than production, and on individual health rather than social justice. And yet, *the current policy environment is a result of political choices, not consumption choices. Therefore, to make different political choices requires much more attention to the broader injustices that the cheap food dilemma rests on and perhaps less attention to what's on the menu.* We cannot change the world one meal at a time.

As for the problem of obesity, it needs rethinking both medically and discursively, especially given the effect of a barely regulated food system on the body. We should give a rest to the idea that "something must be done" to reverse trends in obesity per se. At the very least, we need to consider a broader range of body sizes as nonpathological and to distinguish what's pathological from what's simply not normal (as in average). More to the point, we need to recognize that, even when obesity is pathological, efforts to fix it at the individual level may do more harm to health and well-being than letting it be. A harm-reduction perspective may be in order, which would entail refraining from disciplining people whose health outcomes are not easily determinable by their size and exercising more compassion for those whose condition cannot be cured. More fundamentally, then, we need

to understand that, like the ecologies affected by global warming, bodily ecologies are indeed being remade as a result of unregulated capitalism in ways that we don't entirely know or understand. But, also like global warming, the issue is not the fact that we are getting bigger—things change—but what it means for those most likely to be adversely affected by it.

Given the profits that have been made on the binge and purge economy and the inattention to regulating body-changing pollution, it is clear that we must turn away from the current obsession with individual consumption habits and body sizes and engage more deeply with policy. Rather than complicity in market logics, we need to harness this exploding interest in food and use the power of public politics to change food systems. Given the competing imperatives of food production—to support producers and to feed consumers—we need to admit to the need for subsidies, but subsidies of a different kind: subsidies that allow farmers to grow in the most ecologically and socially responsible ways without having to overtax the environment; subsidies that allow all eaters to buy what they want and need. And we need to remove the subsidies of a free regulatory ride. The "free market" will not do.

To their credit, some organizations in food movements have already begun this shift. The discussions that led up to the 2008 farm bill saw unprecedented participation from this movement, which both critiqued the commodity subsidy programs and demanded more programs that encourage fresh fruit and vegetable production, soil conservation practices, and support for low-resource farmers. Community food security activists have redoubled their efforts to expand entitlement support. And those in the nutrition and public health communities have had a modicum of success in banning sodas from public schools and discouraging the use of trans fats through either local ordinances or more generalized shaming. These are all places to start, although policies must be carefully crafted to change the practices of the producers rather than tax and scold people who can least afford it.

Still, in my view, policy must go to an even deeper place. I have tried to show that the availability of cheap food is a deeply structural problem having to do with the logics of capitalism that the neoliberal "fix" has worsened and made our bodies be the site for that fix. The systematic production of inequality has taken place not only through farm and food policy but also through trade, labor, immigration, health care, economic development, taxation, and financial policy—in other words, just about all policies that have kept American capitalism (barely) afloat. While some in the alternative-food movement have been content to use capitalism to change food, others are returning to the idea of using food, the most essential of human needs, to change capitalism. They are rejecting the limited tools of the market and thinking about other ways in which food issues can galvanize social movements for global justice—because, ultimately, what needs to be put on the table is not only fresh fruits and vegetables (and, really, whatever you want to eat), but capitalism.

Note

1 For the record, I agreed with most of the recommendations and even take some credit for them. This is because I, along with some of my colleagues, participated in a special issue of the journal *Gastronomica* on the politics of food in which we took Pollan to task for his disengagement from policy work. It was after that was published and circulated that Pollan began fervently discussing the farm bill.

The Body, Disability, and Sexuality

Thomas J. Gerschick

We do not express or even show our wishes, because we have learned that in our condition of disablement or disfigurement, no one could (or should) find us sexually attractive.

(*Zola 1982: 215*)

People with disabilities face formidable challenges in establishing self-satisfactory sexualities; yet despite these challenges, they are increasingly doing so. This chapter conveys a range of scholarship from advocates, researchers, and other interested parties regarding the relationship among the body, disability, and sexuality. I begin with a brief contextualization of disability and then turn my attention to the role of the body in social life using the experiences of people with disabilities to highlight key social dynamics. Subsequently, I provide an overview of the challenges that people with disabilities face in determining self-satisfactory sexualities and conclude with a discussion of their active responses to those challenges.

Disabled bodies

Those who are characterized as disabled experience a wide range of medically defined conditions, some readily visible, others much less so. These conditions are conceptualized in a variety of ways by doctors and scholars, but generally they are grouped under physical and psychological conditions. Examples include deafness, blindness, spinal cord injury, multiple sclerosis, muscular dystrophy, developmental disabilities, bipolar disorder, and mental illness. These definitions serve to distinguish people with disabilities from the temporarily able-bodied in society. I inten-

tionally utilize the term temporarily able-bodied to highlight the fact that aging is disabling and many of us will live long enough to develop a disability during our lifetime. Such language highlights the fact that human variation reflects a continuum, rather than a dichotomy of being disabled or not.

As many scholars have noted, it is exceedingly difficult to determine the size of the population of people with disabilities globally due to lack of consensus regarding definitions of disability and differential abilities within countries and regions to count their populations. One well-informed researcher, Gary Albrecht (2004), placed the number at approximately 500 million worldwide, the vast majority of whom live in the developing world. Reflecting our limited understanding of the scope of the population, there is much we do not know regarding the circumstances, conditions and treatment of people with disabilities. As a consequence of this, the bulk of this chapter will focus on the existing scholarship which largely attends to the West, especially the United States. Furthermore, given the relatively new attention to disability and sexuality, not much attention has been paid to the intersection of these with other social factors such as race, class, gender, sexual orientation, and ethnicity. Wherever possible, I include available understandings of these intersections.

The importance of the body in social life

The body is central in social life. People are privileged by the degree to which they approximate the cultural ideal. Bodies physically exist along a continuum. Given the large amount of human variation across time and culture and the array of expectations and standards, the body must be framed in terms of degrees of normativity: from more normative to less (Gerschick 2005). There are many ways in which a body can be less normative. Characteristics such as race, ethnicity, class, age, physique, weight, height, ability, disability, appearance, and skin color predominate. People can be less normative by being too light, too dark, too fat, too skinny, too poor, too young, too old, too tall, too short, too awkward, and/or too uncoordinated. Scholars have noted that the degree to which one is bodily-normative matters considerably because it helps place one in the stratification order. The degree to which bodily variation has been accepted has also varied across time and culture. The societal treatment one experiences, then, depends on the degree of normativeness, one's resources, and the particular historical, cultural, and structural contexts in which one lives (Gerschick 2005). For example, consider the resources available to the late actor, Christopher Reeve, following his injury in 1995, due to his celebrity and wealth. Although his injury was severe, he received the highest quality of care possible and became a cultural icon for his work on behalf *of* others with spinal cord injuries. Many other people with disabilities, lacking Reeve's status and resources, are treated much more poorly. Their opportunities are also much more limited.

The negative treatment experienced by most people with disabilities can be understood by considering how bodies are symbolic. One's body serves as a type of social currency that signifies one's worth. Consequently, people with less-normative bodies, such as people with disabilities, are vulnerable to being denied social recognition and validation. People respond to one another's bodies, which initiates social processes such as validation and the assignment of status. Summarizing the research, Patzer (1985: 1) observes:

> Physical attractiveness is the most visible and most easily accessible trait of a person. Physical attractiveness is also a constantly and frequently used informational cue . . . Generally, the more

physically attractive an individual is, the more positively the person is perceived, the more favorably the person is responded to, and the more successful is the person's personal and professional life.

Thus, researchers maintain that to have a less-normative body, such as having a disability which is perceived by most to be unattractive, is not so much a physical condition as it is a social and stigmatized one.

This stigma is embodied in the popular stereotypes of people whose bodies are less normative. People with disabilities, for instance, are perceived to be weak, passive, and dependent. The English language exemplifies this stigmatization; people with disabilities are de-formed, dis-eased, dis-abled, dis-ordered, ab-normal, and in-valid (Zola 1982: 206). Having a disability can also become a primary identity that overshadows almost all other aspects of one's identity.

This stigma is embedded in daily interactions among people. People are evaluated in terms of normative expectations and, because of their bodies, are frequently found wanting. As demonstrated by the social responses to people with disabilities, people with less-normative bodies are avoided, ignored, and marginalized. They experience a range of reactions from subtle indignities and slights to overt hostility and outright cruelty (Gerschick 2005, 1998). This treatment creates subtle but formidable physical, economic, psychological, architectural, and social obstacles to their participation in all aspects of social life.

A hierarchy of bodies exists in any particular historical, cultural, structural, and global context. The degree to which one's body is devalued is also affected by other social characteristics including social class, sexual orientation, age, and race and ethnicity. The type of disability – its visibility, the severity of it, whether it is physical or mental in origin, and the contexts – mediate the degree to which a person with a less-normative body is socially compromised (Gerschick 2005, 1998). For instance, a severe case of Chronic Fatigue Syndrome can disable someone, thereby creating a less-normative body; however, typically the condition is not readily apparent and as a consequence does not automatically trigger stigmatization and devaluation. Conversely, having quadriplegia and utilizing a wheelchair for mobility is highly visual, is perceived to be severe, and frequently elicits invalidation. One of the challenges facing researchers is to develop a systematic theory to address the degrees of non-normativity and the circumstances that lead to different levels of stigmatization and marginalization and how these differ for different groups of people based on their gender, race, ethnicity, social class, sexual orientation and origin (Gerschick 2005).

People with less-normative bodies, such as people with disabilities, are engaged in an asymmetrical power relationship with their more-normative bodied counterparts, who have the power to validate their bodies and their identities (Gerschick 2005, 1998). An example comes from Jerry, aged sixteen at the time of his interview, who lived with Juvenile Rheumatoid Arthritis:

> I think [others' conception of what defines a man] is very important because if they don't think of you as one, it is hard to think of yourself as one or it doesn't really matter if you think of yourself as one if no one else does.
>
> (*Gerschick and Miller 1994: 50*)

In order to be validated, each person in a social situation needs to be recognized by others as appropriately meeting the situated expectations. Those with whom we interact continuously assess our performance and determine the degree to which we are meeting those expectations. Our "audience" or interaction partners then hold us accountable and sanction us in a variety of ways in order to encourage compliance. Our need for social approval and validation further encourages conformity. Much is at stake in this process because one's sense of self rests precariously upon the audience's decision to validate or reject one's performance.

Successful enactment bestows status and acceptance; failure invites embarrassment and humiliation (West and Zimmerman 1987). This point is illustrated by Kit, one of researchers Shakespeare, Gillespie-Sells and Davies's informants:

> I actually think my being a disabled lesbian is a very . . . it's a struggle, I don't mean that it's a struggle in that I don't want to be a disabled lesbian, it's a struggle in that you are completely, you are completely insignificant and denied any identity or importance.
>
> (*Shakespeare, Gillespie-Sells and Davies 1996: 154*)

It is challenging to maintain one's dignity and sense of self under such circumstances.

Challenges to sexual satisfaction

Before turning my attention to the ways in which people with disabilities seek sexual self-determination, I want to focus on five particular challenges to developing self-satisfactory sexualities: the medicalization of disability, the attitudes of the temporarily able-bodied, internalized oppression, fetishists, and physical and sexual abuse.

The medicalization model of people with disabilities

Historically, disability has been defined in part in medical terms. It has been perceived as an individual, physical problem requiring a medical or mechanical solution. Scholars point out that the emphasis in this model is on deficiency, pathology, tragedy and loss that can, with medical intervention, be remedied. This mindset locates the problem solely in the individual, not in society. As such it is apolitical. The person with a disability is defined as passive, dependent and infant-like, one who needs others to care for them. It reinforces the power of others, especially care professionals, to define people with disabilities and their circumstances. While there is no doubt that medical attention has significantly improved the lives of people with disabilities over the last several decades, the attendant mindset has also undermined disabled people's ability to self-determine their lives, including their sexuality.

Associated with this is the view that people with disabilities are asexual. As a consequence, scholars maintain that medical practitioners tend not to provide information to people with disabilities about sexual functioning or sexual healthcare. In denying them information about sexual pleasure, medical practitioners send a tacit but powerful message about how people with disabilities are perceived as sexual beings. They are, apparently, not entitled to this kind of pleasure, as explained by then 53-year-old essayist, Nancy Mairs:

> . . . the general assumption, even among those who might be expected to know better, is that people with disabilities are out of the sexual running. Not one of my doctors, for example, has ever asked me about my sex life. Most people, in fact, deal with the discomfort and even distaste that a misshapen body arouses by disassociating that body from sexuality in reverie and practice. "They" can't possibly do it, the thinking goes; therefore, "they" mustn't even want it; and that is *that*. The matter is closed before a word is uttered. People with disabilities can grow so used to unstated messages of consent and prohibition that they no longer "hear" them as coming from the outside, any more than the messengers know they are "speaking" them. This vast conspiracy of silence surrounding the sexuality of the disabled consigns countless numbers to sexual uncertainty and disappointment.
>
> (*Mairs 1996: 51–2*)

One can easily imagine, then, how debilitating this mindset can be in cultures that emphasize sex and sexuality.

Attitudes of people with disabilities as sexual partners

Successfully creating and maintaining self-satisfactory sexualities and identities under these challenging social circumstances is an almost Sisyphean task. Consequently, sexuality is threatened when corporeal appearance and performance are discordant with cultural expectations, such as in the case of having a disability (Gerschick 1998). Depending on the degree of their difference, people with disabilities contravene many of the beliefs and expectations associated with being desirable and sexual. For instance, in the contemporary West, to be perceived as physically attractive is to be socially and sexually desirable. Due to their invalidated condition, however, women and men with disabilities are constrained in their opportunities to nurture and to be nurtured, to be lovers and to love, and to become parents if they so desire (Gerschick 1998). These dynamics are particularly acute in subcultures where a premium is placed on bodily appearance. Poet Kenny Fries, in his memoir, discusses what it is like to be a man with a disability within a gay culture that idealizes bodies:

> . . . in bars I would plant myself at a table or on a stool at the bar and stay in one place as long as possible. When I saw someone I would like to get to know, I would stay put. And even when I had to go to the bathroom I would put it off for as long as I could to avoid making my disability noticeable by standing up and walking. By deciding to remain stationary, I rarely met the men I wanted to meet, the men I was attracted to. Those I met would have to come over to me, or I would meet them by chance when they happened to take an empty seat near where I sat at a table or at the bar.
>
> (*Fries 1997: 131*)

Thus people with disabilities, many with few social resources, face deeply entrenched prejudice and stereotypes when seeking to establish self-satisfactory sexualities. They rarely have the power to challenge the dominant discourse which infantilizes them and perceives them to be asexual (Shakespeare, Gillespie-Sells and Davies 1996).

Internalized oppression

Sexuality and a sense of oneself as a sexual being are not created in a vacuum. Frequently people with disabilities internalize societal negative stereotypes and act on them as if they were true. In the following quote, writer and filmmaker Billy Golfus, who was disabled due to a motorcycle accident, illustrates the insidiousness of internalizing asexual stereotypes about people with disabilities when he discusses a woman for a potential relationship:

> Even though she is attractive, I don't really think about her that way partly because the [wheel]chair makes me not even see her and because after so many years of being disabled you quit thinking about it as an option.
>
> (*Golfus 1997: 420*)

The woman *in* this illustration was as invisible to him as his own sexuality was. This example reveals how deeply some people with disabilities internalize societal standards of desirability and sexuality, which then makes them complicit in their sexual oppression (Gerschick 1998).

Similarly, people with disabilities internalize the belief that their degree of function, attractiveness and desirability determines their self worth. Author and cartoonist John Callahan explained:

> I can remember looking at my body with loathing and thinking, Boy, if I ever get to heaven, I'm not going to ask for a new pair of legs like the average quad does. I'm going to ask for a dick I can feel. The idea promoted in rehab of the socially well-adjusted, happily married quad made me sick. This was the crudest thing

of all. Always, I felt humiliated. Surely a man with any self respect would pull the plug on himself

> (*Callahan 1990: 121*)

The lack of self-esteem in this crucial human arena leads people with physical disabilities to limit themselves at times, as Nancy Mairs (1996: 52) describes:

> . . . my wheelchair seals my chastity. Men may look at me with pity, with affection, with amusement, with admiration, but never with lust. To be truthful, I have so internalized the social proscription of libido in my kind that if a man did come on to me, I'd probably distrust him as at least a little peculiar in his erotic tastes.

As the following section demonstrates, Mairs has reason to be concerned.

Fetishists

One of the paradoxical issues facing people with disabilities are devotees: temporarily able-bodied people who are attracted to them because of their disabilities. Because most devotees are heterosexual males pursuing women with disabilities, especially women amputees, this section focuses on them.

There are many websites and magazines devoted to community, companionship, relationships, and picture and DVD exchange and sale between temporarily able-bodied men and women with disabilities. These forums provide locales where women with disabilities can meet and interact with their followers. They can run, or respond to, personal ads and arrange to meet potential suitors in person. Many of these forums are controlled by women with disabilities (Kafer 2000).

The social meanings and ramifications of these sites, communities, and behaviors are difficult to discern. In a society which does not value emotional, mental, or physical difference, relationships between people with disabilities and their devotees are created in an environment of vast power differentials. However, many of the women involved in these communities experience their participation as empowering. Additionally, if we define the attraction of devotee men as deviant, what does that say about the social desirability of women with disabilities? Is it problematic to find women with disabilities attractive? If we define these relationships in this way, are we defining women with disabilities as victims in need of protection, thereby further infantilizing them (Kafer 2000)?

Read another way, these communities challenge the dominant cultural stereotype of women with disabilities as being unattractive and asexual. Some women with disabilities report enhanced self-esteem, self-confidence, and comfort with their bodies since joining devotee communities. These communities and associated social gatherings can be a source of revenue as well, since they provide a market for women with disabilities to sell photos and DVDs of themselves. Supporters claim that this phenomenon allows women with disabilities more power to define and control their sexuality (Kafer 2000).

While some women with disabilities experience a positive effect, these communities simultaneously sexually objectify women with disabilities. The degree to which devotee communities challenge or alter the social structure is highly debated (Kafer 2000). This is especially true regarding power relations between people with disabilities and the temporarily able-bodied. As of now, these communities are relatively small and have had little apparent effect on the perceptions or actions of the temporarily able-bodied. Furthermore, one cannot ignore that devotees are almost entirely temporarily able-bodied men, most of whom are heterosexual, some of whom are gay. There are very few women devotees seeking men or women with disabilities (Kafer 2000). This raises further concerns about power differentials. For instance, these relationships cannot be understood outside of a patriarchal culture which empowers men at the expense of women. Thus, it would be difficult to create an egalitarian relationship when male devotees have cultural and structural power as men while women with disabilities are devalued.

Although women and men with disabilities share similar experiences of devaluation, isolation, marginalization, and discrimination, their fortunes diverge in important ways. One of these ways is in terms of the violence they face.

Physical and sexual abuse

Although there is much that we do not know regarding the extent of violence that people with disabilities experience, research suggests that children with disabilities are 70 percent more likely to be physically or sexually abused than their able-bodied counterparts (Crosse, Kaye, and Ratnofsky 1993). Researchers report that this abuse is more likely to be chronic than episodic and perpetuated by someone the victim knows, such as a family member or personal attendant. Furthermore, this abuse is gendered; females with disabilities are more likely to be sexually assaulted, whereas males with disabilities are more likely to experience physical abuse (Sobsey, Randall, and Parrila 1997). Thus, having a disability exacerbates one of the worst elements of oppression and does untold amounts of damage to disabled people's sense of and experience of their sexuality (Gerschick 2000).

Claiming their own sexualities

As the preceding pages have demonstrated, people with disabilities face formidable challenges to creating self-satisfactory sexual experiences and identities. However, we would be making a grave mistake if we did not simultaneously highlight the agency of people with disabilities to fight the beliefs and social dynamics that hinder the development and expression of their sexualities (Shakespeare *et al.* 1996).

Scholars point out that the Disability Rights Movement, while slow to address issues of sexuality, has for several decades championed a sociopolitical understanding of people with disabilities as a minority group with all the attendant human rights. Movement members have fought for the access and employment rights of people with disabilities. As a result, they have created a social space for activists and scholars to address sexuality by publishing books, educating, and advocating. Key to these efforts is reframing issues of bodily difference as problems with societal definitions, accommodations, and expectations, rather than with people with disabilities themselves. As a consequence, prejudice and discrimination towards people with disabilities are likened to other forms of political, cultural, and social oppression such as racism, sexism, and heterosexism. Thus, the emphasis in the Disability Rights approach is on the cultural, attitudinal, and structural barriers that people with disabilities face rather than on their physical differences. Physical differences, such as disabilities, are only limitations to the degree that society makes them so.

Activists' and scholars' work takes place on multiple levels. On the individual level, they are facilitating people with disabilities' redefinition of their bodies and their relationship with them. They encourage them to embrace their bodily differences and increase self-esteem about them. In so doing, they create positive images and role models that acknowledge, nurture, and promote self-esteem and sexuality for other people with disabilities. This redefinition is clearly illustrated by Penny, one of Shakespeare *et al.*'s informants:

> For me, sex is about pleasure, humour and respect. It is with these factors in mind that I approach any seeming "difficulty" my impairments present me. Of course there are techniques and positions I will never manage to do. But I know this is true of most people, along that huge scale of human variety that in reality exists in human beings. Some activities I choose not to do, because I have no taste for them. This is as it should be. But I also know my open attitude to my sexuality, arising because I am a disabled person, often defines sex for me as a much more celebratory and explorative experience than for many non-disabled people.
>
> (*Shakespeare* et al. 1996: 205)

On an individual and societal level, scholars and activists challenge the limited definition of what constitutes sexuality and sexual behavior, especially the emphasis on heterosexual intercourse. People without genital sensation, from a spinal cord injury for instance, can have orgasms through the stimulation of other parts of their bodies. It is well known that the skin and the brain are two of the largest sources of sexual pleasure.

On a societal level, activists and scholars recognize that the formation of their own culture is key to developing their sexual freedom, for it is in this culture that they can develop their own images, beliefs, and standards, and from this social space they can challenge those of the dominant culture. They emphasize that the pursuit of sexuality and sexual happiness regardless of the condition of one's body is a fundamental human right. They argue that people with disabilities must have the power to define sexuality for themselves. Movement members also seek to shatter the stereotypes associated with people with disabilities, including that they are infantile and asexual. Finally, they are strong advocates for reproductive freedom and contraception for people with disabilities.

Conclusion

Disability has a profound effect on people's sexuality. The barriers are great, but so is the agency challenging them. Yet there is still much we do not know about this process. For instance, we have scant information regarding how disability intersects with other social characteristics like sexual orientation, race, class, ethnicity and gender, to shape sexualities. Furthermore, we know little about global variations. As a consequence, there are many opportunities for scholars to add to our understanding. I close this chapter with encouragement to take up these issues, so that we may better understand the social factors and dynamics that shape the sexualities of people with disabilities today, and so that we may eradicate the social, cultural, and political barriers to their sexual self-definition and self-satisfaction.

References

Albrecht, Gary L. 2004. "Disability as a Global Issue", in George Ritzer (ed.), *Handbook of Social Problems: A Comparative International Perspective*. Thousand Oaks, CA: Sage.

Callahan, John. 1990. *Don't Worry, He Won't Get Far on Foot*. New York: Vintage.

Crosse, Scott B., Elyse Kaye, and Alexander C. Ratnofsky. 1993. *A Report on the Maltreatment of Children with Disabilities*. "Washington, DC: National Center on Child Abuse and Neglect.

Fries, Kenny. 1997. *Body, Remember: A Memoir*. New York: Dutton.

Gerschick, Thomas J. 2005. "Masculinity and Degrees of Bodily Normativity in Western Culture," in Michael S. Kimmel, Jeff Hearn and R. W. Connell (eds), *Handbook of Studies on Men and Masculinities*. Thousand Oaks, CA: Sage.

——2000. "Toward A Theory of Disability and Gender," *Signs*, 25 (4): 1263–8.

——1998. "Sisyphus in a Wheelchair: Men with Physical Disabilities Confront Gender Domination", in Judith Howard and Jodi O'Brien (eds), *Everyday Inequalities: Critical Inquiries*. New York: Basil Blackwell.

Gerschick, Thomas J. and Adam S. Miller. 1994. "Gender Identities at the Crossroads of Masculinity and Physical Disability", *Masculinities* 2 (1): 34–55.

Golfus, Billy. 1997. "Sex and the Single Gimp", in Lennard J. Davis (ed.), *The Disability Studies Reader*. New York: Routledge.

Kafer, Alison. 2000. "Amputated Desire, Resistant Desire: Female Amputees in the Devotee Community". Paper presented at the Society for Disability Studies Conference, Chicago Sheraton, June 29–July 2.

Mairs, Nancy. 1996. *Waist-High in the World: A Life among the Nondisabled*. Boston, MA: Beacon Press.

Patzer, Gordon L. 1985. *The Physical Attractiveness Phenomena*. New York: Plenum.

Shakespeare, Tom, Kath Gillespie-Sells, and Dominic Davies. 1996. *The Sexual Politics of Disability: Untold Desires*. London: Cassell.

Sobsey, Dick, W. Randall, and Rauno K Parrila. 1997. "Gender Differences in Abused Children with and without Disabilities." *Child Abuse and Neglect* 21 (8): 707–20.

West, Candace and Don Zimmerman. 1987. "Doing Gender", *Gender and Society* 1(2): 125–51.

Zola, Irving. 1982. *Missing Pieces: A Chronicle of Living with a Disability*. Philadelphia, PA: Temple University Press.

"National Security" and the Violation of Women

Militarized Border Rape at the US-Mexico Border

Sylvanna Falcón

The US–Mexico border represents an uneasy "union" of the First and Third Worlds. Due to disparaging levels of nation-state power, it is a contentious region that has been militarized to violently reinforce the territory of the United States. In this region, daily attacks occur against border crossers in the form of brutal beatings and assaults—including rape and harassment—by the state and by racist vigilantes. Due to the hypermasculine nature of war and militarism, the use of rape as a tactic against women is well documented.

In this article, I explore documented rape cases involving Immigration and Naturalization Service (INS) officials or Border Patrol agents[1] at the US–Mexico border by accessing data from nongovernmental organizations, government committees, and US newspapers.[2] Each of the women in the case studies took some action against the INS;[3] with some of them using an advocate to move their cases forward through an investigation. (Data indicate that some men report being raped at the border, but the vast majority of rapes involve women victims/survivors, at this border and throughout the world.)[4] In this article, I argue that rape is routinely and systematically used by the state in militarization efforts at the US–Mexico border, and provoked by certain factors and dynamics in the region, such as the influence of military culture on Border Patrol agents.

US–Mexico border militarization rests on two key elements: the introduction and integration of military units in the border region (the war on drugs and national security concerns provide primary justification for involving military units); and the modification of the Border Patrol to resemble the military via its equipment, structure, and tactics. At one time, domestic duties were not part of the US military's mandate. But this regulation changed with the approval of numerous Department of Defense (DOD) authorization acts which facilitated the integration of military units in the border region and loosened restrictions placed on the military for domestic duties.

The 1982 DOD Authorization Act nullified a one-hundred year statute prohibiting cooperation between the army and civilian law enforcement, and changing the role of the military in domestic affairs. This act encouraged an alliance between civilian law enforcement and the military, and subsequent DOD Authorization Acts advanced and expanded this cooperation. Ideological and institutional shifts have also had a role in border militarization. Transferring the INS from the Department of Labor to the jurisdiction of the Department of Justice in 1940.[5] altered the classification of immigration as an issue of labor to one of national security. And more recently, by moving the INS to the Department of Homeland Security (the INS has been renamed "US Citizenship and Immigration Services"), the link between immigration and national security issues has intensified.

Sociologist Timothy Dunn draws on low-intensity conflict (LIC) military doctrine to contextualize the militarization of the US–Mexico border. LIC doctrine advocates for "unconventional, multifaceted, and relatively subtle forms of militarization" and emphasizes "controlling targeted civilian populations." The US military-security establishment drafted this doctrine to target Third World uprisings and revolutions, particularly in Central America. LIC doctrine is characterized by the following:

an emphasis on the internal defense of a nation; an emphasis on controlling targeted civilian populations rather than territory; and the assumption by the military of police-like and other unconventional, typically nonmilitary roles, along with the adoption by the police of military characteristics.[6]

Dunn's study demonstrates that these aspects of LIC doctrine have been actualized in the border region, indicating that a form of "war" exists there. And in every war, in every military conflict, rapes occur because sexual assault is in the arsenal of military strategies; it is a weapon of war, used to dominate women and psychologically debilitate people viewed as the "enemy."

In the context of mass war rape in the former Yugoslavia, Susan Brownmiller likens female bodies to territory.[7] "Rape of a doubly dehumanized object—as woman, as enemy—carries its own terrible logic. In one act of aggression, the collective spirit of women *and* of the nation is broken, leaving a reminder long after the troops depart." Beverly Allen extends this analogy to the imperialist practice of colonization.[8]

Acts of sexual violence which target undocumented (primarily Mexican) women at the US–Mexico border are certainly informed by a legacy of colonialism, which dates back to the forced imposition of a border in 1848.[9] More than 150 years later, migrant women's bodies continue to denote an "alien" or "threatening" presence subject to colonial domination by US officials. Many women who cross the border report that being raped was the "price" of not being apprehended, deported, or of having their confiscated documents returned. This price is unique to border regions in general; while militarized rapes are part of a continuum of violence against women, I call these violations militarized *border* rapes because of the "power" associated with the border itself. In this setting, even legal documentation can provide a false sense of security, because militarization efforts have socially constructed an "enemy" and Mexican women and other migrants fit that particular profile.

My goal in this article is to make visible a form of military rape which has not been previously considered in the range of military rapes by feminist scholars. Militarized border rape is overlooked because many of the world's border regions are not considered war zones. For example, the US–Mexico border conflict is not typically thought of as a "war," because opposing military forces (or insurgents) are not trying to kill each other. But a war is underway at the US–Mexico border, facilitated by cooperating military and civilian units, and the adoption of a militaristic identity in border patrolling efforts. Furthermore, the stance of the US government on immigration suggests that the United States views itself in some form of war with undocumented migrants. Calls to "shut down" the border, or to build an entire wall along the two-thousand mile border, are frequently reported in the news and supported by members of Congress as a way to "protect" the United States.[10] And when engaged in any form of war, women are always disproportionately affected.

Feminist scholar Cynthia Enloe explores three conditions under which rape has been militarized. Observes Enloe, "'recreational rape' is the alleged outcome of not supplying male soldiers with 'adequately accessible' militarized prostitution; 'national security rape' as an instrument for bolstering a nervous state; and 'systematic mass rape' as an instrument of open warfare."[11] She also contends that certain conditions which allow militarized rapes are in place on the US–Mexico border:

A regime is preoccupied with national security; a majority of civilians believe that security is best understood as a military problem; national security policy making is left to a largely masculinized policy elite; and the police and military security apparatuses are male-dominated.[12]

In my view, a variation of national security rape and systematic rape characterize the reality in this border region. First, national security entails the control of labor, migration, and women. In the 1990s, the US government expanded the definition of national security to include "domestic political concerns and perceived threats to culture, social stability, environmental degradation, and population growth."[13] During this time, immigrants and refugees became top national security issues.[14] And in the aftermath of 9/11, the US–Mexico border was completely shut down for several days due to national security reasons, reifying the classification of the US–Mexico border as an area of national security.[15] With a masculinized elite emphasizing the normalcy and role of militarism with regards to "national security," broader definitions of security have become marginalized. For example, the provision of basic necessities—such as shelter, health care, and food—is not seen as a "security issue" by the US government, though international human rights standards and laws do characterize the meeting of basic human needs in this way.

The cases of militarized border rape discussed here can be categorized as a form of "national security rape" for two reasons: first, the absence of legal documents positions undocumented women as "illegal" and as having committed a crime. Thus, law-abiding citizens need "protection" from these criminals; the existence of undocumented women causes national *insecurity*, and they are so criminalized that their bodily integrity does not matter to the state. Second, national security rape privileges certain interests; in other words, Arizona ranchers who pick up arms to "protect" their property, or recently formed "Minutemen patrols" along the US–Mexico border (specifically in Arizona and California) are seen as legitimate because they are protecting their property, land, and families. Their actions are supported by the state because they are literally taking the issue of national security into their own hands.[16]

Occurrences of rape are systematic if they fall into a pattern, suggesting that they have not been left to chance, according to Enloe. "They have been the subject of prior planning. Systematic rapes are *administered* rapes."[17] In the cases highlighted here,

the planning involved is palpable. These were not random acts of violence against women; they were violent crimes which involved planning and efforts to avoid being caught. Additionally, the rapists capitalized on their institutional power over undocumented women, and each man followed their own "script" in attacking these women. These individual patterns became clear during court testimonials by victims/survivors.

Notably, because of the prevalence of sexual violence at the border, a Mexican immigrant woman told the National Network for Immigrant and Refugee Rights in Oakland, California that women heading north routinely use birth-control pills because they anticipate possible sexual assaults. This suggests border rapes are neither random, nor isolated.[18]

Militarized Border Rape at the US-Mexico Border

If they decide to prosecute, women who have been sexually assaulted in the US–Mexico border region confront not only an individual, but directly challenge several powerful institutions— the INS (INS officials tend to conduct these investigations), the US government, the US legal system. And even in more "fair courts," proving rape is extremely difficult.[19] Undocumented women are further disadvantaged because of unfamiliarity with the US judicial process and language or communication barriers.

The rape cases detailed below occurred between 1989 and 1996, and all involved INS or Border Patrol officials.

Juanita's Story

Juanita Gómez and a female cousin crossed through the hole in the border fence between Nogales, Sonora, and Nogales, Arizona, on September 3, 1993.[20] They were on their way to meet two male friends at a nearby McDonald's to go shopping. Larry Selders, a Border Patrol agent, stopped all four people, but only detained Gómez and her cousin in his Border Patrol vehicle. According to both women, Selders told them that he would not take them to the Border Patrol station for processing and deportation to Mexico if they would have sex with him. Both women refused. He eventually asked Gómez's cousin to step outside of his vehicle. When he drove off alone with Gómez, Selders raped her.

Gómez and her cousin eventually found each other at the Mexican consulate in Nogales, Arizona, and informed officials at the Mexican consulate. The consulate immediately contacted the Nogales Police Department and Border Patrol to inform them of the situation. But one of the Nogales detectives did not believe the women's statements, asked them if they were prostitutes, and threatened them with jail time if they failed to pass a lie detector test. However, after this questioning, Gómez and her cousin identified Selders in a photo lineup. Despite their identification, the incompetence of the police led to the loss of other important evidence such as Selders's clothes. In addition, the police seized the wrong Border Patrol vehicle and realized the error a week and a half later.

Selders eventually entered a "no contest" plea on a reduced charge on July 25, 1994. The county attorney decided to reduce the original charge of "rape and kidnapping" to "attempted transporting of persons for immoral purposes . . . while married." This crime is the lowest felony class, and the charge upset many immigrant rights advocates. Selders received a one-year prison sentence on October 7, 1994, and served only six months of the sentence. But he resigned from the Border Patrol in August 1994.[21]

Selders also attempted to secure immunity from prosecution on federal charges, but he was unable to plea-bargain with the US attorney in Arizona because investigators found Gómez's story to be credible. In April 1995, a federal grand jury in Tucson, Arizona, indicted Selders for Gómez's rape.[22] He plead guilty in federal court to violating Gómez's civil rights, and received a fourteen month sentence in the federal trial, receiving credit for time served.

Despite the unfairness of his sentence, on October 13, 1999 Gómez received a $753,045 settlement.[23] Her attorney successfully argued the rape could have been prevented if Selders had been held accountable for previous acts of violence against women; three other women testified at Gómez's trial that Selders attacked them as well.[24] Unlike Gómez, these women had been afraid to file charges, and the statute of limitations in their cases expired by the time of her trial. Since Selders was a government employee at the time of the incident, the US government paid the monetary award to Gómez.

Edilma, Maria, and Rosa

On October 6, 1989, Edilma Cadilla, a US citizen, was driving her car on the highway in Imperial County, California, and was stopped at a checkpoint in the area. Border Patrol agent Luis Santiago Esteves began to question her during this routine stop, but allowed her to continue driving. Further down the road, Esteves pulled her over, asked her additional questions, and then talked about himself, eventually getting her phone number. Edilma believed these questions were official.

Edilma's boyfriend called Esteves's supervisor in El Centro to report the suspicious stop, and the supervisor told him that she should notify the office if Esteves attempted to call her. Three days later, on October 9, Esteves called and purportedly requested a date for the weekend. When she turned him down,

> Esteves told her that was "too bad" because he wanted to take her out dancing, get drunk, and have her "sexually abuse his body." She told him she had a boyfriend and he then asked if she could fix him up with one of her friends.[25]

After Edilma reported the phone call to Esteves's supervisor, the Border Patrol relocated Esteves to the Calexico, California, border crossing point. But Esteves received no disciplinary action for his inappropriate behavior towards Edilma,[26] and he remained as a Border Patrol employee where his new position enabled him to continue having contact with women.

On December 16, 1989, Esteves had problems in Calexico. He stopped Maria, a young woman from the area, and asked to see her immigration papers. While on duty, he asked for her phone number and for a date later that evening. She initially agreed to the date, but called him later to say she could not go out with him. Esteves looked for her at her workplace and then pursued her at a shopping center. Maria agreed to the date on the condition that they first stop at her house to get her mother's approval. He agreed to the request, but indicated he wished to stop at his place to change out of his Border Patrol uniform before going to her house.

According to the court records,

Esteves told her he wanted her to "be with him." At this point, Maria describes him "changing" his attitude and he became angry. He told her she had to have sex with him. He told her to take a shower. Esteves positioned a gun on each side of the bed on two nightstands . . .[27]

Fearful for her life, Maria complied with Esteves's sexual orders. According to Maria's testimony at the trial, Esteves "force[d] an object into her vagina, placed his hands into various parts of her body, orally copulated her and forced her to have intercourse with him."[28] She testified that none of these sexual acts were consensual. She escaped from his apartment when he left the room after the rape. Maria received assistance from people passing in a car. The police were immediately notified, and Esteves was subsequently arrested. But Maria did not show up to the preliminary hearing in court, and the charges against Esteves were dropped. He resumed active duty as an agent.

The third incident in June 1991 involved Rosa, a minor. Rosa was talking to family members at the US–Mexico border fence.

She and her mother were on the US side, and family members were on the Mexico side. Esteves approached them for documentation. During the conversation, Esteves learned from Rosa's mother that Rosa had an upcoming deportation hearing. Esteves informed them he could be of assistance to Rosa in that hearing.

He reportedly took Rosa out a few times after meeting her at the border. On June 28, 1991, he took Rosa out around 10:45 p.m. and bought her alcoholic drinks before taking her to the vacant apartment of a coworker. At this time, Esteves apparently instructed her to take off her clothes. She stated in her testimony that Esteves "ordered her to masturbate." At first she refused, but eventually complied when "he placed his hand on his gun." She testified that throughout the encounter Esteves assaulted her.

[Esteves] repeatedly slapped her and at one point, he punched her. Rosa contends that Esteves then sodomized her. At one point he told her, "I know what I'm doing. And I am capable of everything and if I want I can rape your mother." According to Rosa's testimony, Esteves then told her that he wanted to sell Rosa to his friends. Finally, he told her that he wanted to have sex with her and another woman.[29]

The police arrested Esteves again in July 1991 and prosecuted him for the rapes of Maria and Rosa. He was acquitted for Rosa's rape, but convicted in Maria's case, and Rosa's testimony likely played a role in securing this conviction. In July 1992, Esteves received a twenty-four year prison sentence for the felony rape charge. However, he was released on December 22, 1994.[30]

Like Selders and Riley, Esteves used the threat of revealing the lack of legal documents to gain the upper hand with these women, even suggesting he could be of assistance in a deportation hearing. Legal documents quite literally control the lives of immigrants, so when a US official "seems" helpful regarding matters which may determine your future, it adds another layer of vulnerability. Esteves manipulated this reality to his advantage.

Edilma's story also reflects Esteves's violent past with women; he allegedly beat his first wife, raped his second wife, and threatened to rape the second wife's ten-year-old daughter.[31] Esteves continued to target young women; he understood how his official position provided him with sufficient discretion and authority.

Luz and Norma

Luz López and Norma Contreras filed an INS complaint against an El Paso Border Patrol agent who sexually assaulted them on March 7, 1996. The agent arrested them near the Rio Grande River and detained them in his vehicle. López and Contreras, both from Guatemala, were each twenty-three years old at the time of the assault. According to the complaint the women filed against the agent:

> [The agent] lifted up Contreras' dress, pushed her legs open, pulled aside her underwear and stuck his fingers in her vagina. The other woman, López, was told to undo the buttons on her jumpsuit and the agent put his hands inside her top and felt her breasts. The two women said they stared at each other, paralyzed by terror.[32]

López said: "We feared the worse. We didn't know where he was going to take us. Just the sight of him with a badge and a gun was enough to intimidate anyone." The agent briefly left the women in the car. He spoke to another agent, who was alone in a different vehicle nearby. Both men returned to the car. At this time, "in full view of the second agent, the arresting agent assaulted both women again." The women were then taken to the Border Patrol office. At the office, the same agent allegedly committed a third sexual assault by the same agent "in a detention cell and in a bathroom." After torturing them for several hours, "the agent gave the women one dollar each and released them" into the United States.[33]

Following the ordeal, López and Contreras filed a formal complaint against both agents. The women stayed in El Paso in order to cooperate with the investigation. They recounted the attacks to male Office of Inspector General (OIG) investigators, identified the agent from photographs, and received rape counseling. The OIG began an investigation, but did not pursue the complaints, accusing López and Contreras of "lying and threatened to prosecute them."[34] The women then filed a lawsuit, which is still pending, against the Border Patrol. As in all cases of rape, the women were severely traumatized from the ordeal, and Contreras attempted to commit suicide later that same year.

This case demonstrates the systematic nature of militarized border rape; the officer reportedly raped López and Contreras in different locations, indicating some prior planning. Furthermore, the agent was protected during an OIG investigation which retraumatized the women; officials questioned the women's credibility, and attempted to discredit their story. Contreras attempted suicide in 1996 largely due to this insensitive investigation.

While documenting rape cases in the former Yugoslavia, UN officials described the risks of subjecting women to repeated interviews about their sexual assaults:

> Health care providers are concerned about the effects on women of repeatedly recounting their experiences without adequate psychological and social support systems in place. The danger of subjecting women to additional emotional hardship in the course of interviews is a real one. There have been reports of women attempting suicide after being interviewed by the media and well-meaning delegations.[35]

Factors Associated with Militarized Border Rape

With the integration of aspects of LIC doctrine in its border enforcement efforts, for example, the occurrence of militarized border rapes is not surprising because systematic rapes occurred in the war zones throughout the Central American region where this doctrine was initially implemented. The access to wide, discretionary (and unaccountable) power and an ineffective complaints protocol are factors that perpetuate militarized border rape. And the hiring of military personnel and the "code of silence" ensure that militarized border rapes continue and remain central to border enforcement.

• The level of militarization produces warlike characteristics that make rape and other human rights violations an inevitable consequence of border militarization efforts.

Several aspects of LIC doctrine apply to the militarization efforts at the US–Mexico border.[36] UN monitors have documented the systematic rape of women during war, and have categorized rape as a war crime, a weapon of war, and a form of torture. War-like conditions at the border reinforce a climate in which rape and the systematic degradation of women are fundamental strategies. Furthermore, agent impunity and the absence of institutional accountability have created a border climate in which rape occurs with little consequence.

• The recruitment of former military personnel to join the border enforcement staff reinforces the militarization of the border.

The 1996 federal immigration policy increased the presence of agents at the border and the INS hired individuals at an unprecedented rate. In addition to hiring "agents with dubious pasts, including criminal records and checkered careers with police agencies and the military,"[37] the INS engaged in an effort to recruit former military officers. San Diego's INS is among the most successful in hiring former military officers.[38] A high concentration of former military agents in the Border Patrol tends

to make border enforcement more compatible with the maintenance of a war zone.

• The "code of silence" found in law enforcement and military culture prevents agents from reporting on each other.

Law enforcement and military cultural norms obfuscate human rights violations because agents do not report one another during or after incidents of wrong-doing. The "code of silence" is integral to the militarized border system because it maintains the system's legitimacy. The code is difficult to penetrate and if an individual breaks it, they will likely experience negative consequences.

• Border enforcement agents have wide discretionary power while on the job.

Since "much of their work is unsupervised," border enforcement agents have a great deal of discretion on the job.[39] It is impossible to micro-manage the agents' work and conduct when in the field. This unaccountability can produce an environment of impunity.

For example, since 1989, the INS has reported "only one registered complaint for every 17,000 arrests."[40] Furthermore, Human Rights Watch, Amnesty International, the Citizens' Advisory Panel (organized by the INS), and the state advisory committees to the US Commission on Civil Rights all concluded no effective or useful mechanisms exist to enable victims of human rights violations to file formal complaints against border enforcement agents.[41] According to the Citizens' Advisory Panel, "in 1996, 99% of the complaints received by the Justice Department's Civil Rights Division were not prosecuted. Furthermore, most cases investigated by the Federal Bureau of Investigations do not result in criminal charges or presentation to a grand jury."[42]

The nonexistence of a standardized complaints form and appeals process are systematic and structural shortcomings that allow the INS to minimize the situation at the border. Moreover, the lack of a standardized process and the option of reporting incidents to duty supervisors of the local Border Patrol offices lead to underreporting of abuses. The existing format presents overwhelming obstacles in getting complaints properly investigated.[43] In addition, an increase in border enforcement agents is never met with a proportionate increase of investigative staff.[44]

According to the INS-organized Citizens' Advisory Panel, the INS complaint protocol is completely inadequate for what it is meant to do—investigate allegations of civil rights abuses.[45] Since complaints must be provable beyond a reasonable doubt before proceeding with an investigation, the likelihood of achieving this standard is difficult, leading to a low number of thorough investigations. (Thus, the evidence against the border enforcement agents or INS officials in the rape cases included here was clearly convincing, or they would not have been investigated at all.)

Human Rights and US Accountability

Women all over the world migrate for several reasons: to reunite with family members, to seek economic opportunities via employment, to flee domestic violence,[46] or to escape political strife and instability in their homelands.[47] Human rights treaties seek to ensure basic security and protection—including the right to be free from the threat of sexual violence—in border regions. Yet, the US–Mexico border system supports, protects, and reinforces an environment where militarized border rape routinely occurs.

Human rights establish international standards and "allow groups to hold the US government accountable for its acts of commission and omission with regard to the violation of the human rights of women."[48] Given the actors involved in this region—undocumented people, US officials, and, in some cases, US citizens or residents "mistaken" as undocumented people by US officials—these standards may challenge the system at the US–Mexico border because they provide "a counter-hegemonic language through which the self-justifications of the rich and powerful can be discredited, and the system's legitimacy contested."[49]

Indeed, the desire to protect national (capitalist) interests, institutions, and structures is integral to the legitimacy of the US–Mexico border system. And the strategies employed by the US government to protect state military institutions from international laws and standards are brazen examples of US exceptional-ism.[50] Not surprisingly, the US government has grown increasingly dismissive and undermining of international laws and treaties which support human rights. Nevertheless, a human rights framework has great potential for facilitating cross-border alliances and for placing the border situation in its rightful context; the border crisis is clearly an international matter because of who is involved, as well as the factors—trade, militarism, violence, and political instability—which spur migration.

Conclusion

Rape is among the most underreported crimes in peacetime throughout the world. Shame and secrecy often silence the victims because of the stigma attached to rape. Rape continues to be under-reported during wartime . . . Many women will not talk about their experience of rape for fear of reprisals. Some were reluctant to tell the experts the names of the perpetrators because of fear for their own and their family's safety.[51]

This UN report addressed the specific situation in the former Yugoslavia, but many of its arguments are relevant to all forms of rape.[52] As Beverly Allen argues, rape occurs when fear and insecurity are joined with power and immunity from prosecution in a sexist social system. All rape is related in that "it derives from a system of dominance and subjugation that allows, and in fact often encourages, precisely the violent crime of rape as a way of maintaining that system."[53]

Militarization requires militarized border rape. My goal in highlighting actual cases of militarized border rape is to highlight the humanity of migrant women; rape statistics can be useful in conveying the crisis' severity, but they can also create a sense of detachment from the victims/survivors themselves. The women in these cases displayed courage and agency, and their bold acts revealed some realities about how rape is used as a weapon at the US–Mexico border. Their stories represent an urgent call to hold the United States accountable for human rights violations.

My warmest thanks and appreciation to Clarissa Rojas for her support, encouragement, and feedback on this piece. Mil gracias hermana. Thanks also to Jill Petty and to South End Press for their dedication and assistance, as well as Matthew and Aracely Lehman for their love and support.

Notes

1 This article is concerned with human rights violations committed by US officials and does not discuss the role of Mexican officials in committing acts of rape.

2 For this article, I selected a few cases that were representative of other cases of abuse. Due to space limitations and underreporting, I can provide only a glimpse of human rights violations regarding violence against women. The small number of cases discussed here does suggest important directions for future research. My intent is to exemplify the violation of women's human rights via cases of militarized border rape.

3 For the purposes of this article, I refer to INS officials as INS officials because that was their identity at the time of the incidents even though in reality, the INS does not exist anymore. That said, the militarization efforts continue to grow in a post-9/11 world so that the US public can feel the state is providing them with security, which is why the creation of the Department of Homeland Security is the new home for immigration issues.

4 Amnesty International, United States of America: Human Rights Concerns in the Border Region with Mexico, 1998, http://web.amnesty.org/library/Index/engAMR510031998 (accessed March 13, 2006).

5 Timothy Dunn, *The Militarization of the U.S-Mexico Border 1978–1992: Low-Intensity Conflict Doctrine Comes Home*, (Austin, TX: University of Texas, Center for Mexican American Studies, 1996), 13.

6 Dunn, *The Militarization of the U.S-Mexico Border*, 21.

7 Susan Brownmiller, "Making Female Bodies the Battlefield." *Newsweek*, January 4, 1993.

8 Beverly Allen, *Rape Warfare: The Hidden Genocide in Bosnia-Herzegovina and Croatia* (Minneapolis: University of Minnesota Press, 1996), 159.

9 The Chicana/o saying "We didn't cross the border; the border crossed us" is a powerful reminder to all of us about this colonial legacy.

10 Nicole Gaouette, "Immigration Proposals Include Arizona Fence," *Los Angeles Times*, March 10, 2006, Part A, 1.

11 It is not my intention (nor Enloe's) to suggest that militarized prostitution is not also violent and a form of rape. Militarized prostitution has a history of being forced and inflicted on women from all sides of a military conflict.

12 Cynthia Enloe, *Maneuvers: The International Politics of Militarizing Women's Lives* (Berkeley, CA: University of California Press, 2000), 111.

13 Enloe, *Maneuvers: The International Politics of Militarizing Women's Lives*, 124.

14 Susanne Jonas, "Rethinking Immigration Policy & Citizenship in the Americas: A Regional Framework." *Social Justice* 23 (1996): 72.

15 *Time Magazine*, "Day of Infamy," September 12, 2001, at http://www.time.com/tirne/nation/article/0,8599,174502,00.html (accessed March 13, 2006).

16 Dan Glaister, "Schwarzenegger backs Minutemen," May 2, 2005, http://www.guardian.co.uk/international/story/0,3604,1474559,00.html (accessed March 13, 2006).

17 Enloe, *Maneuvers: The International Politics of Militarizing Women's Lives*, 134.

18 Elizabeth Martínez, *De Colores Means All of Us: Latina Views for a Multi-Colored Century* (Cambridge, MA: South End Press, 1998), 58.

19 Rape convictions in the United States are extremely low [see Catherine Mackinnon, "Reflections on Sex Equality Under the Law," *Yale Law Journal* 100 (1991): 1281].

20 Human Rights Watch (1995) acquired the information in this account through interviews with the victim, her lawyer, the Office of the Inspector General, and press reports.

21 Human Rights Watch, *Crossing the Line: Human Rights Abuses Along the US Border with Mexico Persist Amid Climate of Impunity* (New York, NY: Human Rights Watch, 1995), 12–13.

22 "Ex-Border Guard Indicted on Federal Charges," *Phoenix Gazette*, April 6, 1995.

23 "Women Raped by Border Patrol Agent Awarded $753,000" *Associated Press, State and Local Wire*, October 14, 1999.

24 Ibid; Human Rights Watch, *Frontier Injustice: Human Rights Abuses Along the US Border with Mexico Persist Amid Climate of Impunity,* (New York, NY: Human Rights Watch, 1993), 13.

25 "INS Officer Pleads Not Guilty in Rape, Kidnapping," *Los Angeles Times*, May 16, 1990.

26 Michael Connelly and Patricia Klein Lerner, "INS Agent Faces More Sex Charges," *Los Angeles Times*, June 15, 1990.

27 Ibid.

28 Refer to http://www.ins.usdoj.gov/graphics/glossary.htm#E (accessed March 13, 2006).

29 Michael Connelly, "Jury Acquits INS Officer in Rapes," *Los Angeles Times*, February 28, 1992.

30 Human Rights Watch, "Frontier Injustice," 8. See also *People v. Luis S. Esteves*, Case number 14855, Imperial County, CA, 1992.

31 Human Rights Watch "Frontier Injustice," 8 and Patrick J. McDonnell, and Sebastian Rotella. "Crossing the Line: Turmoil in the US Border Patrol," *Los Angeles Times*, April 23, 1993.

32 Amnesty International "Human Rights Concerns in the Border Region."

33 Ibid.

34 Ibid.

35 United Nations Economic and Social Council. "Question of the Violation of Human Rights and Fundamental Freedoms in Any Part of the World, with Particular Reference to Colonial and Other Dependent Countries and Territories. Rape and Abuse of Women in the Territory of the Former Yugoslavia. Report of the Secretary-General." Document E/CN.4/1994/5, June 30, 1993, 5.

36 Dunn, *The Militarization of the U.S-Mexico Border*, 31.

37 State Advisory Committees to the United States Commission on Civil Rights (Arizona, California, New Mexico and Texas), *Federal Immigration Law Enforcement in the Southwest: Civil Rights Impacts on Border Communities* (Washington, DC: US Government Printing Office, 1997), 24), [CR 1.2: IM6]. See also McDonnell and Rotella, "Turmoil in the US Border Patrol."

38 In San Diego, the Border Patrol launched an aggressive recruitment campaign geared toward military officers. In March 1999, the INS organized the "Southern California All-Military Recruiting Events," where teams of Border Patrol recruiting agents visited 5 to 10 military-bases to talk about the Border Patrol as a possible career. Following this intensive recruitment effort, the INS stated, "with the advent of new

initiatives such as the 'all-military' campaign in the San Diego sector, we hope to see an even greater number of applicants from this key group in the coming year" (US Immigration and Naturalization Service, "INS Recruiting Update: Spotlight on San Diego Sector Recruitment Efforts," communiqué, February, 1999: 11).

39 State Advisory Committees 10. See also US Congress, House Committee on Government Operations, *The Immigration and Naturalization Service: Overwhelmed and Unprepared for the Future.* 193rd Congress, First session, H.R. Rep 216 (Washington, DC: US Government Printing Office, 1993), 2), [Yl. 1/8:103–216].

40 Human Rights Watch "Crossing the Line," 21.

41 Ibid.; Amnesty International "Human Rights Concerns in the Border Region"; State Advisory Committees "Federal Immigration Law Enforcement in the Southwest"; and US Immigration and Naturalization Service, *Citizens' Advisory Panel Report to the Attorney General* (Washington, DC: US Government Printing Office, 1997) [J 21.2:C 49/10].

42 US Immigration and Naturalization Service, "Citizens" Advisory Panel Report," 6.

43 On September 29, 1993, the House Subcommittee on International Law, Immigration, and Refugees held a hearing on the House of Representatives (H.R.) 2119 bill. This bill wanted to establish an independent review commission to investigate complaints of civil rights abuses in the border region. US Congress, House. Committee on the Judiciary, Subcommittee on International Law, Immigration, and Refugees, *Border Violence* (Washington, DC: US Government Printing Press, 1993), [Y4.J 89/1:103/14]. As of October 7, 1994, the bill was stalled in committee (Lexis-Nexis, *Bill Tracking Report*, HR 2119, 1995). Establishing an independent review commission to investigate border violence continues to be an important goal for immigrant rights groups.

44 Amnesty International "Human Rights Concerns in the Border Region."

45 US Immigration and Naturalization Service, "Citizens' Advisory Panel Report."

46 The overwhelming theme of migration literature is people migrate for labor. However, women may be fleeing from domestic violence and therefore, once in the United States, are in search for employment. Therefore, it is important to not reduce their narratives to be one of searching for work when the motivation may actually be escaping domestic violence.

47 Leo Chavez, *Shadowed Lives: Undocumented Immigration in American Society* (Orlando, FL: Harcourt Brace College Publishers, 1998), ix. See also Vicki Ruiz and Susan Tiano, eds., *Women on the US-Mexico Border: Responses to Change* (Boulder, CO: Westview Press, 1991).

48 Mallika Dutt, *With Liberty and Justice for All: Women's Human Rights in the United States* (New Brunswick, NJ: Center for Women's Global Leadership, 1994), 6–7.

49 R. W. Connell, "Sociology and Human Rights," *The Australian and New Zealand Journal of Sociology* 31 (1995): 26.

50 The US efforts to exempt its military units from prosecution in the International Criminal Court (ICC), a court that investigates war crimes as of July 1, 2002 of which gender-based violence such as military rape is prosecutable, is deeply troubling and problematic. Even though President Clinton signed the ICC Treaty to begin the process of institutionalizing the court, Bush "unsigned" the United States's name to the treaty (Neil A. Lewis, "US Is Set to Renounce Its Role in Pact for World Tribunal," *The New York Times*, May 5, 2002), a blatant act of defiance to the international community and a clear message that the United States is accountable to no one. However, the international community responded back to the United States and moved forward with the ICC by obtaining sufficient signatories for

official approval. Although the United States initially hoped to halt the creation of the ICC altogether, the international community continued to move forward to conduct the world's affairs without the United States. Hoping for permanent exclusion from all ICC prosecutions, the United States received an annual approval from the UN Security Council for exclusion from the ICC, which is renewable (William M. Reilly, "Analysis: US, UN Dent Int'l Court," *United Press International (UPI)*, June 12, 2003) meaning that the UN Security Council will not require the ICC to investigate and prosecute the actions of the US military. To clarify, the International Criminal Court and the United Nations operate separately. First, for the court to have jurisdiction, the state where the crimes occurred must have agreed to the treaty or the (accused) individual's country (of nationality) must have agreed to the treaty. Second, prosecutors can initiate an investigation on their own as long as the state (or states) involved has already agreed to the treaty. A 3-judge panel reviews the case to ensure it meets with the requirements of the court. Third, the United Nations Security Council can refer a case to the court, even if a country has not ratified the treaty; the court's jurisdiction is broadest with the UN Security Council. So the United States is ensuring that it is protected from all angles, which is why they pushed for the immunity from the UN Security Council and are for the bi-lateral agreements with other states. The United States is also in the process of passing legislation, which would prevent federal and state agencies from cooperating with the ICC unless the Court is trying Osama Bin Laden, Sadaam Hussein, and/or Slobodan Milosevic. For more information, please refer to Women's Initiatives for Gender Justice (formerly the Women's Caucus for Gender Justice) based in The Hague, The Netherlands at www.iccwomen.org.

Furthermore, as another layer of protection for the US military, the government obtained official bi-lateral agreements from other governments confirming that they will not attempt to prosecute the US military through the ICC either. Obtaining these exemptions to the ICC is a result of US government manipulation and not from a conviction that the US military should be above international law. The United States threatened to remove peacekeeping troops in Bosnia and withhold foreign aid to countries who refused to the agreement. See Serge Schmemann, "US May Veto Bosnia Force In a Dispute Over New Court," *The New York Times,* June 29, 2002 and Thom Shanker and James Dao, "US Might Refuse New Peace Duties Without Immunity," *The New York Times,* July 3, 2002.

51 UN Economic and Social Council "Situation of Human Rights in the Territory of the Former Yugoslavia, Report on the Situation of Human Rights in the Territory of the Former Yugoslavia Submitted by Mr. Tadeusz Mazowiecki, Special Rapporteur of the Commission on Human Rights," Document E/CN.4/1993/50, 10 February 1993, 67.

52 The Statute of the International Criminal Tribunal for the Former Yugoslavia of May 1993 identified rape as a crime against humanity. This statute took an important step toward recognizing armed conflict affects women differently from men, but did not take the issue far enough. That is, the statute characterized rape in a limiting manner by considering it within the context of ethnic cleansing, rather than serving "purposes which are central to the enterprise of war-making" (Liz Philipose, "The Laws of War and Women's Human Rights," *Hypatia* 11 (1996): 46–62.

53 Allen, *Rape Warfare: The Hidden Genocide in Bosnia-Herzegovina and Croatia,* 39.

Chapter Five

Places

Imagine the following scenario: You're driving across the country, maybe on your way to university for the first time or on some other road-trip adventure. You're crossing multiple states, provinces, and territories, many different landscapes, taking it all in: from urban areas to small towns to rural farmlands, from densely populated areas to broad expanses of land cut through only by the road you're on, from mountains to lakes to flatlands. And there are signs everywhere—from road signs to billboards to highway markers—inviting you to stop awhile, attempting to sell you something, enticing you to experience a particular location in a specific way: "Hike our old-growth forest!" or "Dine on our authentic regional cuisine!" or "Go back in time at Old West Town!"

As you cross the country, reading these signs, you start to think about how they are locating you not just geographically, but historically and socially as well, positioning you within particular relationships to these places. You can see in the signs an acknowledgment of what's been here for tens of thousands of years (such as waterways and rock formations) as well as what is newer, created by humans. And yet, you note, in all of these sites and sights, some histories are highlighted, while others remain silent. What was there before the strip malls, highways, subdivisions, oil refineries, or even before the farms and parks? What are the stories you are asked to learn about in these varied locations? And, by implication, what stories are you asked to forget? For instance, some landmarks commemorate battles that are part of the nation's history—the dominant narrative told about a country's formation. But, you think as you stop there, it is also a selective narrative: Where are the highway markers of important sites of Indigenous people's histories? What about their contact—perhaps in battle and perhaps in cooperative arrangements—with each other and with European settlers? Where are the signs that speak of immigrant groups' often-varied experiences of coming to Canada or the United States? Presumably, these are also important moments in the story of what happened in this place. But they are not marked.

Other questions come to mind, too. Why do some places seem to instill a sense of belonging for you, while others seem strangely uncomfortable? Why do some places make you want to stay and others seem to drive you away? What are the things located in this space that make you feel at home: the built environment, the landscape, the people, the businesses, or the various artifacts that mark the presences (or absences) that you hold dear? And what makes you feel like a stranger? As you encounter each place, you wonder: Does everyone experience place in the same way? What about those who used to live here but left, either voluntarily or forcibly? What about those who work here but can't afford to live where they work? And what about those who simply travel through here, never stopping because this place seems to have nothing to offer in terms of diversions, inclusions, or even safety? And, of course, does every-one have the same choice to stop, the same possibility of mobility, to move to and from this place and others—and if not, why not? Does the option to leave or stay make a difference in how people experience a place? Clearly, you realize, a cross-country drive raises a lot of questions about the places you experience!

The Public and the Private

To speak of *place* is to speak of the many meanings attributed to the spaces we, and others, inhabit. Place in Women's and Gender Studies is important to explore, because it both produces and reflects our intersecting identities. The same place—a police station, a cafe, a church, a bar, or a classroom—can be experienced quite differently by different groups depending on their combination of identity categories. Place is always contested; it always reflects multiple uses and interpretations, and sometimes those can be at odds with each other. Place is both literal (an actual physical location) and symbolic (a set of associations we, or others, make about our relationships to particular sites). Another way to think about it is to say that place is both material and imagined; that is, it is about both concrete locations and about people's various emotional connections to those locations. Our thinking about identities, as well as about expected or possible behaviors, attitudes, and relationships, is always influenced by the varied meanings associated with any place.

One common way to think about place and its multiple meanings is to think about it as either *private* or *public*—that is, as personal space intended for one's intimate life, emotions, and activities or as larger social spaces associated with work, leisure, consumption, and politics. For many of us, making a distinction between private and public seems important, given that each of us could probably think of things that we would say or do in spaces we consider private that we would never think to do in spaces we consider public. However, there is nothing natural or innate about this division, and we would probably disagree on where the line is drawn between these spheres. Examining some of the complexities embedded in what are thought of as private and public spaces thus demonstrates how much these locations are always also reflective of the social relations and hierarchies explored throughout this text.

Until very recently, most people in the world lived in rural spaces and worked in those same spaces. This means that the divide between the private, intimate spaces of domestic life and the public, labor-intensive spaces of work has, for most of human history, been nonexistent; these spaces were mostly one and the same. And obviously, for some people, that connection remains today (i.e., people who work out of their home or who telecommute). But even without these obvious examples, the idea that public spaces are distinct from the intimate spaces of our private lives rarely holds up under scrutiny. Think, for example, of the coffee shop, a public space where many of us like to go to have some time alone or to have private conversations with friends. Or, think about social media spaces like Facebook, Tumblr, Twitter, Snapchat, and Instagram, where there is plenty of debate over whether posts on these sites are private or public. Think, too, about the expectations we have about privacy in public spaces such as bathrooms—expectations that can lead to intensely fraught moments about who "belongs" in that space and what they should be doing there. Finally, consider something as supposedly private as displays of sexual desire; even though sex might typically occur in an intimate setting in the home, it often starts with public displays of mutual attraction at a bar, restaurant, or dance club. But, in these examples, identity matters when it comes to how people think public and private are distinct. Not just anyone can display in public what they intend to do in private; for gay men and lesbians in socially conservative contexts, for example, such displays can be met with subtle or overt disapproval, and can even be dangerous in a number of ways[1].

[1]**KNOW ABOUT:** In 1986, the U.S. Supreme Court upheld as constitutional a state law that criminalized oral and anal sex between "homosexuals," even in private. This ruling, known as *Bowers v. Hardwick*, was overturned in 2003 (in another ruling known as *Lawrence v. Texas*), but it is a famous legal case that demonstrates how assumptions about private spaces and behaviors are often unequally applied, and how often it is only particular groups of people that are accorded those rights to privacy.

And even the assumption that sex is ultimately private is further complicated by the fact that for many people, sex is work: e.g., for sex workers. For other people, sex is a public leisure activity: e.g., consuming paraphernalia at a sex shop or watching strippers at a bar.

This public/private divide is a shifting boundary that reflects ideas about who has what kinds of rights and responsibilities in particular places. Think, for instance, of what happens when something that is assumed to be private or personal occurs in a space thought of as public: an escalating fight between a couple on the street, a child being yelled at or hit in the supermarket, or even a public display of affection that seems to cross some line of acceptability (of course, the interesting question is: for whom?). In being a public witness to such seemingly private events, there is often a sense of discomfort in not knowing whether to look away or to intervene. Does the presumed "privateness" of what is happening in these scenarios prevail? Or does the difference of location influence our sense of whether and how to respond? Is there an obligation to intervene, even in cases where something may not be against the law—as in a public conflict? And if this is the case, why shouldn't the same intervention also occur when those behaviors take place behind closed doors[2]?

While there are some instances where intervention, regardless of location, has become more acceptable and even legally required—as in domestic violence or child abuse—private spaces can still seem off-limits for such interventions. But who and what determines a decision to intervene or not? Who is allowed privacy, and whose lives are considered to benefit from closer scrutiny? Think, for instance, of how some families are subject to more surveillance about how they raise their children based on the neighborhood where they live, their immigrant status, their religion, and their cultural affiliations. Who takes it upon themselves to assume that these children are in need of "protection" from familial practices, kinship arrangements, economic statuses, or choices about educational and religious instruction? And whose familial practices are simply taken for granted and left unchallenged? Questioning these distinctions is important—and troubling—because different understandings of private rights and public scrutiny are always culturally specific and wielded quite differently against different groups of people[3].

The differences between public and private space can be further complicated to

[2]**TALK ABOUT:** Some other examples of the blurry lines between private and public behaviors might include: drinking alcohol while visibly pregnant, not wearing seatbelts in taxis, and nursing babies in public spaces. What is the line you would draw between those instances where it's all right to intervene and those where it isn't? Why do other people's private behaviors, when done in public, attract attention—and who is helped or hurt by this attention? Why is there so often a sense of discomfort in intervening in other people's private behaviors? And how much is that discomfort shaped by the identities of people involved (e.g., their gender, race, or age)?

[3]**TALK ABOUT:** What kinds of families are more likely to have direct contact with agents of the state (e.g., law enforcement, children's services, schools)? How much does economic

status, race, citizenship status, sexuality, disability, and religion come up in examples that you have generated? For instance, how might parents' decisions about children walking to school, dating, and what they wear be perceived differently based on issues of place (where families are from and in what neighborhoods they live)?

(4)**TALK ABOUT:** What are other examples where spaces that are seemingly public turn out to in fact not be for everyone? Consider, for example, bus shelters, train stations, food courts, public bathrooms, parking lots? Who is encouraged to use these spaces and who isn't? What activities are permitted and by whom? What does this suggest to you about how "public" public spaces really are and about what other kinds of invisible adjectives are in play?

highlight their political dimensions, that is, how place evokes power differences between individuals or groups of people. Think, for instance, of the shopping mall. Malls are open to all kinds of people who occupy their premises for various reasons: shopping, recreation, socializing, exercise, eating, employment, or just hanging out. But they are not public spaces, if what is meant by public is a place for all members of a community or for the welfare of the community in general. Malls are typically private property, spaces clearly owned, and therefore controlled, by a person or corporation that has the right to refuse entry to anyone for any reason. This fact becomes quite relevant if, for instance, you seek to disagree—in a public manner—with the way a store in the mall does business. Free speech rights—to leaflet about a clothing store's labor practices, to educate consumers about the environmental degradation wrought by the fast food they are about to eat, to demonstrate about how girls are hypersexualized through advertising and fashion, or just to get people's attention on any issue—do not necessarily apply to the spaces where, ironically, the public actually congregates. Instead, protesters in malls are regularly accused of trespassing (and sometimes even arrested for it), implying a criminal misuse of the property and a violation of the property owner's rights. Thus, the apparently public space of the shopping mall is really a private (or, more accurately, privatized) space, where only some activities are permitted.

Another way to think about the tensions between public and private is to consider what kinds of supposedly private activities are nonetheless allowed or even encouraged in public spaces—and whether those are the same for everyone: Sleeping on a park bench, sitting on a sidewalk, hanging out a little too long in front of a store are activities that depend on our social identities or how we might be identified by others. People who are read as middle-class white people, tired from a day of running errands, will probably be much less challenged when they take a break on that park bench than someone who is read as homeless, or young, or otherwise as not "belonging" in that space. Examples like this make clear that public space (as with everything else we talk about here) clearly has invisible adjectives attached to it, demarcating ideas about whose public space it is, whose comfort and safety is valued, and whose isn't[4]. Likewise, consider an earlier example about the tensions around whether social media constitute public or private spaces. Should what we consider to be our private posts, status updates, tweets, and photo uploads be available more publicly to prospective employers, insurance companies, or law enforcement? What are the consequences when expectations of private and public lives clash, and how are those different assumptions about when we are sharing private parts of our lives, even if in public venues, negotiated? Thus, even while public and private might be handy labels for thinking about who is doing what, where they are doing it, and whether what they're doing is okay, the divide between the two terms—and spaces—breaks down quickly and unevenly. So why, then, is place still so often thought of in terms of public and private? And what are the implications of these distinctions about place for operations of power and privilege[5]?

Home and Community

Breaking down the private/public binary—or at least challenging its universality—means first exposing the number of complexities that occur even in a single physical location. Think, for instance, about *home*. It is both a physical space (e.g., house, apartment, mansion, trailer) and a symbolic place of belonging. Both materially and emotionally, home is different for all of us, located in various kinds of geographical and physical spaces and made up of different combinations of people and relationships. And it reflects different meanings: acceptance, exclusion, safety, danger, comfort, estrangement, refuge, trap. It may be a place to return to or a place to escape from. For most of us, home is some combination of these, in an ever-changing (and sometimes fraught) blend of material spaces and emotional connections.

While home is often thought of as synonymous with the private sphere, it can never be easily isolated from its connections to the public world outside of its physical boundaries. For instance, think about the example of how a house becomes a home. What kind of work produces emotional ties and connections to that space and the relationships within it? Who does this work? And what are the often uneven impacts of this labor on the various people who occupy that space? Or think about how particular jobs in the home are often gendered, that is, assumed to belong more appropriately to one gender than another. Research continues to indicate that what we tend to call housework is still not evenly distributed in nuclear families headed

[5]**TALK ABOUT:** A good example to challenge the distinction between public and private is religious expression. What are some of the ways in which religion is both? Consider dress, behavior, places of worship, food choices, social and leisure activities. Are there degrees of comfort and discomfort with public religious expressions (especially if you don't share them)? Where is religion located on your campus, whether it is considered to be a secular campus or one with a more overt religious affiliation? For instance, how is the semester calendar organized: Which religious holidays are also school holidays and which are not? Where is religion's (your own or others) "proper" place? Even though religiosity is an important identity category (just like gender, race, and sexuality), in what ways might it be treated differently than those categories?

(6)KNOW ABOUT: The so-called nuclear (and usually thought of as traditional) family is both a recent arrangement, representing only a short period in mid-20th century Canadian and U.S. history, and quite specific only to particular parts of the world. More common throughout history and currently in most parts of the world are extended families or kinship arrangements that include multiple generations and combinations of cohabitation through births, marriages, and other kinds of communal connections.

(7)THINK ABOUT: In response to the fact that many white-collar workers increasingly don't separate work from leisure, some workplaces are now building in time-outs of various kinds—encouraging workers to take breaks, go for walks, take their lunch, go on holiday without responding to e-mail—all in the name of returning as more productive

by heterosexual couples(6). As such, it is often women's unpaid labor that "reproduces" the family and its members' ability to go into the public or world of paid work. Through the enormous range of domestic activities, such as cleaning, cooking, organizing, task management, consumption, and caretaking, family members are able to do what is required of them outside the home. This unpaid work is often explained as an outgrowth of familial attachments, and is usually revered as an expression of love; indeed, housework is often not even recognized as work, since we more usually think of work only as that which takes place outside of the home and for which one receives a paycheck.

To supplement unpaid labor in the home, families who can afford it sometimes hire people from outside the family—house cleaners, gardeners, nannies, health aides, home managers—turning what was previously unpaid work into paid work (albeit poorly paid work). But this practice of paying others to help manage the home presents a number of tensions, further exposing contradictions between public and private. For example, the nanny hired to care for and form close relationships with children is nonetheless likely to experience the home of the employer—the place of her (and it is overwhelmingly women who are nannies) paid work—as a space of both belonging and not belonging at the same time. As an activity that is usually deemed private, but that she is being paid to do, home is now both public and private, a space where some labor-related rights (a salary) apply but where others (regular breaks during the day) are unrecognized(7). And as the one charged with doing most of the relational work with children in the home when the parents are not there, she is likely to spend more time with the children than anyone else in the family: taking care of their daily needs, preparing nutritious food, keeping their bodies clean, offering stimulating play for their cognitive development, teaching them right from wrong in their interactions with other children, disciplining them when they violate family rules, and offering them comfort and security and love when they are in need—everything expected of parents. And yet, when it comes to justifying her working conditions, this same attachment to the children can be used to frame the nanny's labor as something less than real work: She is "just like family" and doing the same thing the mother did for free. So how much could that labor really be worth? Or, when she is let go, the "work" part of her care work often takes precedence over the "caring" part; the result is that the impact of her departure (on children and on herself) is often not taken as seriously. It was only temporary; it was only a job, after all.

These same assumptions about who is better equipped to do certain kinds of care work in the home influence how similar work outside the home is perceived. The caring for children in daycare facilities or attending to the basic needs of the sick and the elderly in hospitals, nursing homes, and hospices, for instance, shifts the location of that care work from the home to a public institution. But the work of caring, no matter where it occurs, still carries the connotation of not really being work, because caring continues to be thought of as something that people are supposed to do out of emotional attachments. And the typically low wages of this kind of work reflect this lack of presumed worth[8].

To complicate this idea of home even more, though, let's return to how the word home is used to talk about a range of emotions and attachments and not just about the actual physical spaces where we live. We speak of "feeling at home" in a neighborhood, at a political gathering, or among people with whom we have similar interests. This sense of comfort is often what we mean by the term *community*: the symbolic place where we feel we belong and the people with whom we share some affinity. But while the concept of community seems to be about inclusion or identifying commonalities that bring people together, it is also used to draw borders around who is a part of this place, and, importantly, who isn't. In this way, community denotes a site where both belonging and exclusion occur at the same time (much as identity categories were discussed in the "Identities" chapter). This unevenness around defining home and community illustrates how place is always the site of multiple meanings and is, therefore, always contested. Think, for instance, about how neighborhoods in urban areas are so often differentiated from each other along the lines of identity categories such as race and class, and then called "good" neighborhoods or "bad" neighborhoods, regardless of the level of well-being or quality of social relations that may (or may not) be present in either or both. Nevertheless, this discourse of good/bad neighborhoods tends to set up unwritten rules about who can go where safely and without suspicion versus who is seen as—and is made to feel—out of place. The ways we talk about the differences of these places—gated communities, "ghettos," subsidized housing, financial districts, upscale shopping streets, strip malls with discount

workers. When leisure time is considered as part of work time, though, is it work or leisure? And does it matter? How is the supposed distinction between work and home also challenged in other kinds of workplaces (factories, fast food, retail stores)?

[8]**KNOW ABOUT:** Many people argue that the scarcity of affordable nursing homes and hospices means that the care of sick or elderly people falls back onto the family (if there is one) to do in the home. This re-privatization of care work tends to be distributed unevenly, becoming the responsibility all too often of women in the family and removing them from the paid workforce. (Note how this presumes heteronormative family arrangements.) The privatization and individualization of this work is one aspect of what is known as *neoliberalism*.

(9)TALK ABOUT: What are some examples—in the news, in pop culture representations, from your own experiences— of this assumption of someone being in the wrong place? What led to the assumption that they were in the wrong: e.g., self-presentation, behaviors, alone or in groups? What are some responses when places that were assumed to be accessible to some groups suddenly become contested: for instance, when Indigenous peoples attempt to delimit access to their traditional lands by companies interested in resource extraction or by state law enforcement?

(10)KNOW ABOUT:
Environmental racism describes the act of locating environmentally degrading development (waste management sites, sewage plants, refineries) in low-income or minority areas. It argues that the location of these projects in particular areas is as

liquor stores and fast food—are not simply expressions of benign diversity among places and the groups of people within them. Different places produce inclusion and exclusion of particular identity groups, creating a sense of community for some and rendering others who "don't belong" dangerous—and thus, ironically, often putting them in danger[9].

The privilege to occupy a place also determines who can move in and around it freely and whose belonging becomes more precarious. Consider, for example, the effects on poor neighborhoods when higher-income people move in, buy up property and set up businesses that reflect their own tastes and income levels, rather than those of long-time residents whose personal histories are tied to that location. Gentrification—a term derived from "gentry" (elite landed class)—often involves identity groups who seek city amenities adjacent to highly stressed neighborhoods. They invest in real estate but are less concerned about investing in local infrastructure like neighborhood schools. While this sort of mobility could be considered an opportunity to create more diverse living communities, too often the low-income residents become economically displaced by the increase in rents and taxes that result from this higher-income influx into the very community that used to be theirs.

This kind of displacement doesn't only work at the level of people being edged out, however. Consider how displacement is at work when more privileged groups of people and communities require a location to put what they don't want around. The resistance to having "unpleasant" things—landfills, hazardous waste facilities, oil refineries, prisons, cell phone towers, wind farms—in some neighborhoods results in officially or unofficially sanctioning the idea that they do belong in other people's neighborhoods. The desire and power to locate these things somewhere else is captured by the expression NIMBY ("not in my backyard"), a derogatory acronym used to describe the objection, largely of middle- and upper-class communities, to the siting of something perceived as unpleasant or potentially dangerous in their own neighborhoods, and their efforts to have those removed or relocated elsewhere[10]. Few groups would welcome something like a landfill in their neighborhood, but not all groups have equal power to refuse it. What NIMBY points to, then, is a sense of ownership and control over particular places by some groups of people who have the power (e.g., through voice in government, economic clout, high tax brackets) to make their desires happen; thus, even while more powerful communities maintain unsightly infrastructure may be necessary, they insist that it needs to be located somewhere else.

Interestingly though, the externalizing of environmental and social hazards to "other" neighborhoods can be a catalyst for the formation or expression of community in those places, too. In the face of such hazards, people often come together to resist these common external threats, arguing for recognition of their attachments to that place and insisting that their neighborhoods be given the same respect as others. In other words, people aren't just identified with particular places by others; they identify themselves with those places, too, as their neighborhood, their homes, their lands, their heritage, their shared experiences. The resulting struggles not only draw our attention to the construction of communities that resist and redefine their place in the world but they also point out how contested place always is. Thinking of community as a home, then, points to how much we are identified with and through place, how much place both reflects and produces us as subjects, and how place is never simply a neutral location we occupy.

Nation

Probably the place that is most reflective of these tensions around drawing boundaries and constructing commonality is the *nation*. Often used as a synonym for state or country, nation is as much an abstract idea as it is a specific place. One way to think about nation is as a concept capable of transforming a physical territory into a "homeland," a place of belonging and attachment. Nation connects groups of otherwise disparate people to each other and to a physically bounded territory as well as to an assumed set of shared characteristics, a sense of connection referred to as *nationalism*. The nation is always "imagined" in that its perceived coherence—as a place with common ideas about its identity, as a place with a shared history, as a place that must be protected—is socially constructed. Saying the nation is imagined captures the idea that there is no necessary connection between all the members of any particular community, no matter its size[11]. Instead, the sense of being a nation depends on the constant narration of common origins and rituals of belonging; think of how

an expression and perpetuation of racism. Many people also use this term to describe the movement of toxic materials to other countries for disposal.

[11]**KNOW ABOUT:** To say that the feeling of connection is socially constructed, though, is not to say that it is simply made up or easily gotten rid of. Our attachment to nation and a sense of national belonging is as much a part of who we are (as both individuals and groups of people) as are other identity categories such as gender, race, or sexuality (as discussed in the "Identities" chapter). The key question for those of us interested in challenging particular definitions of identity categories thus always becomes how to recognize those attachments and challenge them at the same time.

nations come together around national holidays and celebrations, symbols (such as flags), food, and dress. These narratives and rituals work to produce a national identity that its members can call their own, no matter the other differences between them; they become the common ways that "we" are reminded of who "we" are. As such, nation combines notions of home and community in ways that continuously promote a sense of belonging by and for its members. In the nation, "we" protect our borders, "we" take care of our own, and "we" honor our traditions.

Of course, the key question when we recognize this kind of nationalist discourse is who exactly does this "we" refer to? And what happens when our origin narratives and rituals of belonging conflict or when they cannot contain everyone within them? Do all citizens of a nation belong at all times? After all, nations always consist of competing narratives, symbols, even flags, reflecting the many different groups of people who inhabit their regions and have distinct histories and cultures. For instance, think about in times of war or during international sports competitions: the nation is assumed and spoken of as encompassing everyone within its borders, so that belonging to the nation means everyone within its physical territory. But even during these moments of intense nationalism, there are still plenty of groups who can be or are considered outside that nation: those who don't support the war efforts ("if you're not with us, you're with them") or those who question whether that nation represents them when the sports event is over. The conflicts inherent in national belonging mean that even in these apparently universal moments of "we," people still identify themselves in ways that are at odds with that "we."[12]

Constructing a "we," however, always requires a "they." In other words, the nation depends on that which is not part of it, outside of and excluded from it, and perhaps even a threat to it. Also important to explore, then, is who and what is identified as a threat. For instance, there is a long history of characterizing particular identity groups within the physical nation's borders as a threat, as the "them" that poses a risk to "us." Think about the long and sordid history in both Canada and the United States of particular groups of people designated to be a threat from within: Japanese Americans who were placed in internment camps during the Second World War, or gay men who were seen as communists during the Cold War and therefore denied rights to employment, housing, parenthood, and privacy. More recently for citizens who are practicing

[12]KNOW ABOUT: During the 1968 summer Olympics, for instance, the African American gold and bronze medalists in the men's 200m race raised black-gloved fists—a symbol of the Black Power movement of the time—while the U.S. national anthem was playing. They were subsequently stripped of their medals. Similarly, boxer Mohammed Ali was also stripped of his heavyweight championship title when he refused to be inducted into the U.S. army during the Vietnam War. These two examples illustrate some of the competing senses of belonging to the "we" of the nation.

Muslims or of Middle Eastern descent (or those who are perceived—however erroneously—to be), getting on an airplane in this post-9/11 "war on terror" era can be anything from a tense ordeal to an absolute impossibility. (Note, too, how often the language of "war" is mobilized to position particular identity groups as those internal threats.) The resulting focus on mitigating threats all too often ranges from stigmatizing and stereotyping particular groups of people to more draconian measures, such as increased government surveillance, large police budgets, violent crackdowns on protest, and martial law. Constructing the threat as emanating from within the nation's boundaries highlights the ways in which not everyone occupying the same territory or even legally designated as a citizen of that nation actually belongs to the nation.

Finally, the question of national belonging is especially fraught when a nation, as in the case of the United States or Canada, was formed by settlers from outside these physical locations and when there were already large numbers of people living on these lands. *Settler colonialism* describes what results from a group of people immigrating to a place with the express purpose of occupation and building a new homeland. The subsequent elimination of indigenous communities can also become an organizing principle in the formation of the colonizing community's national identity. For instance, in the United States, think about the romance of the "frontier" and the logic of "manifest destiny" as narratives that justified westward expansion into Native American lands and the formation of Indian reservations. The fact that the territory required to create the new nation had to be taken by force—sustained, brutal, genocidal force—is a story whose scope and complexity are rarely told in the national narratives of either of these countries[13].

Instead, the stories told to explain indigenous presence and absence in the place of the nation include: treaties and ceded territories, reserves and reservations, land allotments, assimilation, trusted guides, "noble" savages, Indian "princesses," and "vanishing" races. Like the paradoxical separation and blurring of public and private spaces discussed previously, the places of indigeneity in the United States and Canada are both domestic and yet somehow foreign: "present" in the names of cities, provinces, states, street names, and sports teams, and yet "absent" in how most non-native Americans and Canadians think of themselves in relation to their national identity and these troubled histories. The irony here is that while both nation-states speak

[13]**KNOW ABOUT:** *Settler colonialism* doesn't only describe North American colonial histories. In addition to the U.S. and Canada, we can speak of various forms of settler colonialism—both historical and contemporary—in Israel, much of Latin America, India, and many parts of Africa and southeast Asia.

of colonialism in their founding stories, in these stories the contemporary nation is the victim of colonial rule, not its perpetrator; both countries recount stories of European settlers having to separate and gain their independence from colonial rule by England and France. These national origin stories do the ideological work of connecting people to, and disconnecting them from, the territory claimed; as a result, they overlook other stories of how colonialism was experienced, especially by the indigenous peoples. They also work to absolve European settlers from being perceived (or perceiving themselves) as those doing the colonizing, as those who perpetrated a wrong, since they position those settlers as the ones who were themselves wronged by European rule from the "home" countries.

The Concept at Work: Prisons and the "War on Drugs"

Prisons are unique places constructed to physically restrict the mobility of the bodies of those deemed criminally deviant by the state. Prisoners are forcibly contained by bars, walls, and barbed wire away from their homes, families, and communities, in sites that are frequently located in isolated rural areas. They are there for "correction," hence the name "Department of Corrections" (in the United States) or "Correctional Services" (in Canada). But what is it that is being corrected? And how can we account for the disparities of who ends up in prisons, which, in both countries, is overwhelmingly people of color? What is the logic of segregating people deemed to be criminal away from the rest of society anyway?

One way to think about what prisons correct is to look at where various kinds of social problems are made visible or invisible. By observing who ends up in prison and what constitutes (and contributes to) the crimes that put them there, it becomes apparent that prisons offer a mechanism to make the highly stigmatized conditions of poverty, mental illness, homelessness, drug addiction, domestic abuse, immigration, and unemployment more visible in some communities than in others. While such conditions can be found in any community, privilege (by way of class, race, gender expression, citizenship status, ability, and even age) can offer various forms of protection from police observation and criminal investigation, rendering these social issues less criminally consequential in some people's lives. For example, while young people across all race and class demographics use illegal drugs with about the same frequency, those locked up in prison for drug-related crimes are disproportionately poor people and people of color. This is, in part, because some neighborhoods are targeted for more police surveillance, intervention, and violence. It is not surprising, then, that the "war on drugs" (as it was termed more than a generation ago) has disproportionately—and negatively—impacted already socially stressed and marginalized communities in both Canada and the United States.

Prisons thus become places that produce dominant ideas of justice and injustice, safety and danger, stories that every society must speak to. But if we consider the fact that most people currently in prison are not there for violent crimes and that a significant number have some form of mental illness (including addictions), then their imprisonment may in fact endanger them—by putting them in violent settings or by withholding treatment, for instance. And the stakes are extremely high. Incarceration can have lifelong effects on people, even once they are released; for example, in the United States, people who have been convicted of felonies have a lifetime ban on receiving federal student loans, and, in many states, lose voting rights for life. And finally, as compared to costs associated with education, housing, medical care, and nutrition (all demonstrated to directly or indirectly reduce criminal behaviors), prisons are vastly more expensive to build and maintain. Why then, given their costs and inefficiencies, are prisons so often seen as the primary location to address social problems and promote public safety?

One way to address this question is to think about the popularity of detective novels and murder mysteries, or of crime dramas on television and in film, where particularly violent crimes (statistically less frequent than popular culture representations would have us believe) are routinely represented as entertainment. Or consider how sensationalizing any crime is a source of ratings spikes for news organizations. And even as violent crime rates are lower in Canada and the United States than they have been in decades, the political imperative for those running for public office to be "tough on crime" has been practically a requirement for the past generation or so; very few politicians tell (or, it seems, want to tell) stories about people convicted of crime as instead deserving of public resources, social support, and second chances. (As a result, the United States locks up more of its citizens than any other country in the world.) But there are other possible stories to tell about justice besides that of prisons as the most appropriate place for those engaged in criminal behavior. What about alternate stories that emphasize justice and safety as produced through a drug rehabilitation center, a mental health clinic, a classroom, a job training program, a hospital, or even a home? Instead of contextualizing the social problems that prisons are set up to supposedly solve, the reasons and justifications for prisons too often turn on a very limited framework for understanding the complexity of such social issues.

Furthermore, even more than just in stories about justice, think about how implicated prisons have become in the larger economy of many countries, producing what is referred to as the *prison industrial complex*. Prisons have become big business as multinational, for-profit corporations (whose shareholders expect growth and dividends) have expanded their wealth through contracting with states and governments. And even though a single prisoner in these privatized corporate institutions costs the state tens of thousands of dollars each year to house, these same corporations profit when prisoners become extremely cheap labor to be farmed out to other corporate and state agencies without the inconveniences of benefit packages, overtime pay, unemployment insurance, unionization, minimum wages, complaints about working conditions, labor actions, or strikes. Thus, to begin to understand the multiple meanings of prisons, we have to ask broader questions about the concept of place: How do prisons reflect notions of inclusion and exclusion and of who belongs where? What difference do identity categories make to the roles prisons play? How are prisons implicated in other social institutions, structures, and practices that are not usually part of the dominant narratives told about them?

Preview of Readings

Imrie, Rob. 2014. "Disability, Embodiment and the Meaning of the Home." In *The People, Place, and Space Reader*, edited by Jen Jack Gieseking and William Mangold, with Cindi Katz, Setha Low, and Susan Saegert, 156–162. New York, NY: Routledge.

Parreñas, Rhacel Salazar. 2009. "The Globalization of Care Work." In *Service Work: Critical Perspectives*, edited by Marek Korczynski and Cameron Lynne Macdonald, 135–152. New York, NY: Routledge.

Meiners, Erica R. 2011. "Awful Acts and the Trouble with Normal." In *Captive Genders*, edited by Eric Stanley and Nat Smith, 113–121. Oakland, CA: AK Press.

Puri, Jyoti. 2011. "Sexuality, State, and Nation." In *Introducing the New Sexuality Studies* (2nd ed.), edited by Steven Seidman, Nancy Fischer, and Chet Meeks, 401–407. New York, NY: Routledge.

Abdulhadi, Rabab. 2011. "Where Is Home?: Fragmented Lives, Border Crossings, and the Politics of Exile." In *Arab and Arab American Feminisms: Gender, Violence, and Belonging*, edited by Rabab Abdulhadi, Evelyn Alsultany, and Nadine Naber, 315–328. Syracuse, NY: Syracuse University Press.

In "Places," we examine the complex meanings we associate with various sorts of locations we move through everyday. Locations like "home" reflect multiple dimensions: labor and leisure, safety and exploitation, who cares and who is cared for. Place—from neighborhood to nation—can also be a source of community building or community rupture, as various identity groups struggle for power, ownership, and sovereignty in and through ideas about place. These place-based attachments provide justifications on the part of some groups to define the terms of inclusion and of belonging to a home, community, or nation.

Rob Imrie delves into the intimate yet, for some, often alienating space of home in "Disability, Embodiment and the Meaning of the Home." That home design and architecture assume upright bodies to maneuver through small kitchens, bedrooms, and bathrooms means that the world is reproduced in the image of the temporarily able-bodied, with the result that the impaired body is experienced as "alien." This means that the dominant disposition of impaired bodies—even in the location constructed to be the sanctuary from the outside world—is one of "making do."

- How do our homes produce disability for some bodies? What might have to be altered to make home accessible for a variety of different kinds of bodies?
- In what ways is alienation produced by various built environments that we move through on a daily basis? Think about the campus bookstore or cafeteria, your favorite coffee shop or fast food restaurant. What assumptions are made about bodies through the built environment?

In "The Globalization of Care Work," Rhacel Parreñas focuses on the international flow of domestic workers and care workers, and in particular on "global care chains" in which North American women purchase care for their children from migrant women with fewer resources. Such care chains illustrate not just the oppression of women in the global south, but also the ways in which families in the global north are burdened by decreased wages and the increased privatization of care work.

- Who is doing the labor of care around us? What value—monetary and in terms of social status—is that labor afforded?
- Whose care seems to matter most in the various institutions you encounter on a daily basis? Whose well-being seems less worthy of paid care work?
- If society valued care work more, how might our personal and national economies be altered?

"Awful Acts and the Trouble with Normal" is Erica Meiners' account of the discourse of "stranger danger" and its arbitrary applications. She recounts childhood memories of how those who didn't seem to "belong" were defined, surveilled, and legally punished for perversion, while someone who did belong—and who she knew to be a sexual predator—went unnoticed and unpunished. The increased use of Sex Offender Registries that don't permit sex offenders within 500 feet of a school have become mechanisms for constructing borders of safe and dangerous spaces for children. Given that 90 percent of childhood sexual predators were known to their victims and the vast majority of violence against women is perpetrated by (ex-) spouses and (ex-)lovers, Meiners argues that the intense focus on protecting children and women from strangers is tragically misplaced.

- What messages about locations of danger did you receive growing up?
- How is "stranger danger" talk circulated and used (or not) on campus or in other contexts in our lives?
- How can locating danger as happening only (or mostly) in particular places perpetuate various forms of violence? What is overlooked in this limited way of thinking about where violence occurs?

Jyoti Puri's "Sexuality, State, and Nation" asks that we consider the role of the state in shaping sexuality. While nationalism's promise is that, as citizens, we are the same and therefore pretty much equal, the reality, argues Puri, is that sexuality—normative or deviant—is shorthand for figuring out who is a good citizen and who is an outsider in need of purging. Using both Indian and U.S. nationalisms to make her points, she notes how rape, HIV/AIDS, homosexuality, and gender "deviance" increase suspicions and evoke heightened surveillance and regulation on the part of the state.

- In what ways does the state promote or discourage various sexualities? What sexualities are rarely or never talked about? Why aren't they talked about?
- How might we think about sexuality as a hierarchy? What practices, identities, and/or contexts influence who ends up where on that hierarchy?

- What are some ways that we might resist state involvement in its citizens' sexualities?

Rabab Abdulhadi's "Where Is Home?: Fragmented Lives, Border Crossings, and the Politics of Exile" illustrates how fraught the notion of "going home" can be in a diasporic community whose history is marked by forced exile. Living in New York City during 9/11 presents her with yet another experience of estrangement as she recounts her deliberate attempts to hide her Arab identity from other New Yorkers. Despite equality under the law and her legal status, she documents the personal stress, pain, and experiences of violence that perceptions of "not belonging" unleash on her, her family, and her various communities.

- What makes us feel at home in an institutional setting, a community, or a nation?
- How does a lack of belonging seem to influence people's personal behavior and psychic lives?
- In considering your own experiences of belonging or estrangement, can you recount reasons that others might consider you to be on one side or other of a community border, one of "us" or one of "them?"

Disability, Embodiment and the Meaning of the Home

Rob Imrie

It has been well established in housing studies that the home is one of the fundamental places that gives shape and meaning to people's everyday lives. A burgeoning literature has, in various ways, explored the social, health and psychological effects of the home. For example, Sixsmith and Sixsmith (1991) note that the home is a symbol of oneself or a powerful extension of the psyche. It is a context for social and mental well-being or, as Lewin (2001) suggests, a place to engender social psychological and cultural security. For others, the home is the focus for personal control and a place that permits people to fashion in their own image. In this sense, the domestic setting is, for Lewin (2001), a mirror of personal views and values (also, see Cooper, 1995).

Gilman's (1903; reprinted 2002, p.3) seminal text suggests that the home, ideally, should offer a combination of rest, peace, quiet, comfort, health and be a place for personal expression. Indeed, throughout the 20th century, the home has been counterpoised to work, as a place of retreat, social stability and domestic bliss far from the travails of everyday life. From builders' marketing brochures that seek to sell the dream of the ideal home, to television programmes about selling a place in the sun, the home is popularly portrayed as the focus of convivial social relationships and a source of human contentment. It is, first and foremost, a place for family interaction and the setting for personal seclusion and intimate behaviour free from public comment or restraint. The home is also the setting for the development of personal values, and patterns of socialisation and social reproduction more generally.

These characterisations of the home, however, do little to reveal the complexity of the cross-cutting variables that imbue domestic space with meaning. For Saunders and Williams (1988), the meaning of the home is not fixed but varies, potentially, between different household members, especially in terms of gender and age, and between households, especially in relation to differences in social class. They also suggest that people's experiences of, and meanings attributed to, the home may differ according to geographical context or setting.

Such studies indicate that the meaning of the home is unstable and transitory. For Gilman (2002, p. 8), despite the prevailing wisdom that homes were "perfect and quite above suspicion", the home was a potential source of repression. In particular, she referred to women's exclusive confinement to the home as leading to 'mental myopia' in which the individual was made into 'less of a person'. Likewise, a range of feminist writers have sought to deconstruct ideal images of the home by suggesting that the home, for some women, is a place of captivity and isolation (Allan, 1985; McDowell, 1983). Others note that the home is as much about the focus for the drudgery of domestic work as for personal pleasure, and a place of fear where, potentially, domestic violence takes place.

While these, and related, studies have done much to destabilise popular representations of the home, they tend to refer to abstract categories (e.g. gender, ethnicity, etc.) that rarely relate to, or reveal, how specific bodily or physiological phenomena interact with dwellings to produce personal experiences of, and generate particular meanings about, the home. Indeed, as Gurney (1990) notes, it is problematical to explain the meaning of the home with reference only to generalised categories, such as class, income or tenure. Rather, for Gurney, the significance of the home is influenced by different personal experiences. Foremost, it is contended, it relates to the body in that, as Twigg (2002, p. 436) comments, the body is a necessary condition of life in as much that "social life cannot proceed without this physiological substratum".

Others concur in noting that the body is the most significant referent of a person or, as Merleau-Ponty (1962, p. 150) notes, "I am not in front of my body, I am in it, or rather I am it". For Merleau-Ponty (1963, p. 5), the "body is not in space like things; it inhabits or haunts space . . . through it we have access to space". Here, the body, as a sensory and physiological entity, is constitutive of space or, as Lefebvre (1991, p. 174) comments, "the most basic places and spatial indicators are first of all qualified by the body". Physiological substratum is also core to domestic life in that the home is the focus for the care of the body, including washing, dressing, grooming and preparation for entry to the world beyond the front door. The physical design of dwellings is 'thoroughly embodied' in that each part of the domestic environment can be thought of as a 'body zone', or where particular bodily functions, both physical and mental, are attended to. Thus, the bathroom is the place for washing the body, while the bedroom is the place for physical and mental recuperation.

While such functional demarcations are neither inevitable nor unchangeable, they are part of a broader and powerful, social and cultural encoding of what constitutes appropriate domestic space and their legitimate (bodily) uses. Such encoding, however, rarely relates to impairment, or to bodies that may require an integration of rooms and/or functions, or more flexible forms of domestic design. In particular, disabled people often experience the home as a series of 'disembodied spaces', or places that are designed in ways that are rarely attentive to their physiological and bodily needs and functions. Thus, interactions between features of bodily physiology, such as muscle wasting, and domestic design, such as heavy doors, can combine to demarcate domestic spaces that are off limits to (particular types of) impaired bodies. For Hockey (1999, p. 108), such embodied experiences, in which people are excluded from participation "in the performance of home as idealised, is to undermine a view of home as a sanctuary or 'place of secure retreat'". Insights into disabled people's experiences of, and meanings associated with, the home, ought to proceed, however, by rejecting reductive conceptions of disability and impairment. Thus, the body is neither a naturalistic organic entity, unaffected by socialisation, nor a socialised entity, unaffected by physiology. Rather, the body, and its interactions with domestic space, reflects a complex conjoining of physiological and social and cultural relations to produce specific, person-centred, meanings of the home. For instance, doorsteps have long been part of the aesthetic decor of dwellings, and reflect values about what constitutes appropriate design. However, for wheelchair users, steps prevent ease of entry to homes. In such instances, the experience, and potential meaning, of the home as a form of embodied encounter, is influenced by the interplay between physiological matter (i.e. the absence of use of limbs) and those social and cultural relations that give rise to, and legitimate, particular design features (i.e. steps).

Disability, Domestic Design and the Home Environment

In investigating disabled people's feelings about disability and domestic design, two research methods were adopted. First, two focus groups were held in October 2002 with members of a disabled persons user group located in a south coast conurbation. This was followed, over the course of the next five months, by interviews with 20 individuals living in three different towns.

The subjects are all individuals with various mobility impairments, ranging from those with problems of balance due to the early onset of Parkinson's disease, to individuals with advanced stages of multiple sclerosis that render them dependent, for some of the time, on a wheelchair.

The respondents live in a mixture of different types of dwellings including flats (5 respondents), detached homes (4), institutional care settings (3), and terraced and semidetached dwellings (8).

Corporeal Dys-appearance and Privation in the Home

The physical design of housing tends to reflect a particular conception of corporeality based around a body that is not characterised by impairment, disease and illness. For instance, most kitchen units in homes are provided as a standardised package in which tabletop and cupboard heights are reachable only by an upright person. People who are dependent on a wheelchair, or whose mobility is such that they have to hold onto a support structure to stabilise themselves, often find it impossible to use their kitchen unless it is adapted to meet their needs. Thus, as Ann recounted, about her kitchen before it was adapted:

It was too high, I couldn't have used the wheelchair, the cupboards were too high, the cooker was completely unusable, I would leave the thing on and oh, it just went on and on and on. . . . As a mum it totally demoralised me.

The design of most dwellings is also underpinned by values that rarely relate to, or incorporate, the needs of wheelchair users. Some respondents were angry that their homes were short of space to permit them ease of movement from one room to another, or even within rooms. For John, his bedroom is an apt example of where design values have been applied without relating to impairment. As he recalled:

There are some basic assumptions. I'm just talking about a very simple basic thing like there is no way on this earth that my wheelchair can go to the other side of my bed. It doesn't matter what you do you can't configure the bedroom any other way, so

the assumption must be that I'm not going to make my bed, that I don't need to get to the other side of the room.

Others commented on the lack of space as the most important factor in preventing them from getting access to rooms and living as they please in their homes. As Carol said:

The kitchen is really very small and when you're manoeuvring a wheelchair you do need a bit of space. You can hardly get your furniture in the lounge and you have to eat in it. It's things like this, and I'm thinking to myself, you've got a life and you want to lead your life and this isn't really helping you.

Similarly, Janet was unhappy with the shortage of space in her WC which, she felt, compromised the quality of her life:

If my loo had been built eighteen inches longer it would've meant I could've got my whole wheelchair in, but as it is I can't use it with the wheelchair . . . I have to leave the door open, and it just brings it home to you about what you can't do in your own home.

Such examples serve to illustrate what Leder (1990, p. 84) refers to as the "dys-appearing" body or where, as he suggests, "the body appears as a thematic focus of attention but precisely in a dys-state" (also, see Paterson and Hughes, 1999). What Leder (1990) is inferring is that, in everyday life, consciousness of *the* body, either by oneself or by others, is minimal or nonexistent. That is, the body has, more or less, disappeared from consciousness. It only reappears, explicitly, in a context of pain, disease or bodily dysfunction. Its reappearance is characterised by encounters with the embodied norms of everyday life, or those that are reflective of, primarily, non-impaired forms of carnality. Such norms serve to reproduce a world in the image of non-impaired bodies, with the consequence that, in Paterson and Hughes'

(1999, p. 603) terms, the impaired body is experienced "as-alien-being-in-the-world".

The body is simultaneously there but not there, characterised by material practices (i.e. moving from room to room, bathing, etc.) which draw attention to 'out-of-place' bodies, or bodies unable to operate wholly in environments characterised by the embodied norms of society.

For most respondents, living in the home is achieved by accepting, and adapting to, the standards of design that reflect the primacy of non-impaired bodies. White respondents often expressed anger about this, they felt that there were few options open to them. For instance, Joe commented on the unfairness of imposing on him domestic design that tended to amplify, and draw attention to, his impairment: "If I try and use that room then it only shows up that my body isn't up to it . . . it's not me though, it's the lack of space in there." However, he felt he had no option but to compromise, although he felt it was all one-sided in that disabled people are the ones who have to take what is on offer. As he said; "You compromise all the time. I hear people all the time saying 'It's good, I can get by, I make do, I'm quite happy'. I don't hear that from temporarily able-bodied people. They're not saying that about their homes."

The feelings of a state of body-out-of-place in the home were, more often than not, related to design details, or the micro-architecture, of the dwelling. Thus, it was often the subtle aspects of the design of the home environment that caused most problems. For instance, John referred to the fitting of an electric window to permit ease of opening of windows by the use of remote control. However, as he said:

I mean, my electric window is beautiful, wonderful, but the switch is on the pelmet [laughter] and out of reach. It's like when they fitted it they didn't look at me or ask me if it was OK. They just did it.

Impairment and De-stabilising the Meaning of the Home

Binns and Mars (1984, p. 664) suggest that the ideal of the home as sanctuary is undermined in circumstances where the home environment becomes "the product of withdrawal from wider social networks". Indeed, for some respondents, broader social, attitudinal and environmental circumstances, beyond the immediate confines of their home, had led them to 'stay-at-home', rarely venturing beyond the front door. For instance, Harry recounted demeaning reactions from 'friends' concerning his inability to access, unaided, stepped thresholds into their homes: "they think I'm being awkward . . . it's not as friendly an atmosphere as what it used to be, when I was up and walking . . . people say I'm seeking attention or whatever. They're wrong about that [laughs]." For Harry, it has become easier not to visit friends or to expose himself to possible ridicule or suggestions that 'he's putting it on'. Rather, as Harry said, "I spend most time indoors, and it feels like I'm confined to quarters."

In other instances, social interactions have been curtailed or have stopped altogether. As Harry noted, "I don't get invited to some of the parties any more, as they've got to lift me into the house."

Likewise, Elaine said that because of her weakening muscles, and physical impediments on the pavement and the lack of access into the local shops, she had stopped going out. For her, 'it all stops at the garden gate'.

Others recalled the loss of independence and personal control in their home due to interactions between impairment and physical design.

For Trish, the home became associated with a complete loss of independence and the performance of personal acts in degrading situations. As she said:

My husband used to carry me upstairs and there were so many practical issues. He had to get my dresses from upstairs and I had to use a bucket for a toilet and I had to be bathed on towels downstairs in the living room. The experience made me realise that the correlation between psychological and physical states should not be underestimated.

For others too, the home was less a place of independence and more a context in which things had to be done for them. Thus, everyday household activities became, with the onset of impairment, more or less impossible to do without some assistance. Moreover, the idea that the home might provide for personal privacy is not always the case.

Such experiences were destabilising for these respondents and left them feeling that they had little control over circumstances. This, then, suggests that the nature of privacy in the home is never stable or guaranteed and, as Allan and Crow (1989, p. 3) suggest, "an individual's ability to secure some degree of privacy is conditional". Likewise, the idea of the home as a retreat, haven, or place of sanctuary and security is not always borne out, particularly in a context where a deteriorating body requires third party care and attention.

Insecurity was also felt by those who said that they had attracted negative comment when outside, and did not want to draw attention to the fact that an impaired person lived in the house. For Harry: "you want to blend in and not reveal that you can't walk. It makes you a target." Others concurred and some respondents were wary about fitting a ramp up to their front door for fear of it labelling them as 'defective' and 'different'. As Carol said:

> I mean, I want to be able to live in my home but I don't want it to be screaming at anybody that walks in, to be inhibited because a disabled person lives here. That's the other thing, you know. I'm very, very conscious of this because one of my sons particularly found it very, very difficult to come to terms with it, and I don't want it screaming 'Oh dear, this poor woman lives on her own, she's in a wheelchair'.

This, then, illustrates, the point, that the external physical features of the house convey subtle shades of meaning and act as signifiers to the outside world.

Resisting Domestic Design and Generating Usable Spaces

In concurring with Allen (2000), I suggest that disabled people are not passive victims of insensitive design, nor necessarily resigned to dependence on others to facilitate aspects of their home lives. Far from it, the experiences of disabled people in this study, and elsewhere, illustrate the capacity to generate usable spaces out of the social and physical impediments that are placed in their way. For instance, Allen *et al.* (2002, p. 65) note that parents of vision-impaired children do not necessarily see them as victims of the built environment. This is because most are able to construct what Allen *et al.* (2002) refer to as 'memory maps' or guides of their home and neighbourhood environment that permit them to navigate, with relative ease, from one space to another.

The strategies deployed by respondents were, in part, dependent on income and social class. For respondents on low incomes, and living in council or housing association property, it was often a struggle to get things changed. As Jenny observed:

> If you've got no income and Social Services are making the alterations for you, you will have had a fight that's probably gone on three or four years to get it, and the chances of you succeeding again getting it if you move to another house is not very high, so you never want to move, you stay where you are.

Others concurred in expressing their frustration with delays in getting adaptations done. As Stan noted, "this is one of the arguments I've had with Social Services for years and years and years. If you need handrails and a ramp, or a toilet adapted, you need it quickly . . . you know, when you're disabled you need help quickly."

In contrast, those with higher incomes, and who owned their home, had more choice about how and when to adapt the domestic environment. Jenny expressed a common view; "If you're middle class and you can afford to do it in the manner that I have, and you've got an income, you're earning money . . . then you do it."

Regardless of income or tenure, respondents were able to rearrange layout by, primarily, 'clearing up the clutter' and making space to facilitate ease of movement and use of rooms. Jenny moved into her house when she could walk and furnished it throughout. As she said: "the house was designed for no more than a walking disabled person . . . and now it's inconvenient for me." However, her more or less constant use of a wheelchair now means that "if I wanted to get into a room I have to push chairs out of the way to get to the far wall . . . there was furniture everywhere". For Jenny, the solution was to sell the furniture, or, as she said: "I've just chucked everything out and we're now in a situation where there's not even any chairs for anybody to sit on." Others have done similar things and Heather, living in housing association property, "got rid of the big furniture and put up grab rails everywhere".

Like Heather, other respondents have changed aspects of the micro-architecture of their homes that had previously made a big difference to their mobility around the home. For Carol, the floor surface had to be changed when she became dependent on a wheelchair. Likewise, Jim persuaded the local authority to provide a grant to adapt the downstairs toilet door, so that it now slides open and permits easier access than was hitherto the case.

For most respondents the need to think ahead is paramount because of the knowledge that bodily deterioration will necessitate different ways of using the home. Jenny bought her present house when she was able to walk without the use of a wheelchair, but knew that, in time, she would be dependent on a wheelchair to get around. As she explained:

I bought the house because it was very flat. I was actually going round saying to my relatives 'Oh, this will do for a wheelchair'. And they were going 'Don't be stupid, you'll never go in a wheelchair'. And I always sort of knew my limitations; I knew it was on the cards.

However, such behaviour and/or actions appear to be no more than 'little victories' in a context whereby the design of most homes remains resistant to the needs of impaired bodies. Indeed, respondents were of the view that the only way to (re) claim domestic space for impairment is if professional experts, such as builders, architects and occupational therapists, respond to experiential information and guidance provided by disabled people themselves. Others concurred, with Jane expressing her frustration at the attitudes of the builders who had adapted her house: "that's the interesting assumption about disabled people, isn't it, we obviously have got nothing to contribute back."

Conclusions

The testimonials in this paper suggest that there are tensions between ideal conceptions of the home and the material, lived, domestic realities of disabled people. While aspects of the home may well provide for privacy, sanctuary, security and other aspects of 'ideal' domestic habitation, such provisions are always conditional, contingent, never secure, and likely to be challenged by, amongst other things, the onset and development of bodily impairment. However, explorations of the meaning of the home, and housing studies more generally, rarely consider the body and impairment and its interactions with domestic space. This is curious because impairment is a significant, and intrinsic, condition of human existence and can affect anyone at any time. In this sense, a person's feelings about, and experiences of, the home cannot be dissociated from their corporeality or the organic matter and material of the body.

Indeed, dominant representations of the meaning of the home, propagated by builders, architects and others, are underpinned by specific conceptions of embodied domestic spaces that do little to acknowledge the possibilities of bodily impairment as part of domestic habitation. Such representations revolve around the home as part of the ideal of family life, in which non-impaired bodies with relative independence of movement and mobility are paramount. The dominance of non-impaired carnality is reflected in physical design that, as the testimonials suggested, rarely includes the fixtures, fittings or spaces to enable the ease of use of domestic spaces by disabled people. Rather, such spaces, for many disabled people, are potentially disembodying in the sense that they deny the presence or possibility of bodily impairment and, as a consequence, are likely to reduce the quality of their home life.

Bodily impairment is neither fixed nor static, or something that acquires meaning or function independent from social context or setting. Rather, as respondents noted, their home lives revolved around resolving issues relating to functioning in restrictive spaces, in contexts whereby bodily changes, particularly organic deterioration, were manifest realities. Housing quality, then, cannot be understood or defined separately from an understanding of the interactions between organic matter and the domestic setting, of which physical design is a component part. This should be one focus for seeking to develop an approach to housing studies that recognises the importance of embodiment in influencing people's experiences of, and meanings attributed to, the home.

References

Allan, Graham. 1985. *Family Life: Domestic Roles and Social Organisation* (Oxford, Blackwell).

Allan, Graham and Crow, Graham. (eds) 1989. *Home and Family: Creating the Domestic Sphere* (London, Allen and Unwin).

Allen, Chris. 2000. On the 'physiological dope' problematic in housing and illness research: towards a critical realism of home and health, *Housing, Theory and Society*, 17, pp. 49–67.

Allen, Chris. 2003. On the socio-spatial worlds of visual impaired children, *or*, Merleau-Ponty + Bourdieu = the socio-spatiality of the habitus, *Urban Studies*, 41(3), pp. 487–506.

Allen, Chris, Milner, Joe and Price, Dawn. 2002. *Home is Where the Start is: The Housing and Urban Experiences of Visually Impaired Children* (York, Joseph Rowntree Foundation).

Binns, David and Mars, Gerald. 1984. Family, community and unemployment: a study in change, *Sociological Review*, 32, pp. 662–695.

Cooper, Marcus Clare. 1995. *House as a Mirror of Self* (Berkeley, CA, Conan Press).

Gilman, Charlotte Perkins. 2002. *The Home: Its Work and Influence* (London, Alta Mira Press).

Gleeson, Brendan. 1998. *Geographies of Disability* (London, Routledge).

Goldsack, Laura. 1999. A haven in a heartless world? Women and domestic violence, in: T. Chapman and J. Hockey (eds) *Ideal Homes? Social Change and Domestic Life*, pp. 121–132 (London, Routledge).

Gurney, Craigh. 1990. *The meaning of the home in the decade of owner occupation*. Working Paper 88 (Bristol, School for Advanced Urban Studies, University of Bristol, SAUS Publications).

Gurney, Craigh. 2000. Transgressing private–public boundaries in the home: a sociological analysis of the coital noise taboo, *Venereology*, 13, pp. 39–46.

Gurney, Craigh, undated. 'The neighbours didn't dare complain': some taboo thoughts on the regulation of noisy bodies and the disembodied housing imagination. Available at <www.cf.ac.uk/uwcc/cplan/enhr/files/Gurney-C2.html>.

Hockey, Jenny. 1999. The ideal of home, in: T. Chapman and

J. Hockey (eds) *Ideal Homes? Social Change and Domestic Life*, pp. 108–118 (London, Routledge).

Imrie, Rob. 2003. Housing quality and the provision of accessible homes, *Housing Studies*, 18, pp. 395–416.

Imrie, Rob and Hall, Peter. 2001. *Inclusive Design: Developing and Designing Accessible Environments* (London, Spon Press).

Leder, Drew. 1990. *The Absent Body* (Chicago, IL, Chicago University Press).

Lefebvre, Henri. 1991. *The Production of Space* (Oxford, Blackwell).

Lewin, Fereshtah. 2001. The meaning of home amongst elderly immigrants: directions for future research and theoretical development, *Housing Studies*, 16, pp. 353–370.

McDowell, Linda. 1983. Towards an understanding of the gender divisions of urban space, *Society and Space*, 1, pp. 59–72.

Merleau-Ponty, Maurice. 1962. *The Phenomenology of Perception* (London, Routledge and Kegan Paul).

Merleau-Ponty, Maurice. 1963. *The Primacy of Perception* (Evanston, IL, Northwestern University Press).

Millen, Dianne. 1997. Some methodological and epistemological issues raised by doing feminist research on non-feminist women, *Sociological Research Online*, 2. Available at <www.socresonline.org.uk>.

Oldman, Christine and Beresford, Bryony. 2000. Home sick home: using the housing experience of disabled children to suggest a new theoretical framework, *Housing Studies*, 15, pp. 429–442.

Oliver, Michael. 1990. *The Politics of Disablement* (Basingstoke, Macmillan).

Paterson, Kevin and Hughes, Bill. 1999. Disability studies and phenomenology: the carnal politics of everyday life, *Disability and Society*, 14, pp. 597–611.

Saunders, Peter. 1989. The meaning of 'home' in contemporary English culture, *Housing Studies*, 4, pp. 177–192.

Saunders, Peter. 1990. *A Nation of Home Owners* (London, Unwin Hyman).

Saunders, Peter. and Williams, Peter. 1988. The constitution of the home: towards a research agenda, *Housing Studies*, 3, pp. 81–93.

Sixsmith, Andrew and Sixsmith, Judith. 1991. Transitions in home experience in later life, *The Journal of Architectural and Planning Research*, 8, pp. 181–191.

Twigg, Julia. 2002. The body in social policy: mapping a territory, *Journal of Social Policy*, 31, pp. 421–439.

The Globalization of Care Work

Rhacel Salazar Parreñas

"Migration has a woman's face," announces a recent educational poster released by the United Nations. The poster declares that close to 70 percent of Filipino and Indonesian emigrants are women, while half of labor migrants around the globe are women. In 2002, approximately 175 million people – 2.3 percent of the world's population – lived outside their country of birth (United Nations Population Division, 2002). Women have historically migrated as wives and dependents of men (Donato, 1992; Hondagneu-Sotelo, 1994). Today, marriage still motivates the migration of women. Contemporary marriage migrants include but are not limited to "pen pal" brides that relocate West from Asia and Eastern Europe, military brides, as well as co-ethnic brides who subsequently follow male migrants abroad (Constable, 2003; Thai, 2003; Yuh, 2002). Yet, more than brides, women now migrate mostly as independent labor migrants. The majority of them are provisional migrants with temporary working visas that allow them to do the care work necessary to maintain the population of richer nations of Asia, the Americas and Europe (Anderson, 2000; Parreñas, 2001). From their performance of elderly care, housecleaning and childcare, migrant care workers arguably meet all of the dependency needs of many industrialized nations.

Because of the dependence of industrialized nations on the care work of migrant women, no longer do men who seek low-wage jobs in construction or heavy manufacturing solely lead the flow of workers from poorer to richer nations in the new global economy. Men still seek labor migration. For instance, they respond to the demand for agricultural workers in richer countries in the North and West. For example, in Spain, 99 percent of Algerian men, 83 percent of Moroccan men, and 86 percent of Senegalese men are in the agricultural sector (Ribas-Mateos, 2000: 176–7). Yet, with or without them, women are relocating across nation-states and entering the global labor market independently. Migrant women do not just respond to the demand for care work but also for low-wage manufacturing work, for instance as garment workers and factory assembly line workers in richer nations the world over (Chang, 2000; Parreñas, 2001; Gamburd, 2000; Hondagneu-Sotelo, 2001). Migration occurs mostly from South to South (Oishi, 2005) but also takes place from South to North and from East to West. As such, a global flow of domestic workers and care workers has emerged with women from Mexico and Central America relocating to clean the households of working families, take care of the children and elderly, in the United States (Hondagneu-Sotelo, 2001); Indonesian women to richer nations in Asia and the Middle East (Silvey, 2004); Sri Lankan women to Greece and the Middle East (Gamburd, 2000); Polish and Ukrainian women to Germany and other nations of Western Europe (Misra *et al.*, 2004); and Caribbean women to the United States and Canada (Bakan and Stasiulis, 1997).

In a much wider and greater scale, women from the Philippines have also responded to the demand for migrant care workers. Providing their services in more than 160 countries, Filipino women are the domestic workers par excellence of globalization (Parreñas, 2001). In Europe alone, a fairly large number of them work in the private households of middle to upper-income families in Great Britain, France, the Netherlands, Spain, Greece, and Italy. While in Asia, they toil in private households in Taiwan, Singapore, and Hong Kong (Lan, 2006;

Constable, 1997). The flow of migrant domestic workers from poor to rich nations speaks of what Pierrette Hondagneu-Sotelo (2001) calls a "new world domestic order," meaning an unequal division of care labor between the global south and global north. This flow of labor raises our attention to new forms of inequalities between women; particularly care labor inequalities that result in the "international division of reproductive labor"[1] or "global care chains" of women purchasing the care of their children from women with lesser resources in the global economy (Parreñas, 2000; Hochschild, 2000). Freed by migrant workers of their care responsibilities in the family, employing women in turn can avoid the penalty of the "mommy tax" or more generally the "caregiver tax" that stalls the advancement of women in the labor market (Crittenden, 2001). As such, migrant care workers enable them to pursue careers without penalty.

The rise in the labor migration of domestic workers speaks of the globalization of care work or what we could more specifically refer to as the global flow of care workers. This flow speaks of a different aspect of the globalization of service work than the outsourcing of service jobs, such as of call-center operators, addressed by George Ritzer in this volume. In this chapter, I do not address the movement of jobs but of workers. As Ritzer (this volume) acknowledges, certain service jobs cannot be off-shored as they depend on face-to-face interaction. Certainly the care of children and elderly are examples of such work.

In this chapter, I address what the global flow of domestic workers tells us about the status of women in the family as well as relations between women in globalization. As I establish, the globalization of service work generates unequal relationships between women across nation-states. This is because to unleash the burden of housework, women, as Evelyn Nakano Glenn (1992) points out, rely on the commodification of this work and purchase the low-wage services of poorer women. This bears significant consequences for relations between women. The advancement of one group of women is at the cost of another group of women. At the same time, as I wish to show in this chapter, the globalization of service work, i.e. the demand for migrant domestic workers, also speaks of women's oppressions in neoliberal states and the failure of states to meet the needs of women who choose to enter the labor force. Across nations, caring for the family remains a private and not a public responsibility, but more precisely a private responsibility designated to women (Conroy, 2000). Despite the increase in their labor market participation in both developing and advanced capitalist countries, women still remain primarily responsible for housework (Hochschild and Machung, 1989; Rai, 2002). Men have not taken up their share of housework, and likewise, states with neoliberal regimes have failed to respond to the welfare needs of the rising number of women in the labor force. Consequently, the gendered burden of housework plagues the possible advancements of women in the labor market and places them at a disadvantage vis-à-vis men.

In this chapter, I explain the social implications of the globalization of service work by first explaining the relations of inequality it engenders with a discussion of the international division of reproductive labor and the exportation of care. Then, I explain how neoliberal regimes contribute to the globalization of service work, and continue with an explanation of how the exclusion of foreign domestic workers locks the inequality of the international division of reproductive labor. I end by analyzing the implications of the inequalities engendered by the globalization of service work to transnational feminist relations between women.

The International Division of Care Work

The flow of migrant domestic workers from poor to rich nations generates troubling care inequities that speak of race and class hierarchies between women and nations. First, it gives rise to the inequality of the international division of reproductive labor, a three-tier transfer of care among women in sending and receiving countries of migration (Parreñas, 2001). Second, it leads to the exportation of care and the consequent unequal distribution of care resources in the global economy.

In the international division of reproductive labor, women with privilege in rich countries pass down the care of their families to migrant domestic workers as migrant domestic workers simultaneously pass down the care of their own families – most of whom are left behind in the country of origin – to their relatives or sometimes even poorer women who they hire as their own domestic workers. The case of Carmen Ronquillo, a domestic worker in Rome, provides us with a good illustration of the international division of carework. Carmen is simultaneously a domestic worker for a professional woman in Rome and an employer of a domestic worker in the Philippines. Carmen describes her relationship to each one of these women:

When coming here, I mentally surrendered myself and forced my pride away from me to prepare myself. But I lost a lot of weight. I was not used to the work. You see, I had maids in the Philippines. I have a maid in the Philippines that has worked for me since my daughter was born twenty-four years ago. She is still with me. I paid her three hundred pesos before, and now I pay her 1000 pesos. I am a little bit luckier than others because I run the entire household. My employer is a divorced woman who is an architect. She does not have time to run her household so I do all the shopping. I am the one budgeting. I am the one cooking. [Laughs.] And I am the one cleaning too. She has a twenty four and twenty six year old. The older one graduated already and is an electrical engineer. The other one is taking up philosophy. They still live with her . . . She has been my only employer. I stayed with her because I feel at home with her.

(Parreñas, 2001: 74–5)

It is quite striking to observe the formation of parallel relationships of loyalty between Carmen (the employer) and her domestic in the Philippines and Carmen (the domestic) and her employer in Italy. Also striking is the fact that Carmen's domestic worker does exactly the same work that Carmen does for her own employer. Yet, more striking is the wide discrepancy in wages between Carmen and her own domestic worker.

Their wage differences illuminate the economic disparity among nations in transnational capitalism. A domestic worker in Italy such as Carmen could receive U.S.\$1,000 a month for her labor. As Carmen describes,

I earn 1,500,000 (U.S.\$1000) and she pays for my benefits. On Sundays, I have a part-time. I clean her office in the morning and she pays me 300,000 lira (U.S.\$200). I am very fortunate because she always gives me my holiday pay in August and my thirteenth month pay in December. Plus, she gives me my liquidation pay at the end of the year.

(Parreñas, 2001: 75)

Carmen's wages easily enable her to hire a domestic worker in the Philippines, who on average only earns what is the equivalent of \$40 during the time of my interviews. Moreover, the domestic worker in the Philippines, in exchange for her labor, does not receive the additional work benefits that Carmen receives for the same labor.[2]

Under the international division of care work, there is a gradational decline in the worth of care. As sociologist Barbara Rothman poignantly describes, "When performed by mothers, we call this mothering . . .; when performed by hired hands, we call it unskilled" (Rothman, 1989: 43). Commodified care work is not only low-paid work but declines in market value as it gets passed down the hierarchical chain. As care is made into a commodity, women with greater resources in the global economy can afford the best-quality care for their families. Conversely, the care given to those with fewer resources is usually worth less.

Consequently, the quality of family life progressively declines as care is passed down the international division of care work. Freed of household constraints, those on top can earn more and consequently afford better-quality care than the domestic workers whom they hire. With their wages relatively low, these domestic workers cannot afford to provide the same kind of care for their family. They in turn leave them behind in the Philippines to be cared for by even lesser paid domestic workers. Relegated to the bottom of the three-tier hierarchy of care work, domestic workers left in the Third World have far fewer material resources to ensure the quality care of their own family.

Another inequality that emerges in the globalization of care work is the exportation of care from the sending countries of migrant domestic workers. For example, in the Philippines, care work is now the largest export and source of foreign currency for the country. In fact, the migrant flow of domestic workers indicates a contemporary colonial trade relationship with the global south, sending neither raw materials nor manufactured goods but rather a (female) labor supply of care workers to the global north. Remittances – mostly from migrant care workers – to the Philippines totaled almost $7 billion in 1999 and generated more foreign currency than manufactured exports including garments and electronics (Bureau of Employment and Labor Statistics, 1999). Most migrant workers from the Philippines, more than half of them, are women and the labor that they provide to the citizenry of other nations is mostly care work.

As a result of the systematic extraction of care from the Philippines, a great number of children are growing up without the physical presence of their (migrant) parents. Assuming that women with children can provide better quality care than other women, employers often prefer their migrant nannies to be mothers themselves. What this means is that migrant mothers who work as nannies often face the painful prospect of caring for other people's children while being unable to tend to their own. Rosemarie Samaniego, a transnational mother working in Rome, describes this predicament.

When the girl that I take care of calls her mother "Mama," my heart jumps all the time because my children also call me "Mama." I feel the gap caused by our physical separation especially in the morning, when I pack (her) lunch, because that's what I used to do for my children . . . I used to do that very same thing for them. I begin thinking that at this hour I should be taking care of my very own children and not someone else's, someone who is not related to me in any way, shape, or form . . . The work that I do here is done for my family, but the problem is they are not close to me but are far away in the Philippines. Sometimes, you feel the separation and you start to cry. Some days, I just start crying while I am sweeping the floor because I am thinking about my children in the Philippines. Sometimes, when I receive a letter from my children telling me that they are sick, I look up out the window and ask the Lord to look after them and make sure they get better even without me around to care after them. [Starts crying.] If I had wings, I would fly home to my children. Just for a moment, to see my children and take care of their needs, help them, then fly back over here to continue my work.

(Parreñas, 2001: 119)

For a large number of women, the experience of migration involves the pain of family separation. This emotional burden is one that directly results from the exportation of care and its consequent effect of transnational motherhood. In pointing out the pain of transnational mothering, I do not intend to naturalize mothering. Instead, I point to the fact that transnational mothering is not a preferred choice for many low wage migrant workers, but a result of the structural inequalities that limit the labor market choices of women from poor countries such as the Philippines to foreign domestic work. Because foreign domestic work is often not a preferred choice in the global labor market, distance mothering engenders feelings of pain and loss for many of those who pursue this type of work.

It is not just mothers but also children who lose out from this separation. Between 2000 and 2002, I spent 18 non-continuous months in the Philippines where I conducted 69 in depth interviews with children of migrant workers. Among these children, I found a great number have come to expect a lesser amount of care from their migrant mothers. This includes Ellen Seneriches,[3] a 21-year-old medical student in the Philippines and daughter of a domestic worker in New York. She states,

> There are times when you want to talk to her, but she is not there. That is really hard, very difficult . . . There are times when I want to call her, speak to her, cry to her, and I cannot. It is difficult. The only thing that I can do is write to her. And I cannot cry through the e-mails and sometimes I just want to cry on her shoulders.

Children such as Ellen, only 10 years old when her mother left for New York, often repress their longing to reunite with their mothers. Understanding the limited financial options available to families in the Philippines, they sacrifice by putting their emotional needs aside. This is often done with the knowledge that their mother diverts her care to other children in the global economy of care work. As Ellen describes,

> Very jealous. I am very, very jealous. There was even a time when she told the children who she was caring for that they are very lucky that she was taking care of them, while her children back in the Philippines don't even have a mom to take care of them. It's pathetic, but it's true. We were left alone by ourselves and we had to be responsible at a very young age without a mother. Can you imagine?

While their mothers give their care and attention to other children, children such as Ellen receive a lesser amount of care from their mothers, a sacrifice made more painful by their jealousy over these other children.

As shown by the story of Ellen, geographical distance in transnational family life engenders emotional strife among children. By asserting this claim, I do not mean to imply that migrant mothers do not attempt to ease the difficulties of children. Yet, despite these efforts of migrant mothers, children in transnational families still do suffer as they lose out in family intimacy. They can only wait for the opportunity to spend quality time with migrant parents. Yet, waiting tends to be a painful process. As Theresa Bascara, an 18 year old college student whose mother has worked in Hong Kong since 1984, describes:

> When my mother is home, I just sit next to her. I stare at her face, to see the changes in her face, to see how she aged during the years that she was away from us. But when she is about to go back to Hong Kong, it's like my heart is going to burst. I would just cry and cry. I really can't explain the feeling. Sometimes, when my mother is home, preparing to leave for Hong Kong, I would just start crying, because I already start missing her. I ask myself, how many more years will it be until we see each other again?

In general, children in transnational families do lose out. They are denied the intimacy of the daily routine of family life. Theresa continues,

> Telephone calls. That's not enough. You can't hug her, kiss her, feel her, everything. You can't feel her presence. It's just words that you have. What I want is to have my mother close to me, to see her grow older, and when she is sick, you are the one taking care of her and when you are sick, she is the one taking care of you.

Sacrificing the routine pleasures of receiving and giving emotional care is what a great number of children in the Philippines are doing to help keep their families intact. This sacrifice works to the benefit of those at the receiving end of the global transfer of care work – the employer, their family, and the local economies that utilize the freed employer's labor.

Regressive State Welfare Regimes

In various industrialized countries around the world, the number of gainfully employed women has climbed dramatically in the last 40 years. For instance, in France, an additional 2 million women entered the labor force between 1979 and 1993, a 21 percent increase in the number of employed women (Conroy, 2000). Mothers are also more likely to work. For instance, in the United States, three out of four mothers with school-age children are in the paid labor force, the majority working fulltime (Coltrane and Galt, 2000). This is also the case in Italy, where an increasing number of married women are in the labor force (Goddard, 1996). In Italy and Spain, women tend to keep their full-time jobs even when they have young children at home (Conroy, 2000).

For the most part, men have not responded to women's income contributions to the household with a marked increase in housework. This is the case in countries such as the United States (Hochschild and Machung, 1989) as well as in countries known to have gender egalitarian welfare policies such as those in Nordic countries (Orloff, 2006). For instance, women more so than men are likely to take advantage of parental leave options in countries such as Sweden. A multi-country study of the division of labor in European families shows that women still do the majority of parental childcare. In Denmark, Belgium, and Spain, for instance, women bear the responsibility for 65 to 87 percent of care work (Ghysels, 2004: 248). As such, they are more likely to hold part-time jobs than men, or less likely to seek high ranking positions than men. This is for instance the case in Nordic countries, which are considered to provide women with more progressive support to balance work and family responsi-

bilities than countries with neoliberal welfare regimes (Orloff, 2006).

Socialist welfare regimes differ from most other countries as they, unlike countries with neoliberal regimes, provide extensive access to publicly supported care. Support begins with highly subsidized parental leave periods in the first three years of a child's life and continues with the provision of centralized care services in centers or through supervised family child-minders. Moreover, children have the option of spending all or part of the day in preschool programs (Gornick and Meyers, 2003). Universal entitlement for care is provided in Finland and Denmark. In Sweden, children have access to publicly subsidized or public care until the age of 12.

Yet, state welfare support for the family in most other countries does not reflect the generous childcare provisions in Nordic countries. For the most part, the state has not adequately responded to the changes brought by the entrance of women, particularly mothers, to the labor force. Instead, in various countries in Europe, Asia, and the Americas, the state has imposed neoliberal policies in response to women's labor market participation. Welfare support in many countries does not provide the new familial needs of single-parents as well as dual-earning or dual-career couples (Heymann, 2000).[4] Examples of such support would include long postpartum family leaves, afterschool programs and extended school days for children in the year (Conroy, 2000; Heymann, 2000; Tronto, 2002). Without a "public family welfare system," government assistance keeps childcare a private and not public responsibility (Conroy, 2000). For instance, in the United States, government assistance for the childcare needs of dual income households remain restricted to an income tax credit. Notably, the private sector usually does not pick up the slack of the welfare system. In the United States, employers often penalize members of working families instead of providing working families with the flexibility to handle their caring needs. For instance, non-managerial employees often do not have the flexibility to take a sick relative to the doctor or to meet their child's teacher during work hours (Heymann, 2000).

In countries such as the United States, the inadequacy of state welfare support is one of the greatest burdens of women in the labor force. Moreover, it instigates care inequalities between women and nations. Privatization engenders the commodification of care and the search for affordable care workers. Many of these care workers are from poorer countries in the global south. This is the case in the United States, which notably has the least welfare provisions among rich nations in the global economy as families are without access to universal health care, paid maternity and parental leave, government-provided childcare, or family care giving allowances (Cancian and Oliker, 2000: 116). Although generally boasting a more social democratic welfare regime than that in the United States, European nations are not immune to the growing trend of privatization. Domestic workers are present in European countries such as: the United Kingdom, where markets have assumed a greater role in welfare regimes; the Netherlands, where single mothers are forced to seek paid employment and are without choice but to remunerate lower paid workers for the care of their children; the Mediterranean region, e.g. Greece, Italy, and Spain, where dual wage earning families do not have market options for care; and France, where the universal care for children by the state is not mirrored in elderly care provisions (Daly and Lewis, 2000: 292). Generally, domestic workers can be found in regions where care is kept a private family matter, which includes most developed nations in the world today.

Countries with high welfare provisions are not exempt from this group, as we more and more see them implement a less universal, more privatized form of welfare with the reduction in publicly controlled care services for families and the increase in the use of cash subsidies as well as paid care leave for mothers (Morgan and Zippel, 2003). Addressing how the state assists time pressed dual earner couples in their efforts to negotiate child care, Rianne Mahon (2002) notes that state welfare assistance largely maintains the privatization of care and fails to secure a gender egalitarian system for employed women. For instance, the new familialism approach found in nations such as France features a decrease in publicly funded collective child care provisions and an increase in cash benefits. A system that truly secures public responsibility for care, one that provides generous parental leaves and universal non-parental childcare services, is adopted in very few countries (e.g. Denmark).

In addition to the absence of public accountability for care, gender inequities in the family also fuel the need for domestic workers. As I noted earlier, the division of labor in most families still does not mirror the increase in women's labor market participation. For instance, a recent survey of dual wage earning families with children in Canada found that women were still responsible for all of the daily housework in 52 percent of households (Rai, 2002: 101). The increase in women's labor market participation usually translates to the dwindling supply of family care providers (Hochschild and Machung, 1989) and consequently goes hand in hand with the commodification of care work. We see this in France, where the comprehensive publicly funded preschool system stabilizes the family life of dual wage earning couples, but still where women suffer from the burden of daily housework as well as elderly care falling mainly on their shoulders, as the latter responsibility is not supported with residential care provisions (Koffman *et al.*, 2000: 143). This burden has created an economic niche for privately hired care workers (Mozère, 2003). In contrast, socially democratic Scandinavian nations depend less on domestic workers as they provide the most gender-sensitive public benefits for families including gender-neutral parental leave and universal entitlements in the form of allowances, subsidies, and direct services for the elderly and single parent households (Cancian and Oliker, 2000: 18).

Ruth Milkman and her colleagues note that economic inequities direct the flow of domestic workers: they found that urban centers with the greatest economic inequities in the United States have a higher rate of domestic service employment (Milkman *et al.*, 1998). I would add to their observation that social patterns of welfare provisions also influence the direction of the migratory flows of foreign domestic workers. Looking at the migration patterns of migrant Filipina domestic workers, the more countries keep the care of the family a private responsibility, the greater the reliance on the low wage work of migrant care workers. This seems to be the case in the Americas and Europe, where the presence of migrant Filipina domestic workers is more strongly felt in countries with the most inadequate welfare provisions. Nations with very low welfare provisions, i.e. nations that keep the care of the family a private responsibility, particularly the United States and southern European nations such as Spain, Greece, and Italy have a greater presence of foreign domestic workers (Koffman *et al.*, 2000). We also see their presence in countries where comprehensive publicly funded welfare programs are threatened by being replaced with the use of cash subsidy benefits such as France (Misra *et al.*, 2004). In contrast, countries with social democratic regimes such as those in Scandinavia, where the benefit system abides by universalism and provides large-scale institutional support for mothers and families, are less likely to rely on foreign domestic workers.

Thus, it seems that the less public accountability there is for the family the greater the need for the labor of foreign domestic workers. This suggests that a movement against neoliberal state regimes would lead to greater recognition of the high worth of care and the lesser burden of the double day on women in the labor force. It would also mean a lesser need to devalue into low-paid labor the caring work required in the family. The implementation of a public family welfare system, as feminist scholars have argued, would not only benefit double burdened women in the labor force and give greater value to the work of privately hired care workers but would translate to the good of society as a whole (Folbre, 2001; Tronto, 2002). As economist Nancy Folbre

argues, public responsibility for parental support would optimize the care of children and consequently increase the likelihood of their healthy and productive labor force participation in the future (2001: 111). This translates to the greater ability of children to physically care for us in the future and pay the taxes needed to cover the social security benefits we are working for today (Folbre, 2001: 110). As had been recognized with the implementation of universal public education in the nineteenth century, the optimal care of children translates to the welfare of society as a whole. It cuts to the core of democracy, helping provide equal opportunities for children to succeed so they may contribute the most to the economy.

The inadequacy of welfare support for dual income families goes against the principles of democracy and universal educational opportunities for our children. As Joan Tronto (2002) further argues, individual accountability for children increases competition between mothers and families and concomitantly decreases the ethic of care. Hiring private domestic workers, tutors, and other care workers creates incredible disparities between families. Those with private care workers can ensure that their children are those best equipped and developed to be competitive members of society. In contrast, other children are less likely to succeed as they are left with less guidance and adult supervision. As Tronto states, "individualized accounts of mothering make us inured to the social structures that contribute to the growing gaps among advantaged and less advantaged children" (2002: 48). Thus, the privatization of care reinforces inequalities of race, class, and citizenship among women – employers and employees – as it furthers the disparities in the prospects available to children in industrialized countries.

With the individual responsibility for care imposed upon them, and denied the utmost benefits of a truly democratic regime, women in industrialized countries have come to take advantage of the greater economic resources that they have than women from developing countries: they do this by unloading the care giving responsibilities of their families to these other women. Those who receive less gender-sensitive welfare provisions from the state do so much more than others. And those who are able to negotiate with their male counterparts in the family for a fairer gendered division of labor are equally less likely to do so. Finally, as I show in the next section, those whose governments deny the human rights of migrant workers are also more able to depend on the low wage work of other women.

The Human Rights of Migrant Domestic Workers

The denial of the human rights of migrant domestic workers eases the process of the care chain. By denying migrants their human rights, states avoid the cost and responsibility for care. States do so by securing a pool of privately hired and affordable care workers for working families, an act which also allows states to avoid the need to expand welfare provisions. Despite their economic contributions, migrant domestic workers suffer from their limited incorporation as partial citizens of various receiving nations (Parreñas, 2001). As I have defined elsewhere, this means they face restrictive measures that stunt their political, civil, and social incorporation into host societies (Parreñas, 2001). From an economic standpoint, this is not surprising. Receiving nations restrict the social incorporation of migrants so as to guarantee their economies a secure source of cheap labor. By containing the costs of reproduction in sending countries, wages of migrant workers can be kept to a minimum. This is because migrants do not have the burden of having to afford the greater costs of reproducing their families in host societies. Moreover, by restricting the incorporation of migrants, receiving nations can secure for their economies a ready supply of low-wage workers who could easily be repatriated whenever the economy is low. For instance, countries often recognize that many immigrants illegally fill the demand for various low wage jobs, but they still do not give work visas for some of these jobs (Misra *et al.*, 2004).

This is the case with care work in France and Germany. In France, the increase in individualized private care among upper middle class families and the reliance on migrant women for such private care is not mirrored in immigration policies. Migrant care workers in France do not qualify for temporary work permits and consequently are subject to the insecurities of the informal economy (Misra *et al.*, 2004). In contrast, Germany grants work permits to domestic workers but only to elderly caregivers and not to housecleaners and childcare workers. This restriction keeps a large number of care workers in Germany ineligible for legal residence status.

Other countries of Europe grant legal residence to domestic workers. However, as migrants, they are usually relegated to the status of guest workers limited to the duration of their labor contracts. Often, they cannot sponsor the migration of their families. This is also the case in Middle Eastern and Asian receiving nations, which are much more stringent than other countries. For example, in Taiwan, state policies deny entry to the spouses and children of the migrant worker (Lan, 2006). Singapore even prohibits the marriage or cohabitation of migrant workers with native citizens (Bakan and Stasiulis, 1997). The restriction of family migration comes in different gradations of exclusion. For instance, with European countries more accommodating of their legal migrants than Asian countries, temporary residents in Italy have been eligible for family reunification since 1990 (Koffman *et al.*, 2000).

However, family reunification remains a challenge for many immigrants in Europe. Despite the more inclusive policies for migrants in Europe than in Asia, many European nation-states still restrict migrants to the status of "guest workers." With heightened anti-immigrant sentiments in European nations such as Italy, the basis of citizenship is unlikely to become more inclusive of ethnically distinct migrant groups. As a result, most migrant Filipina workers would still prefer that their children do not join them in Europe, i.e. despite the struggles of transnational family life (Parreñas, 2001). Other migration policies further discourage complete family migration. In France, for instance, migrants are put off by the increase in residence requirements to qualify for family reunion as well as the decrease in the age of eligibility for dependants from 21 to 18 years old (Koffman *et al.*, 2000: 68). Moreover, in Germany, children under 16 years old must obtain a visa to visit their legally resident parents. In the United Kingdom, entry conditions for family visits have become stricter with the rising suspicion of the intent of family members to remain indefinitely (Koffman *et al.*, 2000). In the Netherlands, the state sponsored au pair program, which disguises the flow of migrant domestic workers from the global south, restricts the household helper to a temporary duration of stay that does not allow for family migration (Meerman, 2000).

Eligibility for full citizenship is available in a few receiving nations including Spain, Canada, and the United States. In Spain and Canada, migrant Filipinas are eligible for full citizenship after two years of legal settlement. Despite the seemingly more liberal and inclusive policies in these nations, political and social inequalities still stunt the full incorporation of migrant workers (Bakan and Stasiulis, 1997). In Canada, the Live-in Caregivers Program requires an initial two years of live-in service before foreign domestics can become eligible for landed immigrant status. During this time, foreign domestics are prone to abusive working conditions, subject to split-household arrangements, and restricted to temporary status (Bakan and Stasiulis, 1997). Foreign domestic workers in the United States experience a similar vulnerability. In the United States, obtaining a green card through employer sponsorship, according to Shellee Colen, is like a "form of state-sanctioned indenture-like exploitation" because "the worker is obligated to stay in the sponsored position until the green card is granted (usually two or more years)" (Colen, 1995: 78).

Providing care work often requires migrants to leave their children in the Philippines because the structure and standards of employment in this type of labor[5] and the imposition of partial citizenship usually prevent the migration of kin (Parreñas, 2001). This works to the benefit of employers. The partial citizenship of migrant workers guarantees employers an affordable pool of care workers who can give them the best care for their families, since migrant care workers are freed of care responsibilities in their own families. Yet, the experience of partial citizenship for migrant domestic workers points to an injustice in globalization, one that poses a direct challenge to transnational feminist alliances. Migrant domestic workers care for rich families in the global north as they are imposed with social, economic, and legal restrictions that deny them the right to nurture their own families. The elimination of these restrictive measures would at the very least grant foreign domestic workers the basic human right of caring for their own family.

Conclusion

The global labor migration of domestic workers attests to the globalization of care work. This global flow speaks of a direct relationship of inequality between women, particularly the unequal relationship between migrant domestic workers and their employers. It also speaks to the different positions of women regarding family care work. In both poor and rich nations, class privileged women are increasingly viewing care work as a burden to be passed on to poorer women. Those to whom they pass it on often view care work as a human right denied to them either by restrictive migration policies that prevent the migration of their kin or by heavy work responsibilities that deny them the time and energy to devote to their own families. However, the division of care labor between women does not completely work to the advantage of the employing women. Though freed of the care work for the family, they are still plagued by the structural gender inequities that relieve men and the state of responsibility for care. The international division of care work arises not just from relations of inequality between women but also from neoliberal state regimes. Migrant Filipina domestic workers rarely enter Nordic countries with socialist welfare regimes but in various degrees of concentration work in countries that keep the care of the family a private and not a public responsibility. Without adequate state welfare provisions, dual wage earning families in countries with neoliberal state regimes turn to foreign domestic workers. This tells us that the failure of the state to adequately meet the care needs of working families partially accounts for the rise in the use of foreign domestic work. Without doubt, some families may prefer to provide private exclusive care for their children and elderly rather than centralized public facilities. Yet, many families turn to the low-wage labor costs provided by foreign domestic workers and not necessarily the skilled work of highly trained care workers such as British nannies and registered nurses. They turn to low-cost foreign domestic work due to their lack of choices for balancing work and family. Yet, many foreign domestic workers, at least from the Philippines, are skilled care workers. For instance, many Filipina domestic workers, if not college educated, secure government accredited caregiver certificates with six months of training prior to migration. The training of these workers comes at no cost and to the benefit of the destination countries. This training enables destination countries to continue to ignore providing care provisions for working families. Perhaps then countries that depend on foreign domestic workers should acknowledge the contributions of their labor and bear some of the costs of these workers. Doing so would mean that receiving states would make these workers eligible for permanent residence, grant them a minimum wage rate comparable to native workers, and ensure the protection of their labor by allowing them to report labor violations without penalty or the threat of deportation for illegal workers.

It is likely that the international division of care work would not completely disappear with state acknowledgment of the labor contributions of foreign domestic workers. A marked increase in care work by men, which will only mean a reduction in their working hours, and a notable limit to the working hours of women, would lessen the reliance of families in non-commodified care work. Moreover, only the greater valuation of care work would abolish the inequalities that currently define the international division of care work. State acknowledgment of the high value and contributions of foreign domestic workers would likely mean that the labor conditions of domestic workers would improve and domestic workers would have the option of raising their children up close and not from a distance. If this occurs, the international division of care work and the commodification of care would at the very least not signify severe relations of inequalities between domestic workers and the families that employ them.

References

Anderson, B. (2000) *Doing the Dirty Work? The Global Politics of Domestic Labour,* London and New York: Zed Books.

Bakan, A. and Stasiulis, D. (1997) "Introduction," in A. Bakan and D. Stasiulis (eds.), Not *One of the Family: Foreign Domestic Workers in Canada,* Toronto: University of Toronto Press.

Bureau of Employment and Labor Statistics. "Remittances from overseas Filipino workers by country of origin Philippines: 1997-fourth quarter 1999," *Pinoy Migrants, Shared Government Information System for Migration*. Retrieved 4 April 2004, from http://emisd.web.dfa.gov.ph/~pinoymigrants/.

Cancian, F.M. and Oliker, S.J. (2000) *Caring and Gender,* Thousand Oaks, CA: Pine Forge Press.

Chang, G. (2000) *Disposable Domestics,* Boston: South End Press.

Chin, C. (1998) *Of Service and Servitude,* New York: Columbia University Press.

Colen, S. (1995) "Like a mother to them: stratified reproduction and West Indian childcare workers and employers in New York" in F. Ginsburg, and R. Rapp (eds.), *Conceiving the New*

World Order: The Global Politics of Reproduction, Berkeley, CA: University of California Press.

Coltrane, S. and Galt, J. (2000) "The history of men's caring," in M. Harrington Meyer (ed.), *Care Work: Gender, Labour and the Welfare State*, New York and London: Routledge.

Conroy, M. (2000) *Sustaining the New Economy: Work, Family, and Community in the Information Age*, New York: Russell Sage Foundation Press and Cambridge, MA: Harvard University Press.

Constable, N. (1997) *Maid to Order in Hong Kong*, Ithaca, NY: Cornell University Press.

Constable, N. (2003) *Romance on a Global State*, Berkeley, CA: University of California Press.

Crittenden, A. (2001) *The Price of Motherhood: Why the Most Important Job in the World is Still the Least Valued*, New York: Metropolitan Books.

Daly, M. and Lewis, J. (2000) "The concept of social care and the analysis of contemporary welfare states," *British Journal of Sociology*, 51, 2, 281–98.

Donato, K. (1992) "Understanding U.S. immigration: why some countries send women and others send men," in D. Gabbacia (ed.), *Seeking Common Ground: Multidisciplinary Studies of Immigrant Women in the United States*, Westport, CT: Greenwood Press, 159–84.

Folbre, N. (2001) *The Invisible Heart: Economics and Family Values*, New York: The New Press.

Gamburd, M. (2000) *The Kitchen Spoon's Handle*, Ithaca, NY: Cornell.

Ghysels, J. (2004) *Work, Family, and Childcare: An Empirical Analysis of European Households*, Cheltenham, UK and Northampton, MA: Edward Elgar.

Glenn, E.N. (1992) "From servitude to service work: historical continuities in the racial division of paid reproductive labor," *Signs: Journal of Women in Culture and Society*, 18, 1, 1–43.

Goddard, VA. (1996) *Gender, Family and Work in Naples*, Oxford and Washington, DC: Berg.

Gornick, J. and Meyers, M. (2003) *Families That Work: Policies for Reconciling Parenthood and Employment*, New York: Russell Sage Foundation.

Heymann, J. (2000) *The Widening Gap: Why America's Working Families are in Jeopardy – and What Can Be Done About It*, New York: Basic Books.

Hochschild, A. (2000) "The nanny chain," *American Prospect*, 11, 4. Retrieved 4 April 2004, from http://www.prospect.org/print/VI1/4/hochschild-a.html.

Hochschild, A.R. and Machung, A. (1989) *The Second Shift*, New York: Avon Books.

Hondagneu-Sotelo, P. (1994) *Gendered Transitions*, Berkeley, CA: University of California Press.

Hondagneu-Sotelo, P. (2001) *Doméstica*, Berkeley, CA: University of California Press.

Koffman, E., Phizacklea, A., Raghuram, P. and Sales, R. (2000) *Gender and International Migration in Europe: Employment, Welfare and Politics*, New York and London: Routledge.

Lan, P. (2006) *Global Cinderellas*, Durham, NC: Duke University Press.

Mahon, R. (2002) "Child care: toward what kind of 'social Europe?'" *Social Politics*, 9, 343–79.

Meerman, M. (2000) *The Chain of Love*, Amsterdam, Netherlands: VPRO-TV (U.S. Distributor: First Icarus Run).

Milkman, R., Reese, E. and Roth, B. (1998) "The macrosociology of paid domestic labor," *Work and Occupations*, 25, 4, 483–507.

Misra, J., Merz, S. and Woodring, J. (2004) "The globalization of carework: Immigration, economic restructuring, and the world-system," American Sociological Association Meeting, American Sociological Association, San Francisco, CA. 17 August.

Morgan, K. and Zippel, K. (2003) "Paid to care: the origins and effects of care leave policies in Western Europe," *Social Politics*, 10, 49–85.

Mozère, L. (2003) "Filipina women as domestic workers in Paris: a national or transnational labour-market?" (unpublished paper), Department of Sociology, University of Metz, France.

Oishi, N. (2005) *Women in Motion*, Stanford, CA: Stanford University Press.

Orloff, A.S. (2006) "Farewell to maternalism? State policies and mothers' employment," WP-05–10, Institute for Policy Research Northwestern University, *Working Paper Series*.

Parreñas, R.S. (2000) "Migrant Filipina domestic workers and the international division of reproductive labor," *Gender and Society*, 14:4 (August), 560–80.

Parreñas, R.S. (2001) *Servants of Globalization: Women, Migration, and Domestic Work*, Stanford, CA: Stanford University Press.

Rai, S.M. (2002) *Gender and the Political Economy of Development*, Cambridge: Polity Press.

Ribas-Mateos, N. (2000) "Female birds of passage: leaving and settling in Spain," in A. Floya and G. Lazaridis (eds.), *Gender and Migration in Southern Europe: Women on the Move*, Oxford and New York: Berg, 173–98.

Rothman, B.K. (1989). *Recreating Motherhood: Ideology and Technology in a Patriarchal Society*, New York and London: W.W. Norton.

Silvey, R. (2004) "Transnational migration and the gender politics of scale: Indonesian domestic workers in Saudi Arabia," *Singapore Tropical Geography*, 25(2), 141–55.

Thai, H. (2003) "Clashing dreams: highly educated overseas brides and low-wage U.S. husbands," in B. Ehrenreich and A. Hochschild (eds.), *Global Woman: Nannies, Maids, and Sex Workers in the New Economy*, New York: Metropolis Books, 230–53.

Tronto, J. (2002) "The 'Nanny' question in feminism," *Hypatia*, 17, 2, 34–51.

United Nations Population Division. (2002) International Migration, *United Nations Publication*, Sales Number E.03.XIII.3. October. http://www.un.org/esa/population/publications/ittmig2002/WEB_migration_wallchart.xls Accessed 6 September 2005.

Yuh, J. (2002) *Beyond the Shadow of Camptown: Korean Military Brides in America*, New York: New York University Press.

Notes

1 By reproductive labor, I refer to the labor needed to sustain the productive labor force. Reproductive labor primarily refers to caring work required to sustain the (able-bodied) population. Such work includes the task of feeding and nurturing.

2 Migrant domestic workers usually belong in a higher-class stratum than do domestics left in the Philippines. Often professionals in the Philippines, they use their resources to afford the option of seeking the higher wages offered in more developed nations.

3 Ellen Seneriches and the names of the other children who I quote in this chapter are all pseudonyms.

4 By welfare support, I refer to the government's accountability for the social and material well-being of their citizenry.

5 Labor conditions in domestic work usually discourage family reunification. This is especially true of live-in domestic workers who are isolated in private homes. Moreover, contracts of "guest workers" usually bind them to stay with their sponsoring employer, which leaves them vulnerable to less than par labor standards.

Awful Acts and the Trouble with Normal

Erica R. Meiners

In my Canadian hometown, where the store in my dad's neighborhood, Iron Mountain, still sells WD-40 next to the tampons, Clifford Olson "snatched up girls like you," my principal Mr. Gayle told my best friend Carla and me. "He will capture you and then . . ."

Olson permeated the spring and summer of 1981. School assemblies lectured us on how to recognize the Car of the Stranger. The ice rink, parks, and other public spaces were closed, and the yellow-striped Royal Canadian Mountain Police were everywhere.

One afternoon that summer, Carla and I were illicitly at Mount Crescent Elementary School on the tire swing, and she told me that her uncle—she did not use the words molested or rape or even sex. In fact, I don't even remember what she said. I just remember that day, the dizzy circles on the tire swing, and awkwardly now, that I thought she was bragging.

Caught in "the biggest manhunt in the country," Olson was picked up in late summer 1981, and I later watched Carla's uncle buy her a shot for her birthday.

Hunts for sex offenders and serial killers are a soundtrack to my life.

Registries

Prior to the US Supreme Court's 2003 six-to-three decision in *Lawrence and Garner v. State of Texas*, ruling anti-sodomy laws unconstitutional, sodomy, or simply the intent, was a crime in many states. While penalties varied, a conviction on a sodomy-re-lated charge carried an average maximum prison term of ten years. For example, legal scholar Robert Jacobsen[1] documents that over a three-year period in Los Angeles in the early 1960s, 493 men were arrested for consensual sodomy, with 257 convicted, and 104 imprisoned.[2] While forms of harassment, surveillance, and corresponding data collection by police and other state agencies were not made available to the public, keeping records of "sex offenders"—a malleable category that included "known homosexuals"—flourished throughout urban centers in the United States during the 1940s. Research by historians William Eskridge[3] and Margot Canaday[4] also documents that police collected and centralized information on other charges levied against men perceived to be engaging in non-gender-normative or same-sex sexual practices and activities, including "lewd conduct," "lewd vagrancy," and "outraging public decency," and targeted "fairies, inverts, and cross dressers."

In 1947, as historian William Eskridge documents in *Dishonorable Passions*, the California legislature "unanimously passed a law to require convicted sex offenders to register with the police in their home jurisdictions," and Chief Justice Warren (the author of the Brown desegregation decisions) requested that this law be extended to include those convicted of "lewd vagrancy" to force more homosexuals to register.[5] In 1950, the FBI was collecting from the states information, including fingerprints, for those charged with sodomy, oral copulation, lewd vagrancy (and serious crimes against minors) to create a "national bank of sex offenders and known homosexuals."[6] The category of sex offender was never applied uniformly. For example, "in the 1930s, when only 6 percent of its adult male population was non-white, 20 percent of New York City's sex offenders were black."[7]

As cumbersome, private documents internal to police forces, these practices diminished as the century progressed. Police harassment was less necessary if formal civil penalties, employment, and housing all regulated gender and sexual practices, and by 1953, Eisenhower had barred all gays and lesbians from holding federal employment.[8] Canaday writes that this state regulation was gendered (and racialized), as tracking female bodies (except for those perceived to be engaged in sex work) held less interest for the state: "Male perverts mattered so much more to the state because male citizens did" and apartheid already regulated non-white bodies through prohibitions on citizenship, mobility, employment, and education.[9]

Yet state regulation and harassment by punitive agencies fostered resistances. In tandem with civil rights and gay and lesbian liberation movements, as the homosexual began a tentative move away from "sex offender." By the 1980s, the category of sexual offender and the corresponding structures of surveillance and documentation identified a new target in child predators. Judith Levine[10] and Phillip Jenkins[11] suggest that the phenomenal expansion of sex offender registries (SOR) in the United States to track those convicted of child-related sex offenses was due to multiple factors: the explosion and fetishization of "stranger danger" and child abductions in mass media, escalating and racialized fears of public urban spaces, and the growing anxieties of adults about that achingly empty signifier, "the child."

In the mid-'90s, weighed down with the precious ennui afforded only by universities and cheap marijuana, I lived, worked, and hung out in bars near the "low track" on the downtown East Side of Vancouver.

Like the spring snow melt, female sex workers disappeared.

These women never made the evening news or the front page of the paper, but their photos, usually from high school, were stapled to telephone poles around the downtown East Side.

Sixty-three had disappeared by 2004. Many were indigenous, not from the city, and poor.

Tanya Holyk, 23, last seen October 1996
Olivia Williams, 22, last seen December 1996
Stephanie Lane, 20, last seen March 1997

Despite candle vigils and marches, the police's tepid non-response throughout the 1990s indicated that these were disposable women who did not merit the full protection, let alone the basic interest, of police. If these women got hurt, they were partially culpable. They were not innocent, and they were probably never children. And how do you know they were missing? These kinds of girls just run away.

Safe Spaces

In Illinois, the 1986 Habitual Child Sex Offender Registration Law established the first public registry for those convicted of child sexual offenses. In the subsequent twenty years, registration requirements have been expanded to include a broader range of offenses, including essentially all sex offenses and other crimes against children. Over the years, SORs also increased the information available to the public (the Illinois State Public Sex offender Web site was up by 1999) and amplified the restrictions attached to registration. In 1996, in direct response to the abduction and murder of twelve-year-old Polly Klaas in 1992 and seven-year-old Megan Kanka in 1994 by two men with prior convictions for violent sexual crimes, the federal government passed Megan's Law, establishing a public national sex-offender registry.

SORs require those convicted of a range of offenses, from public indecency and lewdness to aggravated child sexual assault, to register every ninety days for at least ten years. SORs also restrict employment, housing, and mobility, particularly in public spaces where children congregate. The restrictions are specific and local and vary across states and even between cities. As of

2010, registered sex offenders in Illinois were prohibited from living within "500 feet of a school, playground, or any facility providing programs or services exclusively directed toward people under age 18." In Iowa, convicted sex offenders cannot reside within 2,000 feet of schools or places where children congregate, thus effectively prohibiting anyone on the SOR from living in an urban center. SOR restrictions, like most laws, tend to be selectively enforced. For example, a project that I am affiliated with in Chicago has provided temporary housing for a few registered sex offenders for a number of years. The school nearby is more than 500 feet away when measured by the street but under 500 feet when measured "as the crow flies." As the neighborhood gentrifies (and whitens up), the shelter's proximity to a school has been explicitly questioned, though I suspect that none of the new homeowners would ever enroll their children in this school.

Through these mobility and public-space restrictions, SORs construct meanings about what kinds of public space are dangerous for children, where children are most at risk or vulnerable, and by default, what kinds of spaces are safe or risk-free. With the Bureau of Justice documenting that 70 percent of all reported sexual assaults against children are committed in a residence, usually the victim's, this emphasis on "public spaces," namely parks and schools, is clearly misplaced.

SORs and the construction of sex offenses are flexibly deployed in other ways. Journalist Jordan Flaherty highlighted that in 2010, sex workers in New Orleans, Louisiana (often transwomen and/or women of color) were charged under a state-wide law that makes it a crime against nature to engage in "unnatural copulation" (committing "crimes against nature" or acts of oral or anal sex[12]). Conviction requires registration as a SO and to have "sex offender" stamped on their driver's license. The deployment of these laws in New Orleans has little to do with public safety; rather these laws are used to harass sex workers and to "protect" the interests of local businesses and homeowners.

While strangers do hurt children, SORs create a culture in which the perceptions of violence and harm to children and youth occur outside of the child's life. The Bureau of Justice clearly identifies that "acquaintances," and then family members, are the highest risk category for sexually assaulting children, and for children under 18, strangers are consistently the *least likely*—generally significantly less than 10 percent—to be perpetrators of sexual violence.[13] Given that these are reported incidents to law enforcement, and that the sanctions for children (or anyone economically or otherwise dependent) against identifying family or friends as the perpetrators of violence are high, these numbers are conservative.

The real fear for women and children are not strangers, but the men they know.

In 1999, I moved to Chicago, still a full three years before Robert Pickton would be charged with the murders of twenty-seven women, almost all sex workers, from the downtown East Side.

I hauled myself to the neighborhood "block club meeting" (where the debates are usually about who has the most garbage on their lawn), because my landlord is renovating my apartment and I mistakenly think that this group can be effective.

The people in the room, mainly women, mostly mothers, murmured indignantly as a homemade flyer with the title "Child Molester" is distributed in the cool church basement. The discussion, righteous, is about what to do.
Picket his building? Get him to move out!
Leaflet and poster the entire neighborhood?
Absolutely warn the school.

As I looked around the room, I wanted to ask, Which one of you lives in the apartment where I hear a woman scream almost every night? Are you the one I saw being dragged from your car by your hair, in broad daylight, and we knocked on your door and were told it was "nothing?"

What does it mean that we are so willing to notice certain kinds of violence, to picket and organize, but the other, equally devastating and even more intimate harm, is so carefully protected?

Beyond the Good, the Bad, and the Innocent

While problematizing SORs, I do not minimize the persistent, pervasive violence against women, girls, queers, and trans-folk—those viewed as three-fifths human, those without correct documentation, and others on the margins. Rather, the state has always valued the lives and "innocence" of specific children and women more highly, and this is reflected at every level of our systems, from child welfare policies to drug laws, in word and in application.

From reproductive rights for white women that were dependent upon the sterilization of women of color and the premise of their sexual unfitness and immorality, to miscegenation laws that protected the constructed category of whiteness through the criminalization of "inter-racial" marriage and sexual acts, to the lynching of black men to preserve the safety and the racial purity of white women, the sexual innocence of select white women is enshrined in policies and written into the very conception of the nation-state itself as many, from Ida B. Wells[14] to Andie Smith,[15] continue to document. The United States has typically passed laws that protect *their interests* in women's bodies and sexualities; interests explicitly shaped by white supremacy, investments in hetero-gender-normativity, class, and ability.

Just as drug-free zones around schools do not reduce youth drug usage but instead criminalize entire communities as the Justice Policy Institute has identified[16]; and as zero tolerance policies in schools, "tough on crime" laws, and the "war on terror" don't make us any safer, expanding SORs does not reduce persistent, often state-sanctioned violence against women, girls, and others. These laws and policies disproportionately impact poor people and others already under surveillance and targeted by the state.

In a nation without an adequate or affordable childcare system, no universal healthcare, expensive to prohibitive costs for higher education, and a minimum wage that is not a living wage, there are no *registries* for the officials and employers who routinely implement policies that actively damage all people, including or *even particularly* children.

SORs are expanding. Civil commitment laws, passed in a dozen states by 2006 and upheld by the Supreme Court in a 2005 decision, aim to geographically detain and segregate certain categories of sex offenders, *indefinitely*, after release.[17] Escalating housing and employment prohibitions make life difficult for those convicted of sex offenses and, most centrally, do nothing to make our communities safer or better. And, in a nation of compulsory heteronormativity and cissexism, what is *normal* sexual and gender development?

The relative silence from anti-prison activists, feminists, and queers regarding carceral expansion is troubling. Historically, assimilation, or the "price of the ticket" to borrow from James Baldwin,[18] is often promised at the cost of participating in the demonization of those of lesser value. Yet colluding with this framework does nothing to make our lives safer. We need people to ask questions and to dialogue. What are the factors that support and naturalize the expansion of the SOR? Which children (and adults) benefit from the construction of the child as vulnerable and in need of protection and surveillance? How do SORs protect those with the most power and privileges? How do we, especially those most impacted and harmed, humanize the lives of those convicted, or not, of sexual offenses? How might public dialogues about these questions shift ideas about *health* and *safety* in homes and communities, and even perhaps, shift conceptions about *childhood, sexuality, family and gender?*

This analysis is not new. Organizations and individuals are working to make changes, including generation FIVE, that is dedicated to ending violence against children in five generations without state intervention and Critical Resistance that works towards ending the nation's prison industrial complex and for prison abolition. These organizations, and many other small, local, and unfunded collaboratives, work in communities to create alternatives without stigmatizing populations and without using and legitimating punitive systems. This is much easier to write about than to practice.

Martin, the part-time building maintenance worker, can't find any-where to live. Landlords won't take him, he doesn't have enough money, or there is a nearby school or park. Stammering with anxiety, he blurts his crisis, continuously, to those nearby.

Martin is no friend of mine. I rarely make eye contact aside from a breezy and too loud "hello." I justify my exclusion with the ration-ale that I have known too many women in my life that have sur-vived violence from men. When he has his housing crisis I think that someone else will assist him, and of course, in our posse of deviants (queers, nuns, on-again-off-again sex workers) someone else listens. Undereducated, poor, and with a personal history of violence, I know that my exclusion of Martin is illogical, and possibly harmful, yet of all the things to unlearn in my life, somehow this is not a priority.

Notes

In honor of a life of fierceness and brilliance—Carla Salvail 1969–2005
An earlier version of this piece was originally published in AREA Chicago (2007).

1 Robert Jacobson, "'Megan's Laws': Reinforcing Old Patterns of Anti-Gay Police Harassment," *Georgetown Law Journal*, Vol. 87, No. 7, 1999: p. 2431–2473.

2 Ibid., p. 2433.

3 William Eskridge, *Dishonorable Passions: Sodomy Laws in America, 1861–2003* (New York: Viking, 2003).

4 Margot Canaday, *The Straight State: Sexuality and Citizenship in Twentieth Century America* (Princeton, N.J.: Princeton University Press, 2009).

5 Eskridge, p. 82.

6 Ibid.

7 Ibid., p. 81.

8 John D'Emilio and Estelle Freedman, *Intimate Matters: A History of Sexuality in America* (Chicago: University of Chicago Press, 1998): p. 293.

9 Canaday, p. 13.

10 Judith Levine, *Harmful to Minors: The Perils of Protecting Children from Sex* (Minneapolis: University of Minnesota Press, 2002).

11 Phillip Jenkins, *Moral Panic: Changing Conceptions of the Child Molester* (New Haven: Yale University Press, 1998).

12 Jordan Flaherty, "Her Crime? Sex Work in New Orleans," *Colorlines*, Jan. 13, 2010. http://www.colorlines.com/archives/2010/01.

13 Howard N. Snyder, "Sexual Assault of Young Children as Reported to Law Enforcement: Victim, Incident, and Offender Characteristics." *Bureau of Justice Statistics*, July 2000.

14 Ida B. Wells-Barnett, *On Lynchings* (Amherst, N.Y.: Humanity Books, 2002).

15 Andrea Smith, *Conquest: Sexual Violence and American Indian Genocide* (Boston: South End Press, 2005).

16 Greene, K. Pranis, and J. Ziedenberg, *Disparity by Design: How Drug-Free Zone Laws Impact Racial Disparity—and Fail to Protect Youth* (Washington, D.C.: Justice Policy Institute, 2006).

17 A. Feuer, "Pataki Uses State Law to Hold Sex Offenders After Prison." *The New York Times*, Oct. 4, 2005: p. B4.

18 James Baldwin, *The Price of the Ticket: Collected Nonfiction, 1948–1985* (New York: Martin's Press, 1985).

Sexuality, State, and Nation

Jyoti Puri

- Decriminalize homosexuality
- Pakistan does not have any gays
- Brazilian women are hot!
- http://www.missworld.tv/
- Sex with a girl below 16 years is rape
- Our values are strong, ours is a chaste nation
- Don't ask, don't tell, don't pursue
- She's easy, she's American

Familiar phrases bring us face-to-face with sexuality's insepa-rability from the state and the nation. We live with such senti-ments and policies every day without thinking twice about them. Precisely because the impact of nation and state on sexuality is so routine, it all seems unremarkable. Perhaps the spark of sexual desire set off deep within one's core reinforces the belief that sexuality is personal, private. Nothing could be further from reality; social institutions matter tremendously to issues of sex-uality. When pushed to consider which institutions matter, we easily concede the usual suspects – family, media, peer groups, school, and religion. But the above phrases starkly remind us that nations and states are equally important to sexuality, if not more. Think about it; it is easier to ignore parental injunctions about your sexual behavior than what the state sees as sexually legal. This chapter presents a case for how nations and states bear on matters of sexuality and why this is too crucial to ignore.

It is helpful to have definitions of key terms such as nation-alism, nation, and state, and that's where I start each of the sec-tions, before going on to draw the connections with sexuality. The chapter is organized into two main parts, one on nationalism and nation and the other on the state. Even though there is overlap between the two concepts and what I have to say about each of them in terms of sexuality, this is an effective way to remind our-selves that the two concepts are not the same. For examples, I focus mostly on India and the USA. The idea is to blend useful examples that may be less familiar to the primary readers of this book with what seems familiar, but the purpose is the same: to question the links between sexuality, nation, and state.

Nationalism and nation

Let's start by defining the tricky thing that is nationalism, and the sibling concept, nation. You may wish to try this as we go, but, when I think of nationalism, coming up with an associated list of things is far easier than a crisp definition; flags, wars, passports, patriotism, and so on. One reason making it harder to abstract a definition is the near impossibility of imagining a world without nations; they seem so . . . what's the word? . . . normal that stating exactly what nationalism is, or what a nation is, is tough. All the more important to pin down the definition. Consider this: nationalism is the belief and practice aimed at creating unified but unique communities (nations) within a sovereign space (states). Said in a different way, nationalism is the belief that a people = nation = state.

Nationalism comes before nation; the *idea* and belief in the (north) American nation came before the Declaration of Independence and the creation of the nation of America, and the United States of America became the sovereign state. More than one nation co-exists in the USA, although unequally – America,

Nation of Islam, Cherokee Nation, Queer Nation (now almost defunct), among others. Nationalism is inherently neither good nor bad; rather, it is an abstract idea that unifies us but also separates us from others. We are linked as individuals to a broad collective and, along with others, we become part of a nation that seems uniquely ours. The flip side of each nation as a unique unified entity is to specify how it is different from another. It ought to be difficult to come up with 192 national stereotypes (that's how many nations are recognized by the United Nations), but nevertheless we seem to be able to – the British are stoic, Koreans are hard-working, Americans are loud, Chinese are cheap, Jamaicans are lazy.

Nationalism is a powerful principle, a powerful promise. Power is the ability to make things happen, and nationalism's ability to whip up sentiment and movements, to unify people or divide them, and create policy is awesome. Nationalism has inspired movements of independence (for example, Bangladesh), resistance to oppression (Palestine), a sense of community in times of social crisis (terrorist bombings in Madrid and London), but also genocide (Bosnia), invasion (US in Iraq), war (India–Pakistan), and militarism (South Korea). I don't know of anything more precious to a person than her/his life. And what more sobering measure of nationalism's power is there than the fact that sacrificing one's life or taking the life of another in the name of the nation is considered the highest good?

Nationalism is not merely powerful in the sense of the "power of nationalism"; nationalism is itself a form of power. As a form of power, nationalism is a mechanism of social regulation. Why do I say that? Because we cannot imagine our lives without this social structure; because we are told that it is the highest form of community, over family or religion, to which we owe allegiance; because we are raised within the parameters of national cultural values, and draw from within our sense of self/identity; because we experience kinship with other people whom we have never met, and hatred for people from another nation whom also we

have never met, as a result of nationalism; because it works by permeating our desires, not through force, but by making us complicit in policies and ideologies in the name of the nation.

The promise of nationalism is that we are all essentially the same and equal as citizens – a flawed promise, if there ever was one! No nation has been able to ensure genuine equality to its entire people while recognizing differences of race, ethnicity, gender, sexuality, social class, language, religion. It is not a matter of getting it right, of fixing the flaws of nationalism. In fact, the inequalities are not simply incidental but are built into the national social and legal infrastructures; law, military, government, schools, skilled professions in the US, for example, are remarkably skewed in terms of class, gender, and race. And these limitations of nationalism are directly relevant to sexuality.

Nationalism on sex and the nation's sex

Nationalism's greatest impact on matters of sexuality is by defining what is normal and abnormal, what is respectable and what is deviant. The fundamental link between respectable sexuality and nationalism is that ideals or customs of dominant groups are endorsed as national ideals, and are socially and legally enforced. The flip side of this respectable sexuality is what becomes designated as abnormal or deviant. Curiously, heterosexuality frequently corresponds to what is respectable and normal, and deviance to homosexuality.

In India, the norms for adult sexuality are quite unambiguous – it belongs within marriage and is meant to procreate no more than two children. But what lies beneath the marital bed? If this were true, HIV/AIDS would not be affecting young (primarily 15–44 years of age) sexually-active persons mostly through heterosexual contact (85.7 percent of transmissions). Whether true or not, for normal sexuality to have influence, abnormal sexuality must also be whipped up. Perhaps no greater misconception exists than the fact that Indian Muslims, the main minority group, are increasing rapidly. This increase is wrongly attributed to rampant male Muslim sexuality and the desire to increase proportions relative to Indian Hindus. The irony is that Hindus vastly outnumber any other religious group in the population, at more than 84 percent, and the threat posed by Indian Muslims and their male sexuality is fabricated but widely believed. Already declining birth rates among Muslims are expected to stabilize at 14 percent of the nation's population. So much for rampant male sexuality (notice the absence of any regard for Muslim women's sexual desires, or their wish for contraceptives).

Women are especially spotlighted when it comes to specifying respectable sexuality. Rape is undoubtedly seen as a form of sexual deviance, but under particular circumstances it can reveal national ideologies about sexual respectability. In May 2005, a young student in New Delhi was kidnapped and sexually assaulted in a moving car by four men. The incident struck a raw nerve in the city that is now called the rape capital of India. English-language newspapers reporting on the assault showed restraint, and in one case even reported on the brave determination of the young woman to put aside her grief and trauma and help the police in nabbing the suspects. But individual persons were less impressed or felt less constrained about expressing their opinions. What dominated their reactions was that this young woman was from northeastern India and that she was walking with a friend at two in the morning. Offensive stereotypes of women from the northeast, labeling them as sexually promiscuous and as unrespectable, were more pronounced in these reactions than the expectation that each person, and all women, have a right not to be touched without their consent. The implications were that this young woman is un-Indian and un-respectable, which doesn't condone the rape but purports to explain how she became the victim of sexual assault. Such can be the tragic and offensive logic when sexuality is part of the domain of nationalism.

If something is to be underlined here, then it is this: the issue is one of who belongs in the national community and who doesn't, and sexuality – normal, respectable – is the litmus test of belonging. The paradoxical catch is that some, by virtue of their religious affiliation, their ethnicity, their gender, their social class, are never going to be seen as sexually respectable and, therefore, as part of the national community. Norms of Indian sexuality, or for that matter North American sexual respectability, are specific to class-, gender-, race-, and sexual-orientation. It is curious to me that college-going women in the US worry about how many sexual partners they can have and under what circumstances (one-night stands, for example) before they need to consider their reputations. Interestingly enough, these are worries shared by some friends in India who are older than the college girls by several years.

Nowhere are the issues of belonging to the national community more precarious than for those who identify as lesbian, gay, bisexual, transgender, or queer. How national communities include or exclude their sexual minorities varies; the recently-won right of lesbians and gays to marry, in Spain (2005) and Canada (2005), is about equal citizenship and recognition in the eyes of the nation. More frequently, though, people are excluded either explicitly or through omission on the basis of sexual orientation or because they are transgendered. When was the last time a presidential address in the US made mention of gays and lesbians as an essential and equal part of the national community? This is omission. Current US President Bush has only mentioned them in the context of direct exclusion, by saying that marriage can only exist between a man and a woman.

The disturbing paradox is that, even as lesbians, gays, bisexuals, and transgendered people may be omitted, made invisible in the national community, they are also subject to unusual scrutiny. Another crime committed in New Delhi in 2004 starkly illustrates this point. This time, an upper-class gay man, Pushkin Chandra, and his friend were brutally murdered by two working-class men – as it turned out, over an argument about documenting their sexual activities. The English-language media brought to bear tremendous pressure on the police to solve the crime, but in an outrightly scurrilous manner. Inflammatory articles about "gay lifestyles," their deviant, upper-class, Westernized and, therefore, un-Indian sexual behaviors, littered the newspapers. The police, in their turn, went on a witch hunt within the gay networks *of* New Delhi, surveilling gay men, browbeating, threatening, and tracking them. The police officer who supervised the solving of the crime confirmed this in a conversation. Sexuality rights activists rightly questioned the role of the media in whipping up a voyeuristic revulsion against gay men in general and placing them at the edges of the national community. As Pramada Menon poignantly said, "One person's death has brought an entire community into focus. Newspapers are suddenly full of stories about homosexual life – and not in a celebratory way. . . . A stray incident has been used to stereotype them all and an already marginalized community is being pushed further into the margins."

What I have been doing in this section is noting the obvious ways in which nationalism and sexuality are connected, even though their specific connections will vary by case. I have been also making connections where they may not be so obvious. The idea is that if we start to recognize how nationalism and sexuality are connected, we are more likely to question and undo them. By way of that, here is a summary of the key points made in this section. First, nationalism shapes sexuality by defining what is normal, indeed, respectable. Second, the dominant groups determine the norm of respectable sexuality, which establishes who belongs to the national community. Third, gender, sexual orientation, race, religion, class are among the key social dimensions to determine belonging to national community. Fourth, the nation itself can take on sexual meanings. For example, citizens may associate national identity with exclusively heterosexual citizens. What I am getting at in this point is that, implicitly and sometimes explicitly, nations are seen as heterosexual. This is exactly what happens when the nation is thought of as a community of heterosexuals or when the nation becomes personified as a young desirable woman or as the heroic soldier fighting for family, community, and nation.

State

It is time to underscore a point that is couched in the above discussion, and to segue to the state. We don't think anything of using the concepts of nation and state interchangeably, but any attentive political science student will remind us they are different. The linking together of nation and state, or the equation that a people = nation = state, is itself a modern artifact of nationalism. That's why the terms seem confusing, redundant. The state is a sovereign demarcated territory, and more. It is a set of cultural institutions that generate ideologies (for example: the state is all-powerful), establish administrative policies and procedures (for example: monitoring populations), and enforce them through direct and indirect violence (for example: police and the law). A mouthful of a definition for something that seems awfully boring, no? For all the passion and love the nation inspires, one is hard pressed to find an ode *to* the state.

So, let's see if we can get to the importance of the state in another way. A student wakes up one morning and goes about her routine. As she gets dressed and heads out of the door, she will not recall that the building she inhabits, her apartment, the kitchen appliances and bathroom fittings, the car that she drives, the university that she attends, are all made possible by fulfilling a long list of state and federal laws. She will not note the police on the streets (for the most part), the post office that she drives by, and the traffic lights at the intersection. She is less likely to forget about the taxes that are withheld from her weekly paycheck or the year's financial aid package. All of this has to do with the presence of the state in our lives, and this is just the start of the list.

The TV that she watches, and the communication and broadcast laws, are easier to forget, but it's harder for her to ignore that the content is monitored. The point is that so fundamental a structure is the state in our lives that we see it selectively, and it would have to stop functioning for us to fully appreciate its relevance. This, its semi-invisibility, along with the more obvious institutions such as police, military, law, and government, is what gives the state tremendous power.

State on sex

Sexuality is no exception to the impact of the state in our lives. If one is eligible to have sex, with whom, of what kind, under what circumstances, where, whether sex aids or contraceptives are used, are all matters subject to regulation by the state. And we think sexuality is a personal matter! My point is not that the state is an evil big brother; Hollywood movies have already contributed enough to that myth. That we imagine the state as the evil monster is only a means of working through our anxieties about its impact in our lives. I would rather have us recognize the power of state ideologies, the institutionalization of power in state institutions, and the impact of an intricate administrative machinery. This does not happen in tandem or function smoothly, but can be messy, inconsistent, even contradictory (what happens when a lesbian couple gets married in Massachusetts but the marriage is not recognized in another US state, or under some federal laws?).

Nothing better illustrates the power of the state on issues of sexuality than the mobilization against Section 377 of the Indian Penal Code. The law can be summarized as the "sodomy law," which prohibits "sex against the order of nature." That is really to say, it prohibits anal and oral sex. This poses a problem for heterosexual couples who incorporate a range of sexual techniques. This most certainly poses a problem for gay men and lesbian women, because "sex against the order of nature" is thought to inherently include consenting sex between two adult women or two adult men. Not just anal or oral, but any sex between them could be interpreted as unnatural. Introduced by the British in 1860, this law is not just out of date but it is inconsistent with a cultural past that did not impugn persons with alternative sexualities. Notably, the law is not widely used to prosecute individuals but it contributes to a contemporary culture of violence and intolerance of transgenders, lesbians, gays, and bisexuals in India. It is most typically used by the police, thugs, and opportunists to harass, threaten, blackmail, and extort money and sex. Section 377 of the Indian Penal Code indicates how sexuality is regulated by the state; how it institutionalizes intolerance for some sexualities; how the belonging of lesbians, gays, transgenders and bisexuals in the Indian national community might be unjustly precarious but the state has the power to enforce the injustice through the police, the courts, HIV/AIDS policies, etc. Is it any wonder that there is gathering momentum across India to change Section 377 and to decriminalize homosexuality? Here's hoping.

Earlier, I noted that same-sex sexualities are more systematically targeted; this would include state institutions. Notwithstanding a few nations, gay, lesbian, and bisexual women and men are the objects of regulation by the state through denial. What do I mean by that? In the US, the fact that same-sex couples cannot marry outside the state of Massachusetts, or openly serve in the military, is deeply problematic not just because it limits personal choices. These prohibitions withhold the benefits of citizenship that the state extends to married couples or citizen-soldiers. The other side of this denial is the promotion of heterosexuality by the state. And is it easier to concede the point that gay, lesbian, bisexual, and transgendered people are often denied the privileges enjoyed by heterosexual women and men? Is it harder to concede that heterosexuality is openly or subtly promoted by the state? If so, the reason is that we don't *see* the privileges of heterosexuality. The power of the norm is what makes it disappear from sight: precisely because it is normal, we stop noticing it. Think about the innumerable laws and procedures – inheritance, marriage, birth and adoption, health proxy, death, tax exemptions, parenting, work-related insurance and benefits, home ownership and loans that implicitly say – for heterosexuals only! This is the unequal impact of the state on sexuality.

Sexualizing the state

So far, in this section, the discussion has focused on the state's impact on sexuality. What if we were to turn the lens around? What if we were to look at the state through the lens of sexuality; to sexualize the state, as it were? I think it is an exercise worth doing. For one thing, it would tell us more about how the state promotes and privileges heterosexuality. I am sure you've noticed or heard of the rising tide of Christian right-wing backlash against sexual and gender minorities in the US which began in the 1990s and continues to date. The backlash is unabated but not unchallenged. One such challenge to the right comes from scholar Lisa Duggan (1994), who calls for "disestablishment strategies." This is how Duggan explains disestablishment strategies: to show how the state constantly privileges heterosexuality; and to take the position that the state ought to *stop* its promotion. To make this point, she draws a parallel to why the state ought to remain secular. Think about it: if one of the founding principles of the US state is that it is secular, and not partial to any one religion, then why not have the same approach to sexuality? Why privilege a certain form of sexuality constantly and systematically? The state should divest itself of such heterosexist biases, Duggan rightly declares.

For a second, I think it's important to sexualize the state because it takes us beyond a oneway analysis of the impact of the state on sexuality. We typically see the impact of the state on same-sex sexualities, commercial sex workers, and on other marginalized groups. But, why not analyze the state? Sexualizing the state makes us do the hard work of analyzing how it is thoroughly

infused with issues of sexuality. By this, I don't mean just the laws, policies, and ideologies regulating sexuality, heterosexuality, and same-sex sexualities. I mean all of the same that don't appear to be directly about sexuality but whose pre-occupations with issues of sexuality are never far behind (for example, US citizenship laws that are not obviously related to sexuality but, in fact, privilege heterosexuals). This approach moves us away from treating the state as a singular cohesive unit that unrelentingly privileges heterosexuality and marginalizes all else.

This is not meant to be confusing. In this section, I have argued that the state is implicated in privileging and promoting certain sexualities. I have also argued that the state is not cohesive, monolithic, or a singular unit; indeed, it is a messy, inconsistent and contradictory set of institutions. The additional point that I am making here is that it is politically important to see the state as inconsistent, and to identify when and where the state does not privilege heterosexuality (for example: the decriminalization of homosexuality in the US through Lawrence vs Texas, June 2003; the August 2005 ruling by the California Supreme Court that both lesbian parents are to be seen as a child's mothers even after their relationship is over). To take the position that there are no inconsistencies in the state would be to see it as all-powerful (which it is not), would ignore social change (which has occurred), and would identify strategies for further change (in all spheres of life). Put another way, sexualizing the state is necessary for seeing how state power operates, and for challenging it.

Conclusion

It is hard to predict how familiar you are with the concepts of nationalism, nation, and state. It is equally hard to predict to what degree these concepts interest you. I hope this chapter has been successful in its aim to help you see the intertwining of sexuality with nationalism, nation, and state. I also hope that understanding connections of sexuality to these concepts has tweaked or enhanced your interest in issues of nation and state. What I would like to underscore is that nation and state have an impact upon sexuality in ways that affect our personal and collective lives. In the same vein, it is important to recognize the ways in which matters of sexuality are diffused into the nation and the state. It's a matter of recognizing the complex intertwining of sexuality with nation and state, precisely so that we can question how sexuality is regulated by these social structures. If there is one thing I would like you to take away from this chapter, then it is this: we need to challenge how nation and state create ine-

qualities between normal and abnormal sexuality on the backs of women, transgenders, and men, who are socially marginalized because of their sexual orientation, race, gender, social class, or religion.

References

Duggan, Lisa. 1994. "Queering the State", *Social Text* 39: 1–14.

Hobsbawm, Eric J. 1990. *Nations and Nationalism since 1780: Programme, Myth, and Reality,* Cambridge: Cambridge University Press.

Where Is Home?
Fragmented Lives, Border Crossings, and the Politics of Exile
Rabab Abdulhadi

For the politically exiled, "going home" means more than taking a journey to the place where one was born. The ability to go, the decision to embark on such a trip, and the experience of crossing borders to one's "native" land involve an examination of the makeup of the individual and the collective self, a definition and a redefinition of the meaning and the location of *home*, and a reexamination of one's current and former political commitments. In the Palestinian case, *going home* assumes further complications, especially in view of the Israeli Law of Return that bestows automatic citizenship on Jews arriving in Israel while denying the indigenous Palestinian population the right to return to Palestine and to the homes from which they have been uprooted since 1948. For the Palestinian exiled, then, *going home* brings back memories of one's worst nightmares at international borders: interrogation and harassment, suspicion of malintent, and rejection of one's chosen self-identification. Going *home* ceases to be just about traveling to where one was born; instead, going home is transformed into a politically charged project in which the struggle for self-identification, self-determination, freedom, and dignity becomes as salient as one's physical and mental safety.

Do We Belong? Home Is a Safe Space

When life under Israeli occupation became worse in Palestine, my siblings and I began a campaign to convince our parents to leave. We felt that they should relocate either to the United States, where I lived, or to England, where my sister, Reem, is based. My parents would refuse again and again. Whenever pressed, they would invariably say, "Illi waqe' 'ala nass waqe' aleina" (Our fate is not different from others), or "Who ibna absan min ennas?" (Do you think that we are better than others?). When we persisted, they would respond by invoking Palestinian dispossession, "Ma hada be-3eid illi sar fil '48!" (No one will ever think of repeating what happened in 1948!).

My brother and sister-in-law shared my parents' sentiments. They were nonetheless contemplating a relocation to give their daughters a better education, safe environment, and an innocent childhood. Nasser and Lana felt that they had to make the sacrifice and risk their residence in Jerusalem. The "situation on the ground," as Palestinians refer to their daily reality, was becoming unbearable: Israeli tanks were holding Palestinian towns under siege. Violence was on the rise; and Palestinians were criminalized for being Palestinians or just for being.

Nasser, Lana, and the girls never left Israeli-annexed Jerusalem. With the closure of U.S. borders to Arab and Muslim immigrants, it did not look like they would make it to New York anytime soon. But I did. On August 27, 2001, I came back from a year in Egypt where I taught at the American University in Cairo. I returned "home" to this anonymous city to take in its cultures, to thrive in its rhythms, to disappear and reappear in a sea of accents, tongues, cultures, and lifestyles. Two weeks later, my life came to a standstill, and so did the lives of hundreds of thousands of Arabs, Arab Americans, Muslim Americans, and Central and South Asians.

An earlier version of this essay was published in *Radical History Review* 68 (2003): 89–101. Copyright 2001, MARHO: Radical Historians Collective. Reprinted by permission of the publisher, Duke University Press.

Besides the fear for our loved ones whom we could not locate for several hours on that infamous day, we no longer feel safe: no longer could we draw on New York City's rich, vibrant, and diverse cultural scene, and no longer could we enjoy the anonymity of this city in the manner in which we enjoyed before. We rationalize things to make ourselves feel better. We are alive! Our loved ones are alive! It is more than what many other New Yorkers could say. We should be grateful. My mother's words ring in my ear, "Illi waqe' 'ala nass waqe' aleina" (Whatever happens to other people will happen to us—we are not *alone* in this!).

True, we are not alone. Along with thousands of New Yorkers, we felt miserable, sad, hurt, and wounded. But in more profound ways than one, it was not so: my mother's assurances do not apply here—we were alone, very much so!

The experience of diasporic and fragmented lives in which our souls and concerns are split between here and there sets us apart: we who have a particular skin shade, a particular accent, a certain last or first name, or markings on the body that betray some affiliation with the enemy.

> Be careful if you happen to be named Osama, or even if you own a restaurant named "Osama's Place!"
> You should worry if your last name is Abdul, Ahmad, Mohammad, or Masoud!
> Change your name if you can, from Mohammad to Mike!
> If you're Jamal, Jimmy might be a safer bet! Americanize!
> Be thankful for winter: Wear a heavy long coat and a big hat. It allows you to hide your beliefs from the public space that is supposed to accommodate all beliefs: If you are a Sikh man or a devout Muslim woman, do not parade your convictions in public—the public is too narrow for you.

> Do not speak up. Save your words. Try not to use words with a "P" if you are an Arab. If you may mix it up with a "B," someone will ask, "Where are you from?" Do you really want to answer?

> Try to avoid situations in which you have to present an ID: do not drive a car, do not use a credit card, pay in cash. Money laundering is not a priority for law and order now. No one will check if you present big bills.

> Avoid as much as you can Being You
> *Pass* if you can
> Melt in this melting pot!
> Do not cry multi-culturalism and diversity! This is not the time . . . better save your life!
> Better yet: "Go home," foreigner![1]
> What if you have no home to go back to? What if this is your home?
> Divided loyalty? Not a real American? But what do you mean when you say real American? Are you speaking of those to whom these lands belonged before anyone else? How many "real" Americans are left after the civilized European arrived?

Crossing Borders: Passing and Passing Through

September 11, 2001

I am stuck on Ninety-sixth Street and Lexington Avenue. I cannot get home No trains are running. I desperately need to hear Jaime's voice, to know that he is alive. I cannot reach him. A long line is getting longer at the phone booth. I begin walking aimlessly, hoping to find an available phone to call my mother-in-law. Right in front of me, a woman pushing a baby carriage starts to cross the street. Her head is covered. I am debating whether to say something. Finally I decide to approach her: "Go home!" Immediately I realize how awful I must have sounded. She looks at me with a mix of fear and resentment, too polite to ask me to mind my own business and probably too afraid to fight back. I come closer and declare a part of me I thought I would never claim: "I am a Muslim like you! Go home now. You cannot run with a baby.

When they realize what has happened, they will attack." I am already bracing myself for "their" attacks against "us."

My hand instinctively goes to my neck to hide the chain with the Quranic inscription my students Ghalia and Hedayat gave me before I left Cairo. Luckily I had forgotten to put it on today. My split lives are on a collision course again: I feel like such a traitor for *passing*. But wouldn't it be better to *pass* today? Do I want to identify with "them," though? Do I want to escape the collective guilt by association, the fate of my fellow Arabs, Palestinians, and Muslims? Should I renege on my roots? There is this nagging feeling that I need some sort of a symbol to shout to the world who I am. I want so much to defy this monolithic image.

> *Better tread lightly,* I conclude! "Don't be foolish. Today is not the time for bravado!" I tell myself. The thought of what will happen to women with the *hijab* sends shivers down my back. "But we all make choices," one part of me says. "Not always as we please," the radical in me shouts back. *Passing* is a survival mechanism.
> Lay low until the storm has passed and hope for the best.

I find a Caribbean taxi driver who agrees to take me home. Four white businessmen jump in on 125th street. They do not ask if they could join me; I would not have said no had they asked. Everyone needs to get home. It is becoming very dangerous to be out in the streets. As the only passenger who knows the back roads around blockaded bridges,[2] I begin to give him directions. Then I begin to worry that someone may notice my accent and ask where I came from. I am not sure I want to declare my activist credentials as I usually do and take advantage of the opening to explain the plight of the Palestinian people. A passenger next to me says, "So this is how it feels to live with terrorist bombings." I am certain that he is referring to Palestinian suicide bombings in Israel. There is no way he could

be relating to how Palestinian towns are being bombarded all the time, most recently in Gaza. I almost say something about the value of Palestinian life. I want to share what I have personally experienced this past year alone, but I am not sure that it is such a good idea. I keep my mouth shut and try to *pass* for a professional "American" woman. Another passenger, I realize from his accent, is Iranian. But we somehow bond in survival, making a silent pact not to out each other. We both pretend not to notice each other's accents.

Police cars are stationed at the bridges and on different checkpoints along the highway. I should be calm. I have seen this situation before. But West Bank memories add to, rather than alleviate, my anxiety: what if they stop us now to check our IDs? They *will* surely notice my last name. Would I be safe? What if a cop became trigger happy, as happens to Palestinians at Israeli checkpoints? Would it do me any good if they were to apologize to my family afterward?

I shudder to remember Nasser and Lana telling me about a "road incident" they experienced. A few months before Yasmeen's first birthday, they were driving from Israeli-annexed Jerusalem to our parents' home in Nablus with the baby in the backseat. At an Israeli checkpoint, a large rock flew at them out of nowhere, shattering the windshield and almost killing them. Twice privileged for having a Jerusalem ID and for being employed for a UN agency, Lana got out of the car full of rage and lashed out at the Israeli soldiers who controlled the human traffic in and out of Palestinian Authority areas. "It is not our fault!" yelled an eighteen-year-old soldier. "It was the settlers. What am I supposed to do?" was all he could say, shrugging away Lana's fears and contributing to her sense of helplessness.

For Nasser and Lana and the three million Palestinians living in the West Bank and Gaza, "road incidents" are a daily routine. There is no ordinary travel. If you live under Israeli control, you are never sure whether you will make it to your destination alive. "You were given a new life," Palestinians say to each other whenever one succeeds in making it home safely across the never-ending checkpoints.

It was what happened on a recent drive to Nablus that finally convinced Lana and Nasser that it was time to make the move to the United States.[3] During my visit to Nablus in July 2001, Lana was bringing the girls over to see me. As they were about to get out of their Jerusalem apartment, then four-year-old Yasmeen asked her mother if she could bring along their kitten, Nadia, named for her youngest sister. It was not the request, but rather the way Yasmeen asked that broke Lana's heart: "Do you think the army will let her pass through, Mama?"

September 13, 2001

I am working at home. No one is allowed below Fourteenth Street in Manhattan unless she or he can prove a legitimate reason, the mayor of New York City declares. I am so grateful that I cannot get to work. I still do not have a valid ID. September 11 was the day on which my New York University paperwork was to be completed and the date of my first lecture in Introduction to Women's Studies. I am spared the trouble of having to go through checkpoints or to reveal my identity.

A police car stops in front of the house. Almost automatically I begin to suspect that they have come for me. Rationally, I am aware that I should not be concerned since I have done nothing wrong. But deep down I am worried. I start thinking of the reasons: Maybe a neighbor called and said that a Palestinian lives here. Maybe because our house has no flags while the neighborhood is full of them—flags are everywhere, on the cars, doors, windows, poles . . . Our next-door neighbor has two flags on the front of her house, two on the back porch, one on a planter, and two on her car; her husband has three flags on his van.

The only public symbol of Palestine we could speak of is a sticker my dad had given us with the phrase, "Falasteen fil qalb" (Palestine in my heart).[4] Palestinians made it in 1994 when they thought they would soon have a state. Better remove it immediately. The next day, Jaime says after he came back from work, "I am glad we removed the sticker. There were so many roadblocks. The car was searched twice. They even asked me to open the trunk." Any sense of security I might have had is wiped out. This *home* is becoming so similar to what happens *back home*.

I share this experience with non-Arab friends, but I sense skepticism in their eyes, at least a flicker of disappointment. I should not be jumping to conclusions, they seem to be cautioning. My loneliness deepens.

Another Road—"Back Home"—May 14, 1998

I am leaving Ramallah on the eve of the fiftieth anniversary of Nakbah, or Palestinian dispossession. My cousin's children ask if I want to hoist a Palestinian flag with the slogan of the occasion, "So we will not forget," on the car. "Sure, why not?" I say, not really thinking things through. I exit Palestinian Authority "Area A" and drive through "Area B" with joint Israeli-Palestinian patrol (Palestinians control the population, and Israel controls everything else, according to Oslo Accords) to catch the highway to Nablus. It is a beautiful summer day. I should make it home in thirty minutes or so. So far, so good! At the fork, one direction leads to Ofra, a Jewish settlement built on a sparsely olive tree-dotted hilltop. The other road, to which I am allowed passage, because of my U.S. citizenship, leads to "Area C" (part of the West Bank 1967 borders but under total Israeli control) and 'Aber Samera. 'Aber Samera, or the Samaria Bypass, is a modern highway carved out of West Bank mountains by then Israeli minister of infrastructure Ariel Sharon to shorten the commute to

West Jerusalem and Tel Aviv and thus attract "ordinary" and "secular" Israelis who are not "ideologically" drawn to the settlements to make their homes there.[5] Winding through Palestinian towns and villages whose residents are not allowed to use it, the Samaria Bypass also links the network of Israeli Jewish settlements, sparing the almost two hundred thousand settlers from the constant reminders of the Palestinians whose land was seized to construct these privileged gated colonies with their lush gardens, children's playgrounds, and Palestinian-style red rooftops.

Along the highway, electric poles are covered with Israeli flags. It is Israel's sixtieth birthday as a state and as a haven, we are told, for diasporic refugees escaping discrimination, intolerance, and the Holocaust. But there is no space in this celebration of Jewish diversity for the indigenous inhabitants of these lands. Neither I nor my lonely flag is welcomed. Cars with Israeli license plates packed with settlers honk in annoyance and make obscene gestures at me. Palestinian drivers steer away from my provocative car.

Passing is a survival strategy.

September 24, 2001

A day before traveling from New York to Washington, D.C., to speak at an anti-globalization teach-in, a scholar of a certain descent reserves the train ticket over the phone and begins to suspect that the agent placed her on hold while the FBI checked her name.

She begins packing, going through her wallet, cleaning it up, a product of her familiarity with the ritual of trying to pass under the radar. She finds a Home Depot receipt that she sets aside lest an unexpected search raise questions as to why certain tools were bought! She takes out her U.S. passport. With a name like hers, a driver's license and a faculty ID from a major university might not be enough to prove her legality or "Americanness." After all,

equality does not mean total equality; it only means that some of us are more equal than others!

She goes through her briefcase. Should she take her laptop along? Would it be searched, causing a delay and humiliation in front of other passengers? It is a short trip. She has a lot of work to do. Take the laptop, but better leave early to avoid embarrassment. Better ask someone to go with her to the station: what if she is held? Someone needs to notify the organizers of the teach-in—someone needs to call a lawyer!

She arrives at the station one hour early. She approaches the window to pick up her ticket. She slips in the credit card and driver's license under the glass ever so discreetly, hoping that the clerk would not address her by her last name. It is taking a while to print the ticket. All the while, she is wondering whether a camera above the window is taking her photo. She picks up the ticket with no incident and goes to the tracks. Five policemen are standing on the platform. She is convinced that they are looking directly at her. She begins rehearsing what to say when approached—not *if* but *when* approached: what she is doing here, why she is going to D.C. "Did I bring the formal invitation on the official letterhead?" she wonders. She treads ever so lightly, moving away from the eyes of the cops burning her back to the center of the station. She gets more nervous and starts babbling away. Her companion warns, "You are attracting attention. Relax!" to no avail.

The train pulls into the station. She gets on and finds a seat. Now it is the turn of the conductor to check her ticket. What is he going to do when he sees her name? She opens the briefcase to take out a paper to read. *Al-Hayat*? You cannot read *Al-Hayat* here! She puts it away before anyone notices the Arabic script. She turns on the laptop. "Can the passenger behind me see what I am working on?" Like a little third grader who guards her work from cheaters, she wraps her arms around her laptop before she gives up and puts it away.

The train arrives. The D.C. station is full of military and police personnel; she cannot tell what units, rank, or specialty. Will someone pull her aside for questioning? Nothing happens! She is free to go where she wants. Why does she feel so choked? Is this paranoia? She has not done anything wrong!

Her mind travels to another time, another place, and another continent a few months earlier.

June 10, 2001

The plane is approaching the airport. Butterflies in the stomach: excited to arrive, soon to be "home," soon to see parents and the sixteen nieces and nephews. She disembarks and gets on the bus. A short distance and they are at border control, standing in a line marked "Foreign Passports."

Butterflies in the stomach: fear and anxiety: "Did I clean up my wallet? Did I remove all business cards from the briefcase? Is my calendar clean? Did I erase suspect dates? What should I say if they ask about the letters from the kids in Shatila to their friends in Dheisheh?" She rehearses her story and reminds herself to limit her answer to yes or no. No need to elaborate: this is where they try to trick you; it only prolongs the interrogation. Do I smile or keep a straight face, be rude or docile? Which image should I present to the world here today? What do I do when asked again and again the same question?

Here it comes, here we go again . . .

King Hussein Bridge: July 1994, Going In / Ben-Gurion Airport; July 2001, Getting Out

"Rabab, what is the purpose of your visit to Israel?" a young Israeli woman behind the counter asks. I am a bit annoyed for being addressed by my first name, almost wanting to say, "Do I know you?" but I bite my tongue and maintain my calm. I respond that I am visiting the Palestinian areas to see my family. She asks again: "You have family in Israel? Where do they live?" I answer, "In Nablus." She retorts, "Shekhem?"

(the Hebrew name Israel assigned to my hometown). I calmly say, "Nablus, yes." Now, I am directed to step aside so that my luggage will be searched. I remember, a bit too late, that I should have said that I was staying in Jerusalem or Tel Aviv to prevent the hassle of luggage search. I am taken, along with my luggage, aside.

An undercover intelligence officer approaches me, declaring that he is from Israeli security and wants to ask me a few questions, and that it is for my safety. I do not bother to question his concern for my safety; I have been through enough Israeli border crossings to know not to waste my time. I am too tired; I just want to get *home*. He and a young female soldier search my bags, taking everything out and spreading my clothes on the table. My underwear is there for everyone to see. An elderly Palestinian man is being searched at the next table. We pretend not to notice each other's intimate belongings, but my face is getting very hot with embarrassment. They wave an electrical device over all my stuff. Having as usual found nothing dangerous, they attempt to put my things back as they found them, but it is not possible either to replicate the manner in which I packed my stuff or to restore my dignity.

Exile and Exclusion: Home–October 5, 2001

News Bulletin: *"reconstruction of the downtown area is being discussed"*
Who moves back?
Who goes home?
Who returns?
And who is left behind?

Homelands–June 2001

Beirut is a city reconstructed—with a beautiful, fashionable downtown. The "Paris of the Orient" is resurrected!

Shatila is a sad place. It is a crowded area of one square kilometer on which seventeen thousand people live and where expanding the livable space is not an option. People in Shatila, though, are resourceful. To make space, "they buy air," says Nohad Hamad, director of the Shatila Center for Social Development. I first dismiss what she said, thinking that she was making a joke. "Do not dwell on it!" I think to myself. But then she repeats the same statement. So, I ask. "It is very simple," she says. "There are more [Palestinian] people than land" to the extent that "the only choice left for camp residents is to expand vertically," buying the roof of a house and building another house on top of it—the towers of Babel without the glory! The geography of dispossession in action!

The streets of Shatila—alleys would be more accurate—are narrow. Sewage is open to the eye to see, and the garbage is piling up. In the winter, rain and cesspools flood the alleys. In the summer, the acrid smell of the garbage threatens to suffocate you. Residents do what they can to take care of their camp, but there are barely any services. UNRWA, the only body responsible for Palestinian refugee camps, does not have the resources or the human power to clean up or to maintain the camp. It was supposed to be a temporary solution until the people could return to their homes anyway. If you lived here, you might want to move too!

The people of Shatila have nowhere to go. The only place to which they want to return is a home:

Rabie's Saffouriah is erased from the map
Rut you hold it tenderly in your heart
Your memories embrace it, refusing to let go
You'd like to go home
but the Borders are closed today!

Home–September 21, 2001

News Bulletin: "Artists, developers and families discuss how to memorialize 9/11 victims."

Back Home–July 2001

We are walking toward the mass grave. This grave is where most of the victims of the massacre are buried. A sign at the gate announces: "Here lie the martyrs of the Sabra and Shatila Massacre." We enter through the gate. A lone man is watering the plants: Adnan, the custodian, is not a Palestinian; he came with his family from the South of Lebanon to escape Israeli incursions. With little access to resources, Adnan's family could only afford to live in the Palestinian neighborhood, viewed as a ghetto in dominant Lebanese discourse. Their fate was not much better than the fate of their Palestinian neighbors. The Miqdadis, thirty-eight members of Adnan's family, were slaughtered during the 1982 massacre. To honor them and other victims, Adnan planted flowers and greeneries but "not the tomatoes," he said. "I did not plant the tomatoes; they grew out all on their own."

Home–October 20, 2001

A mobile phone message with the last words is saved. Cellular companies offer it to families free of charge.

Back Home–July 2001

We are sitting in the living room of Maher Srour as he remembers what happened to him and his family nineteen years ago. He speaks in matter-of-fact tones, and a ghost of a smile comes across and slowly disappears on his face as he tells us how fifteen-month-old Shadia, his youngest sister, was ordered to stand and put her hands up in surrender, like the rest of her family members. "'But she cannot walk! She is still crawling!' we told them. Their leader said, 'Yes, she can.' Sure enough, she walked. It was her first time walking . . . Shadia walked just like the rest of us. She stood in line with her hands up and walked.

They shot her, and she fell right there between the bodies of my mother and my father. You see? Right there on the floor. That is Shadia." Maher points out to the television and the homemade video he assembled from newspaper cuttings and fading copies of family photos he collected from exhibits organized to remember Palestinian refugees killed in the 1982 massacre at Sabra and Shatila camps on the outskirts of Beirut.

Tears are flowing down our cheeks; none of us can stop. Each one is trying very hard to stop, but it is impossible as Maher re-members, or tries to reassemble the memories of his family that was broken forever; the only remaining memories are faded photos and a broken heart. As Maher remembers, my mind drifts to another setting. Ciraj Rassoul, a cofounder of the District 6 Museum in Cape Town, recounts how this community was completely razed to the ground by apartheid's Group Area Act, save for a mosque and a church. "Remembering," Ciraj says, "is re-membering, putting together. District 6 Museum is all about re-membering our community, putting it together."

A video of faded pictures here, a Museum there: People do
    remember. And people do memorialize.
The question is
Whose memories are considered valid?
For whom memorials are built?
Does your life, as a Palestinian, count if you are dispossessed?

Home—October 25, 2001

"478 people are confirmed dead at the World Trade Center."
New York grieves for people with a mix of names, cultures, professions, lifestyles, religious beliefs and family arrangements.

Grieve New York, Grieve!
Can you grieve for the Pakistani man who died in the
    INS detention center of a heart attack while awaiting

deportation: Prisoners are not entitled to adequate
    healthcare! What does his family say or feel? Do we get to
    know?
Grieve for the Egyptian who moved to New York in search of a
    safer life but found no peace of mind. Does he count?
Grieve for the West African who used to pray in the Bronx.
    Where does he hide?
Grieve for all those anonymous beings whose labor no one
    credits, names no one remembers, and bodies no one dares
    to claim . . .
Grieve for the mothers and fathers, the daughters and the
    sons, the lovers and the beloved, the friends and the
    coworkers . . .
Grieve for shuttered dreams, for lives lost, for closed
    possibilities
Grieve for a loss of human life and Remember!

Remember, New York!
If I tell you about them, would you remember?
Would you remember Iman Hajou, the 15-month-old baby
    girl whose brains were splattered on the back seat of her
    father's car as he went looking for help?
No hospital for Iman
No passing through checkpoints . . .
The "road situation" is bad today!

Grieve for Mohamed el-Dura
A boy with a father who could not protect his son from
    death
The way fathers ought to do
Bullet after bullet after bullet
Ribbed the boy
The father watches
Crying like a baby
A Palestinian Amadou Diallo?

Grieve, New York
Search your heart
Is there a small spot there to grieve for all?
Then, grieve, if you will, for the Afghans whose screams of
    pain no one seems to hear . . .
Grieve . . .

Where Is Home?

I once believed that the restoration of my dignity was possible in New York. In theory at least, people are supposed to be equal before the law. I am not naive: I am fully aware of subtle and not so subtle systems of domination and discrimination. But no longer can we pretend that equality before the law applies to us as well.

As we continue to be ethnically and racially profiled, thousands of Arabs, Arab Americans, Muslims, and Muslim Americans are feeling foreign at home: we do not feel welcomed, nor do we feel safe. Call it what you want, but the melting-pot theory fails as "America" insists on grinding the coarse kernels of our foods, refusing to name them what they are and accept them on their own terms: garlicky, oniony, spicy, strong, and fulfilling. Beneath the facade of liberal multiculturalism lies an ethnocentric New York that continues to deny our existence except as bloodthirsty and suspect male villains, helpless female victims, and exoticized alien others. Our cultures are erased, our lives flattened to fit neatly in the folds of "Americanness." No longer can we draw on New York City's rich, vibrant, and diverse cultural scene: red, white and blue may be a safety blanket to some, but to the rest of us, they symbolize exclusion. Safety in this anonymous city is a precious commodity reserved for some, achieved only by those persons who *pass* for something other than the multiplicities and complexities in which we are embedded.

Rationalizing exclusion is a Band-Aid solution to dull the pain. But when thousands are detained and thousands more are "voluntarily" coerced into interviews, New York and indeed the United States feel suspiciously like occupied Palestine. But it is not Palestine, though, where most Palestinians are subject to misery and terror. As my mother would say: "Illi waqe' 'ala nass waqe' aleina."

We are very alone here
Our diasporic lives—fragmented!
Our souls bleed!
It is perhaps time to go home
To where?
Homeland erased, nowhere to go!
Yet
"falasteen fil qlab"/"Palestine in the heart"
My father's sticker insists
Memories of him, of Amer and of the land
Green, dry, barren, and mountainous
Locked, loved, guarded
A secret, cheapened if shared
"falasteen fil qalb"
My father's sticker reminds me
Of a homeland erased
Return to sender?
No such address exists?
But we insist
"falasteen fil qalb"

Chapter Six

Representations

Imagine the following: You and some friends decide to attend an event in celebration of International Development Week at your university, a panel of speakers talking about the importance of girls' education for the economic development of different countries. It's a topic you find interesting and believe in, and you're looking forward to going. As you walk in, you see a number of your classmates, although most of the crowd is made up of people you don't know. You notice the panel, the members of which appear to be two women of color, a man of color, and a white woman. The crowd seems to be mostly students, with a sprinkling of faculty, almost everyone seems to be white, and most are fairly young. And you think to yourself as you look around the room that this is something that you didn't use to notice: the composition of a crowd. It is interesting how this WGS class has made you aware of identity categories and how you now find yourself paying particular attention to which aspects of identity are visible—and which are invisible—at events like this.

As the speakers make their arguments for the education girls need in these different countries, though, you find yourself questioning which girls are being talked about, and whether the girls they are focusing on represent all girls in that country. Are there different educational needs for girls in urban versus rural areas? Does social class or religion make a difference to what is meant by education? What about access issues, such as tuition costs and transportation or education for girls with disabilities? In contemplating all these questions, you think also about the role of the expert and about whether any one person—as knowledgeable as they may be—could fully account for these girls' educational needs. How could 15 minutes cover what's important to know? Is this what the girls themselves think of as important?

Just as interesting to you, though, are the differences in what the speakers advocate. From the speaker who talks about "our" responsibility to help others who don't have the resources that "we" do, to the speaker who notes that we should be looking to the communities themselves to decide what is needed, you realize that there are very different possible approaches to this issue. The first approach is one you've heard before, but the second one is new. You find yourself interested in the questions being raised in these different approaches: about who gets to speak for whom and about our responsibility "over here" for something happening "over there." You and your friends leave the event, intrigued by the speakers' comments, but even more captivated by the questions their presentations evoked about the difficulties in representing others.

Meaning Making as Negotiation

Women's and Gender Studies, from its inception as a knowledge project, has been concerned with issues of representation. As we discussed in the "Knowledges" chapter, questions of who is present and who is absent, and the difference that makes, are key to understanding who and what is considered meaningful. The concept of representation thus refers to a process that is always more than simply mirroring something that already exists in the world. Instead, framing the term as *re-presentation,* as we do throughout this chapter, emphasizes that there is a gap between the "re" and the "presentation" and explores what goes on in that gap (a lot!). Re-presentation focuses our attention on the complex processes by which meaning is always both produced and negotiated.

For instance, think of something like news reports about supermodels or violent crime or health care. The tendency is to not only imagine that these reports are about things we can point to in the world but also that those things then easily align with how they are being reflected in that news report. What we write or say or show, then, merely stands in for the thing itself (much like a political representative who stands in for their constituents). With this understanding of *representation* (without the hyphen), all that is required to make representation "real" or "true" is its accuracy or alignment with that reality. To think about *re-presentation,* however, means not taking at face value that anything can be reflected in only one way, or that the way it is reflected through mediums such as language or visual images, through photos or videos or narrative accounts or official histories, is either real or true or the same for everyone[1]. Rather (and sticking with the example of these news reports), it is through the processes of interviewing, writing, speaking, filming, and photographing as well as through the subsequent processes of reading, listening, and seeing, that those things

[1]**KNOW ABOUT:** To clarify, there is a distinction between how the terms *medium* and *media* are used. We use the term *medium* here to refer to the ways in which information or ideas about the world are conveyed to us: for instance, historical narratives or laws or policies or textbooks are all mediums, in that they are ways of re-presenting the world to us. We will use the term *media* to refer to specific modes of mass communications: e.g., newspapers, magazines, radio, film, television, the Internet.

(2)THINK ABOUT: It is important to consider what the medium is, and how the information in it is translated and shaped. For example, think about how moving images are different from still photographs: for instance, a news photograph of a battle scene versus a documentary video about that battle. Consider how the difference in what can be presented in these mediums then shapes our own emotional reactions and connections to those images. Even in this comparison of two very closely related visual media, the difference between how they re-present something is clear. And imagine how complex this becomes the more sites and modes of re-presentation we look at!

in the world are produced as real for an audience. What we encounter in reading or listening or seeing is also filtered through our various experiences, backgrounds, and identities, shaping how the world comes to us and the meanings we make of our encounters with it. And even the medium itself is never a neutral conduit that simply transfers information to us, but is itself a translation of that information, too[2].

What we think or know about the world out there is thus never just a simple, unmediated reflection of some reality of that world. Instead, understanding re-presentation forces our attention onto a process that consists of several stages. So, to think of a few examples, while global warming, gun violence, and birth control all exist in the world, their re-presentations—and what we all come to believe about them—are the result of connecting and overlapping steps: their constructions in particular mediums (as images or words, for instance), those modes of transference themselves and how they might shape understandings (e.g., as fiction versus news reporting), and all of us and our various interpretations of those re-presentations (often related to our various identity categories and social locations). The result of these many steps is that no single meaning of global warming, gun violence, or birth control can be fixed; instead, each takes on varied meanings, often at odds with each other. Images, words, and sounds tell us what's important, whom to listen to, and what to feel about everything from breakfast cereal to taxes, from family structures to popular music. Re-presentation is thus always referring to a struggle over the meaning of something or over meaning-making as a process. And this emphasis on process and struggle means that re-presentation is always political; that is, it's always about power.

To say that re-presentation is a struggle over meaning, though, or that there are many possible meanings of something, is not to deny that there are nonetheless dominant meanings that seem to circulate about events, people, or practices. The many re-presentations we encounter seem to indeed often be quite similar, repeating the same ideas over and over again, within a number of different contexts, so that what they signify becomes common sense or true or "the way things are." Think, for instance, of something like the claim that women are more emotional than men, a belief that is replicated across any number of mediums from popular film to news stories to political debates, from doctors' offices to self-help literature. It's such an oft-repeated and re-presented idea that the dominant perception comes to be that there really is a difference between women and men. In this way, we can say that this idea about gendered emotions reflects an *ideology*, that is, it is a set of common and shared beliefs, a way of looking at the world that is all the more powerful for its taken-for-grantedness.

However, we can also raise a number of questions about ideologies to expose their taken-for-grantedness and help us note how they in fact reflect particular values about the way the world should be. Think, for example, of claims such as "freedom is good," "religion is a private matter," or "meat: it's what's for dinner"—three everyday ideological beliefs that are re-presented to us in numerous ways as unproblematic. While freedom might be good, what does it mean if someone isn't able to visit a doctor or travel to visit a dying relative? For whom is freedom good? Likewise, religion may be private, but one particular religion—Christianity—is more privileged in the United States and Canada, where public holidays such as Christmas and Easter align with Christian, rather than other religious, calendars. And while meat is on many dinner plates, given predictions about the increase in the world's population and the environmental and labor (to say nothing of animal welfare) costs of producing it, there are good reasons to reconsider its primacy on the dinner plate[3]. Dominant ideological claims about particular visions of the world require that they be presented as a kind of common sense; given their instability, though, that is, that they can be questioned, it takes work to maintain those dominant meanings.

For example, one of the ways that ideologies work to produce these common-sense understandings of what things mean is through the process of linking our emotional states to things in the world around us. As such, ideologies build relationships between feelings (such as desire, loneliness, happiness, alienation, pleasure, belonging, abandonment, hope, fear) and associate those with a range of people, products, events, and situations (celebrities, deodorant, chain restaurants, charity organizations, blue jeans, alcohol, political parties) that we encounter every day. In producing these associations, the world becomes meaningful in particular ways and we are positioned as certain kinds of people. Think for example, of the popularity of media images of starving children somewhere else in the world who stare at the camera with tear-filled eyes, and the voiceover talks about how you can help save this child. Such an image

[3]**THINK ABOUT:** Many people argue that the multiple costs and consequences of meat eating—especially given its uneven distribution across the globe—make its levels of production and consumption ultimately unsustainable. Some of the problems identified include: i) its environmental impact in terms of water consumption, land use to grow grain for animals, and manure disposal sites; ii) the dependence on fossil fuels for the large-scale transport of animals for slaughter; iii) the use of pesticides for food growth and hormone and antibiotic use in factory-farmed animals; iv) the working conditions of the laborers, both on the farms that produce the grain and animals, and in the abattoirs; v) the treatment of animals by agribusiness; and vi) the inequitable distribution of resources, where what it takes to produce one large animal for meat could feed many more people, at a far lower cost, than that animal would.

(4)TALK ABOUT: Can you identify images or narratives—in advertising, for example—that work to position you as a certain kind of person: giving, generous, caring, politically astute, desirable, adventurous? How do these examples accomplish this work? What emotions are being mobilized and to what are they connected? Do you (or your classmates) feel any conflicts about how you are positioned? How might you respond to these conflicts? For instance, think about car commercials that seem to always take place in expanses of nature (rather than in cities)? To what kind of person does this ad appeal?

calls upon a number of emotions: compassion, desire to help, sorrow, fear, and worry, as well as on a long history of narratives about who helps and who is in need of help. And there is clearly an appropriate response called for by this particular ideological construction: donate to the cause. And yet, for many of us, there are other possible meanings made of these images. For instance, those of us who have ever been hungry or know poverty intimately understand quite readily that it doesn't just happen only to children halfway around the world. Or, we might be concerned about this limited presentation of that place and know that this is an image that reflects only some of the children there. Thus, while we might recognize that these images are trying to make us feel a particular way about a situation, we also recognize that this is just one re-presentation of poverty. As much as some meanings take on a dominant status, then, we don't have to accept those as accurate or true or the way things are. And indeed, people often don't. Our interpretations of these images of children, for instance, are influenced by other things in our lives—intersecting identity categories, geographical locations, life experiences—that all lead us to question those images' dominant meaning and to negotiate other meanings for ourselves(4).

As these multiple possible interpretations make clear, then, no one meaning of any of these images is assured or the same for everyone, as much as they work to perpetuate only particular understandings of these children. Relating to the re-presentations we see in the world is thus complicated; not only is one interpretation not likely, but our interpretations (or, readings) may also conflict, and lead to conflict in us. If there are other possible interpretations of those images of the children, though, what do we do when faced with them? We can neither accept them unquestioningly nor reject them outright, since either response would force us to negate the complexity of our reactions and the questions they raise. But do these contradictory responses mean we're being unethical or not true to our convictions? Are we being duped in some way, falling for something we actually don't believe in? Or rather, is it precisely in the contradictoriness of these responses that we see also the complexity of ideology—as part of what goes on in that gap between "re" and "presentation," as part of the constant struggle over what images, words, and sounds mean to us and others.

A number of ideas about representation have emerged so far. First, because representation is really re-presentation, no image, sound, or word can ever simply reveal the world around us in a way that could be agreed upon as real or accurate to everyone; as such, re-presentations are never neutral, but always political, or invested in particular views of the world. Second, precisely because their meanings can never be set or stable, the work of re-presentation engages us all in a constant struggle over the meaning(s) reflected in the world around us, although some of those meanings do get more taken for granted than others. Finally, the meaning behind any re-presentation is always contingent, partial, and highly dependent on how the producer(s) and the consumer(s) of those re-presentations are positioned and position themselves. Meaning or interpretation depends both on identities and on how those identities have been shaped in relation to various social structures, processes, and institutions, in addition to how individual people claim and live those identities.

Visibility and Invisibility, Presence and Absence

One of the major ways re-presentation can be thought of is as an issue of presence or absence, visibility or invisibility—that is, of who is there (and is not) in the texts, images, or organizations around us. For many of us, especially those who occupy marginalized identity positions, re-presentation often means we are either completely absent, or only present in limited ways. Where are the same-sex families or non-normative gender presentations in advertising images? How come news shows so seldom show people of color as experts on anything that isn't specifically about race? Why are the struggles of working-class families on television and film so stereotypical? How come Aboriginal peoples are barely talked about in histories of nation-states, or are only talked about as victims (or survivors) of the actions of European settlers? Why are so many political figures in Canada and the United States white men, even in areas where the populations are much more diverse? Looking for re-presentations of these identity groups on the cultural landscape too often means disappointment, as they are simply not found, not found in great numbers, or found only in ways that seem inadequate. This invisibility doesn't mean that these groups don't exist out there; instead, it speaks to how institutions like the media, the state, and the educational system shape only some re-presentations as worth knowing about, others as only worthy in limited ways, and still others as not worthy at all.

The call for more inclusion of these invisible groups has taken many forms. It's important, this argument goes, that we see the greatest variety of people reflected in the world around us—in settings they already occupy and doing things that they already do—as a way of reflecting our complicated realities; we want to see ourselves in the world, and the stories, images, and organizations around us all need to better capture our perspective on that world. So, for example, the call for increased visibility makes demands such as: queer youth need to be featured on a television serial drama; black people should be talk show hosts, interviewing national leaders (of every racial group); and university presses should establish a focus on Indigenous Studies' books and articles. In each case, the problem of the invisibility of marginalized groups would then be solved, according to some, as those identities would be recognized and made visible. These kinds of changes would "make things better," because there would now be more gay characters on television shows, or people with disabilities included in advertising[5]. But, to return to the argument made previously, if re-presentation is always about meaning-making as a process of negotiation among many possible meanings, then it probably isn't a surprise that even these inclusions too often fall short. The queer youth is so often a gender-normative, white, middle-class, and well-supported-by-family-and-friends person; the black talk show host is lauded for her interviews, but has trouble getting white politicians on the show, and is assumed to only be interested in issues of race; the new indigenous scholarship is publicly celebrated but then rarely referred to, remaining tokenized and largely unused in mainstream education. In other words, there too often remains a gap between the production of these re-presentations, and their reception by various identity groups; the measures taken might aim to include, but that inclusion doesn't capture the complexity of experiences of those ostensibly being re-presented.

The point, then, is that inclusion is not enough. It is not the same thing as the ability to decide on the *terms of inclusion,* or on how any group is reflected in those re-presentations. Simply because a group is made visible does not mean that their re-presentation isn't still a limited version of their experiences. And it certainly doesn't mean that those re-presentations don't repeat and perpetuate stereotypes. They do. Visibility is always dependent on the very knowledges that previously rendered some groups unworthy of knowing about in the first place. For instance, in a context in which gender normativity is assumed, then the queer youth (as in the previous example) so often simply repeats that gender normativity, even as their sexuality is now included. Inclusion can thus result in continued marginalization—for instance, of other gender, racial, class, and age expressions of that queerness. The irony (or tragedy) of re-presenting previously invisible identity categories is that the re-presentation rarely reflects the intersectionality of that category. All too often, the opposite is the case, as attempts at inclusion nevertheless perpetuate rigidly defined versions of any identity category[6].

Remaking Meanings

Despite what we have discussed to this point, we are never simply stuck with the re-presentations around us; they are never fixed. In fact, dominant meanings are always being challenged and remade. *Subversion, resistance, cultural appropriation*, and *co-optation* are related terms that help us explore the ways that meanings are constantly renegotiated. One way of challenging the limits of re-presentation is through *subversion*. To *subvert* something means to resist and transform a dominant meaning and thereby put it to other uses. Subversion captures both an intentionality and a political rationale for that other use, a deliberate attempt to redirect meanings associated with that re-presentation. As one example, think about how people have used the iconic toy, Barbie, to point out the limitations and constructedness of rigidly defined, dominant, white norms of femininity: for instance, by putting her in contexts ("white trash" Barbie) or outfits (dominatrix Barbie) that are clearly not part of those norms nor of the marketing of this toy[7]. These kinds of interventions are important to consider, because they remind us that the gendered, racialized, nationalized, or sexualized re-presentations that tell us what the world means depend on our consent. In short, subversion happens when people actively resist re-presentations, when they make conscious decisions—big or small—to demonstrate how particular re-presentations are impossible, unhealthy, outdated, boring, and, especially, unjust.

People have of course always resisted dominant social and political structures and definitions of their identity groups, often loudly and publicly. For example, the history of the U.S. South in the mid-twentieth century is a powerful example of African

explored, though, all identities are always intersecting, and the sexuality of these two men is clearly tied to their racial and class positions, too.

[6]**TALK ABOUT:** Generate examples from popular culture that include previously marginalized identity groups. What is being included? And what is still excluded in these examples? What might be the consequences of this limited inclusion, especially for those who claim these identities? Is there disagreement among your classmates about these consequences? If so, what is that disagreement about? How does the idea of "terms of inclusion" help you talk about these disagreements?

[7]**KNOW ABOUT:** Barbie is a great example to explore the idea of subversion, because of both her ubiquity and her

longevity as a popular toy and American icon. Children have clearly always played with Barbie in ways that are probably not what the toy's makers imagined (cutting her hair, leaving her undressed, having her have lots of sex with Ken or Skipper or some other toy). But the theory of subversion goes further than this idea of using the toy otherwise than intended. One of the best examples of the subversion of Barbie occurred in the early 1990s, when a group that called itself the "Barbie Liberation Organization" took talking Barbies and GI Joes from stores, transplanted their voice boxes, and returned them to the stores–where unsuspecting consumers then purchased Barbies who intoned "dead men tell no tales" while GI Joes said "I love to shop" and "math class is tough"–a subversion that drew attention to the role of toys in perpetuating a rigid gender dichotomy. This kind of intervention into pop culture is also known as *culture jamming*.

American *resistance*—through boycotts and protests and in the face of violent retaliation by white power structures—to their racialized re-presentation as second-class citizens in the Jim Crow era (before the Civil Rights movement of the late 1950s). Likewise, in the 1980s and 1990s, HIV/AIDS activists (in both the United States and Canada) fought against the (in)actions of politicians, religious authorities, and drug manufacturers for the ways in which they constructed same-sex desire as criminal, actions that both created and perpetuated the idea that some lives are less worthy than others. In both cases, activists used signs ("I Am A Man" or "Silence = Death"), slogans ("We Shall Overcome" or "Act Up, Fight Back, Fight AIDS"), and actions (sit-ins or kiss-ins) to intervene in dominant re-presentations of black and gay identities, to make them mean something else, to resist the dominant re-presentations of who they were. This is not to suggest that these counter re-presentations weren't also inadequate to that group's intersectionality, however. It is important to note their limitations: the often-stifling heteronormativity embedded in those resistant re-presentations of black citizenship or the overwhelming whiteness and masculinity embedded in those re-presentations of same-sex sexuality. Resistance and subversion are thus related actions, in that each is an attempt to consciously and actively speak back to dominant re-presentations; they are both protests against power, even as they refer to different kinds of protest. Both are interventions in cultural structures and practices that aim to expose and challenge dominant ideologies.

But it is not just marginalized identities in politically charged historical contexts that demonstrate resistance. In our own personal lives, many of us negotiate and struggle over re-presentations of identities we claim or care about. Think about how we mount our own resistances at the micro-level of self-presentation—for instance by using piercings or hair dye as ways to resist social, familial, and maybe even peer-culture ideas about appropriate representations of gender, class, age, or national identity (practices also explored in the "Bodies" chapter). These acts of taking a practice that signifies something in one context and attempting to alter its meaning by placing it in another are examples of subverting that practice, of making it mean "otherwise." Challenging dominant meanings can thus be as big and public as social movements that resist structural inequality or as intimate as attempts to change the meanings of what we do to and with our bodies in private spaces.

These acts of individual resistance, of subverting dominant meanings by actively working against them through doing the unexpected or "wrong" thing, can also become the basis for bringing groups of people together. Consider, for example, dominant re-presentations of masculinity that place a tremendous burden on most people who identify as men to be (or at least seem to be) straight, young, muscular, physically strong, able-bodied, in charge, competitive, capable of violence, rich, resourceful, well endowed, and sexually desirous of women—a set of expectations which few men meet entirely. Taken together, these are the characteristics of "real men" consistently re-presented around us, in everything from popular culture (film, TV, music videos) to the workplace; indeed, there is a long history of such re-presentations of what has been called *hegemonic masculinity*. But how many "real" men do any of us know? Of course, we know plenty of people who call themselves men. But chances are most of those people are probably failing (in some way) at that identity given all the required characteristics. And while for so many men the social consequences for deviating from these characteristics can be quite severe—name calling, humiliation, discrimination, social isolation, physical threats, even violence and death—there are nonetheless many ways in which this version of masculinity is actively subverted.

For instance, consider the example of an identity that seems completely counter to hegemonic masculinity: the "nerd," an identity that for some people is self-consciously constructed out of failed masculinity, subverting those values by inverting them or deliberately doing their opposite. Most of us probably know this identity in a general kind of way; nerds (supposedly) spend inordinate amounts of time on unpopular, obscure, or non-mainstream activities (either highly technical or relating to topics of science fiction and fantasy) to the exclusion of more mainstream masculine activities (like sports or working on cars). They favor intellectual pursuits over those that demonstrate physical strength or social connection, becoming instead boringly studious. Despite coming from dominant racial and class positions, they are (or at least have been) extremely "uncool." And yet, many of us would also admit that our everyday lives have been transformed by these same technological obsessions, and that activities that were formerly relegated to the realm of nerdiness have become much more widespread—for instance, fantasy and role-playing online games. Somehow, nerds became cool (not to mention rich), and lots of different kinds of people, activities, practices, and cultures now fit into the nerd category. As a result, dominant culture's re-presentation of desirable and hegemonic masculinities has been challenged, and nerdiness has been increasingly taken up, adopted, and adapted by even more men (and women), further expanding who and what belongs in that category.

Not every act of giving new meaning to something is an example of subversion, however; some acts can, in fact, simply perpetuate other kinds of marginalization, becoming examples of cultural appropriation. *Cultural appropriation* expresses the idea that particular practices and artifacts more "authentically" belong to some people than to others and that their adoption by these others demonstrates uneven power relations between identity groups. Cultural appropriation is an accusation that disregards intent—in other words, whether that adoption is meant respectfully and with admiration or simply for "fun" is not the issue. Think, for instance, about the wide availability of Halloween "Indian" costumes or of popular brands that reflect stereotypes about indigeneity: the Washington Redskins, the Jeep Cherokee, or, most egregiously (the now discontinued) Crazy Horse Malt Liquor. Re-presentations of Native American and First Nations cultures have long been appropriated (taken up and re-used) by the dominant societies of the United States and Canada, but in ways that may not undermine so much as perpetuate those stereotypes. Traditions, symbols, stories, artifacts, images, music, and styles are in regular circulation within sites ranging from Hollywood film to New Age religions. Such uses of native cultures raise difficult questions about intent, about visibility, and about authenticity: Is this kind of recognition celebratory and complimentary, or derogatory and denigrating? Who gets to decide how people should be re-presented, and whether an adoption and adaptation is an act of subversion or an act of cultural appropriation? What happens if the people being re-presented take issue with the ways in which they are made visible by someone else? How do members of a culture arbitrate disagreements to these questions by people who claim these as authentic to their cultural identities? Appropriation is not necessarily conscious or malicious, and is often even an attempt to use something that is admired from another group[8]. However, it can have any number of effects, both for those identities that are appropriated and for those doing the appropriating,

(8)**TALK ABOUT:** What are some examples of cultural practices that are appropriated? Who is doing the appropriating and for what purposes? For instance, what about how some people like to dress for music festivals by wearing "Indian" headdresses? What are some of the struggles over appropriation you see in the news around you? Are there limits to this argument about appropriation? That is, can you think of examples where a practice may "come from" another culture but is so incorporated that it now feels like "ours"—e.g., yoga? How would you argue for or against these kinds of practices as also being examples of cultural appropriation?

because these re-significations ultimately don't change dominant meanings so much as perpetuate them.

Finally, remaking meanings can also occur when a dominant group or institution adopts what was a subversive practice or artifact and gives it another meaning by integrating it back into the dominant culture. *Co-optation* is a term that is commonly used to talk about how consumer capitalism adopts and adapts a wide range of alternative cultural practices, remaking those into new items for purchase. What used to be subversive or alternative, then, and a commentary on the limitations of capitalism, now gets incorporated back into capitalism, becoming simply another product. Think, for instance, of something like ripped jeans. Ripping, bleaching, acid washing, or adding safety pins or other adornments to jeans are all examples of subverting the fashion industry's elevation of a functional fabric (with farming and working-class histories) into an expensive marker of status. Those subversions—by people deliberately using jeans to make political statements about the fashion industry, about how much jeans cost, or about the labor conditions of their production elsewhere in the world—are co-opted by the fashion industry, with the result that ripped, bleached, and reconstructed jeans become available in high-end fashion stores, again at great expense. Much as with our discussion of reclaiming words in the "Knowledges" chapter, though, those high-fashion ripped jeans still carry traces of their subversive meanings; spending a lot of money and wearing fashionable ripped jeans, for many people, is also a recognition of how the initial ripping of that item of clothing came from outside that industry and was about making other kinds of political statements. Co-optation and subversion can thus be thought of as flip sides of the same coin; people adopt and adapt items from dominant culture and alter their meanings by using them otherwise; those same items are then reintegrated into that culture but still carry vestiges of those subversive meanings in their new appearance[9].

Resistance, subversion, cultural appropriation, and *co-optation* are related terms that help us think about how meanings of any artifacts or practices are never stable; instead, they are constantly being produced and negotiated. As they circulate through a number of contexts, those meanings are adopted, adapted, altered, re-adopted, readapted, re-altered in an endless cycle and through many audiences and end-users, a process that demonstrates how fluid and contested meaning always is. This lack

[9]**THINK ABOUT:** As with many other processes we explore here, co-optation is not simply capitalism's benign reuse of products and practices that originally challenged it. Think for instance of the example of "green" products. Twenty-five years ago, buying green products largely meant going to small specialty stores, set up as alternative co-ops or grassroots efforts. There were no green products widely available at large supermarkets. Today, however, green products are much more mainstream and one can easily purchase them at big grocery stores, with the result that those small alternative venues have largely shut down.

of certainty points to how complex structures and processes of meaning making are—not every act of resistance is empowering, not every re-use changes dominant cultures, not every co-optation is worth mourning. But exploring indeterminacy or ambiguity of meanings and charting some of the shifts and changes in the meanings of artifacts and practices can help us imagine and implement new ways of thinking about and being in the world.

However, it is also important to highlight how inseparable these processes always are. Perhaps one of the best examples to explore this complexity is to look at what has come to be known as *DIY*, or *do-it-yourself*, culture. DIY is an idea that eschews dependence on "experts" or "professionals," and embraces self-sufficiency in building, modifying, repairing, or creating things for our everyday use: reconstructed clothing and craft jewelry (as opposed to designer labels or fast fashion), indie media or pirate radio (as opposed to professional journalism or licensed broadcasting), and even Etsy shops and barter economies (as opposed to retail and cash exchange). This DIY ethic of self-sufficiency reworks capitalism's class hierarchies that tend to denigrate manual labor and glorify the expert as sole producer of our cultural products. Instead, DIY champions the average person's production and consumption outside of resource-intensive factory spaces and retail supply chains to instead emphasize the importance of community, personal relationships, and even the environment. As with all remaking of meanings, though, it is important to remember—even in the midst of admiration for resistant and subversive practices—that they never completely escape that which they protest.

Take, for example, the kind of DIY networks, practices, and identities that have formed around food production and consumption in the past decade or so: organics, community gardening, food co-ops, community shared or supported agriculture, vegans, farm-to-table restaurants, and locavores. The attempt in such alternative food networks is to resist buying and selling food produced by corporations that exploit agricultural workers (often migrant labor), degrade the planet with unsustainable farming practices, and contribute to the suffering of animals. In one sense, this particular DIY ethic embraces the practices of communities that had to grow, barter, and sell just to survive. Thus, there can be a nostalgic element at work in DIY practices, upholding a simplicity and sense of local networks that were historically formed out of necessity. Yet, as these networks have taken hold, it is often more privileged communities who have the ability to participate in this kind of resistant food politics. Organic food and locavore products are typically more expensive than mass-produced and distributed food. And the desire to opt out of corporate capitalist structures is not necessarily the same thing as seeking and achieving solidarity with those who use the same practices for survival. Indeed, eating organic or local might be an expression of such privilege, a means of distinction and a quest for purity in one's body and life practices that can be achieved by very few of us.

For many people, these kinds of alternative agricultural and consumer practices also perpetuate invisible adjectives or assumptions about race and class. The idea of eating more simply or "eating like your grandparents did" begs the question: "Whose grandparents are being referred to here?" Likewise, ideas such as going back to the land, getting one's hands dirty, or the universal good of bypassing agribusiness too often overlook that the historical (and contemporary) connections to food production are not the same for everyone; for many African Americans and other ethnic and immigrant groups, for instance, a long history of being forced to work the land reflected their lower social and economic status (and even enslavement)—a different historical connection to the idea of farming that nostalgic or romanticized views ignore. This is not to suggest that an interest in alternative food practices doesn't cross multiple identity categories; it does. Rather, it is to argue for the necessity to always think about how universal and "good for everyone" claims are in fact socially and historically situated.

Re-presentation, then, refers to an immensely complicated set of practices. Re-presentations are simultaneously sites of struggle, products of histories, and negotiated within institutional settings; their meanings circulate in different contexts, are never fixed or stable, and are constantly challenged and changed. Exploring how re-presentations are always complex and contradictory, however, offers us a way to imagine ourselves and our worlds otherwise.

The Concept at Work: Hip-Hop and the Politics of Style

Both the history and current status of hip-hop as a mainstream popular cultural form provide numerous examples of how the politics of re-presentation are in play in our everyday lives. One way to think about hip-hop music is as a formal innovation that has created a unique style of political speech by and for specific communities marginalized by race, class, region, and culture. First developed in the South Bronx (in New York City) in the late 1970s, this innovative style was subsequently translated throughout the 1980s and 1990s across multiple race, class, and national borders to foment youth movements and document the oppressions, frustrations, and hopes of a new generation—the hip-hop generation. At the same time, it is a stylistic form that often involves rapping over other recorded music, sampling and scratching records on a turntable, and reaching back into the musical vaults of U.S. and other world music movements for its raw material. In other words, hip-hop's formal innovations are re-uses of previously produced (and, famously in the early days, copyrighted) work of others, a stylistic subversion that became part of a larger social protest.

At the same time, the question of "who can speak for whom" has been the hallmark of this style. Because it was—and often still is—associated with a particular location in the heart of a disenfranchised, often poor, and racially divided, urban landscape, notions of who can claim to authentically belong to the hip-hop generation rise and fall on perceptions of identity. As such, an artist's creative expressions may be considered more authentic if they are grounded in experiences common to a particular marginalized community, social location, and consciousness. Often, these claims depend on directly experiencing these hardships in a particular body—i.e., most often young, male identified, of color, and heterosexual. But what is also interesting is that as hip-hop travels around the globe, the criteria for authenticity also morph to fit other geographies of struggle. Thus, what is considered authentic in Palestine is different than in Dar es Salaam, Mexico City, and the Maori territories in New Zealand. Hip-hop's representational power, then, is a flexible cultural form that enables direct engagement with localized systems of power and authority. But that power can be—and often is—readily contested by other producers and consumers who may consider themselves to have more authority to judge who and what is authentic.

Even though the earliest practices of hip-hop were far removed from the epicenters of the commercial music industry, this industry is always in need of something new to sell and hip-hop was subsequently co-opted. As it moved from street parties in

New York to recording studios of record companies, debates arose about the changing meanings of this style of expression. In the 1990s, hip-hop's commercial success in Canada and the United Stated crossed over to white, class-privileged, suburban youth, who now make up the majority of hip-hop consumers. So what are these white kids buying? Does the musical form offer them frameworks for understanding the deep racism, poverty, violence, and economic inequalities that produced hip-hop in the first place? Or, does the most lucrative of hip-hop's subgenres—gangsta rap—actually reinforce for white listeners racial stereotypes already firmly in place in their social contexts? Does a protest movement lose or compromise its politics when it gets taken up in commercially successful ways? Or, can protest be about both subversion and mainstream public appeal at the same time?

Preview of Readings

Gamson, Joshua. 2011. "Popular Culture Constructs Sexuality." In *Introducing the New Sexuality Studies* (2nd ed.), edited by Steven Seidman, Nancy Fischer, and Chet Meeks, 27–31. New York, NY: Routledge.

Nemoto, Kumiko. 2011. "Interracial Romance: The Logic of Acceptance and Domination." In *Introducing the New Sexuality Studies* (2nd ed.), edited by Steven Seidman, Nancy Fischer, and Chet Meeks, 221–228. New York, NY: Routledge.

Nakamura, Lisa. 2008. "Cyberrace." *PMLA* 123.5: 1673–1682.

Reger, Jo. 2012. "DIY Fashion and Going *Bust*: Wearing Feminist Politics in the Twenty-First Century." In *Fashion Talks: Undressing the Power of Style*, edited by Shira Tarrant and Marjorie Jolles, 209–225. Albany, NY: SUNY Press.

Kafer, Alison. 2013. "A Future for Whom?: Passing on Billboard Liberation." In *Feminist, Queer, Crip*, 86–102. Bloomington, IN: Indiana University Press.

"Representations" argues that the words, images, ideas, and meanings we encounter on an everyday basis are mediated through various cultural forms (e.g., journalism, television, photography) as well as through our own experiences, understandings, and investments in the worlds around us. Rather than offering up facts or a singular truth, we discuss representation (or *re-presentation*, as we term it) as a process that is always a struggle over meanings; therefore, it is also a process implicated in identities and power, differences and unfairness. None of us stand outside these operations of meaning making; in our daily encounters with re-presentations, we are always resisting along with acquiescing, subverting along with silencing, and appropriating along with approving. As such, the concept of re-presentation allows us a way to think about the messiness, complexities, and paradoxes of our lived experiences.

Joshua Gamson's "Popular Culture Constructs Sexuality" speaks to the importance of popular culture as that which shapes our everyday lives even as it is, by definition and design, superficial. Because popular media is saturated with the sexual (even if its definition of that category is limited), we imagine ourselves as sexual beings through the images and narratives we encounter there. Gamson argues that while the visibility of marginalized sexual identities has tended to rely on stereotypes, sensationalism, and conflict to boost ratings, the people featured in popular genres have nevertheless been able to speak for themselves and win over mainstream sympathies.

- What are the limits of genres such as talk shows as a way of educating people about marginalized identity categories?
- How is Gamson illustrating the struggles over meaning in talk shows that represent marginalized sexualities?
- How is desire represented in the popular culture we consume? What practices do we employ that illustrate either our resistance or our acquiescence to those re-presentations?

In "Interracial Romance," Kumiko Nemoto focuses on how racialized scripts play out in the intimate relationships of Asian American and white heterosexual couples. Although these relationships would seem to testify to increased understanding and acceptance of multiple racialized identities, Nemoto points out that the terms of acceptance often demand rigid adherence to normative gender and sexuality categories. Stereotypes about the hyper-femininity and subservience of Asian American women play a role in what white husbands admire in their wives and in the social acceptability of their cross-racialized unions. However, white women who marry Asian American men report less social acceptance.

- How is the importance of intersectionality illustrated in the couples that Nemoto interviews?
- How is heterosexual romance mobilized in popular culture in ways that negotiate the larger struggles around race and racism in our society?

- To what extent can we be held accountable for who and what we desire? Can or should our desires be critiqued in terms of acceptance and inclusion? Or, are desires all our own and something separate from how we treat others in our everyday lives?

Lisa Nakamura's "Cyberrace" raises questions about the enthusiasm we may have about the virtual worlds we inhabit. While the internet's implicit promise is to put "the world at our fingertips," Nakamura cautions against seeing these online spaces as somehow leaving behind the problems—like racism—of real life. Instead, she argues, experiencing the internet as a location where we can "choose" our race or gender (through, for example, constructing and adopting avatars) constitutes a kind of "identity tourism." Just like regular tourism, this online version gives a false sense of understanding a place and its people through highly mediated versions of a culture and makes it even more difficult to represent issues like racism or sexism or homophobia. In short, our stereotypes travel with us.

- How are racism, sexism, and homophobia represented (or not) in the popular culture we consume? How much does the visibility of various identity categories matter in how you respond to this question? How might you begin to talk about the terms of inclusion in your favorite popular culture?
- Does it matter who produces the various cultural forms—like video games—that we consume? Do representations always follow the perspectives of their producers?
- Since we consume different forms of popular culture, what are some favorites from your own life and those of others in the class? In what ways do you see identity categories at play in your examples?

Jo Reger's "DIY Fashion and Going *Bust*: Wearing Feminist Politics in the Twenty-First Century" examines empowerment through fashion and femininity. Her primary question is about the effects (and effectiveness) of an oppositional politics of style in the pages of *Bust* magazine. Is it a challenge to societal norms of feminine respectability and investments in economic status? Or, is it an individualistic indulgence that brings about little social change but is nevertheless easily co-opted by a consumer society in a constant quest for the next new thing? Through these questions, Reger stages a classic debate about strategies and tactics within the field of Women's and Gender Studies, bringing together social movement scholarship, fashion studies, and feminist theorizing.

- How important is developing a sense of style in your own life or in the lives of other members of the class? What statements about identity are referenced in how people dress and adorn themselves?
- What is political about style? Have you used style in ways to communicate your own political beliefs?
- What are the various ways in which the social world is changed? Where do we locate this change? How do we know that change has happened?

In "A Future for Whom?: Passing on Billboard Liberation," Alison Kafer alerts readers to the taken-for-granted assumptions embedded in the billboards produced by the Foundation for a Better Life. The Foundation's implicit message throughout the dozens of highly visible billboards—many depicting people with disabilities—is that people overcome adversity by taking personal responsibility and demonstrating strength of character. These individual characteristics guarantee better futures for all. What is obscured here, Kafer points out, are the collective efforts and outcomes of the disability rights movement, recent civil rights legislation, and the networks of family and care workers—in short, entire communities—that support the lone individuals depicted in the billboards. Ultimately, the billboards both reinforce the idea that disability can (and should) be overcome and depoliticize the situations of people living with adversity that cannot be overcome by individual effort alone.

- How is disability represented as a personal problem in popular culture? Can you identify other examples of these kinds of representations?
- What are the political impacts of a focus on individual triumph that otherwise obscures the contributions of community networks and other institutional and structural supports?
- How would our culture change if people understood themselves to be only temporarily able-bodied, that is, accepting the fact that all of us—if we live long enough—will fit the identity category of disabled?

Popular Culture Constructs Sexuality

Interview with Joshua Gamson

You wrote two books on popular culture. What is it about popular culture that fascinates you?

I'm first of all just interested in everyday life, and so much of everyday life gets its texture from popular culture – whether it's from commercial culture, or from more organic, self-created forms of culture. Pop culture is a common currency, and in this society there aren't that many things the whole population shares; the United States is so diverse, and just so huge, that commonalities are relatively rare, and mostly they come from pop culture. I also find thinking about popular culture challenging, because it so often combines social significance with tremendous superficiality. It's important almost by definition – it's the sea in which we swim, and to a large degree it sets the terms and boundaries of imagination; it is where discussions central to social life take place. But often the experience of pop culture, especially commercially produced culture, is thin, fleeting, and not that deeply felt or thought through. I find that combination intriguing. And finally, I'm interested in the politics of pop culture. There's this interesting tension between a sort of "top down" version of popular culture, in which people who control major cultural institutions create and manage what gets out there, and a "bottom up" version of popular culture, in which people at a more grassroots level make up their own stuff. I think those dynamics are important and interesting to understand.

In general, how do you see popular culture influencing or shaping sexuality?

There are a few ways this happens. Sexual statuses, populations, behaviors, and so on, all get processed through popular culture. Some become visible in it, others are rendered invisible; some are celebrated or treated as legitimate, others are denigrated or delegitimated. So popular culture affects who and what gets on the cultural map in the first place, and proposes ways of thinking about sexualities. (Some people think popular culture *determines* how people think about sexuality, but I don't think that's quite right.) So, for instance, for a long time there were just very few stories being told publicly about homosexuality, and those that were – in movies, in novels, and so forth – were mostly about the tragic lives of people presented as diseased. Obviously, gay people are now far from invisible in popular culture – right now there are at least two television shows with "queer" in their titles, advertising now explicitly targets lesbians and gay men, and I cannot possibly keep track any longer of all the films and books with gay content. Before that change in the popular culture, it was hard to make the argument for gay rights and respect, since people who don't exist don't get rights, and people who are sick are usually put away. Now, with the change in popular culture, we face a radically different environment with a different set of challenges: the conservative backlash against gay visibility; the commercialization and sanitizing of a lot of lesbian and gay life; the attempt to set off "good" gays (monogamous, gender-normative) from "bad" ones (promiscuous, gender-nonconforming).

Popular culture also is the main site of public discussion of sexualities, whether in the form of fictional or nonfictional representations – a "60 Minutes" report on same-sex marriage or an episode of "Will and Grace" – or in the sorts of public controversies that are a cultural constant. Pop culture is a kind of forum – a structured one, in which only some people get to speak, but a forum none the less. Ideas about sexuality are proposed, and people take those into everyday life. Even things like the exposure of Janet Jackson's breast at the 2004 Superbowl Halftime show, or the periodic complaints that this or that cartoon character is gay, silly as they are, are also significant moments when people are publicly debating whether and how sex should be publicly visible, battling out sexual norms. These discussions are also important for affecting what gets on the policymaking agenda around sexuality, and often also in how policy decisions are resolved. How sexuality is framed is especially crucial here, I think. So when African-Americans' sexuality is framed in popular culture as "out of control," for example, it is easier for policymakers to justify something like forced sterilization.

I also think popular culture is simply a central source of how people imagine themselves as sexual beings: they see images and hear stories about what sex can or should look like, what kinds of relationships are available to be had, and so on, and these become the source material for building their sexual identities and practices. For example, in recent years popular culture has involved much, much more open discussion of women's sexuality, and not just of women as passive servants to male sexual needs. It's one thing for a woman to grow up with the "happy homemaker pleasing her man" images and stories that dominated pop culture of earlier decades, and quite another for a woman to see hookups on "The Real World" and reruns of "Sex in the City" in which women discuss masturbation and orgasms, and are shown, literally, pursuing their own pleasure.

What do you think are some of the big changes in the way popular culture views sexuality over the last few decades?

It's been a strange few decades. On the one hand, there has been a massive opening up of pop-cultural images and discussions of sexuality, to the point where homosexuality – while still obviously controversial – is presented on television, for instance, in a diverse set of genres, with an increasingly diverse range of gay and lesbian characters, and in storylines or formats that are quite flattering to gay people. This is a hugely dramatic change, given that in the fifties and sixties homosexuality was barely visible in popular culture, and when it was, it was usually presented as a sad, sick, stigmatized existence. Homosexuality is out of the pop-culture closet, to the degree that we've got entire TV shows, and now even TV networks, built around gay life. Similarly, as I suggested earlier, while a few decades ago the idea that women could be sexual subjects rather than only objects, that women could be in control of their own sexuality, was not all that prevalent in popular culture, now, images of women making decisions about who and how to be, sexually, are commonplace. On the other hand, the last few decades have also seen both a huge backlash – with consistent attempts to desexualize popular culture, to re-closet the ideas and images that have become part of pop culture – and a major expansion of exploitation of sexuality, especially women's sexuality, for selling.

You study daytime talk shows in Freaks Talk Back. Why?

Mainly because daytime talk shows were among the first significant sites of consistent discussion of lesbian, gay, bisexual, and transgender issues in popular culture, and also because they are places where people actually speak for themselves – sometimes edited, always constrained, often distorted, but at least speaking. I thought talk shows would be a great place to go to understand how stigmatized sexualities became visible in popular culture, what kinds of visibility were available and why, what happened to the sexuality discourse when the genre changed (becoming, in the case of talk shows, more "tabloid"), and just how public discussions and spectacles of sexuality operated.

Many people think that talk shows promote either degrading views of sexual minorities or portray them as exotic and bizarre. What did your research find?

I found that, although there was certainly plenty of degrading and exoticizing and stigmatizing content in the shows, that was neither the most significant nor the most interesting aspect of them. After just a little while into the research process, I began to take the exploitation of sexual and gender minorities as a starting premise. Of course, shows built on conflict, taboo subjects, sensationalizing, and so on, were using their guests for entertainment purposes. But one of the most interesting findings was that exploitation and voice were not mutually exclusive, and that the people presented on the shows as "freaks" were often given, and took, plenty of space to talk back, and they often got a lot of support from the studio audiences for doing so. In fact, in the earlier version of the genre, the more middle-class debate shows like "Donahue," people were invited to testify and demystify their sexual identities, and were treated as experts on their own experience. Even in the newer version of the genre, the louder, scrappier, nastier shows like "Springer," oftentimes the anti-gay bigots were the ones who really got raked over the coals. Another interesting finding was that the kind of gay, lesbian, bisexual, and transgender visibility on the more tabloid shows was much, much more diverse in terms of race and class than on the older, more staid shows, which were almost exclusively white and middle-class. Sexual minorities also became, oddly, more incidental, mixed into programming that was about something else. For instance, a show on "You stole my boyfriend!"

would have a gay storyline thrown into the mix. Finally, I found that, when I looked more closely at just who was being degraded and treated as bizarre, it was really not sexual minorities in general, but people who departed from conventional gender norms or monogamy norms. None of this means we should celebrate talk shows as advocates for sexual minorities, but that the picture was much more complicated than degrading or bizarre portrayals.

Some researchers argue that the media today promotes stereotyped views of gay men and lesbians; others argue that the media champions images of gays and lesbians as normal or ordinary Americans. What view is supported by your research?

As I implied in my response about talk shows, it seems obviously to be both, and the important question – at the center of a lot of my research – has to do with the conditions and forces that drive in one direction or the other. You have to break it down, I think: how the stereotype vs. normalized process plays out has to do with which particular medium and industry and genre you're looking at. For instance, various wings of the media have clearly discovered that images of gays and lesbians can be profitable, for attracting both a gay niche audience and straight audiences. But there are different strategies for doing so. If you look at advertising images aimed directly at gays and lesbians, you see more "normal" images, partly because advertisers have an interest in seeing lesbians and gay men as normal and predictable consumers; if you look at films marketed to teenaged boys, you still see a fair amount of gratuitous and old-fashioned gay stereotyping, since that's familiar and comfortable to the market being pursued. Oftentimes, you get both normalization and stereotyping at once. For instance, "Queer Eye for the Straight Guy" has none of the sick-and-self-hating stereotypes, no interest whatsoever in the closet, and the gay men there are emulated by the straights they're in charge of transforming. Their sexuality itself is uncontroversial. But the show also promotes certain old stereotypes (gay men are more "cultured" than straight ones) and generates new ones (gay men are in charge of instructing straight men in how to be good consumers). The news coverage of gay marriage countered the stereotype of lesbians and gay men as "different," while also further stigmatizing those gays and lesbians who choose different relationship frameworks. All that complicated stuff aside, though, I think the overall trend has been towards images of certain gays and lesbians (gender-conforming ones, in particular) as normal, ordinary, even possibly boring.

What are your chief criticisms of the way the mass media presents sexuality, and especially sexual minorities?

My chief criticisms are just that the mass media have not yet made enough room for all kinds of sexualities to be visible and thoughtfully considered; that they still proceed, for the most part, from a heterosexist worldview, in which they speak to their audience as if everyone were heterosexual; and that the images of sexual and gender minorities currently available are still quite narrow racially and class-wise. The coverage still tends to center around sexual minorities as sources of controversy and conflict (always a good way to attract an audience, but not always so in touch with the actual experience being presented), or on "good gays" versus "bad gays."

Is there a TV show that comes close to what you would like to see in its presentations of sex and sexualities?

The one that comes closest, for me, is "Six Feet Under." Sex is complex and visible on that show, but not overly burdened with significance. It's an integrated part of the characters' lives – or

when it's unintegrated, that's because sex has taken on some unusual role in their lives, as a way of acting out or testing boundaries or working through some emotional issue. There's a remarkable diversity of sexual practices and sexual persons on the show. The sex isn't always sexy, and it's only presented as "dirty" if the character is feeling shame. That's quite different from elsewhere on television, where sexuality seems to be simultaneously suppressed as something shameful and exposed as something titillating, which in both cases inflates the significance of sex.

As a researcher of television and sexuality, what is your response to recent government efforts to impose stricter regulations on sexual content?

I find it mostly misplaced and intensely hypocritical. Let's just say that my research suggests it is unlikely that Janet Jackson's exposed breast is a significant threat to Western civilization. I understand people not wanting their kids exposed to hypersexualized images early in life, and I think there is a lot of very irresponsible sexual content on television, especially sexualized images of girls; and I'm not against regulation. My objection is more that, in the context of other attempts to impose "traditional" sexual norms – in schools, for instance – the strict regulations on sexual content seem to be more about social control than about protection of kids. (I might see it differently were there similar attempts to regulate violent content.) Also, I'm just not convinced that such regulation is a very effective option, if the goal is to create a climate for people to think about sexuality and integrate it into their lives in the most satisfying and emotionally and physically healthy manner. I would like to see efforts to make sexual content more honest, humane, funny, and open, rather than efforts to shut people up or to generate shame. Rather than the current "morality"-based attempts to keep sexuality tightly reined in, I'd love to see more efforts to present sexuality as a natural aspect of human existence, and to present information about the various ways people use their bodies with each other for pleasure and how to do so without endangering oneself. Even if it's more messy, I think that would serve both children and adults much more effectively. I can dream, right?

Interracial Romance
The Logic of Acceptance and Domination
Kumiko Nemoto

With globalization and an increasing immigrant population in the United States, the surge in interracial relationships might not be a surprising trend. In fact, the increase in intermarriage and interracial relationships should be a welcome sign in the changing landscape of love, romance, and family, as it fits America's racial-melting-pot image and atmosphere of steadily greater multi-culturalism. However, interracial relationships are still far from the norm. While many Americans date someone of another race, fewer marriages cross racial lines. While about 92 percent of all interracial marriages include white partners, only 4 percent of married whites have non-white spouses (Qian 2005:34). In fact, many white Americans remain uncomfortable about interracial intimacy and tend to disapprove of their family members' interracial relationships (Qian 2005:33). Skin color also greatly influences patterns of interracial marriage. The lighter the skin color, the higher the rate of intermarriage with white Americans (Qian 2005:31). Hispanics who label themselves as racially "white," Asian Americans, and American Indians have high rates of marriage with whites compared to those of African Americans. Also, there are distinct gender patterns: 74 percent of the black–white couples involve a black husband and a white wife, and 58 percent of the Asian American–white couples involve an Asian American wife (Qian 2005:36).

The increase in interracial relationships gives the impression that racism and discrimination are lessening in our society. However, the types of interracial couples that are deemed acceptable and desirable continue to be shaped by society's dominant racial and gender beliefs. An increase in dating and marrying across racial lines may not be explained entirely by a decline in racism. Patricia Hill Collins (2004:250) writes, "Crossing the color line to marry interracially challenges deep-seated American norms, yet such relationships may not be inherently progressive." By the same token, Henry Giroux (2006:32) argues that some seemingly oppositional or counter-normative behaviors in fact reveal the logic of domination more than they represent the logic of protest or resistance to the system, much less the logic of liberation. So, what are the dominant images of interracial relationships? What are the ingrained messages in them? In this chapter, I will examine some popular images and interracial relationships and how they express dominant ideologies. Then, drawing on my research on Asian American–white couples, I will explore the racial and gender ideologies that shape these couples and the challenges that are faced by them.

Whiteness and images of interracial couples

Popular culture daily sells hypersexualized racial images and offers aesthetic consumption of racial differences as if such consumption were synonymous with the end of racism and sexism. The cultural images are ambiguous, blurring the line between oppression and nuanced celebration of racial diversity. The images of interracial romance continue to be shaped by traditional themes of white normalcy, whites' exoticization of people of color, male authority, and distinct differences between masculinity and femininity. In many images, white manhood and womanhood continue to represent the norm, with people of color portrayed alongside in an exoticized way.

Even though the popular media claim that "racial mixing" represents an ideal of racial integration, it has also denoted whiteness as a sign of normalcy and ascendancy. In 1993, a multiracial female cyborg appeared on the cover of *Time* magazine as "The New Face of America." Her image metaphorically characterized a future America as increasingly comprising multiracial individuals and couples. At the same time, this young female cyborg represented future multicultural citizenship in a state that would continue to enforce conventional norms of heterosexuality, family values, and white privilege. The "white-enough" appearance of the cyborg, as the face of America, evoked the image of "the future as what will happen when white people intermarry" (Berlant 1997:207), and insinuated that whiteness would remain central to America's race relations. Also, by highlighting race within the private realms of "love," "sex," and "marriage," the cover ensured the continuation of heterosexual unions and family love as solutions for the "problems" of race and immigration (Berlant 1997). Almost 15 years later, media portrayals of interracial couples and multiracial families still reflect what the female cyborg represented at that time: interracial relationships depicted in terms of their approximation to heterosexual unions and the ideal white middle-class family in which traditional male authority figures rule and female caretaker figures serve.

Recent images of interracial couples have apparently gained wide media attention not just because these couples transgress racial lines, but also because they express exotic yet traditional versions of femininity and masculinity. Couples in the media often consist of a white partner with a light-skinned partner of color such as Halle Berry or Jennifer Lopez (Childs 2009). Non-white partners often appear to mirror the white fantasy of hypermasculine or hyperfeminine racial minority images. By portraying interracial couples that represent traditional gender and racial messages, these popular images tell us that interracial couples can be acceptable when they embody attractive racialized femininity and masculinity in which male authority is embraced, whiteness is retained, and American middle-class ideology is sustained.

In addition, images of interracial romance, while aesthetically and romantically appealing in terms of their potentially positive effect on race relations, can erase realities of racial violence and racial hierarchy. They reduce racial differences to a matter of physical appearances and conventional heterosexual romantic norms. Instead of challenging hierarchies and inequalities, these interracial images re-order signs of race and gender according to traditional ideologies, and perpetuate the display of white manhood and white womanhood as dominant – in other words, white men and women as figures served by men and women of color.

Considering the fact that over 90 percent of screenwriters are white (Childs 2009:70), it might not be surprising that images of, and storylines about, interracial relationships in television and film reflect white male desires and fantasies. Interracial relationships are also often portrayed as "race-less" in white-dominated settings (Childs 2009), and race is often represented as a matter of superficial physical differences. Such color-blindness or race-less-ness is a unique aspect of American multiculturalism, and it often entails the exoticization of racial minorities or white-centered assimilation messages (Perry 2002). Neither approach critically engages the issue of power (Nylund 2006). Also, the analysis of interracial couples in contemporary films (Childs 2009) finds repeated instances of the message that white people are not racist; it is racial minorities and their communities, not whites, who oppose and complain about interracial relationships. In many TV programs and films, interracial romances are represented as doomed to fail, thus perpetuating the safe normalization of white couples and same-race unions. The images are also gendered: interracial relationships that appear in the media reinforce white male heroism, with white men depicted as liberal and progressive, certifying their goodness, kindness, and superiority over others (Childs 2009:87).

Popular discourses about Asian American women

Given the dominant hierarchies of race and gender implicit in popular images of interracial relationships, this section looks at how racial and gender ideologies have been historically played out in Asian American–white relationships. Compared to African Americans, a higher number of Asians and Asian Americans marry whites. There are various social factors that could explain the high rate of intermarriage between Asian American women and white men: Asian Americans' overall high education and income, compared to whites and other racial minorities, may be one. But such factors do not explain why Asian American women have a higher intermarriage rate than Asian American men. Also, while Asian Americans are often seen as a "model minority," the question of how Asian American men and women fare as intimate or marital partners of whites has not been much discussed.

Racial stereotypes play a critical role in the dynamics of gender in interracial relationships. Like the stereotype of black men's hypermasculinity, long-existing stereotypes of Asian women as submissive, subservient, passive, and/or hypersexual may serve as critical components in heterosexual attraction. Also, in a culture that automatically equates long dark hair and a thin body with being "feminine" regardless of race, images of the Asian female body are easily marked as representative of a non-threatening femininity. In contrast, Asian men have been often de-sexed and feminized, or hypermasculinized as martial artists or oriental villains. As many researchers have discussed (e.g. Espiritu 2000), these stereotypes of hyperfeminine Asian women and de-sexed Asian men contribute to the maintenance of conventional orders of race and gender centered on the normalcy of whiteness and the dominance of men.

Exotic and hyperfeminine images of Asian American women have long flourished in the United States, Images of Asians and Asian Americans as hyperfeminine have been popular pre-cisely because they complement social and cultural beliefs about American manhood and American family values, in which white men serve as the dominant patriarchal figures and women serve as caretakers of the family. Images of subservient Asian women were repeatedly circulated on military bases in Asian countries during World War II, the Korean War, and the Vietnam War. When a large number of Asian military brides entered the United States in the post-World War II period, interracial marriage was still banned in many states; the images served to reduce racial anxieties stemming from the large influx of Asian women and facilitated these women's assimilation. Hyperfeminine and sexual images of Asian women continue to play a critical role in the transaction of desires and fantasies in cross-border marriages (Constable 2003).

In the 1970s, the model minority stereotype took hold. Asian Americans were viewed as educated and upwardly mobile. Asian and Asian American woman, still imagined as submissive, were increasingly viewed as upwardly mobile and therefore as desirable. These women were good substitutes for white women (who were often viewed as challenging) (Koshy 2005). As a result, Asian American women emerged as exemplars of an alternative femininity which could help men regain the confidence they lost after feminism marked white femininity as more independent and masculine (Koshy 2005).

Subservient images of Asian immigrant women have also complemented America's paternalistic images of nation. That is, these women are welcomed in part because they celebrate America while condemning the patriarchal and non-democratic countries they left. Immigrant women are valued for having the courage to pursue freedom and to escape from their home country's patriarchal constraints (Berlant 1997:195). The women, with few distinctions among them with regard to whether they are "immigrants," "aliens," "minorities," "illegal," or whatever, and who want to "escape" the constraints of their patriarchal families, are seen as suitable markers of model migrant citizens who will be devoted to America (Berlant 1997). Such a gendered immigration discourse has long framed Asian female–white male sexual relationships, especially in the context of military brides who have entered the United States. Thus, the stereotypes associated with Asian women and the immigration discourse have historically served to validate Asian American female–white male couples as "acceptable" gendered unions that can sustain the traditional orders of gender, nation, and family in the United States.

Asian American–white couples

In order to understand the impact of race and gender on the dynamics of interracial relationships, I conducted interviews with 42 Asian Americans and whites who were either in interracial relationships at the time of the interview or had previously been involved in such relationships (Nemoto 2009). I explored couples' race consciousness and social receptions, racialized desires, and gender dynamics. The Asian Americans I interviewed included Chinese, Filipino, Japanese, Korean, and Vietnamese Americans. The individuals ranged in age from their early twenties to their early fifties, and all were heterosexual.

White men interviewed for the study often viewed Asian American women as ideal partners because of their racialized femininity and model minority traits. The stereotypes of Asian American women as hyperfeminine and subservient were frequent responses I received. Likewise, white women referred to Asian American men as having model minority traits or as being domineering. But there are some interesting differences among the couples consisting of an Asian American woman and a white man, relating to whether the woman was a native-born or foreign-born Asian American. Foreign-born Asian American women who lack class mobility, language skills, and a thorough knowledge of US racism and sexism were more likely to adhere to traditional gender arrangements in their dating or marriages, while second-generation Asian American women

who date white men often have more education and/or a higher socio-economic status than their white partners. The second- and higher-generation young Asian Americans saw themselves as upwardly mobile and independent, and different from stereotypical Asians. They expressed a preference for white men who possess "egalitarian" traits, which they mentioned were often lacking in Asian American men. Interestingly, many Asian American women, including young second- and higher-generation women who described themselves as being egalitarian and independent, projected highly gendered images onto white men, describing them as being protective breadwinner figures or liberators. Thus, it seems that racial and gender hierarchies have greatly influenced Asian American–white couples. But stereotypes could also be surmounted. For example, Asian American men who possess high class status could repudiate negative stereotypes by exercising power over white women.

In the following section, I discuss some of the findings of my research, with a particular focus on the ways Asian American–white couples were received by family and friends. The Asian American female–white male couples I interviewed reported little social hostility or familial opposition, especially when compared to Asian American male–white female couples; in other words, Asian American women coupled with white men seemed to be much more socially accepted than Asian American men with white women. Some men stated that having an Asian wife was not a problem because of their reputation as good wives. Gary, a 58-year-old businessman who is married to a Korean woman, said, "American men like Asian women. . . . I think there's a great acceptance of the Caucasian man marrying an Asian woman. In fact, many of my friends, non-Asian friends, actually say that they envy me because they understand that Asian women are very good wives and very nice ladies." His comment demonstrates the culturally shared notion that Asian women possess the qualities of good wives and also, therefore, reinforce men's sense of masculinity. Gary said, "I think [Asian women] respect the [traditional] values and they tend to be pretty loyal. They exhibit qualities that a lot of American women don't seem to have [such as being] family oriented. [They are] good mothers and good parents."

Some white men noted that the Asian American woman's exotic appearance and small physique is part of their attraction. Peter, a 27-year-old, said that he likes dark-skinned women, and Asian women often caught his eye because of their distinct physical features which he described as "more beautiful than those of whites." Peter associated his second-generation Chinese American girlfriend's thin body with stylish urban femininity, which he thought suited his lifestyle as a musician who performs underground electronic music. Possessing a young Asian woman was a sign of cultural hipness. Peter added, "If you are dating Asian girls, probably it is cooler than if you are dating black girls."

Some men mentioned that, even though they were attracted to Asian women, they were not attracted to other women of color. Patrick, a 28-year-old engineer, had dated a variety of Asian women whom he met in Asian countries when he traveled for work. "I kind of acquired the taste for or the inclination of liking Asian woman," he said. "Black women and Mexican women are different, too. But for some reason, I'm never attracted [to them]." In all likelihood, he has never been attracted to other women of color because his interest lies not in their color but rather in racialized images of traditional womanhood. Of his Filipino engineer wife, Patrick said, "Her nature is [to] try to take care of her husband. I don't think that most American women I've met have been that way . . ." Foreign-born Asian American women were often characterized by their white partners as being family-oriented, loyal, and caring. These characteristics apparently played a critical role in some men's attraction to them. The image of Asian women as enhancing men's masculinity bolsters their sense of themselves as authority figures and also contributes to the positive social reception of Asian and Asian American women.

In addition to the stereotype of hyperfemininity, the stereotype of the model minority also adds to the positive image of Asian American women. In my interviews, Asian American women, especially those born in America, associated being Asian with being a disciplined "model minority" and believed this is the reason why they are welcomed by whites. Victoria, a second-generation 26-year-old Chinese American medical student, pointed out that Asian American female–white male couples are extremely common. She said, "All the Asian girls I know have gone out with white guys, basically . . . because it's almost popular for white guys to go out with Asian girls." Victoria emphasized that Asian women are desirable for white men. "I know my boyfriend's parents are happy because I'm a lot different from the girls he's gone out with before . . . I don't think American girls are quite as respectful as far as how [they] treat another person's family." Victoria's comment illustrates that Asian American women are not merely associated with domestic femininity but also are exemplars of disciplined, respectable womanhood. Peter, a 27-year-old white man, said, "A lot of white women are like spoiled brats. . . . A lot of the white women I dated have had codependency issues. They were just overly demanding." Peter says his current Chinese American girlfriend is from an intact family and is professionally ambitious and tenacious, qualities that his white former girlfriends lacked. While these descriptions of model minority traits are well-meant, some of the descriptions, such as "not overly demanding," "not complaining too much," or "not sexually promiscuous," indicate that these men value a conservative, somewhat submissive image of womanhood. They apparently feel that they have more control in their intimate relationships than with white women.

While the white men I interviewed reported few negative responses from their family and friends with regard to their Asian or Asian American girlfriends, many of them did note that things would have been different if they had brought a black woman home. Peter, a 27-year-old multimedia designer, said,

"No one ever said anything about Vivian [his Asian girlfriend] . . . But had I come home with a black girlfriend, then some . . . of my uncles or somebody might have said something about not liking it." Thus, it is not that race does not matter in interracial relationships; it is just that certain racialized femininities, ones that adhere to more traditional gender roles, are more acceptable than others.

Many of the Asian American women I interviewed expressed a preference for white men over men of other ethnic and racial groups, including Asian American men. A 58-year-old first-generation Korean woman believed that American husbands treat women better than Korean husbands do. Similarly, a 38-year-old first-generation Filipina American, who is a mother of two biracial children whom she referred to as "white," talked about her childhood dream to marry a white man. White men, she believed, embody an authentic American middle-class ideal. Considering the fact that whiteness (and its associated Anglo-Saxon middle-class lifestyle) has been circulated globally as a sign of power and an object of desire (Kelsky 2001), foreign-born Asian women's preference for white men over men of other races might not be surprising.

However, most second- or higher-generation Asian American women also explicitly expressed their aversion to Asian and Asian American men, sometimes much more strongly than foreign-born Asian women did. Victoria, a 24-year-old medical school student, was adamant that she would never date anyone other than a white man. She said, "I never dated an Asian guy. . . . I think that Asian guys are not courteous to women." Grace, a 26-year-old engineer, also never dated Asian men. Grace described them as incapable of dealing with "independent women" like herself. "I am not attracted to Asian guys. . . . They are not gentlemen. . . . They are not affectionate. At least the ones I've met. I think my personality clashes with a lot of them. Because I think I'm too independent. I'm too outgoing. A lot of Asian guys like Asian women . . . Either they are dainty or they are

pretty or they are. . . . submissive . . ." Second- or third-generation Asian American women portrayed white men as being egalitarian, tall, and capable of providing them with what they deserve. Many Asian American women were particularly willing to date or marry white men because they believed these men could provide evidence that they are assimilated, authentic "Americans" who are also independent. Thus, Asian American women's valuing whiteness and white manhood has promoted a mutual attraction between them and white men, bolstering existing racial stereotypes and gender hierarchies.

In the relationships between Asian American men and white women, some of the more successful couples adhered to very traditional gender arrangements. In many of these cases, the Asian American men possessed professional jobs, class status, or career prospects. When minority men exhibit or possess class privileges, and follow the male breadwinner model, they are likely to exercise leverage and power in their relationships with white women, and possibly repudiate the negative racial stereotypes associated with them. However, many negative stereotypes of couples consisting of Asian/Asian American men and white women persist. In contrast with the social acceptance of Asian American female–white male couples, a few white women dating Asian American men reported negative reactions from their families and friends. Emily, a 38-year-old schoolteacher married to a Cambodian American man, used to invite her friends to their home, but eventually stopped. "We had made friends from work, then tried to invite them to dinner. But there's always an air of uncomfortableness that we both detect from these people." Emily has been disowned by her family members since she married her husband; he has rarely met her kin. Karen, a 20-year-old student coupled with a Chinese American man who is studying engineering, remembered her parents mentioning something about their future child. "It wasn't extremely derogatory, but I didn't really like it. They said something like, our children may have a hard time because they will be half-white, half Asian." Karen's friends also expressed concern about her boyfriend. "I said, you know, I am dating somebody and he is Asian. One of my friends made fun of it, and made an Asian joke. The other one said OK. They didn't say oh, that's great. They just said OK. One of them asked me how my parents felt about it." Tracey, a 26-year-old waitress married to a 29-year-old Japanese man, remembered her friends' comments. "They asked me if he had a bad temper or drank too much."

These experiences show that white women coupled with Asian American men encounter less social acceptance than Asian American women with white men. However, this does not mean that Asian American women do not encounter racism. In the same study, most Asian American women described individual encounters with racism, such as name-calling or being dismissed as "foreigners." But the long-popular stereotypes of subservience combined with the logic of patriarchy, in which white men are imagined as protectors and authority figures, validate Asian American female–white male couples and provide them with far more social acceptance than is granted to other types of interracial couples. As I mentioned previously, the public presence of white husbands serves as a buffer or reduces general suspicion toward these women, reducing the likelihood that they will be seen as immigrants, foreigners, or racial minorities (Nemoto 2009:71). Meanwhile, white women with Asian American men are deemed most acceptable when they follow traditional gender arrangements – and even then they might be seen as deviant because they haven't adhered to the logic of white male authority.

In this chapter, I have argued that the dominant racial and gendered ideologies embedded in images and discourses of interracial relationships make certain couples more socially acceptable than others. Even though the rise of interracial dating and marriage gives the impression that racism and sexism are in decline, our images of interracial romance continue to be constructed by traditional ideologies of race and gender. Discourses and the realities of interracial romance do not signify a public welcome for random cross-race relationships. In the case of Asian American–white couples, the high intermarriage rate of Asian American women may largely derive from the dominant stereotype of these women as hyperfeminine and subservient. This stereotype reinforces men's authority, and traditional norms of marriage and the family. These unions therefore do not contradict the dominant ideologies of whiteness, white privilege, or gender inequality. Seen this way, interracial romances may be a more exotic version of the traditional heterosexual union that sustains white privilege, male authority, and America's traditional norms of heterosexual marriage and family values.

References

Berlant, Lauren. 1997. *The Queen of America Goes to Washington City: Essays on Sex and Citizenship*. Durham, NC and London: Duke University Press.

Childs, Erica Chito. 2009. *Fade to Black and White: interracial Images in Popular Culture*. Lanham, MD: Rowman & Littlefield.

Collins, Patricia Hill. 2004. *Black Sexual Politics: African Americans, Gender, and the New Racism*. New York: Routledge.

Constable, Nicole. 2003. *Romance on a Global Stage: Pen Pals, Virtual Ethnography, and "Mail-Order" Marriage*. Berkeley: University of California Press.

Espiritu, Yen L. 2000. *Asian American Women and Men: Labor, Laws, and Love*. Walnut Creek, CA: Alta-Mira Press.

Giroux, Henry A. 2006. *The Giroux Reader*, ed. Christopher G. Robbins. Boulder, CO: Paradigm.

Kelsky, Karen. 2001. *Women on the Verge: Japanese Women, Western Dreams*. Durham, NC: Duke University Press.

Koshy, Susan. 2005. *Sexual Naturalization: Asian Americans and Miscegenation*. Stanford, CA: Stanford University Press.

Nemoto, Kumiko. 2009. *Racing Romance: Love, Power, and Desire among Asian American/White Couples*. New Brunswick, NJ and London: Rutgers University Press.

Nylund, David. 2006. "Critical Multiculturalism, Whiteness, and Social Work: Towards a More Radical View of Cultural Competence." *Journal of Progressive Human Services* 17(2): 27–42.

Perry, Pamela. 2002. *Shades of White: White Kids and Racial Identities in High School*. Durham, NC and London: Duke University Press.

Qian, Zhenchao. 2005. "Breaking the Last Taboo: Interracial Marriage in America." *Contexts* 4(4): 33–37.

Cyberrace

Lisa Nakamura

Remember *Cyber*? Surely one of the most irritating and ubiquitous prefixes of the nineties, *Cyber* quickly became attached to all kinds of products (the Sony Cybershot camera), labor styles (cybercommuting), and communicative practices (cyberspace) that have now become so normalized as already digital that the prefix has dropped out of the language. Photography, work, and social discourse no longer need be flagged as cyber since we can more or less assume that in postindustrial, informationalized societies they usually are. *Cyber* migrated widely during the nineties, but the legal scholar Jerry Kang's article "Cyber-race," which appeared in the *Harvard Law Review* in 2000, was the first to attach this prefix to race. Kang answers the question "can cyberspace change the very way that race structures our daily lives?" with an affirmative: "race and racism are already in cyberspace." He then proposes three potential "design strategies" for lawmakers to deal with the problem of race and racism in cyberspace: the abolitionist approach, in which users take advantage of the Internet's anonymity as a means of preventing racism by hiding race; the integrationist approach, in which race is made visible in online social discourse; and the most radical one, the transmutation approach. Strategies for transmuting race in cyberspace reprise some of the discourse about identity and performativity that was often associated with Judith Butler—"it seeks racial pseudonymity, or cyber-passing, in order to disrupt the very notion of racial categories. By adopting multiple racialized identities in cyberspace, identities may slowly dissolve the one-to-one relationship between identity and the physical body" (1206).

The notion that racial passing is good for you and, what's more, good for everyone else since it works to break down the rigidly essentialist notion of the body as the source and locus of racial identity legitimated a widespread practice in the pregraphic Internet period. In the days before widely supported graphic images generated on the fly using Web browsers became a common aspect of Internet use, the Internet was effectively a text-only space, and conversation by e-mail, chat, bulletin board, or MUD (multiuser dungeon—these were early social games in digital space) was the most popular way to communicate. Users' racial identities could not be seen as they interacted with others, yet as Kang rightly predicted, technological innovations and user desire would change that, and "it [would] become increasingly difficult to delay the disclosure of race" (1203). Improvements in interfaces, video devices, and bandwidth have made us more visual social actors; Kang claims, "as we move from communications that are text-only to text-plus, avatars will become more popular," and they have (1151). The wide range of imaging practices available to users such as profile photographs on social-network sites like *Facebook* and graphic avatars created by using the extremely popular Simpsons avatar-building engine guarantee that racial identity is now often visually signified as part of users' self-presentational practices. Yet while it lasted, the pregraphic Internet overlapped with the rise of digital utopianism, the beginnings of a Clinton-led neoliberal political dynasty in the United States, and a concomitant strategy of addressing racial problems by refusing to see race—Kang's abolitionist strategy writ large, which Patricia Williams identifies as the "colorblind" approach. At the same time, in the academy theories of social constructionism strongly challenged and indeed displaced essentialist understandings of race by asserting that race is an effect of social performance, thus empowering the individual agent to "jam" race through playful acts of recombining, confounding, and cutting and pasting existing identity markers. This a form of pastiche characteristic of "participatory media" such as mashups, animutations, and other contemporary forms of Web-user production, practices that fall under the umbrella term *Web 2.0*.

Indeed, the notion of identity as variable, modular, and granular, resembling most closely a program in perpetual beta release rather than a stable object, recalls the logic of new media as defined by Lev Manovich and others. As Manovich puts it, "new media technology acts as the perfect realization of the utopia of an ideal society composed of unique individuals" because the variability of a new-media object guarantees that every user will generate and receive her or his own version of it. New media appeals to us so powerfully partly because it satisfies our needs in post-industrial society to "construct [our] own custom lifestyle from a large (but not infinite) number of choices" (42). Manovich questions this rosy picture of new media as infinite choice by calling attention to the bound quality of choice in digital interactive environments, and Jennifer Gonzalez extends this notion by questioning the nature of the objects themselves. If identity construction and performance in digital space is a process of selection and recombination much like shopping, another privileged activity of the nineties, what types of objects are on offer, what price is paid, who pays, who labors, and who profits? Gonzalez calls out neoliberal digital utopians by characterizing bodies as an infinitely modifiable assemblage defined by "consumption, not opposition" (48). The illusion of diversity through digitally enabled racial passing and recombination produces a false feeling of diversity and tolerance born of entitlement:

> What this creation of this appended subject presupposes is the possibility of a new cosmopolitanism constituting all the necessary requirements for a global citizen who speaks multiple languages, inhabits multiple cultures, wears whatever skin color or body part desired, elaborates a language of romantic union with technology or nature, and moves easily between positions of identification with movie stars, action heroes, and other ethnicities of races.
>
> (48)

If cyberrace was distinguished from "real" race by its anonymity, composability, variability, and modularity, the task of debunking it as inherently liberatory was linked to critiquing new-media utopianism generally. It was necessary for new media to be discussed in a more critical way, in the light of structural constraint, industrial imperatives, and global inequality, for race to be viewed as a salient category in what was then known as cyberspace. This was an uphill battle in the nineties, however, because the fetish of interactivity had yet to be exposed either as a marketing strategy or as a racial ideology.

The fetish of interactivity is alive and well—my students frequently claim that "the world is at their fingertips" when they use the Internet, a formulation that recalls television's vast claims to "give us ten minutes, and we'll give you the world"—but it was even more alive and well ten years ago. The ability to manipulate the "look and feel" of race by online role-playing, digital gaming, and other forms of digital-media use encouraged and fed the desire for control over self-construction and self-representation. This was quite an empowering ideology, and scholars such as Sherry Turkle, in her influential 1995 *Life on the Screen: Identity in the Age of the Internet*, claimed that the cyberspace was postmodern because it permitted unprecedented fluidity and composable identities. (Edward Castronova makes similar claims for MMORPGs—massively multiplayer online role-playing games—as a radically level playing field and thus as radically democratic.) Turkle's psychoanalytic approach took identity play extremely seriously, as identity work: this first wave of theoretical writing confirming the formative and subversive influence of online subjectivity, which included Julian Dibbell's important "A Rape in Cyberspace" article, attempted to persuade us that virtual life and gender were real, not a difficult feat since many of us were already convinced. Yet this brought up a vexing question—if life online is real, are race and racism online real too?

In 1995 I published an article entitled "Race in/for Cyberspace: Identity Tourism and Racial Passing on the Internet" that discussed cross-racial role-playing and passing in MUDs as a form of identity tourism. Drawing on Edward Said's work on tourism, racial passing, and travel in the imperial context, in *Cybertypes* I discussed how MUD users who created orientalist avatars such as samurai and geisha were able to temporarily "appropriate an Asian racial identity without any of the risks associated with being a racial minority in real life" and how online communities often punished users who wished to discuss race and racism (40). Identity tourism resembled off-line tourism because it gave users a false notion of cultural and racial understanding based on an episodic, highly mediated experience of travel, an experience rhetorically linked with digital technology use as the "information superhighway" and the "cyberfrontier," as well as with the burgeoning travel industry.[1] Community hostility toward discussions of race and racism in LambdaMOO reflected the color-blind attitude held about race that characterized nineties' neoliberalism, where neither asking nor telling was encouraged. Race in virtual space was "on you" in more than one sense: when users "wore" race in the form of a racialized avatar or performed it as racialized speech or conveyed it by sharing their "performance of tastes (favorite music, books, film, etc)," or "taste fabric," this form of display was viewed as a personal decision, an exercise of individual choice. It was also "on you" because users were considered to be solely responsible for any negative consequences—such as racism.[2]

Identity tourism let users "wear" racially stereotyped avatars without feeling racist, yet it also blamed users who revealed their real races and were victims of racism online. The logic of identity tourism figured race as modular, ideally mobile, recreational, and interactive in ways that were good for you—part of the transmutation strategy with the supposed potential to "break" race as a concept and break its hold on our imaginations and bodies. However, the narrow range of racialized performance visibly enacted in many online social spaces—gangstas, samurai, geisha, Latin lovers and hot Latin mamas—attested to the problem with seeing digital interactivity as infinite rather than bounded. "The illusory nature of choice in many interactive situations" contributed toward the conviction that the Internet was a postracial space because it was possible to "choose" a race as an identity tourist, as well as to withhold, or "cover," racial identity; however, these choices were preconstituted by existing media texts (Patterson 117). Cultural images of race—our database of bodies, discourses, behaviors, and images—resemble all database-driven new-media objects in that they are experienced by users as much more profuse and open than they really are. As Zabet Patterson writes, "we often find this compensatory rhetoric and narrative of free choice, a cornerstone of American cultural ideology, inhabiting precisely those situations that, on a basic structural level, admit of little or no choice at all" (116). The limited interactivity available to identity tourists online promoted a comforting amnesia in regard to the lack of choice racial minorities faced in everyday life.

In 2001 Tiziana Terranova advocated a turn toward the political economy of digital culture and away from reveries of idealized Internet digital identities ("Free Labor"). Though race is not discussed overtly in her analysis, this turn is useful to new-media scholars because it enables a grounded discussion of race, power, and labor in digital culture. If post-racial cosmopolitans refused to acknowledge the ways that unequal access, limited forms of representation in digital culture, and images of race under globalization were shaping cyberrace, it could not be denied that labor in postindustrial societies is racialized and gendered. She urged us to examine how the "outernet"—the network of social, cultural and economic relationships which criss-crosses and exceeds the Internet— surrounds and connects the latter to larger flows of labour, culture and power. It is fundamental to move beyond the notion that cyberspace is about escaping reality in order to understand how the reality of the Internet is deeply connected to the development of late postindustrial societies as a whole.

(*Network Culture* 75)

Seeing the Internet as a virtual space that was like real life while being separate from it—a second life—figured it as a place to escape from reality, especially racial realities. Several new-media scholars studying race and gender before 2002 challenged this state of exemption. In 1996 Cameron Bailey wrote:

Faced with the delirious prospect of leaving their bodies behind for the cool swoon of digital communication, many leading theorists of cyberspace have addressed the philosophical implications of a new technology by retreating to old ground. In a landscape of contemporary cultural criticism where the discourses of race, gender, class, and sexuality have often led to great leaps in understanding—where, in fact, they have been so thoroughly used as to become a mantra—these interpretive tools have come curiously late to the debate around cyberspace. (334)

In the nineties and after, the Internet was pitched as a curative to racism, which was always framed as a problem of too much visibility by the telecommunications and computing industries and scholars alike, since the Internet permitted users to hide their race or pass as a different one. *Cyberrace* was thus deemed an oxymoron at that time, a useful strategy for a computer industry and for a political regime that was struggling to get users to invest in, purchase, and believe in this technology. Updating the Internet's image as a clubhouse for hobbyists and geeks involved

representing it as a solution to especially knotty social problems like racism. As Alondra Nelson wrote in 2002,

Public discourse about race and technology, led by advertisers (and aided and abetted by cybertheorists), was preoccupied with the imagined new social arrangements that might be made possible by technological advance. Advertisers relied on a shared message about race and ethnicity—the disappearance of the DuBoisian "color line"—to promote their products. (5)

As Nelson notes, this digital racial-abolitionist strategy was waged on two fronts—the commercial and the academic. Much of the important critical scholarship on race and new media noted this alliance and traced its trajectory through close readings of technology-industry texts such as advertisements.

Advertisements, films, novels, and the Internet itself produced a rich stream of content during this period that depicted racialized bodies in exotic locales juxtaposed with digital technologies. This advertising blitz was a result of the "thriving and competitive market for high-speed nationwide computer networking services" that quickly developed in the early nineties (Abbate 197). In 1995 the Internet's backbone became a series of networks run by private companies (Shah and Kesan). IBM, Cisco, MCI, Worldcom, and others produced almost only this type of image, but it was a staple as well in cyberpunk science-fiction film, television, and literature. Wendy Chun's, Tom Foster's, and Alondra Nelson's critiques of postracial utopianism analyze digital-networking advertisements and cyberpunk films and fiction and explain why race and cultural difference are continually invoked in them. Chun's adept unpacking of digital racialization in telecommunications-company commercials from the nineties such as MCI's "anthem" identifies how a

[r]ewriting of the Internet as emancipatory, as "freeing" oneself from one's body, also naturalizes racism. The logic framing

MCI's commercial reduces to what they can't see, can't hurt you. Since race, gender, age, and infirmities are only skin-deep (or so this logic goes), moving to a text-based medium makes them—and thus the discrimination that stems from them—disappear. (132)

This racial-abolitionist rhetoric advocated technologically enabled disembodiment as a solution to social problems; Foster's cogent critique of this strategy in *The Souls of Cyberfolk: Posthumanism as Vernacular Theory* discusses this discourse's roots in cyberpunk science fiction such as William Gibson's *Neuromancer*. Simply put, race and racism don't disappear when bodies become virtual or electronically mediated. In his discussion of the Deathlok comic-book series, he writes, "neither becoming a cyborg nor accessing cyberspace is conceptualized as escaping the body, but rather in terms of a more complex relationship that is both productive and problematic" (156).

Critical race theory and political-economic approaches caught up to the Internet around the turn of the century, at a time when it was particularly ready to be caught—shortly after the stock-market crash of 2001 and right around the time when the term *cyber* started to vanish. It was only after the digital bloom was off the dot-com rose that it became possible to discuss cyberspace as anything other than a site of exception from identity, especially racial identity. Several collections such as *Race in Cyberspace* (Kolko, Nakamura, and Rodman), *Technicolor: Race, Technology, and Everyday Life* (Nelson, Tu, and Hines), *Asian America.Net: Ethnicity, Nationalism, and Cyberspace* (Lee and Wong), and *Learning Race and Ethnicity: Youth and Digital Media* (Everett) have been published since 2000, and, just as important, general new-media and cyberculture anthologies started to include chapters on race, such as David Trend's widely taught *Reading Digital Culture;* David Bell and Barbara M. Kennedy's *Cybercultures Reader,* now in its second edition; *Handbook of Computer Game Studies* (Raessens and Goldstein); Chun and Thomas Keenan's

New Media, Old Media, as did popular-culture anthologies such as *Popular Culture: A Reader* (Guins and Cruz) and *The Visual Culture Reader* (Mirzoeff). Digital media, an area of study that an entire generation of undergraduate students experienced as the last couple of weeks of their courses on writing, media literacy, television and film, and literature, not only came to the fore as a discipline that merited its own courses but also began to integrate discussions of racial identity in digital media and online social space.[3] The publication of several monographs signaled the growth of the field—my *Cybertypes: Race, Ethnicity, and Identity on the Internet* was published in 2002, Chun's *Control and Freedom* and Foster's *The Souls of Cyberfolk* in 2005, Adam Banks's *Race, Rhetoric, and Technology* in 2006, Christopher McGahan's *Racing Cybercultures* and my *Digitizing Race: Visual Cultures of the Internet* in 2007–08.

The "larger flows of labour, culture and power" that surround and shape digital media travel along unevenly distributed racial, gendered, and class channels (Terranova, *Network Culture* 75). As Caren Kaplan wrote in *PMLA* in 2002: "Questions about divisions of labor cannot be left out of an inquiry into representational practices in information and communication technologies. . . . [T]here is no discussion of the people who make the devices that are used to achieve the dream of subjectivity" (40).

Coco Fusco, Donna Haraway, Toby Miller, and Kaplan all urge us toward a concern with labor and embodiment, one less about fleeing, refashioning, and augmenting bodies with technology and more about viewing bodies within technophilic, informationalized societies—and noting the costs paid by racialized bodies. In contrast with the Internet's early claims to transform and eliminate both race and labor, digital-communication technologies today racialize labor, employing "virtual migrants" who perform tasks such as help-line staffing, online gamers who sell their virtual gold and leveled-up avatars to busy Americans and Europeans to use in MMORPGs, and a class of truly miserable workers who "pick away without protection at discarded

First World computers full of leaded glass to find precious metals" (Miller 9). Significantly, these workers are primarily Asian, a phenomenon that has led to robust anti-Asian racism in MMORPGs such as World of Warcraft (WoW), where "gold farmers" are despised and abused as their services are used promiscuously among its ten million players. Most players condemn gold selling as the rankest form of cheating yet purchase virtual gold in such quantity that they have turned the secondary market in virtual property into a massively profitable industry, one that is predicted to outstrip the primary digital-games market in the years to come.[4] The anti-Chinese gold-farmer media produced by WoW players and distributed through *Warcraftmovies.com* and *YouTube* is especially salient in the United States context because it echoes anti-immigration discourse. The racialization of this type of digital labor as Asian, abject, and despised bears comparison with the ways the other forms of racialized labor are controlled and managed.

Around 2005 the Internet entered a new industrial, historical, and cultural period: Web 2.0.[5] The software publisher Tim O'Reilly first circulated this term in his article "What Is Web 2.0: Design Patterns and Business Models for the Next Generation of Software." The article claims that the Web as we use it today is a much more participatory and potentially profitable medium than it was before 2005, and indeed there has been a renewed interest in and faith in the Web as a renascent source of capital, as well as a new utopianism regarding user interactivity. Of course in semantic terms, today's 2.0 is tomorrow's cyber, but it is worth unpacking it to see what kind of ideological baggage it has. Web 1.0, or "cyber" space, conceptualized the Internet as an alternative reality, a different place in which one could exercise agency and live out fantasies of control. This control extended to all aspects of personal identity, including and especially race. Web 2.0 comes with a different imaginary. While it neither posits a postracial utopia based on racial abolitionism online nor envisions racialized others and primitives as signs of cosmopoli-

tan technofetishism, it does make claims to harness collective intelligence by allowing everyone to participate in a more or less equal fashion. These claims are implicitly postracial, and many contemporary advertisements for telecommunications hardware and software visually address the stubborn problem of digital inequality by showing "global kids" broadcasting video of themselves on the Internet in the most meaningful way possible—to be famous.

Cisco's "Human Network" ad campaign, running since 2007, figures racialized performance and publicity through digital video broadcasting as both the ends and the means to a radical Web 2.0-inflected democracy. Its thirty-second video spot "Fame" depicts children of color in the United States and "global" children broadcasting digital video of themselves to ubiquitous digital screens viewed by their parents, red-robed monks in Tibet, other children around the world, and an idealized global public. In a reprise of famous viral performance videos such as the Chinese boys who lip-synched to the Backstreet Boys' "I Want It That Way," the "Human Network" Web site depicts an African American boy popping and locking for his father's cellphone camera (fig. 6.1), a Latina girl flamenco dancing, a Russian man performing a "Russian" dance while his PC's camera captures the performance (fig. 6.2), buskers in Europe playing violins, and an Asian woman in a kimono dancing with a fan, with the subtitle "one dance moves and grooves the world."[6] Uncannily, one of these video ads is entitled "Anthem," harking back to the MCI ad from the nineties and conveying a similar message of digital-cultural triumphalism with a 2.0 twist: it reads "welcome to the network where anyone can be famous—welcome to the human network." Yet while, as Chun notes, the original MCI-anthem ad touted cyberspace's ability to hide users' bodies and races, Cisco's "Anthem" 2.0 works differently, by selling the network as a site of racialized performance and visibility. The site's users are also invited to contribute content in the form of stories, which are incorporated into the site in the true spirit of user-generated

Figure 6.1

Figure 6.2

content. The work of racialization, or making race through digital means, is passed on and eagerly accepted by the children in these ads, just as the logic of Web 2.0 passes on and accepts all kinds of software and content-development work. The performance of stylized images of race and ethnicity is industriously undertaken by children of color in the Cisco "Human Network" campaign and is accepted as an inevitable and natural part both of the compulsory immaterial labor of becoming "famous" and of being seen on the multiple mediated screens embedded in everyday life—on cellphones; PDAs; PCs; televisions; and, in the "Myles" commercial, on the megascreens on tall buildings in Times Square. This is a privilege figured as an entitlement of digital citizens and as a justification for our continuing faith in the Web—so long as those citizens are able to labor properly, performing race in ways that will appeal to other users.

As Terranova notes in her pre-Web 2.0 article "Free Labor," "The Internet does not automatically turn every user into an active producer, and every worker into a creative subject" (34). The question of what constitutes a creative subject in our current digital culture is racialized in terms of Web 2.0 entrepreneurship, the grueling immaterial labor of "making yourself." Tila Tequila, the Vietnamese American star of the 2007 VH1 reality television program *A Shot at Love with Tila Tequila*, is most likely the first Internet star, for the "signal reason for [her] breakout success may also be the basis for Ms. Tequila's unconventional fame, her boast that she has 1,771,920 MySpace friends" (Trebay). Tequila's immense popularity on a widely used social-network site (she has 2,940,387 friends as of 19 March 2008 on *MySpace*—a number that has grown since Guy Trebay wrote his article, partly because of the new audience generated by A *Shot at Love*) was leveraged on "the classic show-business redemption narrative" but, more important, also on constant claims of possessive individualism and rehabilitation through digital racial self-fashioning. Tequila's profile is, like any Web 2.0 object, in perpetual beta release. It is a valuable new-media object because it employs the labor of her "friends," using the posts both as a sounding board for Tequila and as unique content, and it capitalizes on her own racial and sexual ambiguity. The profile captures the sense of liveness characteristic of digital media that has migrated across so many other genres and platforms; it maps the development of Tequila's "deeply disoriented" identity growing up in a Houston housing project after emigrating from Singapore (Trebay). In an interview with *Car Tuner Magazine*, she explains, "I was really confused then, because at first I thought I was black, then I thought I was Hispanic and joined a cholo gang" (qtd. in Trebay).

Though Tequila's story has been read as a symptom of a radical change in the nature of media celebrity—as Trebay puts it, "a shift from top-down manufactured celebrity to a kind of lateral, hyper-democratic celebrity"—Tequila emphasizes her own digital labor in the manufacture of her celebrity on *MySpace*, a celebrity that is racialized as diasporic and polysexual. Tequila depicts herself as a bisexual Asian woman fleeing religious repression, poverty, and urban violence—a modern day Horatio Alger in a G-string—and her constant references to her "fans" on *MySpace* as the source of her visibility and fame highlight the ways in which she needs to construct herself as "user generated" as well as self-made. Clearly Tequila's *MySpace* profile exemplifies what Celine Parreñas Shimizu terms the "hypersexuality of race"—it describes an Asian woman who will "friend" anyone and everyone, and who is endlessly responsive, invoking Asian American porn megastars such as Annabel Chong. Like other Asian female stars such as Anna May Wong, Nancy Kwan, and Lucy Liu before her, whose "hypersexuality is essentialized to their race and gender ontology and is constructed in direct relation to the innocence and moral superiority of white women" (Shimizu 62), Tequila is unfavorably compared to Paris Hilton by Trebay. Tequila's purported lack of talent is articulated to her racialized hypersexuality, digital promiscuity, and racio-sexual ambivalence.

Tequila's Web 2.0 narrative repeats the message of the Cisco "Human Network" campaign—digital fame accrues to racialized performance. Instead of "routing around" race, Web 2.0 creates Race 2.0 (Silver 138). Tequila and Cisco's human network demonstrate that while Race 1.0 was understood as socially constructed, a process that at least acknowledges that race and gender are historical formations, Race 2.0 is user-generated. Once again race is "on *us*," as Web 2.0 rhetoric positions us all as entrepreneurial content creators. The Internet's resurgence and rebranding as Web 2.0 incessantly recruits its users to generate content in the form of profiles, avatars, favorites, comments, pictures, wiki postings, and blog entries. Cyberrace has gone the way of the Cybershot, cybercommuting, and cyberspace, and for much the same reason: racialization has become a digital process, just as

visual-imaging practices, labor, and social discourse have. The process of racialization continues on both the Internet and its outernet, as the "dirty work" of virtual labor continues to get distributed along racial lines.

Works Cited

Abbate, Janet. *Inventing the Internet.* Cambridge: MIT P, 1999.

Aneesh, A. *Virtual Migration: The Programming of Globalization.* Durham: Duke UP, 2006.

Bailey, Cameron. "Virtual Skin: Articulating Race in Cyberspace." Trend 334–46.

Banks, Adam J. *Race, Rhetoric, and Technology: Searching for Higher Ground.* NCTE-LEA Research Ser. in Literacy and Composition. Mahwah: Erlbaum; Urbana: Natl. Council of Teachers of English, 2006.

Bell, David, and Barbara M. Kennedy, eds. *The Cybercultures Reader.* 2nd ed. London: Routledge, 2007.

Boler, Megan. "Hypes, Hopes, and Actualities: New Digital Cartesianism and Bodies in Cyberspace." *New Media and Society* 9.1 (2007): 139–68.

Castronova, Edward. *Synthetic Worlds: The Business of Culture and of Online Games.* Chicago: U of Chicago P, 2005.

Chun, Wendy. *Control and Freedom: Power and Paranoia in the Age of Fiber Optics.* Cambridge: MIT P, 2005.

Chun, Wendy Hui Kyong, and Thomas Keenan. *New Media, Old Media: A History and Theory Reader.* New York: Routledge, 2006.

Cisco Systems, Inc. "The Human Network." *Cisco.* 21 May 2008 <http://www.cisco.com/web/about/humannetwork/>.

Consalvo, Mia. *Cheating: Gaining Advantage in Videogames.* Cambridge: MIT P, 2007.

Dibbell, Julian. "A Rape in Cyberspace." *Scribble, Scribble, Scribble: Selected Texts, Published and Unpublished.* 23 Dec. 1993. 11 June 2008 <http://www.juliandibbell.com/texts/bungle_vv.html>.

Ellison, Nicole, and Danah Boyd. "Social Network Sites: Definition, History, and Scholarship." *Journal of Computer Mediated Communication* 13.1 (2007). 11 June 2008 <http://jcmc.indiana.edu/vol13/issue1>.

Everett, Anna. *Learning Race and Ethnicity: Youth and Digital Media.* John D. and Catherine T. Macarthur Foundation Ser. on Digital Media and Learning. Cambridge: MIT P, 2007.

Foster, Tom. *The Souls of Cyberfolk: Posthumanism as Vernacular Theory.* Minneapolis: U of Minnesota P, 2005.

Fusco, Coco. The Bodies That Were Not Ours *and Other Writings.* London: Routledge, in collaboration with inIVA, Inst, of Intl. Visual Arts, 2001.

Galloway, Alexander. "Starcraft; or, Balance." *Grey Room* (2007): 86–107.

Gonzalez, Jennifer. "The Appended Subject: Race and Identity as Digital Assemblage." Kolko, Nakamura, and Rodman 27–50.

Guins, Raiford, and Omayra Zaragoza Cruz. *Popular Culture: A Reader.* London: Sage, 2005.

Haraway, Donna. *Simians, Cyborgs, and Women: The Reinvention of Nature.* London: Routledge, 1991.

Kang, Jerry. "Cyber-race." *Harvard Law Review* 113 (2000): 1130–208.

Kaplan, Caren. "Transporting the Subject: Technologies of Mobility and Location in an Era of Globalization." *PMLA* 117 (2002): 32–42.

Kolko, Beth E., Lisa Nakamura, and Gilbert B. Rodman. *Race in Cyberspace.* New York: Routledge, 2000.

Lee, Rachel C., and Sau-ling Cynthia Wong. *Asian America.Net: Ethnicity, Nationalism, and Cyberspace.* New York: Routledge, 2003.

Lovink, Geert. *Zero Comments: Blogging and Critical Internet Culture.* New York: Routledge, 2007.

Manovich, Lev. *The Language of New Media.* Cambridge: MIT P, 2001.

McGahan, Christopher. *Racing Cybercultures: Minoritarian Art and Cultural Politics on the Internet.* Routledge Studies in New Media and Cyberculture. New York: Routledge, 2007.

Miller, Toby. "Gaming for Beginners." *Games and Culture* 1.1 (2006): 5–12.

Mirzoeff, Nicholas. *The Visual Culture Reader.* 2nd ed. London: Routledge, 2002.

Nakamura, Lisa. *Cybertypes: Race, Ethnicity, and Identity on the Internet.* New York: Routledge, 2002.

———. *Digitizing Race: Visual Cultures of the Internet.* Minneapolis: U of Minnesota P, 2007.

———. "Race in/for Cyberspace: Identity Tourism and Racial Passing on the Internet." *Works and Days* 13.1-2 (1995): 181–93.

Nelson, Alondra. "Introduction: Future Texts." *Social Text* 20.2 (2002): 1–15.

Nelson, Alondra, and Tuy Tu, with Alicia Hines. *Technicolor: Race, Technology, and Everyday Life.* New York: New York UP, 2001.

O'Reilly, Tim. "What Is Web 2.0: Design Patterns and Business Models for the Next Generation of Software." *O'Reilly.* 30 Sept. 2005. 1 May 2008 <http://oreillynet.com/pub/a/oreilly/tim/news/2005/09/30/what-is-web-20.html>.

Patterson, Zabet. "Going On-line: Consuming Pornography in the Digital Era." *Porn Studies.* Ed. Linda Williams. Durham: Duke UP, 2004.105–23.

Raessens, Joost, and Jeffrey H. Goldstein. *Handbook of Computer Game Studies.* Cambridge: MIT P, 2005.

Shah, Rajiv C., and Jay P. Kesan. "The Privatization of the Internet's Backbone Network." *Journal of Broadcasting and Electronic Media* 51.1 (2007): 93–109.

Shimizu, Celine Parreñas. *The Hypersexuality of Race: Performing Asian/American Women on Screen and Scene.* Durham: Duke UP, 2007.

Silver, David. "Margins in the Wires: Looking for Race, Gender, and Sexuality in the Blacksburg Electronic Village." Kolko, Nakamura, and Rodman 133–50.

Terranova, Tiziana. "Free Labor: Producing Culture for the Digital Economy." *Social Text* 18.2 (2000): 33–58.

——. *Network Culture: Politics for the Information Age*. London: Pluto, 2007.

Trebay, Guy. "She's Famous (and So Can You)." *New York Times* 28 Oct. 2007. 5 June 2008 <http://www.nytimes.com>.

Trend, David. *Reading Digital Culture*. London: Blackwell, 2001.

Turkle, Sherry. *Life on the Screen: Identity in the Age of the Internet*. New York: Simon, 1995.

Williams, Patricia. *Seeing a Colorblind Future: The Paradox of Race*. New York: Noonday, 1997.

Notes

1 In her analysis of cyberspace's advertising discourse, Megan Boler describes this false sense of cultural understanding as "'drive-by difference' [that] presents difference and the other as something that can be 'safely' met or experienced—at a distance" (146).

2 In their study of friend connections in social-network sites, Liu, Maes, and Davenport formulated the term "taste fabric" to describe users' creation of alternative networks for community formation (qtd. in Ellison and Boyd).

3 See Boler; Galloway for two excellent examples of new-media critique that incorporate critical race theory.

4 "The International Game Exchange states that the '2005 marketplace for virtual assets in MMOG's is approaching 900 million,' and that 'some experts believe that the market for virtual assets will overcome the primary market—projected to reach 7 billion by 2009—within the next few years'" (Consalvo 182).

5 Lovink writes that "by 2005, the Internet had recovered from the dot-com crash and, in line with the global economic figures, reincarnated as Web 2.0" (ix).

6 The "Chinese Backstreet Boys" have been viewed over 6 million times on *YouTube* as of 26 March 2008. When a user types in "Backstreet Boys" as a search query on this site, the Chinese video for "That Way" comes in as number 7, ahead of some of the "official" Backstreet Boys content.

DIY Fashion and Going *Bust*
Wearing Feminist Politics in the Twenty-First Century
Jo Reger

She stands on the street posing for the Fashion Nation feature in *Bust,* a magazine geared toward young contemporary feminists. Her hair is streaked multiple colors and worn in a ponytail. Her homemade green dress has an overlay of dollar-bill printed material. On her feet are Converse tennis shoes and around her neck is a necklace made of brass knuckles. From her ears hang white plastic pistol earrings.[1]

Longtime feminist activist Letty Cottin Pogrebin addressed young feminists at the 2002 Veteran Feminists of America conference by saying, "Being able to bare your midriff . . . is fine as an expression, but it doesn't mean things are going to change."[2] Feminist views on fashion range from adopting dominant dress codes as a political tactic, to disavowing fashion as oppressive and patriarchal, to seeing fashion as something that can be selectively incorporated and empowering.[3] In this chapter, I discuss how contemporary feminists embrace and reclaim aspects of femininity and sexuality as a form of empowerment.[4] To explore the idea of fashion and feminism, I draw on three theoretical frameworks and related key concepts: fashion theory and the concept of oppositional dress, feminist theory and the embodiment of the political, and tactical repertoires as articulated by social movement theorists. Using a content analysis of *Bust* magazine, I argue that the contemporary feminists featured in *Bust* magazine are creating and embracing an oppositional fashion and reclaim femininity as empowering.

Bust runs a reoccurring section on fashion and carries a variety of articles and advertisements related to clothing, jewelry, and general issues of style.[5] I selected the magazine because of its visibility within feminist networks and its attention to fashion and dress. By adopting a style that resists mainstream consumer culture, privileges individuality, and incorporates sexuality, women profiled in *Bust* make dress and appearance a form of political resistance. However, this resistance through fashion is made problematic with the commodification of style and the perception (among some) that dress is an inadequate (and therefore controversial) form of feminist activism. I first discuss how various theories address contemporary feminist appearance and beauty norms, and then examine the relationship between feminism and fashion.

Social Movements, Protest, and Fashion

Social movements at their core are oppositional in nature, and social movement actors are seen as engaging in forms of resistance for the sake of social change. Social movement scholars have struggled to define what qualifies as a social protest.[6] Some argue that opposition to the state is what matters,[7] while others propose that changing participant identities and culture, and state policies are desired outcomes.[8] Nancy Whittier argues that political activism is legitimated on multiple levels because inequality operates at the levels of individual subjectivity, culture, and policy.[9]

Drawing on Whittier's multilevel analysis, I argue that dress as a form of political protest blends individual subjectivity and culture by signifying one's membership in a group or subculture.[10] In fact, "dress is a subculture's most powerful means of communication."[11] The importance of community building through oppositional dress has been documented in both social movement and fashion studies. Marginalized groups in society such as black Americans, members of techno culture, and particularly youth use dress as a way to "make the community stronger, thus empowering its members."[12] For example, gays and lesbians wear rainbow-colored clothing and jewelry, black triangles, or equal signs (=) as a way of signifying that they belong to a LGBTQ "family" or are "in the know."[13] Yet by these examples, if dress is clearly such an important political component of oppositional cultures and social movements, then why hasn't it been taken more seriously?

One reason is that fashion is traditionally linked to the feminine as a pursuit that engages mostly women, where "the feminine" is devalued or easily dismissed.[14] Samantha Holland argues that fashion is seen as frivolous and anti-intellectual, and historically women's dress was seen as a form of wasteful consumption.[15] Despite the view of fashion as inconsequential, dress (defined as modifications to the body), has embedded in it signifiers of power and resistance.[16] One of the most powerful ways to see the importance of dress is through the construction of anti-fashion or oppositional dress. Oppositional dress takes on mainstream society by rejecting, parodying, satirizing, or neglecting contemporary appearance norms.[17] Reinventing or creating an oppositional style has the ability to challenge all sorts of societal norms including those of propriety, class position, sexuality, racial-ethnic, and economic status. In particular, oppositional dress can challenge gender norms, both feminine and masculine. In this chapter, I focus on how feminist dress reclaims and reinvents norms of femininity.

Feminism, Femininity, and the Politics of Fashion

Many feminist scholars are concerned that traditional and often corporate-driven beauty norms disempower women by sapping their energy, time, and money. While women can gain some limited hedonic power through dress,[18] Holland's study of women and dress found many respondents concluded that to be "traditionally attractive you have to be malleable and not independent."[19] Some feminist critiques of fashion view feminine dress as primarily a form of enslavement, displaying women's bodies for a male gaze and giving them a false sense of power.[20] Part of this sense of enslavement is the idea that women are forced by social dictates to adopt certain fashions.[21] For instance, Adrienne Rich argues high heels and feminine dress are in the same categories as purdah, rape, veiling, and foot binding.[22] This perspective was reflected in the 1968 Miss America pageant protest by feminists who threw objects of female "oppression" such as high heels, bras, and girdles into a "freedom trash can."

Many of the debates within the women's movement focused on notions of political efficacy. Scholars document how more liberal feminists, represented by such women as Betty Friedan, clashed with younger or more radical feminists over the issue of appearance in the 1960s and 1970s.[23] Radical feminists often adopted a style that included jeans, loose shirts, no bras, and no makeup. This "natural" style was based on the political ideology that women were beautiful without unnecessary endeavors or patriarchal adornment. Other feminists believed this political fashion countered the goals of the movement and described it as "scruffy," wondering why women would go to lengths to make themselves ugly.[24] For feminists like Friedan, presenting oneself fashionably and attractively was a tactic reflecting the belief that the women's movement fit within dominant mainstream society. The liberal feminist goal was for women to align with cultural norms of feminine dress, (i.e., pumps, pantyhose, and suits) as a way to fit into and make change within institutions.

As the media picked up on the radical feminists' politicized appearance, the idea of a feminist uniform became a part of the popular culture. Fashion scholar Kate McCarthy describes how women coming into feminism in the 1960s dealt with the matter of appearance:

One approach to this problem [the critique of fashion by feminists], of course, is to empower women to quit making such inscriptions on their bodies. Those of us who grew into feminism in the 1970s are familiar with this effort, often caricatured as mandates, to disavow lipstick, shaving, and ideally male sexual partners.[25]

While some followed those mandates, radical feminist dress was disavowed by other feminists who felt it sent the wrong message, and by the larger public who saw radical style as evidence of the "man-hating" deviant identities of all feminists. Despite these divisions, all feminists were stereotyped as disavowing or ignoring fashion. This led *New York Times* fashion writer Ingrid Sischy to conclude that fashion will continue outside of feminism because feminists' views are "knee jerk and programmatic."[26]

Contemporary feminists continue this history of politicizing fashion. In their article, "Feminism and Femininity: Or How We Learned to Stop Worrying and Love the Thong," authors Jennifer Baumgardner and Amy Richards argue that girlie culture, one aspect of twenty-first century feminism, reclaims what past periods of (primarily radical) feminism have discarded. Girlie culture revalues femininity and embraces "girlieness as well as power."[27] Baumgardner and Richards explain that "Girlies' motivations are along the same lines of gay men in Chelsea calling each other 'queer' or black men and women using the term 'nigga.'"[28] Contemporary feminists engage in the politics of fashion through the concept of embodied politics as a creative act of resistance to disrupt power.[29] Here the female body is a site of both oppression and resistance "where cultural expectations about gender are rehearsed but also, at least, potentially, manipulated and resisted."[30] One form of embodied resistance is a process of reclaiming what mainstream culture has defined as femininity and feminine sexuality, an act that Judith Taylor describes as taking ownership of group stereotypes rather than

simply conforming to them.[31] The body can therefore become a site of resisting cultural norms by reclaiming femininity through fashion. This differs from simply following cultural norms for acceptance and instead is the intentional creation and reaffirmation of femininity through dress. These politicized statements not only serve to take back the feminine in a reinvented and empowered manner, but can also serve to establish membership in a feminist community. Therefore, the relationship between fashion and femininity makes dress and appearance grounds for feminist ideology and activism.

Oppositional Feminist Fashion

So what is political about wearing a spandex dress made out of dollar-bill printed fabric, Converse tennis shoes, a necklace made of brass knuckles, and white pistol-shaped earrings? The outfit is a DIY (Do It Yourself) creation a homemade dress and jewelry. At the same time this outfit refutes beauty norms (Converse tennis shoes versus high heels) and subverts consumer culture (using fabric with a dollar-bill motif). Symbols of physical power and sexuality—a tight bodice combined with a brass knuckles necklace and pistol earrings—further upend the expectations of feminine beauty. This carefully constructed outfit illustrates how aspects of femininity have been reappropriated and combined with feminism to create a look that defines the wearer as different from other women who are following dominant fashion norms. In the pages of *Bust*, the wearer is portrayed as a self-styled woman and not a fashion "don't." She plays with feminine norms without wholesale adoption (or rejection) of them. Her outfit is meant to resonate with the reader as both representing an individual *and* an identifiable collective feminist style.

Many of the contemporary feminists profiled in *Bust* use a consciously constructed look as a way to live out, on an everyday basis, their politics and ideologies.[32] As such it becomes a signifier of their feminist beliefs. Based on the content analysis, three themes emerge that incorporate these beliefs; the focus on individuality, sexualized dress, and the resistance of consumer culture.

FASHION NATION
Kerin Weinberg
Student/Music Promoter
PHOTO BY SHANNON SINCLAIR

HOW WOULD YOU describe your style? I like to refer to myself as a biological drag queen—I dress like a drag queen even though I was born a woman. Tell me about this outfit: I made the money dress myself. I bought the fabric for about $12 at Spandex House, one of my favorite fabric stores in the garment district. It's two floors of spandex fabric! The dress underneath is from H&M; it was probably around $20. The shoes are Chuck Taylors. I hand-applied 2700 Swarovski crystals to them. It took me eight hours to do, over the course of a week. How did you make the shoes? Well, I'd rhinestoned a bunch of things—my cell phone, my iPod. Then I realized that Converse are made out of canvas and they'd make a good surface. I had to buy two full gross of rhinestones, and I glued them on with E6000 Adhesive. The shoes only cost $30, but the crystals cost about $165. They're spaced really close together; you can't see the shoe at all. What about your jewelry? The jewelry is a mixture of H&M and Griprops. The brass knuckles (worn as pendant) were given to me as a gift from the owner of Made Clothing. The hoop earrings are either from H&M or Griprops; they're white and plastic and probably cost about $7. I'm also wearing earrings with guns, because white plastic pistols hanging from your ears definitely lets people know you're dangerous. DEBBIE STOLLER

Figure 6.3 *Looks* feature, *Bust*, Fall 2004

Focusing on Individuality

One paradox of feminist fashion exemplified by *Bust,* is that while this dress creates an intentional and oppositional collective style (vintage, funky, and/or DIY), it does so in a way that values individuality. Gwendolyn O'Neal notes that oppositional subcultures on the margins often resist the status quo through clothing norms. While it may appear all members of a group are dressing the same, O'Neal argues that in fact what the members are doing is making a statement as to who they are as individuals.[33] This dynamic is captured by classical sociologists who argue it is only the collective that allows us to act individually.[34] By acting collectively, contemporary feminists complicate the dominant standards of fashion and appearance while embracing their individualism.

Feminist fashion encompasses a variety of individual styles and the women profiled in *Bust* have a wide range of style descriptors including "'70s scholar," "Dyke-alicious," "Art Nouveau punk," and "Over-the-top glamour, 1950s thrift shop, and couture." In the words of one profiled woman:

> Be comfortable in your clothes. Wear it like you own it and not the other way around. Don't be afraid to mix and match. And definitely never walk out of a store with the exact same outfit you saw in the window.[35]

This focus on individuality and dress aligns with scholars' descriptions of contemporary feminism as focused on everyday activism and cultural change.[36]

By prizing both collectivity and individuality through contemporary style, dress becomes a way to create community by constructing a feminist identity that seeks to unsettle dominant ways of seeing femininity. Feminist fashion is both accommodationist by accepting certain in-group community aesthetics, and resistant by refusing to completely abide by dominant femininity and fashion norms. It is interesting to note that one Asian woman describes her look as "Dragon lady disguised as Japanese bubblegum pop" claiming not only her individuality (complete with pink boa) but also reclaiming (and acknowledging) racist stereotypes of Asian women in her assertion of self.[37] What is unclear here, as many of the *Bust* outfits portray, is how the viewer understands the wearer's intent, highlighting the tension between refuting and reinforcing stereotypical dress. This tension is particularly apparent in sexualized dress.

Sexualizing Dress

Sexualized dress has long been a fashion staple; however it is growing increasingly more popular in the dominant culture. Stephanie Rosenbloom notes that Halloween has become a time for young women to "go bad for a day" with costumes that are more "strip club than storybook."[38] Ariel Levy points to the same phenomenon happening in women and girls' everyday fashion, and "Girls Gone Wild" antics where women bare their breasts or make out with heterosexual girlfriends in order to win a baseball cap or appear in a video.[39] However, the move toward hypersexualized clothing is more than a trend pushing women to present themselves for the male gaze. By politicizing sexuality as a part of femininity and feminism, contemporary feminist fashion is unabashedly sexual. The focus of the gaze is turned inward with women expressing their sexuality for their own gratification rather than male approval. As with individualized style, however, the intention of sexualized dress is subject to different interpretations by the wearer and the viewer. In creating sexualized fashion, there are two forces at work: reacting to perceptions of earlier feminists and reclaiming one's own sexuality from the dominant mainstream.

In Jane Sexes It Up, feminist scholar Merri Lisa Johnson writes that the goal for contemporary feminism is to press forward "sex-positive in a culture that demonizes sexuality, and sex-radical

Figure 6.4 *Looks* feature, *Bust,* Dec. 2004/Jan. 2005

in a political movement that has been known to choose moral high grounds over low guttural sounds."[40] Yet Stephanie Gilmore reminds us that these struggles with conceptualizing and living out sexuality are not new. Sex and sexuality were debated issues in the so-called second wave from the infamous anti-lesbian "lavender menace" in the National Organization for Women (NOW) to the claim by Radicalesbians that women should forgo sex with men for true liberation. At the same time, Gilmore notes, NOW allowed ads for *Playgirl* and *Venus* magazines at early conventions and heterosexual members openly wrote about their desire and "kinky sex wishes."[41]

Despite the diversity of 1960s and 1970s feminist approaches to sex and sexuality, contemporary feminist activists and scholars often presume these feminist generations were anti-sex and see their own youth-oriented actions as sex-positive. To that end, many feminists in *Bust* incorporate a sense of sexiness into their dress. In the *Bust* profiles several of the women are dressed in ways that can be interpreted as sexual (e.g., fishnet stockings, camisoles, bustiers, short skirts, and shorts). For example Jamie, a designer, is profiled wearing a pair of knee-high boots, a see-through lace camisole, a pair of butt-hugging denim shorts, and white jacket tied with a bow at her neck. She says of her look, "I like to wear short shorts in the summer, together with a feminine blouse. It's professional, but fun."[42] Others describe their look with terms such as "flirty and feminine."[43] This sexualized way of dress, revealing the body and wearing lingerie as outerwear is done with a sense of play. As Kelsey, a young feminist in Johannesburg, South Africa comments, "My friends never know what I'm going to look like, because one day I'll be wearing baby dolls and the next, I'll be wearing Doc Martens."[44] By adopting sexualized fashion, contemporary feminists incorporate sexiness into their appearances as a choice, while sidestepping the unequal sexual relationships between girls and boys, which strip girls of their own innate desires and sexuality.[45] Acting as subjects playing with being objects of sexuality, desire and sex become ways to state one's empowerment. As evidenced in the multitude of advertisements and features in *Bust*, being sex-positive through purchasing sex toys and openly discussing sexual desire and dysfunction is a part of a contemporary feminist sexual ethos.[46]

Resisting Consumer Culture

One of the main critiques of fashion is that it encourages women to consume goods, diminishes women's economic status, and supports capitalism and host of other evils including sweatshop labor and unfair trade practices.[47] One of the most evident ways oppositional fashion resists consumer culture is through buying clothes and jewelry as cheaply as possible. Frugal shopping is a mainstay of many of the women profiled in *Bust*. Almost all of the women profiled bought various pieces of clothing and shoes at thrift stores, resale shops, and street vendors. Many report that they also shop at discount or "big box" stores such as H&M, Target, and Kmart for their clothes. For example, a waitress and aspiring documentary filmmaker details where she purchased her outfit:

> I got the boots at the Salvation Army—on half price day—so they were like $2. I've had the skirt for like four years; I think I got it in Italy. The belt I've had since I was 13. The red shirt is from the 40s; a friend's mother gave it to me. The jacket I bought in a flea market on the Lower East Side for $1. I got the tights in Italy too. The bag I got at a yard sale.[48]

It is tempting to see this trend toward frugal shopping as solely the outcome of students or young women starting their careers purchasing what they can afford. While this might be the case for many of those profiled, it is important to note that many of the women also wore individual pieces of clothes that ranged from $80 to $350, illustrating how thrifty shopping is more than finding affordable clothing. Thrifty shopping only functions as political resistance when one does not have to shop frugally. By mixing expensive pieces such as a silk blouse or custom-made jewelry with articles of clothing which cost less than $10 can be viewed as a political statement against a consumer culture that encourages the consumption of high-end (and high cost) outfits, regardless of the wearer's income.[49]

Many of the items purchased in thrift or discount stores were then reinvented as part of the DIY ethic. DIY is not a new phenomenon, but grew out of punk culture and the notion that creating something oneself (e.g., earrings from safety pins or reworking a garment) is a rejection of mainstream capitalist consumerist society.[50] Ricia Chansky adds that current trends in doing needle works (i.e., knitting, crocheting) is a reaction to the standardization of goods and can be seen historically throughout U.S. culture, notably the Arts and Crafts Movement of the late nineteenth and early twentieth centuries.[51] DIY as a leisure activity is only available to social classes who have the time and resources to create goods not necessary for daily survival.

In *Bust*, women alter their clothing in a variety of ways that range from adding more decoration (e.g., rhinestones or crystals) to remaking clothing so that it fits better or expresses their own style. Chansky writes:

> In a time when many women are actively trying to work against culturally regimented ideals of feminine beauty and have healthy body images, the act of creating one's own clothes is a way to have funky, expressive clothing that fits well despite the limitations of mass produced clothing that tends to be made for specific body sizes and shapes.[52]

Two of the profiled women, one a jewelry designer and the other an illustrator, describe how they reinvented their clothing:

> *Jo:* I made the jacket from the satin of an old 1930s wedding dress. The embroidery depicts the story of P. T. Barnum, who had a traveling circus in the 1800s. He was famous because he created a fake merman—half ape, half salmon.
> *Janet:* The Hello Kitty shirt I got from Target, I just cut off the neck. Luckily I fit into a children's size large.[53]

The importance of social class is particularly evident in Jo's description of remaking the wedding dress into a unique silk jacket. Not only does it take resources to remake the dress (i.e., purchasing the gown, sewing equipment, and embroidery supplies) but it also takes leisure time to devote to learning the skill and doing the activity.

A third way in which consumer culture is resisted is through the selection of vintage clothing. One reason is that vintage clothing is often available at thrift and resale shops and is economical and easily altered. Dirty Martini, a burlesque performer, notes:

> I have an awful habit of collecting 1950s underwear; my closets are stuffed with the most insane lingerie. It's hard to find a bra in double-D that's pretty these days but back then it was a common size.[54]

Purchasing vintage fashions can be seen as rejecting the constantly changing nature of fashion by focusing on a particular period of dress. When asked to describe their style, many of the women highlighted styles of different periods, such as 1920s flappers, "'70s proggy-rock bands," early Lucille Ball (1940s and 1950s) or in the fashion of eighteenth century women.

In sum, through thrift shopping, reinventing clothing, and adopting vintage styles, the feminists profiled in *Bust* create a form of embodied politics that rejects some of the norms of mainstream fashion and is identifiable to other feminists. This is not to argue that adopting alternative forms of dress means one is a feminist. However, dressing with a political intent to reject mainstream fashion and cultural norms and reclaim aspects of femininity is one tactic of contemporary feminism. However, for each of the ways in which dress is made feminist, through individuality, sexuality, and anti-consumerism, there arise a series of complicated outcomes.

Complications of Politicized Fashion

Refashioning appearance through feminist ideologies has multiple, complicated outcomes. When a way of presenting oneself is associated with a movement, it can serve in a positive manner by drawing together community.[55] There may also be negative unintended outcomes such as stereotyping or labeling the movement in a way that dissuades potential members. In the earlier periods of feminism, the "natural" fashion (e.g., no makeup, unshaven bodies, and peasant shirts with jeans) was picked up by the media as the uniform of all feminists and came to be viewed as a series of stereotypes (e.g., ugly, man hating, lesbian) that still repels some women (and men) from the movement today. Feminists also deal with these stereotypes, fearing that to adopt a fashionable appearance means to disavow "true" feminist activism. In the 1990s, Jennifer Allyn wrote of the tension between feminism and fashion:

> I felt a part of a new generation of feminists. We wanted to make room for play in our lives—dyeing our hair, shaving our legs, dressing in ways that made us happy—without sacrificing a commitment to political activism.[56]

Yet the concern is that when any subculture creates a new way of dressing, it can be commodified, co-opted, and absorbed into the larger culture. One example is how tattoos moved from being oppositional statements by prisoners, gang members, or the modern primitives movement to becoming fashionable in the mid-to-late 1990s. Sociologist Michael Messner writes that feminism itself has been commodified through commercials for products such as Nike which exhort women to "Just do it" as a form of true empowerment.[57] Feminist DIY trends are similarly commodified. In the early twenty-first century the "handcrafted" as well as the "vintage" look became a part of mainstream fashion. Popular brands Urban Outfitters, Ugg boots, and Ann

Taylor all offered crocheted or vintage-style clothing in the early 2000s. This follows a similar trend in which hip-hop, slacker, grunge, and Goth styles went from subculture dress to becoming available at any mall.

These co-opted fashion trends are without overt political statements and may diffuse the political meaning in similarly styled clothes. Further complicating the politics of feminist fashion is the way in which crafting has become an entrepreneurial endeavor for many young feminists whose goods may be purchased and consumed without a political understanding of DIY or feminism. Feminist or progressive crafting fairs are common around the country and magazines such as *Bust* run regular features on how to do certain crafts. Debbie Stoller, the editor-in-chief of *Bust*, is also the author of several books on knitting with titles such as *Stitch 'N Bitch: The Knitter's Handbook* and *Stitch 'N Bitch Crochet: The Happy Hooker*, These books, with a feminist edge, are popular with many knitters who do not claim a feminist identity. When crafts (or crafting instructions) created as aspects of feminine resistance are sold in the mainstream, the feminist political impact can become diluted.

Why, then, is fashion featured so prominently in *Bust* magazine and evident in so many contemporary feminist communities, given the potential drawbacks and complications of using fashion as a feminist statement?

Whittier argues that as repression from the state shifts in form, so does the resistance from social movements.[58] The contemporary women's movement is made up of a generation of feminists who have seen the constant chipping away of the policy and legislative gains of earlier feminists. Title IX, reproductive rights, sexual harassment, and workplace protections have been subject to attack, particularly by the presidential administrations of George Bush, Sr. and George W. Bush, although these incursions threaten to continue. Whereas U.S. feminism has always worked to change cultural norms (e.g., the Bloomer "Turkish pants" movement of the 1800s), earlier generations of feminists had periods in which the political arena was more open to institutional change.[59] In a time when the institutional avenues of making change are not as open, contemporary feminists focus on culture as one way of making change. Fashion addresses in significant cultural ways the manner in which we understand femininity and masculinity in society. When women begin to alter their presentations of femininity, as represented in *Bust*, it has cultural significance. In examining the ways in which fashion is being constructed by some young feminists it is clear that a feminist identity is being asserted and ideologies on issues such as sexuality are being elaborated. The body becomes the location where larger issues are played out (i.e., sweatshop labor and anti-consumerist values) and where connections to other social movements are made.

By drawing on three theoretical frameworks seldom used together, feminist-, fashion-, and social-movement theory, this essay illustrates that dress is one of the most evident aspects of a cultural tactical toolbox that activists use.[60] The concepts of oppositional fashion and embodied politics are important in understanding movements that engage in lifestyle, culture-focused politics. Adding these concepts to a social movement vocabulary opens new directions of study, challenging the way in which we define political protest as well as how we understand the dynamics of tactics, innovation, co-optation, and commodification. By narrowly defining movement tactics and politics as focused only on policy efforts, scholars miss the opportunity to see how micro-level, personal action functions within social movement contexts. Vibrant debates about the current state and strategies of contemporary feminism continue, yet the evidence is clear that contemporary feminists present a form of social resistance written on the body and expressed both communally and individually, dynamics of social movement protest that are informative to scholars and important to activists.

In conclusion, I return to the feminist concerns exemplified by Letty Cottin Pogrebin's statement that opened this chapter:

Does fashion create social change? Is contemporary feminism more than "baring one's midriff?" When a group of people articulates the norms of the status quo and seeks to reclaim definitions of themselves through cultural means, does this alter society? Is this forging social change? To many who view social movements as only collectively making change through direct engagement with the state, contemporary feminism's focus on fashion, as illustrated by *Bust* magazine, falls short. However, if we open the definition of the political to encompass work to bring about cultural shifts, I argue that by dressing in a way to reclaim femininity and sexuality as powerful, while working to negate the forces of overconsumption, contemporary feminists enact a form of social change. However, this argument is tempered by the knowledge that mass social change is difficult when a primary tactic of social movement actors is individual choice. When individual agency, as in feminized and politicized dress, is done in a culture of commodification, the impact of the tactic is often diluted and misunderstood in the larger culture and within the movement.

Notes

1   *Bust*, "Fashion and Booty," Fall 2004, 37.

2   As cited in Stephanie Gilmore, "Bridging the Waves: Sex and Sexuality in a Second Wave Organization," in *Different Wavelengths: Studies of the Contemporary Women's Movement*, ed. Jo Reger (New York: Routledge, 2005), 97.

3   While there are many definitions of "feminist" and "feminism," I identify *Bust* magazine and its contents as feminist for several reasons. First, *Bust* is often referred to as a contemporary feminist magazine because of the philosophy of the founders (among them Debbie Stoller, who often appears in the media and documentaries as a voice of feminism and is the author of several knitting books). Second is the magazine's overall philosophy of self empowerment

and the critique of patriarchy. Evidence of this is in the magazine's tagline, "For Women with Something to Get off Their Chests." Third, the fashion focus of the magazine often refers specifically to feminism, such as the cover headline "Be a Feminist or just dress like one," *Bust*, August/September 2006, cover.

4 See Jennifer Baumgardner and Amy Richards, "Feminism and Femininity: Or How We Learned to Stop Worrying and Love the Thong," in *All About The Girl-Culture, Power And Identity,* ed. Anita Harris (New York: Routledge, 2004), 59–68; Beth Kreydatus, "Fashion," in *The Women's Movement Today: An Encyclopedia of Third-Wave Feminism,* ed. Leslie Heywood, vol. 1 (Westport, CT: Greenwood Press, 2006), 59–68.

5 The analysis was conducted using the Fall 2002 to Oct./Nov. 2007 issues with the magazine increasing its publications from four times a year to bimonthly publications in 2005. The magazine was founded in 1993 as a feminist 'zine (self-produced magazine). A standard feature of the magazine is called "Looks—Fashion and Booty." The feature is similar in each issue with women describing their outfits, where they got individual pieces, why they put them together the way they did, and how it made them feel. I coded each issue by analyzing the hair, outfit, race-ethnicity, occupation, style descriptors used, the reworking of the clothing, and the adjectives in the copy, A total of twenty-two features were analyzed.

6 See Verta Taylor and Nella van Dyke, "'Get Up, Stand Up': Tactical Repertoires of Social Movements," in *The Blackwell Companion to Social Movements,* eds. David Snow, Sarah Soule, Hanspeter Kriesi (Malden MA: Blackwell Publishing, 2004), 262–293.

7 Charles Tilly, *Social Movements, 1768–2004* (Boulder, CO: Paradigm Publishers, 2004).

8 David Meyer, "How Social Movements Matter," *Contexts 2,* no. 4 (2003): 30–35; Suzanne Staggenborg, "Can Feminist

Organizations Be Effective?" in *Feminist Organizations: Harvest of the New Women's Movement,* eds. Myra Marx Ferree and Patricia Yancey Martin (Philadelphia: Temple University Press, 1995), 339–355.

9 Nancy Whittier, *The Politics of Child Sexual Assault: Emotions, Social Movements and the State* (Malden, MA: Oxford University Press, 2009).

10 Verta Taylor and Nancy Whittier, "Collective Identity in Social Movement Communities: Lesbian Feminist Mobilization," in *Frontiers in Social Movement Theory,* eds. Aldon D. Morris and Carol McClurg Mueller (New Haven, CT: Yale University Press, 1992), 104–129.

11 Gwendolyn O'Neal, "The Power of Style: On Rejection of the Accepted," in *Appearance and Power,* eds. Kim K. P. Johnson and Sharron J. Lennon (New York: Berg, 1999), 127–137; 141.

12 O'Neal, "The Power of Style: On Rejection of the Accepted," 129. Also see Suzanne Szostak-Pierce, "Even Further: The Power of Subcultural Style in Techno Culture," in *Appearance and Power,* 141–151; Samantha Holland, *Alternative Femininities: Body, Age and Identity* (New York: Berg, 2004).

13 Jane Ward, "Diversity Discourse and Multi-Identity Work in Lesbian and Gay Organizations," in *Identity Work in Social Movements,* eds. Jo Reger, Daniel J. Myers, and Rachel L. Einwohner (Minneapolis: University of Minnesota Press, 2008), 233–255.

14 Shari Benstock and Suzanne Ferriss, "Introduction," in *On Fashion,* eds. Shari Benstock and Suzanne Ferriss (New Brunswick, NJ: Rutgers University Press, 1994), 1–17; Holland, *Alternative Femininities.*

15 Holland, *Alternative Femininities.*

16 Kim K. P. Johnson and Sharron J. Lennon, "Introduction: Appearance and Social Power," in *Appearance and Power,* 1–10; O'Neal, "The Power of Style: On Rejection of the Accepted."

17 Holland, *Alternative Femininities.*

18 See Ariel Levy, *Female Chauvinist Pigs: Women and the Rise*

of Raunch Culture (New York: Free Press, 2006); Nancy A. Rudd and Sharron J. Lennon, "Social Power and Appearance Management among Women," in *Appearance and Power*, 153–172.

19 Holland, *Alternative Femininities*, 81.

20 Kate McCarthy, "Not Pretty Girls?; Sexuality, Spirituality, and Gender Construction in Women's Rock Music." *The Journal of Popular Culture* 39, no. 1 (2006): 69–94; Adrienne Rich, "Compulsory Heterosexuality and Lesbian Existence," in *Bread, Blood and Poetry* (New York: W. W. Norton, 1994), 23–75; see also discussion in Linda Scott, *Fresh Lipstick: Redressing Fashion and Feminism* (New York: Palgrave MacMillan, 1994).

21 Baumgardner and Richards, "Feminism and Femininity."

22 Rich, "Compulsory Heterosexuality and Lesbian Existence."

23 See Rachel Blau DuPlessis and Ann Snitow, *The Feminist Memoir Project: Voices from Women's Liberation* (New York; Three Rivers Press, 1998); Karla Jay, *Tales of the Lavender Menace: A Memoir of Liberation.* (New York: Basic Books, 1999); Scott, *Fresh Lipstick;* Deborah Siegel, *Sisterhood Interrupted: From Radical Women To Grrls Gone Wild* (New York: Palgrave Macmillan, 2007).

24 As cited in Siegel, *Sisterhood Interrupted*, 85.

25 McCarthy, "Not Pretty Girls?," 71.

26 Ingrid Sischy, "Will Feminism's Fourth Wave Begin on the Runway?" *New York Times Style Magazine*, February 25, 2007, http://www.nytimes.com/2007/02/25/style/tmagazine/25tbody.html?ex=1173330000&en=1506c56f789e38fd&ei=5070.

27 Baumgardner and Richards, "Feminism and Femininity," 59.

28 Ibid., 61.

29 Patricia Hill Collins, *Black Feminist Thought: Knowledge, Consciousness, and the Politics of Empowerment* (Boston: Unwin Hyman, 1991).

30 McCarthy, "Not Pretty Girls?," 70; See also M. Evans and C. Bobel, "'I am a Contradiction:' Feminism and Feminist Identity in the Third Wave," *New England Journal of Public Policy* 1 and 2 (2007): 207–222; Natalie Fixmer and Julia T. Wood, "The Personal is Still Political: Embodied Politics in Third Wave Feminism," *Women's Studies in Communication* 28, no. 2 (2005): 235–257.

31 Judith Taylor, "The Problem of Women's Sociality in Contemporary North American Feminist Memoir." *Gender & Society* 22, no. 6 (2008): 705–727; Chris Bobel, "'Our Revolution Has Style:' Contemporary Menstrual Product Activists 'Doing Feminism' in the Third Wave." *Sex Roles* 54 (2006): 331–345; Ricia Chansky, "A Stitch in Time: Reclaiming the Needle in Third Wave Feminist Visual Expression" (paper presented at the National Women's Studies Association meeting, St. Charles, IL, 2007).

32 Because of their inclusion in a magazine that focuses on feminism and links feminism and fashion, I am assuming that the people profiled are feminists even though the limited copy does not identify them as so. Even if some do not choose to identify as feminists, they are clearly being presented as feminist fashion models.

33 O'Neal, "The Power of Style: On Rejection of the Accepted."

34 I thank David Maines for this insight.

35 *Bust*, Dec./Jan. 2007, 33.

36 Bobel, "'Our Revolution Has Style;'" Evans and Bobel, "'I am a Contradiction;'" Fixmer and Wood, "The Personal is Still Political."

37 Illustration 2, *Bust*, Dec. 2004/Jan. 2005, 39.

38 Stephanie Rosenbloom, "Good Girls Go Bad, for a Day," *New York Times*, October 19, 2006, http://www.nytimes.com/2006/10/19/fashion/19costume.html?scp=8&sq=stephanie%20rosenbloom&st=cse.

39 Levy, *Female Chauvinist Pigs.*

40 Merri Lisa Johnson, "Jane Hocus, Jane Focus," *in Jane Sexes It*

Up: True Confessions of Feminist Desire, ed. M. L. Johnson (New York: Four Walls, Eight Windows, 2002), 9.

41 As quoted in Gilmore, "Bridging the Waves," 106.

42 *Bust,* April/May, 2005, 33.

43 *Bust,* October/November, 2005, 33.

44 *Bust,* April/May, 2007, 42.

45 See Deborah Tolman, *Dilemmas of Desire: Teenage Girls Talk about Sexuality* (Cambridge MA: Harvard University Press, 2002).

46 See also Jo Reger and Lacey Story, "Talking About My Vagina: Two College Campuses and the Vagina Monologues," in *Different Wavelengths: Studies of the Contemporary Women's Movement,* 139–160.

47 Kreydatus, "Fashion."

48 Transcribed as written, *Bust,* Winter 2002, 27.

49 For example consider the designer jean fad of the 1980s in the United States with the designer label prominently displayed on the back pocket as a status symbol.

50 Bobel, "'Our Revolution Has Style.'"

51 Chansky, "A Stitch in Time," 6.

52 Ibid., 5.

53 *Bust,* Aug./Sept. 2007, 37 and Dec./Jan. 2004/2005, 39, respectively.

54 *Bust,* Oct./Nov., 2006, 37.

55 Staggenborg, "Can Feminist Organizations Be Effective?" 339–355.

56 Jennifer Allyn and David Allyn, "Identity Politics," in *To Be Real: Telling the Truth and Changing the Face of Feminism,* ed. Rebecca Walker (New York: Anchor Books, 1995), 144.

57 Michael Messner, *Taking the Field: Women, Men and Sports* (Minneapolis: University of Minnesota Press, 2002).

58 Whittier, *The Politics of Child Sexual Assault.*

59 For example see Karla Jay's memoir *Tales of the Lavender Menace* for a description of the rush of accomplishments of the movement in the 1970s.

60 Ann Swidler, "Culture in Action: Symbols and Strategies," *American Sociological Review* 51 (1986): 273–286.

A Future for Whom?
Passing on Billboard Liberation
Alison Kafer

[Advertising] is a world that works by *abstraction*, a potential place or state of being situated not in the present but in an imagined future with the promise to the consumer of things "you" will have, a lifestyle you can take part in.

—Marita Sturken and Lisa Cartwright, "Consumer Culture and the Manufacturing of Desire"

"SUPER MAN," THE billboard exclaims, the unfamiliar gap between the two words emphasizing both the noun and its adjective. Below this phrase is the word "STRENGTH," followed by the imperative *"Pass It On"* At the bottom, in small print, runs the name and web address of the organization behind this public relations campaign: Values.com/Foundation for a Better Life. The "super man" referenced in the caption is, of course, the late Christopher Reeve, the white actor who starred in a series of *Superman* films in the 1980s before becoming a quadriplegic in a riding accident in 1995. A black-and-white photograph of Reeve's head and shoulders consumes the left half of the billboard; the only marker of Reeve's disability is the ventilator tube that is just visible at the bottom of the frame. Reeve smiles slightly, looking thoughtfully into the camera and the eyes of passersby.

Quadriplegics are not often presented as the embodiment of strength, but this sign suggests that, in Reeve's case, such a designation is accurate. According to the billboard, although Reeve was no longer able to run or jump or climb, he remained a strong man; his strength simply lay more in his character than in his body. Prior to his injuries, Reeve was "Superman," a fictional hero capable of leaping buildings and bending steel. Later, as a disabled person, Reeve was not Superman but a *super* man. The

billboard informs its audience that Reeve's masculinity not only remained intact postinjury but increased, an improvement due primarily to his strong character and integrity. Indeed, his masculinity, disability, and strength are presented in the billboard as intricately related, each supporting the other: it was his disability that provided him the opportunity to prove his strength, and his strength testified to his masculinity. Reeve's ability to triumph over his disabilities, to continue living and working even after a life-changing injury, marked him as strong, and this strength in turn marked him as a super man. The billboard urges viewers to preach this message of self-improvement, to spread the word about the importance of developing and maintaining strength of character, even in, or especially in, the face of adversity.

According to the organization's website, "The Foundation for a Better Life is not affiliated with any political groups or religious organizations" but is rather an apolitical organization interested in fostering individual and collective betterment through values education and engagement.[1] It is this positioning that I want to examine here; this attempt to depoliticize notions of community, this assumption of shared values, and this articulation of what a better life entails. By presenting these concepts as apolitical, the Foundation for a Better Life (FBL) renders them natural, accepted, commonsense, and therefore beyond the scope of debate or discussion. The FBL operates on the assumption that we all know and agree what a better life entails, and what values are necessary to achieve it; there is no need for argument or critique. Representations of disability and illness play a large role in this campaign, with a significant number of billboards praising individuals with disabilities for having the strength of character to "overcome" their disabilities. The depoliticization mandated by these billboards and the FBL itself is made possible through reference to the disabled body; in other words, it is not just that the FBL depoliticizes disability, but that it does so in order to depoliticize all the values featured in its campaign. Indeed, the presence of the disabled body is used to render this campaign not as ideology but as common sense.

In order to show that the depoliticization mandated by these billboards is made possible through reference to the disabled body, I first examine the parameters of this "better life" sketched out by the FBL, highlighting the exclusions inherent in such articulations. Not all bodies, practices, or identities are welcome in this better life, especially those figures deemed too queer, or too political, or too dependent to be of value. Next, I uncover the ways in which these billboards strategically deploy this depoliticized view of disability to present their entire ideology as beyond reproach. Finally, I want to explore the possibility of queering and cripping these billboards, of offering alternative, and multiple, conceptions of what constitutes a better life. How might we turn this iconography back on itself, making apparent its political assumptions about "community values" by challenging its deployment of disability and disabled bodies?

Super Man's Values and the Quest for a Better Life

Persuading passersby of the importance of self-improvement, and encouraging them to engage in values-oriented conversations, is the raison d'être of the Foundation for a Better Life, the sponsor of the Reeve billboard and others like it. A privately funded nonprofit organization based in Colorado, the FBL uses its website and a series of billboards, bus shelter posters, and television public service announcements to advocate personal responsibility and character development.[2] According to the website, the FBL's mission is to remind people of the importance of "quality values." In order to promote these values, each of the

organization's print pieces celebrates a different value, from ambition to self-respect, by highlighting a person or event that embodies that trait. The celebrities and private citizens featured in the campaign donated their images to the FBL in support of its efforts to foster values-based communities and individuals. In addition to the Reeve piece on strength, there are billboards of a New York City firefighter on 9/11 (who modeled *courage*), Benjamin Franklin (displaying *ingenuity*), and even the animated figure Shrek (who encourages you to *believe in yourself*), among others. All three of the "courage" signs are illustrated with an adult male figure (a 9/11 firefighter, a protestor at Tiananmen Square, and Muhammad Ali), suggesting that the values of the FBL's community adhere, at least partly, to traditional gender roles.[3] The values "helping others," "volunteering," "compassion," and "love," for example, are represented by women.

There are fifty-eight different billboards in the group's portfolio, almost a third of which feature disabled people[4] who, as the captions make clear, have overcome the limitations of their minds and bodies through the development of individual values: Muhammad Ali, whose face is shown in a black-and-white photograph edged by darkness, embodies *courage* in recognizing that, as someone with Parkinson's disease, "His biggest fight yet isn't in the ring"; Adam Bender, who lost a leg to cancer, stands one-legged in his baseball uniform as a symbol of *overcoming* ("Threw cancer a curve ball"); Brooke Ellison, smiling as she poses in her wheelchair and wearing her graduation gown, was able to graduate from Harvard ("Quadriplegic. A-. Harvard") because of her *determination*; Michael J. Fox, depicted in black-and-white with his face partly in shadow, models *optimism* ("Determined to outfox Parkinson's"); Whoopi Goldberg, pictured with lowered head, furrowed brow, and her eyes looking up at the camera through her dreadlocks, "Overcaem [sic] dyslexia" through *hard work*; Bethany Hamilton, a young surfer who lost an arm during a shark attack, demonstrates *rising above* adversity ("Me, quit? Never") as she poses on the beach next to her bitten surfboard; Dick Hoyt models *devotion* by pushing his adult son Rick in a modified racing wheelchair along a wooded path ("Dad's been behind him for 65 marathons"); Helen Keller, depicted as a young girl reading Braille and wearing an abundantly frilly dress, is praised for her *foresight* because she "could only see possibilities"; Christopher Reeve, as noted above, is a "Super man" because of his *strength;* Alexandra Scott, a young girl pictured sitting behind her homemade lemonade stand, is a figure of *inspiration* for raising millions of dollars for pediatric cancer research ("Raised $1M to fight cancer. Including hers"); Marlon Shirley, poised to begin a race with his sleek prosthetic leg, epitomizes *overcoming* ("Lost Leg. Not heart"); and Eric Weihenmayer, a blind hiker photographed in profile on a snowy mountaintop, succeeded ("Climbed Everest. Blind") thanks to his *vision.*[5]

In keeping with the foundation's focus on personal accountability, most of the people featured in these billboards are pictured alone, several of them depicted against an empty dark background. The accompanying text makes clear that whatever successes these people have achieved, whether graduating from college or reaching Everest, were achieved solely through an individual adherence to "community-accepted values." Within this individualist framework, disability is presented as something to be overcome through personal achievement and dedication. Although the Hoyt father-son team seemingly departs from this iconography of individualism, disability in this image remains firmly within a private familial framework; not only is a family member the only community imagined for Rick Hoyt, "devotion"—a virtue laden with notions of private faith and individual rather than social action—is presented as the operative value here. Moreover, despite their label "Team Hoyt," the father is positioned as the virtuous one; he is the agent of devotion and his disabled son its passive recipient.

In case the message of the billboards is too ambiguous, the FBL's website clearly delineates the group's perspective: by

encouraging "adherence to a set of quality values through personal accountability and by raising the level of expectations of performance of all individuals regardless of religion or race," the FBL places a high premium on individual responsibility. The billboards are intended "to remind individuals they are accountable and empowered with the ability to take responsibility for their lives and to promote a set of values that sees them through their failures and capitalizes on their successes."[6]

This narrative of overcoming is made explicit in the texts featuring Adam Bender, Whoopi Goldberg, Bethany Hamilton, and Marlon Shirley but it underlies the other signs as well: Eric Weihenmayer, for example, overcomes the limitations of his eyesight by relying on his metaphoric *vision,* an intangible virtue that permits him to achieve a difficult feat, while Brooke Ellison and Christopher Reeve overcome quadriplegia through their respective *determination* and *strength.*[7] Disability appears as an individual physical problem that can best be overcome (and should be overcome) through strength of character and adherence to an established set of community values.

This focus on personal responsibility precludes any discussion of social, political, or collective responsibility. There are no billboards touting solidarity, or social change, or community development; none of the images celebrate disparate groups coming together to engage in coalition work. There is no recognition of ableism or discrimination or oppression in these materials, only an insistence that individuals take responsibility for their own successes and failures. As a result, disability is depoliticized, presented as a fact of life requiring determination and courage, not as a system marking some bodies, ways of thinking, and patterns of movement as deviant and unworthy.

This depoliticization is exacerbated by the campaign's erasure of the work of disability rights activists. In the FBL worldview, disabled people thrive not because of civil rights laws and protection from discrimination, but because of their personal integrity, courage, and ability to overcome obstacles. Thus, Ellison's ability to go to Harvard is attributed solely to her individual determination, which, although a factor in her success (and certainly a factor in her A- average), was surely facilitated by accessible buildings, antidiscrimination policies, and laws mandating equitable and inclusive education for disabled people. Her education was, in key ways, made possible by the disability rights activists who struggled before, and after, her.

Disability rights activists, however, aren't the only ones erased in this particular billboard, and it is worth sitting with the Ellison image a little longer in order to highlight the gendered assumptions of this campaign. Brooke Ellison's mother, Jean, was surely as determined as her daughter when it came to Brooke's education. Jean Ellison lived with Brooke during her tenure at Harvard, attending classes with her, helping with her personal care, and serving as her scribe during exams: doing whatever it took, in other words, to help Brooke survive and flourish at Harvard. Ellison's profile on the FBL website does acknowledge that she excelled at Harvard "[w]ith the tireless help of her mother," but this help is made invisible by the billboard image and text. Unlike Dick Hoyt, who is publicly celebrated for the (alleged) sacrifices he has made to assist his son, and lifted up as the embodiment of devotion, Jean Ellison is nowhere to be found in the image of her daughter. Comparing the representations of these two parent-child teams, one could easily argue that gender plays a role here: we expect women, as mothers, to devote their lives to their children, an expectation that then renders their devotion banal and uninteresting; but male, fatherly, devotion continues to be treated as an anomaly and therefore deserving of surprised celebration.

The FBL's attention to individual virtue obscures the ableist attitudes inherent in these billboards. Reeve appears strong and "super" to many Americans, and Ali "courageous," simply by virtue of their living with a disability. In the logic of ableism, anyone who can handle such an (allegedly) horrible life must be strong; a lesser man would have given up in despair years

ago. Indeed, Reeve's refusal to "give up" is precisely why the FBL selected Reeve for their model of strength; in the "billboard backstories" section of their website, they praise Reeve for trying to "beat paralysis and the spinal cord injuries" rather than "giv[ing] up." Asserting that Goldberg is successful because of her hard work suggests that other people with dyslexia and learning disabilities who have not met with similar success have simply failed to engage in hard work; unlike Whoopi Goldberg, they are apparently unwilling to devote themselves to success. Similarly, by positioning Weihenmayer's ascent of Everest as a matter of vision, the FBL implies that most blind people, who have not ascended Everest or accomplished equivalently astounding feats, are lacking not only eyesight but vision. The disabled people populating these billboards epitomize the paradoxical figure of the supercrip: supercrips are those disabled figures favored in the media, products of either extremely low expectations (disability by definition means incompetence, so anything a disabled person does, no matter how mundane or banal, merits exaggerated praise) or extremely high expectations (disabled people must accomplish incredibly difficult, and therefore inspiring, tasks to be worthy of nondisabled attention).

The individuals featured in these billboards have been decontextualized and their lives have been depoliticized. They have been removed from the realm of health-care inequalities, inaccessible buildings, and discriminatory hiring practices. Those who have succeeded do not need legislative assistance because they have strong values; those who have failed simply lack those values and are in need not of a more equitable society but of character education. According to the FBL and its billboards, disability is not a political issue but a character issue, and should be addressed as such. There is no mention of the ways in which these individuals differ by race, gender, or class, presenting everyone as equally capable of succeeding, as possessing equal opportunities and resources. Reeve's many accomplishments, for example, are presented as solely the result of his immense inner strength of character; his reliance on a huge staff of attendants, therapists, and doctors—all made possible because of his personal wealth and quality insurance coverage—go unmentioned. All it takes is strength to survive, and thrive.

In this focus on individual virtue and personal responsibility, every other aspect of these individuals' lives is stripped away, making disability, and the overcoming of that disability, the only salient characteristic of their lives. Muhammad Ali's well-known battles with racism and his public protests against US imperialism in Vietnam—surely instances in which he embodied courage by speaking his conscience and challenging injustice—are erased in the presentation of Parkinson's disease as his biggest fight yet, or as his only fight outside of the ring.[8] To address those fights, the FBL would have to expand its vision of a better life to include not simply individual virtues but collective action. It would necessitate a contextualizing of disability as only a part of the fabric of people's lives, one always already inflected by categories of race, class, and gender. Such a portrayal would then require a reckoning with the politics of disability, thereby challenging the FBL's positioning of disability as mere fact of the mind/body, a presentation that enables their depiction of the entire Pass It On campaign as apolitical, noncontroversial, and commonsense. In other words, the campaign relies heavily on a depoliticized vision of disability in order to depoliticize the entire campaign.

A Better Life for Whom? Foundational Foreclosures

According to the FBL's website, the group is concerned about the current state of American culture and the direction in which the country is moving. It offers these billboards as part of its vision for what a better America would look like and what values it would embody. The very name of the organization—the Foundation for a Better Life—establishes the group's concern with the future and testifies to its belief that the principles it celebrates are integral to achieving this "better life." In an early version of the FAQ section of its website, the organization argues that the future depends on individual Americans dedicating themselves to "community values" and values-based education:

> The Foundation encourages others to step up to a higher level and then to pass on those positive values they have learned. These seemingly small examples of individuals living values-based lives may not change the world, but collectively they will make a difference. And in the process help make the world a better place for everyone. After all, developing values and passing them on to others is the Foundation for a Better Life.[9]

The FBL mission statement claims that the organization's sole purpose is to remind people of the importance of the "quality values" that "make a difference in our communities." In recent years, the website has become increasingly interactive, and there is now a section where visitors can suggest people and values for future billboards. At first glance, this shift seems to signal a new openness on the part of the organization, a willingness to see the values we live by as subject to debate and disagreement, but the FBL continues to define the terms of the debate. Commentators must choose from a select list of values in making their recommendations: "perseverance" is an acceptable virtue, for example, while "resistance" is not; values-based communities apparently have room for "volunteering" but not "activism." Moreover, every posting on the site is subject to the organization's terms and conditions, and there is not a single negative or critical post on the FBL site. A values-based life may be key to the health of the community, but it is the FBL, not local communities, that determines what those values are. Nor, for that matter, is there any discussion of what "community" means in this context and whom the term was intended to include. Nonetheless, the Pass It On campaign has been running on billboards, on television stations, and in movie theaters nationwide for over a decade, suggesting that the

FBL envisions a coherent national community with a single set of shared values. But what are these community values? Who constitutes the community imagined here, and based on what criteria? Whose better life is this?

Wholly absent from the website are details about the FBL itself: there is no address given for the organization, nor is there a description of its history or a directory of its members. According to Gary Dixon, identified in press releases as the president of the FBL, the family who created and funded the FBL wants to remain anonymous, but media reports and tax returns link the organization to billionaire developer Philip Anschutz and the Anschutz Family Foundation.[10] Since its inception in 1982, the Anschutz Foundation has supported a range of conservative organizations. In the early 1990s, it supported the antigay organization Colorado for Family Values, which was one of the driving forces behind Colorado's Amendment 2; declared unconstitutional by the US Supreme Court in 1996, this amendment to the state constitution would have prohibited local antidiscrimination laws on behalf of gays, lesbians, and bisexuals. More recently, the Anschutz Foundation has provided financial support to the Institute for American Values, which runs antipornography campaigns, warns of the dangers of single-mother households, supports reforms to make divorces more difficult to acquire, and favors marriage incentives for low-income people. If these affiliations provide a hint of what the "better life" promised by the FBL entails, then the future they envision is certainly a heteronormative one.

Although individuals with disabilities play a starring role in the Pass It On campaign they are not the primary or intended audience for these billboards. They appear in these billboards to inspire—and contain—the nondisabled, who are the target audience for these spots. "If even severely disabled people like Christopher Reeve and Brooke Ellison can develop these values and improve themselves," the signs imply, "then so can you. Unlike them, you have no excuse. Stop complaining, buck up, work hard and overcome."

Visitors to the FBL website can post comments on each billboard, and even a cursory reading of the posts makes clear that (nondisabled) viewers respond in exactly this way to these images. As one respondent wrote regarding the Bethany Hamilton sign, "[She] is a inspiration. For all those who blame others or circumstances, I will say—'look at Bethany Hamilton.'" R. H. in Utah internalizes this message, writing in response to the Reeve billboard: "I printed this out/cut it out and thumbtacked it to my pod wall at work. I see it everyday and I am reminded that I am not paralyzed and I can do this! . . . My life isn't so hard—just somedays it feels like it is." Many of the comments regarding the disability billboards echo this notion that (nondisabled) viewers should be grateful for what they have because things could be much worse, a "much worse" best illustrated by the disabled body.[11]

The billboard format exacerbates this contrast. Each of these images is located far above ground level, so that passersby literally have to look up at the pictures of the virtuous people towering over them. This difference in scale mimics the difference in scale nondisabled viewers trace between themselves and the disabled people in the billboards: "Their problems are huge—paralysis, blindness, amputation—and mine are small because I'm not disabled."

Through these messages of individualism and compliance, the disabled bodies in these billboards are used to push other disabled bodies aside, beyond the margins of these texts. Populating the margins of the FBL billboards are those other disabled people, the ones who haven't managed to graduate from Harvard, or climb Mount Everest, or sport high-tech prosthetic limbs. The ones who demand and require access to quality elementary education, or who protest the institutionalization of mostly low-income disabled people, or who refuse to accept quietly the cultural narratives of cure and assimilation. The ones who aren't interested in easy celebrations of community values but rather in the right to live within one's community, on one's own terms. The ones who recognize that the marginalization of disabled people is due not to a lack of determination or hard work or courage but to pervasive and persistent economic, political, and social exclusions. These disabled bodies are relegated to the margins of the better futures promised by the FBL: we're admitted only insofar as we promise not to complain but only to inspire.

This articulation of a better life, illustrated through the strategic use of disabled bodies, conjures not only an able-bodied future, but a heteronormative one. Joining the failed disabled bodies on the margins of these billboards are the failed bodies of queers and other deviants. If the possession of already-agreed-upon and extrapolitical values are necessary for inclusion in the FBL dreamscape, then queers will be excluded by default. If, as David Halperin argues, queerness entails "a social space for the construction of different identities, for the elaboration of various types of relationships, for the development of new cultural forms," then queerness cannot—and would not—coexist with the FBL.[12] Rather than simply accepting such values as self-evident, queer theory would insist upon an interrogation of such values. Whose values are these, and whose experiences do they take for granted?

Although the FBL presents itself as committed to and concerned about diversity and tolerance of difference—two values highlighted on the organization's website—it is a diversity that is used to consolidate a white able-bodied heteronormativity. Images on the FBL website are carefully composed of people of all ages, religious affiliations, and racial/ethnic groups, but the insistence on shared community values constrains and contains that diversity. There is no recognition that different communities might value different characteristics at different historical moments and in different contexts. On the contrary, the FBL argues that its values, and its entire campaign, "transcend any particular religion or nationality," evoking a unified global community coming together to lead values-based lives. The FBL's "better life" and "positive values" rhetoric takes for granted the

notion that "we" all agree what constitutes a better life, what values we hold dear, and, for that matter, who "we" are.

This taken-for-grantedness is made possible, at least in part, through strategic recourse to the disabled body. While the few FBL billboards that draw explicitly on 9/11 or make direct calls to patriotism have met with some criticism, the remainder of the billboards, and particularly those in what I call the disability series, serve to shield the entire FBL campaign from scrutiny. Images of inspirational cripples, from Reeve to Ellison, are used to testify to a shared set of values with which we can all easily agree. Who would publicly dispute the description of Mohammad Ali as courageous, or Alexandra Scott as inspirational, or Brooke Ellison as the embodiment of determination? Who would deny the value of perseverance, or inner strength, or foresight, particularly when embodied by people from a marginalized group? As one of my students said when I mentioned this campaign to her, "What kind of person says bad things about a billboard praising a little girl with cancer?"

Indeed, I can find little public criticism of the billboards, the "Pass It On" campaign, or the FBL itself.[13] A LexisNexis search turns up a few exposés on Philip Anschutz (his business deals, particularly his ownership of Qwest Communications, have sparked a handful of lawsuits), but nothing critical about the billboards themselves. Even in the context of an extended profile of Anschutz, the *New York Times*, for example, argues that these billboards are "largely noncontroversial, apolitical, and multi-faith," ending the discussion there.[14] Anschutz, in other words, merits critical attention by the press, but the billboards apparently do not. There is no need for a critical look at these billboards because there is nothing there, no agenda, no politics, no exclusions. In the words of the FBL, "In this day and age, it can be hard to believe that an organization's only goal is to encourage others to do good—but that really is why we exist."

If this lack of critical attention is any indication, the FBL is being taken at their word, understood as existing only to foster good works and character development. But the predominance of disabled bodies in these billboards demands greater attention. What work does disability do in this campaign, and what are the assumptions on which these signs rely?

In order to address these questions, I want to deconstruct two more billboards, one that clearly belongs in the disability series of images, and one that, at least on the surface, seems not to be about disability at all. I first saw the Marlon Shirley billboard in 2006, three years into the US occupation of Iraq.[15] Shirley's amputation is not war-related; as his FBL backstory makes clear, his left foot was amputated in 1984 as the result of a childhood accident. The billboard itself, however, doesn't give any details of Shirley's injury, and it seems likely that at least some viewers will imagine this young black male amputee as one of the 45,329 US service members injured in Iraq and Afghanistan.[16] Shirley's age, gender, and race, together with his athleticism, feed into this misperception of him as an injured veteran; young men continue to be the image of the US military, news profiles of disabled athletes tend to focus on disabled veterans, and Shirley's youthful muscularity suggest his amputation was the result of accident rather than illness. Moreover, the nature of Shirley's impairment increases the likelihood that he will be read as an injured veteran. Although an astonishing number of veterans are returning from Iraq and Afghanistan with traumatic brain injuries and/or PTSD, the figure of the amputee remains the predominant image of the disabled veteran in the media.[17]

What are we to make of the fact that this image surfaced in this particular moment, as many wounded soldiers were returning home and attempting to claim disability assistance and health care? Or at a time when soldiers with PTSD were being denied treatment and discharged because they allegedly had preexisting conditions? What might "overcoming" mean in such a context? Or a focus on personal responsibility and individual character development? To be clear: I'm not suggesting that the Pentagon is behind the FBL, determining which images appear when; nor

do I mean to suggest that the FBL is opposed to granting any medical care or social services to disabled veterans. But I do want to draw attention to the ideological frameworks and effects of these billboards. Given the other billboards in this campaign, and the responses viewers have had to such billboards, it seems reasonable to assume that many viewers will read Shirley's body and the accompanying text (Lost leg, not heart / OVERCOMING / Pass It On) as a reminder that all people, including wounded veterans, need to pull themselves up by their own bootstraps. The sign's imperative to overcome, and then to pass on such overcoming to others, makes clear that such personal achievement is the only acceptable response to tragedy; only then will we have the foundation for a better life.

To make clear how much the effectiveness of this message relies on the disabled body, I turn now to a billboard that doesn't appear to have anything to do with disability. In this billboard, Liz Murray, a young white woman, is seated in a classroom, holding a psychology textbook and smiling slightly at the camera. "From homeless to Harvard," the billboard proclaims, "AMBITION." I first saw this billboard in Austin, Texas, in the northern part of the city. The sign was directly over a clothes donation box and a bus shelter—two sites marked by poverty and homelessness— at an intersection with panhandlers on each corner. Looking up at the sign and down at the donation box, the insidiousness of this campaign hit me hard. How might the sight of this billboard affect drivers' responses to the panhandlers at the stoplight? Or how might it affect their responses to the city of Austin's changes to its panhandling laws, changes intended to push the homeless away from city streets and neighborhoods? More broadly, how might it influence their stance toward the public sector itself, and moves to further shrink public services? Does a values-based life mean that we should preach ambition to the homeless? Is ambition all that the homeless lack? Surely Murray's journey to Harvard was more complicated than that, but the juxtaposition of her smiling face and the donation box suggests otherwise.

Although this particular billboard does not seem at first to fit in my disability series, I want to position it as such. Not only are many homeless people disabled, homelessness is a threat all-too-real for many disabled people; homelessness is a disability issue. But even Murray's own "billboard backstory" draws a link with disability. Her parents were both drug addicts when she was a child, and it was their addiction that caused them to lose their housing. Her mother eventually died of AIDS, and Murray nursed her father through a long illness. These details emerge in reading her story on the FBL website, as do examples of the many kinds of assistance she received in her childhood. The sound-bite format of the billboard eclipses these details, however, completely removing her story from any social or political context.

Responses to the billboard suggest that this removal of context has been effective. Rafael, in Salinas, California, writes on the FBL website: "Thank you for this wonderful billboard and its prime location. I saw this billboard driving along highway 99 in California's Central Valley where unemployment and poverty is at double digits. Ambition lets us all know that everything is possible if you go after it." But can ambition really solve the problem of unemployment? How is Murray's story being used to push other bodies—disabled and nondisabled—out of the margins of the billboards, those who haven't managed to ride the wave of personal responsibility to success? Personal responsibility becomes the only factor that matters, the only thing standing between the homeless and a Harvard education.

What I want to suggest is that the predominance of disability billboards in the FBL campaign makes it easier for most people to read this kind of decontextualized paean to personal responsibility as apolitical and benign. Queer theorists Lauren Berlant and Lee Edelman suggest that the figure of the child is used to render certain positions as extrapolitical, as beyond the realm of politics, and I suggest that the disabled body performs a similar function within the logic of the FBL. To quote Edelman,

Such "self-evident" one-sidedness—the affirmation of a value so unquestioned, because so obviously unquestionable, as that of the Child whose innocence solicits our defense—is precisely, of course, what distinguishes public service announcements from the partisan discourse of political argumentation. But it is also, I suggest, what makes such announcements so oppressively political . . . shap[ing] the logic within which the political can be thought.[18]

In the case of the FBL, the "unquestioned because so obviously unquestionable" position is that of praising disabled people for overcoming their disabilities. What could possibly be wrong with highlighting the character of people who have worked hard and succeeded?

This question runs throughout online discussions of the billboard campaign. Anytime someone challenges the neoliberal demands of the billboards, there are readers who respond with calls for more trust and less cynicism. As one commentator puts it, "Take the message you are given and stop trying to decipher hidden intentions. [I]'ll do you a lot of good."[19] Even some of those who are suspicious of Philip Anschutz's involvement with the FBL (and who therefore worry that there might be "hidden intentions") make distinctions between Anschutz's politics and the values he promotes. Maria Niles of *BlogHer*, for example, is wary of Anschutz's involvement, casting her politics as far different from his, but admits to liking and appreciating the uplifting messages of the billboards.[20] Justin Berrier, writing on the *MediaMatters* blog, stresses that he has "no problem with the Foundation for a Better Life's values messages" even as he condemns the secrecy surrounding Anschutz's involvement with the organization.[21] Respondents to a critical story on Portland's Indymedia site react similarly, with one explaining that his "concerns are hardly the message, but clearly the messenger"; another notes that, "while the info on Anschutz is disturbing to me, and I don't like the Unity/Spirit of

America stuff, I thought the other messages passed along were good."[22]

There are bloggers challenging the FBL billboards, and some of them challenge the campaign for its exclusionary notions of community, much as I do here. But their critiques are almost always leveled at the explicitly, or recognizably, political billboards, those that make explicit reference to patriotism and nationalism. The disability billboards are given a pass, either not discussed at all or critiqued only for their "saccharine" or "cheesy" tone. Yet, as I detail here, the disability series is also political, and those images play a significant role in creating the exclusionary, and coercive, notions of community that pervade the campaign as a whole. We need to recognize and challenge this strategic deployment of disability, acknowledging that rhetorics of disability acceptance and inclusion can be used to decidedly un-crip ends.[23]

Advertising, including public service announcements, works by "reflect[ing] preexisting ideological narratives," and the FBL billboards are successful because they draw on commonsense, familiar understandings of disability.[24] The use of realistic photographs facilitates the reception of these billboards as truth. As Rosemarie Garland-Thomson explains, "Photography's immediacy and claim to truth intensify what it tells viewers about disability, at once shaping and registering the public perception of disability."[25] Seeing disability as the site of and for personal struggle, overcoming, and triumph—one of the dominant frames for understanding disability in this culture—makes it easier to overlook the ideological underpinnings of this campaign.

As these responses suggest, most of the FBL billboards—and by extension, the entire Pass It On campaign—are seen to be not about politics but about hope and community and goodness. And it is the presence of disabled minds/bodies that makes this message possible, not because disabled minds/bodies are recognized as embodying hope, community, or goodness, but because we assume that anyone who finds Christopher Reeve inspiring or wants to say kind things about Marlon Shirley must embody

these characteristics. These ads are effectively cast as beyond reproach because what oppositional stance could one possibly take to these texts? There is no need to explore whose values are celebrated in this campaign, whose bodies are seen as belonging to the community, whose practices are valued. As a result, those failed disabled bodies inhabiting the margins of the billboards remain on the margins, as do the bodies of others unable to meet the FBL's standard of virtue, unwelcome in the FBL community.

But "community" rests on the notion that people can come together in consensus and unity, putting aside their differences in order to create a unified whole grounded in common experiences and common values. This presumption of unity, however, excludes differences and dissent, thereby creating a self-perpetuating homogeneity.[26] Attempts to determine in advance how to adjudicate community values run the risk of solidifying existing understandings of community, thereby making it much more difficult to shift or expand definitions of "community" in the future. Current understandings of such concepts then become the standard against which to measure future articulations, potentially keeping in place barriers to access that are not as yet recognized as such, thereby prohibiting or marginalizing other bodies, identities, and practices. Instead, following Judith Butler, I propose "open[ing] up the field of possibility . . . without dictating which kinds of possibilities ought to be realized."[27]

Queercrip Futures

There is another billboard in the Foundation for a Better Life's disability series that I have yet to address. Their final disability-related sign features a young baseball player dressed in his team uniform and holding a baseball bat. He sits proudly in his wheelchair, and his fellow wheelchair-baseball teammates are in a semicircle behind him, with a few nondisabled spectators standing in the borders of the photo. The word OPPORTUNITY appears on the right side of the billboard, over the phrase "A league of their own." According to the text, these young baseball players are flourishing thanks to their being given the opportunity to play in a "league of their own."

Drawing on the tools of feminist, queer, and disability studies scholars, I want to read this billboard differently, to crip and queer its representations. My oppositional reading begins by contrasting the picture in this billboard with the others in the disability series. This piece touting "opportunity" is the only one in which a disabled person is situated in a community, surrounded by other disabled people and their friends and family. Unlike Ali, Scott, Reeve, Keller, Goldberg, Ellison, Hamilton, Shirley, Fox, Bender, and Weihenmayer, all of whom are depicted alone, or Hoyt, who is featured with his "devoted" father, the baseball player is presented as part of a much larger community, one in which he is an active participant. He has gained recognition not for an individual achievement but for teamwork and collective action. Such a depiction seems appropriate, as this billboard is the only one to tout a value that hints at a larger social and political context. Unlike courage, determination, and hard work, each of which typically describes the character of an individual person, opportunity positions someone within a larger field of social relations. This sign, then, can be interpreted as a recognition that disabled people (like nondisabled people) need opportunities and resources in order to thrive. Rather than preaching a message of charity or individual accountability, this sign can be interpreted as a call for increased social responsibility, for working to ensure that all people have access to opportunity.

But this kind of reading requires working hard against the grain, and, as feminist and queer scholars have long noted, such readings can be far from satisfying.[28] For, even as I describe my imagined interpretation, I know that most viewers read this image through a heavily sentimental lens. Rosemarie Garland-Thomson argues that images of disabled children epitomize the sentimentalization of disability, a process by which disability appears as "a problem to solve, an obstacle to eliminate, a chal-

lenge to meet," thereby motivating the viewer to act on behalf of the "sympathetic, helpless child."[29] Within such a framework, it makes sense that the billboard backstory for this image includes quotes only from the parents of these children, not from the children themselves. We learn that the boy in the center of the frame is Justin, and that he has cerebral palsy, but we learn these facts only through the words of Justin's (unidentified) parent. Justin's visible presence in the billboard but verbal absence in the backstory suggests yet again that it is the nondisabled whom the FBL most wants to reach. Rather than read this billboard as a story about increased social responsibility, or about the vibrant communities that exist among and with disabled people, viewers are to discover yet another paean to personal virtues such as charity and tolerance. "Opportunity" reads not as part of a collective responsibility, as something tightly woven in structures of privilege and oppression, but as a personal obligation to those imagined as less fortunate than oneself, a private gift completely divorced from ableism, discrimination, or inequality.

Instead of resigning myself to the existing images, then, I want to imagine another disability series, another set of billboards that trumpet "a better life." My disability series imagines "community values" not in the FBL understanding, in which discrete individuals manifest a set of already-agreed-upon values in their own private lives, but in a feminist/queer/crip understanding of community and *coalition* values, in which both the parameters of the community and the values praised within it are open to debate. What does "courage," "determination," or "opportunity" mean? What kinds of practices and attitudes do they include, and which do they exclude? Who is involved in determining the characteristics valued in a particular community? Who is included in—or excluded from—the community itself? How can different communities come together to form coalitions? Rather than accepting the FBL proclamation that *unity* is "what makes us great," I envision a media campaign that favors *dissent* at least as much as unity, that recognizes political protest and activism as signs of courage, that is as concerned with collective responsibility and accountability as personal.

I am not the first to suggest alternate billboards to the ones created by the FBL. Billboard activists across the country have "liberated" some of these signs, with the "What makes us great/ UNITY" billboard attracting the most attention. In the FBL version of this billboard, a young white girl waves an American flag while sitting on the shoulders of an adult male, perhaps her father. There are other people and flags in the background, suggesting a patriotic rally of some kind; the "billboard backstory" confirms this characterization, describing it as a rally in Arizona on September 12, 2001. In the reimagined versions, posted on Indymedia, one has been changed to read "What makes us great/ IMPUNITY," while another states that "what makes us great" is "PROFIT$ AT ANY COST."[30] Such efforts literally and metaphorically disrupt the borders of the billboard, making the billboard itself into a contested and contestable site, positioning the message contained therein as part of a larger debate. The "us" invoked in the billboard is apparently not so unified after all.

As far as I know, however, these activists have yet to liberate the billboards in the disability series, and this fact supports my contention that the presence of disability positions these billboards—and, effectively, the overall Pass It On campaign—as beyond reproach. Unlike the UNITY billboard, which has consistently been claimed as a political space and statement, the disability billboards are assumed to be devoid of any political content, and therefore not in need of debate or dialogue. The combination of words such as "determination," "inspiration," and "courage" with the images of disabled people creates an appeal seen as impossible to refuse.[31] And this lack of debate is precisely my point: through the use of the disabled body, and the long history of representations of disability as natural, individual, and apolitical, the FBL casts its entire campaign as impossible to refuse.

In the face of this denial of politics, my extended disability series features Leroy Moore, a disabled African American poet and activist whose *courage* is evident in his writings condemning racism, ableism, and their interrelationships; Corbett O'Toole, a white lesbian polio survivor who models *coalition building* as she bridges queer, lesbian, and disability communities and concerns in her activism; disability rights activists from ADAPT crawling up the steps of the Supreme Court building who illustrate the vital importance of *dissent;* the coalition of genderqueer and disability activists involved in PISSAR—People In Search of Safe and Accessible Restrooms—who embody *direct action* when they map gender-neutral and disability-accessible restrooms on college campuses; and Mia Mingus, a disabled queer woman of color practicing *solidarity* in her work on reproductive justice. And, in order to challenge the realm of "positive thinking" mandated by the FBL billboards—itself a kind of ablemindedness—I also imagine billboards acknowledging *anger* over discriminatory policies and billboards *mourning* the loss of community activists.[32] Disability in these images is not something to be overcome through adherence to "community values" but an identity to be claimed and reinterpreted through collective action and coalition work. In this worldview, disabled people do not lack strength of character but legal protections, access to public spaces, adequate and affordable health care, and social and political recognition.

I call for a queer/crip team of billboard liberators, scrawling the word "pity" or "tokenism" underneath the word "overcoming" on the Marlon Shirley billboard. I want to pair "inspiration"—a word that has long been the bane of disabled people's existence—with Nomy Lamm's description of a prosthetic leg as an effective, and certainly inspired, sex toy.[33] I want to see Tee Corinne's famous photograph of two naked dykes getting it on in a wheelchair plastered over the picture of Bethany Hamilton: "Me, quit? Never." Or let's replace Helen Keller as the model of "only see[ing] possibilities" with Loree Erickson, a young activist pioneering the development of radical crip porn through her film *Want*. Not only would these text/image combinations trouble the staid, assimilationist images of disabled people favored by the

FBL, they would also insist upon queer sexuality as valued.

After delivering an earlier version of this chapter at a talk in Berkeley, I joined two local crips in a small guerrilla campaign to kickstart these dialogues. We departed from the more established practice of billboard liberation and decided to liberate a bus shelter sign. With two of us in wheelchairs, and the third disabled by chronic fatigue syndrome and environmental illness (EI), the ground-level sign was easier to reach from our particular embodiments than a billboard would be. Moreover, the bus shelter seemed closer to crip communities and histories of crip activism than the billboard; public transit systems have long been targets of civil disobedience, with activists engaging in continuing struggles for accessible buses, bus and train stops, and stations.[34] We found a bus shelter in southwest Berkeley that featured the Marlon Shirley image, and, armed with spray paint and stencils, we began the liberation. Although we had not discussed it in advance, we each took on the task best suited to our impairments: Ellen Samuels served as lookout, because her EI required her to stay at a distance from the paint; my limited hand control made wielding the spray paint impossible, so I held the stencils in place, blocking the sign from public view with my body; and Anne Finger transformed the original caption "Lost Leg, Not Heart: Overcoming" into "Lost Leg, Not Rights: Overcoming Pity." Ellen snapped a quick picture of the liberated sign with her phone, and we hurried away.

In hindsight, our careful surreptitiousness was probably unnecessary. The depoliticization of disability that I trace in this chapter likely made our political acts unintelligible; no one would suspect three white women, two of them in wheelchairs, of vandalism or destruction of property. Indeed, as we moved away from the sign, we noticed two women waiting on the other side of the shelter, neither one of whom seemed to even notice what we were doing, despite our immediate proximity and excited conversation about our intent and action. Unfortunately, our liberating text was removed within days, and not long after that the FBL poster was replaced with an advertisement for *America's Next Top Model,* a different manifestation of heteronormative able-bodiedness.

I want to close with one more tweaked billboard to drive home the point that simply substituting the FBL billboards with my own, tempting though that may be, is not a permanent solution, as the *America's Top Model* ad suggests, nor is it an unambiguous one. In this final billboard, courtesy of the Billboard Liberation Front, we have the familiar image of the young white girl waving an American flag, but the text has been radically altered. NATIONALISM, the reworked ad now exclaims, "What Makes Us Blind." The billboard liberators have managed to highlight and challenge the nationalism inherent in the original advertisements, but only by relying on the same kind of normalizing logic found within the campaign as a whole. By figuring "blindness" as the sign of ignorance and exclusion, the alleged liberators of this billboard remained trapped in the ableist logic of the FBL. This time, rather than using disability to foreclose debate, the text's creators have used disability as a sign of such foreclosure. Either way, the better life heralded by the billboard isn't welcoming of disabled people.

Taking my cue from the work of queer cultural critics who remind us that "queer" is not always transgressive, I want us to reckon with the inevitability that in dealing with notions of a better life, of a better future, it is not enough to simply insert new billboards in the place of old ones; that, too, would signal a foreclosure of other potentialities and possibilities.[35] I am not merely arguing for a progress narrative of images, moving from "bad" images of disability to "good" ones.[36] I offer these cripped, queered billboards not as the real tools of a better life, not as the real future, but as a catalyst to get us thinking about what might equal a more livable life, and for whom, under what conditions and at what costs.

Notes

1 The Foundation for a Better Life, February 7, 2010, http://www.values.com/.

2 All of the billboards can be viewed on the foundation's website, which also features "inspirational stories," "good news stories," and short vignettes about specific values. See the Foundation for a Better Life, February 7, 2010, http://www.values.com.

3 The image of the Tiananmen Square protestor has been removed from the organization's website, but I am unsure as to when it disappeared. It was still on the site in 2007, but by 2010 it was gone, and there is no mention of it on the organization's website.

4 Of course, as any disability studies scholar (or social services gatekeeper) will note, determining who is and who is not disabled is easier said than done. For the purposes of this discussion, I have focused only on those figures who are widely recognized as disabled, who have publicly identified as disabled, and/or whose illnesses and disabilities are highlighted in the campaign itself.

5 The italicized words are the values highlighted in each billboard; on the billboard, the value is in white bold capitals, inside a red text box. The phrases in quotation marks are the captions on the billboards.

6 The Foundation for a Better Life, "About FBL," June 30, 2004, http://www.forbetterlife.org/main.asp?section=about&language=eng.

7 Amy Vidali offers a useful analysis of the relationship between vision and knowledge, critically examining the assumption that "knowing is seeing." Amy Vidali, "Seeing What We Know: Disability and Theories of Metaphor," *Journal of Literary and Cultural Disability Studies* 4, no. 1 (2010): 33–54. See also Georgina Kleege, *Sight Unseen* (New Haven: Yale University Press, 1999). Both the FBL billboards ("VISION") and the stylistic conventions of footnotes (e.g., "see Kleege") rely on this history of representation and this epistemology.

8 It is useful here to read the FBL's representation of Muhammad Ali in light of Anna Mollow's discussion of overcoming. Mollow rightly notes that a story of overcoming illness or disability does not have to be "a denial of political realities" but can instead be "an assertion of personal strength amid overwhelming social oppression." In the case of the FBL, however, their overcoming narratives do not highlight "individuals' power in relation to oppressive political and economic structures"—Mollow's criteria for understanding overcoming narratives differently—but rather deny that such oppression exists at all. Anna Mollow, "'When *Black* Women Start Going on Prozac': Race, Gender, and Mental Illness in Meri Nana-Ama Danquah's *Willow Weep for Me*," *MELUS* 31, no. 3 (2006): 89, 68.

9 Foundation for a Better Life, "Our Mission Statement," accessed February 7, 2010, http://www.values.com/about-us/mission-statement.

10 The FBL's Internet domain name is registered to the Anschutz Exploration Corporation, an oil and gas exploration company owned by Anschutz. See Nathan Callahan, "Corporate Vulture: Philip Anschutz Tries to Thread His Way into Heaven," *OC Weekly* 8, no. 35 (2003), accessed September 18, 2004, http://www.ocweekly.com/ink/03/35/news-callahan.php; Stuart Elliott, "A Campaign Promotes Noble Behavior," *New York Times*, November 9, 2001; Colleen Kenney, "Lincoln Receives Several Messages of Hope from Up Above" *Lincoln Journal Star*, February 5, 2004; Jerermy David Stolen, "Foundation for a Better Life," Portland Independent Media Center, accessed July 4, 2004, http://portlandindymedia.org/2002/02/7617.shtml; and Jeremy David Stolen, "Big Money behind 'Inspirational' Billboard Campaign," accessed April 15, 2006, http://

www.theportlandalliance.org/2002/april/billboard.html. See also Sandra Thompson, "Billboards Marketing Virtues We Can Use Now," *St. Petersburg Times*, February 2, 2002, http://saintpetersburgtimes.com/2002/02/02/Columns/Billboards_marketing_.shtml.

11 These kinds of responses likely feel familiar to many of us with visible disabilities. I have more than once been stopped by a stranger who wanted to tell me that seeing me made their day. As one woman put it, "I was feeling so sorry for myself today, but then I saw you and realized how lucky I am."

12 David M. Halperin, *Saint Foucault: Toward a Gay Hagiography* (New York: Oxford University Press, 1995), 67.

13 There has been some attention to the campaign in the blogosphere, and I address those responses below. Thus far scholars have largely ignored the billboards, and most news coverage has been positive.

14 Graham Bowley, "Goal! He Spends It on Beckham," *New York Times,* April 22, 2007, http://www.nytimes.com/2007/04/22/business/yourmoney/22phil.html?pagewanted=i&_r=1&ref=media&adxnnlx=1313886061-H/sYx4pZH4V3t39yunqx3A.

15 The billboards are not dated on the FBL website, making it difficult to determine when each billboard debuted nationwide. The Shirley billboard was not one of the original images.

16 The Iraq and Afghanistan Veterans of America organization (IAVA) includes official casualty statistics from the Department of Defense on its website, but it also encourages visitors to research the statistics provided by private organizations and individual researchers. Available at http://iava.org, accessed August 10, 2011. For additional statistics, see, for example, the website http://icasualties.org, accessed August 10, 2011.

17 For example, *Newsweek's* editors chose an image of an amputee to illustrate their cover story, "Failing Our Wounded," March 5, 2007, on newly disabled veterans and their troubles with Veterans Affairs.

18 Lee Edelman, *No Future: Queer Theory and the Death Drive* (Durham, NC: Duke University Press, 2004), 2. In focusing on the figure of the child in American politics, Edelman draws on the work of Lauren Berlant's *The Queen of America Goes to Washington City: Essays on Sex and Citizenship* (Durham, NC: Duke University Press, 1997). Berlant traces the ways in which the ideal American citizen is imagined through the figure of the child.

19 Katie, August 29, 2005, http://majikthise.typepad.com/majikthise_/2004/11/what_is_the_fou/comments/page/2/#comments, last accessed July 29, 2010. The "majikthise" blog is no longer active and this link now leads to a blank page. (I first saw the entry in April 2006.)

20 Niles eventually decides that the ads make her too uncomfortable, but that discomfort seems to stem from her distrust of Anschutz rather than the content or rhetoric of the billboards themselves. Maria Niles, "Am I Too Cynical for a Better Life?" *BlogHer,* June 7, 2008, http://www.blogher.com/am-i-too-cynical-better-life.

21 Justin Berrier, "Fox Hides Anti-Gay, Right-Wing Background of Foundation for a Better Life," *MediaMatters,* December 16, 2010, http://mediamatters.org/blog/201012160022.

22 *Observer,* May 4, 2002, http://portland.indymedia.org/en/2002/02/7617.shtml; JYPD, May 1, 2002, http://portland.indymedia.org/en/2002/02/7617.shtml.

23 Robert McRuer offers necessary caution about disability rhetorics and frameworks, noting that they can and are being used in ways counter to radical crip politics. See, for example, Robert McRuer, "Taking It to the Bank: Independence and Inclusion on the World Market," *Journal of Literary Disability* 1, no. 2 (2007): 5–14.

24 Noël Sturgeon, *Environmentalism in Popular Culture: Gender,*

Race, Sexuality, and the Politics of the Natural (Tucson: University of Arizona Press, 2009), 28.

25 Rosemarie Garland-Thomson, "Seeing the Disabled: Visual Rhetorics of Disability in Popular Photography," in *The New Disability History: American Perspectives*, ed. Paul K. Longmore and Lauri Umansky (New York: New York University Press, 2001), 338.

26 Iris Marion Young, *Justice and the Politics of Difference* (Princeton, NJ: Princeton University Press, 1990), 227–34; Betty Sasaki, "Toward a Pedagogy of Coalition," *Twenty-First-Century Feminist Classrooms: Pedagogies of Identity and Difference*, ed. Amie A. MacDonald and Susan Sánchez-Casal (New York: Palgrave, 2002), 33.

27 Judith Butler, *Gender Trouble: Feminism and the Subversion of Identity*, 10th anniversary ed. (New York: Routledge, 1999), viii. See also Judith Butler, "Contingent Foundations," in *Feminist Contentions: A Philosophical Exchange*, ed. Seyla Benhabib, Judith Butler, Drucilla Cornell, and Nancy Fraser (New York: Routledge, 1995), 50–51; and Chantal Mouffe, *The Return of the Political* (London: Verso, 1993), 8.

28 Susan Stewart, of the Kiss and Tell Collective, notes, "Some of us have been reading across the grain for so long that our eyes have splinters." Kiss and Tell, *Her Tongue on my Theory* (Vancouver: Press Gang, 1994), 51.

29 Rosemarie Garland-Thomson, "The Politics of Staring: Visual Rhetorics of Disability in Popular Photography," *Disability Studies: Enabling the Humanities*, ed. Sharon L. Snyder, Brenda Jo Brueggemann, and Rosemarie Garland-Thomson (New York: Modern Language Association, 2002), 63.

30 Photographs of these altered billboards are available on the Portland Independent Media Center's website, accessed July 4, 2004, http://portland.indymedia.org/en/2002/02/7617.shtml.

31 Edelman, *No Future*, 2.

32 I am influenced here by Heather Love and her insistence that we attend to negative affect. Heather Love, *Feeling Backward: Loss and the Politics of Queer History* (Cambridge, MA: Harvard University Press, 2007).

33 Nomy Lamm, "Private Dancer: Evolution of a Freak," *Restricted Access: Lesbians on Disability*, ed. Victoria A. Brownworth and Susan Raffo (Seattle: Seal Press, 1999), 152–61. For an incisive critique of the inspiring disabled person, see John B. Kelly, "Inspiration," *Ragged Edge Online* (January/February 2003), accessed February 7, 2010, http://www.raggededgemagazine.com/0103/0103ft1.html.

34 The disability rights organization ADAPT was a key player in transportation struggles in the 1980s; ADAPT originally stood for American Disabled for Accessible Public Transit. For more information on ADAPT, see http://www.adapt.org. For a more extensive history of disability rights activism, including transit battles, see, for example, Sharon N. Barnartt and Richard K. Scotch, *Disability Protests: Contentious Politics, 1970–1999* (Washington, DC: Gallaudet University Press, 2001); (Doris Zames Fleischer and Frieda Zames, *The Disability Rights Movement: From Charity to Confrontation* (Philadelphia: Temple University Press, 2001); and Joseph Shapiro, *No Pity: People with Disabilities Forging a New Civil Rights Movement* (New York: Three Rivers Press, 1994).

35 See, for example, Jasbir Puar's analysis of homonationalism. Jasbir Puar, *Terrorist Assemblages: Homonationalism in Queer Times* (Durham, NC: Duke University Press, 2007). See also McRuer, "Taking It to the Bank."

36 As Robert McRuer shows in his analysis of disability imagery, it is not enough to frame some images of disability as "positive" and others as "negative." McRuer, *Crip Theory*, 171–98.

Now What? The (Anti) Conclusion

Imagine the following scenario: You are on break from university, a holiday from the grind of classes and exams. Back with family and friends, you probably feel a sense of relief. But things have also changed since you were home last—or, more specifically, you seem to have changed. You realize you're thinking a lot more about differences between people and the injustices in the world, about issues like sexism and ableism and colonialism. And you're seeing these "-isms" in play around you, recognizing how much your own sense of self, your multiple identities, are part of these -isms in some way, too. Over the past few months at school, you helped organize events about some of these issues: a class project to raise awareness about accessibility to public bathrooms; an invited speaker for the Student Union's "Sex Week" to challenge its otherwise unspoken heteronormativity; a march with Indigenous peoples about missing and murdered Aboriginal women. In short, you've been learning and doing so much, and you want to raise consciousness among your peers and make real and lasting change in the world around you.

And now you're home and talking with your friends and family about all of this—at the dinner table, while watching TV, as you're riding around town—and their response isn't always what you hope for. Often they're surprised, occasionally they're impressed, but sometimes they're just offended. In all cases, however, you recognize that you're increasingly perceived as being out of step, perhaps even as a bit of a "downer." You find yourself thinking they don't really want to have these conversations, or hear what you've learned about the injustice that is now so obvious (to you at least). This new knowledge, which really excites you, also seems to isolate you. Even as your acceptance into an institution of higher education, your professional ambitions, and your expanding horizons are exactly what your family hoped for, these seem to also be the very things that are alienating you from them. And all this talk about feminism or anti-racism or settler colonialism—the things you now think of as really important— seems to have become the source of some uncomfortable feelings from the place you once belonged and the people with whom you once felt "at home." Now what?

Complicating Matters

Now what, indeed! You are near the end of your Women's and Gender Studies course, an experience that (we hope!) has provided some new insights and a more developed sense of why it is that people are different and how it is that the world isn't fair. But now, you may be thinking: "What do I do with all these new ideas?" or, "Now that I know, how shall I live?" By now, it's clear that WGS is a discipline that revolves around some basic concepts—knowledges, identities, equalities, bodies, places, representations—that are applicable to just about everything around you. They really are concepts with everyday uses, handy tools to rethink a number of issues you've probably encountered before; and now, those same issues have been rendered somewhat strange. (And that's a good thing!) The examples presented in the chapters, in addition to other readings and resources you've encountered throughout this course, have demonstrated just how far reaching this field is and how it contributes to richer and more complicated understandings of the various worlds we inhabit. We think that's one of the most exciting things about WGS: It has something to add to just about every conversation[1].

But you've probably also been struck by the attention to the development of these concepts themselves as much as by what they can do in analyzing the world. These chapters, additional readings and resources, and discussions with classmates and friends have illustrated that these concepts are also always being tested and refined. They are never simply established conclusively and then applied in the same way forever. Rather, one of the central mandates of WGS is to continuously ask questions about the assumptions and implications of our own thinking. And this self-reflexivity is important, because complicated issues are rarely settled once and for all, and easy answers are hard to come by. As this book (and this course) has made clear, it's not easy to think about something like identities or places or bodies without recognizing how often those concepts lead us to contradictory conclusions—conclusions that also never quite seem conclusive at all. In addition, though, working with these concepts forces us to recognize how much, even in the midst of all this complexity, we still tend to nonetheless take certain ideas about those same concepts for granted, still tend to leave some questions unasked. For instance, why do so many of us remain invested

[1] **THINK ABOUT:** What are some new perspectives you've gained in this class? What ideas or examples did you find most instructive? What readings or discussions provided you with useful frameworks for thinking about the world in a different way? Most importantly, how will you apply those frameworks in the future?

in the idea of identities, even as we recognize how constructed they are, how multiply they are defined, how exclusionary they can be, and how they so often limit our lives? And even while we're focused on better futures for greater numbers of people, on what we've been calling *more equitable outcomes*, how do we know when we get there? Whose version of equality of outcome is recognized, and whose is sidelined? And how far in the future do we have to look to see when, or if, it happens? Can some knowledges or views of social justice cancel out others?

Think, for example, of how often arguments for abortion rights draw on claims that abortion has to be available in cases of fetal "deformity." And even many people who argue for more restricted access to abortion nonetheless agree that it might be necessary in some cases, such as the potential, or even certainty, of disability. Both of these positions rest on and perpetuate ideas about disability as an unwanted tragedy. Is there another way to think about this issue that doesn't depend on this kind of hierarchy of desired bodies, that doesn't see arguments for reproductive justice and disability justice as opposed, but can hold them together at the same time? No matter what one thinks about abortion, this example clearly illustrates how working towards social change can often be contradictory and conflicted, where different narratives of change cannot simply be added together, but instead, can and do counter each other. When one narrative becomes a dominant mode of knowing the world, another might become impossible to articulate: In this case, reproductive rights are articulated at the cost of perpetuating disability as always unwanted. Thus, paying attention to which narratives of a socially just future are told and find an audience—and which aren't and don't—has important ramifications for how we think about social justice.

Finally, think all the way back to a claim we made in the "Knowledges" chapter that knowing the world differently will make the world different, more fair, more accessible, more accepting for more people. This claim captures the belief that how knowledge is constructed is foundational to thinking about how identities are formed and negotiated, how differences between us "make a difference," and how social justice is defined and then attained (or not). However, as this book has illustrated, that relationship between what we know and what we do is far from direct or obvious. We may have many different knowledges. Even having the same knowledges may lead us to contemplate different social changes. And even if we agree on a needed change, we may still feel hesitant about it or resist it outright. Surely, doing the right thing shouldn't be this complicated. But very often, of course, it is. So, what to do?

Negotiating Attachments

Consider these common experiences:

> You love the ways that hip-hop—the music, the style, the social critiques, the positive value placed on what the rest of society tends to find too transgressive—moves you to imagine a better world; it is where you locate your political consciousness. But that music, style, and positive value seems to also be intertwined with plenty of misogyny, homophobia, ableism, and ageism—that are not part of your politics. Now what?

> Most of us are very attached to our cell phones, so much so that it is hard to imagine even going a full class period without being able to check them. But we also know that there are all kinds of inequities associated with their production, from the working conditions and labor rights in overseas factories to the mining of the minerals used in their construction and their connections to war, child labor, and environmental degradation. Now what?

If, too often, our knowledges and actions don't always align and may in fact pull us in different directions, then we need to explore both what produces that contradiction and how we come to be at odds with the social change we also claim to want. On the one hand, the reason people hang on to knowledges that perpetuate various kinds of unfairness can be explained pretty easily: Some groups of people benefit from their privileged position inherent in such knowledges. White privilege, male privilege, citizenship privilege, able-bodied privilege, heterosexual privilege—they are all around us, and many of us gain so much from them. As we examined in the "Equalities" chapter, these are privileges that pay off for some of us in various contexts: for instance, having access to buildings because of the ability to walk up the steps. The idea of privilege, however, doesn't completely account for the gap between knowledge and action. If there is so often a gap between what we know, what we want, and what we are willing to do to get what we want, how can we negotiate these tensions? What else might we have to recognize to account for that gap?

One way to respond to these questions is to also consider the importance of *attachments*, the emotional investments we make in ideas about what's "right" or "good" or "desirable." These investments range from what we like about the things we consume (hip-hop, cell phones) to ideas like wanting a more just world for more people. As illustrated in the above two examples, though, these investments come into conflict with each other. Even more, they are exacerbated by our attachment to particular versions of ourselves—as innocent, as good, as doing the right thing—that frame the ways we see and experience these tensions. For example, think about some fairly common attachments to desired lifestyles: wanting everyone to live in a "safe" neighborhood; to attend a "good" school; or to practice particular forms of consumption (such as wearing fashionable clothes or buying sustainable products). Many of these reflect values that seem related to social justice and a more just life for many people—that is, they seem like good or positive values. But their pursuit might very well produce effects that work against other values in which we are also invested, producing moments of contradiction between what we know and want, and what we say and do. Suppose, for instance, that certain material sacrifices are necessary (tax increases, perhaps) in order to ensure that every person's neighborhood is safe. Or, suppose that we have to pay more out of our limited monthly budget in order to ensure that every consumer good is sustainably produced and that the people who produced our fashionable clothes or green products make a living wage and have dignified working conditions. That these seem like choices with definite consequences for us—about which we often have uncomfortable ambivalences—demonstrates the power of our emotional investments in a particular set of social relations. Few people consciously set out to contribute to the pain of others. But the ideas to which we attach ourselves contain contradictions that can produce these results nevertheless. And they can be hard to let go of, even when those unintended consequences are identified. For many of us, examining our emotional investments too closely can also invoke fears about loss and about what we might need to give up, whether those are our consumption pleasures or our beliefs in ourselves as people who want to do the right thing[2].

If we acknowledge that our attachments are contradictory, then perhaps we need to temper our impulse to "do good" with equal amounts of reflection about how what

(2)**TALK ABOUT:** Can you think of other examples where you experience these kinds of tensions and contradictions—that is, where something you believe in or do has other associations you find problematic? Think about large social institutions—education, religion—as well as smaller more everyday practices—clothing, eating, sports. What are some of the issues that account for these tensions, that become the ways in which we negotiate these choices for and to ourselves? What do we mean when we use the expression "guilty pleasure," for instance? What do we tell ourselves (if anything) about what is okay (or not okay) about this guilty pleasure?

we do is seldom good for all. Determining a course of action rarely offers certainty that we in fact are doing the right thing, or that what constitutes the right thing is equally shared by all. And yet, even doing nothing isn't an option either, because simply acquiescing to the world as it is means perpetuating a version that is also never neutral. Our presence in the world and the decisions we make in our everyday lives always have an impact on the lives of others, resulting in tensions that are not necessarily reconcilable. It is this recognition of the complexity of the relationship between knowledge and social change that demands a habit of constant reflection (and humbleness) in our pursuit of making the world a more just place for more people.

The Concept at Work: University Attachments

Think about your university or college. All academic institutions tell stories—their official narratives—about what they are, where they come from, and how their existence is vital to their various stakeholders (e.g., students, faculty, staff, parents, alumni, donors, the state, employers). And these stories in turn shape ideas about how people in the institutions act, and on whose behalf, in the present and future (whether they enthusiastically adopt and promote, or resist and question, these stories). These narratives are a way of telling an institutional history—of highlighting some events while diminishing others while completely rejecting still others. As such, they're a way to attract particular students, faculty, and staff as well as garner donations and enhance reputations. And as with all stories, they create a sense of belonging for some people while simultaneously indicating how other people just don't fit[3].

Suppose, for instance, that a university was established 40-odd years ago, out of two existing schools that were already well over 100 years old, and renamed as a "new" university (which is actually the case for one of the authors). Which story of its origins does this new university tell? Does it tell a narrative of how it has over a century-long history of providing university education to the people and community around it? While evoking a sense of tradition, commitment to that community, and permanent presence in that location, it might also bring along with it a history of exclusion, elitism, and colonialism. Or does it tell a story that stresses its newness, its

[3]**TALK ABOUT:** What are the ways that your university or college cultivates attachment to the institution? Think about artifacts like mascots, sports uniforms, school colors, plaques and statues, paintings (of past presidents or big donors for instance). Or think about events like sports, speakers, and ceremonies (such as convocation). What narratives about the institution are evoked on these occasions? What stories about the institution are not told?

modernity, perhaps even its edginess, thereby claiming that it has always been open to all? But this is a story that doesn't account for a past of limiting admission only to white men and offers no historical basis to talk about why many groups of people are still excluded from the university. What are the emotional attachments to these very different origin stories for students, faculty, administration, alumni, and donors?

If we think of each of these narratives as contradictory frameworks through which to see and know the university, then we see how the stories it tells frame our attachment to it. Neither of these stories is inherently truer or more accurate, but both clearly lead in quite different directions. And in some contexts, and for some audiences, one might be a better or at least more useful narrative than the other to tell. But it's probably also clear that all of us would find ourselves preferring one story over the other, feeling more invited into one narrative because it lines up more with how we think of ourselves (as modern or traditional). The recognition of these attachments allows us to understand why we articulate, promote, and even fight for some versions of the university over others.

Or, let's take another example a little closer to home: the discipline of Women's and Gender Studies. As discussed in the "Knowledges" chapter, the predominant story told about this field is that it emerged out of the feminist movements of the 1960s and entered the university to make women and their experiences both part of the curriculum and members of recognized and endorsed knowers. Forty-five years later, when the majority of students at most universities in Canada and the United States are women, when feminist scholarship is required learning in many fields (especially in the humanities and social sciences), when WGS as a stand-alone field exists in more universities and colleges than not, and when there are many more women faculty and administrators, this narrative of WGS's origins from feminist social movements is clearly a success story, a story of progress.

But let's return to that question of the implications of institutional origin stories. The question of which women have been included in this success and how their inclusion has made a difference in the story (or not) is just as important to ask, since it might lead to a different interpretation of this (apparent) progress. Another way to think about it is this: What are the invisible adjectives in this story of WGS? Does the story of progress hold true if we speak of Native American and First Nations women, transwomen, working-class women, women of color, immigrant women, or disabled women? Are there different terms of inclusion for different groups of women (or men) hidden within this disciplinary narrative of progress? How might this difference make a difference in understanding various attachments to the field of WGS and its versions of social justice, or to university educated people who want to make the world a better place? In short, for whom is this progress narrative actually "progress?"

And Now . . .

To sum it all up: Now that this course has just about come to an end, how might your everyday life be affected by what you've learned? What are your most compelling new WGS knowledges? And how might you choose (or not choose) to put them to work in the world? Neither this nor any other book can point to some universal, definitive path toward a more just world. Even when we are certain of our social justice intentions, the work has only just begun. Reflecting on our intentions in relation to our privileges and oppressions, our multiple social locations and contexts, and our attachments and those of others, is really more of an approach—as opposed to a formula—for social justice. It always assumes that one clear-cut path to a better world does not (and probably should not) exist. What certainly does exist, though, is a world more full of complexity and contradiction than we might have thought. It is a world where the knowledge of how *People are different, and the world isn't fair* moves us to always ask, *Now that we know, how shall we live?*

Preview of Readings

Chess, Simone, Alison Kafer, Jessi Quizar, and Mattie Udora Richardson. 2008. "Calling all Restroom Revolutionaries!" In *That's Revolting! Queer Strategies for Resisting Assimilation*, edited by Mattilda Bernstein Sycamore, 216–233. Berkeley, CA: Soft Skull Press.

Edwards, Gemma. 2014. "From Collective Behaviour to Misbehaviour: Redrawing the Boundaries of Political and Cultural Resistance." In *Social Movements and Protest*, 213–234. New York, NY: Cambridge University Press.

Coulthard, Glen Sean. 2014. "Lessons from Idle No More: The Future of Indigenous Activism." In *Red Skin White Masks: Rejecting the Colonial Politics of Recognition*, 165–179 [excerpt]. Minneapolis, MN: University of Minnesota Press.

In this final chapter, we consider the question of what to do with the new insights learned in the introductory Women's and Gender Studies course. Or, as we have talked about it throughout this text: Now that we know the various ways in which people are different and the world isn't fair, how shall we live? The new understandings produced through the concepts explored in this book—knowledges, identities, equalities, bodies, places, representations—are constantly being rethought within the field of WGS. In other words, the field always interrogates its own knowledge production at the same time as it questions the world around us. Part of that interrogation is to consider our own attachments, investments we make to particular ways of being in our various worlds, that have an impact on our attempts to "do good." We consider how such attachments to a lifestyle, to an institution, to a narrative, or to a discipline mean social justice solutions can only ever be partial and temporary, always giving way to being rethought—and we insist on that process as both necessary and productive.

"Calling All Restroom Revolutionaries!" is a collaborative piece that illustrates the power of political coalitions. In this case, public bathrooms are analyzed as locations where people with disabilities, trans and genderqueer people, people who menstruate, and parents of small children all have needs that are not accounted for in a typical public restroom. This article makes bathroom accessibility an activist project that can be replicated in public spaces everywhere.

- In what ways are public bathrooms reflective of assumptions about identity categories?
- How would you assess your institution's bathroom accessibility? How could you change that accessibility, if you find issues with it?
- What are other spaces we encounter in our everyday lives that are also in need of an accessibility evaluation? How might we go about identifying and creating a coalition of people to engage in accessibility work? What would work best at your institution?

The excerpt from Glen Sean Coulthard's chapter, "Lessons from Idle No More: The Future of Indigenous Activism," assesses a social movement that is still unfolding. While specific in its references to this recent indigenous activism (mostly in Canada), Coulthard points out some object lessons about tactics and strategies that could prove useful in the context of other social movements. In exploring the value of direct action to coalition work with other identity groups, as well as the consequences of working from the assumption that the nation-state is both predicated on stolen land and is a legitimate starting place for negotiations, Coulthard argues that the unique accomplishments of Idle No More have provided new perspectives to both First Nations and settler colonizers in conceptualizing their respective futures together.

- Have you heard of Idle No More? If so, how have their actions been talked about in what you've heard? What assumptions seem to be at work (in media reports, on internet sites, in your discussions) in deciding whether or not their demands are legitimate?

- If you haven't heard of them, why do you think that is? How do we tend to hear about dissent and protest? Are the outlets that we have now (e.g., network news, social media, newspapers) adequate for the task of monitoring and accounting for groups of people who have grievances against the nation-state?
- What are your responses to direct actions of groups like Idle No More? Do they prompt you to rethink your own attachments? Why or why not?

"From Collective Behaviour to Misbehaviour: Redrawing the Boundaries of Political and Cultural Resistance" is Gemma Edwards' consideration of how individual resistance works in the name of collective action. She argues that organized public protest is not the only way to engage in making social change. Rather, she argues, we must also focus on "misbehaviour," even if it sometimes seems unintentional and its meanings shift across various contexts.

- What does Edwards mean by the term misbehaviour? Thinking about the various institutions of which you are a part, can you remember an occasion where someone's misbehavior resulted in changing that institution?
- What are the potential risks of utilizing misbehavior as a social change mechanism? What else might need to be considered in taking up this term as a way to explore social justice actions?
- What new perspectives might misbehavior offer us as a political practice in our everyday lives?

Calling All Restroom Revolutionaries!

Simone Chess, Alison Kafer, Jessi Quizar, and Mattie Udora Richardson

CALLING ALL RESTROOM REVOLUTIONARIES: People In Search of Safe and Accessible Restrooms (PISSAR) needs you! We are a coalition of queer, genderqueer, and disabled people working toward greater awareness of the need for safe and accessible bathrooms on campus and in the dorms. BE A RESTROOM REVOLUTIONARY! Join PISSAR as we develop a checklist for genderqueer safe spaces and create teams to map safe and accessible bathrooms around campus.[1]

Everyone needs to use bathrooms, but only some of us have to enter into complicated political and architectural negotiations in order to use them. The fact is, bathrooms are easier to access for some of us than for others, and the people who never think about where and how they can pee have a lot of control over how using restrooms feels for the rest of us. What do we need from bathrooms? What elements are necessary to make a bathroom functional for everyone? To make it safe? To make it a private and respectful space? Whose bodies are excluded from the typical restroom? More important, what kind of bodies are assumed in the design of these bathrooms? Who has the privilege (we call it pee-privilege) of never needing to think about these issues, of always knowing that any given bathroom will meet one's needs? Everyone needs to use the bathroom. But not all of us can.

And that's where People in Search of Safe and Accessible Restrooms (PISSAR) comes in. PISSAR, a coalition of UC-Santa Barbara undergrads, grad students, staff, and community members, recognizes that bathrooms are not always accessible for people with disabilities, or safe for people who transgress gender norms. PISSAR was formed at the 2003 University of California Student of Color Conference, held at UC-Santa Barbara. During the lunch break on the second day of the conference, meetings for the disability caucus and the transgender caucus were scheduled in adjacent rooms. When only a few people showed up for both meetings, we decided to hold a joint session. One of the members of the disability caucus mentioned plans to assess bathroom accessibility on the campus, wondering if there was a similar interest in mapping gender-neutral bathrooms. Everyone in the room suddenly began talking about the possibilities of a genderqueer/disability coalition, and PISSAR was born.

For those of us whose appearance or identity does not quite match the "man" or "woman" signs on the door, bathrooms can be the sites of violence and harassment, making it very difficult for us to use them safely or comfortably. Similarly, PISSAR acknowledges that, although most buildings are required by the Americans with Disabilities Act to provide accessible bathrooms, some restrooms are more compliant than others and accessible bathrooms can often be hard to find. PISSAR's mission, then, is threefold: 1) to raise awareness about what safe and accessible bathrooms are and why they are necessary; 2) to map and verify existing accessible and/or gender-neutral bathrooms on the campus; and 3) to advocate for additional bathrooms. We eventually hope to have both web-based and printed maps of all the bathrooms on campus, with each facility coded as to its accessibility and gender-safety.[2] Beyond this initial campaign, PISSAR plans to advocate for the construction or conversion of additional safe and accessible bathrooms on campus. To that end, one of our long-term goals is to push for more gender-neutral bathrooms and showers in the dormitories, and to investigate the feasibility of multistall gender-neutral bathrooms across the campus as a whole.

As it turned out, we weren't the only restroom revolutionaries on campus. We soon joined forces with a student-run initiative to stock all campus tampon and pad machines, a group called, appropriately enough, Aunt Flo and the Plug Patrol. Aunt Flo's goal is to use funds garnered from the sale of tampons and pads in campus bathroom dispensers (blood money, if you will) to support student organizations in a time of tremendous budget cuts. We liked their no-euphemism approach to the bathroom and the body and joined their effort to make the campus not only a safer and more accessible place to pee but also to bleed.[3] We also expanded our focus to include issues of childcare, inspired in part by one of our members' experiences as a young mom on campus. PISSAR decided to examine whether campus bathrooms featured changing tables, a move that increased our intersectional analysis of bathroom access and politics.

By specifically including the work of Aunt Flo and concerns about childcare, PISSAR challenges many of the assumptions that are made about genderqueer and disabled bodies. Why shouldn't every gender-neutral restroom have a tampon/ pad machine? Putting tampon/pad machines only in women's rooms, and mounting them high on the wall, restricts the right to menstruate conveniently to those with certain bodies. It suggests that the right to tampons and pads is reserved for people who use gender-specific women's rooms and can reach a lever hanging five feet from the ground. This practice reinscribes ideas about disabled bodies being somehow dysfunctional and asexual (as in, "People in wheelchairs get their periods too?") and perpetuates the idea that genderqueer folks are inherently unbodied (as in, "Only real women need tampons, and you don't look like a real woman").

So how exactly does PISSAR work? Picture a team of people taking over a bathroom near you. They're wearing bright yellow T-shirts stenciled with the phrase "free 2 pee" on the back. They're wearing gloves. They're wielding measuring tape and clipboards, and they're looking very disappointed in the height of your toilet. What you've seen is PISSAR in action. We call this a PISSAR patrol, and it's our way of getting the information we need in an unapologetically public way. We gather this information with the help of the PISSAR checklist, a form featuring questions about everything from the height of a tampon dispenser to the signs on the door, from the number of grab bars beside the toilet to the presence of a diaper-changing table.

From the information garnered in the PISSAR patrols, we are in the process of making a map that will assess the safety and accessibility of all the bathrooms on campus. The map is vital to our project because it offers genderqueer and disabled people a survey of all the restrooms on campus so that they can find what they need without the stigma and frustration of telling a possibly uninformed administrator the details of their peeing needs. For people who have never had to think about bathrooms, the map's detailed information suggests the ways in which our everyday bathrooms are restrictive and dangerous. Thus the map also functions as a consciousness-raising tool, educating users about the need for safe and accessible restrooms.

PISSAR patrols aren't simply about getting information. They're also a way to keep our bodies involved in our project. PISSAR is, after all, a project about bodies: about bodily needs, about the size and shape of our bodies, and about our bodily presentation. The very nature of our bathroom needs necessitates this attention to the body. So it makes sense that when we tried to theorize about what a safe, respectful restroom might look like, we realized we needed to meet in the bathroom. Because the bathroom is our site, and the body in search of a bathroom is our motivation, we recognized early on the need to be concerned with body and theory together. PISSAR's work is an attempt at embodying theory, at theorizing from the body.

We do this work partly through our name. The name PISSAR avoids euphemism and gets right down to business. We are here to talk about peeing and shitting, and what people need in order to do these things with comfort and dignity. Both PISSAR's name and the goals of the group come down to one unavoidable fact: When you've got to go, you've got to go. The name endeavors both to avoid abstraction and to highlight the embodied experiences that make bathroom accessibility so pressing when one needs to pee. PISSAR's name isn't an accident, it's a tool. We use our funny name to demand attention to our basic and critical needs. We warn with our name: We're about to talk about something "crude." We take it seriously—you should, too.

Our concern with body/theory is also evident in our insistence that bathroom accessibility is an important issue for a lot of different people. Everyone should be able to find a bathroom that conforms to the needs of their body. Everyone should be able to use a restroom without being accused of being in the "wrong" place. Everyone should have access to tampon dispensers and facilities for changing diapers, regardless of gender or ability. Homeless folks should have access to clean restrooms free of harassment.[4] Bathroom activism is, from the outset, a multi-identity endeavor. It has the potential to bring together feminists, transfolks, people with disabilities, single parents, and a variety of other people whose bathroom needs frequently go unmet. It creates a much needed space for those of us whose identities are more complicated than can be encompassed in a single-issue movement. Viewed in this light, restroom activism is an ideal platform from which to launch broader coalition work. In PISSAR, we tend to think about "queerness" as encompassing more than just sexual orientation; it includes queer bodies, queer politics, and queer coalitions.

On Bodies In Bathrooms: Pissar Politics

There is tremendous social pressure to avoid talking about bodies in bathrooms. First, such talk is not considered polite. We're trained from an early age not to talk publicly about what happens in the bathroom; we don't even have language for what happens in there; many of us still rely on the euphemisms our parents used when we were three. Second, the topic is not appropriately academic. For the most part, scholars do not tend to theorize about bathrooms and what bodies do in them.[5] Bathrooms are somehow assumed to be free of the same institutional power dynamics that impact and shape the rest of our lives. Finally, bathroom talk is considered politically dangerous, or at least irrelevant, because of a fear that it will be seen as a trivial issue, prompting the mainstream culture to not take us seriously. Political activism is supposed to be about ideas, the mind, and larger social movements, not about who pees where.

PISSAR is tired of pretending that these polite, academic, political bodies don't have needs. We resist the silencing from mainstream communities that want to ignore our queerness and our disability, while simultaneously challenging the theories that want to pull us away from the toilet seat. We refuse to accept a narrow conception of "queer" that denies the complexities of our bodies.

Keeping this focus on our particular bodies is no easy task. Mainstream culture, with its cycles of acceptance and disapproval of homosexuals (and we use this rather limited term intentionally), has always presented a rather narrow view of queer life. In order to be portrayed in the mainstream media, for example, queers must either fit into acceptable stereotypes of gay appearance and behavior, or be visibly indistinguishable from heterosexuals. These positions are highly precarious and strictly patrolled: Mainstream gay characters can only exhibit limited amounts of "gayness," a restriction epitomized in the lack of any sexual contact, even kissing, between gay characters. Those few gay characters that do exist in the mainstream media obey very strict norms of appearance. Unfortunately, this stance is becoming increasingly pervasive within mainstream gay culture as well. One need only glance at the covers of magazines such as *the Advocate* to discover that members of the gay community are supposed to be young, thin, white, nondisabled, and not genderqueer. In fact, mainstream gay media has often contributed to pressure on the gay community, particularly gay men, to be hyper-able and gender conforming. Images of big, beefy, muscle-bound bodies decorate the ads in gay publications and the words "no fats or fems" frequently appear in gay personal ads. We believe that this disavowal of queers that are too queer—those of us who are trans-identified, genderqueer, too poor to afford the latest fashions, disabled, fat, in-your-face political—is the result of internalized shame.

The gay community has internalized the larger culture's homophobia and transphobia, which has made us ashamed of our visible queerness, especially any signs of genderqueerness. We have internalized the larger culture's ableism, which has made us ashamed of our disabilities and illnesses. This shame has marginalized many trans and genderqueer folks and many people with disabilities, casting them out of the mainstream gay community. Internalized self-hatred, a distancing from the bodies of those who do not fit the idealized norms, an insistence on assimilation: All of these lead to and result from a sense of shame in our bodies—a shame that pervades our conversations, our relationships, and our politics. This tendency to move away from the body, to drop the experiences of bodies out of conversations and politics, is evident in many queer organizations.[6] We lack the language to say what needs to be said; we don't have the tools to carry on this level of conversation.

Because we lack this language, because of our internalized self-hatred and shame in our bodies, the politics of the bathroom—a potentially transgressive and liminal site—have not been given priority within the mainstream gay rights movement. This inattention has particularly strong real-life effects on disabled and genderqueer folks. The need for a safe, dignified, usable place to pee is a vital, but too seldom addressed, issue. It has gone unaddressed because it is so much about the body, particularly the shameful parts and shameful acts of the body. This shame,

and the resulting silence, is familiar to many in the disability community. In striving to assimilate to nondisabled norms, many of us gloss over the need for the assistance some of us have in using the bathroom. We are embarrassed to admit that we might need tubes or catheters, leg bags or personal assistants—or that some of us may not use the bathroom at all, preferring bedpans or other alternatives. Particularly in mixed company (that is, in the presence of nondisabled folks), we are reluctant to talk about the odd ways we piss and shit. But this reticence has hindered our bathroom politics, often making it difficult for us to demand bathrooms that meet all of our needs.

Queer bathroom politics have been similarly affected by this kind of ashamed reticence. Our reluctance to talk about bathrooms and bodies and our sense that discussions about pissing and shitting are shameful colors our responses to the potential violence facing many genderqueer people in the bathroom. Such acts aren't to be discussed in polite company because they occur in and around the bathroom, itself a taboo topic; because of homophobia and transphobia, these acts aren't seen as worthy of conversation because "those kinds of people" don't really matter; and because they conjure thoughts about public sex in bathrooms.

Indeed, public sex has often been the target of surveillance, and those implicated in such practices have been publicly humiliated, arrested, and abused. In 1998, several local news organizations around the country sent hidden cameras into public restrooms to film men engaged in sexual activities; these tapes were often turned over to local authorities, many of whom used them as the basis for sting operations. A station in San Diego, for example, justified its use of this stealth tactic in campus restrooms at San Diego State University by stressing the need to protect students from these deviant activities. The prevalence of these kinds of news stories and the presence of surveillance equipment in campus restrooms serve to police sexual behavior: Threats of public exposure and humiliation are used to enforce "normative" sexuality. At the University of California in Berkeley, this policing was taken a step further when some bathrooms on campus were locked in an effort to eliminate public sex. Only certain people were given keys to these restrooms, literally locking out some bodies and behaviors. These practices, privatizing public spaces and placing them under surveillance, demarcate the boundaries of appropriate and permissible behavior, thereby policing both bodies and bathrooms.

This surveillance of deviant bodies and practices in bathrooms all too often takes the form of brutal physical violence. Genderqueer and trans-identified folks have been attacked in public restrooms simply because their appearance threatens gender norms and expectations. This issue of bathroom violence is consistently delegitirnized in both queer and non-queer spaces as not important or sexy enough to be a "real" issue. In many gay activist circles, there seems to be a pervasive sentiment that no one (read: no straight people) will take us seriously if we start talking about bathrooms. Additionally, there is tremendous cultural shame around the violence itself—either you should have been able to protect yourself or you must have deserved it or both.

In the genderqueer community we know how often our bodies cause anxiety and violence. We have been systematically and institutionally discouraged from talking about that violence or from linking it to these bodies. When a woman in our local community was attacked by strangers because of her androgynous appearance, local police insisted that she was injured in a "lesbian brawl." It was easier for them to talk about (and assume) her sexuality than to admit that it was her queer body, her race, and her confusing gender that led to both her original attack and the subsequent neglect of local law enforcement, who failed to follow protocol in her case. Internalized shame about her body led our friend to take on responsibility for her attack, to allow the police to mistreat her and make false assumptions, and to feel that she had no right to talk about how her attack was based in her refusal of racial, sexual, and gender norms. She

was ashamed to talk about her body, about the violence done to it, and about how its needs were ignored. The community felt the impact of our own shame. We stood beside her, outwardly supportive, but unable to gather enough energy to mobilize a collective demand that her story be heard and that the police investigate the crime.

Sadly, as this story illustrates, our shame isn't always directed outward, toward the society and institutions that helped create it. It often drives wedges between communities that might otherwise work together. And it is precisely this kind of embodied shame—the shame that we feel in our bodies and the shame that arises out of the experience and appearance of our bodies—that drives the divisions between queer and disability communities. PISSAR initially had trouble bridging this gap, in that some of our straight disabled members worried about the political (read: queer) implications of our bathroom-mapping work. Indeed, many queer disability activists and scholars have drawn attention to the ableism that thrives within queer communities, and the homophobia and heterocentrism that reside within disability circles.

Due to the fact that disabled people are discriminated against on the basis of our disabilities, some of us may want to assert our "normalcy" in other aspects of our lives, including our sex lives. Although this impulse is understandable in a culture that constantly pathologizes our sexuality, this assertion in some cases takes on a homophobic/transphobic quality. Heterosexuals with disabilities may thus distance themselves from disabled queers and transfolk in an attempt to facilitate their assimilation into an ableist and heterocentric culture. Similarly, because of the ways in which queer desires, identities, and practices have been pathologized, cast as unnatural, abnormal, and most importantly, "sick," some LBGTIQ-identified people may want to distance themselves from disabled people in an effort to assert their own normalcy and health. As a result, queers and people with disabilities have been set up by our own communities as diametrically opposed, a move that has been particularly problematic—and painful—for queers with disabilities. For all of us balancing multiple identities, this kind of thinking enacts a dissection, first separating us from the realities of our bodies through shame and a lack of language, then further cutting apart our identities into separate and distant selves.

We suggest, however, that bathroom politics can potentially lift us out of this polarization. Advocating for bathroom access and repeatedly talking openly about people's need for a safe space to pee helps us break through some of this embodied shame and recognize our common needs. It is through the process of going on PISSAR patrol while wearing bright T-shirts and reporting on our findings in loud voices that we begin to move beyond a shamed silence.

Our attention to the body (the pissing and shitting body) and our insistence that we talk about the specificities of people's embodied experiences with humor rather than shame challenges the normalizing drive found within both queer and disability communities. Rather than mask our differences or bolster our own claims to "normalcy" by marginalizing others as shameful and embarrassing, we insist on a coalition that attempts to embrace all of our different needs. PISSAR is built around queerness, but a queer queerness, a queerness that encompasses both sexually and medically queer bodies, that embraces a diversity of appearances and disabilities and needs. The PISSAR checklist—a manifesto of sorts—models queer coalition-building by incorporating disability, genderqueer, childcare, and menstruation issues into one document, refusing single-issue analysis. It entails a refusal to assimilate to the phantasm of the "normal" body by explicitly incorporating the allegedly abnormal, the freakish, the queer. The body evoked in the checklist is a real body, a menstruating body, a body that pees and shits, a body that may not match its gender identity, a body subjected too often to violence and ridicule, a body that may have parts missing or parts that don't function "properly," a body that might require

assistance. Bathroom politics and organizations such as PISSAR resist the normalization of "queer," striving to acknowledge and embrace all these different bodies, desires, and needs that are too often ignored, obscured, or denied out of shame and internalized self-hatred.

Raising Consciousness and Doing Theory on the Pissar Patrol

The disability access-related activities required by the checklist, such as measuring door widths, counting the number of grab bars, and checking for visual and auditory fire alarms, train PISSAR patrol members in different people's needs, a training that extends far beyond concepts of "tolerance" and "acceptance!" In stark contrast to "disability awareness" events that blindfold sighted people so that they can "feel what it is like to be blind" or place people without mobility impairments in wheelchairs so they can "appreciate the difficulties faced by chair users," the PISSAR patrols turn nondisabled people's attention toward the social barriers confronting people with disabilities. Rather than focusing on the alleged failures and hardships of disabled bodies—an inability to see, an inability to walk—PISSAR focuses on the failures and omissions of the built environment—a too-narrow door, a too-high dispenser. The physical realities of these architectural failures emphasize the arbitrary construct of the "normal" body and its needs, and highlight the ability of a disabled body to "function" just fine, if the space would only allow for it. This switch in focus from the inability of the body to the inaccessibility of the space makes room for activism and change in ways that "awareness exercises" may not.

Although disability "awareness" events are touted as ways to make nondisabled people recognize the need for access, we have serious doubts about their political efficacy and appropriateness. Sitting in a wheelchair for a day, let alone an hour, is not going to give someone a full understanding of the complexities and nuances of chair-users' lives. We think such exercises all too often reinforce ableist assumptions about the "difficulty" of living with a disability, perpetuating the notion of disability as a regrettable tragedy. They reduce the lives of people in wheelchairs to the wheelchair itself, distancing the bodies of chair-users from those without mobility disabilities. PISSAR, by virtue of its coalitional politics, focuses attention on the ways that a whole variety of bodies use restrooms and the architectural and attitudinal barriers that hinder their use or render it potentially dangerous.

The educational experience of being in the bathroom on PISSAR patrol, of imagining what different kinds of bodies might need to fully utilize a space, extends beyond the issue of disability access. Just as measuring the width of doors enables nondisabled people to recognize the inaccessibility of the built environment, going on bathroom patrol facilitates an awareness among non-trans and non-genderqueer folk of the safety issues facing genderqueer and trans people. As we began instituting our bathroom patrols, we had to make a variety of decisions in the interest of safety: PISSAR patrols would consist of at least three people; there would be no patrolling after dark; at least one member would wear a yellow PISSAR shirt, thereby identifying the group; and each group would ideally consist of a range of gender identities. Through this decision-making process, all of us—particularly those of us who are not genderqueer or trans-identified—increased our understanding of the potential dangers that lie in not using a restroom "properly." As empowering as our patrols sometimes feel, we have also experienced stares, some hostility, and a general public bewilderment about what our business is in that protected space. Being in groups on "official" business probably mitigated most of those risks, but the experience of entering bathrooms that we might not ordinarily enter helped us recognize the need for safety in these public/private spaces.

Thus, one of the most revolutionary aspects of the checklist is its function as a consciousness-raising tool, particularly within PISSAR's own ranks. It was not until we first began discussing the need for a group like PISSAR that one of our nondisabled members realized that the widedoored stalls were built for wheelchairs. Another acknowledged that she had never realized how inaccessible campus and community buildings were until she began measuring doors and surveying facilities; going through the PISSAR checklist caused her to view the entire built world through different eyes. Many nondisabled people stopped using accessible stalls, realizing that they might be keeping someone with a disability from safe peeing. By the same token, one of our straight members with disabilities had always ridiculed the push for gender-neutral bathrooms until he began to understand it as an access issue. Realizing that gender-specific signs and expectations for single-gender use are barriers to some genderqueer and trans people's use of a space—because of the ever-present threat of harassment, violence, and even arrest—enabled him to make the connection between disability oppression and genderqueer oppression. A space for multiple identity organizing was forged. The PISSAR checklist allowed all of us to understand the bathroom in terms of physical and political access; people with disabilities and transfolk are being denied access because of the ways in which their/our bodies defy the norm.

Now picture this: a boardroom at UC-Santa Barbara, filled with the chancellor and his team of advisors. We're talking about gender, and we're taking about bathrooms. We've been talking about gender for quite a while, and no one has asked for any definitions or terms. Now, with the reality of bathrooms on the table, the chancellor needs some clarification about the differences between sex and gender. What he is saying is, "What kinds of bodies are we talking about here?" PISSAR and the PISSAR checklists facilitate an open and impolite conversation about pissing, shitting, and the organs that do those things, right there in the boardroom. Because PISSAR is talking about something concrete—bodies, bathrooms, liability—administrators want to understand all the terms. They start to learn the issues: what exactly is preventing this otherwise accessible bathroom from being fully accessible (often something simple—and inexpensive—like moving a trash can or lowering a dispenser); why do genderqueer folks need unisex bathrooms, and what does that even entail (again, often something simple—and inexpensive—like changing the signs or adding a tampon/pad dispenser). And they learn the issues in a way that makes sense to them and that works for us politically. They are being trained by a group of folks devoted to the issue, they are being given specific details and facts, and all the work is being done on a volunteer basis by folks committed to the campus and the causes. What's more, because the realities of bathroom needs and restroom politics forced this table of administrators to ask about gender, sex, disability, barriers, and so forth, the administrators are now better equipped to tackle more abstract issues around trans and disability inclusion on campus and in the larger UC community (for example, when adding gender identity to the nondiscrimination clause happens at the state-wide level, we'd like to think our chancellor will be on board . . .)

Through the PISSAR checklist, we bring both the body and the bathroom into the boardroom. We challenge the normalizing impulse that wants to ignore conversations about attendant care or queer-bashing or inaccessibility. We refuse the expectation that chancellors' offices are places for polite topics of conversation and abstract theorizing, rather than discussions about who does and who does not have the right to pee. We demand a recognition of the body that needs assistance, the body that is denied access, and the body that is harassed and violated. And we insist on remembering the body that shits, the body that pees, the body that bleeds.

Where will you be when the revolution comes? We'll be in the bathroom—come join us there.

From Collective Behaviour to Misbehaviour

Redrawing the Boundaries of Political and Cultural Resistance

Gemma Edwards

The Ethiopian peasant's fart certainly does not blow the passing lord off his horse, and yet: it is part of the substratum of negativity which, though generally invisible, can flare up in moments of acute social tension . . . This layer of inarticulate non-subordination, without face, without voice . . . is the materiality of anti-power, the basis of hope.

(John Holloway, 2010b, 159–60)

We began the book with a consideration of 'collective behaviour' (CB), and in this penultimate chapter, we embark upon a consideration of 'misbehaviour'. 'Misbehaviour' literally means not behaving in the way in which you are required to behave. 'Good behaviour' (compliant behaviour) is the basis of the social order. We learnt from Blumer in Chapter 2 that behaviour that subverts the 'cultural pattern' (society's rules, norms, and expectations) rather than conforming to it, is the secret to changing the social order. In this chapter, we employ the concept of 'misbehaviour', taken from organizational studies, to consider not only organized forms of resistance, but 'every impulse to dissent' (Ackroyd and Thompson, 1999, 39).

We have come across a number of indications in the book as to why looking at protest outside social movement organizations (SMOs) could be important. Sometimes, social movements do not engage in direct confrontations with the state, but focus upon symbolic struggles instead (see Chapter 5). This means that, excepting for a few visible moments of public protest, social movement activity can be 'submerged' (Melucci, 1980, 1989), and can involve individuals in constructing cultural alternatives, which, while not divorced from collective efforts at change, can involve them in carrying out collective action 'on their own'.

We continued to detect this 'lifestyle' activism (Haenfler et al., 2012) and attempts to construct alternative cultural values in the alternative globalization movement (AGM) (see Chapter 6), where confrontations with the state not only lost salience in a globalized context, but were also radically critiqued as a social movement strategy. The suggestion instead was that all the small things we *do* in our daily lives can be important to the alter-global/anti-capitalist struggle if only we would *do* differently (Holloway, 2010a [2002], 2010b). Even in the last chapter on terrorism, we were given a useful reminder that not all forms of social movement activity, and not all protest strategies, are about making frequent public 'noise'. Some, quite self-consciously, involve covert activities that operate 'underground', and are all the more successful when they do take the public stage.

In this chapter, we pick up the threads left by previous debates to push our conceptualization of social movements and protest one final step further to look at the surging 'underbelly' of defiance (J. Scott, 1990, 17) that has interested social movement scholars for decades (Piven and Cloward, 1977; Scott, 1985, 1990; Jasper, 1997; Holloway, 2010a [2002], 2010b), but has rarely been given the place it should in our conceptualizations of social movements and protest. By the end of the chapter you should understand why it is important for social movement scholars to look outside SMOs and public protest events. You should be able to appreciate the ways in which individual and non-organized forms of protest relate to collective efforts at social change. You will therefore be able to critically engage with the notion that participation in social movements and visible protest events is the only way in which people in society are engaged in challenging the social order.

The concept of misbehaviour

By turning to organizational studies to borrow concepts for social movement studies, we are hardly trail-blazing. In fact, we are following the first generation of social movement theorists who in the 1960s and 1970s found in organizational studies a rich array of concepts and ideas to help them think about social movements as 'organizations' (Zald, 2005). What is somewhat ironic is that I am now suggesting that turning to concepts in organizational studies can help us to conceptualize social movements and protest *beyond* SMOs.

Stephen Ackroyd and Paul Thompson (1999) introduce the concept of 'misbehaviour' to organizational studies (a field also known as 'organizational behaviour'). They do so for two reasons: first, 'organizational studies' has not given a very accurate picture of what workplaces are really like. They paint a portrait of workers as passive, submissive and compliant in the face of workplace management, when in reality, workers are anything but. Instead, workers frequently engage in 'misbehaviour': while retaining an overall stance of compliance, they are, in fact, finding ways to not do what they are required to do, in the way they are required to do it.

Misbehaviour is therefore a concept that, strictly speaking, can only apply in a context of power inequalities in which there are attempts to direct behaviour as part of maintaining control. In such contexts, 'directions' are given and certain 'responses' are expected. Misbehaviour is about breaking the link between direction and expected response, and can be seen in the context of control as small and often trivial-looking – but nevertheless significant – attempts to assert autonomy (Ackroyd and Thompson 1999, 12).

The kinds of misbehaviour that Ackroyd and Thompson (1999) identify within workplaces include: sabotage, pilfering, joking, sexual misconduct (i.e. forging romantic relations at work rather than professional ones), go-slows, absenteeism, and whistleblowing (also see Jasper, 1997 on whistleblowing, and Roscigno and Hodson, 2004 on individualized worker resistance). Misbehaviour along these lines, they suggest, is the reality of most workplaces. Sabotage in particular has been well-researched in industrial sociology. A famously amusing study of worker sabotage was presented by Laurie Taylor and Paul Walton (1994 [1971]). It involved a worker at a Blackpool rock factory (which makes those sticks of colourful hard candy that you buy at the sea-side and break your teeth on). One worker, in defiance of his employer, substituted the cheery holiday message that normally runs through a stick of rock with one of his own:

> They had to throw away half a mile of Blackpool rock last year, for, instead of the customary motif running through its length, it carried the terse injunction 'Fuck Off'. A worker dismissed by a sweet factory had effectively demonstrated his annoyance by sabotaging the product of his labour.
>
> (Taylor and Walton, 1994 [1971], 321)

Acts of workplace sabotage, among other ways in which workers – short of open defiance – mess around to express their non-compliance to management control, are therefore acts of 'misbehaviour' that show that workers are not passive receptacles of 'direction' from above.

The second reason why Ackroyd and Thompson offer the concept of misbehaviour as important for organizational studies is one that social movement studies should pay particularly close attention to: they note the growing absence of studies about *worker resistance* from academics in the field (Thompson and Ackroyd, 1995; Ackroyd and Thompson, 1999). Trade union membership, as we know from Chapter 5, has declined, and so have incidences of strike action. Studies about the growing power and control of management and the passivity of workers abound.

These studies make a mistake, however, according to Ackroyd and Thompson (1999), in equating worker resistance with only organized collective action, like trade unions. Just because workers are not so active in trade unions, or busy staging strikes, it does not mean that they are compliant. In order to appreciate all the ways in which workers resist control, however, we need to broaden our vision as to different forms that non-compliance can take – not just in terms of 'organized non-compliance' (e.g. strikes), but the non-compliance that is represented by acts of organizational 'misbehaviour' (Thompson and Ackroyd, 1995; Ackroyd and Thompson 1999, 22).

I suggest here that the two reasons that Ackroyd and Thompson have given for why it is important to bring the concept of 'misbehaviour' into organizational studies also stand for social movement studies. We, too, would benefit from adopting a concept of misbehaviour. It could be applied to broaden our vision to the resistance that takes place outside SMOs and public protest events; and it can help us move beyond the rather black-and-white picture we currently have of people as *either* participating in outright, organized, public activism (e.g. in SMOs and public protest events), *or* doing nothing at all. As James Scott states:

> A view of politics focused either on . . . consent or open rebellion represents a far too narrow concept of political life – especially under conditions of tyranny or near-tyranny in which much of the world lives.
>
> (J. Scott, 1990, 20)

In repressive regimes, for example, it can often appear that people are doing nothing at all to resist if we focus purely on public protest events. We often get a rather pessimistic picture of protest, too, when political scientists measure the 'levels' of par-

Question: About a government action which you thought was unjust and harmful. Have you ever . . . Gone on a protest or demonstration?
(0) Never Done
(1) Ever done

Percent answering 'Ever done'

Age group	1983	n	2000	n	2011	n
<25	4.5	222	1.7	241	7.4	241
25–44	2.2	640	11.7	879	7.1	879
45–64	1.6	514	12.6	728	9.6	728
65+	0.6	338	3.6	439	6.1	439

Figure 1 Percentage of British people who have ever gone on a protest or demonstration, by age
Source: British Social Attitudes 1983, 2000, 2011. ©CCSR, University of Manchester

ticipation in conventional activities in Western democracies, like voting, writing to MPs, signing petitions, or going on demonstrations. Figure 1 shows the percentage of British people who have ever gone on a protest or demonstration in response to government action that they perceived as unjust or harmful. You can see from the results that only a minority of the population (less than 10 per cent across all age groups) had ever gone on a demonstration or protest when asked in 2011. You can also see that these levels have stayed consistently low over time, and across different age groups.

What should we take from these statistics? That the 90 per cent who are silent and inactive are happily complying: either successfully coerced or passively duped into a 'false consciousness'? Or are these people sometimes aware of power inequalities, and the control that is exerted over how they must act in society, such that what they show is a superficial 'posturing' of consent while, in private, find ways to defy and subvert it (J. Scott, 1990)? In the next section I will flesh out an answer to this question, and the role I foresee misbehaviour as a concept playing in social movement studies. I do this by looking at misbehaviour and its function in different historical, social, and political contexts. Before we turn to this, however, it is necessary to make three rather important disclaimers about the concept of 'misbehaviour'.

(a) *Misbehaviour is not a 'new' form of 'individualized' protest.*

The first disclaimer is this: the concept of 'misbehaviour' is not meant to suggest that the 'protest' that happens outside SMO and public protest events is *individualized* rather than collective, or that it is something 'new' to the contemporary context. Whilst misbehaviour – not behaving as you are required to do so – is an individual act, it can also be part of a collective strategy for expressing discontent or struggling for social change, and is most analytically interesting and relevant for social movement studies when it is viewed as such (Piven and Cloward, 1977, 5). While some have argued that in contemporary 'post-modern' society efforts at social change themselves must shift from collective to individualized forms, namely from the realm of collective organizations to individualized 'life politics' (Giddens, 1991) or 'sub-politics' (Beck, 1997), this is not the argument being made here. Fewer instances of visible, organized, collective action should not be confused with no *collective* action at all. Indeed, the point of the concept of 'misbehaviour' is to look at how *collective* challenges can exist, hidden from view, and in different forms. Misbehaviour can, then, be a collective strategy (Ackroyd and Thompson, 1999). Misbehaviour is not by any means condemned to be, or remain, an *individualized* response to power in contemporary society because, for example, we are now supposed to live in an *individualized* world in which collectivist efforts at change are no longer possible (as the post-modernists argue). Misbehaviour, then, is no post-modern treatise on individualized resistance.

(b) *Misbehaviour is related to, but distinct from, Foucauldian 'resistance'.*

This is clear to see in the arguments of the authors of the misbehaviour concept, Stephen Ackroyd and Paul Thompson (1999), and is one of the reasons I suggest it is so attractive. 'Misbehaviour' is a concept preferred to that of 'resistance', offered by Michel Foucault. The French social theorist Michel Foucault (1926–84) is perhaps the obvious starting point for considering political struggles at the level of culture. This is because Foucault can offer us an alternative 'cultural politics' that locates struggles against power in the realms of everyday life, discourse, and identity, rather than state-society interactions (Nash, 2001). Rather than identifying power with the state and political institutions and their interventions into everyday life, Foucault argues that 'power is always already there' (Foucault, 1980, 141).

What this means essentially is that power is already part of the social relations and cultural discourses that construct us as particular types of people in the first place. Our identity is already shaped by power because it has been socially and culturally constructed (Fraser, 1989). While this sounds like we are condemned forever to be the prisoners of power, Foucault also argues that wherever there is power, there is resistance (Foucault, 1982). Attempts to construct and mould our 'subjectivity' (our very sense of who we are) in particular ways are felt as limitations to our choices, autonomy and freedom (Foucault, 1982). 'Resistance' therefore refers to all the small, individual acts of non-compliance that people commit in an effort to refuse the social construction of their identity as a particular kind of identity, which limits who they might otherwise be. If this sounds very Meluccian, then we should note that Melucci does draw upon Foucault, as does Habermas, although both refrain from fully embracing his theory (Melucci, 1999; Habermas, 1987).

Importantly, the social construction of persons does not stop at the level of their psyche and identity, but particular kinds of 'human bodies' are also inscribed by dominant cultural discourses and the normative expectations attached to them. Bodily deportment and appearance, for example, are moulded by power relations. Sandra Lee Bartky (1988) gives a good example of this by looking at how patriarchal power relations shape the very 'bodily activity' of women so as to produce 'gendered bodies' (Bartky, 1988, 62). Women internalize the normative expectations around feminine beauty and shape their bodily practices in relation to them, such as what they wear, how they sit, exercise and diet regimes, make-up and beauty regimes, and so forth.

Foucault (1977) argues therefore that the body is a battlefield for power/resistance. We are socially constructed to be 'docile and useful bodies' in modern society, such that our compliance to forms of control is built into the material fabric of our being and symbolized by it. This is useful for noticing the role played by the 'protesting body' in everyday acts of misbehaviour. Natasha Walter (1998) notes, for example, how practices around applying make-up, which are seen by Bartky (1988) as oppressive in the Western context, can be subversive acts elsewhere, such as when Afghan women apply lipstick in resistance to the Taliban regime.

Acts of body modification have also been analysed as politically significant in this context, representing a desire to withdraw conformity to prevailing social values and reclaim the body as a site of autonomous self-expression. Tattooing and piercing, according to Lauren Langman (2008, 657) can be 'understood as a way of claiming agency to resist domination':

> Body modifications, tattoos, piercings . . . have become fashion statements indicating a moment of resistance, a rebellion against capitalist modernity, the regulation by rational rules and mass produced selfhood . . . Many of the adherents of such body modification regard their embrace of the grotesque as a rejection of the alienation, sterility, emptiness and inauthenticity of modernity.
>
> (Langman, 2008, 664)

Attempts to reject ascribed identities and bodies that comply to expected norms can be seen as important kinds of 'resistance', undertaken outside any organized attempts at social change, and by individuals in their everyday lives.

Foucault is useful, then, for thinking about daily resistance undertaken by individuals. Power is everywhere and operates in a myriad of ways; it does not just come 'top down' from the state, but is part of cultural discourses, norms, identities, and bodies (Nash, 2001). Resistance is therefore everywhere, too, and comes in a myriad of forms that are about subverting cultural discourses and norms, ascribed identities and bodies. Although Foucault (1982) has useful insights into cultural resistance, and has been a necessary reference point for other theorists I will come on to discuss (Scott, 1985, 1990; Holloway, 2010a [2002], 2010b), here I consciously employ the concept of 'misbehaviour' *instead* of Foucault's 'resistance'.

'Misbehaviour' was conceived by Stephen Ackroyd and Paul Thompson (1999) as an alternative to Foucault's theory of resistance. An alternative is necessary, they suggest, because Foucault has, by and large and especially in organizational studies, been employed to much better effect to analyse power and domination in modern societies rather than resistance. The idea that 'power is everywhere' may mean, on the one hand, that we can see 'resistance' everywhere too, but it also complicates our idea of the 'subject' – the human being – who *does* the resisting. According to Foucault, power produces this subject in the first place – their identity and material existence are socially constructed by relations of power. The question is: how then are subjects able to rebel? (Habermas 1990; Ackroyd and Thompson, 1999).

I suggest here, in line with James Scott (1990), that while individuals may give a public performance of compliance and conformity in their daily lives, and may do all the bodily and discursive 'posturing' necessary to look like they comply to the cultural discourses and normative expectations that maintain power relations, this does not mean that they are *nothing* but the product of power. People are not merely filled up with the 'false consciousness' and delusion that the Frankfurt School theorists thought were keeping the working classes politically docile (Adorno and Horkheimer, 1979 [1944]). Instead, we keep a ceremonial distance from the act we perform, we engage in 'impression management', and beneath that – or 'off-stage' argues James Scott by invoking Erving Goffman's terms – we retain a core of self-autonomy that expresses itself in many small acts of defiance when power is not looking (Scott, 1985, 321). Power may be productive of subjectivity in that subjectivity is socially constructed (Nash, 2001), but we are not merely the effect of power, the puppet dolls of dominant cultural discourses, the empty bodily vessels that are marked with whatever society wishes to inscribe upon us.

There *is* something underneath, a person who does the 'doing', who puts on the performance, and can therefore 'do' this 'doing' differently, as John Holloway argues (2010a [2002], 40–2). In the process, people can subvert or withdraw the performance on which power depends (Scott, 1990; Holloway, 2010a [2002]). This 'doing' subject can, as Holloway argues, be an essential part of dismantling power relations (what he calls 'anti-power') and in that sense can create the kind of transformation of society that Foucault thought was not possible (Holloway, 2010a [2002], 40).

Since the first two disclaimers have been long we had better pause to summarize before moving on: while there are overlaps with some 'post-modern' theories of resistance, the concept of misbehaviour is not one. Unlike Foucault's concept of 'resistance', misbehaviour does not relegate collective struggle to individual resistance that can never transform society. That is why I talk of 'misbehaviour' and not 'resistance' (Ackroyd and Thompson, 1999).

(c) *Misbehaviour is meant to open up 'a can of worms' about political intentionality.*

The third disclaimer surrounds a recurrent problem when looking at 'protest' as acts of non-compliance that take place outside SMOs, and which puts many off undertaking the task: there is a danger that we end up focusing upon the whole range of 'deviance' (and what in other terms might be called 'anti-social' behaviour) to which we cannot impart *any political* motivation whatsoever, and which is better off left to the psychologists, criminologists and so forth (Cloward and Piven, 1979). Indeed, in our enthusiasm for detecting 'every impulse to dissent', we may end up ascribing political intentions to deviants who do not have any. Social deviance may be a wide-ranging and problematic category, but it is not, however, a territory that social movement theorists have no right to enter. As Melucci (1984) pointed out, social movements belong to the same category as other kinds of social deviance in that they are behaviours that the system cannot integrate.

Once in this territory, however, Ackroyd and Thompson (1999, 52) refer to the very real problem of what to do with the 'rebel without a cause'. While what we mean by 'political intentionality' is certainly a 'can of worms' which is opened by this approach, this is, in fact, the point of it. The purpose of looking outside SMOs is to be sensitized to 'every impulse to dissent' (Ackroyd and Thompson, 1999, 39), in order to be able to analyse the relationship that there might be between these acts and the collective strategies used by certain groups to challenge power (including the public, organized, and more obviously political efforts at social change) (Ackroyd and Thompson 1999, 25).

Only by separating out the 'rebels' seemingly 'without a cause', and the rebels with one, can we explore the possibility of a relationship between the two. As James Jasper argues, if our conceptualizations of social movements omit what goes on outside SMOs and says it is beyond our interest then 'this choice renders invisible all the ways that individual acts of protest do or do not feed into more organized movements' (Jasper, 1997, 5).

James Scott (1990) for example has argued that small acts of insubordination committed 'off-stage' (i.e. out of public view) are very much interconnected with the public, organized rebellions that we usually look at in social movement studies. Scott suggests that they form the 'cultural and social infrastructure' of organized protest events and movements, such that he refers to them as 'infrapolitics' (Scott, 1990, 184). John Holloway makes a similar point by arguing, as he puts it, that without looking at all the small, individual acts of non-compliance that take place in daily life we end up concentrating on 'only the smoke rising from the volcano' rather than the layers of sediment beneath it that caused the eruption in the first place (Holloway 2010b, 159). Opening the can of worms so that – clutching them – we fall down the slippery slope of considering all forms of deviance as *potentially* politically significant, is therefore the point.

I suggest however that because the concept of 'misbehaviour' – unlike that of 'resistance' – retains the notion that such deviance can sometimes be a collective strategy used to express collective discontent, and/or employed in collective efforts towards social change, we do keep some analytic purchase and can unpick individual forms of deviance (that arise for other reasons) from the kind of misbehaviour that interests social movement theorists. Piven and Cloward highlight how when they state that 'the problem . . . is to identify the features of social context which lead people to defy the particular norms they do' (Cloward and Piven, 1979, 651). It is the context, then, through which we determine whether an act is 'misbehaviour', not the act itself (Ackroyd and Thompson, 1999).

This means that there is no universal or definitive list of behaviours that would count as 'misbehaviour'. It wholly depends upon the context in which the behaviour takes place (and of course, the content of the behaviour). While in the next section we will look at examples of misbehaviour that include sabotage, folk tales, grumblings, graffiti, jokes, subversive talk on Facebook, and so forth, this is not to say that these kinds of acts are *always* to be thought of as 'misbehaviour' as if it were some inherent quality of them. Misbehaviour, then, is an analytic category, not an empirical one. Unpicking 'movement' significant deviance from the range of deviance, I admit, is a messy and far from clear-cut process that may take us down mistaken paths. Without engaging in this task, however, we cannot look at the bits of misbehaviour that represent hidden collective strategies and might be politically significant or, indeed, have the potential to be. We will now turn to several examples of misbehaviour in context.

Misbehaviour in context

This section takes seriously the adage – now some three and half decades old – that people can only do what they can do, in the ways that they can do it, and that the times when it is possible for them to succeed in achieving their full objectives are rare (Piven and Cloward, 1977). What this means – and the key argument here – is that the *form* of protest depends upon the political and social circumstances in which people find themselves.

Piven and Cloward (1977) argue, for example, that because poor people often lack the means to launch formally organized political struggles, they have to rely upon individual acts of defiance in which they withdraw their conformity to social order. These acts can nevertheless be viewed as part of a collective effort to achieve social change. Indeed, the 'unorganized' forms of protest that involve individual acts of non-compliance have been referred to by James Scott (1985) as 'weapons of the weak'.

It is true that some social circumstances give people more reason to protest, but it is equally true that some contexts provide more culturally visible means of expressing discontent. In modern Western democracies this means that discontented people often take to the streets with placards, or join SMOs (on- and offline).

In Eastern Europe and the Middle East, where such activities are readily and sometimes violently repressed, it may mean that individuals can only express what they really think in semi-protected spaces within their everyday lives, including perhaps the 'subversive' political talk that takes place via Facebook and Twitter. While Russian and Nigerian youth have in the past been forced to communicate political messages via graffiti in the context of a repressive regime (as I will discuss later in the section), youth today can instead scribble on the walls of their Facebook pages and have their say in tweets, subverting authority with political talk online that they would not be permitted to use in public spaces offline (see debate point).

Debate point: will the revolution be Facebooked?

Do Facebook and Twitter provide new spaces for people to misbehave by engaging in 'subversive political talk' in semi-public virtual spaces? Moreover, can this talk add to a seething 'underbelly' of resistance that can sometimes fall out onto the streets in public protest or be mobilized by SMOs? In considering these questions, let us take the case of the Egyptian revolution of 25 January 2011 (part of the Arab Spring) which overthrew President Mubarak. It has been suggested that Facebook and Twitter boosted an online surge of outrage and dissent which fed into the street demonstrations and the occupation of Tahrir Square (Vargas, 2012). Facebook pages set up by young people in support of the protesters, and publicizing the brutality of the police response to them, helped to raise awareness of the oppression of Egyptian people and point towards the wider corruption of the regime (Ghonim, 2010).

The first point to note is that internet access is not universally available in the Middle East, and that some regimes (like China) have blocked people's access to Facebook and Twitter. In Egypt, about 13.6 million people have got access to the internet (Ghonim, 2010), out of a population of around 82.5 million (World Bank

figure, 2011). We need to be careful therefore about overstating the role that social media can play in mobilization because it tends to be a minority of the wealthy and educated in the population who have access to the internet. Armando Salvatore (2013) also challenges the perception that isolated young people in Egypt started the revolution by setting up their own Facebook pages about police brutality towards protesters. Instead, a longer-term view shows that social media had been used by educated and discontented Egyptians for some time before the revolution as an alternative sphere of political communication and solidarity-building between different groups. It was a sphere in which they were able to escape the repression of the state authority and the censored media (Iskander, 2011). It was really the long-term networks that had formed between different activist groups through online communication over a period of time that made mobilization at the time of the revolution possible, rather than the impromptu Facebook pages set up by individuals (Salvatore, 2013).

- Have you been converted to a political cause or mobilized for a protest via Facebook?
- Can subversive political talk on Facebook and Twitter *cause* a revolution?
- Do Facebook and Twitter mean that we can all be political activists now, whether we are members of SMOs or not?

Tactics, Blumer (1951 [1946]) pointed out, can never be universal, but must always be adapted to the social and cultural context. Using one tactic everywhere is not only bound to fail, but certain styles of protest would surely be inconceivable to people in very different cultural contexts. What I suggest therefore is that in certain contexts, particularly those which are repressive of collective political struggles, misbehaviour might be the only strategy available to people.

The first example of this is already famous in social movement studies. James Scott (1985) studied a small peasant village in Malaysia in 1978–80, which he fictionally named 'Sedaka'. The peasants relied for their livelihood on rice production. Changes imposed to the way in which rice was produced undermined their livelihood and increased poverty in the village. Scott looked at the ways in which peasants resisted the powerful landowners and officials who drove through these adverse changes. As the power differential between the landowners and the peasants was so great, the peasants knew that there was no point in engaging in a public rebellion. Any attempts at organization or public protest would be quashed. The peasants did not even attempt to use such means since they could not win a confrontation with landowners.

Did this mean that the Malaysian peasants merely acquiesced? Scott argues that if we look at protest just in terms of public, organized protest then it would seem that they did. His research however went beyond the 'public performance' of consent and compliance shown by peasants to unearth what he calls 'the hidden transcript' of resistance (J. Scott, 1985). Peasant resistance revealed itself in covert, anonymous, and everyday acts of defiance that reclaimed some control and autonomy over life and subverted authority but which, at the same time, could not get anyone in trouble.

The 'hidden transcript' was found in subversive folk tales, poems, songs, gossip, rumour, jokes, and grumblings, which contributed to 'steady grinding efforts to hold one's own against overwhelming odds – a spirit and practice that prevents the worst and promises something better' (Scott, 1985, 350). Let us pause to consider jokes as an example of misbehaviour in the 'case point' because, I suggest, there are overlaps here with forms of protest currently used in Western democratic contexts against the power of neoliberal global capitalism (see Chapter 6).

Case point: just joking!

It may strike you as odd to be considering jokes in a book about social movements and protest. There is however a growing literature about humour and social protest, suggesting that it plays a crucial role in several different contexts in framing, collective identity formation, and resource mobilization (Bos and t'Hart, 2008). In terms of misbehaviour, jokes have also been accorded a significant place by Ackroyd and Thompson (1999), who consider joking around at work as one way to subvert authority and create a distance between the direction from above and the expected behavioural response. Indeed, jokes rupture the link between directions and response in contexts of domination and control by providing the last response that those exerting authority expect or desire: laughter. Laughter has a way of puncturing the legitimacy of authority like no other tactic and can therefore be used as a tactic of subversion (Downing, 2001, 107). Studies on the subversive role of humour frequently refer to the work of Mikhail Bakhtin (1984) who considered the function played by carnivals and festival days in medieval Europe (like All Fools' day and the Harvest Festival). Bakhtin argues that festive holidays and carnivals provided moments of pleasure, laughter, and comedy which created an atmosphere in which the usual social structures and power relations were momentarily suspended. Carnivals included clowns and fools, whose mocking of authority, religion, and social superiors provided a space in which to experience a more equal relationship to those who usually ruled over you, providing you with a moment of freedom (J. Scott, 1990, 172–82). It is interesting to note that Herbert Blumer (1951 [1946]) referred to carnival as one of the forms that 'crowds' can take. Carnival crowds play an important expressive function according to Blumer, seen in the dancing and singing which provides an opportunity for unconventional behaviour to be enacted. We see this carnival crowd on public protest events organized by alter-globalization activists in recent years. There are samba bands, dancing, and 'tactical frivolity', for instance (which includes dressing up as fairies and dancing in front of riot police)

(Chesters and Welsh, 2006). The alter-global group 'The Insurgent Clandestine Rebel Clown Army' are also illustrative here. They not only embrace humour as a strategy of subversion and protest, but also adopt the characters of the 'fool' and the 'trickster', which James Scott argues have played important subversive roles in folklore history in Malaysia, Thailand, West Africa, India, and North America (J. Scott, 1990, 162). The Rebel Clowns state that they adopt the character of the fool 'because nothing undermines authority like holding it up to ridicule' (www.clownarmy.org/about.html).

- Do you think that jokes can be used to subvert authority in the workplace or in other contexts of life? Can you think of any examples from your own life?
- Why might carnival crowds create moments of freedom?
- Do you think that 'clowning around' is an effective strategy of protest?

In the cases of Malaysian peasants, then, protest had to take the form of misbehaviour – a cultural struggle which involves attempts to subvert authority and directed behaviour – in other words, to *not* say and do (at least in private) what you are required to say and do in public.

Cihan Tugal (2009) argues that similar methods have to be employed in contexts where there is a repressive state authority that tries to control and shape personal identities and everyday practices. In such contexts, Tugal (2009) argues, cultural struggles that involve not behaving in the way that is directed 'from above' (in this case, the Turkish state), can be even more effective strategies of challenging state power compared to direct confrontation. In Turkey, a secular state is locked in attempts to reshape the daily practices of its Muslim population away from religious authority by undermining prayer times, making difficult the separation of men and women in public spaces, and curbing the authority of mosques and controlling the content of sermons. In response, the Islamist Movement in some parts of Turkey does not directly engage the state in public confrontation, but involves individuals in attempts to wrestle back control over their daily lives and identity by reasserting the centrality of religious creed and practices. Islamism consciously 'avoids noisy protest' (Tugal, 2009, 423) and employs 'silent movement work on everyday practices' instead (Tugal, 2009, 451).

Methods point: ethnography and the 'intentionality' of protest

We have seen that 'misbehaviour' is not inherent in particular kinds of human acts, but can only be determined analytically by relating these acts to the context in which they arise, and by looking at the content of them. It is no surprise therefore, that studying misbehaviour requires, first and foremost, an ethnographic research strategy. Ethnography is a method widely employed by anthropologists seeking to explore the way of life of a particular cultural group. It often requires a long period of participant observation, in which the researcher joins the group and observes their day to day lives, like, for example, the two years that James Scott (1985) spent in the Malaysian peasant village he named 'Sedaka'. In this respect, ethnography is known as an 'insider' technique, which aims to understand the everyday lives of groups *in their own terms*. It looks at the meaning structures that are employed by the group and how they make sense of the world. Ethnographic methods have been seen as particularly valuable for appreciating the complexities of social movement mobilization and participation; taking what is often presented as a straight-forward linear process and – by adopting a 'grassroots' perspective – showing the inherent 'messiness' of the action involved (Plows, 2008). Importantly for studying misbehaviour, ethnography has also been seen as a method that can problematize and challenge how social movement theorists think of 'political intentionality' (Wolford, 2006). We have seen earlier in the chapter that one of the 'can of worms' opened up by the misbehaviour concept is the question of intentionality and the problem of the 'rebel without a cause'. Wendy Wolford's ethnographic study of the Brazilian landless movement, Sem Terra, is particularly instructive here (Wolford, 2006). She interviewed Brazilian plantation workers over a number of years, exploring how their commitment and involvement in the movement changed. Wolford found that her ethnography complicated the dominant way in which social movement studies view participation as a conscious decision-making process (involving either rational or emotional forms of reasoning). Instead, her data suggested that there was little clear, conscious reasoning at all surrounding involvement with the movement. Instead people's relationship to activism lacked an overall coherence, and their actions were often contradictory. Wolford therefore criticizes social movement scholars for perpetrating the idea that 'believing in agency has come to mean believing in intentionality' (Wolford, 2006, 338). While ethnography can, therefore, be a valuable research method for exploring misbehaviour because it looks in detail at the relationship between context, meaning, and everyday behaviour, it may be especially useful when studying 'misbehaviour' because it can consider agency without transferring onto it social-scientific notions of 'political intentionality'.

It can be said, therefore, that people will only protest in the ways available to them within a specific historical, political and social context. Misztal (1992), for example, shows how the Orange Alternative in Poland was forced to rely upon performance art and humour in public spaces, which attempted to subvert the cultural meanings of everyday life, because it was unable to mount an organized political struggle against the state. In repressive regimes historically people have had to find different ways of protesting and asserting their defiance, which are covert and anonymous in nature rather than public.

Another good example of this is graffiti. We think of graffiti as antisocial behaviour, as the vandalism of public space. It some cases it may be. In other contexts, however, graffiti can be an important medium through which to communicate politically subversive messages. Downing (2001) cites several examples of the political use of graffiti, particularly in the context of repressive regimes in which people cannot protest in more overt ways. The first of these comes from Moscow in the 1970s and 1980s, where young Russians wrote the names of their favourite football teams and rock bands in English on the walls of their apartment blocks (Bushnell, 1990). At the time, the Soviet regime had outlawed Western rock music from America and Britain, viewing it as a harmful outside influence that was eroding Russian cultural values and traditions. Downing states:

> the use of English in these graffiti simply but very directly challenged the bureaucrats' stultifying cultural policies . . . The graffiti neatly and effectively blew off core Soviet propaganda, and invited passers-by to do so, too. The radiant Soviet future – its young people – were blowing the regime a radiant raspberry.
>
> (Downing, 2001, 122)

The second example is from Nigeria in 1991, when Nigerian students – subject to state surveillance and the threat of physical harm if they had spoken out publicly – communicated political opinions through graffiti in university toilets, constructing one of the more unusually sited public spheres of political debate (Nwoye, 1993).

The means of expressing protest, then, varies, and not just across national boundaries but within them as well. The cultural expression of protest differs markedly by class, as the subcultural theorists of the 1960s were adept at showing when they noted the distinctive style of rebellion of working-class youth subcultures

(Hebdige, 1979). Working-class youth expressed their resistance to existing social arrangements in the way that they dressed, the values they lived their lives by, and, in the case of the mods and the rockers, the music that they listened to.

In some contexts, therefore, misbehaviour – expressed in gossip, grumbling, jokes, individual acts of defiance, and non-compliance at work and in daily practices, subversive folk tales, poetry and songs, performance art, and graffiti – is all people can do. Sometimes oppositional acts have to be covert, hidden, silent, but the examples provided here should be enough to illustrate that misbehaviour does not have to be seen as an individualized strategy; it can be a collective strategy for expressing discontent, retaining some personal autonomy, and, importantly, for trying to seek social change.

The everyday troublemaker

I have mentioned in the discussion of James Scott's work that, at times, he draws upon the American Sociologist, Erving Goffman (1922–82). Scott talks for example about the 'public performance' that those in subordinate positions have to put on. This is a public performance of compliance and deference – but, he points out, this cannot be equated with their entire sense of self. This is a useful point to make in reply to both Melucci and Foucault, who sometimes make it sound as if power has got us at the very core, despite out attempts to resist. Instead, people embark upon 'impression management' in social situations; they put on an act (Goffman, 1959). Scott argues that what powerless groups do in private, or 'off-stage' as Goffman puts it, is to engage in defiance and subversion (the 'hidden transcript' that we discussed earlier). In this section, I want to pause to consider how the work of Erving Goffman might also be relevant to the misbehaviour that takes place in *public* places, and is therefore not covert or anonymous.

We have come across one of Goffman's concepts once before: in Chapter 4 when we considered the efforts of social movements to break away from dominant understandings of social situations and instead 'frame' them in terms of injustice (Gamson, 1992). Goffman's work was the origin of 'frame analysis' which, as we saw, has had an important role to play in how we understand the activity that social movements undertake to construct particular cultural meanings of the world (Benford and Snow, 2000). Goffman does however offer a wider tool-kit of concepts that could be useful for opening up the realm of protest. These may be particularly helpful for considering exactly how people manage to misbehave in public as a way of subverting existing social relations. This is because, as Pierre Bourdieu put it, 'Goffman's achievement was that he reintroduced sociology to the infinitely small, to the things which the object-less theoreticians and concept-less observers were incapable of seeing' (Bourdieu, 1983, 112). By engaging with the task of placing the 'infinitely small' acts of daily life under the telescope, Goffman provided a portrait of the everyday troublemaker, who, through misbehaviour in public encounters, could be the 'destroyer of worlds' (Goffman, 1961, 72; Edwards, 2003).

Goffman was interested in the rules of interaction in public encounters. He suggested that social situations have very clear moral codes of conduct attached to them: normative rules that map out how you are expected to behave and how you are not, such that interaction takes on a 'structured' appearance (Goffman, 1967). Our freedom to act is constrained therefore by the rules of the interaction order to which our public performances must conform. Relationships of domination and subordination are symbolically and ritually reproduced in public encounters, through, for example, 'deference patterns' (Goffman, 1967, 65), the struggle to avoid 'stigma' (Goffman, 1967), and 'avoidance rituals' (Goffman, 1969, 11).

These ideas are significant for the study of misbehaviour in public places because they point to the expressive mechanisms that people can employ in social situations to invert the meaning of those situations and their symbolic relationships to others. The everyday troublemaker, for example, is the person who subverts the rules of the interaction order and therefore fails to keep their place within the encounter. Goffman is useful because he tells us how this effect is achieved. People misbehave when they commit 'situational impropriety' (Goffman, 1967), through, for example, their non-compliance to normative rules, their bodily appearance and comportment (Goffman refers to the 'delinquency strut which . . . communicates an authority challenge', 1969, 191), and their manner and gestures (we can include uses of humour here). Interestingly, because they similarly engage in 'situational impropriety', Goffman draws a parallel between those defined as mentally ill and the members of social movements (perhaps explaining something of the early association between protesters and those 'mad people with mad ideas' we looked at in Chapter 2):

> In the last few years . . . situational improprieties of the most flagrant kind have become widely used as a tactic by hippies, the New Left and black militants, and . . . they seem too numerous, too able to sustain collective rapport, and too facile at switching into conventional behaviour to be accused of insanity.
>
> (Goffman, 1971, 412)

Situational impropriety is not only used as a tactic by people who misbehave in public outside SMOs, but can also be employed by activists staging public protest events as part of SMOs. Nevertheless, dipping into Goffman's conceptual tool-kit beyond the framing concept helps us to understand how seemingly trivial acts of non-compliant behaviour (through body, dress, comportment, performance) in public situations can have destabilizing effects for the symbolic relationships between dominant and subordinate parties, and why therefore, they might be employed as tactics in politically significant struggles. Misbehaviour does not just take place 'off-stage' in private domains of life (J. Scott,

1990), but the rules of the interaction order in public situations can provide a public stage for non-compliance and the protesting body. It is really in public realms that the everyday troublemaker realizes her potential to be the 'destroyer of worlds' – at least symbolically.

Summary

In times marked by a recurring public discourse about apathy and indifference in Western democratic societies, and by repressive regimes which afford little opportunity to publicly protest at all, it is all the more important to look at what people actually *do* when it comes to the question of protest. In ways sometimes very small, and sometimes very large, ordinary people somewhere are engaged in resisting existing social arrangements, envisioning new ones, and putting their plans into practice. Public commentators, and some sociologists, however, start out with a very particular image of what 'protest' or 'social movements' should look like and, moreover, what a 'successful' movement should achieve. They are very often disappointed therefore with the actual level of interest, participation, commitment, and persistence of 'the people' who must drive them.

In this chapter, I have suggested that social movement studies would benefit from importing another concept from organizational studies, that of 'misbehaviour' (Ackroyd and Thompson, 1999). The reasons for this are threefold:

- 'Misbehaviour' may help us to detect protest in contexts outside Western democratic societies, but also within them.
- It can help us to detect non-organized protest that takes place covertly, as well as in public spaces.
- The emphasis is on looking for what ordinary people actually *do* and not simply to focus upon *either the* hard-core

activists or the indifferent majority who seemingly acqui-esce.

Engaging in this task takes the unwieldy category of 'social deviance' and picks away at it to find moments of political significance. Such a task will always raise challenging ques-tions about political intentionality, about what to do with the 'rebels without a cause' (Ackroyd and Thompson, 1999). Nevertheless, these rebels without a cause might be the *mobi-lization potential for* rebels who do have a cause, or they might have been inspired by them.

The main argument of this chapter has not been that we need to move from CB to misbehaviour as such, but that we need to explore the relationship between the two:

- the relationship between individual and collective cultural struggle and organized political struggle
- the relationship between hidden/silent protest and public/noisy protest.

Misbehaviour, then, does not mean that protest today merely rests in individualized, multiple, and ultimately futile resist-ances in everyday life. It means that the acts of non-compli-ance that exist outside SMOs and public protest events are neither politically insignificant, nor our only hope. To stretch our conceptualization of social movements and protest to include 'misbehaviour' is (to invoke John Holloway's met-aphor once again) to pay attention to the volcano before it erupts, as well as fixing our eyes on the smoke that rises.

Discussion Point

- Do you think that there are circumstances in which acts of body modification (tattoos, piercings), graffiti, sabotage, and jokes can be considered as forms of protest?
- Are acts of protest that take place outside SMOs important to efforts to change society?
- Will social movement studies benefit from looking at 'misbe-haviour' or should it be outside our field of interest?

Further Reading

The concept of 'misbehaviour' as it is presented in organiza-tional studies comes from Ackroyd and Thompson (1999) *Organizational Misbehaviour*. To put this in context of debates in organizational studies, also see Thompson and Ackroyd (1995) 'All Quiet on the Workplace Front? A Critique of Recent Trends in British Industrial Sociology', *Sociology* 29(4): 615–33. James Scott's (1985) *Weapons of the Weak: Everyday Forms of Peasant Resistance*, is already a classic in Social Movement Studies, while his (1990) *Domination and the Arts of Resistance* outlines his theory of the 'hidden transcript'. For a lively and engaging read, see John Holloway's (2010a [2002]) *Change the World without Taking Power: The Meaning of Revolution Today*. On joking and protest in varied historical and national contexts, including after-globalization, see Dennis Bos and Marjolein t'Hart (2008) (eds.) *Humour and Social Protest*.

Lessons from Idle No More

The Future of Indigenous Activism

Glen Sean Coulthard

As a conclusion to this study I want to critically reflect on the Idle No More movement in light of what we have discussed up to this point. With this as my aim, I will organize my thoughts around five theses on Indigenous resurgence. These theses are not meant to be overly prescriptive or conclusive. Instead I propose them with the aim of both consolidating and contributing to the constructive debates and critical conversations that have already animated the movement to date. They also indicate areas where future research is required.

Thesis 1: On the Necessity of Direct Action

I am going to structure my comments on direct action around a discursive restraint that has increasingly been placed on movements like Idle No More (both from within and from without) since the debates that emerged leading into the January 11 meeting with Prime Minister Harper and the January 16 national day of action. This constraint involves the type of tactics that are being represented as morally legitimate in our efforts to defend our land and rights as Indigenous peoples, on the one hand, and those that are increasingly being presented as either morally illegitimate or at least politically self-defeating because of their disruptive, extralegal, and therefore potentially alienating character, on the other hand.

With respect to those approaches deemed "legitimate" in defending our rights, emphasis is usually placed on formal "negotiations"—usually carried out between "official" Aboriginal leadership and representatives of the state—and if need be coupled with largely symbolic acts of peaceful, nondisruptive protest

that abide by Canada's "rule of law." Those approaches that are increasingly deemed "illegitimate" include, but are not limited to, forms of "direct action" that seek to influence power through less mediated and sometimes more disruptive and confrontational measures. In the context of Indigenous peoples' struggles, the forms of "direct action" often taken to be problematic include activities like temporarily blocking access to Indigenous territories with the aim of impeding the exploitation of Indigenous peoples' land and resources, or in rarer cases still, the more-or-less permanent reoccupation of a portion of Native land through the establishment of a reclamation site which also serves to disrupt, if not entirely block, access to Indigenous peoples' territories by state and capital for sustained periods of time. Even though these actions may be oriented toward gaining some solid commitment by the state to curtail its colonial activities, I think that they still ought to be considered "direct action" for three reasons: first, the practices are directly undertaken by the subjects of colonial oppression themselves and seek to produce an immediate power effect; second, they are undertaken in a way that indicates a loosening of internalized colonialism, which is itself a precondition for any meaningful change; and third, they are prefigurative in the sense that they build the skills and social relationships (including those with the land) that are required within and among Indigenous communities to construct alternatives to the colonial relationship in the long run. Regardless of their diversity and specificity, however, most of these actions tend to get branded in the media as the typical Native "blockade." Militant, threatening, disruptive, and violent.

The following positions are typical of those that emerged in the wake of the January 11 meeting regarding use of these direct action tactics to defend Indigenous peoples' land and interests. The first position is drawn from a statement made by the former national chief of the Assembly of First Nations, Ovide Mercredi, at an Aboriginal leadership gathering in the spring of 2013. In his speech Mercredi boldly stated that it is "only through talk, not through blockades that [real] progress will be made."[47] The assumption here, of course, is that the most productive means to forge lasting change in the lives of Indigenous people and communities is through the formal channels of negotiation. The second example is slightly more predictable. It is drawn from a statement made by Prime Minister Stephen Harper: "People have the right in our country to demonstrate and express their points of view peacefully as long as they obey the law, but I think the Canadian population expects everyone will obey the law in holding such protests."[48]

There are three arguments that typically get used when critics rail against the use of more assertive forms of Indigenous protest actions. The first is the one clearly articulated by Mecredi in the statement I just quoted: negotiations are, objectively speaking, simply more effective in securing the rights and advancing the interests of Indigenous communities. This is simply false. Historically, I would venture to suggest that all negotiations over the scope and content of Aboriginal peoples' rights in the last forty years have piggybacked off the assertive direct actions—including the escalated use of blockades—spearheaded by Indigenous women and other grassroots elements of our communities. For example, there would likely have been *no* negotiations over Aboriginal rights and title in British Columbia through the current land claims process (as problematic as it is) if it were not for the ongoing commitment of Indigenous activists willing to put their bodies on the line in defense of their lands and communities. There would have likely been *no* Royal Commission on Aboriginal Peoples without the land-based direct actions of the Innu in Labrador, the Lubicon Cree in Alberta,

the Algonquin of Barrier Lake, the Mohawks of Kanesatake and Kahnawake, the Haida of Haida Gwaii, the Anishanaabe of Temagami, and the countless other Indigenous communities across Canada that have put themselves directly in harm's way in the defense of their lands and distinct ways of life. Likewise, there would have likely been *no* provincial inquiry (there has yet to be a national one) into the shameful number of murdered and missing Indigenous women in Vancouver and across the province if it were not for the thousands of Native women and their allies who have formed lasting networks of mutual care and support and taken to the streets every year on February 14 for more than two decades to ensure that state-sanctioned sexual violence against Indigenous women ends here and now. All of this is to say that if there has been any progress in securing our rights to land and life—including through the largely male-dominated world of formal negotiations—this progress is owed to the courageous activists practicing their obligations to the land and to each other in these diverse networks and communities of struggle.

The second argument that gets used to denounce or criticize more "disruptive" forms of Indigenous direct action involve these actions' supposedly "self-defeating" or "alienating" character.[49] The idea this time is that insofar as these tactics disrupt the lives of perhaps well-intentioned but equally uninformed non-Indigenous people, First Nations will increasingly find themselves alienated and our causes unsupported by average, working-class Canadians. I have two brief points to make here.

First, I think that getting this reaction from the dominant society is unavoidable. Indigenous people have within their sights, now more than ever, a restructuring of the fundamental relationship between Indigenous nations and Canada. For more than two centuries the manifestations of this relationship have run roughshod over the rights of Indigenous peoples, which has resulted in a massive stockpiling of power and privilege by and for the dominant society. Land has been stolen, and significant amounts of it must be returned. Power and authority have been unjustly appropriated, and much of it will have to be reinstated. This will inevitably be very upsetting to some; it will be incredibly inconvenient to others. But it is what needs to happen if we are to create a more just and sustainable life in this country for the bulk of Indigenous communities, and for the majority of non-Indigenous people as well. To my mind, the apparent fact that many non-Indigenous people are "upset" or feel "alienated" by the aims of decolonization movements like Idle No More simply means that we are collectively doing something right.

My second point is that this criticism or concern smells of a double standard. I suspect that equally "disruptive" action undertaken by various sectors of, for example, the mainstream labor movement, including job actions ranging from the withdrawal of teaching, transit, and healthcare services to full-blown strike activity, does not often undergo the same criticism and scrutiny by progressive non-Natives that Indigenous peoples' movements are subjected to. When these sectors of society courageously defend their rights outside of the increasingly hostile confines of imposed labor legislation—actions that also tend to disproportionately "disrupt" the lives of ordinary Canadians—it is crucial that we educate ourselves about the causes that inform these efforts. All Indigenous people ask is that the same courtesy and respect be offered our communities in our struggles.

The third critique involves what we might characterize as a neo-Nietzschean concern over the largely *reactive* stance that such acts of resistance take in practice. On the surface, blockades in particular appear to be the epitome of *reaction* insofar as they clearly embody a resounding "no" but fail to offer a more *affirmative* gesture or alternative built into the practice itself. The risk here is that, in doing so, these *ressentiment-laden* modalities of Indigenous resistance reify the very structures or social relationships we find so abhorrent. In Nietzsche's terms, insofar as this "No" becomes our "creative deed" we end up dependent on the "hostile world" we have come to define ourselves *against*.[50] We

become dependent on "external stimuli to act at all—[our] action is fundamentally *reaction*."[51]

This concern, I claim, is premised on a fundamental misunderstanding of what these forms of direct action are all about. In his own creative engagement with Nietzsche at the end of *Black Skin, White Masks*, Frantz Fanon exclaims that, yes, "man is an *affirmation* . . . and that we shall not stop repeating it. Yes to life. Yes to love. Yes to generosity." "But man," he continues on to insist, "is also a *negation*. No to man's contempt. No to the indignity of man. To the exploitation of man. To the massacre of what is most human in man: freedom."[52] Forms of Indigenous resistance, such as blockading and other explicitly disruptive oppositional practices, are indeed *reactive* in the ways that some have critiqued, but they are also very important. Through these actions we physically say "no" to the degradation of our communities and to exploitation of the lands upon which we depend. But they also have ingrained within in them a resounding "yes": they are the affirmative *enactment* of another modality of being, a different way of relating to and with the world. In the case of blockades like the one erected by the Anishinaabe people of Grassy Narrows in northwest Ontario, which has been in existence since 2002, they become a *way of life*, another form of *community*. They embody through praxis our ancestral obligations to protect the lands that are core to who we are as Indigenous peoples.

Thesis 2: Capitalism, No More!

What the recent direct actions of First Nation communities like Elsipogtog in New Brunswick demonstrate is that Indigenous forms of economic disruption through the use of blockades are both a negation and an *affirmation*.[53] They are a crucial act of negation insofar as they seek to impede or block the flow of resources currently being transported to international markets from oil and gas fields, refineries, lumber mills, mining operations, and hydroelectric facilities located on the dispossessed lands of Indigenous nations. These modes of direct action, in other words, seek to have a negative impact on the economic infrastructure that is core to the colonial accumulation of capital in settler-political economies like Canada's.[54] Blocking access to this critical infrastructure has historically been quite effective in forging short-term gains for Indigenous communities. Over the last couple of decades, however, state and corporate powers have also become quite skilled at recuperating the losses incurred as a result of Indigenous peoples' resistance by drawing our leaders off the land and into negotiations where the terms are always set by and in the interests of settler capital.

What tends to get ignored by many self-styled pundits is that these actions are also an affirmative gesture of Indigenous resurgence insofar as they embody an enactment of Indigenous law and the obligations such laws place on Indigenous peoples to uphold the relations of reciprocity that shape our engagements with the human and nonhuman world—the land. The question I want to explore here, albeit very briefly, is this: how might we begin to scale up these often localized, resurgent land-based direct actions to produce a more general transformation in the colonial economy? Said slightly differently, how might we move beyond a resurgent Indigenous politics that seeks to inhibit the destructive effects of capital to one that strives to create *Indigenous alternatives* to it?

In her recent interview with Naomi Klein, Leanne Simpson hints at what such an alternative or alternatives might entail for Indigenous nations: "People within the Idle No More movement who are talking about Indigenous nationhood are talking about a massive transformation, a massive decolonization"; they are calling for a "resurgence of Indigenous political thought" that is "land-based and very much tied to that intimate and close relationship to the land, which to me means a revitalization of sustainable local Indigenous economies."[55]

Without such a massive transformation in the political economy of contemporary settler-colonialism, any efforts to rebuild our nations will remain parasitic on capitalism, and thus on the perpetual exploitation of our lands and labor. Consider, for example, an approach to resurgence that would see Indigenous people begin to reconnect with their lands and land-based practices on either an individual or small-scale collective basis. This could take the form of "walking the land" in an effort to refamiliarize ourselves with the landscapes and places that give our histories, languages, and cultures shape and content; to revitalizing and engaging in land-based harvesting practices like hunting, fishing, and gathering, and/or cultural production activities like hide-tanning and carving, all of which also serve to assert our sovereign presence on our territories in ways that can be profoundly educational and empowering; to the reoccupation of sacred places for the purposes of relearning and practicing our ceremonial activities.

A similar problem informs self-determination efforts that seek to ameliorate our poverty and economic dependency through resource revenue sharing, more comprehensive impact benefit agreements, and affirmative action employment strategies negotiated through the state and with industries currently tearing up Indigenous territories. Even though the capital generated by such an approach could, in theory, be spent subsidizing the revitalization of certain cultural traditions and practices, in the end they would still remain dependent on a predatory economy that is entirely at odds with the deep reciprocity that forms the cultural core of many Indigenous peoples' relationships with land.

What forms might an Indigenous political-economic alternative to the intensification of capitalism on and within our territories take? For some communities, reinvigorating a mix of subsistence-based activities with more contemporary economic ventures is one alternative.[56] As discussed in chapter 2, in the 1970s the Dene Nation sought to curtail the negative environmental and cultural impacts of capitalist extractivism by proposing to establish an economy that would apply traditional concepts of Dene governance—decentralized, regional political structures based on participatory, consensus decision-making—to the realm of the economy. At the time, this would have seen a revitalization of a bush mode of production, with emphasis placed on the harvesting and manufacturing of local renewable resources through traditional activities like hunting, fishing, and trapping, potentially combined with and partially subsidized by other economic activities on lands communally held and managed by the Dene Nation. Economic models discussed during the time thus included the democratic organization of production and distribution through Indigenous cooperatives and possibly worker-managed enterprises.[57]

Revisiting Indigenous political-economic alternatives such as these could pose a real threat to the accumulation of capital on Indigenous lands in three ways. First, through mentorship and education these economies reconnect Indigenous people to land-based practices and forms of knowledge that emphasize radical sustainability. This form of grounded normativity is antithetical to capitalist accumulation. Second, these economic practices offer a means of subsistence that over time can help break our dependence on the capitalist market by cultivating self-sufficiency through the localized and sustainable production of core foods and life materials that we distribute and consume within our own communities on a regular basis. Third, through the application of Indigenous governance principles to nontraditional economic activities we open up a way of engaging in contemporary economic ventures in an Indigenous way that is better suited to foster sustainable economic decision-making, an equitable distribution of resources within and between Indigenous communities, Native women's political and economic emancipation, and empowerment for Indigenous citizens and workers who may or must pursue livelihoods in sectors of the economy outside of the bush. Why not critically apply the most egalitarian and participatory features of our traditional governance practices to all of our economic activities, regardless of whether they are undertaken in land-based or urban contexts?

The capacity of resurgent Indigenous economies to challenge the hegemony of settler-colonial capitalism in the long term can only happen if certain conditions are met, however. First, all of the colonial, racist, and patriarchal legal and political obstacles that have been used to block our access to land need to be confronted and removed.[58] Of course, capitalism continues to play a core role in dispossessing us of our lands and self-determining authority, but it only does so with the aid of other forms of exploitation and domination configured along racial, gender, and state lines. Dismantling all of these oppressive structures will not be easy. It will require that we continue to assert our presence on all of our territories, coupled with an escalation of confrontations with the forces of colonization through the forms of direct action that are currently being undertaken by communities like Elsipogtog.

Second, we also have to acknowledge that the significant political leverage required to simultaneously block the economic exploitation of our people and homelands while constructing alternatives to capitalism will not be generated through our direct actions and resurgent economies alone. Settler colonization has rendered our populations too small to affect this magnitude of change. This reality demands that we continue to remain open to, if not actively seek out and establish, relations of solidarity and networks of trade and mutual aid with national and transnational communities and organizations that are also struggling against the imposed effects of globalized capital, including other Indigenous nations and national confederacies; urban Indigenous people and organizations; the labor, women's, GBLTQ2S (gay, bisexual, lesbian, trans, queer, and two-spirit), and environmental movements; and, of course, those racial and ethnic communities that find themselves subject to their own distinct forms of economic, social, and cultural marginalization. The initially rapid and relatively widespread support expressed both nationally and internationally for the Idle No More movement in spring 2013, and the solidarity generated around the

Elsipogtog antifracking resistance in the fall and winter of 2013, gives me hope that establishing such relations are indeed possible.

It is time for our communities to seize the unique political opportunities of the day. In the delicate balancing act of having to ensure that his social conservative contempt for First Nations does not overwhelm his neoconservative love of the market, Prime Minister Harper has erred by letting the racism and sexism of the former outstrip his belligerent commitment to the latter. This is a novice mistake that Liberals like Jean Chrétien and Paul Martin learned how to manage decades ago. As a result, the federal government has invigorated a struggle for Indigenous self-determination that must challenge the relationship between settler colonization and free-market fundamentalism in ways that refuse to be coopted by scraps of recognition, opportunistic apologies, and the cheap gift of political and economic inclusion. For Indigenous nations to live, capitalism must die. And for capitalism to die, we must actively participate in the construction of Indigenous alternatives to it.

Thesis 3: Dispossession and Indigenous Sovereignty in the City

In Canada, more than half of the Aboriginal population now lives in urban centers.[59] The relationship between Indigenous people and the city, however, has always been one fraught with tension. Historically, Canadian cities were originally conceived of in the colonial imagination as explicitly non-Native spaces—as *civilized* spaces—and urban planners and Indian policy makers went through great efforts to expunge urban centers of Native presence.[60] In 1911, for example, Prime Minister Wilfrid Laurier announced in Parliament that "where a reserve is in the vicinity of a growing town, as is the case in several places, it becomes a source of nuisance and an impediment to progress."[61] This developmentalist rationale, which at the time conceived of Native

space, particularly reserves, as uncultivated "waste" lands, justified an amendment to the Indian Act a month later, which stipulated that the residents of any "Indian reserve which adjoins or is situated wholly or partly within an incorporated town having a population of not less than eight thousand" could be legally removed from their present location without their consent if it was deemed in the "interest of the public and of the Indians of the band for whose use the reserve is held."[62] This situated Indian policy in a precarious position, as by the turn of the nineteenth century the reserve system, originally implemented to isolate and marginalize Native people for the purpose of social engineering (assimilation), was increasingly being seen as a failure because of the geographical distance of reserves from the civilizational influence of urban centers.[63] Here you have the economic imperatives of capitalist accumulation through the dispossession of Indigenous peoples' land come into sharp conflict with the white supremacist impulses of Canada's assimilation policy and the desire of settler society to claim "the city for themselves—and only themselves."[64]

The civilizational discourse that rationalized both the theft of Indigenous peoples' land base and their subsequent confinement onto reserves facilitated a significant geographical separation of the colonizer and the colonized that lasted until the mid-twentieth century.[65] As Sherene Razack notes, the segregation of urban from Native space that marked the colonial era began to break down with the increase in urbanization that took hold in the 1950s and 1960s, which resulted in a new racial configuration of space. Within this new colonial spatial imaginary,

> The city belongs to the settlers and the sullying of civilized society through the presence of the racialized Other in white spaces gives rise to a careful management of boundaries within urban space. Planning authorities require larger plots in the suburbs, thereby ensuring that larger homes and wealthier families live there. Projects and Chinatowns are created, cor-

doning off the racial poor. Such spatial practices, often achieved through law (nuisance laws, zoning laws, and so on), mark off the spaces of the settler and the native both conceptually and materially. The inner city is racialized space, the zone in which all that is not respectable is contained. Canada's colonial geographies exhibit this same pattern of violent expulsions and the spatial containment of Aboriginal peoples to marginalized areas of the city, processes consolidated over three hundred years of colonization.[66]

The dispossession that originally displaced Indigenous peoples from their traditional territories either onto reserves or disproportionally into the inner cities of Canada's major urban centers is now serving to displace Indigenous populations from the urban spaces they have increasingly come to call home. To this end, I suggest that the analytical frame of *settler-colonialism* developed throughout the previous chapters offers an important lens through which to interrogate the power relations that shape Indigenous people's experiences in the city, especially those disproportionately inhabiting low-income areas. As we learned in previous chapters, defenders of settler-colonial power have tended to rationalize these practices by treating the lands in question as *terra nullius*—the racist legal fiction that declared Indigenous peoples too "primitive" to bear rights to land and sovereignty when they first encountered European powers on the continent, thus rendering their territories legally "empty" and therefore open for colonial settlement and development.

In the inner cities of Vancouver, Winnipeg, Regina, Toronto, and so forth, we are seeing a similar logic govern the gentrification and subsequent displacement of Indigenous peoples from Native spaces within the city. Commonly defined as the transformation of working-class areas of the city into middle-class residential or commercial spaces, gentrification is usually accompanied by the displacement of low-income, racialized, Indigenous, and other marginalized segments of the urban population.[67] Regardless

of these violent effects, however, gentrifiers often defend their development projects as a form of "improvement," where previously "wasted" land or property (rooming houses, social housing, shelters, small businesses that cater to the community, etc.) and lives (sex-trade workers, homeless people, the working poor, mentally ill people, those suffering from addictions, etc.) are made more socially and economically productive. This Lockean rationale has led scholars like Neil Smith, Nicholas Blomley, and Amber Dean to view the gentrification of urban space through a colonial lens, as yet another "frontier" of dispossession central to the accumulation of capital.[68] Through gentrification, Native spaces in the city are now being treated as *urbs nullius*—urban space void of Indigenous sovereign presence.

All of this is to say that the efficacy of Indigenous resurgence hinges on its ability to address the interrelated systems of dispossession that shape Indigenous peoples' experiences in *both* urban and land-based settings. Mi'kmaq scholar Bonita Lawrence suggests that this will require a concerted effort on the part of both reserve- and urban-based Indigenous communities to reconceptualize Indigenous identity and nationhood in a way that refuses to replicate the "colonial divisions" that contributed to the urban/reserve divide through racist and sexist policies like enfranchisement.[69] Although Lawrence's work has shown how Native individuals, families, and communities are able to creatively retain and reproduce Indigenous traditions in urban settings, she also recognizes the importance for urban Native people to have "some form of mutually agreed upon, structured access to land-based communities."[70] Access to land is essential.

Similar struggles are seen in land-based communities, which would no doubt benefit from the numbers and human capital offered through the forging of political relations and alliances with the over 50 percent of Indigenous people now living in cities.[71] For Lawrence, all of this suggests that urban Native people and First Nations need ways of forging national alliances strategically in a manner that does not demand that First Nation governments endlessly open their membership to those who grew up disconnected from the life and culture of their original communities, or urban Indigenous people having to engage in the arduous struggle of maintaining an Indigenous identity cut off from the communities and homelands that ground such identities.[72] In other words, we need to find ways of bringing together through relations of solidarity and mutual aid "the strengths that urban and reserve-based Native people have developed in their different circumstances, in the interests of our mutual empowerment."[73]

Thesis 4: Gender Justice and Decolonization

According to Anishinaabe feminist Dory Nason, if Idle No More showed us anything, it is the "boundless love that Indigenous women have for their families, their lands, their nations, and themselves as Indigenous people." This love has encouraged Indigenous women everywhere "to resist and protest, to teach and inspire, and to hold accountable both Indigenous and non-Indigenous allies to their responsibilities to protect the values and traditions that serve as the foundation for the survival of the land and Indigenous peoples." Nason is also quick to point out, however, that the same inspirational power of Indigenous women's love to mobilize others to resist "settler-colonial misogyny's" inherently destructive tendencies has also rendered them subjects of "epidemic levels of violence, sexual assault, imprisonment and cultural and political disempowerment."[74]

The violence that Indigenous women face is both systemic and symbolic. It is systemic in the sense that it has been structured, indeed institutionalized, into a relatively secure and resistant set of oppressive material relations that render Indigenous women more likely than their non-Indigenous counterparts to suffer severe economic and social privation, including disproportionately high rates of poverty and unemployment, incarceration, addiction, homelessness, chronic and/or life-threatening health problems, overcrowded and substandard housing, and lack of access to clean water, as well as face discrimination and sexual violence in their homes, communities, and workplaces.[75] Just as importantly, however, the violence that Indigenous women face is also "symbolic" in the sense that Pierre Bourdieu used the term: "gentle, invisible violence, unrecognized as such, chosen as much as undergone."[76] Symbolic violence, in other words, is the subjectifying form of violence that renders the crushing materiality of systemic violence invisible, appear natural, acceptable.

As we saw in chapter 3, the symbolic violence of settler-colonial misogyny, institutionalized through residential schools and successive Indian Acts, has become so diffuse that it now saturates all of our relationships. The misogyny of settler-colonial misrecognition through state legislation, writes Bonita Lawrence, "has functioned so completely—and yet so invisibly—along gendered lines" that it now informs many of our struggles for recognition and liberation.[77] In such contexts, what does it mean to be "held accountable" to our "responsibilities to protect the values and traditions that serve as the foundation for the survival of the land and Indigenous peoples"? To start, it demands that Indigenous people, in particular Native men, commit ourselves *in practice* to uprooting the symbolic violence that structures Indigenous women's lives as much as we demand *in words* that the material violence against Indigenous women come to an end. This is what I take Nason to mean when she asks that all of us "think about what it means for men, on the one hand, to publicly profess an obligation to 'protect our women' and, on the other, take leadership positions that uphold patriarchal forms of governance or otherwise ignore the contributions and sovereignty of the women, Indigenous or not."[78] Here, the paternalistic and patriarchal insistence that we "protect *our* women" from the material violence they disproportionately face serves to reinforce the symbolic violence of assuming that Indigenous women are "ours" to protect. Although many Native male supporters of Idle No More have done a fairly decent job symbolically recognizing the centrality of Indigenous women to the movement, this is not the recognition that I hear being demanded by Indigenous feminists. The demand, rather, is that society, including Indigenous society and particularly Indigenous men, stop collectively *conducting ourselves* in a manner that denigrates, degrades, and devalues the lives and worth of Indigenous women in such a way that epidemic levels of violence are the norm in too many of their lives. Of course, this violence must be stopped in its overt forms, but we must also stop practicing it in its more subtle expressions—in our daily relationships and practices in the home, workplaces, band offices, governance institutions, and, crucially, in our practices of *cultural resurgence*. Until this happens we have reconciled ourselves with defeat.

Thesis 5: Beyond the Nation-State

We are now in a position to revisit the concern I raised at the end of chapter 1 regarding a problematic claim made by Dale Turner in *This Is Not a Peace Pipe*. Turner's claim is that if Indigenous peoples want the political and legal relationship between ourselves and the Canadian state to be informed by and reflect our distinct worldviews, then we "will have to engage the state's legal and political discourses in more effective ways."[79] This form of engagement, I claimed, assumes that the structure of domination that frames Indigenous–state relations in Canada derives its legitimacy and sustenance by excluding Indigenous people and voices from the legal and political institutional/discursive settings within which our rights are determined. Seen from this light, it would indeed appear that "critically undermining colonialism" requires that Indigenous peoples find more effective ways of "participating in the Canadian legal and political practices that determine the meaning of Aboriginal rights."[80]

Yet, I would venture to suggest that over the last forty years Indigenous peoples have become incredibly skilled at participating in the Canadian legal and political practices that Turner suggests. In the wake of the 1969 White Paper, these practices

emerged as the *hegemonic* approach to forging change in our political relationship with the Canadian state. We have also seen, however, that our efforts to engage these discursive and institutional spaces to secure recognition of our rights have not only failed, but have instead served to subtly reproduce the forms of racist, sexist, economic, and political configurations of power that we initially sought, through our engagements and negotiations with the state, to challenge. Why has this been the case? Part of the reason has to do with the sheer magnitude of discursive and nondiscursive power we find ourselves up against in our struggles. Subsequently, in our efforts to *interpolate* the legal and political discourses of the state to secure recognition of our rights to land and self-determination we have too often found ourselves *interpellated* as subjects of settler-colonial rule.

What are the implications of this profound power disparity in our struggles for land and freedom? Does it require that we vacate the field of state negotiations and participation entirely? Of course not. Settler-colonialism has rendered us a radical minority in our own homelands, and this necessitates that we continue to engage with the state's legal and political system. What our present condition does demand, however, is that we begin to approach our engagements with the settler-state legal apparatus with a degree of critical self-reflection, skepticism, and caution that has to date been largely absent in our efforts. It also demands that we begin to shift our attention away from the largely rights-based/recognition orientation that has emerged as hegemonic over the last four decades, to a resurgent politics of recognition that seeks to practice decolonial, gender-emancipatory, and economically nonexploitative alternative structures of law and sovereign authority grounded on a critical refashioning of the best of Indigenous legal and political traditions. It is only by privileging and grounding ourselves in these normative lifeways and resurgent practices that we have a hope of surviving our strategic engagements with the colonial state with integrity and as Indigenous peoples.

Chapter Genealogies

The list that follows includes some of the texts that inform our thinking and writing in this book. While not comprehensive, it is a genealogy that provides a rough outline to the Women's and Gender Studies' intellectual history we chose to emphasize throughout this text. Clearly many of these readings could be listed under several different chapter titles. And, no doubt, there are important thinkers and important writings that we have left out. Nevertheless, we offer this partial list as a starting point for those who want to know more about our influences.

NOTE FOR INSTRUCTORS

- Ahmed, Sara. 2014. "Problems With Names." *feministkilljoys: Killing Joy as a Worldmaking Project.* http://feministkilljoys.com/2014/04/25/problems-with-names/
- Baxandall, Rosalyn. 2001. "Re-visioning the Women's Liberation Movement's Narrative: Early Second Wave African American Feminists." *Feminist Studies* 27.1: 225–45.
- Braithwaite, Ann. 2004. "'Where We've Been' and 'Where We're Going': Reflecting on Reflections of Women's Studies and 'The Women's Movement.'" In *Troubling Women's Studies: Pasts, Presents, and Possibilities,* Ann Braithwaite, Susan Heald, Susanne Luhmann, and Sharon Rosenberg, 91–146. Toronto, ON: Sumach Press.
- Gluck, Sherna Berger, Maylei Blackwell, Sharon Cotrell, and Karen S. Harper. 1997. "Whose Feminism, Whose History? Reflections on Excavating the History

of (the) U.S. Women's Movement(s)." In *Community Activism and Feminist Politics: Organizing across Race, Class, and Gender*, edited by Nancy Naples, 31–56. New York, NY: Routledge.

- Hemmings, Clare. 2005. "Telling Feminist Stories." *Feminist Theory* 6.2: 115–139.
- Henry, Astrid. 2012. "Waves." In *Rethinking Women's and Gender Studies*, edited by Catherine M. Orr, Ann Braithwaite, and Diane Lichtenstein, 102–117. New York, NY: Routledge.
- Luhmann, Susanne. 2005. "Questions of the Field: Women's Studies as Textual Contestation." In *Open Boundaries: A Canadian Women's Studies Reader* (2nd ed.), edited by Barbara Crow and Lise Gotell, 28–38. Toronto, ON: Pearson Education Canada.
- Mapayaran, Layli. 2012. "Feminism." In *Rethinking Women's and Gender Studies*, edited by Catherine M. Orr, Ann Braithwaite, and Diane Lichtenstein, 17–33. New York, NY: Routledge.
- Newman, Louise Michelle. 1999. *White Women's Rights: The Racial Origins of Feminism in the United States*. New York, NY: Oxford University Press.
- Tuck, Eve. 2015. "Decolonizing Our Theories of Change." Keynote talk at annual WGSRF (Women's and Gender Studies et Recherches Féministes) conference, Ottawa, ON, May.
- Wiegman, Robyn. 2010. "The Intimacy of Critique: Ruminations on Feminism as a Living Thing." *Feminist Theory* 11.1: 79–84.

INTRODUCTION

- de Certeau, Michel. 1984. *The Practice of Everyday Life*. Berkeley, CA: University of California Press.
- Genz, Stephanie and Benjamin A. Brabon. 2009. *Postfeminism: Cultural Texts and Theories*. Edinburgh, Scotland: Edinburgh University Press.
- Hemmings, Clare. 2011. *Why Stories Matter: The Political Grammar of Feminist Theory*. Durham, NC: Duke University Press.
- Lefebvre, Henri. 2014. *The Critique of Everyday Life (Volumes 1-3)*. New York, NY: Verso.
- Rifkin, Mark. 2013. "Settler Common Sense." *Settler Colonial Studies*, 3.4: 322–340.

- Sedgwick, Eve Kosofsky. 1990. *Epistemology of the Closet*. Berkeley, CA: University of California Press.
- Smith, Dorothy. 1987. *The Everyday World as Problematic: A Feminist Sociology*. Boston, MA: Northeastern University Press.

KNOWLEDGES

- Ahmed, Sara. 2000. "Whose Counting?" *Feminist Theory*, 1.1: 97–103.
- Bonilla-Silva, Eduardo. 2013. *Racism Without Racists: Color-blind Racism and the Persistance of Racial Inequality in America* (4th ed.). Lanham, MD: Rowman and Littlefield.
- Braziel, Jana Evans and Kathleen LeBesco, eds. 2001. *Bodies Out of Bounds: Fatness and Transgression*. Berkeley, CA: University of California Press.
- Butler, Judith. 1990. *Gender Trouble: Feminism and the Subversion of Identity*. New York, NY: Routledge.
- Foucault, Michel. 1972. "The Discourse on Language." In *The Archaeology of Knowledge and The Discourse on Language*. 215–237. Translated by A.M. Sheridan Smith. New York, NY: Pantheon.
- Hammonds, Evelynn M. 1997. "Towards a Genealogy of Black Female Sexuality: The Problematic of Silence." In *Feminist Genealogies, Colonial Legacies, Democratic Futures*, edited by M. Jacqui Alexander and Chandra Talpade Mohanty, 170–182. New York, NY: Routledge.
- Haraway, Donna. 1988. "Situated Knowledges: The Science Question in Feminism and the Privilege of Partial Perspective." *Feminist Studies* 14.3: 575–599.
- Henry, Astrid. 2004. *Not My Mother's Sister: Generational Conflict and Third-Wave Feminism*. Bloomington, IN: Indiana University Press.
- Illouz, Eva. 1997. *Consuming the Romantic Utopia: Love and the Cultural Contradictions of Capitalism*. Berkeley, CA: University of California Press.
- Piontek, Thomas. 2006. *Queering Gay and Lesbian Studies*. Urbana, IL: Illinois University Press.
- Smith, Linda Tuhiwai. 2012. *Decolonizing Methodologies: Research and Indigenous Peoples* (2nd ed.). London, England and New York, NY: Zed Books.
- Wiegman, Robyn. 2012. *Object Lessons*. Durham, NC: Duke University Press.

IDENTITIES

- Anzaldúa, Gloria. 1987. *Borderlands/La Frontera: The New Mestiza.* San Francisco, CA: Aunt Lute Press.
- Back, Les and John Solomos, eds. 2000. *Theories of Race and Racism: A Reader.* London, England: Routledge.
- Cohen, Cathy. 1997. "Punks, Bulldaggers, and Welfare Queens: The Radical Potential of Queer Politics?" *GLQ: A Journal of Lesbian and Gay Studies* 3.4: 437–465.
- Combahee River Collective. 1982. "Black Feminist Statement." In *All the Women Are White, All the Blacks Are Men, But Some of Us Are Brave: Black Women's Studies,* edited by Gloria T. Hull, Patricia Bell Scott, and Barbara Smith, 13–22. New York, NY: The Feminist Press.
- Crenshaw, Kimberlé. 1989. "Demarginalizing the Intersection of Race and Sex: A Black Feminist Critique of Antidiscrimination Doctrine, Feminist Theory and Antiracist Politics." *University of Chicago Legal Forum* 140: 139–167.
- Deliovsky, Katerina. 2010. *White Femininity: Race, Gender, and Power.* Halifax, NS: Fernwood.
- Driskill, Qwo-Li, Chris Finley, Brian Joseph Gilley, and Scott Morgensen, eds. 2011. *Queer Indigenous Studies: Critical Interventions in Theory, Politics, and Literature.* Tucson, AZ: University of Arizona Press.
- Duggan, Lisa. 1995. "Making It Perfectly Queer." In *Sex Wars: Sexual Dissent and Political Culture,* Lisa Duggan and Nan Hunter, 155–172. New York, NY: Routledge.
- hooks, bell. 1988. *Talking Back: Thinking Feminist, Thinking Black.* Boston, MA: South End Press.
- Jakobsen, Janet R. and Ann Pellegrini, eds. 2008. *Secularisms.* Durham, NC: Duke University Press.
- Laqueur, Thomas. 1990. *Making Sex: Body and Gender from the Greeks to Freud.* Cambridge, MA: Harvard University Press.
- Mattilda a.k.a. Matt Bernstein Sycamore, ed. 2006. *Nobody Passes: Rejecting the Rules of Gender and Conformity.* Berkeley, CA: Seal Press.

- May, Vivian. 2015. *Pursuing Intersectionality: Unsettling Dominant Imaginaries*. New York, NY: Routledge.
- Pendleton, Eve. 1997. "Love for Sale: Queering Heterosexuality." In *Whores and Other Feminists*, edited by Jill Nagle. 73–82. New York, NY: Routledge.
- Reeser, Todd. 2010. *Masculinities in Theory: An Introduction*. West Sussex, UK: Wiley-Blackwell.
- Rubin, Gayle. 1993 (1984). "Thinking Sex." In *The Lesbian and Gay Studies Reader*, edited by Henry Abelove, Michele Aina Barale, and David Halperin, 3–44. New York, NY: Routledge.
- Rupp. Leila J. 2001. "Towards A Global History of Same-Sex Sexuality." *Journal of the History of Sexuality* 10.2: 287–302.
- Stryker, Susan. 2008. *Transgender History*. Berkeley, CA: Seal Press.
- Wilchins, Riki. 2004. *Queer Theory, Gender Theory: An Instant Primer*. Los Angeles, CA: Alyson Books.
- Zimmerman, Bonnie and Toni McNaron, eds. 1996. *The New Lesbian Studies: Into the 21st Century*. New York, NY: The Feminist Press.

EQUALITIES

- Ahmed, Sara. 2012. *On Being Included: Racism and Diversity in Institutional Life*. Durham, NC: Duke University Press.
- Alcoff, Linda. 1988. "Cultural Feminism vs. Post-Structuralism: The Identity Crisis in Feminist Theory." *Signs* 13.3: 405–436.
- Cohen, Cathy. 2012. *Democracy Remixed: Black Youth and the Future of American Politics*. New York, NY: Oxford University Press.
- Collins, Patricia Hill. 1990. *Black Feminist Thought: Knowledge, Consciousness, and the Politics of Empowerment*. New York, NY: Routledge.
- Duggan, Lisa. 2003. *The Twilight of Equality?: Neoliberalism, Cultural Politics, and the Attack on Democracy*. Boston, MA: Beacon Press.
- Puar, Jasbir. 2007. *Terrorist Assemblages: Homonationalism in Queer Times*. Durham, NC: Duke University Press.

- Rothenberg, Paula. 2004. *Invisible Privilege: A Memoir about Race, Class, and Gender.* Kansas, KS: University of Kansas Press.
- Scott, Joan W. 1988. "Deconstructing Equality-Versus-Difference: Or, the Uses of Poststructuralist Theory for Feminism." *Feminist Studies* 14.1: 33–50.
- Spade, Dean. 2011. *Normal Life: Administrative Violence, Critical Trans Politics, and the Limits of Law.* Brooklyn, NY: South End Press.
- Wendell, Susan. 1996. *The Rejected Body.* New York, NY: Routledge.

BODIES

- Bordo, Susan. 1993. *Unbearable Weight: Feminism, Western Culture, and the Body.* Berkeley, CA: University of California Press.
- Butler, Judith. 1988. "Performative Acts and Gender Constitution: An Essay in Phenomenology and Feminist Theory." *Theatre Journal* 40.4: 519–531.
- Dreger, Alice. 2005. *One of Us: Conjoined Twins and the Future of Normal.* Cambridge, MA: Harvard University Press.
- Foucault, Michel. 1995 (1977). *Discipline and Punish.* Translated by Alan Sheridan. New York, NY: Vintage.
- Halberstam, Judith. 1998. "Transgender Butch: Butch/FTM Border Wars and the Masculine Continuum." *GLQ: A Journal of Lesbian and Gay Studies* 4.2: 287–310.
- Heyes, Cressida J. 2007. *Self-Transformations: Foucault, Ethics, and Normalized Bodies.* New York, NY: Oxford University Press.
- Roberts, Dorothy. 1997. *Killing the Black Body: Race, Reproduction, and the Meaning of Liberty.* New York, NY: Vintage.
- Thomson, Rosemarie Garland. 1996. *Extraordinary Bodies: Figuring Physical Disability in American Culture and Literature.* New York, NY: Columbia University Press.
- Wann, Marilyn. 2009. "Foreword: Fat Studies: An Invitation to Revolution." *The Fat Studies Reader*, edited by Esther Rothblum and Sondra Solovay, xi-xxvi. New York, NY: New York University Press.
- Wright, Alexa. 2013. *Monstrosity: The Human Monster in Visual Culture.* London, England: I.B. Tauris.

PLACES

- Alexander, Michelle. 2012. *The New Jim Crow: Mass Incarceration in the Age of Colorblindness.* New York, NY: The Free Press.
- Anderson, Benedict. 1983 *Imagined Communities: Reflections on the Origin and Spread of Nationalism.* New York, NY: Verso.
- Arat-Koc, Sedef. 2002. "Imperial Wars or Benevolent Interventions? Reflections on 'Global Feminism' Post September 11th." *Atlantis* 26.2: 53–65.
- Bell, David and Gill Valentine. 1997. *Consuming Geographies: We Are Where We Eat.* London, England: Routledge.
- Davis, Angela Y. 2003. *Are Prisons Obsolete?* New York, NY: Seven Stories Press.
- Johnston, Lynda and Robyn Longhurst. 2010. *Space, Place, and Sex: Geographies of Sexualities.* Lanham, MD: Rowman and Littlefield.
- Narayan, Uma. 1997. *Dislocating Cultures: Identities, Traditions, and Third World Feminism.* New York, NY: Routledge.
- Razack, Sherene, ed. 2002. *Race, Space, and the Law: Unmapping a White Settler Society.* Toronto, ON: Between the Lines.
- Sibley, David. 1995. *Geographies of Exclusion: Society and Difference in the West.* New York, NY: Routledge.
- Smith, Andrea. 2008. "American Studies without America: Native Feminisms and the Nation-State." *American Quarterly* 60.2: 309–315.
- Sudbury, Julia, ed. 2004. *Global Lockdown: Race, Gender, and The Prison Industrial Complex.* New York, NY: Routledge.

REPRESENTATIONS

- Baumgardner, Jennifer and Amy Richards. 2004. "Feminism and Femininity: Or How We Learned to Stop Worrying and Love the Thong." In *All About the Girl: Culture, Power, and Identity*, edited by Anita Harris, 59–68. New York, NY: Routledge.
- Deloria, Phillip. 1999. *Playing Indian.* New Haven, CT: Yale University Press.
- Fraser, Nancy and Linda Gordon. 1996. "The Genealogy of Dependency: Tracing a Keyword of the U.S. Welfare State." In *For Crying Out Loud: Women's Poverty in*

the *United States*, edited by Diane Dujon and Ann Withorn, 235–267. Boston, MA: South End Press.

- Gill, Rosalind. 2006. *Gender and the Media*. Cambridge, England: Polity Press.
- Hall, Stuart. 1997. "The Work of Representation." In *Representation: Cultural Representations and Signifying Practices*, edited by Stuart Hall, 15–64. Thousand Oaks, CA: Sage.
- hooks, bell. 1992. *Black Looks*. Boston, MA: South End Press.
- Khan, Shahnaz. 2005. "Reconfiguring the Native Informant: Positionality in the Global Age." *Signs: Journal of Women in Culture and Society*, 30.4: 2017–2037.
- Milestone, Katie and Anneke Meyer. 2011. *Gender and Popular Culture*. Cambridge, England: Polity Press.
- O'Brien, Susie and Imre Szeman. 2013. *Popular Culture: A User's Guide* (3rd ed.). Toronto, ON: Nelson Education.
- Pullen, Christopher and Margaret Cooper, eds. 2010. *LGBT Identity and Online New Media*. New York, NY: Routledge.
- Watson, Elwood and Marc E. Shaw, eds. 2011. *Performing American Masculinities: The 21st Century Man in Popular Culture*. Bloomington, IN: Indiana University Press.
- Zeisler, Andi. 2008. *Feminism and Popular Culture*. Berkeley, CA: Seal Press.

NOW WHAT? THE (ANTI) CONCLUSION

- Ahmed, Sara. 2005. *The Cultural Politics of Emotion*. New York, NY: Routledge.
- Ahmed, Sara. 2004. "Declarations of Whiteness: The Non-Performativity of Anti-Racism." *borderlands* 3.2. www.borderlands.net.au/vol3no2_2004/ahmed_declarations.htm
- Ahmed, Sara. 2010. "Killing Joy." *Signs: Journal of Women in Culture and Society* 35.3: 571–594.
- Berlant, Lauren. 2011. *Cruel Optimism*. Durham, NC: Duke University Press.
- Kafer, Alison. 2013. *Feminist, Queer, Crip*. Bloomington, IN: Indiana University Press.
- Mahrouse, Gada. 2010. "Questioning Efforts that Seek to 'Do Good': Insights from Transnational Solidarity Activism and Socially Responsible Tourism." In *States of*

Race: Critical Race Feminism for the 21st Century, edited by Sherene Razack, Malinda Smith, and Sunera Thobani, 169–190. Toronto, ON: Between the Lines.

- Orr, Catherine M. 2012. "Activism." In *Rethinking Women's and Gender Studies*, edited by Catherine M. Orr, Ann Braithwaite, and Diane Lichtenstein, 85–101. New York, NY: Routledge.
- Srivastava, Sarita. 2005. "'You Callin Me a Racist?' The Moral and Emotional Regulation of Antiracism and Feminism." *Signs: Journal of Women in Culture and Society*, 31.1: 29–65.
- Thompson, Becky. 2002. "Multiracial Feminism: Recasting the Chronology of Second Wave Feminism." *Feminist Studies* 28.2: 336–360.
- Wiegman, Robyn. 2002. *Women's Studies on Its Own*. Durham, NC: Duke University Press.

Readings Chart

The chart below indicates several options for most of the readings included in this book. While we put a group of five readings together for every chapter in the text, we also think that many of them could be used with other sections of the book, too. Where we included them is marked with a "✖"; other possible chapters they could be used with are marked with a "●".

Article title	Chapter One: Knowledges	Chapter Two: Identities	Chapter Three: Equalities	Chapter Four: Bodies	Chapter Five: Places	Chapter Six: Representations	Now What? The (Anti) Conclusion
Abbas, Ali. "Death By Masculinity."			✖		●		
Abdulhadi, Rabab. "Where Is Home?: Fragmented Lives, Border Crossings, and the Politics of Exile."	●				✖		
Abu-Lughod, Lila. "The Muslim Woman: The Power of Images and the Danger of Pity."	✖					●	
Angel, Buck. "The Power of My Vagina."		✖		●			
Bailey, Moya. "'The Illest': Disability as Metaphor in Hip Hop Music."	✖						●
Carbado, Devon W. "Privilege."			✖				

Article title	Chapter One: Knowledges	Chapter Two: Identities	Chapter Three: Equalities	Chapter Four: Bodies	Chapter Five: Places	Chapter Six: Representations	Now What? The (Anti) Conclusion
Chess, Simone, Alison Kafer, Jessi Quizar, and Mattie Udora Richardson. "Calling All Restroom Revolutionaries!"			●				✖
Coulthard, Glen Sean. "Lessons from Idle No More: The Future of Indigenous Activism." [excerpt]	●						✖
Coyote, Ivan. "The Rest of My Chest."		●		✖			
DeMello, Margo. "Racialized and Colonized Bodies."		✖		●			
Edwards, Gemma. "From Collective Behaviour to Misbehaviour: Redrawing the Boundaries of Political and Cultural Resistance."	●						✖
Falcón, Sylvanna. "'National Security' and the Violation of Women: Militarized Border Rape at the US–Mexico Border."				✖	●		
Gamson, Joshua. "Popular Culture Constructs Sexuality."		●				✖	
Gavey, Nicola. "Viagra and the Coital Imperative."		✖		●			
Gerschick, Thomas J. "The Body, Disability, and Sexuality."		●		✖			
Guthman, Julie. "What's on the Menu?"				✖			●
Huff, Joyce L. "Access to the Sky: Airplane Seats and Fat Bodies in Contested Spaces."			✖	●			
Imrie, Rob. "Disability, Embodiment and the Meaning of the Home."			●		✖		
Ingraham, Chrys. "One Is Not Born a Bride: How Weddings Regulate Heterosexuality."	✖					●	

Article title	Chapter One: Knowledges	Chapter Two: Identities	Chapter Three: Equalities	Chapter Four: Bodies	Chapter Five: Places	Chapter Six: Representations	Now What? The (Anti) Conclusion
Kafer, Alison. "A Future for Whom? Passing on Billboard Liberation."			●			✖	
Meiners, Erica R. "Awful Acts and the Trouble with Normal."					✖		
Nakamura, Lisa. "Cyberrace."			●			✖	
Nemoto, Kumiko. "Interracial Romance: The Logic of Acceptance and Domination."			●			✖	
Parreñas, Rhacel Salazar. "The Globalization of Care Work."					✖		
Pascoe, C. J. "'Guys Are Just Homophobic': Rethinking Adolescent Homophobia and Heterosexuality."		✖					
Pershai, Alexander. "The Language Puzzle: Is Inclusive Language a Solution?"	✖	●					
Puri, Jyoti. "Sexuality, State, and Nation."					✖		
Reger, Jo. "DIY Fashion and Going *Bust*: Wearing Feminist Politics in the Twenty-First Century."						✖	
Spade, Dean. "Their Laws Will Never Make Us Safer."			✖				
Titchkosky, Tanya. "'Where?': To Pee or Not to Pee." [excerpt]			✖		●		
wallace, j. "The Manly Art of Pregnancy."	✖	●					
Walters, Suzanna Danuta. "The Medical Gayz."		✖		●			
Wilson, Bianca D. M. "Widening the Dialogue to Narrow the Gap in Health Disparities: Approaches to Fat Black Lesbian and Bisexual Women's Health Promotion."		●		✖			

Index